PROGRAMMING 16-BIT MACHINES

MACHINES

The PDP-11, 8086, and M68000

William H. Jermann
Memphis State University

Prentice-Hall
Englewood Cliffs, N.J. 07632

Library of Congress Cataloging-in-Publication Data

Jermann, William H.   (date)
    Programming 16-bit machines.

    Bibliography: p.
    Includes index.
    1. PDP-11 (Computer)—Programming.   2. Intel 8086
(Microprocessor)—Programming.   3. Motorola 68000
(Microprocessor)—Programming.   I. Title.   II. Title:
Sixteen bit machines.
QA76.8.P2J47 1986   005.26   85-16960
ISBN 0-13-729161-2

Editorial/production supervision
and interior design: Tracey L. Orbine
Cover design: 20/20 Services, Inc.
Manufacturing buyer: Rhett Conklin

Printed in the United States of America

10   9   8   7   6   5   4   3   2   1

ISBN 0-13-729161-2   025

Prentice-Hall International (UK) Limited, *London*
Prentice-Hall of Australia Pty. Limited, *Sydney*
Prentice-Hall Canada Inc., *Toronto*
Prentice-Hall Hispanoamericana, S.A., *Mexico*
Prentice-Hall of India Private Limited, *New Delhi*
Prentice-Hall of Japan, Inc., *Tokyo*
Prentice-Hall of Southeast Asia Pte. Ltd., *Singapore*
Editora Prentice-Hall do Brasil, Ltda., *Rio de Janeiro*
Whitehall Books Limited, *Wellington, New Zealand*

This book is dedicated to the hope that humankind will utilize its technological advances for its betterment rather than its termination.

Contents

Preface

A colleague of mine from Japan recently commented on what he considered to be unusual about electrical engineering education in the United States. He stated that our typical curricula consisted of just "hardware" engineering. Perhaps this observation was made because universities in Japan include software-oriented courses in electrical engineering curricula, whereas similar courses are frequently taught in computer science programs in the United States.

Although hardware and engineering component concepts are indeed important, the evolution and applications of large-scale and very-large-scale integrated circuits have resulted in an increased need for engineers to develop and improve programming skills. On the other hand, hardware requirements for interfacing components to 4-bit or 8-bit microprocessor based systems are not too much different from those required to interface components to 16-bit and 32-bit microprocessor systems.

The material for this textbook evolved from a course traditionally referred to as a Minicomputer Systems course. Early textbooks that surveyed various existing minicomputer systems have been obsolete for some time. However, texts illustrating development of assembly-language programs and use of minicomputers for real-time applications are still utilized.

The rapid changes in the computer industry have resulted in almost continuous curriculum changes in our universities. It is generally accepted that universities should teach principles rather than attempt to have students develop very specific skills. However, attempts to teach computer-related principles independent of particular machines have, at best, led to questionable outcomes. Furthermore, a wide variety of different courses has evolved, and these courses are offered at various levels within engineering and computer science curricula.

This textbook deals primarily with architecture and assembly-language programming of 16-bit machines. This category of machines was selected because it is thought that in the foreseeable future, this is the class of computer systems most likely to be devoted to real-time applications. Although concepts related to computer architecture are dispersed throughout the text, the textbook does not display the depth of material contained in several popular books on computer architecture. However, this textbook offers the student examples and review questions with answers on virtually all major subjects. We believe this is essential for favorable educational outcomes.

Chapters 1 to 4 contain material that is nearly machine independent. Chapters 5 to 9 relate to the PDP-11 family of computers. The first nine chapters may be used for an introductory course, such as Minicomputer Systems, Assembly-Language Programming, or Introduction to the PDP-11. Student access to a PDP-11 is required in order that skills related to assembly-language programming be developed. Access to a PDP-11 is not required for development of skills in PDP-11 machine-language programming. Feedback in this area may be obtained through use of a simulator. A FORTRAN listing of a PDP-11 simulator is included in the Instructor's Manual.

Chapter 10 is a self-contained unit relating to the 8086/88 processor and its assembly language. Access to an IBM Personal Computer is all that is required for developing the related concepts and skills. We have found the material covered in this chapter to be sufficient for a student to appreciate the architecture and to develop assembly-language programming skills related to the 8086/88 processor. On the other hand, use of certain popular textbooks devoted entirely to this processor has not been sufficient for learning and developing the related skills.

Chapter 11 is devoted to the M68000 processor. Feedback is obtained through use of a Motorola-developed Cross Assembler and Simulator. These FORTRAN programs are furnished to educational institutions at a nominal cost. The material covered in the first nine chapters of this text significantly facilitates the mastery of the material in Chapters 10 and 11.

All material in this textbook has been developed for use at an introductory level. The only prerequisite is some knowledge and moderate skills related to computer programming.

This text may be used for an introductory course in microprocessors offered at the precircuits level. For such a course, it is suggested that the first four chapters be covered and that selected segments of Chapters 5 through 9 be introduced. Then emphasis can be placed on Chapters 10 and 11. A more traditional course in microprocessors is generally offered later in an electrical engineering curriculum. It certainly appears to be advantageous if students already have an appreciation of the architecture and skills in assembly-language programming of popular machines before taking such a course.

Virtually all of the material used in this textbook has been taught in the format presented in the textbook. Appreciation is expressed for the numerous contributions made by students related to the development of this material. Although it is impractical to mention all of these students. I particularly recall contributions made by the following: Amy Reinhardt, Tunney Dong, Chris Hannekin, Brian Hopkins, Michael Trombley, Raymond Ng, Eva White, Bill Dabbs, Surendra Desai, and Portia King. Student-generated enthusiasm for this subject matter has indeed been rewarding.

William H. Jermann

1

Introduction

A *computer program* is a well-defined sequence of instructions capable of being executed by a target machine. We may define *computing* as the execution of computer programs. Computing activities involve a wide variety of applications, including scientific and mathematical applications, business and related information-retrieval activities, and the monitoring and controlling of external operations.

Use of computers has permeated virtually all activities in highly technological societies. The impact of computing activities has been so great that our present period has been called the postindustrial revolution era or the *information era*. This classification has emerged because of the numerous activities related to information processing. The role of the computer in the information era is so well recognized that a highly respected publication recently assigned its "man-of-the-year" award to the computer.

During the late twentieth century, computing machines have been developed and used for a variety of applications. These machines have served to enhance human capabilities previously classified as *intellectual* capabilities. Such terms as *memory, information retrieval, information processing, artificial intelligence, learning machines,* and *decision-making devices* are now used to describe attributes related to computers and computer applications. Use of computers to enhance the highest levels of human activities is very exciting. Any difficulties or frustrations encountered in the development of hardware or software that is necessary to configure computing machines to perform such activities are clearly well worth the effort.

1.1 THE TECHNOLOGY EXPLOSION

The significant growth in technology occurred primarily in the latter half of the nineteenth century and throughout the twentieth century—a relatively small period of time in comparison to the length of time that human beings have inhabited earth. These relatively recent technological advances have served to amplify and reinforce significantly the capabilities of human beings. As an example, Figure 1.1 illustrates the exponential increase in travel speed that has been obtained by human beings. The achievements made during the twentieth century are truly phenomenal. As a result of developments in travel speeds, we have been able to visit the moon. Recently, an instrumented satellite has left our solar system and thereby offers a potential for exploring truly new frontiers.

The physical strength of human beings probably has not varied much throughout recorded history, but the development of weapons and explosives has served to enhance their strength. Figure 1.2 illustrates the exponential growth of explosive power during the past 600 years. If we measure such power in terms of explosive power that can be actuated throughout the world within a brief time, say one day, then the projected exponential increase shown in this figure is justified.

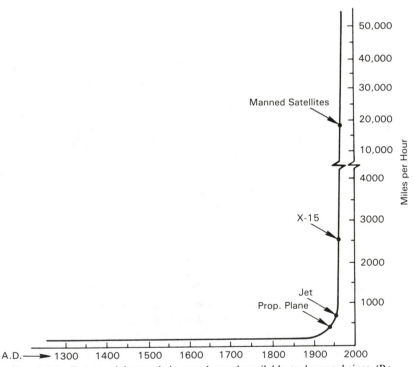

Figure 1.1 Exponential growth in travel speed available to human beings (Reprinted by permission of Department of Technology and Society, SUNY-Stony Brook, N.Y.)

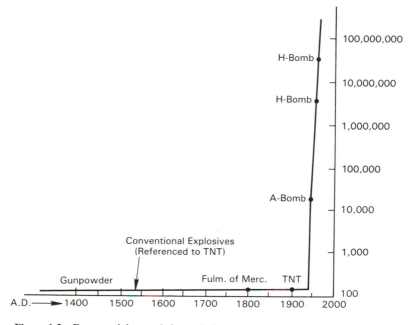

Figure 1.2 Exponential growth in explosive power (Reprinted by permission of Department of Technology and Society, SUNY-Stony Brook, N.Y.)

Although the topic of this textbook is modern computer systems, it is worthwhile to reflect on the potential of such explosive power. The increase in such power continues even though the dimensions of the planet and the elastic limits of the ecological systems remain fixed. To this date, no serious study has been conducted concerning the maximum disturbance that the ecological system can endure before catastrophic environmental effects will occur.

Figure 1.3 illustrates the exponential growth in published books. Before the development of the computer, the number of printed books might be considered as closely related to the growth of available information. It is now visualized that an era of information management and knowledge processing is emerging, and that this era is very closely related to the expanding capabilities of digital computers.

The exponential growth in the development and use of digital computers has occurred primarily within the last three decades. Curves similar to those displayed in Figs. 1.1, 1.2, and 1.3 related to exponential growth in the computer industry can be displayed. The size of a megabyte of computer memory has decreased exponentially during this interval, and the cost of this block of memory has similarly decreased. Furthermore, the speed in which a fixed set of calculations can be performed has likewise increased. The number of computing machines and the number of active users have increased in a similar manner. There are different projections related to continued development and use of digital computers. As fifth-generation computer systems are being developed, the most popular projections state that the

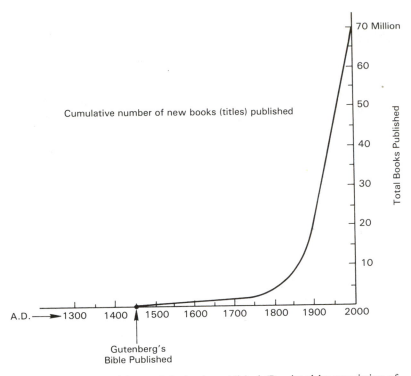

Figure 1.3 Exponential growth in books published (Reprinted by permission of Department of Technology and Society, SUNY-Stony Brook, N.Y.)

present use of computers is just the tip of the iceberg in comparison to anticipated use.

1.2 EVOLUTION OF DIGITAL COMPUTERS

It is difficult to identify the very beginning of computer technology. Because applications of computing are sometimes considered to be extensions of the central nervous system of humans, the origin of computers may be linked to the development of prehistoric man. Some computer users equate computer applications to the storage, retrieval, and manipulation of information. From this perspective, the ancestors of modern computers are considered primitive information storage and retrieval systems.

It is convenient to associate computing activities with computer hardware. Evidence of early development of such hardware has been found in all the populated continents. Perhaps one of the first computers that was similar to modern digital computers was the analytic machine developed in England by Charles Babbage (1791–1871). Mechanical devices were used in the machine. Values of variables corresponded to the positioning of gear wheels. The analytic engine was different from previous calculating machines in that it was designed to operate on algorithms or sequential computational rules. Algorithms were to be entered into the machine as a sequence of punched cards. Thus, in a sense, a computer program could be entered into the machine, stored in the machine, and executed. The development of this early stored program digital computer was very expensive. Partly because of expiration of funds, the machine was never satisfactorily completed.

Countess Augusta Ada Byron, daughter of Lord Byron, was a contributor to the development of the analytic machine. As a mathematician, she assisted in developing concepts related to its utilization. In addition, she made financial contributions to assist in the development of the project. Later she transformed notes on the programming of the analytic machine into readable script. Because of her contributions, she is considered by some to be the first computer programmer. The modern programming language ADA is named in honor of her work.

With the evolution of the electronics industry came the true development of modern digital computers. In 1906, Lee de Forest invented the three-grid vacuum tube. This device was used in early radio and television circuitry as well as in the first electronic computers. In 1948, John Bardeen and Walter Brattain developed the point-contact transistor at Bell Telephone Laboratories. Concurrently, William Shockley developed the first junction transistor. The limitations of vacuum tube computers were already becoming apparent as *solid state,* or transistorized, circuits were being developed. Although the idea of incorporating many different components on a single device was not new, commercial *integrated circuits* were not developed until the 1960s. An integrated circuit consists of a number of electronic elements or a number of logic gates fabricated on a single silicon chip.

Shortly after the development of these devices, integrated circuits were classified according to the number of electronic components contained in a single package. Classifications include SSI (small-scale integration), MSI (medium-scale integration), LSI (large-scale integration), and VLSI (very-large-scale integration). The particular classification depends on the number of components within the package or on the chip. Modern computers are composed primarily of LSI and VLSI chips. Sophisticated computer processing units, such as that of the IBM 370, have been fabricated on a single integrated circuit. It is estimated that within a very short period, integrated circuits containing more than a million and a half components will be commercially available.

Many other individuals not associated with electronic hardware have contributed to the development of digital computers. In 1854, George Boole developed a mathematical formulation related to the laws of propositional logic. In 1938, Claude Shannon applied these principles of Boolean algebra to the description and simplification of switching circuits that were used in telephone communications networks. This application of Boolean algebra was extended to describe the type of circuitry found in digital computers.

In 1936, A. M. Turing published a paper related to "computability." This paper described the types of problems considered to be "solvable" by a digital computer. Later, Turing investigated other computer-related ideas, such as whether or not a computer can "think." In 1945, John von Neumann presented a series of lectures on computer concepts at Princeton University. Perhaps the most significant concept developed was that the same memory used for data storage on a computer can also be used for program storage. A program command can be *fetched* from memory and *executed*. Then the subsequent command is fetched and executed and so on. Data needed by the program can be stored *any where* in the same memory unit in which the program statements are stored. Such a computer is called a von Neumann computer or a Princeton-type machine.

The first electronic stored-program digital computers were developed during World War II. One of the first commercial digital computers became available about 1950, the UNIVAC I developed by Remington Rand. The logic components of this machine consisted of vacuum tube circuits. During the same period, IBM, as well as several other vendors, marketed general-purpose digital computers. Although the early computers consisted of vacuum tube circuits, transistorized, or solid-state, computers were soon developed.

Programming early computers was very tedious. Programs had to be developed in machine code, and entering the programs into computers was time-consuming. At least one digital computer was programmed by patching conducting cords into holes on a removable patchboard. The patched wires related to specific machine-language instructions.

Because machine-language programming is very tedious and difficult to document and to debug, tools became available for developing programs. One such tool was the *assembler*. An assembler translates simple English-type statements or mnemonics into the corresponding machine code. Some shortsighted enthusiasts visualized assemblers as the last tool that would be required for assistance in program development. It was even speculated that professional computer programmers would no longer be required, as anyone could develop programs using an assembler.

During the 1960s, more sophisticated programming languages were developed. These include FORTRAN (*FOR*mula *TRAN*slation), BASIC (*B*eginners *A*ll-purpose *S*ymbolic *I*nline *C*ode), and COBOL (*CO*mmon *B*usiness *O*riented *L*anguage). Enhancements of these languages are still popular and very widely used.

In 1965, the Digital Equipment Corporation introduced a small computer, the PDP-8. This computer was packaged within a single cabinet, had relatively simple input/output devices, and was considered relatively inexpensive. Such a computer generally did not require the services of a full-time staff and often was dedicated to standalone applications. The term *minicomputer* was used to describe this computer. A number of manufacturers entered the minicomputer marketplace. Two of the most popular minicomputers were the PDP-11 family manufactured by the Digital Equipment Corporation and the NOVA family manufactured by the Data General Corporation.

The minicomputers that were developed in the 1960s utilized only solid-state components. Furthermore, it appeared likely that integrated circuits would soon be developed such that an entire computer CPU could be fabricated on a single chip.

In 1971, two computer CPUs, each fabricated on a single chip, were made available for commercial applications by the Intel Corporation. These devices were referred to as *microprocessors*. They were the 4-bit machine, the 4004, and an 8-bit machine, the 8008. These two devices were soon enhanced. Initially, 4-bit machines were very popular, especially in applications related to point-of-sale terminals. By the middle of the decade, a number of popular 8-bit machines had emerged. By the end of the decade, at least five different 16-bit microprocessors had been developed, and preliminary work had been completed on the development of 32-bit microprocessors. In the early 1980s, several 32-bit machines were developed.

It is relatively easy to package a general-purpose digital computer using one or more microprocessors, some memory chips, and some input-output and interfacing chips. Such computers are referred to as *general-purpose microcomputers*. Many of these computers were developed in the 1970s. Virtually all of these were based on 8-bit microprocessors. Three very popular families of such computers were the Apple computers, the Commodore Pet computers, and the Radio Shack TRS-80 computers.

Late in 1981, IBM entered the marketplace with its Personal Computer (PC), based on a 16-bit microprocessor, the Intel 8088. This machine rapidly emerged as a leader in the field. Many other 16-bit microcomputers, including a line of Japanese microcomputers, were developed during this time.

Precise classification of digital computers is difficult. Some classification categories that have historically been used include the following:

1. Mainframe computers, minicomputers, and microcomputers
2. Business computers and scientific computers
3. Home computers and office computers
4. 8-bit, 16-bit, 32-bit, 36-bit, 64-bit (etc.) computers

At present, general-purpose stored-program digital computers supported by at least one high-level language can be procured for well less than $100. Similarly, top-of-the-line mainframe computer systems are sold for amounts ranging into the multimillion-dollar categories.

This textbook is related to relatively small computers and computing systems. It is concerned with "typical" 16-bit machines. In particular, it is concerned primarily with the computing capabilities possessed by the central processing units of these typical machines. Further discussion related to classification of computers as 16-bit machines is given in Chapter 12.

1.3 OBJECTIVES

This textbook is intended for use in an introductory course related to the use of a certain class of computers. Introductory skills in programming in a high-level language serve as a sufficient prerequisite for the material covered in this textbook.

The overall objective of this textbook is to introduce to readers typical capabilities and attributes of small 16-bit computers. The specific objectives are to enable users of this textbook to

1. Become familiar with the attributes and machine capabilities of typical popular 16-bit computing machines.
2. Develop skills in formulating and testing software at the assembly-language level. Such computing skills are to include development of software for real-time monitoring and controlling applications, as well as for data-manipulating operations.
3. Be introduced to real-world computer components that are used for a variety of applications.

To achieve the specified objectives, the use of three particular 16-bit machines is introduced: the PDP-11 minicomputer (or the LSI-11, T11, or F11 microprocessor), the 8086 (or 8088) microprocessor, and the M68000 microprocessor. There is no intention to endorse any of these products.

The PDP-11 is covered because of its very extensive usage, its acclaimed architecture, and its apparent entrenchment due to the massive amount of software already developed. The 8086 is currently the most popular of the 16-bit microprocessors. Its use in the IBM PC and in recently developed Japanese computers virtually ensures its use over an extended period of time. Consistent with Intel's previous policies, enhancements of this machine that have been developed are upward compatible with the original machine. The M68000 is also emerging as a popular machine. It appears that it will be relatively easy to develop true 32-bit machines that are compatible enhancements of this machine. Furthermore, both the 8086 and the M68000 have been designed to support readily parallel processing.

In order for the reader to obtain the desired skills, the review questions that appear at the end of most sections should be answered. Answers to all review questions are given in Appendix D. It is also suggested that the selected exercises at the end of the chapters be worked.

Computing involves the formulation of programs. In Chapter 2, concepts related to development of programs are covered. Most of these concepts are independent of both the particular computer architecture and the programming language selected. In Chapters 3 and 4, concepts fundamental to understanding any computer architecture are introduced. In Chapter 5, the PDP-11 architecture is introduced, and readers are given the opportunity to develop programs at the machine-language level.

It is anticipated that users of this textbook will have some previous programming experience using a high-level language. It is not expected that they already have skills in assembly-language programming. In Chapter 6, assembly-language programming of the PDP-11 is introduced. The fixed-point and floating-point operations available to users of high-level languages are frequently not directly supported by machine-code operations. Use of assembly-language techniques to implement these numerical operations is covered in Chapter 7.

In order to utilize a small computer effectively, the user must be familiar with certain capabilities related to external hardware and devices. Input/output operations are treated in Chapters 8 and 9. Concepts related to monitoring and controlling external devices are introduced. Considerations related to programmed data transfers on PDP-11 systems are treated. In order to use a digital computer to monitor and control external analog systems, hybrid peripheral components are introduced. The use of an analog-to-digital converter and a digital-to-analog converter is illustrated.

The shortcomings of the use of programmed data transfers, especially in multiuser systems, will become apparent. The use of external interrupts and programmed traps is introduced in Chapter 9. Similarly, the implementation of DMA (direct memory access) data transfers is introduced. Although software for implementing such input/output operations is emphasized, formulation of computer hardware for these operations will not be difficult for a reader who comprehends the material in the related sections. Specific integrated circuits related to each of the desired tasks are generally available for use in appropriate microcomputer implementations.

In Chapter 10, the 8086 (or 8088) microprocessor is covered, and in Chapter 11 the capabilities of the M68000 microprocessor are discussed. At first glance, it may appear that there is an excessive amount of material in each of these chapters; however, by this time, the reader is already familiar with basic concepts. Chapter 12 presents an overview of the three 16-bit machines that have been covered.

REFERENCES

DORF, R. C., *Computers and Man*. San Francisco: Boyd and Frazier, 1974.

FEIGENBAUM, E. A., and P. McCORDUCK, *The Fifth Generation*. Reading, Mass.: Addison-Wesley, 1983.

JERMANN, W. H., *The Structure and Programming of Microcomputers*. Palo Alto, Calif.: Mayfield, 1982.

The Man Made World. ECCP Project, Polytechnic Institute of Brooklyn. New York: McGraw-Hill, 1971.

MAYOH, B., *Problem Solving with ADA*. Chichester, England: John Wiley, 1982.

2

Programming

A digital computer is composed of a number of components, some of which will be discussed in detail in this textbook. Virtually any popular digital computer is used for a wide variety of applications. Frequently, the physical components or *hardware* related to a computer system are either identical or very similar to the components contained in corresponding systems at other locations. Yet the applications for which similarly configured systems are utilized may be entirely different. Even the various tasks performed by a single computer in one day may cover a wide spectrum of activities.

Most computer configurations are originally designed as general-purpose systems. That is, a single set of hardware may be used for a variety of applications. Each application is identified by a specific set of software. The related software may be a single program or it may consist of a large collection of computer programs.

At one time, computer hardware was very expensive. Programmers were required to adapt their programs to the idiosyncrasies of the related computer hardware. Good programs were identified as those that ran very rapidly and required a minimal amount of memory space. Although these characteristics are still desirable, they are no longer the only attributes associated with good programs. Frequently, these attributes are not the most important considerations in program development.

At present, the cost of developing computer software is frequently greater than the cost of the related hardware. For some applications it has been estimated that software computer costs entail up to 90 percent of the total cost of computer-related projects. As a result, several important factors should be considered when software is being written. These concepts are generally independent of the programming lan-gauge that is being used. The concepts are relevant for software developed at the machine-language level, as well as for software developed using high-level lan-guages.

2.1 PROGRAMMING CONCEPTS

Regardless of the computer utilized, program planning is essential. Frequently, nov-ice programmers think that good programming techniques are not really important because only the individual programmer will ever use the particular program. How-ever, poorly written programs can lead to very serious difficulties, even for the pro-grammer. For example, such programs are difficult to debug. If modifications or changes are to be made, the programmer finds them difficult to implement, and someone else may find them nearly impossible to implement.

The following steps are important in the development of a program or a set of programs.

1. Determine precisely what you would like your program to do.
2. Unless the program is very simple, make appropriate plans for achieving the objectives of your program.
3. Using a suitable programming language, write your program.
4. Test your program. It probably doesn't work! Debug your program. Exten-sively test your program to ensure it works properly for the types of appli-cations for which it was designed.
5. Shortly after your program has been satisfactorily tested, you will probably want to improve it and extend the scope of its applications. Such activities are referred to as *program maintenance*. Program maintenance continues throughout the useful life of a program.

In the development of useful programs, step 3 often requires the least amount of time and effort. In many applications, step 1 requires the greatest expenditure of effort. For some computer-related efforts, it is estimated that 50 percent of the budgeted person-hours be allocated to project planning. Estimates have been made that program maintenance efforts in "typical" programs require approximately twice as much effort as is required in the initial creation of a program. If steps 1 and 2 are not properly satisfied, debugging can become unwieldy.

The following is an enumeration of several desirable attributes for computer programs. The relative importance of each of these attributes is dependent on the demands of the particular task.

1. *A program should have a well-defined purpose.* Furthermore, the purpose or the function of the program should be stated within the program text.

2. *The program should be well documented.* A long program should be supported by one or more documentation manuals. All programs should include internal documentation that defines what aspect of the program mission is being achieved by a particular program segment. The internal comments should not be used to restate the commands of the particular programming language. Such documentation is readily available.

3. *The program code should be readable.* Comments can be written in a variety of styles and may be interpreted differently by different individuals. On the other hand, a program code has well-defined interpretations. A program may be made more *readable* by assigning meaningful variable names. For example, in a program that computes interest on a bank deposit, use of the variable names PRINCIPAL, RATE, and TIME will tend to increase the readability of the program. A program serving an identical function could be written using unrelated variable names, such as X, BIRD, and CAT. This will seriously decrease the readability of a program. The portions of a program corresponding to separate subtasks should be clearly isolated. All *loops* should be clearly identified. Frequently, this is accomplished by indenting statements in a loop that are enclosed by another loop.

4. *Any long program should be developed in several independent segments. Each segment should be well documented. Such a program is said to be modular or well structured.* It is significantly easier to debug and maintain a program written as a collection of several small independent blocks than it is to debug or make changes in a long program. Furthermore, some of the program segments or blocks may be useful components of other, unrelated programs.

5. *Both the source code and the object code should be efficient.* This efficiency implies that neither the source code nor the resulting machine code should be excessively long. Furthermore, neither the compilation time (if a compiler is utilized) nor the typical program execution time should be excessive.

6. *Programs should be written in such a manner to facilitate program maintenance requirements.* In the program planning phase, some consideration should be given to the types of modifications or improvements that may eventually be required. Such planning may result in identification of some separate program blocks. In some cases, variables may be defined and used in place of constants. This may significantly decrease the necessary efforts required for program modifications or enhancements.

7. *In many cases, program transportability is highly desirable.* This attribute is especially applicable when long programs are developed. Use of standardized languages facilitates running programs on computers other than those on which they were developed. When developing programs that are not to be restricted to operation on a specific machine, programmers should be conscious of the transportability requirement. Use of architectural attributes of a particular machine should be avoided. A standard programming language, such as FORTRAN or COBOL, should be used. Use of enhancements of these languages

that are unique to a particular class of machines should be avoided. Even use of new statements in the latest version of an upward compatible standard language should be avoided unless such statements significantly facilitate program development.

8. *Any program should be developed, tested, and documented within a reasonable interval of time.* Perfect programs do not exist. In many commercial enterprises, it is more important to have a product available for use prior to a specified deadline than it is to continue to improve the product. Furthermore, improvements on a functioning program can be developed after the program is in use. However, the known practical limitations of a program should be clearly enumerated.

9. *A completed program should be easy to use.* Most programs are utilized by people who are neither electrical engineers nor computer science majors. Therefore, any actions required by a program user should be very clearly specified and relatively easy to implement.

Example 2.1

Refer to the following BASIC program:

```
100 REM PROGRAM FINDS INTEREST
110 READ X,Y
120 FOR I=1 TO 10
130 IF I>1 THEN 150
140 PRINT " 0        ",Y
150 Y=Y*(1+X)
160 PRINT I,Y
170 NEXT I
180 DATA .06,1000
190 END
```

Comment on the shortcomings of this program.

Solution   The purpose of the program is not well defined. The program is not well documented. No effort has been made to produce an easily readable program. As a result, changes or modifications of this program are not easy to implement. The program is certainly not easy to use in its present form. An improved version of this program is presented in Fig. 2.1.

Review

1. Refer to the BASIC program in Fig. 2.1. The readability of this program can be improved by using variable names PRINCIPAL, INTEREST RATE, and TIME instead of *P, I,* and *J*. Furthermore, several versions of BASIC, such as the IBM PC Advanced BASIC, will support such variable names. What is a disadvantage of using such descriptive variable names?

2. Refer to the program in Fig. 2.1. Perform the necessary modifications (or program maintenance) so that the value of interest rate may be entered as a percent value rather than as a decimal number.

```
100 REM   ******************************************************************
110 REM         THIS PROGRAM COMPUTES AN ANNUAL BALANCE.
120 REM   SUPPOSE A FIXED PRINCIPAL IS DEPOSITED IN AN ACCOUNT.
130 REM     THIS BALANCE ACCRUES INTEREST AT A FIXED ANNUAL RATE.
140 REM     THIS PROGRAM WILL FIND THE ANNUAL BALANCE FOR THIS PRINCIPAL
150 REM     THAT IS DEPOSITED AT THE SPECIFIED INTEREST RATE.  THE
160 REM     INTEREST IS COMPOUNDED ANNUALLY.
170 REM
180 REM******************************************************************
190 REM                    VARIABLE NAMES
200 REM         I              INTEREST RATE EXPRESSED AS A DECIMAL
210 REM         P              PRINCIPAL EXPRESSED IN DOLLARS
220 REM         N              THE NUMBER OF YEARS FOR WHICH AN OUTPUT
230 REM                        IS DESIRED.
240 REM ######## BEGIN   "ENTER-DATA" SEGMENT" ####################
250 PRINT " ENTER THE NUMBER OF DOLLARS DEPOSITED"
260 INPUT P
270 PRINT
280 PRINT " ENTER THE INTEREST RATE AS A DECIMAL NUMBER"
290 INPUT I
300 PRINT
310 PRINT  "  ENTER THE TOTAL NUMBER OF YEARS"
320 INPUT N
330 PRINT
340 PRINT
350 REM  ####### END ENTER-DATA SEGMENT ############################
360 REM  $$$$$$$$$$$$$$$ START COMPUTE SEGMENT $$$$$$$$$$$$$$$$$$$$$$$$
370 I1= 100*I
380 PRINT  " YOUR DEPOSIT IS",P
390 PRINT  " THE INTEREST RATE IS ";I1;"% COMPOUNDED ANNUALLY."
400 PRINT
410 PRINT
420 PRINT " ELAPSED TIME        "; "       CURRENT BALANCE"
430 PRINT
440 PRINT " 0                  " ,P
450               FOR J=1 TO N
460               P=P*(I+1)
470               PRINT J,P
480               NEXT J
490 REM $$$$$$$$$$$$$ END OF COMPUTE SEGMENT $$$$$$$$$$$$$$$$$$$$$$$$$
500 REM   ---------- BEGIN TERMINATE SECTION -------------------
510 PRINT
520 PRINT " WOULD YOU LIKE TO TRY ANOTHER CASE???"
530 INPUT A$
540 IF A$="YES" THEN 250
550 REM  ---------- END TERMINATE SECTION -------------------
560 END
```

Figure 2.1   An improved program for Example 2.1

3. Refer to the program in Fig. 2.1. Modify the program so that the current year may be entered. Then make modifications so that the actual year and the corresponding balance are printed for each of the specified number of years.

2.2 ILLUSTRATIVE PROGRAMS

In order to illustrate the concepts presented in Section 2.1, certain illustrative programs will be presented. These are given in three programming languages: BASIC, FORTRAN, and Pascal. Even though you may not be familiar with these languages, the *readability* attribute of each of these programs should assist you in following the flow of the programs.

The programs presented in this section are *sorting* programs. A modified *bubble sort* algorithm is utilized. The sorting algorithm that is employed may be used for character strings as well as for numbers. Sorting a set of character strings into ascending order is equivalent to alphabetizing the words represented by these character strings.

Suppose you wish to sort a set of numbers or a set of words. The following procedure may be used. Suppose there are *N* numbers or strings. Refer to these elements as STRING(1), STRING(2), . . . , STRING(N).

1. Set a FLAG or a KEYWORD to "NOT SORTED."
2. Set a limiting number, NUM, to 1 less than the number of strings to be sorted.
3. If the value of FLAG is "SORTED," exit from the sorting procedure.
4. Set the value of FLAG to "SORTED."
5. Set an index variable *I* to a value of 1.
6. IF STRING(I) has a larger value (or alphabetically follows) STRING(I + 1), then
   a. SWITCH or exchange positions of the two strings.
   b. Set the value of FLAG to "NOT SORTED."
7. Add 1 to the value of *I* (proceed to next string).
8. If *I* is not greater than NUM, go to statement 6.
9. Subtract 1 from the value of NUM.
10. If NUM = 0 (no more cases), exit from the sorting procedure. Otherwise, go to statement 3.

Examination of the above algorithm shows that the elements are always compared two at a time. By the time step 9 is executed for the first time, the largest element, or the one that will be last on an alphabetized list, will be placed in a position identified by the highest subscript or index number. There is no need to do any other comparisons with this string. Consequently, the number of elements still to be sorted has been reduced by 1. Suppose at some intermediate stage in the sorting process that the entire set of elements is properly sorted. Then the algorithm will proceed from step 4 to step 8 without any switches or exchanges being made. The sorting procedure will then either terminate at step 10 or proceed to step 3 and then terminate.

Example 2.2

Consider a set of character strings in which each string consists of eight characters (for example, a set of names in which each name is eight letters long). Write a program that
(a) Reads the names from a file called CLASSROLL.
(b) Prints the names.

```
100 REM    THIS PROGRAM READS A SET OF CHARACTER STRINGS FROM A FILE CALLED
110 REM       CLASSROLL.  THE STRINGS ARE PRINTED.  THEN THE STRINGS ARE
120 REM       ARRANGED IN ALPHABETICAL ORDER AND ARE PRINTED AGAIN.  THE NUMBER
130 REM       OF STRINGS IS LIMITED TO 100.  THE LIST OF STRINGS IN CLASSROLL IS
140 REM       TERMINATED WITH THE SYMBOLS, "$$$$$$$$$"
160 REM    #########   START MAIN PROGRAM   ##############################
170 DIM A$(100)
180 OPEN CLASSROLL FOR INPUT AS FILE 1
185 REM               READ STRINGS FROM FILE CLASSROLL
190 GOSUB 250
195 REM             PRINT UNSORTED STRINGS
200 GOSUB 310
205 REM             SORT STRINGS IN ALPHABETICAL ORDER
210 GOSUB 350
220 PRINT
225 PRINT "               SORTED STRINGS               "
226 PRINT
227 REM             PRINT SORTED STRINGS
230 GOSUB 310
240 STOP
245 REM #########   END MAIN PROGRAM   ##############################
246 REM $$$$$$$$$ START READ-CLASSROLL ROUTINE $$$$$$$$$$$$$$$$$$$$$$$$$$$$$$
250 I=0
260 INPUT FROM 1: B$
270 IF B$ = "$$$$$$$$$" THEN RETURN
280 I = I + 1
290 A$(I) = B$
300 GO TO 260
305 REM $$$$$$$$$$$$ END READ-CLASSROLL ROUTINE $$$$$$$$$$$$$$$$$$$$$$$$$$$$$
306 REM %%%%%%%%%%% START PRINT-ARRAY ROUTINE %%%%%%%%%%%%%%%%%%%%%%%%%%%%
310 FOR J=1 TO I
320    PRINT A$(J)
330 NEXT J
331 RETURN
335 REM %%%%%%%%%% END PRINT-ARRAY ROUTINE %%%%%%%%%%%%%%%%%%%%%%%%%%%%%%
345 REM &&&&&&&&&&& START SORTING ROUTINE &&&&&&&&&&&&&&&&&&&&&&&&&&&&&&
350 N=I-1
360 F$= "NOTDONE"
370     IF F$ = "DONE" THEN RETURN
380        F$ = "DONE"
390           FOR K=1 TO N
400              IF A$(K)>A$(K+1) THEN GOSUB 450
410           NEXT K
420        N = N - 1
430        IF N = 0 THEN RETURN
440        GOTO 370
445 REM &&&&&&&&&&&&& END SORTING ROUTINE &&&&&&&&&&&&&&&&&&&&&&&&&&&&&
446 REM *********** START SWITCH-STRING ROUTINE *********************
450 B$ = A$(K)
460 A$(K) = A$(K+1)
470 A$(K+1) = B$
480 F$ = "NOTDONE"
490 RETURN
495 REM ************ END SWITCH-STRING ROUTINE *********************
500 END
```

Figure 2.2   A solution to Example 2.2 using BASIC

(c) Alphabetizes the names.

(d) Prints the alphabetized list of names.

Solution   A BASIC program satisfying the above requirements is given in Fig. 2.2. A corresponding FORTRAN program is given in Fig. 2.3, and a corresponding Pascal program is given in Fig. 2.4. The attributes of these programs are discussed below.

Refer to the BASIC program in Fig. 2.2. This program possesses several of the attributes suggested in Section 2.1: The purpose of the program is stated, and documenting statements are included. Also, attempts have been made to provide a reasonable degree of readability. However, due to the limitations of most versions of the BASIC language, it is difficult to choose meaningful variable names.

The program has been divided into relatively simple segments. Separate segments or subroutines have been provided to read the names from a file into an array, to print the names in an array, and to sort or alphabetize the names in the array. An additional subroutine is provided to "off-load" the sorting routine. The SWITCH-STRING routine exchanges the position of two adjacent names whenever it is invoked by the sorting routine.

Although this program is developed in well-defined segments that satisfy specific requirements, the segments are *not independent*. Variable names and line numbers used within each segment are not unique to that particular segment. This is another limitation to the use of BASIC.

No consideration was given to developing this program in such a manner as to facilitate future program modifications. However, the fact that the program is written in short, well-defined segments tends to support future maintenance requirements. In developing this program, attempts were made to use "standard" BASIC statements. However, the transportability of BASIC programs is not particularly good. Program commands such as those given in lines 180 and 260 are not unique on different implementations of this language. In fact, some older implementations of BASIC will not permit standard assignment statements such as $X = 1$. These versions require a "LET" prefix with each assignment statement.

The FORTRAN program in Fig. 2.3 is structured in a manner similar to the corresponding BASIC program. Observe in both programs that the *main program* serves primarily to call or direct the working routines. Use of FORTRAN enables more meaningful names to be assigned both to the subroutines and to the variables used within these subroutines. The subroutines shown in Fig. 2.3 are *independent* modules. Variable names and statement numbers refer only to quantities within a subroutine. The same variable names and statement numbers may be used in other subprograms, as well as in the main program. Thus, once a subroutine is written and tested, it should serve as a reliable component of a larger system or program. In many cases, individual subroutines are written and *compiled* or translated into *object code*. Then the various subroutines are linked with the main program before it is executed.

The FORTRAN IV programming language does not possess string variables (such as A$) like those illustrated in the BASIC program. Handling strings in FORTRAN is somewhat more tedious. Generally four characters are contained in a single word, so an eight-character string involves the use of two words. When this FORTRAN program was developed, it was anticipated that future modifications might be required. In order to implement these modifications easily, a variable NSIZE was utilized and assigned a value of 2. The strings utilized in this program

```
*     THIS PROGRAM READS A SET OF CHARACTER STRINGS FROM A FILE CALLED
*      CLASSROLL.  THE STRINGS ARE PRINTED.  THEN THE STRINGS ARE
*      ARRANGED IN ALPHABETICAL ORDER AND ARE PRINTED AGAIN.  THE NUMBER
*      OF STRINGS IS LIMITED TO 100.  THE LIST OF STRINGS IN CLASSROLL IS
*      TERMINATED WITH THE SYMBOLS, "$$$$$$$$$"
      DIMENSION NAMES (100,8)
*     SET SIZE OF STRING I
      NSIZE = 2
      CALL GETDAT (NAMES,NUMBER,NSIZE)
      CALL PNTDAT (NAMES,NUMBER,NSIZE)
      CALL SORT (NAMES,NUMBER,NSIZE)
      WRITE(6,99)
99    FORMAT(//,'         SORTED STRINGS',/)
      CALL PNTDAT(NAMES,NUMBER,NSIZE)
      STOP
      END
* *****************************************************************
      SUBROUTINE GETDAT(N1,NUM,NSIZE)
      DIMENSION N1(100,8)
      DATA NTERM/4H$$$$/
* READ IN DATA ON UNIT 10. (ASSIGN CLASSROLL TO UNIT 10)
      I=1
99    READ(10,98) (N1(I,J),J=1,NSIZE)
98    FORMAT (8A4)
      IF (AND(N1(I,1),N1(I,2)).EQ.NTERM) RETURN
      NUM = I
      I=I+1
      GO TO 99
      END
* *****************************************************************
      SUBROUTINE PNTDAT(N1,NUM,NSIZE)
      DIMENSION N1(100,8)
      WRITE (6,98)
98    FORMAT(/)
        DO 99 I=1,NUM
99      WRITE (6,97) (N1(I,J),J=1,NSIZE)
97    FORMAT (10X,8A4)
      RETURN
      END
* *****************************************************************
      SUBROUTINE SORT(N1,NUM,NSIZE)
      DIMENSION N1(100,8)
      N=NUM-1
      IFLAG=1
97    IF(IFLAG.EQ.0) RETURN
      IFLAG=0
      DO 99 K=1,N
      J=1
98    IF(N1(K,J).GT.N1(K+1,J)) CALL SWITCH(N1,K,NSIZE,IFLAG)
      IF(N1(K,J).LT.N1(K+1,J)) GO TO 99
      J=J+1
      IF(J.GT.NSIZE) GO TO 99
      GO TO 98
99    CONTINUE
      N=N-1
      IF (N.EQ.0) RETURN
      GO TO 97
      END
* *****************************************************************
      SUBROUTINE SWITCH(N1,I,N,IFLAG)
      DIMENSION N1(100,8)
      DO 99 J=1,N
      ITEMP = N1(I,J)
      N1(I,J) = N1(I+1,J)
99    N1(I+1,J) = ITEMP
      IFLAG = 1
      RETURN
      END
```

Figure 2.3   A solution to Example 2.2 using FORTRAN

```
(*** THIS PROGRAM READS, SORTS AND PRINTS A SET OF
       CHARACTER STRINGS COMPOSED OF 8 LETTERS IN EACH STRING *)
PROGRAM SORT_NAMES (INPUT,OUTPUT,CLASSROLL);
TYPE NAMES = PACKED ARRAY[1..8] OF CHAR;
     LIST = ARRAY[1..100] OF NAMES;
     STATUS = PACKED ARRAY[1..2] OF CHAR;
VAR      N:INTEGER;
         CLASS: LIST;
         CLASSROLL: TEXT;
(*-----------------  PROCEDURES  ------------------------*)
PROCEDURE READ_NAMES(VAR NUMBER_OF_NAMES: INTEGER;
                     VAR CLASSLIST: LIST);
VAR  I,J:  INTEGER;
     NAME:  NAMES;
     TERMINATOR_TEST: PACKED ARRAY[1..8] OF CHAR;
BEGIN
       J:=1;           NUMBER_OF_NAMES:=0;
          WHILE NOT EOF(CLASSROLL) DO
               BEGIN
          FOR I:=1 TO 8 DO READ(CLASSROLL,NAME[I]);
          READLN(CLASSROLL);
          FOR I:= 1 TO 8 DO TERMINATOR_TEST[I]:=NAME[I];
          IF TERMINATOR_TEST<>'$$$$$$$$' THEN BEGIN
                             NUMBER_OF_NAMES:=NUMBER_OF_NAMES+1;
                             CLASSLIST[J]:=NAME;
                             J:= J+1;
                                           END;
               END;
END;
(***********************************************************)
PROCEDURE WRITE_NAMES(VAR NUMBER_OF_NAMES:  INTEGER;
                     VAR CLASSLIST: LIST);
VAR  I:  INTEGER;
  BEGIN
          WRITELN;
              FOR I:=1 TO NUMBER_OF_NAMES DO
                  WRITELN('          ',CLASSLIST[I]);
END;
(***********************************************************)
PROCEDURE SWITCH_NAMES(I:INTEGER; VAR CLASSLIST: LIST;
                       VAR SWITCH_FLAG: STATUS);
VAR TEMP: NAMES;
      BEGIN
          SWITCH_FLAG := 'UP';
          TEMP:=CLASSLIST[I];
          CLASSLIST[I]:=CLASSLIST[I+1];
          CLASSLIST[I+1]:=TEMP;
    END;
(***********************************************************)
PROCEDURE ALPHABETIZE_NAMES(VAR NUMBER_OF_NAMES: INTEGER;
                     VAR CLASSLIST: LIST);
VAR I,N:  INTEGER;
   FLAG: STATUS;
   BEGIN
   N:= NUMBER_OF_NAMES - 1;
   FLAG := 'UP';
   REPEAT
        FLAG := 'DN';
        FOR I:= 1 TO N DO
                IF CLASSLIST[I]>CLASSLIST[I+1] THEN
                     SWITCH_NAMES(I,CLASSLIST,FLAG);
        N := N-1;
   UNTIL (N=0) OR (FLAG='DN');
END;
(***********************************************************)
(***********  END PROCEDURES     ***************************)
```

Figure 2.4   A solution to Example 2.2 using Pascal

```
(*$$$$$$$$$$$$$$ START MAIN PROGRAM $$$$$$$$$$$$$$$$$$$$$$$$$$$$*)
BEGIN
        RESET (CLASSROLL);
        READ_NAMES(N,CLASS);
        WRITE_NAMES(N,CLASS);
        ALPHABETIZE_NAMES (N,CLASS);
        WRITELN;
        WRITELN('          SORTED LIST OF NAMES');
        WRITE_NAMES(N,CLASS);
END.
```

Figure 2.4   (*cont.*)

have an NSIZE, or two-word, attribute. In order to enlarge the size of the character strings, only the value of NSIZE needs to be changed.

The Pascal solution in Fig. 2.4 is quite similar to the FORTRAN solution. However, this program is probably easier to read and to comprehend. Variable names and procedure names can be significantly longer. Thus, they can be selected to be more descriptive. All procedures and variables must be explicitly identified or *declared* before they are used. Therefore, a reader who reads from top to bottom and from left to right will encounter variable names and procedure names before they are actually used in a program execution statement.

The Pascal procedures, like the FORTRAN subroutines, are independent *blocks* or modules. The function or purpose of the *main program* is merely to invoke or direct these procedures. Observe the format of the main program in Fig. 2.4. The major program statements given in this program are very similar to the four statements in the description of task requirements given in Example 2.2.

Example 2.3

Refer to the task requirements given in Example 2.2. Suppose the input file CLASS-ROLL is to be changed to a file of names in which each name contains 16 characters. Modify each of the solution programs so they will handle these new strings. The file terminator is still the string $$$$$$$$.

Solution   The BASIC program requires no modification. The FORTRAN program merely requires that the value of NSIZE be changed to 4. The Pascal program requires that the size of the packed arrays be changed from 8 to 16. Thus the number 8 in line 4 of the program and the number 8 in line 10 of PROCEDURE READ_NAMES should each be changed to 16. In addition, at least eight characters should be appended to the terminating string in the file CLASSROLL.

Review

1. Refer to the ten-step sorting algorithm described at the beginning of this section. For certain arrays of elements, this algorithm will terminate execution at step 10.
   (a) What characteristics must the array of elements possess in order for termination to occur at step 10?
   (b) Under what conditions will the algorithm execute the loop between steps 4 and 8 just once?

2. Refer to the FORTRAN solution to Example 2.2. Suppose only the value of NSIZE is to be changed.
   (a) How large can a set of strings be in order to be sorted by this program?
   (b) How long can each of these strings be?
3. Refer to the Pascal sorting routine in Fig. 2.4.
   (a) Suppose this routine has been modified to sort strings containing 16 characters. Why is it necessary to append at least eight characters to the eight-character terminating string?
   (b) What must these characters be?
4. Modify the three sorting programs so that they will perform the following functions:
   (a) The BASIC program is to sort a set of 200 nonnegative numbers in ascending order.
   (b) The FORTRAN program is to sort a set of 50 nonnegative integers in ascending order.
   (c) The Pascal program is to sort a set of 100 positive integers in descending order.

2.3 FLOWCHARTING

A *flowchart* is a symbolic representation of the sequencing or flow of a set of simple instructions. Flowcharts are generally used to describe the sequencing of a computer program. Standard symbols are utilized for specific functions within a flowchart. Some commonly used symbols are illustrated in Fig. 2.5.

A flowchart should be a general representation of a particular task. It should be clear and easy to follow. The text within the flowchart should be relatively simple, closely related to the task to be performed, and generally independent of the syntax of any particular programming language. The development of the final version of a flowchart may involve a higher level of abstraction than the development of the corresponding program. In this sense, it may appear that development of flowcharts is a very formidable task. In fact, novice programmers frequently complain that they cannot develop a flowchart until after the corresponding program has been written.

It is essential that the specifications and limitations of a particular task be thoroughly understood before a computer code related to this task is developed. Use of flowcharting is beneficial in precisely defining the particular task. One should not expect to develop a complete and final version of a flowchart on the first attempt. Several refinements may be required before a flowchart that adequately identifies the programming tasks is completed. However, expenditure of such efforts is quite necessary. We cannot expect to develop a program related to the solution of a complex task unless we can first clearly define the task.

Although use of flowcharting techniques is extremely valuable for program development, certain limitations and difficulties are involved in the formulation of flowcharts. General statement blocks are used in flowcharting to represent simple or nonlooping program tasks. Similarly, subroutine blocks are used to represent well-defined independent tasks that can be performed by independent procedures. It is often difficult to describe adequately such tasks within the confines of the

Symbol   Function

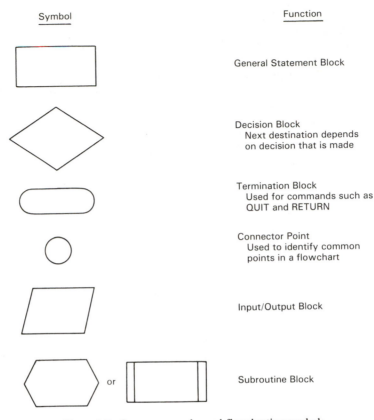

General Statement Block

Decision Block
   Next destination depends
   on decision that is made

Termination Block
   Used for commands such as
   QUIT and RETURN

Connector Point
   Used to identify common
   points in a flowchart

Input/Output Block

or   Subroutine Block

Figure 2.5   Some commonly used flowcharting symbols

standard sized blocks. Decision blocks are essential to most flowcharts. Very simple questions must be posed within these blocks, and program flow depends on a simple yes–no or true–false response to these questions. Again, it is sometimes difficult to formulate such questions precisely, especially with the additional restriction that such statements should be independent of any particular programming language.

Furthermore, branching capabilities used in modern programming languages are considerably more sophisticated than the binary-type branching options represented by decision blocks. For example, "computed GO TO" statements enable program control to branch to any location in a specified set of destination addresses. On standard flowcharts, such a simple operation is often represented as a sequence of binary branches.

Flowcharting is not the only tool used in developing and documenting software. Use of *structured programming* techniques also facilitates program development. Refinement of programming tasks using small sequences of simple statements is referred to as use of *pseudo code,* which can be of considerable value during the various phases of program development. Illustrations of these concepts are introduced in Section 2.4.

Although use of flowcharts certainly has its limitations, such structures are valuable to a programmer. Properly developed flowcharts can serve as excellent program documentation. They are both compact and relatively easy to read. An experienced programmer can easily convert a flowchart to efficient code, regardless of the programming language selected. A less experienced programmer may attempt to convert each block of a flowchart to a corresponding statement or to a sequence of statements. Such one-to-one translations may be very inefficient. This process is analogous to attempting to translate from one natural language to another by utilizing one-to-one word mappings.

Use of flowcharts may be very convenient in program planning or even in allocating tasks for a major project. Such flowcharts may be imperfect and may not serve as suitable program documentation. They may not even adequately satisfy the definition of flowcharts, as defined by computer science purists. However, programmers should not hesitate to use such programming aids if they are useful in initial program planning.

Example 2.4

Suppose you wish to alphabetize a set of N character strings. Formulate an appropriate flowchart.

Solution   The flowchart developed will depend on the sorting algorithm utilized. For this example, a modified bubble sorting algorithm is utilized. A solution is shown in Fig. 2.6. The flowchart was formulated by following the sequence of operations described at the beginning of Section 2.2.

Example 2.5

Suppose a file contains N names or character strings. A program is to be developed that searches the file for a particular name. If the name is found in the alphabetized list of names, an appropriate identifying index is to be returned. Formulate an appropriate flowchart related to this program requirement.

Solution   A flowchart satisfying these specifications is given in Fig. 2.7. Formulation of this flowchart did not follow directly from the statement of the problem. Several intermediate steps were involved. Discussion related to these intermediate steps is presented in the next section of this chapter.

Review

1. Refer to the following FORTRAN statement:

```
GO TO (10,20,30,40,50) NEXT
```

Formulate a flowchart representing program flow corresponding to this statement.

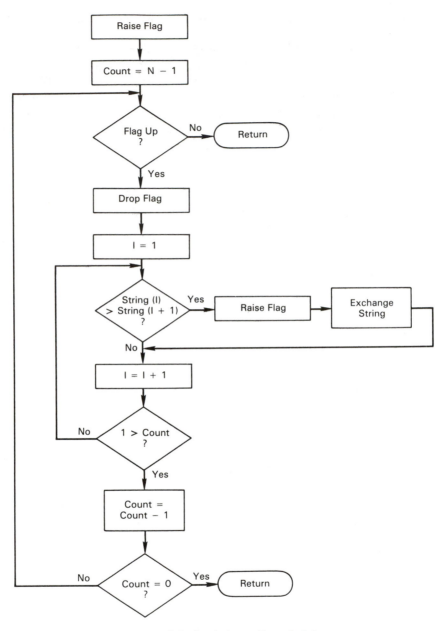

Figure 2.6   A solution to Example 2.4

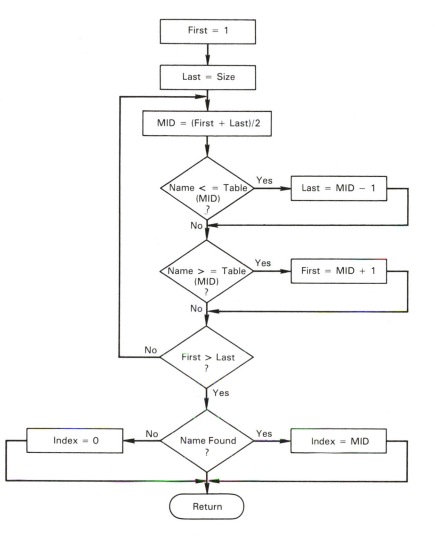

Figure 2.7   A solution to Example 2.5

2. In Fig. 2.7, refer to the decision block containing the statement "NAME FOUND?" In order for the answer to this question to be yes, what must be the value of the variable FIRST?

The following list of names refers to Review questions 3 and 4:

```
TURKEY,THANKSGIV
RABBIT,EASTER...
DOG,HOT.........
CATFISH,SLIMY...
CAT,SYLVESTER...
TUNA,CHARLIE....
```

3. Suppose this list of strings is sorted by the algorithm given in Fig. 2.6.
   (a) What is the value of COUNT?
   (b) How many times will strings be exchanged during the first pass through the inner loop?
   (c) How many string exchanges will be made during execution of the entire program?
4. Suppose the array of names given above has been alphabetized and placed in an array called TABLE. Refer to Fig. 2.7 and to the decision block containing the statement "FIRST>LAST?" During execution of the corresponding program, how many times will the "no" branch be taken for each of the following values of NAME?
   (a) CAT,SYLVESTER...
   (b) DOG,HOT.........
   (c) HORSE, HERMAN....

2.4 STRUCTURED PROGRAMMING

Concepts related to efficient program development were suggested and illustrated in Section 2.1. In particular, it was suggested that programs be written in well-defined *independent* modules or blocks. A *working routine* or a simple module may consist of a program code that performs just one simple task. Other program blocks may incorporate several working routines to perform more difficult tasks. A main program may invoke just a few blocks or routines. Each routine is responsible for a major independent function. A typical *main program* may have a structure such as indicated by the flowchart in Fig. 2.8.

The executable program code developed may be very similar to the blocks in the flowchart. For example, in Fig. 2.8, the executable statements correspond to

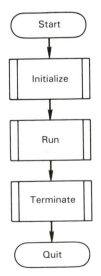

Figure 2.8 A flowchart for a typical main program

just three subroutine calls. The remainder of the main program will consist of declaration and related "typing" statements, space reserving statements, variable initiation statements, and similar nonexecutable statements.

Clearly, the major programming task consists of developing the subroutines INITIALIZE, RUN, and TERMINATE. Each of these routines may represent long and tedious sequences of operations. Similarly, these routines are subdivided into major categories, and specific jobs are assigned to lower-level routines. If possible, these lower-level routines should relate to *independent tasks*. Subordinate routines may be used in performing these tasks, but use of routines on a higher or equal level should generally be avoided. Of course, exceptions to this policy exist.

One way to develop such *structured programs* is to use a *top-down, bottom-up* approach. First it is necessary that all the requirements of the task to be performed are thoroughly understood. Then the general program tasks should be enumerated using, if possible, a set of simple declarative sentences. This set should be limited in size. Frequently, the size of the set is limited to some small number, such as five.

Each of the programming subtasks thus defined should be examined. If implementation of a particular subtask by use of appropriate programming code is obvious, then no further reinforcement of that statement is necessary. Otherwise, the particular task corresponding to a statement should be further refined. That is, a small set of declarative statements should be written describing the subtasks related to a particular task. Refinement should continue until each task can be related to a particular program segment. Such an approach is called a *top-down* approach to structured programming.

Programming code is often written in the inverse order. That is, once the low-level tasks are clearly defined, subroutines related to the implementation of these tasks are developed and tested. Then subroutines corresponding to higher-level jobs are developed using these working routines. Of course, as blocks at each level are written, they are tested and debugged before higher-level procedures are developed. Thus, the program code is actually written using a *bottom-up* approach.

Even if modern high-level languages are utilized, it is still sometimes difficult to convert a simple, well-defined task into a correct and reasonably efficient program code. As an intermediate step, a programmer may specify the task requirements as a combination of simple natural-language statements and the syntax of a particular programming language. Such sequences of statements are referred to as *pseudo code*. Use of pseudo code frequently serves as a valuable intermediate step in software development.

Concepts of structured programming are useful in the development of program code. However, they generally do not enable a programmer to avoid all difficulties in the formulation of a software package. For example, refer to the ten statements describing the tasks required for implementing a modified bubble sort routine that are given in Section 2.2. During a first pass at developing a sorting routine, a programmer may not specify the task requirements correctly. However, it is frequently easier to identify errors in programming logic from a set of written statements such as these than it is to identify such errors from the actual program code.

Example 2.6

Consider the following programming task. Determine if a particular name or character string is contained within the elements of a sequential file of alphabetized names. If so, identify an index number corresponding to the position of the name within the file. Assume that this program will be used to search for a significant number of names in a relatively large file.

Solution   Based on the program specifications, the desired program should perform the following tasks:
1. Read the file of names into an array of names.
2. Enter a particular name. We will search the array for this name.
3. Search to see if a particular name is in the file.
4. Identify the position of the name if the name is in the file.

The statements related to tasks 1, 2, and 4 probably do not require further refinement. Furthermore, task 1 needs to be performed only once for any given set of queries related to the file. Because the method of searching the array has not been specified, the statement related to task 3 should probably be further refined. One way of doing this is as follows:

```
3a)  INDEX = 1
3b)  IF NAME = ARRAY(INDEX) , EXIT ROUTINE
3c)  INDEX = INDEX + 1
3d)  IF NO MORE NAMES, SET INDEX = 0 AND EXIT
3e)  GO TO 3b
```

A flowchart corresponding to this set of steps is given in Fig. 2.9.

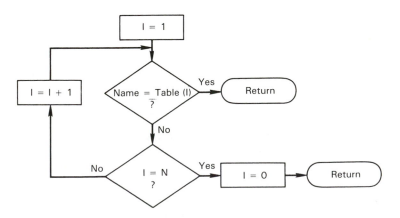

Figure 2.9 Searching a table for a name: linear search

The statements given above and the corresponding flowchart can be easily converted into a programming language code. Before this is done, let us consider the suitability of the search algorithm selected. Suppose the file to be searched contains 10,000 names. Then, to identify the location of any name in the table, an average of 5000 string comparisons would be required. If a name was selected that did not appear in the table, the above linear search would require that the full table be searched before it could be determined whether or not a name was present. The above linear search is suitable for searching an array of names that is not in alphabetical order. However, it is not a good algorithm for searching an alphabetized array.

A *binary* search algorithm is preferable. If such an algorithm is used, the search starts in the middle of the table. If the name is not found at the computed middle, then the search continues at either the lower quarter or the upper quarter of the table. The search continues until either the name is located or the remaining segment of the table can no longer be subdivided. This is illustrated by the following sequence of steps.

```
3a)  Let FIRST = 1 and LAST = N
3b)  Locate middle of table. ie. MID=(FIRST+LAST)/2
3c)  If (NAME >=TABLE(MID)) Let FIRST=MID+1
3d)  If (NAME <=TABLE(MID)) Let LAST= MID-1
3e)  If NOT DONE (ie. FIRST <=LAST) GO TO 3b
3f)  If NAME in Table, Set INDEX = MID and EXIT
3g)  If NAME not in Table, Set INDEX = 0 and EXIT
```

A flowchart corresponding to this sequence of statements is given in Fig. 2.7.

The binary search illustrated above is sometimes referred to as an *optimal* search. This method of searching a table is "optimal" only if some absurd assumptions are made about the contents of the array of names. It is quite easy to develop a better searching algorithm for practical situations. For instance, if the name to be checked for inclusion in the table begins with an *A* or a *B,* the search should start near the beginning of the table. If it starts with a *Z,* the search should start near the very end of the table. Typical frequencies of the first letters of various names can be used for determining an entry point into the table.

Review

1. Consider an alphabetized array of 64 names. The array is to be searched to see if a particular name is present. Actually, this name is not contained within the array.
   (a) How many string comparisons are necessary if a linear search is used?
   (b) How many string comparisons are necessary if a binary search is used?

2. Write a program segment in Pascal that uses a binary search to determine if a particular 16-character name is contained in an array of 16-character names.

3. Consider the following programming problem. Each of four different classes contains 32 individuals. An alphabetized list of each class is contained in the following files:

CLASS1, CLASS2, CLASS3, and CLASS4. Using structured programming concepts, formulate a plan for a program that merges these four files into one alphabetized file, TOTCLASS. Then form an appropriate flowchart. *Note:* Although an optimal solution is not required, try to develop a program plan that will not result in an excessive amount of string swapping.

REFERENCES

CHAPIN, N. *Flowcharts.* Princeton, N.J.: Auerbach, 1971.

HUGHES, J. K., and J. MICHTORN, *A Structured Approach to Programming.* Englewood Cliffs, N.J.: Prentice-Hall, 1977.

JERMANN, W. H., *The Structure and Programming of Microcomputers.* Palo Alto, Calif.: Mayfield, 1982.

MERCHANT, M. *FORTRAN 77 Language and Style.* Belmont, Calif.: Wadsworth, 1981.

MIRATECK, S. L., *BASIC,* 2nd ed. New York: Courant Institute of Mathematical Sciences, 1982.

SCHNEIDER, G. M., S. W. WEINGART, and D. M. PERLMAN, *An Introduction to Programming and Problem Solving with Pascal.* New York: John Wiley, 1978.

UNGER, E. A., and N. AHMED, *Computer Science Fundamentals.* Columbus, Ohio: Ch. E. Merrill, 1979.

YOURDON, E., *Techniques of Program Structure and Design.* Englewood Cliffs, N.J.: Prentice-Hall, 1976.

EXERCISES

1. List some of the attributes associated with a good computer program.
2. What is meant by a *block structured* program? What are the chief benefits of developing a program using independent modules or blocks?
3. Refer to Example 2.1. Develop and test a corresponding program written in FORTRAN.
4. Refer to Review question 3 in Section 2.1. Develop a corresponding program written in Pascal.
5. Refer to the sorting programs given in Section 2.2. Comment on the attributes associated with the BASIC, FORTRAN, and Pascal versions of this program.
6. Modify the BASIC version of this program so that an appropriate message is printed if any name appears more than once in the file CLASSROLL.
7. Refer to Exercise 6. Similarly modify the FORTRAN version of this program.
8. Refer to Exercise 6. Similarly modify the Pascal version of this program.
9. Develop a program plan for the following task:
   (a) Check to see if a particular name is in an alphabetized array of names.
   (b) If the name is present, output an appropriate message.
   (c) If the name is not present, insert the name in the proper place in the array.

10. Formulate a flowchart for the program plan developed in Exercise 9.

11. Implement the program plan developed in Exercise 9 using BASIC. Test your program.

12. Implement the program plan developed in Exercise 9 using FORTRAN. Use eight-character names. Test your program.

13. Implement the program plan developed in Exercise 9 using Pascal. Use 16-character names. Test your program.

14. Develop a program plan for the following tasks:
    (a) Read an alphabetized file of names into an array.
    (b) Enter a small array of names.
    (c) Check each name in the second array to see if it is also in the first array. If it is, delete the name from the first array.
    (d) Restore the updated file.

15. Formulate a flowchart for the program tasks described in Exercise 14.

16. Implement the program plan developed in Exercise 14 using BASIC. Test your program.

17. Implement the program plan developed in Exercise 14 using FORTRAN. Use eight-character names. Test your program.

18. Implement the program plan developed in Exercise 14 using Pascal. Use 16-character names. Test your program.

3

Fundamental Concepts

Virtually all computers are made from very elementary components. These components are essentially *two-state* or *binary* devices. Thus, use of the binary number system is convenient to describe or characterize the state of a set of binary components.

This textbook is primarily concerned with *16-bit machines*. Thus, the various states of the fundamental components of these machines can be related to 16-bit binary numbers. Binary numbers use just two characters, 0 and 1. It is very awkward for human beings to remember, process, and manipulate 16-character binary numbers. It is more convenient to use other numerical representations for these numbers. Traditionally, both the octal (base-8) and the hexadecimal (base-16) number systems have been used to represent sequences of binary numbers. In this textbook, the octal number system is used with the PDP-11 processor. The hexadecimal number system is used with both the 8086/88 microprocessor and the M68000 microprocessor. This is consistent with the documentation produced by the manufacturers of these devices.

Binary numbers are used not only to represent simple positive numbers. They are also used to represent instruction codes, signed integers, decimal numbers or floating points, and encoded elements of character strings. Even computer operations that are referred to as decimal operations are merely operations performed on binary sequences that are encoded to represent decimal numbers. Before we can appreciate the machine capabilities of any computers, including 16-bit machines, it is important that we thoroughly understand these fundamental concepts.

32

3.1 *REVIEW OF NUMBER SYSTEMS*

Consider the base-10 positive integer N. Suppose $N = 732$. We can say that the value of N is

$$N = 7 \text{ hundreds} + 3 \text{ tens} + 2 \text{ ones}$$

Expressed as a function of the base that is being used, we can say

$$N = 7 \times 10^2 + 3 \times 10^1 + 2 \times 10^0$$

Similarly, we can express the number $N = 732.415$ in the following manner:

$$732.415 = 7 \times 10^2 + 3 \times 10^1 + 2 \times 10^0 + \\ 4 \times 10^{-1} + 1 \times 10^{-2} + 5 \times 10^{-3}$$

Suppose we wish to generalize the manner in which we express base-10 numbers. Then the base-10 number N can be written as

$$N = C_j C_{j-1} C_{j-2} \ldots C_0 . C_{-1} C_{-2} \ldots C_k$$

where each C_i is an integer character having a value between 0 and 9. The value of N can then be expressed as

$$N = C_j \times 10^j + C_{j-1} \times 10^{j-1} + \ldots + C_0 \times 10^0 + C_{-1} \times 10^{-1} + C_{-2} \times \\ 10^{-2} + \ldots + C_{-k} \times 10^{-k}$$

Written more compactly

$$N_{10} = \sum_{i=-k}^{j} C_i \times 10^i$$

A quantity need not be expressed as a base-10 number. Indeed for some applications, it is practical to use a different base value, for these cases the use of a negative *base* or *radix* has been explored. In this textbook, however, only positive radix systems will be utilized.

Although any integer greater than 1 may be used as a base for specifying numbers, there are certain difficulties associated with using bases bigger than 10. The valid characters used in a particular system are nonnegative integers that are *smaller* than the base value. For bases larger than 10, standard symbols generally do not exist for such characters. In elementary school textbooks, the symbols T and E are frequently used in base-12 systems, T represents the number 10, and E represents the number 11. When the base-16, or *hexadecimal,* number system is utilized, the symbols *A, B, C, D, E,* and *F* are used to represent the numbers 10, 11, 12, 13, 14, and 15, respectively. In certain computer-related work, the base-64 number system is utilized. It would be inconvenient to designate special symbols to represent each integer between 10 and 63. In this situation, pairs of integers are used as if they were a single symbol.

In general, a number to the base B may be expressed in the following manner:

$$N_B = \sum_{i=-k}^{j} C_i B^i$$

where each C_i is an integer having a value within the range 0 to B $-$ 1.

Example 3.1

Convert each of the following numbers to the corresponding base-10 number:
(a) 010101110101_2 (binary)
(b) 2143_5 (base-5)
(c) 3.33_4 (base-4)
(d) 2565_8 (octal)
(e) 575_{16} (hexadecimal)
(f) $7AC.8_{16}$ (hexadecimal)
(g) 1.2_3 (base-3)

Solution (a) $0 \times 2^{11} + 1 \times 2^{10} + 0 \times 2^9 + 1 \times 2^8 + 0 \times 2^7 + 1 \times 2^6 + 1 \times 2^5 + 1 \times 2^4 + 0 \times 2^3 + 1 \times 2^2 + 0 \times 2^1 + 1 \times 2^0 = 1397$
(b) $2 \times 5^3 + 1 \times 5^2 + 4 \times 5^1 + 3 \times 5^0 = 298$
(c) $3 \times 4^0 + 3 \times 4^{-1} + 3 \times 4^{-2} = 3.9375$
(d) $2 \times 8^3 + 5 \times 8^2 + 6 \times 8^1 + 5 \times 8^0 = 1397$
(e) $5 \times 16^2 + 7 \times 16^1 + 5 \times 16^0 = 1397$
(f) $7 \times 16^2 + 10 \times 16^1 + 12 \times 16^0 + 8 \times 16^{-1} = 1964.5$
(g) $1.2_3 = 1.6666666 \ldots$

Note: Observe that just because a number may be expressible in terms of a small (or finite) set of characters in one number system, it does not necessarily follow that it can be expressed exactly using a finite set of characters in a different number system.

If one number system is an *integral* power of another number system, it is very easy to convert a number from one of these number systems to the other. For example, consider the following base-10 number:

$$N = 1234.56$$

If we wish to express this number as a number in the base-100 system, we can express it as follows:

$$N = \underline{12} \times 100^1 + \underline{34} \times 100^0 + \underline{56} \times 100^{-1}$$

Observe that the conversion was implemented merely by grouping the base-10 characters into pairs. This technique is especially useful for conversion of numbers between the binary number system and the octal number system, and for conversion of numbers between the binary number system and the hexadecimal number system.

This technique may be generalized as follows. Consider two bases, B1 and B2, where $B2 = B1^K$. Then a positive or unsigned number expressed in the base-B1 number system can be converted to the base-B2 number system by the following procedure:

1. Start at the radix point, expressed or implied.
2. Arrange the numbers to the right of the radix point into groups of size K. Trailing zeros may be added if necessary.
3. Arrange the numbers to the left of the radix point into groups of size K. Leading zeros may be inserted.
4. Replace each group of size K with the corresponding base-B2 character.

The inverse of this procedure is also very easy to implement.

Example 3.2

    (a) Convert 0111101.11011_2 to an octal number.
    (b) Convert 0111101.11011_2 to a hexadecimal number.
    (c) Convert $3F34.E_{16}$ to a binary number.
    (d) Convert 765.4_8 to a binary number.

    Solution   **(a)** Since $8 = 2^3$, the value of K is 3, and the binary digits will be grouped in sets of three. Grouping the numbers according to steps 1, 2, and 3 in the above algorithm results in the following representation of the number:

$$000 \quad 111 \quad 101 \quad . \quad 110 \quad 110_2$$

Using step 4, it is seen that the corresponding octal number is

$$0 \quad 7 \quad 5 \quad . \quad 6 \quad 6 \quad = \quad 075.66_8$$

    (b) $K = 4$. Therefore, $0111101.11011_2 = 0011 \quad 1101 \quad . \quad 1101 \quad 1000_2$
$$= \quad 3 \quad D \quad . \quad D \quad 8 = 3DD8_{16}.$$

    (c) $3F34.E_{16} = 0011 \quad 1111 \quad 0011 \quad 0100 \quad . \quad 1110_2$
$$= 011111100110100.111_2.$$

    (d) $111110101.1_2.$

The conversion of a base-B number to a base-10 number is straightforward. Likewise, conversion of numbers among the binary, octal, and hexadecimal number systems presents no difficulties.

It is slightly more involved to convert numbers from the base-10 number system to a base-B number system. This may be done by use of the following algorithm. Consider a positive or an unsigned integer. The following sequence of steps can be used to convert the base-10 number to a base-B number.

1. Divide the number N by the base B. Label the quotient Q and the remainder R.
2. Write the value of R directly above the last value of R that has been written. (*Note*: If no previous value of R has been written, write the value of R on the bottom of the page.)
3. If $Q = 0$, then EXIT from routine.

4. Let $N = Q$.
5. Go to step 1.

After this procedure has been completed, the values of R that have been written on the "STACK-type" structure correspond to the desired base-B number, with the most significant character on the top of the stack and the least significant character on the bottom of the stack. If the base value is greater than 10, it may be necessary to substitute appropriate base-B characters for the values stored on the stack.

Example 3.3

Convert the base-10 number 2220 to the corresponding numbers in each of the following number systems: **(a)** hexadecimal; **(b)** octal; **(c)** base-7.

Solution   **(a)** The required sequence of operations starts at step 1 in the following table:

Step Number	Operation	Q	R	Symbol
3	8/16	0	8	8
2	138/16	8	10	A
1	2220/16	138	12	C

Therefore, $2220_{10} = 8AC_{16}$.
(b) $8AC_{16} = 1000 \quad 1010 \quad 1100_2 = 100 \quad 010 \quad 101 \quad 100_2 = 4254_8$.
(c)

Step Number	Operation	Q	R	Symbol
4	6/7	0	6	6
3	45/7	6	3	3
2	317/7	45	2	2
1	2220/7	317	1	1

Therefore, $2220_{10} = 6321_7$.

Example 3.4

Write a computer program that accepts a base-10 number that is not greater than 99,999 and prints the corresponding hexadecimal number.

Solution   A corresponding Pascal program is given in Fig. 3.1.

The algorithm that we have used to convert base-10 numbers to base-B numbers involves division by the base B. Conceptually, each division by B shifts the corresponding base-B number one position to the right. The remainder corresponds to the base-B character that would be lost if only the quotient portion of each division operation is retained. Likewise, this remainder corresponds to the "current" least significant base-B character.

```
PROGRAM CONVERT_TO_HEX(INPUT,OUTPUT);
(* THIS PROGRAM CONVERTS A POSITIVE INTEGER TO THE CORRESPONDING
   HEXADECIMAL NUMBER.  EXIT FROM THE PROGRAM IF THE BASE-10
   NUMBER ENTERED IS LARGER THAN 99,999. *)
TYPE   HEX_CHAR = 1..15;
       STACK = ARRAY[1..6] OF CHAR;
VAR  NUMBER,I,BASE,COUNT,QUOTIENT,REMAINDER:  INTEGER;
     BUFFER: STACK;
     FLAG,FLAG1: BOOLEAN;
     X:   CHAR;
BEGIN
BASE := 16;
REPEAT
       FLAG := TRUE;
       READLN(NUMBER);
       IF (NUMBER>99999) THEN FLAG := FALSE;
       FLAG1:= FLAG;
       WHILE (FLAG1=TRUE) DO
          BEGIN
           FLAG1:=FALSE;
           WRITE(' THE HEX NUM FOR ',NUMBER:6,' IS ');
           COUNT:=0;
               REPEAT
                  COUNT:=COUNT+1;
                  QUOTIENT:= NUMBER DIV BASE;  REMAINDER:= NUMBER MOD BASE;
                  CASE REMAINDER OF
                     0:  X:='0'; 1: X:='1'; 2: X:='2'; 3: X:='3';
                     4:  X:='4'; 5: X:='5'; 6: X:='6'; 7: X:='7';
                     8:  X:='8'; 9: X:='9'; 10: X:='A'; 11: X:='B';
                     12: X:='C'; 13: X:='D'; 14: X:='E'; 15: X:='F';
                  END(*CASE*);
                  BUFFER[COUNT]:=X;
                  NUMBER := QUOTIENT;
               UNTIL (QUOTIENT=0);
               FOR I:= COUNT DOWNTO 1 DO WRITE(BUFFER[I]);
           WRITELN;
          END;
UNTIL (FLAG=FALSE)
END.
```

Figure 3.1   A solution to Example 3.4

Similarly, multiplying a base-B number by B corresponds to shifting the characters of the number one position to the left. This is useful for converting a base-10 number whose value is less than 1 to the corresponding base-B number. This is illustrated by the following algorithm. Consider a base-10 number whose value is less than 1. The following sequence of steps can be used to obtain the corresponding base-B number.

0. Let P be the desired precision of the number. *Note*: Precision consists of the number of meaningful characters to the right of the radix point.
1. Multiply the number N by the base B.
2. Let N be the number to the right of the decimal point and C be the number to the left of the decimal point of the above product.
3. Convert C to the corresponding base-B value and output this character.
4. If $N = 0$, then EXIT from routine.
5. Let $P = P - 1$. If $P = 0$, then EXIT from routine.
6. Go to step 1.

Consider the general case in which a base-10 number has characters to the left of the decimal point as well as to the right of the decimal point. This number can be expressed as two components, a whole component and a fractional component. The algorithm previously described can be used to convert the whole portion of the number to the corresponding base-B characters. Then the algorithm more recently described can be used to convert the base-10 fractional part to the corresponding base-B fractional part.

Example 3.5

Convert each of the following base-10 numbers to the correspondng hexadecimal numbers. Use a precision of four characters to the right of the radix point: **(a)** 174.8125; **(b)** 0.3.

Solution   **(a)** The whole part of the number is $174 = AE$. The following procedure is used to convert the fractional portion of the number to a base-16 number.

Step Number	Operation	C	N	Symbol
1	16×0.8125	13	0.0000	D

Therefore, $174.8125_{10} = AE.D_{16}$.

(b)

Step Number	Operation	C	N	Symbol
1	16×0.3	4	0.8	4
2	16×0.8	12	0.8	C
3	16×0.8	12	0.8	C
4	16×0.8	12	0.8	C

Therefore, $0.3_{10} \doteq 0.4CCC_{16}$.

Review

1. Convert the following numbers to base-10 numbers:
   (a) 183_9
   (b) $4AC.C_{16}$
   (c) 34.5_8
   (d) 011010.111_3
2. Convert the following numbers to the corresponding octal numbers:
   (a) 1101.0110101_2
   (b) $3A76.BAD_{16}$
3. Convert the following base-10 numbers to the corresponding octal numbers. Use a precision of four characters to the right of the radix point.
   (a) 1349
   (b) 7683.6
   (c) 0.13

4. Convert the following base-10 numbers to the corresponding hexadecimal numbers. Use a precision of four characters to the right of the radix point.
   (a) 37516
   (b) 41412.75
   (c) 0.147

5. Formulate a Pascal program segment that separates a real number into two components. One component is an integer corresponding to the "whole" portion of the number. The other component is a real number corresponding to the "fractional" component of the number.

3.2 OPERATIONS ON BINARY NUMBERS

The arithmetic and logic units of digital computers perform operations on signals that can be represented as binary numbers. It is relatively easy for humans to perform operations on binary characters because there are only two different values for such characters, 0 and 1. Usually, computers perform operations on groups of binary characters. Computers classified as 16-bit machines generally perform operations on groups of size 8, or 8-bit groups, and on groups of size 16, or 16-bit groups. The 8-bit binary numbers are referred to as *bytes*. The 16-bit binary numbers are frequently called *words*.

The addition tables for binary characters are much simpler than those used for base-10 characters. Suppose we wish to add two binary characters together. We can express this operation as

$$Z = X + Y$$

where Z, X, and Y can each have one of two possible values. In order to perform addition operations, two other pieces of information are required. It must be known whether or not there was a *carry* from addition of a less significant set of numbers. Furthermore, it must be recorded whether or not the present addition operation produces a *carry*. The tables defining addition of binary characters are given in Fig. 3.2.

Addition of single binary characters is seldom performed on digital computers, whereas addition of bytes and words is very frequently done. Furthermore, virtually all computers perform operations on just *two* operands. Suppose, for example, that the addition operation is being performed on bytes. This means that the source operands are both bytes or *8-bit* words. It also implies that the result must also be an 8-bit word. Clearly, there are cases in which the sum of two 8-bit words cannot be fully represented as another 8-bit word. That is, it may be necessary to propagate a carry bit out of the most significant bit of the result. In order that information not be lost, there must be an additional 1-bit storage space for the value that is propagated. Such a storage space is called a *carry bit* or a *carry flag*.

An electronic device that is capable of storing a voltage level corresponding to the value of a binary character is called a *flip-flop*. A group of flip-flops, or

PREVIOUS CARRY = 0

Inputs		Output	Carry
X	Y	Z	C
0	0	0	0
0	1	1	0
1	0	1	0
1	1	0	1

PREVIOUS CARRY = 1

Inputs		Output	Carry
X	Y	Z	C
0	0	1	0
0	1	0	1
1	0	0	1
1	1	1	1

Figure 3.2 Addition operation on binary characters

simple electronic storage cells, is referred to as a *register*. For byte operations, binary numbers are stored in 8-bit registers. For word operations, binary numbers are stored in 16-bit registers. The carry bit or carry flag is a 1-bit register. Generally, the carry bit is a *dynamic* register. That is, the value of the binary character stored in this register is only dependent on the most recently executed *arithmetic* or *logic* operation.

Example 3.6

Determine the sums generated and the value stored in the carry flag as the result of each of the following byte operations. *Note*: For convenience, the hexadecimal number system is used to represent the values of the 8-bit binary numbers.

(a) $8B + 13$
(b) $F3 + 2A$
(c) $83 + 94$

Solution   (a) Converting the numbers to their binary number representations, $8B + 13$ corresponds to the sum

$$10001011$$
$$+00010011$$

Using the table in Fig. 3.2 it is seen that the result is

$$10011110$$

Observe that there is no carry propagated out of the most significant bit. The result expressed as a hexadecimal number is $9E$, and the value in the carry bit is 0.

(b) The sum is $1D$, and the value in the carry bit is 1.

(c) The sum is the hexadecimal number 17, and the carry is 1. (That is, the value stored in the carry bit is 1.)

Example 3.7

Determine the sum and carry for each of the following *word* operations. The 16-bit words are expressed in the *octal* number system. Each word is represented by six octal characters. The first or most significant octal character can only have a value of 0 or 1.

(a) $012345_8 + 123456_8$

(b) $100345_8 + 100321_8$

Solution   (a) With the numbers represented in terms of their binary characters, the addition operation can be expressed as follows:

$$
\begin{array}{c c c c c c c}
  & 0 & 001 & 010 & 011 & 100 & 101 \\
+ & 1 & 010 & 011 & 100 & 101 & 110 \\
\hline
  & 1 & 011 & 110 & 000 & 010 & 011
\end{array}
$$

Thus, the sum is 136023_8 and the carry value is 0.

(b) The sum is 000666_8 and the carry value is 1.

Subtraction operations are performed by adding the *negative* value of a subtrahend to a minuend (this technique is defined in more detail in Section 3.3). Multiplication and division operations may be performed in the same manner as they are done in the base-10 number system. However, multiplication tables are much simpler because only values of 0 and 1 are utilized. These operations are illustrated in Section 7.2.

In addition to *arithmetic* operations, virtually all computers can perform certain *logic* operations. Most digital computers can perform the following logic operations on groups of binary numbers, such as *bytes* and *words*.

1. Complementation
2. OR operation
3. AND operation
4. EXCLUSIVE OR operation

The COMPLEMENT operation is a unitary operation. That is, only a single operand is involved. Each of the other three logic operations requires two operands. All of these logic operations are simpler than arithmetic operations. They just involve the corresponding bits in the operands and are not dependent on previous carry values.

The complement of a binary character is a 0 if the character has a value of 1, and it is a 1 if the value of the character is 0. The complement of a group of binary

OR OPERATION (SYMBOL — > +)

X	Y	Z = X + Y
0	0	0
0	1	1
1	0	1
1	1	1

AND OPERATION (SYMBOL — > •)

X	Y	Z = X • Y
0	0	0
0	1	0
1	0	0
1	1	1

EXCLUSIVE OR OPERATION (SYMBOL — > ⊕)

X	Y	Z = X ⊕ Y
0	0	0
0	1	1
1	0	1
1	1	0

Figure 3.3 Logic operations on binary characters

characters consists of the complements of each of the characters. Observe that the sum of an N-bit binary number and its complement is always an N-bit number whose bits are all 1s. The OR, AND, and EXCLUSIVE OR operations on binary characters are defined in Fig. 3.3. The corresponding operations on groups of binary numbers produce results obtained by performing the logic operations on the corresponding binary characters of the two operands.

Example 3.8

Two 16-bit binary numbers A and B are represented using the octal number system in the following manner.

$$A = 143625_8 \qquad B = 035427_8$$

(a) Find the complement of A (Sometimes this is represented as $\overline{A}$).
(b) Find C, where $C = A$ OR B.
(c) Find C, where $C = A$ AND B.
(d) Find C, where $C = A \oplus B$.

Solution (a) $A = 1$ 100 011 110 010 101

$\overline{A} = 0$ 011 100 001 101 010 $= 034152$

(b) A OR $B =>$ 1   100 011 110 010 101

OR 0   011 101 100 010 111

1   111 111 110 010 111 $= 177627_8$

(c) A AND $B =>$ 1   100 011 110 010 101

AND 0   011 101 100 010 111

0   000 001 100 010 101 $= 001425_8$

(d) $A \oplus B =>$ 1   100 011 110 010 101

$\oplus$ 0   011 101 100 010 111

1   111 110 010 000 010 $= 176202_8$

Novices frequently convert octal or hexadecimal numbers to the corresponding binary numbers and then perform the logic operations on the corresponding bits of the binary numbers. The results are then converted back to an octal or hexadecimal representation. Typically, programmers rapidly develop skills so that they can directly operate on octal or hexadecimal representations of the numbers and thus avoid the tedium of working with binary numbers.

Review

Consider the following set of 16-bit binary numbers:

$$P = AF32_{16} \qquad Q = 0123_{16} \qquad R = 43D4_{16}$$

$$X = 124367_8 \qquad Y = 064321_8 \qquad Z = 100263_8$$

1. Find each of the following sums. Also indicate the number in carry bit after the operation has been performed.
   (a) $P + Q$
   (b) $Q + R$
   (c) $X + Y$
   (d) $Z + Q$

2. Find the results of the following logic operations:
   (a) $\overline{Q}$ (Complement of Q)
   (b) $\overline{Y}$
   (c) Q OR R
   (d) X AND Z
   (e) $P \oplus Q$
   (f) $Y \oplus Z$

3. Find the results of the following arithmetic or logic operations:
   (a) $P + X$
   (b) Q OR Y
   (c) R AND Z
   (d) $P \oplus Z$

3.3 REPRESENTATION OF SIGNED INTEGERS

So far, we have been concerned only with the representation of *positive* numbers. Because we will soon define a representation for signed integers, it is more proper to refer to the numbers we have previously represented as *unsigned* numbers. A programmer may wish to perform operations on "pure" binary or unsigned numbers. However, we are frequently required to use *signed* numbers, in particular, *signed* integers. In noncomputer-related applications, we represent a negative number by prefixing the corresponding positive number with a *minus* sign. Numbers without such a prefix, or numbers with a plus sign as a prefix, are considered positive. Of course, it does not matter whether the number 0 is considered positive or negative. When representing numbers on computers, we use only binary representations, that is, only strings of zeros and ones are used. If we wish to use signed numbers, this information must be incorporated within the strings of binary characters.

Several methods have been used to represent binary characters. On modern 16-bit machines, there is just one popular method that is used. A negative number is defined as the *twos-complement* of the corresponding positive integer. Recall that logic complementation was defined in the previous section. Also recall that the sum of any N-bit number and its complement results in an N-bit number whose bits are all 1s. Now suppose a 1 is added to the least significant bit of this sum. The result is an N-bit word that contains all 0 bits. Furthermore, a 1 will be contained in the carry bit.

The complement of an N-character number in a base-B number system is an N-character number such that when this number is added to the original number, the N-character sum contains the character corresponding to B-1 in all of its positions. This complement is sometimes referred to as the *diminished radix complement*. In a base-10 system it is called the nines-complement. Similarly, in a base-16 system, it is referred to as the Fs-complement, and in a base-2 system as the ones-complement. By tradition, the diminished radix complement is called the ones-complement regardless of the number system utilized.

Consider an N-character number X. Suppose the N-character number Y is added to this number, where $Y = \overline{X} + 1$, or the complement (ones-complement) of X plus 1. This addition results in an N-character word in which all the characters are zeros. *Note:* Addition of 1 as represented above corresponds to adding a 1 character at the least significant bit position to the complement of X. If there is an implied radix point associated with the number, this character may not represent a true value of 1.

If $\overline{X}$ is the complement of X, then $Y = \overline{X} + 1$ is defined as the *radix complement* of the number X. In the base-10 number system, this is called the tens-complement. In a base-2 number system, it is referred to as the twos-complement. By tradition, this number is frequently referred to as the twos-complement regardless of the number system utilized. The addition of an N-character number to its twos-complement always results in an N-character number whose value is 0. Thus, the twos-complement of a number satisfies the definition of an *additive inverse* of the original number. Therefore, if X is a positive number, then a representation of $-X$ is

$$-X = \overline{X} + 1$$

If we are working with signed binary numbers, a positive integer is defined as a number whose most significant bit is a 0. The corresponding negative number is the twos-complement of the positive number. Similarly, it generally follows that if we are given a negative number, the corresponding positive number is the twos-complement of the negative number. Consistent with our previous discussions, leading zeros may be affixed to any positive integer. By the definition of twos-complement representation, it follows that leading ones may be affixed to negative integers without affecting their values. When leading characters are properly added to signed integers, these numbers are said to be *sign extended*.

Consider an 8-bit binary number. The smallest unsigned number that can be represented by an 8-bit word has a value of 0. The largest value that can be represented is $2^8 - 1$, or 255. If signed numbers are utilized, it follows that only 256 different numbers can be represented by an 8-bit word. Because a positive number must contain a 0 in its most significant bit, the largest possible positive number consists of a 0 followed by seven 1s. This is a representation of the base-10 number $2^7 - 1$, or 127. The number 0 is also considered *positive* because its most significant bit is a 0. Since 128 out of the possible 256 numbers that can be represented by an 8-bit number are positive, it follows that there are 128 possible negative numbers. These range in value from -1 to -128. In general, an N-bit number can be used to represent any integer within the range of -2^{N-1} to $+2^{N-1} - 1$.

Example 3.9

Consider each of the following 8-bit signed numbers. Refer to each of these numbers as X. Represent $-X$ as a 16-bit number. *Note*: The numbers are expressed in the hexadecimal number system.

(a) $6B$

(b) $D2$

Solution **(a)** $-6B = \overline{6B} + 1 = 94 + 1 = 95$. Sign-extending this number, $-X = FF95$.

(b) $-D2 = \overline{D2} + 1 = 2D + 1 = 2E$. Therefore, $-X = 002E$.

Example 3.10

Express each of the following signed integers as a base-10 integer. The numbers are expressed as hexadecimal numbers.

(a) $X = 7F$ (8-bit number)

(b) $X = FFF3$ (16-bit number)

(c) $X = 8$ (4-bit number)

Solution   (a) $7F$ is a positive number. Therefore, $X = 7 \times 16 + 15 \times 1 = 127_{10}$.

(b) This is a negative number. Therefore, $-X = \overline{FFF3} + 1 = 000C + 1$ $= 000D_{16}$. Therefore, $X = -13_{10}$.

(c) This is a negative number. Expressed as a binary number, $X = 1000$. Therefore, $-X = \overline{1000} + 1 = 0111 + 1 = 1000$. Observe that the twos-complement of this negative number is *not* a positive number.

In order to determine the value of X, let us perform an algebraic operation. We will choose an arbitrary number and add it to X. We select the number 3.

$$X + 3 => 1000 + 0011 = 1011 = Y$$

But Y is negative. Therefore, $-Y = \overline{1011} + 1 = 0100 + 1 = 0101$. Therefore, $Y = -5$. Because $X + 3 = -5$, it follows that $X = -8_{10}$. It should not surprise us that the 4-bit signed number corresponding to -8 does not have a corresponding positive number as its twos-complement. The largest possible number that can be represented by a signed 4-bit number is $2^3 - 1 = 7$.

Because we have defined a method of representing negative numbers, it is now easy to perform the subtraction operation. Frequently computers perform this operation by adding the twos-complement of the subtrahend to the minuend. For example, suppose we wish to perform the operation $7 - 3$ on a 16-bit computer. The number -3 is represented as the 16-bit number $FFFD$. Then the following 16-bit addition operation is performed:

$$
\begin{array}{r}
0007 \\
+\ \underline{FFFD} \\
0004
\end{array}
$$

Note that the carry bit will be set (will have a value of 1) as the result of this operation. A little more exploration will enable us to make the following conclusions related to the subtraction of N-bit numbers.

1. Addition of the twos-complement of the subtrahend to the minuend yields the correct signed result if the correct answer is expressible as an N-bit signed integer.
2. The carry flag will be set if the minuend is greater than or equal to the subtrahend. That is, the carry flag will be set if there is *no* borrow requirement.
3. The carry flag will be cleared if the subtrahend is larger than the minuend. That is, the carry flag is cleared or set to 0 if there *is* a borrow requirement.

Computers generally do not have a borrow flag. During subtraction operations, it would be convenient if the carry flag acted as a borrow flag. That is, it would be convenient if the carry flag were set when there is a borrow requirement and be cleared when there is no borrow requirement. This is just the opposite way in which the carry flag is affected. In order that the carry flag be in the desired state, most 16-bit computers perform the subtraction operation in a manner similar to the following sequence of steps:

1. Add the twos-complement of the subtrahend to the minuend.
2. Then complement the number in the carry bit.

Thus, a value of 1 in the carry bit indicates that a "borrow" is required.

Example 3.11

Refer to the following *signed* 8-bit numbers, expressed using the hexadecimal number system.

$$V = FC \qquad W = 82 \qquad X = 70 \qquad Y = 10 \qquad Z = 05$$

Find the 8-bit result for each of the following operations:
(a) $V + W$
(b) $X + Y$
(c) $W - Z$

Solution   (a) $V + W = FC + 82 = 7E$
               (b) $X + Y = 70 + 10 = 80$
               (c) $W - Z = W + \bar{Z} + 1 = 82 + FB = 7D$

These solutions appear to be straightforward, but let's inspect the results a little more closely. In part (a), we added together two negative numbers and obtained a positive result. In part (b), we added two positive numbers and obtained a negative answer. In part (c) we subtracted a positive number from a negative number and obtained a positive result. Clearly, none of our answers can be correct. The correct answers to each of the problems expressed as base-10 numbers are the following:

(a) $-4 + (-126) = -130$
(b) $112 + 16 = 128$
(c) $-126 - (+5) = -131$

The correct answers *cannot* be expressed as signed 8-bit numbers. Recall that the valid range for 8-bit signed integers is between -128 and $+127$.

The phenomenon illustrated in Example 3.11 is referred to as *overflow*. That is, when the result of an arithmetic operation is not expressible within the valid range of values, numerical overflow is said to occur. Such overflow can occur on any computer. In order that overflow can be readily detected, computers contain an overflow flag or a 1-bit overflow register. Like the carry bit, this is a dynamic flag. That is, each new arithmetic operation affects the state of this flag in a manner that is independent of the previous state of the flag.

Arithmetic operations on integers always produce a result that can be considered either positive or negative. (Recall that the representation of the number 0 is considered a positive number.) Computers have another 1-bit dynamic register referred to as the *sign bit* or *sign flag*. If the result of an arithmetic operation is negative, the sign bit is set. If the result is positive, the sign bit is cleared.

Example 3.12

Determine the state of the carry flag, the sign flag, and the overflow flag after each of the following operations is performed on a typical 16-bit computer. *Note:* All quantities are expressed as hexadecimal numbers.

(a) $F3 - 2A$

(b) $4B - 4B$

(c) $28 + AB$

Solution   (a) $F3 - \overline{2A} = F3 + 2A + 1 = F3 + DB = CE$.

Note: This portion of the subtraction operation leaves the carry flag set. Then the carry flag is complemented. Therefore, the sign flag is set, and the carry and overflags are cleared.

(b) $4B - 4B = 4B + \overline{4B} + 1 = 4B + B5 = 0$, and sets the carry flag. Then the carry flag is complemented. Thus, all three flags are cleared.

(c) The sign flag is set, and the carry and overflow flags are cleared.

Refer to part (b) in Example 3.12. The result of this operation is the number 0. Modern computers also contain a dynamic *zero flag*. This flag or bit is set if the result of the most recent arithmetic operation is zero, and cleared if the result is *not* a zero.

A programmer may wish to perform operations on unsigned numbers rather than on signed numbers. There is no difficulty doing this if the program is developed at the machine-language level. However, the sign flag and the overflow flag will be affected in a manner consistent with operations on the corresponding signed numbers.

Arithmetic operations are not the only type of computer operations affecting the contents of the dynamic status bits. Logic operations, as well as certain other commands, can affect the status of some or all of these flags. How such commands affect the status flags depends on the architecture of the particular computer being utilized.

Review

1. What is the range of the values of signed numbers that can be used for a computer that performs operations on
   (a) 4-bit words?
   (b) 32-bit words?

2. Find the twos-complement of each of the following 8-bit numbers. Express your answer as a 16-bit number using the hexadecimal number system.
   (a) 87_{16}
   (b) 25_{10}
   (c) 45_{16}
   (d) 325_8

3. The following 16-bit operations are performed on a 16-bit computer:

```
A)  FFFF  +  FFFE
B)  A000  +  6000
C)  12AB  -  7ABC
D)  A242  -  7000
E)  0000  -  0000
```

(*Note*: This operation generally will cause the carry flag to be cleared.)

```
F)  4A32  -  23A4
G)  23A4  -  4A32
```

(a) Which operations will raise the carry flag?
(b) Which operations will set the overflow flag?
(c) Which operations will clear the sign flag?
(d) Which operations will set the zero flag?
(e) Which operations produce erroneous results?

3.4 CHARACTERS AND STRINGS

In previous sections we indicated how sequences of binary numbers can be used to represent either unsigned numbers or signed integers. Other data types, such as *real numbers* or *floating points*, are also represented by sequences of binary characters. One very important data type used on computers is the *character*. Sequences of binary symbols are used to represent various characters. Generally, it is necessary to encode all or at least most of the characters found on a standard typewriter keyboard.

Use of sequences of binary symbols to represent characters is not new. Morse code is a very early application of such an encoding technique. However, Morse code does not represent a true binary code, as it uses not only dots and dashes but also requires delays or time intervals between transmission of each encoded character.

Two methods are commonly used for encoding characters for use with digital computers: the EBCDIC and the ASCII representations for characters. *EBCDIC* is an acronym for Extended Binary Coded Decimal Interchange Code. For a relatively long time it was commonly used to represent characters on IBM computers and other mainframe computers. However, today this code is generally not used with 16-bit machines and will not be discussed further in this textbook.

The acronym *ASCII* stands for American Standard Code for Information Interchange. There are several commonly used subsets of the full ASCII code. A table of 7-bit ASCII codes is given in Appendix A. Observe that the hexadecimal number system is used to specify the 7 bits corresponding to a particular character or symbol. It is convenient to represent a 7-bit ASCII code by using a pair of hexadecimal characters. Furthermore, the 7-bit ASCII representation of a particular symbol is generally stored in an 8-bit register segment. In such cases, the most significant bit of the character representation is unspecified, as it takes just 7 bits to encode the character. Frequently, we assume that the most significant bit of an encoded character stored in an 8-bit register segment is a 0. We should be cautious, however, because sometimes this is not a valid assumption.

Because the ASCII representation of a character requires just 7 bits, and in practice resides in a byte of storage space, two such characters may be stored in a single 16-bit word, and four such characters may be stored in a 32-bit word. In these cases, we say the characters are *packed*. Suppose several representations of characters are stored in consecutive bytes of computer memory. Such a data structure is referred to as a *packed array of characters*.

A packed array of characters is frequently referred to as a *string* or as a *character string*. In Chapter 2, manipulation of character strings using high-level languages was illustrated. In subsequent chapters, we will investigate processing strings at the machine-language level. One reason that string manipulations are so important is that most computer *input/output* operations involve the use of character strings.

Example 3.13

Two 16-bit registers contain the following hexadecimal numbers:

                          5241   and   5453

What character string is represented by these numbers?

Solution   Using the table in Appendix A, it is seen that the numbers correspond to the character string RATS.

Example 3.14

Four characters are typed on a console device and entered into consecutive memory locations in a computer. Inspection of these memory locations indicates that they contain the following hexadecimal numbers: *C*D, *C*9, *C*3, and *C*5. What character string was typed on the console?

Solution   The hexadecimal numbers do not seem to coincide with any of the numbers given in the table in Appendix A. Recall, however, that the code being used is a 7-bit code, and the number in the most significant bit position of each of the corresponding bytes is not specified. In this case, a 1 is in the most significant bit position. Therefore, the characters entered correspond to the codes 4*D,* 49, 43, and 45, and the word *mice* was typed on the console.

In many computer programs, numerical data are entered and/or printed. The term *numerical data* is misleading. Suppose we wish to enter the number 1234 into a program written in a high-level language, such as BASIC, Pascal, or FORTRAN. To enter the number, we may type it in on a terminal device. However, we are not really entering a number, instead, we are entering a string of four ASCII characters encoded as the hexadecimal numbers 31, 32, 33, and 34. An internal routine must accept this character string and process or convert it into the binary number corresponding to the base-10 number 1234. Similarly, when it is desired to print an integer, such as one whose value is 1234, it is first necessary to convert this number into a string of ASCII characters.

Example 3.15

Suppose we wish to enter a string of four ASCII characters on a keyboard. The characters to be typed correspond to numbers between 0 and 9. Formulate a program plan that will convert this sequence to the corresponding unsigned binary number. Assume we are using a 16-bit machine.

Solution   The following sequence of steps satisfies the program requirements.
1. Clear register X.
2. Set COUNT = 4.
3. Read character into C.
4. Erase all but four least significant bits in C. That is, $C = C$ AND 000F.
5. Multiply X by 10.
6. Add C to X.
7. COUNT = COUNT − 1. If COUNT = 0, then QUIT.
8. GO TO step 3.

Example 3.16

Using a high-level language, write a program that accepts a string of hexadecimal characters and converts this string into the corresponding real number.

Solution   A program plan for these specifications may be very similar to the one used in Example 3.15. Here, however, we are using the set of hexadecimal characters instead of the set of base-10 characters. Also, we are converting the string to a real number or a floating point rather than to an integer. When using a high-level language, it is awkward to convert directly a statement such as shown in line 4 of the solution to Example 3.15 into appropriate code. However, techniques are available to achieve the same results. A solution written in Pascal is given in Fig. 3.4.

Review

1. What character string is represented by each of the following sets of hexadecimal numbers?
   (a) 48, 4F, 52, 53, 45
   (b) 4249   5244
   (c) $C7C9D2CC$
2. Refer to the solution to Example 3.15, in particular, step 5. Suppose the character string 2764 is entered into this procedure. What will be the value of X each time step 5 is executed?
3. Refer to the solution to Example 3.16 (Fig. 3.4). In particular, refer to the line containing the comment "UPDATE VALUE OF X." Suppose the following character string is read into this program: 01A5.C00.
   (a) What will be the value of X immediately after each execution of this line?
   (b) What value of X will be printed?

```
PROGRAM CONVERT_HEX_STRING(INPUT,OUTPUT);
   (*   THIS PROGRAM CONVERTS A STRING OF HEXADECIMAL CHARACTERS TO THE
        CORRESPONDING REAL NUMBER.  A RADIX POINT MAY BE ENTERED AS
        PART OF THE NUMBER.  TO AVOID FLOATING POINT OVERFLOW, THE
        INPUT STRINGS SHOULD BE RELATIVELY SHORT.  THE EXACT LIMITATION
     TO THE LENGTH OF THE INPUT STRINGS IS DEPENDENT ON THE WAY
        FLOATING POINTS ARE REPRESENTED AT THE PARTICULAR INSTALLATION*)
(* $$$$$$$$$$$$$$$$$$$$$$$$$$$$$$$$$$$$$$$$$$$$$$$$$$$$$$$$$$$$$$$$$$$$$$ *)
VAR X,Y: REAL; C: CHAR; COUNT: INTEGER; FLAG: BOOLEAN;
BEGIN
   COUNT:=0;
     FLAG:= FALSE;
     X:= 0.0;
     READLN;
     WHILE NOT EOLN DO
          BEGIN
          READ (C);
          IF (C='.') THEN FLAG:= TRUE;
          IF ((FLAG=TRUE)AND(C<>'.')) THEN COUNT := COUNT+1;
          IF ((C>='0')AND(C<='9')) THEN
                          CASE C OF
           '0': Y:=0.0;  '1': Y:=1.0;  '2': Y:=2.0;  '3': Y:=3.0;
           '4': Y:=4.0;  '5': Y:=5.0;  '6': Y:=6.0;  '7': Y:=7.0;
           '8': Y:=8.0;  '9': Y:=9.0;
                          END;
            IF ((C>='A')AND (C<='F')) THEN
                          CASE C OF
           'A': Y:=10.0;  'B': Y:=11.0;  'C': Y:=12.0;  'D': Y:=13.0;
           'E': Y:=14.0;  'F': Y:=15.0;
                          END;
              IF (C<>'.') THEN BEGIN
              X:=X*16.0;   X:= X+Y;(* UPDATE VALUE OF X *)
                          END;
     END;
     (* NOW ADJUST X IF A RADIX POINT WAS ENTERED *)
     WHILE (COUNT<>0) DO BEGIN
                   X:=X/16.0; COUNT:= COUNT-1;
                          END;
     WRITELN(X);
   END.
```

Figure 3.4   Solution to Example 3.15

3.5 BINARY CODED DECIMAL NUMBERS

For a large number of applications, inputs to computers consist primarily of numerical data. For example, many cash registers, point-of-sale terminals, automated banking terminals, and similar devices are computer controlled. Such devices receive and display a considerable amount of numerical data. Both the inputs and the outputs of these systems consist of representations of base-10 numbers.

As suggested earlier, computers generally perform operations on numbers expressed in the binary or base-2 number system. In Section 3.4, we illustrated how ASCII representations of base-10 numbers can be converted to binary numbers. After numerical processing is completed, these binary numbers can be transformed back into ASCII representations of the corresponding base-10 results and printed or displayed on an output device. In situations in which there is a considerable amount of input and output operations, such transformation of numbers between two number systems may require a significant amount of a system's computing capabilities. For such cases it would be convenient if computations could be per-

Decimal character	BCD representation	BCD representation represented as a hexadecimal number
0	0000	0
1	0001	1
3	0010	2
3	0011	3
4	0100	4
5	0101	5
6	0110	6
7	0111	7
8	1000	8
9	1001	9

Figure 3.5   Binary coded decimal (BCD) representation of decimal characters

formed directly on the ASCII representations of numbers, or at least on some closely related representation of these characters.

The 7-bit ASCII representation of the base-10 characters between 0 and 9 inclusive corresponds to the hexadecimal numbers between 30 and 39. Suppose we delete the three most significant bits in this 7-bit representation of the base-10 characters. Then the decimal characters 0 to 9 can be represented by the hexadecimal numbers between 0 and 9. Of course, each of these hexadecimal numbers may be represented by four binary characters. Such a code may be referred to as a 4-bit ASCII code for representing base-10 characters—generally referred to as the *binary coded decimal* (or BCD) representation of decimal characters. See Fig. 3.5 for an illustration.

Observe that it takes just 4 bits to represent a decimal character using BCD code. Frequently, a byte-sized register is used to store two characters represented in BCD code. This may be referred to as a *packed* BCD representation, or simply as a BCD representation of two decimal characters. When arithmetic operations are performed on digital computers, these operations are usually performed on binary numbers. Thus, if arithmetic operations are performed on two BCD numbers, the result may not be a valid BCD number. If the result is a valid BCD number, it may still be an incorrect answer.

Example 3.17

The symbols X, Y, and Z are used to represent base-10 numbers expressed in BCD code.

$$X = 20_{16} \Longrightarrow 20_{10} \qquad Y = 78_{16} \Longrightarrow 78_{10} \qquad Z = 89_{16} \Longrightarrow 89_{10}$$

What results are obtained if the following 8-bit addition operations are performed?
(a) $X + Y$
(b) $Y + Z$
(c) $X + Z$

Solution   (a) $X + Y = 98_{16} => 98_{10}$, which is a valid BCD representation and the correct result.
   (b) $Y + Z = 01_{16} => 01_{10}$, which is a valid BCD representation. However, the answer is incorrect if we wish to perform decimal operations.
   (c) $X + Z = A9_{16}$. This is not a valid BCD representation.

Example 3.17 shows that binary addition of packed BCD numbers does not always yield a correct BCD result. Frequently, computer commands are available that *adjust* the results of BCD operations and thus produce a correct BCD result. Such commands are referred to as *decimal adjust* operations. In order to describe the functioning of a typical decimal adjust command for the addition operation, we will first define one additional dynamic status bit or status flag. This is the *half-carry* flag or the *auxiliary carry* flag. Consider an arithmetic operation such as addition being performed on 2 bytes or 8-bit words. Now consider the lower nibble or half byte of each word. The half-carry flag will come up if and only if the sum of the two least significant half bytes is greater than $0F_{16}$.

Now suppose that binary addition is performed on two 8-bit words, as illustrated in Example 3.17. After addition is performed, a decimal adjust command is given. The decimal adjust command will produce the correct BCD sum if it performs the following sequence of operations.

1. If the lower half byte of the sum is > 9 or if the half-carry flag is up, 06 is added to the sum. This addition may set the carry flag but may never clear the carry flag.

2. If the upper half byte of the adjusted sum is > 9 or if the carry flag is up, 60_{16} is added to the sum. This addition may set the carry flag but may not clear the carry flag.

Application of this decimal adjust for addition (DAA) command will produce a valid and correct BCD sum of two packed BCD bytes. If this operation is applied to the result obtained in part (b) of Example 3.17, the hexadecimal number 67 will be the result, and a 1 will be in the carry bit. Similarly, if the decimal adjust command is applied to the result obtained in part (c), the hexadecimal number 09 will be the result, and a 1 will be in the carry bit. The value in the carry bit can be interpreted as a true BCD carry value.

Example 3.18

Consider the following arithmetic operations:
(a) $43_{16} + 59_{16}$
(b) $28_{16} + 39_{16}$
(c) $AB_{16} + BC_{16}$
Suppose each of these operations is followed by a DAA command. What is the value in the auxiliary carry bit before the desired adjust operation is performed? What are the result and the value stored in the carry bit after the DAA operation is performed?

Solution **(a)** The auxiliary carry flag is cleared, but the value of the lower half byte of the sum is > 9. Therefore, 06 is added to the result. Now the value of the upper half byte is > 9, so 60_{16} is added to the result. The final result is 02_{16}, and a 1 is in the carry bit.

(b) The auxiliary carry bit is set and then the decimal adjust operation is performed. This produces a result of 67_{16} with a 0 in the carry bit.

(c) Neither of the original terms is a valid packed BCD number. The addition of these numbers produces a sum of 67_{16} and a 1 in both the carry bit and the auxiliary carry bit. After the decimal adjust operation is performed, the sum is CD_{16}, and there is a 1 in the carry bit.

Some 16-bit machines also include a decimal adjust command for subtraction. That is, binary subtraction is performed between two packed BCD numbers, and then the decimal adjust for subtraction (DAS) command is applied to the resulting difference. After this instruction has been executed, the adjusted difference is a valid and correct BCD result. Such a command may perform the following sequence of operations.

1. If the low-order nibble is greater than 9 or if the half-carry flag is up, subtract 06 from the result. *Note:* The half-carry flag will be up if there had been a borrow requirement from the low-order nibble.

2. If the high-order nibble is greater than 9 or if the carry bit is set, then subtract 60_{16} from the result and set the carry bit. *Note:* This decimal adjust operation may set the carry flag but will never clear the carry flag.

Example 3.19

Refer to the following arithmetic operations:
(a) $53_{16} - 49_{16}$
(b) $28_{16} - 39_{16}$
(c) $AB_{16} - BC_{16}$
Suppose each of these operations is followed by a DAS command. What is the state of the auxiliary carry flag before the decimal adjust operation is performed? What are the result and the state of the carry flag after the DAS operation is performed?

Solution **(a)** The auxiliary carry flag is set. The initial result is $0A_{16}$. Execution of the DAS command causes 06 to be subtracted from $0A_{16}$, yielding 04. The carry flag remains cleared.

(b) The auxiliary carry flag and the carry flag are set, and the initial difference is EF_{16}. Subtracting 66_{16} from this quantity yields 89_{16}, and the carry bit remains set.

(c) Neither of the original terms is a valid packed BCD number. The initial subtraction yields EF_{16} and sets the carry flag and the auxiliary carry flag. After the decimal adjust operation is performed, the result becomes 89_{16}, and the carry bit remains set.

At least one modern 16-bit computer combines the arithmetic operation and the decimal adjust operation into a single instruction. Some machines also provide similar adjustments or operations for multiplication or division of BCD numbers.

Review

1. Convert the following ASCII strings, expressed in base-16, to packed BCD numbers: 35, 37, 38, 39, 30, 31.

2. Consider the following operations. All of the numbers are expressed as hexadecimal numbers.
   (a) 47 + 34
   (b) 98 + 89
   (c) 41 + 60

   After each of the indicated operations is performed, the DAS operation is executed. What is the state of the auxiliary carry flag before the DAS command is executed? After the DAS command is executed, what is the result of each operation, and what is the state of the corresponding carry bit?

3. Repeat Review question 2 for the identical numbers but for the subtraction operation followed by execution of a DAS command.

3.6 REPRESENTATION OF FLOATING-POINT NUMBERS

We have illustrated how sequences of binary characters are used to represent signed integers. Similarly, sequences of binary characters are used to represent decimal or BCD numbers. Another frequently encountered data type is the *real number* or *floating-point* number. A computer user may consider the difference between the integer 6 and the real number 6.0 to be trivial. However, the difference in the manner in which these two numbers are represented on a computer is very significant.

Several methods are used to represent real or floating-point numbers. Even the number of bits required for representing these numbers varies among different installations or for different applications. However, in general, real numbers or floating points are represented in a manner such as illustrated in Fig. 3.6.

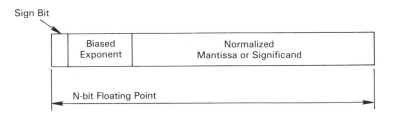

Figure 3.6   Typical representation of an *N*-bit floating point

In a typical representation of a floating point, 1 bit (not necessarily the first bit) is used to specify the sign of the number. A 0 corresponds to a positive number, and a 1 to a negative number. A relatively small number of bits is used to specify the value of the *exponent* or *characteristic*. The size of the exponent is generally expressible by a number of bits that ranges between 7 and 15 for various floating-point representations. The number of bits used to specify the exponent determines the *range* of the floating-point number. The exponent is generally biased; that is, a fixed constant is added to the true value of the exponent. Use of a biasing number is convenient if we wish to use both positive and negative values of exponents. A relatively large number of bits is used to express the value of the *mantissa* or *significand*. This value is typically in a range between 23 bits and 64 bits. The *precision* of a floating point is determined by the number of bits used to specify the mantissa.

The value of a real number or a floating point is given by the following expression:

$$\text{Real number} = \pm \text{ Mantissa} \times \text{Base}^{\text{Exponent}}$$

For computer applications it is important that the base be an integral power of 2. Generally, either a value of 2 or a value of 16 is utilized for the base. The format for one particular floating-point representation, the American National Standards Institute (ANSI) 32-bit floating point, is illustrated in Fig. 3.7. Virtually all floating points that are stored in computer memory are in a *normalized* form.

The ANSI 32-bit floating point is defined as follows. The exponent is a 7-bit number, and it is biased by the base-10 number 64. That is, 64 is added to the true exponent, and the result is stored in bit positions 30 to 24 in the 32-bit representation. The base used is the number 16. The mantissa consists of 24 bits. In order for the floating point to be in normalized form, the mantissa is required to be within the following range of numbers:

$$0.0625_{10} =< \text{mantissa} < 1.0$$

Expressed in the binary number system

$$0.0001_2 =< \text{mantissa} < 1.0$$

There is one exception to this rule: The number 0.0 has a mantissa consisting of all 0 bits. Observe that an implied radix point exists to the left of the most significant character of the mantissa.

b_{31} b_{30} b_{24} b_{23} b_0

| | Exponent | Mantissa |

Sign Bit

Figure 3.7   Format of an ANSI 32-bit floating point

Example 3.20

Express the real number 29.0 as an ANSI floating point.

Solution $29.0_{10} => 11101_2 => 1.1101_2 \times 16_{10}^1 = 0.00011101_2 \times 16_{10}^2$.
Therefore, the sign bit is 0, the true exponent is 2, and the biased exponent is 66_{10}.
Expressed as a binary number, the corresponding floating point is
0 1000010 00011101000000000000000. Expressed in the hexadecimal number system, the corresponding 32-bit floating point is 421D0000.

Example 3.21

Express the number -9.55 as an ANSI floating point.

Solution $9_{10} => 1001_2 => 9_{16}$. In order to express 0.55 in the base-16 number system, we will make use of the algorithm described in Section 3.1.

Number	Number × 16	Character
0.55	8.8	8
0.8	12.8	C
0.8	12.8	C
0.8	12.8	C
0.8	12.8	C
0.8	12.8	C
0.8	12.8	C

Therefore, $9.55_{10} = 9.8CCCCCC_{16} => 0.98CCCCCC_{16} \times 16^1$. The sign bit is 1 and the biased exponent is 65_{10}. Therefore, the corresponding ANSI floating point expressed as a hexadecimal number is $C198CCCC$.

Even computers do not necessarily include machine-language commands for performing arithmetic operations on floating-point numbers. In such cases, programs must be written to implement floating-point operations. Such software is generally included as routines used in high-level languages. Fig. 3.8 illustrates a

1. Identify the number with the largest exponent. Refer to this number as *A* and to the other number as *B*. *Note:* If the exponents are identical, either number may be called *A*.

2. Let *C* = exponent of *A* − exponent of *B*.

3. Shift mantissa of *B* 4*C bits to the right.

4. Add shifted mantissa to mantissa of *A*.

5. ANSWER => exponent of *A* and new mantissa obtained in step 4.

6. Normalize ANSWER.

7. Check for overflow; indicate if overflow occurs.

Figure 3.8 Initial program plan for addition of two positive ANSI floating points

1. Remove bias from exponents. Add the exponents and replace the bias constant.
2. Multiply the mantissas.
3. Normalize the result.
4. Check for overflow; indicate if overflow occurs.

Figure 3.9   Initial program plan for multiplication of two positive ANSI floating points

program plan for the addition of two positive ANSI floating points. Fig. 3.9 suggests a program plan for multiplication of two ANSI floating points.

Normalization of the results obtained by an arithmetic operation implies that the value of the mantissa must be within the specified range. For example, suppose after a multiplication operation has been performed that the 24 most significant bits of the mantissa of the result are 000001110000000000000000. To convert this number to its normalized form, it is required to shift 4 bits to the left and to subtract 1 from the corresponding exponent. Because shifting may be required for normalization, more than 24 bits of precision should be maintained during intermediate steps in floating-point operations.

Just as there are limits to the range of integers that can be expressed using finite-length registers, there are similar limitations to the size of floating-point numbers. These limitations are primarily dependent on the number of bits allocated for use as an exponent. If ANSI 32-bit floating points are used, the largest real number that can be expressed is

$$7FFFFFFF_{16} = 0.7FFFFFFF_{16} \times 16^{63} = 7.237 \times 10^{76}$$

The magnitude of the smallest nonzero number is

$$0.0001_2 \times 16^{-64} = 5.3976 \times 10^{-79}$$

The ANSI standard floating point is merely one of several popular representations of floating points. Recently, a standard has been developed by the Institute of Electrical and Electronic Engineers (IEEE)—the IEEE-754—for representation of floating points. Hardware associated with popular 16-bit machines has been designed to conform with this standard. A floating-point representation closely related to the "short real" portion of this standard is described in Section 7.4.

Review

1. The following hexadecimal numbers represent ANSI 32-bit standard floating points. Express the corresponding real numbers in the base-10 number system.
   (a) $41C00000$
   (b) $C3EA2000$
   (c) $3D800000$

2. Express the following base-10 numbers as ANSI standard floating points:
   (a) 537
   (b) −10.3
   (c) 4×10^{-3}

3. Suppose two positive ANSI standard floating points are multiplied together using the technique described in Fig. 3.9. It may be necessary to normalize the result.
   (a) Under what conditions will normalization be required?
   (b) If during step 3 of this procedure, normalization is required, what modification must be made to the exponent of the result that has already been computed?

4. Which of the following floating-point summations will produce a floating-point overflow?
   (a) $CABC0324 + 4ABC0000$
   (b) $7F02345E + 7FFE0000$
   (c) $8FFFABCD + 7FFFABCD$

REFERENCES

GIBSON, G. A., and Y. LUI, *Computer Logic Design.* Englewood Cliffs, N.J.: Prentice-Hall, 1980.

JERMANN, W. H., *The Structure and Programming of Microcomputers.* Palo Alto, Calif.: Mayfield, 1982.

JOHNSON, D. E., J. L., HILLBURN, and P. M. JULICH, *Digital Circuits and Microcomputers.* Englewood Cliffs, N.J.: Prentice-Hall, 1979.

KRUTZ, R. L., *Microprocessors and Logic Design.* New York: John Wiley, 1980.

MANO, M. M., *Computer Logic Design.* Englewood Cliffs, N.J.: Prentice-Hall, 1972.

SIMINGTON, R. B., "Guaranteed Standard Results with the 8087," *BYTE,* 8, no. 4 (April 1983), 174–75.

EXERCISES

1. Express the following numbers as base-10 numbers:
   (a) 467_8
   (b) ABC_{16}
   (c) 01010111_2
   (d) $79GE_{17}$

2. Express the following numbers as base-10 numbers:
   (a) 0.10101_2
   (b) 4.56_{16}
   (c) 40.61_7

3. Express the base-10 number 321 in the designated number system.
   (a) octal

    (b) hexadecimal

    (c) base-6

4. Express the binary number 010111.10011 in the designated number system.

    (a) base-10

    (b) octal

    (c) hexadecimal

5. Express the octal number 376.2 in the designated number system.

    (a) base-10

    (b) binary

    (c) hexadecimal

6. Express the base-10 number 0.35 as a 16-bit binary number. Assume the radix point is just to the left of the most significant binary character. Express your answer in both an octal representation and a hexadecimal representation.

7. Refer to Review question 5 in Section 3.1. Write a corresponding program using either BASIC or FORTRAN.

       The following numbers refer to Exercises 8 through 16. Assume each number is to be expressed as a 16-bit signed integer and stored in an appropriate register on a typical 16-bit computer.

$$P = 87_{16} \qquad Q = -15_{10} \qquad R = 1A36_{16} \qquad S = 177046_8$$
$$T = 45_{10} \qquad U = 003456_8$$

8. Find each of the following 16-bit results and express your answer using the octal number system.

    (a) $-P$

    (b) $P + Q$

    (c) $Q + R$

    (d) $\overline{T}$

9. Find each of the following 16-bit results and express your answer in the hexadecimal number system.

    (a) P AND Q

    (b) P OR Q

    (c) $S - R$

    (d) $\overline{T} \oplus U$

10. Find each of the following 16-bit results and express your answer in the base-8 number system.

    (a) $-U$

    (b) $T + U$

    (c) U OR $(-Q)$

11. Express each of the following results using the hexadecimal number system.

    (a) $P \oplus R$

    (b) $S \oplus U$

    (c) Q OR S

12. Express each of the following results in the hexadecimal number system.

    (a) $(P - Q)$ AND R

    (b) $(Q - R) \oplus U$

    (c) $(T + U)$ OR $(Q - R)$

13. Which of the following 16-bit operations will clear the carry flag?
    (a) $P + Q$
    (b) $Q - R$
    (c) $S - T$
    (d) $Q + S$
    (e) $R - R$

14. Refer to Exercise 13. Which of these operations will *set* the *zero* flag?

15. Refer to Exercise 13. Which of these operations will *clear* the *overflow* flag?

16. Refer to Exercise 13. Which of these operations will *set* the *sign* flag?

17. Refer to the solution to Example 3.4 given in Fig. 3.1. Modify this program so that it can be used to convert a positive base-10 number to the corresponding octal number.

18. Refer to Exercise 17. Modify this program so that a value of B may be entered from the console, where B corresponds to any base between 2 and 16. The program will print the base-10 number that is entered as a base-B number.

19. Design and test a program that converts a base-10 number with an *expressed* decimal point to a corresponding hexadecimal number.

20. Design and test a program that converts a base-10 number with an *expressed* decimal point to a corresponding octal number.

21. Refer to the solution to Example 3.15 in Fig. 3.4. Modify this program so that it will convert a string of ASCI characters to a real number if the characters correspond to
    (a) octal characters
    (b) base-10 characters

22. Refer to Exercise 21. Modify the routine so it will work for any base-K number system, where, $2 = < K <= 16$.

23. Suppose that the following operations are performed on 8-bit packed BCD numbers represented in the base-16 number system. After these operations are performed, the appropriate decimal adjust operation is performed on the result. What will be the result for each of the following operations?
    (a) $43 + 91$
    (b) $27 + 19$
    (c) $91 - 47$
    (d) $32 - 88$
    (e) $46 - 46$

24. Refer to Exercise 23. What is the state of the zero, carry, and auxiliary carry flags after each of the above operations is completed? *Note:* Assume the decimal adjust operation may set the auxiliary carry flag, but will not clear it.

25. Suppose the following operations are performed on 8-bit numbers represented as hexadecimal numbers. Then the appropriate decimal adjust command is performed. What are the results of each of these operations?
    (a) $97 - 97$
    (b) $DD + 3E$
    (c) $3E - DD$

26. Refer to Exercise 25. What will be the state of the zero, carry, and auxiliary carry flags after each of these operations is completed?

27. Suppose a floating-point representation uses an 8-bit exponent biased by 128_{10} with a base value of 2, and a 24-bit mantissa. In normalized form, the value of the mantissa is
$$0.5_{10} = < \text{ mantissa } < 1.0$$
    (a) What is the value of the largest floating point that can be represented?
    (b) What is the magnitude of the smallest nonzero floating point that can be represented?

28. Convert each of the following base-10 numbers to ANSI standard floating points. Express your answers in the hexadecimal number system.
    (a) 47,352
    (b) 3.14159
    (c) -1.3×10^{-4}

29. The following 32-bit numbers, expressed as base-16 numbers, represent ANSI floating points. Express these floating points as base-10 numbers.
    (a) 4612*ABC*0
    (b) 35800000
    (c) *AB*123456

30. Design a program segment that accepts a real number and prints out a number that corresponds to the true value of the exponent that would be obtained if the number is represented as an ANSI floating point.

31. Design a program segment that accepts a real number and then prints a string of eight characters. These characters correspond to the ANSI representation of the floating point expressed in the hexadecimal number system.

4

The Digital
Computer

Although many different computers have been developed during the last three decades, there are common attributes to most of these machines. Most computers currently in operation are *von Neumann machines*. Such machines fetch instructions from the same computer memory that is used to store data. The instructions are stored in memory in forms that represent sequences of binary characters, in a manner analogous to the way data are stored in memory. The instruction codes may be manipulated in the same manner in which data are manipulated. The instructions, which are encoded as binary numbers, are fetched from memory in orderly sequences, translated, and executed.

The internal components of digital computers are frequently silicon-based integrated circuits. In a modern machine, the primary internal components are either LSI (large-scale integrated circuits) components or VLSI (very-large-scale integrated circuits) components. A single integrated circuit (or a chip) is referred to as a VLSI if it contains more than 100,000 electronic gates.

4.1 ORGANIZATION OF A DIGITAL COMPUTER

Figure 4.1 is a block diagram representation of the organization of a digital computer. The CPU, or central processing unit, is the focal point of the operation of the system. Program sequencing and control emanate from the CPU. Instructions

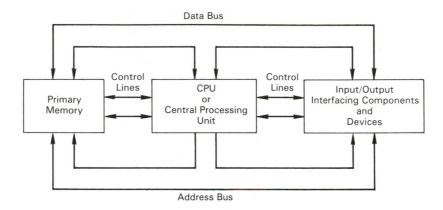

Figure 4.1   Block diagram representation of a digital computer

are fetched from primary memory to the CPU and translated and executed under its control. Generally, instructions to be fetched are stored as sequences of binary characters in primary memory. Similarly, various data types are also stored in primary memory. The binary information that is fetched from memory is *not* fetched one bit at a time. Rather, it is fetched in *groups* of binary digits. Typical arrangements of such groups may consist of 8-bit, 16-bit, or 32-bit groups.

A digital *line* may be considered an electrical connection between two or more points in a circuit. Only binary information is passed along this line. For example, a "high" value of voltage on this line may correspond to a logic 1, and a "low" value of voltage may correspond to a logic 0. A group of such lines is referred to as a *bus.*

Usually a bus is connected to several components. At any instant of time, the value of voltage on a given line may represent either a logic 0 or a logic 1, but not both simultaneously. Therefore, it is essential that only one device at a time is placing voltages corresponding to binary characters on the bus. For this reason, the operation of activity on a bus must be carefully controlled. The bus is *deactivated, turned off,* or *floated* when it is not in use. Because the lines on a bus have levels that correspond to logic 1s or logic 0s, or can be turned off or floated, a bus is referred to as a *tristate* device.

Before the operations of *fetching* an instruction, *reading* data from memory, or *writing* data into memory, an appropriate address must be placed on the *unidirectional* address bus. This address identifies a group of binary characters. Frequently, this group of binary characters is a *byte.*

As a typical case, consider a machine with an 8-bit data bus. Suppose a byte address is sent out on the address bus so that a specific 8-bit word be read by the CPU. Then a corresponding 8-bit word will be read from memory and placed on the *bidirectional* data bus. Suppose, however, that a CPU is to read a 32-bit floating point. Then it is required that four different (usually consecutively stored) bytes of information be read from memory. A machine that addresses 32-bit words and possesses a 32-bit data bus can read this information in approximately one-fourth the time required by a machine with an 8-bit data bus.

In this textbook, we are concerned primarily with 16-bit machines. Sometimes 16-bit machines are defined as machines that have a 16-bit data bus. This is not a very good definition, as some machines very commonly referred to as 16-bit machines have just an 8-bit data bus. Further discussion related to machine classification is presented in Chapter 12.

Peripheral devices are essential components of any computer. Frequently they account for the greatest portion of the cost of a computer system. Furthermore, they are also the only interface between computer users and the system. Typical peripheral, or input/output devices include keyboards, cathode ray display devices, paper tape readers and punches, card readers and punches, hard-copy printers, magnetic tape devices, hard disks, flexible disk units (usually called *floppies* or *floppy disk* units), and graphics display devices. Input/output devices that *monitor* or *control* external operations include *analog-to-digital converters* (ADCs), *digital-to-analog converters* (DACs), and *real-time clocks*. These latter devices are discussed in more detail in Chapter 8.

Refer again to the representation of a digital computer in Fig. 4.1. Input/output components generally are not directly connected to the computer CPU, rather they are connected to the CPU through *interfacing components* or interfacing circuits. An interfacing circuit generally consists of just a single large-scale integrated circuit. Such devices are frequently classified as either *serial* interfacing components or *parallel* interfacing components.

Suppose that a serial printer is part of a computer system. A serial interfacing device receives data words from the data bus, adds appropriate control information, and then, at the proper time, sends this information one bit at a time to the printer. A parallel interfacing device performs a similar function. However, it transmits bits of information received from the data bus simultaneously along parallel lines to the appropriate device. Such interfacing components require appropriate *control* signals from the CPU in order to function properly. Sometimes the set of control lines, or *control bus,* the address bus, and the data bus are collectively referred to as the *system bus.*

The control bus, address bus, and data bus of a computer are physically separate entities. These buses are needed so that information may be passed between the CPU and external devices. Frequently, the CPU is just a single integrated circuit or perhaps a small collection of integrated circuits. In such cases, the CPU may be referred to as a *microprocessor.* It may be awkward or expensive to fabricate a CPU chip if a large number of external pin connections is required in order to provide all the required external signals. Sometimes external pin connections on a chip are shared, or used to perform more than one function. For example, during certain periods of time, a set of pins on a CPU chip may transmit address information to the address bus. During other times, the same pins may be used to send or receive information from a data bus. Such sharing of common facilities is referred to as *multiplexing.*

Because it is the center of operations of a computing system, let us consider the central processing unit in more detail. Figure 4.2 is a block diagram representation of a typical modern computer CPU. Four sub-blocks are contained in this diagram. However, each CPU element is not necessarily uniquely defined to be within a sub-block. Furthermore, data are transmitted between these internal blocks, and control signals communicate among the blocks.

The block labeled ALU represents the arithmetic and logic unit of the CPU. Virtually all arithmetic and logic operations, such as those described in Chapter 3, are performed within this block. It is necessary to route the data operands from memory or from the register group to the ALU, perform the desired operations, and then direct the results to the desired destination. The internal data and the results are moved by way of the *internal data bus*. The width or size of this bus is a primary factor in the classification of a computer. For example, if the internal data bus contains 16 lines, the machine is generally classified as a 16-bit machine.

The control unit of the CPU is responsible for the generation of internal and external control signals. It is also responsible for movement of internal data and the performance of the primary functions of a CPU. That is, fetching instructions, translating instructions, executing instructions and maintaining internal registers and status bits are functions of the control unit. At one time, the details related to performing these tasks depended primarily on a set of specifically fabricated logic circuits that resided within the CPU. On modern machines, the specific functions are *programmed* and executed by a rather general internal machine.

The internal program, or *control program,* resides in the *control memory.* This memory may reside on a CPU chip that contains other CPU functions or on a separate memory chip. In either case, it is required that access to the control memory

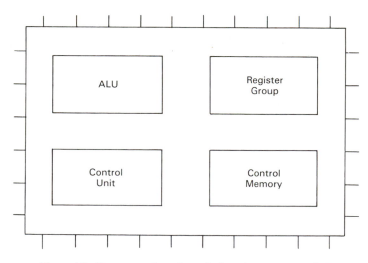

Figure 4.2   Representation of a typical modern computer CPU

be relatively rapid. The program stored in the control memory determines the architecture of the computer. *Computer architecture* may be defined as the set of computer attributes available to a programmer. The architecture includes the instruction set and the functioning of internal registers and flags.

The control program is frequently referred to as *firmware* or *microcode*. The memory in which it is stored is a *control store*. On some systems, a computer user is able to develop her or his own microcode. Such computers are said to be *microprogrammable* or *user microprogrammable*. If the microcode can be varied in a manner similar to the way that data are written into primary memory during program execution, the machine is said to possess a *writable control store*.

Although there is great diversity among various CPUs, there are a number of registers that are common to many computer architectures. Figure 4.3 illustrates some typical registers.

Before a memory location is accessed, an appropriate address must be sent out on the address bus. Addresses are computed internally and stored in a *memory address register*. Computer program segments are typically stored in consecutively labeled memory addresses. The *program counter* is a register that stores the address of the next instruction to be fetched. Frequently, this address is the successor to the address of the previous instruction. However, if *program-control* or *branch-type* instructions are executed, or if *subroutines* or *procedures* are invoked, then a nonsequential transfer must be made. In order to execute such instructions, the appropriate address must be computed and stored in the program counter.

The data register is used to store temporarily any data words that may be read from or written onto the data bus. If a computer instruction is read from the data

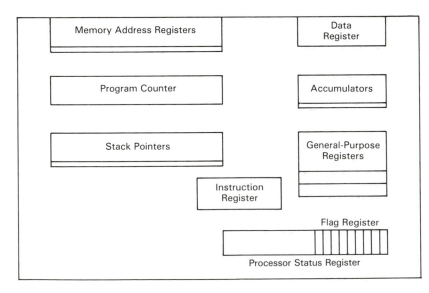

Figure 4.3   Representation of typical CPU registers

bus, it is routed to the *instruction register*. After an instruction code is placed in the instruction register, it is decoded and executed. Many computer central processing units contain general-purpose registers. These registers can be used to store data or to store addresses of certain memory locations. Addresses stored by CPU registers are frequently referred to as *pointers*.

In early computers, certain internal registers were designated as *accumulators*. Accumulators were the destination registers for the results of all arithmetic and logic operations. In modern computers, general-purpose registers or memory registers may serve as destination registers for most arithmetic and logic operations. However, for some specific operations, certain registers may be designated as accumulators and used to store computational results. Arithmetic and logic operations generally affect various status flags. These include a carry flag, a zero flag, a sign flag, and an overflow flag. (The functions of these status bits were discussed in Chapter 3.) A CPU register segment referred to as a *flag register* or as a *condition codes register* is used to store these bits. This register may be a subset of a larger register called a *processor status word* (PSW) register. The PSW contains additional information related to the current state of a machine.

Most machines contain one or more registers specifically designated as *stack pointers,* or, more properly, as *stack pointer registers*. These registers are used to store a *pointer* or an *address* that identifies a data structure stored in memory and referred to as a *stack*. The functions of a stack and of the stack pointer register are discussed in Section 4.3.

Review

1. What is meant by each of the following terms?
   (a) von Neumann machine
   (b) bus
   (c) floating state
   (d) serial interface
   (e) firmware
2. Refer to the three blocks in Fig. 4.1. Associate each of the following terms with one of these blocks.
   (a) computer program
   (b) microcode
   (c) parallel interface
   (d) status flags
3. Refer to the various registers in Fig. 4.3. Associate each of the following terms with one or more of these registers.
   (a) auxiliary carry flag
   (b) computer operation code
   (c) instruction address
   (d) data location
   (e) memory-write operation
   (f) output of ALU

4.2 PRIMARY MEMORY

The primary memory in a computer system has a very significant impact on the overall evaluation of the capabilities of the system. The *size* of a computer memory and the *speed* in which the memory may be accessed are significant factors. Some early computers were utilized as general-purpose machines even though they had only a few thousand words of memory. Some modern microprocessors can readily access memory banks containing several gigabytes of primary memory. (*Note:* A gigabyte is 1000 million bytes, or 1000 megabytes.)

Certain peripheral devices, such as disk units and multitrack magnetic tapes, are used to store either data, program commands, or encoded text. These devices are not primary memory devices but are sometimes classified as *secondary memory* devices. Bytes or words stored on disks cannot be accessed in the same manner that primary memory is accessed. Primary memory can be *randomly accessed*. This means that the address of any memory location can be sent out on the address bus and then that memory location can be immediately accessed. The words stored in secondary memory are *sequentially accessed*. That is, a particular word is not available until preceding words have passed under a magnetic reading device.

There are several desirable attributes associated with primary memory. Some of these attributes are the following:

1. The time required to read or write a word into memory should be very short. (*Note:* Typical memory access times for relatively inexpensive computers range between 0.1 and 1.0 microseconds.)
2. Primary memory capacity should be relatively large.
3. Storage of information in memory should be reliable. That is, the contents of memory should remain unchanged even during periods of external electrical activity or power failure.
4. Under program control, the contents of memory should be easily variable.
5. Memory should be compact; that is, it should require very little physical space.
6. Only a minimal amount of power should be required in order to sustain memory operations
7. The required memory components should be inexpensive.

A variety of memory components are available. No single type of memory component excels in satisfying all of the above requirements. Consequently, a variety of different memory devices may be used on a single computer.

At one time the word *memory* was nearly synonymous with the term *core memory*. That is, computer memory consisted of a large number of ferrite toroids or cores. Each of these small toroids can be magnetized in one of two possible directions and thus is capable of storing one bit of information. Core memory has some desirable attributes. For example, storage of data in core memory is relatively secure. Even if electrical power is disconnected for a relatively long time, core memory retains the stored information. However, with the advent of *integrated circuits,* the use of core memory has greatly diminished.

In modern computers, *semiconductor memory* is more frequently utilized. Thus, a physical unit of primary memory is a large-scale or a very-large-scale integrated circuit. A computer memory frequently consists of just a single printed circuit board or a portion of a board that includes several memory chips. Memory chips are available that contain 4K, 8K, 16K, 32K, 64K, 128K, and 256K bits of storage capacity. (K represents *kilo* or 1000. It more accurately refers to the number 2^{10}, or 1024, when specifying capacity of memory chips.)

Figure 4.4 is a representation of a typical memory chip. Observe that there are 12 address lines connected to this chip. Thus, 2^{12}, or 4096 locations can be addressed within this memory chip. There are eight data lines on the chip. This indicates that each address contains an 8-bit word. Thus, there are 4096 bytes or 32,768 bits of memory capacity on this integrated circuit. Nominally, the device is referred to as a 32K memory chip. In this particular chip, each addressable location stores an 8-bit word. Commonly used memory chips are available that store 1-bit words, 4-bit words, and 8-bit words. Figure 4.5 illustrates how chips that store 4-bit words may be used on a computer that has a 16-bit data bus.

Computer memory devices may be classified into two broad categories: *ROM* memory and *RAM* memory. Both types of devices are used for primary memory, and both types may be classified as *random access memory.* The devices shown in Figs. 4.4 and 4.5 represent either ROM components or RAM components.

ROM is an acronym for *read only memory.* During execution of a computer program, information can be read from ROM memory, but no information can be written into ROM memory. *RAM* is an acronym for *random access memory.* This is not a meaningful descriptor, because it does not differentiate RAM memory devices from ROM memory devices. The acronym *RAM* is actually used to denote *read-write memory.* That is, during execution of a program, information can either be *read from* or *written into* RAM memory.

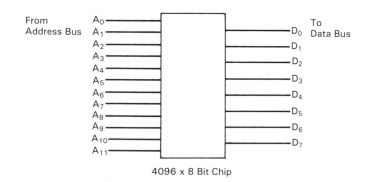

4096 x 8 Bit Chip

Figure 4.4   Representation of a typical memory chip

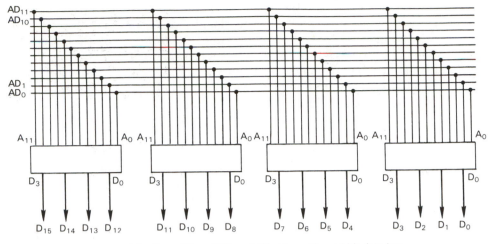

Figure 4.5 Use of four 4096 × 4 bit chips with a 16-bit data bus

There are several types or classes of read only memory, including ROM, PROM, EPROM, and EAPROM memory devices.

ROM usually implies that the bits stored on the corresponding memory chip are incorporated at the time the chip is manufactured. This is done by effectively adding or omitting electrical connections, depending on whether 0s or 1s are stored in particular bit locations. Programs of significant length may be stored in ROM. Some personal computers are sold with BASIC interpreters stored in ROM.

Program storage in ROM devices is permanent. As long as the chip itself is not damaged, the program remains stored on the chip. Unfortunately, the user cannot make any program changes. Because ROM programming is done by the manufacturer, programs should not be placed in ROM until they have been thoroughly tested.

PROM refers to programmable read only memory. A PROM chip is a read only memory device that is user programmable. A *fusable* link is effectively connected between each addressable bit and a reference location. The value stored in each bit position is a logic 0 or a logic 1, depending on whether or not the corresponding fusable link remains intact or is destroyed or burned out. A special device referred to as a *PROM programmer* is used to remove or burn out the particular links. Although a PROM is user programmable, it may be programmed only once, because when an internal link is removed from *any* bit location, it cannot be replaced.

Components referred to as *EPROMs,* or *erasable PROMs,* are also user programmable. These devices are programmed by applying an electrical potential to the designated bit locations. Generally, an EPROM is supplied with all logic 1s contained in storage. By using a special device, an *EPROM programmer,* logic 0s can be written in the designated memory cells. All memory cells may be erased or set back to 1 by exposing the transparent window of an EPROM to ultraviolet light for a reasonably long interval of time, such as 15 minutes. Care should be taken not to inadvertently expose EPROMs to an ultraviolet light source, such as the sun, or stored program bits will be unintentionally erased.

Some EPROMs permit either logic 0s or logic 1s to be placed in specified bit positions by the application of different voltage levels to specified addresses for relatively significant intervals of time. Such devices are called *electrically alterable PROMs,* or *EAPROMs.*

There are also various classifications for RAM or read-write memory chips. Two major classifications are volatile memory devices and nonvolatile memory devices. *Nonvolatile* memory retains its information when electrical power is disconnected from the circuit. Clearly, all ROM-type devices are nonvolatile. Magnetic core memory, which at one time was very popular, is another type of nonvolatile memory.

A more recently developed type of nonvolatile memory is *magnetic bubble memory.* Magnetic bubbles are small magnetic quanta or particles that can be incorporated on integrated circuits. Under appropriate control, these particles can be circulated. Presence of a particle in a particular location may correspond to a logic 1, and absence of such a particle may correspond to a logic 0. A particular memory address corresponds to a position in the queue of circulating bubbles. Thus, to access a particular memory location, a delay is encountered until the particular subsequence can be sensed. Thus, memory access time is relatively long, and the effective use of bubble memory is somewhat limited.

Most currently used RAM or read-write memory is *volatile* memory. That is, if electrical power is disconnected, information stored in memory will be lost. If such information loss is not tolerable, then an *uninterruptible* power supply can be utilized. That is, if the primary source of electrical power is interrupted, a second source is automatically connected. Another technique used to avoid memory information loss is to provide circuitry that senses a power failure as it is occurring. If a power failure is detected, a temporary power source can be used to transfer the contents of volatile memory to a permanent storage device.

Volatile semiconductor memory is subclassified into two major types, static memory and dynamic memory. *Static memory* possesses the attribute that the contents of all memory locations remain fixed until either power is turned off or a program or an external command alters the contents of memory. In *dynamic memory,* electrical charges are placed on devices corresponding to specified memory cells. These charges rapidly decay. Thus, if the information stored in memory is to be retained, all memory cells must be regularly sensed, and those containing decaying charges must be reactivated before the electrical charges decay to a level that is too small to be recognized. Therefore, computers using dynamic memory must include *memory refresh circuitry.* In typical systems, the memory refresh operation occurs about once every millisecond.

Dynamic memory is usually more compact than static memory. Likewise, less electrical power is required to sustain the operation of dynamic memory. An obvious disadvantage of using dynamic memory is that memory refresh circuitry is required. However, such circuitry is often *transparent* in that it may be included as an integral part of a memory board.

Review

1. Suppose a particular computer uses 16-bit words. A full complement of read-write memory consists of 32,768 words of memory. How many memory chips such as those illustrated in Fig. 4.5 are required for this memory?
2. A particular PROM chip is designated as a 32,768 × 8 memory chip.
   (a) How many address pins are on this chip?
   (b) How many data pins are on this chip?
3. What is meant by each of the following terms?
   (a) ROM
   (b) secondary memory
   (c) core memory
   (d) volatile memory
   (e) memory refresh circuitry

4.3 USE OF A STACK

One commonly used data structure is referred to as a *stack,* or an LIFO stack. The abbreviation *LIFO* refers to *last in first out,* which properly describes the function of a stack. Words or bytes are placed in sequentially numbered registers and then retrieved in the inverse order. Thus, in normal stack manipulation operations, only the last word placed on a stack is immediately accessible.

In early computers, stack registers were contained within the CPU, usually resulting in relatively small stack capacity and severely limiting the extent to which a stack could be utilized. In many systems, an option is given for the location of the stack registers. Systems may be configured such that a separate memory is available for use with the system stack. In most cases, however, the same primary memory space used for storing data and instructions is used for stack operations.

We should differentiate between use of *user stacks* and *system stacks*. A computer user may define arrays and construct program access to those arrays so that they satisfy the definition of stack structures. However, our concern is primarily with stack structures that are inherent to the architecture of a machine. In these cases, the stacks that are utilized are identified by the contents of the stack pointer register (or registers) that are part of the CPU.

There are three primary ways in which such stack structures are utilized. Machine-language instructions may be used to add or remove explicit elements from a stack. These commands are frequently identified as PUSH and POP commands. Likewise, commands or operations that *implicitly* affect the stack may be given. Instructions involving the use of subroutines are one such example. When a subroutine is *invoked* or *called,* an apparent return address is automatically placed on a stack. When exiting or returning from a subroutine, the address stored on top of a system stack is transferred into the program counter, and this becomes the true return address.

Interrupt and *trap* operations also affect the system stack. Such events may be externally generated operations, internally generated operations, or programmed commands. They are sometimes referred to as *exception*-type operations because they interrupt the normal sequencing of a computer program.

As an example, suppose an external device sends out a signal requesting service from the computer. Such a signal is referred to as an *external interrupt.* If certain conditions are satisfied, at the conclusion of execution of the current instruction the contents of at least the program counter and the PSW register are placed on the stack. Then program control will branch to an appropriate *interrupt servicing routine.* When execution of this routine is completed, a *return from interrupt* command will be executed. This restores the previous contents of the processor status word register and the program counter and thus permits continued execution of the pre-interrupt program segment. Additional discussion and examples related to interrupts and traps are given throughout the remainder of this text.

Stack operations may be implemented in several different ways. The three machines discussed in this textbook implement these operations in a similar but not identical manner. We will discuss the general way in which these machines implement stack operations. Consider a 16-bit machine, and suppose stack operations are typically done on 16-bit words. However, suppose memory addresses identify *bytes* of memory. Thus, each memory byte in the stack structure must store half of a word. Execution of a PUSH OPERAND command produces the following sequence of events:

1. The number stored in the stack pointer register is decremented. *Note:* This number is called the *stack pointer.*
2. Half of the word operand is stored in the memory location identified by the stack pointer.
3. The stack pointer is again decremented.
4. The other half of the word operand is stored in the memory location now identified by the stack pointer.

There are two ways in which 16-bit words are stored in byte-mapped memory. On some systems the most significant byte is stored in the memory location identified by the lower of the two required addresses. In other systems, the least significant byte is stored in the memory address identified by the lower of the two required addresses. In either case, we may say that the 16-bit word is stored in a memory location identified by the lower of the two addresses. In most systems in which words are stored in byte-mapped memory, it is desirable or sometimes even mandatory that 16-bit words be stored in even addresses. That is, the first byte of the word is located in an even-numbered address.

Example 4.1

On a given 16-bit machine, the contents of register RX are $07A9_{16}$, and the contents of the stack pointer are 1000_{16}. Memory addresses are byte addresses. Then the command PUSH RX is fetched and executed. After execution is completed, identify the contents of register RX, SP (the contents of the stack pointer register), and the contents of memory locations in which data have been changed. Do this for each of the following two cases.

(a) The machine stores words in memory with the most significant byte stored first, or in the lower-numbered memory location.

(b) The machine stores the least significant byte of a memory word first.

Solution   A solution to this example is given in Fig. 4.6

The execution of POP-type operations is similar to that of PUSH-type operations, except the steps are done in the inverse order. Similarly, the stack operations involved in a return from subroutine operation are done in the inverse order of those done in the CALL operation. The stack operations involved in a return from interrupt operation are likewise done in the inverse order of those occurring during an interrupt or a trap execution.

As an example, let us consider the execution of a POP REGISTER command. This results in the following sequence of events:

1. The byte operand stored in the memory location identified by the stack pointer is stored in half of the designated register.

2. The stack pointer is incremented.

3. The byte operand stored in the memory location identified by the stack pointer is stored in the other half of the designated 16-bit register.

4. The stack pointer is again incremented.

Example 4.2

Consider a typical 16-bit machine in which the registers are 16-bit registers and the memory addresses refer to byte addresses. Words are stored in memory with their least significant byte stored first. Suppose each instruction code consists of a 16-bit word. Prior to execution of the following string of commands, the designated CPU registers and memory locations contain the following hexadecimal numbers.

Register	Contents	Memory Address	Contents	Memory Address	Content
R1	89AB	9FA	01	9FE	89
R2	1234	9FB	23	9FF	AB
PC	4400	9FC	45	A00	EF
SP	0A00	9FD	67	A01	CD
				A02	FF

Numbers Expressed in Hexadecimal   Numbers Expressed in Octal

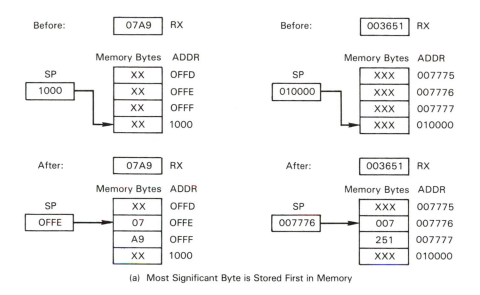

(a) Most Significant Byte is Stored First in Memory

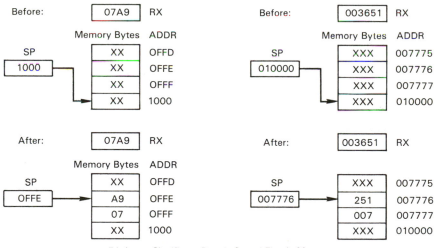

(b) Least Significant Byte is Stored First in Memory

Figure 4.6   A solution to Example 4.1

Then the following sequence of instructions is executed.

POP   R1
PUSH R2
PUSH R2
PUSH R1

After execution of this sequence of instructions is completed, identify the contents of each of the designated registers and memory locations.

Solution   Because four instructions are executed, the number in the program counter at the conclusion of program execution will be 4408. There are three PUSH operations but just one POP operation, so the number in the stack pointer will four less than at the beginning of the program segment. Execution of the first instruction places CDEF in R1. Execution of the second instruction puts 1234 into the memory word identified by address A00. Then 1234 is placed in the memory word identified by the address 9FE, and CDEF is stored in the memory word identified by the address 9FC. These results are summarized below.

Register	Contents	Memory Address	Contents	Memory Address	Contents
R1	CDEF	9FA	01	9FE	34
R2	1234	9FB	23	9FF	12
PC	4408	9FC	EF	A00	34
SP	09FC	9FD	CD	A01	12
				A02	FF

Example 4.3

A 16-bit machine has 16-bit instruction codes, and memory locations are identified by 16-bit byte addresses. The least significant bit of each memory word is stored first, or in the lower of two consecutive addresses. Refer to the following program segment. *Note:* All numbers are expressed in octal.

Memory Location	Instruction	Comment
1000	CALL 1112	Call subroutine at location 1112
——	——	——
1112	CALL 2234	Call subroutine at location 2234
——	——	——
2234	PUSH R1	Push contents of R1 on the stack
2234	HALT	Quit

Prior to execution of this program, the following octal numbers are stored in the following CPU registers.

Register	Contents
PC	1000
SP	1000
R1	4567

Suppose the above program steps are executed. Identify the memory registers used as a stack and the contents of each of these registers.

Solution   During the first subroutine call, the apparent return address 001002 is placed on the stack at locations identified by the address 000776. Then the apparent return address 001114 is placed on the stack in memory locations identified by the address 000774. Finally, the word 004567 is placed on the stack. Then the HALT instruction is encountered. At this time, the number in the stack pointer is 000772, and the stack registers contain the following octal numbers.

Memory Location	Contents
000772	167
000773	011
000774	114
000775	002
000776	002
000777	002

Example 4.4

A 16-bit machine has instruction codes that are all 16-bits long, and memory addresses refer to byte locations. The least significant byte of each memory word is stored first. Refer to the following program segment, where each number is expressed using the hexadecimal number system.

Label	Address	Instruction	Comment
FIRST:	1000	NOP	The NOP instruction does nothing
——	——	——	——
INTPROC:	2000	CALL SERVE	Invoke a subroutine called SERVE
——	——	——	——
SERVE:	2348	HALT	

During execution of the first instruction, an external interrupt occurs. After the NOP instruction is executed, the interrupt causes program control to be *vectored* to the memory location identified by the label INTPROC.

Suppose prior to execution of this program, the following hexadecimal numbers are stored in the designated CPU registers.

Register	Contents
PC	1000
SP	0F00
PSW	0ABC

After the HALT statement is executed, identify the contents of the PC, SP, and each stack register that was utilized. *Note:* On this particular system, an external interrupt or a trap event first causes the processor status word to be saved and then the apparent return address is saved.

Solution   After the HALT instruction is executed, the value in the PC identifies what appears to be the next instruction. Thus, the value in the PC will be the hexadecimal number 234*A*. Because three words are pushed onto the stack and no words are popped from the stack, the value stored in the SP register will be $0F00 - 6 = 0EFA$. The bytes stored on the stack are the following hexadecimal numbers.

Memory Location	Contents
0EFA	02
0EFB	20
0EFC	02
0EFD	10
0EFE	BC
0EFF	0A

Review

1. Refer to the problem statement in Example 4.2. Suppose the same operations are done on a machine that stores the *most significant* byte of a word in the lower-numbered memory location. Identify the contents of each memory location used in the stack.

2. Refer to the "typical" machine described in Example 4.2 and to the numbers initially stored in the designated CPU registers and in memory. Suppose the following sequence of instructions is executed:

```
PUSH  R1
POP   R2
POP   R1
PUSH  R1
PUSH  R2
```

After conclusion of this sequence of instructions, what number or numbers will be in each of the following locations?
(a) the program counter
(b) the stack pointer
(c) R1
(d) R2
(e) each of the designated memory addresses

3. Refer to the machine described in Example 4.4. Suppose the designated registers and memory locations contain the following hexadecimal numbers.

Register	Contents
PC	3002
SP	1002
PSW	ABCD
1000	12
1001	34
1002	56
1003	78
1004	9A
1005	BC
1006	DE
1007	FO

The following command is fetched from memory location 3002 and executed.

Memory Address	Command	Comment
3002	RTI	Return from Interrupt or Return from Trap

After execution of this command, what hexadecimal number will be in each of the following registers?

(a) PC

(b) SP

(c) PSW

4.4 TYPICAL COMPUTER INSTRUCTIONS

One of the most significant attributes of any computer is its *instruction set*. This consists of the set of all possible machine codes that can be fetched, translated, and executed by the machine. Although any instruction set serves to characterize a particular class of machines, the types of instructions available on typical machines are quite similar. There are a variety of ways that similar operations may be performed, different registers and status flags associated with different machines, and a wide variety of memory addressing modes. However, there is a definite commonality of instruction types available for the popular 16-bit machines.

Typical machine-language computer instructions may be classified under the following general headings:

1. Data transfer instructions
2. Arithmetic and logic operations
3. Control transfer instructions
4. Processor control commands
5. Rotate and shift instructions
6. Input/output operations
7. Stack operations
8. Miscellaneous commands

Before we discuss each of these categories, recall that a machine instruction is just a sequence of binary characters. For example, on one popular 8-bit machine the sequence of binary characters $01110110 => 76_{16}$ is the operation code for the HALT instruction. It is impractical to discuss instructions in terms of their binary codes or even in terms of the octal or hexadecimal representations of these codes. Instead, we will consider instructions in terms of one-word descriptors, such as HALT. Such words or shortened forms of these words are called *mnemonics*.

Typical data transfer instructions include the following types of commands: MOVE, LOAD, STORE, and EXCHANGE. The MOVE command implies that the contents of a *source* register or a source memory location are transferred to a *destination* register or a destination memory location. During execution of a MOVE instruction, the contents of the source register generally *are not affected*. A LOAD command is a special type of MOVE command. It implies that the source operand is in memory and the destination address is a CPU register. Similarly, a STORE command transfers the contents of a CPU register to a memory location. An EX-CHANGE command causes the source operand to be transferred to the destination address and the destination operand to be transferred to the source address. The CPU must temporarily store one of the operands when it is executing an EX-CHANGE command.

The arithmetic and logic operations described in Section 3.2 are implemented as machine-language instructions on most 16-bit computers. These instructions may be classified as unitary or binary operations. A *unitary* operation requires just one operand, whereas a *binary* operation requires two operands. Typical unitary operations are COMPLEMENT, NEGATE, INCREMENT, DECREMENT, and DAA (or decimal adjust accumulation). The COMPLEMENT command replaces the operand with its ones-complement, and the NEGATE command replaces the operand with its twos-complement. The INCREMENT and DECREMENT operations cause the operand to be increased or decreased by 1. The DAA command performs the decimal adjust operation in a manner similar to the technique described in Section 3.5.

Most arithmetic and logic operations involve two operands. The address of one of these operands also generally serves as the address or location in which the result will be stored. Usually machine-language commands are available to implement the AND, OR, and XOR or EXCLUSIVE OR logic operations. Similarly, ADD and SUB arithmetic commands are generally available. The SUB command is generally used to subtract the source operand from the destination operand. A COMPARE command performs virtually the same function as a SUB or subtract command. However, the COMPARE command *does not* save the result, and leaves both of the operands undisturbed. It is useful because it affects the *status flags*.

Control transfer instructions are essential to any instruction set. These include JUMP or BRANCH commands, CALL, BRANCH ON CONDITION, RETURN, INTERRUPT, and RETURN FROM INTERRUPT commands. The unconditional JUMP command is analogous to the high-level language GOTO command. *Conditional* branch-type commands perform the designated BRANCH operation if and only if specified conditions related to the current state of the processor are satisfied. Typical examples are BCC, BNE, and BMI commands. These correspond to branch if the carry flag is clear, branch if the zero flag is clear, and branch if the sign flag is set. CALL, RETURN, and INTERRUPT commands may be either unconditional or conditional commands. These commands also involve stack operations as described in the previous section.

Processor control commands include SET status flag commands and CLEAR status flag commands, where specific flags may be specified. They may also include commands that load or modify internal registers, such as the stack pointer. Similarly, a HALT command or other commands that affect the processor state may be classified under this category.

Commands permitting *shifting* and *rotating* of words are included in typical instruction sets. These instructions are frequently designated as ASL, ASR, LSR, ROR, and ROL. Some machines permit only one-bit shifts or rotations, whereas other computers have machine-language capabilities that implement multibit shifts and rotations.

There are two types of shift-right commands: the *arithmetic shift-right* command and the *logic shift-right* command. A logic shift fills in the vacated bit positions of a shifted word with binary zeros. An arithmetic shift left is the same as a logic shift left. An arithmetic shift right fills in these vacated bit positions with values corresponding to the value of the sign bit of the original word. Thus, an arithmetic shift of a signed integer N bit positions to the right corresponds to division of the original signed integer by 2^N. In both types of shift-right operations, bits shifted past the least significant bit position are generally lost.

The rotate command, ROR, is similar to the LSR command, except it causes bits shifted to the right of the least significant bit position to be placed in the most significant bit positions of the adjusted word. Similarly, ROL commands may cause bits shifted to the left of the most significant bit position to be placed in the least significant bit positions. Usually rotate commands are available that produce rotations through the carry bit. That is, the actual word to be rotated includes the value of the carry bit appended to the left of the most significant bit of the operand.

Some computer instruction sets include specific commands used for input/ output operations. Typical command mnemonics are IN and OUT followed by an appropriate address. Other computer instruction sets contain no such commands but use data transfer instructions, such as the MOVE command, to transfer information between I/O devices and the CPU. Most computers have commands that explicitly affect the contents of the system stack. Sometimes these are referred to as PUSH and POP commands. In other cases, stack operations may be specified implicitly by referencing the stack pointer.

Computer instructions that do not fit into categories previously described will be referred to as miscellaneous instructions. The NOP, or no operation, instruction is one such command. Another is the SIGN EXTEND instruction. This instruction may be used to extend the sign bit of an 8-bit signed integer such that the same value is represented as a 16-bit signed integer. Other special commands may exist that specify a particular operating state of the CPU or may specify certain electrical control signals emanating from the CPU.

Example 4.5

Prior to execution of the following program on a typical 16-bit machine, the following registers contain the specified octal numbers.

Register	Number
R0	000000
R1	012345
R2	123456
R3	000004
PC	001000
SP	001000

Then the following program is executed. *Note:* When double operands are specified, the first one is the source operand and the second one is the destination operand.

Location	Label	Command	Operands	Comments
1000	START:	MOVE	R1,R2	
1002	BACK:	ADD	R0,R0	;Double number in R0
1004		INC	R0	;Add 1 to R0
1006		DEC	R3	;Decrement counter
1010		BNE	BACK	;Branch to BACK if Zero ; Flag is not up
1012		HALT		

What octal number will be in each of the specified registers at the conclusion of execution of this program?

Solution   The contents of the SP will not be changed. The octal number stored in the PC will be 1014. The contents of R1 remain the same, but as a result of the MOVE operation, the number in R2 becomes 012345. The first time the command stored at location 1004 is executed, a 1 is placed in R0. Then the number in R3 is decremented and becomes 3, and program control reverts to location 1002, which is labeled BACK. The next time through the sequence of instructions in this loop, the number in R0 is doubled, and 1 is added to it. Then the program executes the steps in this loop twice more. Finally, a 0 appears in R3, and the conditional branch is no longer executed. At this time, the base-10 number 15 or the octal number 17 will be stored in R0.

Example 4.6

Consider a machine with 16-bit registers. Prior to execution of each of the following instructions, the value stored in the carry bit is 0, and the octal number 123456 is stored in R1. After execution of each of the following instructions, what number will be in R1, and what will be the state of the carry flag?

Note: In the following command statements, assume the source operand specifies the number of bits that the destination operand is shifted or rotated.

Note: Rotation operations all involve 17-bit numbers composed of the carry bit followed by the contents of the 16-bit operand.

Note: In both shift and rotate operations, the new state of the carry flag corresponds to the last bit shifted to the left of the most significant bit position of the register or to the right of the most significant bit of the register.

(a) ASR 3,R1

(b) LSR 2,R1

(c) ROL 1,R1

(d) ROR 4,R1

Solution   In order to facilitate our work, let us first write the number stored in R1 as the binary number 1010011100101110.

(a) Because the most significant bit is 1, an arithmetic shift right operation will fill in the vacated bit positions with 1s. Thus, the binary number 1111010011100101 or the octal number 172345 will be in R1, and the carry flag will be up.

(b) The two vacated positions are filled with 0s and a 1 is moved to the carry bit. The number in R1 will be the octal number 024713.

(c) The most significant 1 is shifted into the carry bit, and the 0 that was previously in the carry bit is moved to the least significant bit position. Thus, 047134_8 will be in R1.

(d) The bit that is located four places to the left of the right boundary of the number, a 1, is rotated into the carry bit. The new contents of R1 are 145162_8.

Review

1. Prior to execution of the following program, the following registers contain 16-bit numbers, expressed in octal.

Register	Contents
R1	014315
R2	147762
PC	001000
SP	001000

Location	Command	Operand
1000	MOVE	SP,R1
1002	XOR	R1,R2
1004	PUSH	R2
1006	HALT	

After the program has been executed, what octal number will be in each of the designated registers?

2. What single-operand type of command causes a number to be moved into the program counter?

3. Refer to Example 4.5. Suppose the BNE command is replaced with a BCS (branch if carry set) command. What number will be in R0 after this program is executed?

4. Work Example 4.6 for the case in which a 1 is initially stored in the carry bit and the octal number 176543 is stored in R1.

4.5 COMPUTER EMULATION

During the execution of a single computer instruction, a number of different events must occur in the proper sequence. Let us consider some events that occur during the execution of a typical ADD instruction in which both the source operand and the destination operand are stored in memory. This may be represented by the following symbolic notation:

$$(MEM\_S) + (MEM\_D) => MEM\_D$$

That is, the contents of memory location S added to the contents of memory location D are placed in memory location D. In order to identify a sequence of events necessary to implement this operation, refer to the general representation of a computer in Fig. 4.1 and the representation of typical computer registers in Fig. 4.3. Then it is necessary that the following sequence of events occurs in order that the specified ADD instruction be implemented.

1. (PC) => MAR   ;That is, the contents of the program counter are transferred to the memory address register.

2. (MAR) => ADDRESS BUS

3. Memory is addressed and INSTRUCTION WORD => DATA BUS

4. (DATA BUS) => DATA REG

5. (DATA REG) => INSTRUCTION REG   ;*Note:* Via the *internal data bus.* This step completes a FETCH cycle.

6. Instruction is translated

7. Source operand address is computed

8. Source address => MAR

9. (MAR) => ADDRESS BUS

10. Memory is addressed and OPERAND WORD => DATA BUS

11. (DATA BUS) => DATA REG

12. (DATA REG) => ALU REG_X   ;The internal data transfers are by way of the internal data bus.

13. Destination address is computed.

14. Destination address => MAR.

15. (MAR) => ADDRESS BUS

16. Memory is addressed and OPERAND WORD => DATA BUS

17. (DATA BUS) => DATA REG

18. (DATA REG) => ALU REG_Y
19. ALU is programmed for addition and the operation is done.
20. FLAG REG is updated.
21. Output of ALU => DATA REG
22. (MAR) => ADDRESS BUS
23. (DATA REG) => DATA BUS
24. Memory is accessed and (DATA BUS) is written into memory
25. (PC) => ALU REG
26. ALU increments operand
27. Output of ALU => PC

Recall that in many machines these internal operations may be programmed (refer to Fig. 4.2). If these internal operations are programmed, the corresponding firmware or microcode is stored in the control memory. It is not necessary to identify each of the above operations with a unique program command. Generally, several of the sequential operations are specified within a single word stored in microprogram memory. Observe that, in this particular example, the ADD operation that we described was a valid machine-language instruction only because part of a control program identifies and controls a sequence of internal operations. In this sense, the instruction set available to the user does not exist as part of the machine hardware but is merely being *emulated* by the microcode. Thus, the microprogrammer merely develops firmware that emulates a particular computer architecture. If a *writable control store* is available, different microprograms can be written, and the identical hardware can be used to implement different computers with nonsimilar architecture.

Computer emulation is not done just at the microcode level. Frequently, high-level languages are used to develop programs that simulate the functioning of specified computers. Such programs are useful for developing and debugging software for the emulated machines. In fact, sometimes such emulators are developed for new machines before such machines are available commercially.

The operations needed to emulate a single computer instruction may be summarized as follows:

1. The instruction is FETCHED.
2. The instruction is translated and then associated with a particular task.
3. Addresses of operands are determined. Then the operands are procurred.
4. The desired operations are performed.
5. The dynamic status flags are updated, if necessary.
6. Results are routed to the desired location.
7. The address of the next instruction is determined and placed in the program counter.

Example 4.7 illustrates how some of these tasks are emulated using a high-level language.

Example 4.7 Emulation of a Simple Computer

Consider a computer that has two 8-bit registers available to a programmer—an *accumulator* and a *program counter*. There are also two dynamic status flags—a zero flag and a carry flag. There are just 256 bytes of memory. When this computer is activated, all internal registers are cleared. Thus, the number 0 is stored in the program counter, and the first instruction must be fetched from memory location 0. The instruction set for this computer is defined in Fig. 4.7. Because there is no sign flag, the computer architecture does not identify negative numbers. Using a high-level language, formulate an emulator for this computer.

Solution   An emulator written in FORTRAN is given in Fig. 4.8, and a set of subroutines used by this emulator is given in Fig. 4.9. The instruction is fetched in line 11

SINGLE-BYTE INSTRUCTIONS

Mnemonics	OP code	Flags affected	Comments
CMA	00	None	Complement Accumulator
ROL	01	Z and C	Rotate carry bit and accumulator one bit to the left.
HLT	02	None	Halt

DOUBLE-BYTE INSTRUCTIONS

AND	03 ADDR	Z	(ACC) and (ADDR) => ACC The contents of the specified memory location are ANDED with the contents of the accumulator.
ADD	04 ADDR	Z and C	(ACC) + (ADDR) => ACC
STO	05 ADDR	None	(ACC) => ADDR The contents of the accumulator are stored in the specified address.
DCR	06 ADDR	Z	(ADDR) − 1 => ADDR
BNE	07 ADDR	None	ADDR => PC if Z = 0 Branch to the specified address if the zero flag is not up.

Figure 4.7   Instruction set for the computer emulated in Example 4.7

```
 1 *    COMPUTER EMULATOR !!!!!!!!!!!!!!!!!!!!!
 2         IMPLICIT INTEGER (A-Z)
 3         DIMENSION MEMORY(0:255)
 4         DATA PC/0/,ZERO/0/,CARRY/0/,MEMORY/256*0/,MASK/255/
 5 *  ENTER USER PROGRAM AND DATA USING DATA STATEMENTS!!!
 6 *************************************************************
 7         DATA MEMORY/3,31,5,34,4,33,4,33,5,35,3,31,1,5,34,6,36,6,37,7,15,
 8        &3,31,4,36,0,4,32,5,36,2,0,1,137,0,0,0,8,218*0/
 9 *********** START EMULATION ****************************
10 * FETCH INSTRUCTION
11 50     INSTR = MEMORY(PC)
12         IF (INSTR.GT.7) CALL TRAP(PC)
13 *   INTERPRET AND EXECUTE INSTRUCTIONS
14 *   DETERMINE IF THE INSTRUCTION IS A 1-BYTE OR 2-BYTE INSTRUCTION
15         IF(INSTR.GT.2) GO TO 60
16 *  INTERPRET AND EXECUTE SINGLE BYTE INSTRUCTIONS!!
17         PC = PC + 1
18         GO TO (100,200,300) INSTR+1
19 ******* CMA    ********
20 100    ACCUM = MASK-ACCUM
21         GO TO 50
22 ********* ROL    ********
23 200    ACCUM = 2*ACCUM
24         IF (CARRY.EQ.1) ACCUM = ACCUM + 1
25         CALL CARFIX(ACCUM,CARRY)
26         CALL ZERFIX(ACCUM,ZERO)
27         ACCUM = AND(MASK,ACCUM)
28         GO TO 50
29 ********* HLT    ********
30 300    CALL TERM(ACCUM,PC,ZERO,CARRY,MEMORY)
31         STOP
32 *************************************************************
33 * INTERPRET AND EXECUTE DOUBLE BYTE INSTRUCTIONS
34 60     ADDRES = MEMORY(PC+1)
35         DATA = MEMORY(ADDRES)
36         PC = PC + 2
37         GO TO (302,402,502,602,702)INSTR-2
38 ********* AND    ********
39 302    ACCUM = AND(ACCUM,DATA)
40         CALL ZERFIX(ACCUM,ZERO)
41         GO TO 50
42 ********* ADD    ********
43 402    ACCUM = ACCUM + DATA
44         CALL ZERFIX(ACCUM,ZERO)
45         CALL CARFIX(ACCUM,CARRY)
46         ACCUM = AND(ACCUM,MASK)
47         GO TO 50
48 ********* STO    ********
49 502    MEMORY(ADDRES) = ACCUM
50         GO TO 50
51 ********* DCR    ********
52 602    IF (MEMORY(ADDRES).EQ.0) X=255
53         IF (MEMORY(ADDRES).NE.0) X=MEMORY(ADDRES)-1
54         CALL ZERFIX(X,ZERO)
55         MEMORY(ADDRES)=X
56         GO TO 50
57 ********* BNZ    ********
58 702    IF (ZERO.EQ.0) PC = ADDRES
59         GO TO 50
60         END
```

Figure 4.8 A FORTRAN emulation of the computer described in Example 4.7

```
 61  ************************************************************************
 62  ************************* ROUTINES ************************************
 63        SUBROUTINE TERM(IA,IP,IZ,IC,M)
 64        DIMENSION M(0:255)
 65        WRITE (6,99)
 66  99    FORMAT(//,'      HALT INSTRUCTION ENCOUNTERED!!!!!!!!!',/)
 67        CALL PNTREG(IA,IP,IZ,IC)
 68  1     WRITE(6,98)
 69  98    FORMAT(/,'  MEMORY AVAILABLE FOR INSPECTION.',/,' ENTER 999 TO TER
 70       &MINATE PROGRAM!!',//,'    ENTER FIRST MEMORY ADDRESS TO BE INSPECT
 71       &ED.  USE BASE-10 NUMBERS.')
 72        READ(5,*) I
 73        IF (I.GT.255) GO TO 999
 74        WRITE(6,97)
 75  97    FORMAT('  ENTER LAST ADDRESS TO BE INSPECTED.')
 76        READ (5,*) J
 77        IF ((J.GT.255).OR.(J.LT.I)) GO TO 999
 78        WRITE(6,94)
 79  94    FORMAT('    MEMORY ADDRESS            CONTENTS      (BASE-10)')
 80        DO 998 K=I,J
 81  998   WRITE(6,997) K,M(K)
 82  997   FORMAT (2I20)
 83        GO TO 1
 84  999   WRITE(6,90)
 85  90    FORMAT('  COMPUTER EMULATION COMPLETED!!')
 86        RETURN
 87        END
 88  *************  SUBROUTINE TERM ENDS   *****************************
 89        SUBROUTINE PNTREG(IA,IP,IZ,IC)
 90        WRITE(6,99) IA,IP,IZ,IC
 91  99    FORMAT(5X,'ACCUMULATOR => ',I4,4X,'PC=>',I4,4X,'ZERO=>',I2,4X,'CAR
 92       &RY=>',I2)
 93        RETURN
 94        END
 95  *************  SUBROUTINE PNTREG ENDS   ****************************
 96        SUBROUTINE ZERFIX(N,IZ)
 97        IZ=0
 98  98    IF (AND(255,N).EQ.0) IZ = 1
 99  99    RETURN
100        END
101  *************  SUBROUTINE ZERFIX ENDS   ****************************
102        SUBROUTINE CARFIX(N,IC)
103        IC = 0
104        IF(AND(256,N).NE.0) IC = 1
105        RETURN
106        END
107  *************  SUBROUTINE CARFIX ENDS   ****************************
108        SUBROUTINE TRAP(IPC)
109        WRITE(6,99)
110  99    FORMAT (/,' INSTRUCTION TRAP.  INVALID INSTRUCTION!!!')
111        WRITE (6,98) IPC
112  98    FORMAT(' INVALID INSTRUCTION FETCHED FROM LOCATION ',I3,'!')
113        STOP
114        END
```

Figure 4.9   Subroutines required for the emulator in Fig. 4.8

of the emulator. In line 15, it is determined whether the instruction is a 1-byte or a 2-byte instruction. In lines 18 and 37 the instruction is decoded and associated with a particular task. The desired operations are executed between lines 19 and 29 and between lines 38 and 59. The commands necessary to update the status bits are given in lines 25, 26, 40, 44, 45, and 54. The instruction sequence for each particular code routes the result to the proper destination.

Addresses of operands are determined in line 34. A memory access operation is required to obtain these addresses. Data contained at each of the addresses are obtained from memory in line 35. The data are operands for the AND, ADD, and DCR instructions. The data are not used for the STO or BNE instruction. The address is used as a pointer for the STO instruction and as a possible operand for the BNE command. Lines 17, 37, and 58 are used to update the program counter.

Example 4.8

Refer to Example 4.7. The program to be run must be placed in the designated DATA statement starting at line 7. Document the program that is currently contained in this DATA statement and show results that are obtained if this program is run on the emulator.

Solution   Documentation of this program is given in Fig. 4.10, and results obtained by running the program are given in Fig. 4.11.

Label	Address (base-10)	Mnemonics	Machine code (each 8-bit word is expressed in base-10)		Comments
Start:	00	AND ADR_1	03	31	Clear Accumulator
	02	STO ADR_4	05	34	CLEAR ADR_4
	04	ADD ADR_3	04	33	Load Accumulator from ADR_3
	06	ADD ADR_3	04	33	ADD Numbers
	08	STO ADR_5	05	35	Store LOW of Result
	10	AND ADR_1	03	31	Clear Accumulator
	12	ROL	01		Get Carry Bit
	13	STO ADR_4	05	34	Save HOW of Result
Loop:	15	DEC ADR_6	06	36	Decrement Number
	17	DEC ADR_7	06	37	Decrement Counter
	19	BNE LOOP	07	15	Loop until done
	21	AND ADR_1	03	31	CLA
	23	ADD ADR_6	04	36	Load Number
	25	COM	00		Ones Complement
	26	ADD ADR_2	04	32	Twos Complement
	28	STO ADR_6	05	36	Save Result
	30	HLT	02		Quit
**					Start Data Storage
ADR_1:	31		00		Zero
ADR_2:	32		01		One
ADR_3:	33		137		A Data Number
ADR_4	34		00		Space for HOW of Result
ADR_5	35		00		Space for LOW of Result
ADR_6	36		00		Space for a Result
ADR_7	37		08		Counter

Figure 4.10   Documentation for program included in the emulator in Figure 4.8

```
ENTERING USER PROGRAM


HALT INSTRUCTION ENCOUNTERED!!!!!!!!

ACCUMULATOR =>     8    PC=>  31    ZERO=> 0    CARRY=> 0

MEMORY AVAILABLE FOR INSPECTION.
ENTER 999 TO TERMINATE PROGRAM!!

   ENTER FIRST MEMORY ADDRESS TO BE INSPECTED.   USE BASE-10 NUMBERS.
>31
   ENTER LAST ADDRESS TO BE INSPECTED.
>38
     MEMORY ADDRESS              CONTENTS      (BASE-10)
             31                     0
             32                     1
             33                   137
             34                     1
             35                    18
             36                     8
             37                     0
             38                     0

MEMORY AVAILABLE FOR INSPECTION.
ENTER 999 TO TERMINATE PROGRAM!!

   ENTER FIRST MEMORY ADDRESS TO BE INSPECTED.   USE BASE-10 NUMBERS.
>999
 COMPUTER EMULATION COMPLETED!!
END PROGRAM EXECUTION
```

Figure 4.11   Results obtained by running the program illustrated in Fig. 4.10 on the emulator

Review

1. Suppose a computer instruction is to cause an unconditional branch to a particular address. The address is stored in the memory location immediately following the location in which the operation code for the branch instruction is stored. Indicate a sequence of events that must occur during execution of this instruction.

2. Refer to the sequence of events required for an ADD operation that is specified at the beginning of this section. Among this list of events, there is a subsequence that may be moved to various positions in this queue of events without affecting the results obtained. Identify this subsequence.

3. A computer user finds that the instruction set of the machine specified in Example 4.7 satisfies her requirements, but she needs more memory space. Identify convenient changes that can be made to the computer architecture and to the corresponding emulator so that her requirements are satisfied.

4. Refer to the results obtained from the program run on the emulator shown in Fig. 4.11. The numbers stored in memory locations 34 and 35 are 1 and 18, respectively. What base-10 number is specified by these results?

5. Suppose the following program is run on the emulator described in Example 4.7. At the conclusion of the execution of this program, identify the contents of the accumulator, program counter, zero flag, and carry flag.

Memory Location	Machine Code
00	04 00
02	04 00
04	00
05	01
06	02

REFERENCES

ECKHOUSE, R. H., and R. L. MORRIS, *Minicomputer Systems.* Englewood Cliffs, N.J.: Prentice-Hall, 1975.

GIBSON, G. A., and Y. LIU, *Microcomputers for Engineers and Scientists.* Englewood Cliffs, N.J.: Prentice-Hall, 1980.

KATZAN, H. *Microprogramming Primer.* New York: McGraw-Hill, 1977.

LEVENTHAL, L. A., *Introduction to Microprocessors: Software, Hardware, Programming,* Prentice-Hall, N.J.: Englewood Cliffs, 1978.

Memory Integrated Circuits D.A.T.A. Book, vol. 28, book 7. Electronic Information Series. San Diego: D.A.T.A. Inc., March 1983.

OSBORNE, A. *An Introduction to Microcomputers, vol. 1, Basic Concepts.* Berkeley: Calif. Adam Osborne and Associates, 1975.

EXERCISES

1. A computer CPU has a 16-bit address bus and an 8-bit data bus.
   (a) How many different memory addresses are there?
   (b) How many *bits* of primary memory storage can this system have?

2. What is the difference between a FETCH operation and a memory-read operation?

3. Give a one-word name relating to each of the following descriptions:
   (a) Sharing of common facilities, such as the pins on a CPU chip
   (b) A set of digital lines common to several devices
   (c) A computer CPU fabricated on a single large-scale integrated circuit.
   (d) A large-scale integrated circuit
   (e) The attributes of a computer CPU available to a programmer
   (f) An internal control program

4. Utilizing appropriate references, identify specifically at least one type of each of the following memory chips:
   (a) static RAM
   (b) PROM
   (c) EPROM
   (d) dynamic RAM

   Indicate a unique identifier for each chip as well as its capacity and the pin numbers corresponding to address lines and data lines.

5. How many address lines would you expect to find on a 65,536 × 1 RAM chip? How many pins corresponding to data lines would you expect to find on this chip?

6. How many 2048 × 1 chips are required to implement a memory board containing 16K bytes of memory capacity?

7. When developing a machine-language program, how can a programmer decide how much stack space should be reserved in memory?

The following information refers to Exercises 8 through 11. These conditions hold before the set of specified operations is executed. A 16-bit machine has instruction codes that are all 16-bit codes, and memory addresses refer to byte addresses. The least significant byte of each word is stored in the lower-numbered memory address. The contents of internal registers and memory locations are identified by the following octal numbers.

Register	Contents
PC	1000
SP	700
PSW	1234

Memory Location	Contents
674	01
675	02
676	04
677	06
700	10
701	14
702	16
703	32
704	42

8. Suppose the following two program statements are stored in memory as indicated.

Memory Location	Instruction	Comment
1000	PUSH PSW	Save the status word
1002	JMP 1234	Jump to location 1234

After execution of this program segment, what will be the new values stored in each of the following registers?
(a) the program counter
(b) the stack pointer
(c) the stack registers

9. Suppose the operation codes corresponding to the following two program statements are stored in memory as indicated.

Memory Location	Instruction	Comment
1000	POP PSW	
1002	CALL 2040	Call subroutine starting at location 2040

After execution of this program segment, what will be the new values stored in the following registers?

(a) the program counter

(b) the stack pointer

(c) the stack registers

10. Suppose the code corresponding to the following instruction is stored in location 1000:   INTERRUPT 200. Execution of this statement causes a programmed interrupt, and program control branches to octal location 200. After this command is executed, what octal number will be in each of the following registers? (*Note:* Assume INTERRUPT and TRAP operations function as described in Example 4.4.)

(a) the program counter

(b) the stack pointer

(c) the stack registers

11. Suppose the code for a RETURN FROM INTERRUPT command is stored in octal memory location 1000. At the conclusion of execution of this program statement, what number will be in each of the following registers?

(a) the program counter

(b) the stack pointer

(c) the PSW register

12. Prior to execution of each of the following program commands, suppose the 16-bit number in R1 is 175632_8, and the carry bit is cleared. What number will be in R1, and what will be the state of the carry flag after execution of each of the following instructions?

(a) ASR 3,R1

(b) LSR 3,R1

(c) ROR 2,R1 (*Note:* Assume rotations involve the 17-bit word composed of the carry bit concatenated with the contents of the specified register.)

(d) ROL 5,R1

13. Repeat Exercise 12 for the case in which the number in R1 is initially 037642_8, and the carry bit is initially set.

14. Prior to execution of each of the following instructions, the octal number in R1 is 103432 and the octal number in R2 is 077615. What number will be in R2 after each of the designated instructions is executed?

	Instruction	Operand	Comment
(a)	COM	R2	Complement R2
(b)	NEG	R2	
(c)	ADD	R1,R2	
(d)	SUB	R1,R2	DST $-$ SRC $=>$ DST
(e)	CMP	R1,R2	COMPARE operation
(f)	AND	R1,R2	
(g)	OR	R1,R2	
(h)	XOR	R1,R2	EXCLUSIVE OR operation

15. Refer to parts (c), (d), and (e) of Exercise 14. What will be the state of the sign flag, zero flag, and carry flag after execution of each of these instructions?

16. Refer to Example 4.5. Suppose the BNE command is replaced with a BMI (branch if minus) command. This command produces a branch operation only if the sign flag is

set when the command is being executed. What number will be in R0 after the corresponding program is executed?

17. Using the emulated machine described in Section 4.5, write and test a program segment that replaces the word stored in memory location 255 with its twos-complement.

18. Using the emulated machine described in Section 4.5, design a program that adds together three unsigned numbers stored in consecutive memory locations. The high-order byte of the answer, HOW, and the low-order byte of the answer, LOW, should be stored in consecutive memory locations.

19. Refer to the FORTRAN emulator in Fig. 4.8. It is awkward to enter a program as part of a DATA statement. Modify this FORTRAN program so that an emulated program may be loaded into memory by reading numbers entered from the console.

20. Suppose two additional commands are to be added to the instruction set of the emulated machine. These commands are to be the following:

Mnemonic	Code	Command
INC ———	08 ADDR	Increment number in memory
BCS ———	09 ADDR	Branch if Carry Set

Modify the emulator so it includes these commands.

5

The PDP-11

The letters *PDP* originally were used to represent the words *programmed data processor*, a line of small computers manufactured by the Digital Equipment Company of Maynard, Massachusetts. These small computers were probably the first family of computers to be referred to as *minicomputers*. The PDP-11 was introduced in 1970. Since then the term PDP-11 has been used to represent a *family* of computers and computer components. Even PDP-11 CPUs (central processing units) consist of a family of processors.

In order for a class of computers to be represented as a family, it is desirable that programs written for an early version or simple implementation of the system are able to be run on more sophisticated implementations of the system. Thus, new and improved versions of a computer system or a computer CPU should be *upward compatible* with previous implementations of the machine. It is very important that previously developed software can be run on newer processors without the need for extensive modifications.

5.1 THE PDP-11 FAMILY

The PDP-11 family consists of general-purpose digital computers that perform both 8-bit and 16-bit operations. Some models of the family are the PDP-11/34, 11/40, 11/50, 11/60, and 11/70. In 1976, a PDP-11 processor fabricated on a small number of large-scale integrated circuits was introduced. This microprocessor is referred to as the LSI-11. The LSI-11 consists of either a set of four large-scale integrated circuits or a set of five large-scale integrated circuits, depending on whether or not *extended arithmetic operations* are desired. Two of these chips are used merely to store microcode for the CPU control unit. Discussions in this textbook related to the PDP-11 are based on the LSI-11 implementations of the processor. However, most of the attributes that are discussed relate to all members of the PDP-11 family.

Since 1976, significant enhancements have been made on large-scale and very-large-scale integrated circuits. Single-chip implements of the PDP-11 that are compatible with the LSI-11 have been developed. One such implementation is the T11 integrated circuit. This is a relatively inexpensive implementation of the PDP-11 that has been incorporated on a single 40-pin chip. A more powerful version of the PDP-11 is available on a single 60-pin chip, the J11. This implementation includes a 32-bit internal data bus, extended arithmetic and floating-point capabilities, user-support firmware, and interfacing devices incorporated on the CPU chip.

Figure 5.1 is an illustration of the internal registers associated with the PDP-11 architecture. Only registers that are directly available for use by a programmer are shown. Observe that there are eight general-purpose 16-bit registers and a 16-bit processor status word register. The contents of any of these general-purpose registers may be used either as a source operand or as a destination operand. Registers R0 through R5 may be used to store either data operands or memory addresses. Register R6 serves as the system stack pointer register. When subroutines are invoked or when INTERRUPT or TRAP operations are executed, information will be stored in memory on the stack structure identified by the contents of R6. Register R7 is a program counter.

The PSW (processor status word) register contains four status bits. These bits correspond to the *sign, zero, overflow,* and *carry* flags. (The functions of these flags were discussed in Chapter 3.) The T bit, or *trace trap* bit, is a *control* bit that is set or cleared by a program command. Its use is discussed and illustrated in Chapter 9. Bits 7, 6, and 5 are used to identify the *priority* of a current operating state. Devices having a *higher* priority may interrupt a program currently in progress. The

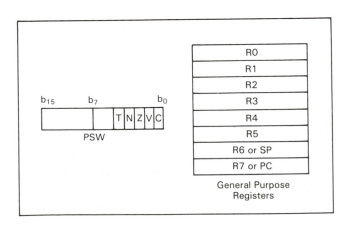

General Purpose
Registers

Figure 5.1   A representation of PDP-11 registers

functions of *interrupts* and priority interrupt levels are also discussed in Chapter 9. Bits 15 to 8 of the processor status word are used only in higher-level implementations of PDP-11 architecture, and will not be discussed further in this textbook.

Addresses on PDP-11 systems are *byte* addresses. All instructions, however, consist of one or more 16-bit *words*. Similarly, data may consist of either bytes, words, or groups of words. When words are stored in memory, the least significant bytes are stored first. Words stored in memory are identified by the address of the least significant byte. Generally this is an *even* address. All instructions must be stored in even-numbered addresses. However, when system software or system firmware is used to display words stored in memory, the word is displayed in the normal manner, that is, the most significant characters are displayed first.

Example 5.1

Prior to execution of an instruction, the internal registers of a PDP-11 contain the following octal numbers.

$$(R3) = 145632$$
$$(R7) = 001016$$

A one-word instruction is fetched and executed. The command is to MOVE the word stored in R3 to memory location 2000_8. After execution of this command
(a) What octal number will be in R7?
(b) What octal number will be in the byte address 2000_8?
(c) What octal number will be in the byte address 2001_8?

Solution   The program counter will be incremented twice, so 1020_8 will be in R7. The low-order byte of the word, 232_8, will be in octal location 2000, and the high-order byte, 313_8, will be in octal location 2001. If we wish to identify the *word* stored in location 2000, we can say that 145623 is in location 2000.

The program counter shown in Fig. 5.1 is a 16-bit register. This suggests that 2^{16}, or 65,536, bytes of memory may be addressed without the need for an external memory management system. On PDP-11 systems, input/output device registers are treated in the same manner as memory locations. That is, to input information from an input device, the same type of machine-language command is utilized as is used for moving words or bytes from memory to CPU registers. Thus, it is necessary to associate some of the address space with memory addresses and some of this space with peripheral devices. The upper 4K (4096) word addresses in LSI-11 implementations are reserved for addressing peripheral device registers.

A PDP-11 *instruction set* is given in Appendix B. Typical instructions may be classified as either *single-operand* instructions or *double-operand* instructions. The format for these typical instruction types is illustrated in Fig. 5.2. Observe that for the single-operand instructions the operand is identified by specifying a *mode* and a *register*. Three bits are used to specify the mode, and 3 bits are used to specify a CPU register. Thus, the location of the operand is identified by specifying one of eight possible modes and one of the CPU general-purpose registers. Similarly, if two operands are required, 6 bits of the instruction code are used to specify the

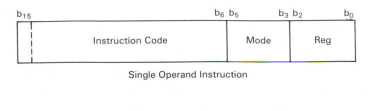

Single Operand Instruction

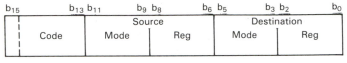

Double Operand Instruction

Figure 5.2   Formats for typical PDP-11 instructions

source operand, and 6 bits are required to specify the location of the destination operand. In most cases the result of the operation will be placed in the location specified by the destination mode and the destination register. The specifics related to operand addressing are covered in the following section.

Review

1. Cite an attribute that is essential in defining a *family* of computers.
2. Suppose the octal number 162543 is in register R0, and a command is given to store the contents of R0 in memory location 3012. Identify the byte stored in location 3012 and the byte stored in location 3013.
3. Suppose the register R1 contains the octal number 177760, and register R2 contains the octal number 140007. A command is given to add the contents of these two registers. Identify the four least significant bits stored in the program status register after this instruction has been executed.
4. Which two CPU registers would you expect to contain only even numbers? Explain.
5. The valid range of word addresses available on a PDP-11 system consists of the even numbers between 000000_8 and 177776_8.
   (a) Identify the range of memory addresses in which instructions may be stored.
   (b) Identify the range of word addresses for I/O registers.

5.2 ADDRESSING MODES

A variety of addressing modes are available on PDP-11 computers. The mode and register identifiers relating to an operand or to two operands are contained within the instruction code word. The manner in which this information is included as part of an instruction was illustrated in Fig. 5.2. Because 3 bits are allocated for mode specification, there are eight possible addressing modes. These are referred to as mode 0 through mode 7. These eight addressing modes are defined in Fig. 5.3.

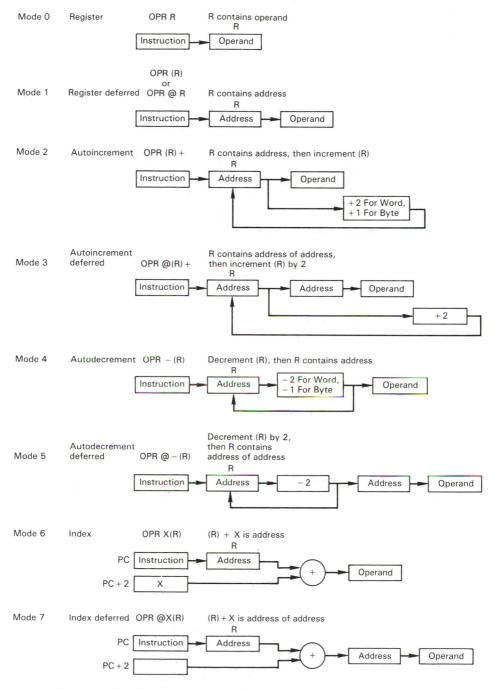

R is a general register, 0 to 7
(R) is the contents of that register

Mode 0   Register   OPR R   R contains operand

Mode 1   Register deferred OPR (R)
                             or
                             OPR @ R   R contains address

Mode 2   Autoincrement   OPR (R) +   R contains address, then increment (R)

Mode 3   Autoincrement
          deferred   OPR @(R) +   R contains address of address,
                                         then increment (R) by 2

Mode 4   Autodecrement   OPR − (R)   Decrement (R), then R contains address

Mode 5   Autodecrement
          deferred   OPR @ − (R) Decrement (R) by 2,
                                         then R contains
                                         address of address

Mode 6   Index   OPR X(R)   (R) + X is address

Mode 7   Index deferred   OPR @X(R)   (R) + X is address of address

Figure 5.3 PDP-11 addressing modes (Copyright Digital Equipment Corporation, 1978. All rights reserved. Reprinted by permission.)

101

Mode 0 and mode 1 addressing modes are referred to as *register addressing* and *deferred-register addressing* modes. In mode 0 addressing, the operand is in the specified register. In mode 1 addressing, the operand is in memory, and the address of the operand is in the specified register. This address is sometimes referred to as a *pointer*.

Recall that PDP-11 architecture supports both *byte* operations and *word* operations. However, not all instructions can be performed on both byte operands and on word operands. The instruction set given in Appendix B clearly identifies instructions that can be used with both types of operands. The instruction code mnemonics specified in Appendix B refer to byte operations if the letter *B* is appended to the code mnemonic. Otherwise, the operation codes refer to word operands.

Refer again to the typical instruction formats in Fig. 5.2. Observe that bit 15, or the most significant bit of an instruction, is segmented from the remainder of the space used for the operation code. If a particular instruction can be used either for byte operations or for word operations, then bit 15 is used to specify the type of operation. A 0 is used to code a *word* operation, and a 1 is used to code a *byte* operation.

Example 5.2

Refer to the following instructions that are identified by the appropriate mnemonics and operands.

(a) COM R2

(b) ADD R1,(R3)

Prior to execution of each of the following instructions, the indicated registers contain the following numbers. (*Note:* In PDP-11 systems, octal numbers are generally used to specify codes, addresses, and the contents of CPU registers and memory registers.)

$$(R1) = 013762 \quad (R2) = 143205 \quad (R3) = 002000$$
$$(R7) = 001000 \quad (2000) = 012345$$

(That is, the contents of memory location 2000 are 012345.)

Identify the operation code for each of the following instructions, and identify the contents of any register or memory location that change during execution of the command.

Solution   **(a)** From Appendix B, it is seen that the code for this instruction is □051DD. Because the instruction is a *word* instruction, its most significant bit is 0. The first *D* refers to the *mode* of addressing the single operand—mode 0. The second *D* refers to the particular CPU register—R2 in this case. Thus, the operation code is 005102. Because the program counter initially identifies location 1000, this operation code must be stored in location 1000. At the end of the execution of this instruction, the address of the next instruction will be in the PC. That is, (R7) = 1002. The operand in R2 will be complemented. Thus, (R2) = 034572.

(b) The operation code for the ADD instruction is 06SSDD. The source operand uses mode 0, register 1 addressing, and the destination operand is identified by mode 1, register 3. Thus, the instruction code is 060113. The instruction causes the word R1 to be added to the word in memory location 2000. Thus, after the instruction is executed, (R7) = 1002, (2000) = 026327, and the contents of R3 are *not* changed.

Example 5.3

Just before execution of the following instruction

    ADD   R2,@R5

the designated registers contain the following numbers.

(R2) = 117563   (R5) = 1234   (R7) = 1234   (1234) = ?

(a) What number will be in memory location 1234 before execution of the instruction?
(b) What number will be in each of the designated registers after execution of the instruction?

Solution **(a)** The instruction code for the designated instruction 060215 must be in memory location 1234 if it is to be the next instruction executed.

(b) This instruction causes the number 117563 to be added to the contents of memory location 1234. Thus, execution of the instruction in this case causes the instruction code itself to be changed. The designated registers will now contain the following numbers:

(R2) = 117563   (R7) = 1236   (R5) = 1234   (1234) = 000000

Addressing modes 2 and 3 are referred to, respectively, as *autoincrement* and *autoincrement-deferred* addressing modes. The autoincrement mode is similar to the register-deferred mode of addressing. The operand is in the memory location identified by the pointer in the designated register. After the operand is selected, the number in the designated CPU register is incremented. The value of the pointer is increased by 1 if the operation is a *byte* operation and by 2 if the instruction is a *word* operation. There is an exception: If the pointer is in either R6 or R7, and if the instruction is a byte operation, the designated byte operation is executed. However, the pointer is increased by 2, as the stack pointer register and the program counter should contain only even numbers.

The autoincrement-deferred mode of addressing is similar to the autoincrement mode. However, the pointer in the CPU register always identifies a memory address in which another *pointer* is stored. This second pointer is the address of the *operand*. The operand itself may be either a word or a byte. However, because the pointer in the CPU register identifies the address of a word, it is always incremented by 2. The first operand fetched from memory is a pointer corresponding to the address of the operand. This pointer may be located anywhere in memory, and its location is not related to the location of the corresponding instruction. After this pointer has been procurred by the CPU, memory must again be accessed in order to procure the operand. Addressing in which memory is first randomly accessed for one or more pointers and then is randomly accessed for an operand is referred to as *indirect addressing*.

Example 5.4

Consider the following command:

ADD @(R3)+, (R2)+

Before execution

(R7) = 1000   (R3) = 1050   (R2) = 1100   (1100) = 2000
(1050) = 2000   (2000) = 012345   (1000) = operation code

After execution of the instruction, what are the contents of each of the registers?

Solution   (R7) = 1002   (R3) = 1052   (R2) = 1102   (1100) = 014345
(1050) = 2000   (2000) = 012345   (1000) = 063322

Example 5.5

Consider the following command:

COMB @(R7)+

Before execution:

(R7) = 1226   (1226) = operation code   (1230) = 1226

After execution of the instruction, identify the contents of each of the registers.

Solution   Before execution of the instruction, the operation code 105137 is stored in memory location 1226. Observe that the pointer for the particular instruction is in R7, which is the program counter. We cannot work this particular exercise unless we know at what stage of a computer instruction the program counter is actually incremented. On PDP-11 computers, *the value in the program counter is incremented by 2 near the very beginning of the sequence of events required for instruction execution.* This means that by the time an instruction code is actually executed, the value in the program counter has already been updated. Thus, during execution of this instruction, the CPU pointer has a value of 1230. Because deferred addressing is used, the pointer stored at location 1230 is fetched, and the value in the designated register is incremented by 2. Thus, (R7) = 1232. The pointer fetched from location 1230 identifies the byte operand stored in byte address 1226. This operand happens to be the least significant byte of the instruction code being executed. Thus, the new word stored in address 1226 is 105240. The contents of memory location 1230 are unchanged.

Modes 4 and 5 are referred to, respectively, as *autodecrement* and *autodecrement-deferred* addressing modes. In a sense, they are inverse operations in comparison with the autoincrement addressing modes. In the autodecrement mode, the pointer in the CPU register is *first decremented,* and then the updated pointer is the address of the operand. The designated CPU pointer is decremented by 1 if the operand is a byte operand and by 2 if the operand is a word operand. This operation is useful for pushing information on user-defined stacks if registers R0 through R5 are used for the appropriate pointers. Similarly, data may be pushed onto the system stack if the register associated with the autodecrement mode of addressing is R6. If either R6 or R7 is used in conjunction with *byte* operations in the autodecrement mode, they are *first* decremented by 2 in order that the numbers in these registers remain even. Mode 5, or the autodecrement-deferred mode, is similar to mode 4 except that indirect addressing is utilized.

Example 5.7

Formulate a command that causes the contents of R2 to be *pushed* onto the system stack.

Solution   Expressed in symbolic form, the command is MOV R2, $-$(SP). The symbol MOV is the mnemonic for the MOVE command. The code for this command is 010246. *Note:* In symbolic code, frequently SP is used to represent R6, and PC is used to represent R7.

Example 5.8

Consider the following command:

```
ADD  -(R2),@-(R3)
```

Before execution:

$$(R7) = 1006 \quad (R3) = 1052 \quad (R2) = 1102 \quad (1100) = 2000$$
$$(1050) = 2000 \quad (2000) = 012345 \quad (1006) = \text{operation code}$$

After execution of the instruction, what number will be in each of the designated registers?

Solution $(R7) = 1010 \quad (R3) = 1050 \quad (R2) = 1100 \quad (1100) = 2000 \quad (1050)$
$$= 2000 \quad (2000) = 014345 \quad (1000) = 064253$$

Example 5.9

Consider the following sequence of instructions:

Location	Mnemonics	Code
1000	ADD @$-$(R7),R0	065700
1002	HALT	000000

Initially, R7 = 1000. What number will be in R7 after the HALT instruction is executed?

Solution   Early during the execution of the first instruction, the number in the program counter is incremented to 1002. Then, when the source operand is being identified, the number in R7 is decremented by 2. The number in location 1000, or 64700, is then added to R0. At the conclusion of this operation, the number 1000 is in R7. Thus, the same instruction continues to be fetched and executed, and the HALT instruction is never encountered.

Modes 6 and 7 are referred to as *index* and *index-deferred* modes of addressing. These addressing modes are essentially different from those previously described, as the location of an operand cannot be determined from a single 16-bit instruction word. For index addressing, the address of the operand is the 16-bit sum of the contents of the specified CPU register, referred to as an *index register,* and a 16-bit *displacement*. The displacement word immediately follows the instruction code word. Thus, to specify complete instructions using index addressing, an instruction consisting of at least two 16-bit words is required. If a two-operand instruction is to be used, and if both the source and the destination operands use a form of index addressing, then the instruction will consist of *three words*. Deferred index addressing differs from index addressing in that the 16-bit sum of the displacement word and the contents of the index register are the address of a pointer to the operand rather than the address of the operand.

Example 5.10

Consider the following command:

    COM 200(R2)

Before execution:

$$(R7) = 1000 \qquad (R2) = 1200 \qquad (1400) = 012345$$

(a) Identify the complete instruction code.
(b) Identify the numbers in the designated registers after execution of the instruction.

Solution   **(a)** The operation code 005162 is stored at location 1000, and the displacement 000200 is stored at location 1002.
(b) $(R7) = 1004 \qquad (R2) = 1200 \qquad (1400) = 165432$

Example 5.11

Consider the following command:

    ADD 100(R2),@200(R3)

Before execution:

$(R7) = 1000 \quad (1000) = 066273 \quad (1002) = 100 \quad (1004) = 200 \quad (R2) = 1000 \quad (1100) = 3000 \quad (R3) = 2000 \quad (2200) = 1004 \quad (3000) = 123456$

After execution of the instruction, what number will be in each of the registers?

Solution   Because two displacement words are required, $(R7) = 1006$. The instruction causes the number in 1100 to be added to the contents of 1004. Thus, the instruction modifies itself, and the new value of the number stored in location 1004 is 3200. The numbers stored in all the other designated registers are unchanged.

Example 5.12

Consider the following command:

    COM 100(R7)   OR   COM 100(PC)

Before execution:

$$(R7) = 1000 \quad (1000) = 005167 \quad (1002) = 100$$
$$\text{(all other memory registers)} = 000000$$

After execution of this command, which memory location will contain the word 177777?

Solution   Both the instruction code and the displacement word must be fetched from memory. After the displacement is procurred from memory location 1002, the value in the program counter will be updated to 1004. Thus, the address of the operand is 1104.

Each of the addressing modes that we have discussed uses one of the eight general-purpose registers in order to specify an operand. Use of register 7, the program counter, is a useful way to specify operand addresses. Four particular cases of program-counter addressing are especially important. Special symbolic code is used to represent these cases. These special program-counter addressing modes are defined in Fig. 5.4.

Two modes of addressing that are used on a number of machines are *immediate* addressing and *absolute* addressing. Immediate addressing implies that the operand is stored in memory immediately following the corresponding instruction code. Absolute addressing implies that the address of the operand is stored in memory immediately after the operation code. In either case, by the time execution of the instruction is completed, it is required that the number in the program counter identify the *next instruction* rather than a data operand or a data pointer.

In order to implement immediate addressing on a PDP-11, mode 2, register 7 addressing is utilized. In order to implement absolute addressing, mode 3, register 7 addressing is used. The symbolic notation OPR #N is used to represent *immediate* addressing. This symbolic notation implies that

1. The operation code for OPR, using mode 2, register 7 addressing, is stored in a memory location.
2. The operand N is stored in the successive memory location.

Similarly, the notation OPR @#A is used to represent *absolute* addressing. The notation OPR @#A implies that

1. The operation code for OPR, using mode 3, register 7 addressing, is stored in a memory location.
2. The address A is stored in the following memory location.

Generally, immediate addressing is used just for source operands. However, the general addressing modes available on the PDP-11 do not enforce this restriction. Absolute addressing is useful for accessing both source operands and destination operands.

Program Counter Addressing   Register = 7

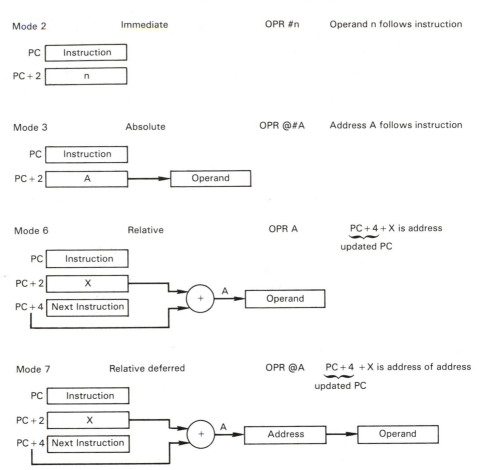

Figure 5.4   Special program-counter addressing modes (Copyright Digital Equipment Corporation, 1978. All rights reserved. Reprinted by permission.)

Example 5.13

Consider the following command:

        ADD #1234, @#2000

Before execution:

$$(R7) = 1000 \qquad (2000) = 123456$$

(a) Determine the complete operation code for this instruction.

(b) After execution of the instruction is completed, what number will be in each of the registers?

Solution (a) Mode 2, register 7 addressing is used to determine the source operand, and mode 3, register 7 addressing is used for the destination operand. Therefore, the instruction code is 062737, and this code is stored in location 1000. The immediate operand 001234 is stored in the successive memory location, or at address 1002. Similarly, the address 2000 is stored in memory location 1004.

        (b) Because the contents of the program counter are first updated and then autoincrementation of the program counter occurs twice, the number 1006 will be in the program counter after instruction execution is completed. The number 124712 will be in memory location 2000.

When the program counter is used as an index register, the addressing mode is referred to as *relative addressing*. Use of relative addressing is very popular because the location of an operand is identified without making reference to an *absolute* address. That is, if a program that uses relative addressing is moved to a different section of memory, operands will still be in the same relative position with respect to numbers in the program counter. Therefore, the relative addresses of these operands will not have to be modified even though the operands are now stored in different absolute addresses. Programs written using relative addressing are said to be written in *position-independent code*.

Mode 6, register 7 addressing is used to implement relative addressing on PDP-11 computers. If a pointer to the operand rather than the operand itself is to be initially accessed, mode 7, register 7 addressing is utilized. This is referred to as *relative-deferred* addressing.

In order to use relative addressing techniques correctly, we must know precisely what number is in the program counter at the time the address of a designated operand is being determined. Suppose either mode 6 or mode 7 addressing is being utilized, and the instruction involves just a single operand. Furthermore, suppose the number P is stored in R7 at the beginning of the corresponding instruction. Then the number $P + 4$ will be in R7 at the time the address of the source operand is computed.

Now consider an instruction containing a double operand. If the source operand uses relative addressing, the number $P + 4$ will be in R7 at the time the address of the source operand is computed. If the destination operand is also identified using relative addressing, $P + 6$ will be in R7 when the address of the destination operand is being computed. However, if the destination operand uses relative addressing, and the source operand does not use either immediate, absolute, or relative addressing, then $P + 4$ will be in R7 when the address of the destination operand is being computed.

Example 5.14

Suppose the symbol FIRST is used to identify memory location 1020, and the symbol SECOND is used to identify memory address 1032. Consider the following instruction that is stored in memory starting at location 1000.

```
    ADD FIRST,SECOND
```

Identify the complete operation code for this instruction.

Solution   Refer to Fig. 5.4. It is seen that we are using symbolic notation to specify relative addressing for both the source operand and the destination operand. The instruction code 066767 must be stored in location 1000, and appropriate displacements must be stored in locations 1002 and 1004. When the address of the source operand is being computed, the number 1004 will be in the program counter, so the source displacement is 1020 − 1004 = 0014. Similarly, when the destination displacement is determined, 1006 is in the program counter. Therefore, the destination displacement is 1032 − 1006 = 0024. Thus, the complete instruction is stored in memory in the following way:

Memory Location	Contents
1000	066767
1002	000014
1004	000024

Example 5.15

Consider the following sequence of computer instructions or *computer program:*

Label	Memory Location	Instruction	Code
FIRST:	1000	COM @(R5)	005115
	1002	ADD #FIRST, @#SECOND	062737
			001000
			001000
	1010	ADD R3,CAT	062767
			000010
	1014	ADD #45,DOG	062767
			000045
			000004
	1022	HALT	000000
CAT:	1024		001111
DOG:	1026		002222

Before execution:

$$(R7) = 1000 \quad (R3) = 003333 \quad (R5) = 1000$$

After execution of the program has been completed, what number will be in each of the following registers?

    (a) R7
    (b) R3
    (c) R5
    (d) Memory location FIRST or location 1000
    (e) Memory location 1024 or CAT
    (f) Memory location DOG

Solution   During execution of this program, the number in location 1000 is complemented. Then 1000 is added to this number. Then the number in R3 is added to the number in CAT, and 45 is added to the number in DOG. The results are the following:

$$(R7) = 1024 \quad (R3) = 3333 \quad (R5) = 1000 \quad (1000) = 173662$$
$$(1024) = 4444 \quad (1026) = 2267$$

Review

1. Find the complete operation code for each of the following instructions.
   (a) ADD R1,(R2)
   (b) COM (R7)+   or   COM (PC)+
   (c) ADD #1234, −(R3)
   (d) ADD #42, 56(R5)
   (e) ADD @#42, #56

2. Prior to execution of each of the following instructions, the following numbers are in the designated CPU and memory registers.

   (R7) = 1000   (R1) = 1200   (R2) = 1400   (R3) = 1402
             (1200) = 1300   (1300) = 1400   (1400) = 1200

   Identify the contents of each of the registers after each of the following instructions has been executed.
   (a) ADD −(R3), (R2)+
   (b) COMB R3
   (c) COMB (R1)+
   (d) ADD #200, 200(R1)
   (e) ADD #200, @200(R1)

3. Prior to execution of each of the following instructions, the following numbers are in the designated registers.

   (R7) = 1000   (R6) = 1000   (R1) = 2002   (R2) = 2000
             (2000) = 2200   (2200) = 123456   (776) = 000000

   Identify the contents of each of the designated registers after each of the following instructions has been executed.
   (a) MOV @#2000, @ −(R1)
   (b) MOV (SP)+, R1
   (c) MOV @200(R2), −(SP)

4. Refer to the following program written in symbolic code:

Label	Instruction
START:	MOV (R5),@#(2000)
NEXT:	MOV #NEXT, R0
	ADD 20(R2),@ −2(R4)
TERM:	HALT

   The program is stored in memory starting at location 1000. Translate the program into machine code, and indicate the address at which each instruction is stored.

5. Refer to the program in Review question 4. Prior to execution of this program, the following registers contain the designated numbers.

   (R7) = 1000   (R0) = 123456   (R2) = 760   (R4) = 2002
             (R5) = 1006   (2000) = 7777   (1004) = 012700

   What number will be in each of these locations after the program has been run?

5.3 THE PDP-11 INSTRUCTION SET

A PDP-11 instruction set is given in Appendix B. Many of these instructions are virtually the same as the typical computer instructions described in Section 4.4, and no further elaboration is required. Several of the instructions described in Appendix B are *extended arithmetic options*. These commands, which include floating-point instructions, will be discussed in Section 7.3.

The MOV command is used for the majority of *data transfer* operations. In addition, this command is used for *input/output* operations and for *explicit stack operations*. The only other commands directly involving data transfers are the MTPS command and the MFPS command. The MTPS command moves a byte operand into the condition code segment of the processor status word register, and the MFPS command moves the byte stored in the condition code register to a destination location. One exception should be noted: The T bit (bit 4) in the processor status register cannot be set using the MTPS command. The data transfer operations that are performed using these move-type operations do not affect the contents of the source address.

Example 5.16

Using symbolic code, formulate a program command for each of the following specifications.
(a) Transfer the word in memory location 2000 to location 3000.
(b) Read the byte located in the input register at location 177756 into CPU register R0.
(c) Send the low-order byte in R0 to the output register located at 177760.
(d) Pop the top 2 bytes stored on the system stack into R5.
(e) Clear the condition codes register.

Solution   (a) MOV @#2000,@#3000
              (b) MOVB @#177756,R0
              (c) MOVB R0,@#177760
              (d) MOV (SP)+,R5
              (e) MTPS #0

There are a number of *arithmetic* and *logic* commands available in the basic instruction set. The arithmetic commands include the ADD, SUB, INC, and DEC commands. The subtract command subtracts the source operand from the destination operand, places the result in the destination address, and sets the carry flag if and only if there is a borrow requirement. The *increment* and *decrement* commands add or subtract 1 from the destination operand but *do not* affect the contents of the carry flag. The ADC, or add-carry, command adds the current value of the carry bit to the destination operand. This command is useful in performing multiple-precision addition operations. The SBC command subtracts the value of the carry bit (or borrow bit) from the destination operand. The CMP, or compare, command produces a subtraction operation. However, the results of the subtraction operation are not saved, and neither the source operand nor the destination is disturbed. The compare command subtracts the destination operand from the source operand. The TST, or test, command produces an arithmetic operation that essentially adds 0 to the destination operand. This does not affect the result but does affect the status flags.

The logic commands included in the PDP-11 instruction set are similar but not identical to those described in Section 4.4. The CLR, or clear, command places all zeros in the destination location. The COM, or complement, command replaces the operand with its ones-complement, and the NEG, or negate, command replaces the operand with its twos-complement. The BIS, or bit set, operation is a logical OR operation. The logic operation is performed between the source operand and the destination operand and is stored in the destination address. The BIT, or bit test, operation is a logic AND operation. The source operand is ANDed to the destination operand. The results are not saved but determine the state of the sign and zero flags. The BIC, or bit clear, command performs the AND operation between the *complement* of the source operand and the destination operand and saves the result in the destination address. The XOR command performs the EXCLUSIVE OR operation between the source operand, which must be stored in a CPU register, and a destination operand.

Example 5.17

Using symbolic code, formulate a program command for each of the following specifications.
(a) Raise the zero flag if and only if the least significant bit in the byte stored at address 177756 is a 0. Do not modify the contents of this location.
(b) Erase or set to 0 all bits in R0 except the four least significant bits.

Solution   **(a)** BITB #1,@#177765
              (b) BIC #177760,R0

Many *program-control* commands are available in the PDP-11 instruction set. The BRANCH commands are an important subset of these program-control commands. Branch-type operations may be *unconditional* or *conditional*. The BR command causes an unconditional branch to be performed. The BNE, BEQ, BPL, BMI, BVC, BVS, BCC, and BCS commands are conditional branch-type commands based on the current setting of a particular status bit. The branch operation related to these commands is executed provided that the specified flag is in the specified state. For example, if a BNE command is fetched, the branch operation is actually executed if and only if the zero bit is cleared. If the BMI command is being executed, the branching operation is actually performed if and only if the sign flag is set.

Branch-type operations *do not* utilize the addressing modes discussed in the previous section. All branch-type operations use a form of *relative* addressing. All branch commands use single-word instruction codes. The most significant 8 bits of a branch command are used to specify the particular command. The least significant 8 bits represent a *signed displacement*. The displacement indicates the number of *words* between the value in the program counter when the instruction is being executed and the *address* at which program control is to continue if the branch operation is performed.

In order to illustrate how a displacement is determined for branching commands, consider the following program segment:

```
        Label           Command

        BACK:           COM   R0
                        COM   R0
        FIRST:          BR  BACK
        SECOND:         BR  AHEAD
        THIRD:          COM  R0
        AHEAD:          HALT
```

Refer to the branching operation at the location labeled FIRST. As this statement is being executed, the number corresponding to the label SECOND is in the program counter. Therefore, the displacement is −3 words. Refer to the program step labeled SECOND. When the branch operation at this address is being performed, the number corresponding to the label THIRD is in the program counter. Therefore, the displacement is +1 word. The machine code for the backward branch operation is 000775, and the machine code for the forward branching operation is 000401. The most significant 8 bits of the code specify the particular branch-type operation, and the least significant 8 bits correspond to the displacement.

Suppose P represents the address of a branch instruction that is being executed. Then P + 2 is in R7 as the instruction is being executed, and the number of *displacement bytes* is DEST − (P + 2), where DEST is the address to which program control may be branching. However, the displacement must be specified in words. Therefore, the displacement used in a branch-type operation is given by the following relationship:

$$\text{DISP} = \frac{\text{DEST} - (\text{P} + 2)}{2}$$

Because the displacement is a signed number, it must have a value in the range between −128 and +127. Therefore, the destination address must be between −254 and +256 *bytes* from the location of the branch instruction.

Example 5.18

Each of the following branch-type instructions is to be fetched from memory location 1232. Encode each of these instructions.

(a) BCS 1200
(b) BCC 1500
(c) BR 2000

Solution   (a) The displacement is

$$\frac{1200 - 1234}{2} = -\frac{34}{2} = -16$$

Recall: *We are using the base-8 number system*. That is why $34 \div 2 = 16$. But

$$-16_8 = -(00010000_2) = 11110000_2 = 360_8$$

The instruction code can be determined in the following manner. Refer to Appendix B for the BCS instruction code. The most significant 8 bits of this code are $\underline{1}\ \underline{000}\ \underline{011}\ \underline{1}$. We will represent this number using the octal characters 1034, where the first and the last characters represent just a single bit.

The instruction code is:	1034__ __	
The displacement is:		__ __ __360
(b) Therefore, the instruction code is:	103760	
The instruction code is:	1030__ __	
The displacement is:		__ __ __122
Therefore, the instruction code is:	103122	

(c) The displacement is 262. Therefore, the instruction cannot be implemented.

Certain branch-type operations utilize more than a single status flag in determining whether or not to execute the conditional branch. The decision of whether or not a branch is to be executed is based on a function of the state of certain status flags. The particular functions are given in Appendix B. Suppose an addition, subtraction, or comparison operation is performed on a pair of *signed* numbers. Immediately following execution of this instruction, suppose one of the following branch-type commands is executed:

BGE   Branch if greater than or equal to 0.

BLT   Branch if less than 0.

BGT   Branch if greater than 0.

BLE   Branch if less than or equal to 0.

Then the conditional branch will be performed if the *true* or *correct* result of the operation satisfies the specified conditions. For example, addition of two positive numbers may produce an overflow condition and result in a negative answer. However, the *true* result is positive. If a BGE or BGT command immediately follows this addition operation, the conditional branch will be executed.

Certain branching commands were developed primarily for use in *comparing* values of *unsigned* numbers. Most of the time these commands are used immediately after a CMP command is executed. These commands are

BHI   Branch if higher.

BLOS   Branch if lower or same.

BHIS   Branch if higher or same.

BLO   Branch if lower.

For example, if a BHI command is executed immediately after a CMP command, the branch will be executed if and only if the unsigned number corresponding to the source operand is larger than the unsigned number corresponding to the destination operand.

Example 5.19

Refer to the entire set of *branch* commands and to the following program segment:

Command	Operand
CMP	R1,R2
A BRANCH COMMAND	SOMEWHERE

Which branch commands will result in a control transfer to location SOMEWHERE if the numbers in R1 and R2 are the following?

(a) (R1) = 123456   (R2) = 042345
(b) (R1) = 010101   (R2) = 010101
(c) (R1) = 123456   (R2) = 111111

Solution   **(a)** Execution of the CMP command affects the status flags in the following manner: (Z) = 0, (C) = 0, (V) = 1, (S) = 0. Therefore, the BR, BNE, BNC, BVS, and BPL commands will result in the branch operation being executed. Because the *true* result of the subtraction operation is a negative number, the BLT and the BLE commands will produce a transfer of program control. The value of the unsigned source operand is greater than that of the unsigned destination operand, so the BHI and BHIS commands will cause program control to branch to SOMEWHERE.

(b) BR, BPL, BCC, BVC, BEQ, BGE, BLE, BLCS, and BHIS

(c) BR, BPL, BCC, BVC, BNE, BGE, BGT, BHI, and BHIS

In addition to branch-type instructions, there are several other control transfer instructions. Unconditional transfers can be made using the JMP, or jump, instruction. This instruction has a single operand and uses the modes of addressing described in Section 5.2. Execution of the JMP instruction causes the *address* of the operand to be moved into the program counter. Clearly, mode 0 is not a valid mode of addressing to be used with jump instructions.

The JSR instruction is used to call subroutines, and the RTS instruction is used to return from subroutines. These instructions function in a similar but not identical manner as the corresponding commands described in Section 4.3.

The JSR command has two operands. The symbolic code for this command is

```
JSR R,DST
```

The destination operand may be specified using one of the seven valid addressing modes. (*Note:* Mode 0 is not a valid mode, as the *address* of the operand will be moved into the program counter.) Any of the registers may be selected as the *linking register,* but generally R6 should not be used. The following internal sequence of events occurs during execution of the above command:

1. (R) => STACK   ; The contents of the linking register are pushed onto the stack.
2. (PC) =>R   ; The apparent return address is placed in the linking register.
3. DEST ADDR => PC   ; Program control transfers to the subroutine.

The RTS, or return from subroutine, command has the symbolic form

    RTS R

where R is the linking register. The following internal sequence of events occurs during execution of this instruction:

1. (R) => PC   ; Return address goes into PC.
2. (STACK) => R   ; The word on top of the stack is popped into R.

Frequently R7, or the program counter, is used as the linking register. For these cases, the second step in the JSR sequence and the first step in the RTS sequence are trivial operations.

Use of linking registers is very convenient if *subroutine arguments* are to be placed immediately after the statement that *calls* or *invokes* the subroutine. In such cases, immediately after control is passed to the subroutine, the number in the linking register (unless the linking register is R7) is a pointer to the argument list. This is illustrated in Example 5.20.

Example 5.20

Write a subroutine that adds two 16-bit numbers together and places the results in memory location 1776. The two arguments carried into the subroutine are values, and they are to be placed immediately after the statement that calls the subroutine. Then write a *test* program that invokes this subroutine.

Solution   We will let R0 be the linking register. Then an appropriate subroutine and a test program are given. We assume that the stack pointer register contains an appropriate number before we execute our test program. That is, the stack pointer register contains a pointer that identifies an area of memory that we may use for a stack. The size of the stack space required for this program is just 2 bytes.

Label	Location	Symbolic Code	Machine Code	Comments
SUBR:	1000	MOV (R0)+,@#1776	012037 001776	;Subroutine starts
	1004	ADD (R0)+,@#1776	062037 001776	
	1010	RTS R0	000200	;Subroutine ends

```
;********** START TEST PROGRAM ****************
START:      1012    JSR R0,SUBR    004067        ;Start main
                                   177762        program
DATA1:      1016                   000001        ;Start argu-
                                                 ment list
DATA2:      1020                   000002        ;End argu-
                                                 ment list
DONE:       1022    HALT           000000        ;End test
                                                 program
```

There is one more class of control transfer instructions—the programmable *interrupt* or *trap* instructions and the related *return from interrupt* and return from trap instructions. These instructions produce transfer of program control in the same manner that external interrupts produce such transfers. This topic was introduced in Section 4.3.

If one of the interrupt instructions is being executed, the following sequence of events occurs:

1. (PSW) = > STACK   ; The processor status word is pushed onto the stack.

2. (PC) = > STACK   ; The apparent return address is pushed onto the stack.

3. (MEMV) = > PC   ; The contents of a specially designated memory location, sometimes referred to as an *interrupt vector,* is placed in the program counter.

4. (MEMV + 2) = > PSW   ; The contents of the memory address following the specially designated location are moved into the PSW register.

Thus, program control is transferred to the memory address stored in the memory vector register. The apparent return address and the value of the processor status word prior to execution of the interrupt command are stored on the stack. A return from interrupt command pops the word on top of the stack into the program counter and the next word into the PSW register.

There are four different interrupt or trap commands available in the instruction set:

Command	Name	Memory vector addresses
EMT	Emulator trap	30 and 32
TRAP	Trap	34 and 36
BPT	Breakpoint trap	14 and 16
IOT	Input/output trap	20 and 22

The low-order byte of the EMT and TRAP commands may be used to carry information into the corresponding trap processing routines.

Example 5.21

Write a trap processing routine that clears R0 if the low-order byte of the invoking TRAP command is odd, and complements R0 if the low-order byte of the corresponding TRAP command is even.

Solution   We will first develop a program to test each case.

Label	Location	Symbolic code	Machine code	Comment
TEST1:	1000	TRAP 15	104415	;ODD Test
	1002	HALT	000000	
TEST2:	1004	TRAP 20	104420	;EVEN Test
	1006	HALT	000000	

Next we will place appropriate words in the corresponding memory vector locations.

Location	Data	Comment
34	2000	;Trap processing routine is to start at location 2000.
36	000000	;New value of program status word.

Now we will develop the appropriate trap processing routine.

Label	Location	Symbolic code	Machine code	Comment
PROCESS:	2000	MOV (SP), R5	011605	;Get return address

; Now we will look at the instruction stored in the memory location preceding that identified by the return address. This is the TRAP instruction.

Label	Location	Symbolic code		Machine code	Comment
NEXT:	2002	BIT	#,1-(R5)	032745 / 000001	;Is TRAP data byte odd?
	2006	BNE ODD		001002	;YES
EVEN:	2010	COM R0		005100	;NO
	2012	RTI		000002	;EXIT
ODD:	2014	CLR R0		005000	
	2016	RTI		000002	;EXIT

The following shift and rotate instructions are available: ASL, ASR, ROR, and ROL. These refer to *arithmetic shift left, arithmetic shift-right, rotate-right,* and *rotate-left* instructions. These commands are essentially the same as those described in Section 4.3. The *arithmetic shift-left* command is identical to a *logic shift-left* command. The rotate commands produce rotations through the carry bit. That is, a *byte* operation involves rotating a 9-bit number, and a *word* operation involves rotating a 17-bit number. These shift and rotate commands produce just a 1-bit shift or rotation.

Certain *processor-control* commands are available. Commands exist to set or clear status bits. One form of such a command does not specify any bit or group of bits to be set or cleared. This command is interpreted as a NOP, or no operation, command.

The remainder of the commands given in Appendix B are classified as *miscellaneous*. The HALT command is one such command. The SWAB command is used to exchange the position of the 2 bytes in a 16-bit word, and the SXT command is used to sign extend a byte into a 16-bit word that has the same signed value. The RESET command is used to send out a specific electrical signal from the CPU. The WAIT command is similar to the HALT command except that instruction sequencing can continue if an external interrupt signal occurs.

The SOB, or subtract one and branch, command is a combination of an arithmetic command and a one-word control transfer command. This command is a very useful for implementing *looping* operations. The command has two operands, a register, and a 6-bit *unsigned* number corresponding to a 6-bit displacement. During execution of the SOB command, 1 is subtracted from the specified register. If the resulting value in the specified register is not zero, the specified branch operation is executed. The branch operation is done in the same manner that is used by the other one-word branch instructions. The only differences are that

1. The displacement is an unsigned number.
2. The displacement is just a 6-bit number.
3. Branching is only done in the *backward* direction. That is, the unsigned displacement is always treated as a negative number.

Example 5.22

Suppose the following SOB command is fetched from memory location 1444.

$$0111111 \quad 010 \quad 000110_2 = 077206_8$$

If the branch operation is executed, at which address will program control continue?

Solution   The specified register is R2, and the unsigned displacement is 000110_2. Therefore, if the branch operation is executed, program control will continue six words before the current value in the program counter, which is 1446. Therefore, the destination address for this instruction is 1432.

Review

1. Prior to execution of each of the following instructions. (R1) = 107342 and (R2) = 013256. Formulate the machine-language code for each of these instructions. Then identify the number that will be stored in R2 and the state of each of the status flags after execution of the corresponding instruction has been completed.
   (a) SUB R1,R2
   (b) CMP R1,R2
   (c) TST R2
   (d) BIS R1,R2
   (e) BIT R1,R2
   (f) BIC R1,R2
2. Suppose each of the following instructions is fetched from memory location 1236. Furthermore, suppose the following labels identify memory addresses as indicated: DOG = 1230, CAT = 1440, MOUSE = 1160, RAT = 1302. Translate each of the following symbolic statements into machine code.

    (a) BVS DOG
    (b) BHIS CAT
    (c) SOB R1,MOUSE
    (d) BMI RAT

3. Prior to execution of each of the following instructions, (R1) = 000420 and (R2) = 170102. After each of the following instructions has been executed, a *branch* instruction is fetched. For each case, identify the subset of branch instructions that will actually produce a transfer of program control.
    (a) CMP R1,R2
    (b) SUB R2,R1
    (c) ADD R1,R2

4. Prior to execution of a program, the designated registers contain the following numbers.
    (1000) = 104052 or (1000) = the EMT 52 instruction   (R6) = 1000   (R7) =
        1000   (R1) = 0000   (30) = 2000   (32) = 000017   (2000) = 000000
    Program execution commences and continues until a HALT command is encountered. At this time, what number will be in
    (a) R1?
    (b) R6?
    (c) R7?
    (d) each of the status bits?

5. Prior to execution of each of the following instructions, (R1) = 032451 and (PSW) = 000015. Identify the contents of R1 and the value stored in the carry bit after each of the following instructions is executed.
    (a) ASL R1
    (b) ASR R1
    (c) ROL R1
    (d) ROR R1
    (e) SWAB R1

5.4 LOADING, RUNNING, AND DEBUGGING MACHINE-LANGUAGE PROGRAMS

Development of machine-language programs has been introduced, and several examples of PDP-11 machine-language programs are given in Section 5.5. Although some machine-language programs may ultimately reside in read-only memory, it is generally necessary to enter these programs into read-write memory at least during the testing phase of program development. Therefore, some facilities are required for entering and debugging these programs.

    Most small computer developmental systems have either software or firmware available for entering, testing, and debugging machine-language programs. PDP-11 systems generally include a firmware package called *console ODT* that is used for such purposes. Originally, ODT, which stands for octal debugging techniques, was a software package that could be used for either entering or debugging machine-language programs or as a tool for debugging programs written in a high-level language. In modern implementations of PDP-11 architecture, many of these capabilities are included as part of the system's firmware. The principal capabilities of console ODT are given in Fig. 5.5.

In order to illustrate the use of ODT for entering and debugging programs, suppose we wish to enter the following machine-language program into computer memory.

Label	Location	Symbolic code	Machine code	Comments
START:	1000	MOV DATA,R1	017701 0000774	
BACK:	1004	DEC R2	005302	;Decrement counter
NEXT:	1006	BNE BACK	001376	;Loop
DONE:	1010	HALT	000000	;Quit
	;...			
DATA:	2000		001000	;Data Pointer

Prior to running this program, we must first place the value of a counter in register R2. Suppose the value of the counter is 3. This number can be placed in R2 by entering ODT and typing the following command. (*Note:* Underlined quantities are those responses typed by the computer.)

@ R2/ Number 3 (RET)

Now the entire program may be entered by typing the following sequence of ODT commands.

@ 1000/ Number 017701 (LF)
1002/ Number 774 (LF)
1004/ Number 5302 (LF)
1006/ Number 1376 (LF)
1010/ Number 0 (RET)
@ 2000/ Number 1000 (RET)

To run the program, we now type 1000G. When the HALT statement is encountered, the computer terminal will type the following number:

001012

This indicates that the HALT mode was entered with 1012 in the program counter. Program control now reverts to the ODT microcode, and the ODT prompt character, @, is printed.

After program execution is completed, the CPU registers and key memory locations may be displayed using ODT commands. In this way, a program may be checked to ensure that it is producing correct results. However, frequently a program in its developmental stage may encounter "infinite" loops or unexpected transfers of control. These occurrences happen because it is easy to make mistakes in selecting addressing modes or computing branching displacements. During initial program development, HALT statements may be inserted in selected locations throughout the program. During program execution, when a HALT statement is encountered, registers and key memory locations may be inspected. If no discrep-

	Command	Name	Function
1.	Number/or RI	Slash (ASCII 057)	Open Memory location Number or Register I for inspection. Note: Alternate notation $I may be used to open register I. ODT responds by printing contents of the opened location.
2.	(CR)	Carriage (ASCII 015) Return	Close opened location. Leave value as it was.
3.	Number (CR)		Change value in opened location to a new value, ''Number.'' Close opened location.
4.	(LF)	Line feed (ASCII 012)	Close opened location. Leave value as it was. Open subsequent location.
5.	Number (LF)		Change value in opened location to a new value, ''Number''. Close opened location. Open subsequent location.
6.	↑	Up arrow (ASCII 135)	Close opened location. Leave contents as it was. Open preceding location.
7.	Number ↑		Change value in opened location to a new value, ''Number''. Close opened location. Open preceding location.
8.	@	At symbol (ASCII 100)	Close opened location. Open a location identified by the contents of the location that has just been closed.
9.	Number @		First change contents of opened location. Then perform @ function.
10.	← or	Back arrow (ASCII 137)	Close opened location. Open location identified by the following sum: 2 + address of location just closed.
11.	Number ←		First change contents of opened location. Then perform ←function.
12.	$S or RS	(ASCII 044 and 123)	Open processor status word.
13.	Number G	GO (ASCII 107)	Start program execution at location ''Number.''
14.	P	Proceed (ASCII 120)	Start or continue program execution at address specified by current contents of PC.

Figure 5.5   A subset of console ODT commands (Copyright Digital Equipment Corporation, 1978. All rights reserved. Reprinted by permission.)

Note: 1. Responses by computer are underlined.
2. ODT prompt is @.
3. Address only even-numbered memory locations.
4. All values are WORD values expressed in octal.
5. Normal methods of entering ODT (Octal Debugging Techniques) are:
a) Executing a HALT instruction
b) Pressing the BREAK key on the system console

ancies are detected, program execution may be continued until the next HALT statement is encountered.

Inserting HALT statements for debugging purposes is rather crude. In subsequent sections, we discuss more refined methods used for programming debugging. These methods include the insertion of *breakpoints* instead of HALT instructions and the use of the TRAP bit in order to obtain a *trace* of the program execution.

Review

1. Refer to the sample program given in this section. After this program is executed, control reverts to ODT. Then suppose the following ODT command is entered: R1/.
   (a) What number will be displayed?
   (b) After this number is displayed, suppose the line-feed key is pressed. What numbers are then displayed?

2. Refer to the sample program. Suppose the corresponding machine-language program has been entered into memory, and we type the following ODT command: 1002/. The number 000774 will be displayed by the computer.
   (a) What ODT command should be entered if we wish to see the pointer identified by this operand?
   (b) After the pointer to the operand has been displayed, what ODT command may be entered to display the value of the operand?

3. In order to facilitate program development, suppose we wish to include a HALT statement within the sample program. Where may this statement be placed so that no modifications of machine codes will be required?

5.5 MACHINE-LANGUAGE PROGRAMMING EXAMPLES

Machine-language programming can be somewhat tedious. However, potential difficulties may be alleviated if programming concepts such as those described in Chapter 2 are incorporated into the development of programs. In particular, it is important that machine-language programs be developed in relatively small independent blocks. Preliminary copies of such programs should be well documented, and, generally, symbolic code and meaningful label names should be included as part of the documentation. As changes are made in the program, this preliminary documentation should be updated to reflect such changes. We shall attempt to illustrate attributes associated with machine-language programming with the following set of examples.

Example 5.23

Write and test a subroutine that adds together ten unsigned 16-bit numbers that are stored in consecutive memory locations. The high-order word of the answer should be stored in memory location 2040, and the low-order word is to be stored in memory location 2042.

Solution   Assume a pointer identifying the array of data words is in R0 when the subroutine is entered. Then we will first *clear* the contents of memory locations 2040 and 2042. Next we add one word at a time to the contents of memory location 2042. Each time an addition operation produces a 1 in the carry bit, the number in location 2040 will be incremented. A solution is given in Fig. 5.6.

Example 5.24

Write and test a subroutine that adds together *N* unsigned 16-bit numbers that are stored in an array. The high-order word and low-order word of the answer are to be

Label	Location	Symbolic Code	Machine Code	Comments
ADD10:	1000	CLR @#2040	005037 002040	;Begin subroutine
	1004	CLR @#2042	005037 002042	
	1010	MOV #12, R1	012701 000012	;Set counter to 10.
BACK:	1014	ADD (RO) +, @#2042	062307 002402	
	1020	BCC UP	103002	
	1022	INC @#2040	005237 002040	;Increment HOW
UP:	1026	DEC R1	005301	;DONE?
	1030	BNE BACK	001371	;NO
	1032	RTS PC	000207	;YES
;* * * * * * * * * * START TEST PROGRAM				
;* *				* * * * * * * * * * * * * * * * *
START:	1034	MOV #ADD10,SP	012706 001000	;Load stack pointer
	1040	MOV #2000,RO	012700 002000	;Load array pointer
	1044	JSR PC,ADD10	004767 177730	;CALL SUBR ADD10
QUIT:	1050	HALT	000000	
;* * * PUT DATA INTO ARRAY				
;* *				* * * * * * * * * * * * * * * * *
DATA:	2000		177777	;DATA Starts
	2002		177777	
	2004		177777	
	2006		000001	
	2010		000001	
	2012		000001	
	2014		000001	
	2016		000001	
	2020		000001	
TERM:	2022		177777	;DATA ENDS

Figure 5.6   A solution to Example 5.23

stored in consecutive memory locations. The argument list for this subroutine should be stored immediately after the statement that is used to call the subroutine. The argument list is to consist of three words. These are the *value* of N, the *address* of the array, and the *address* at which the high-order word of the answer is to be stored.

Solution   We will let R5 be the linking register. Then we will save the values currently in R1, R2, and R3 on the stack. Next we will put the value corresponding to the size of the array in R1, the address of the array in R2, and the pointer to the answer in R3. The true return address will now be kept in the linking register. The addition operation will be performed as shown in Example 5.23, and the results will be placed in the desired locations. The values that were originally contained in R1, R2, and R3 will now be restored to these registers. A solution to this example is given in Fig. 5.7.

The subroutine given in Fig. 5.7 is considerably different from that in Fig. 5.6. Clearly, this second program is more general. Furthermore, although the subroutine requires the use of registers R1, R2, and R3, it initially saves these values

Label	Location	Symbolic Code	Machine Code	Comments
ADDN:	1000	MOV R1,-(SP)	010146	;Push registers on stack
	1002	MOV R2,-(SP)	010246	
	1004	MOV R3,-(SP)	010346	
	1006	MOV (R5)+,R1	012501	;Pull in arguments
	1010	MOV (R5)+,R2	012502	
	1012	MOV (R5)+,R3	012503	
	1014	CLR (R3)	005013	;Clear HOW and LOW
	1016	CLR 2(R3)	005063 000002	
LOOP:	1022	ADD (R2)+,2(R3)	062263 000002	;Add elements of array
	1026	BCC UP	103001	
	1030	INC (R3)	005213	;Increment HOW
UP:	1032	SOB R1,LOOP	077105	;Loop until done
	1034	MOV (SP)+,R3	012603	;Restore registers
	1036	MOV (SP)+,R2	012602	
	1040	MOV (SP)+,R1	012601	
	1042	RTS R5	000205	;EXIT
;****** START TEST PROGRAM ***************				
START:	1044	MOV #ADDN,SP	012706 001000	;Load stack pointer
	1050	JSR R5,ADDN	004567 177724	;Call subroutine ADDN
N:	1054		000004	;Size of array
ARRAY:	1056		002000	;Address of array
ANSWER:	1060		002174	;Address of answer
QUIT:	1062	HALT	000000	

Figure 5.7   A solution to Example 5.24

on the stack and then restores these values before control is transferred back to the program that invoked the subroutine.

A more significant attribute of this subroutine is that it is *reentrant*. The property of *reentrancy* means that the subroutine may be shared by several *different programming tasks*. Suppose, for example, that one program starts to use the subroutine given in Fig. 5.6. Before this task is completed, suppose the contents of all registers are saved and a different program starts to use the same routine. This new program will vary the numbers in memory locations 2040 and 2042. By the time the original program returns to this subroutine to complete its task, information previously accumulated will have been lost.

Development of *reentrant* programs is very useful in *multiuser systems*. In such systems, several users may share a single copy of a reentrant routine. Subroutines that are *self-reentrant* are said to be *recursive*. A subprogram is self-reentrant if it has the capability of calling or invoking itself. Not only must recursive programs be reentrant but they must also possess a mechanism or a conditional branching capability that permits exiting from such routines.

Example 5.25

Write a recursive subroutine that accepts a positive odd integer N as the only input argument. The subroutine is to find the sum of all odd positive integers up to and including N by adding N to the sum of all odd positive integers up to and including N - 2. The latter sum is obtained by letting the subroutine invoke itself as often as necessary.

Solution   We will let the number in R1 define a *user stack*. The input argument to the subroutine will be placed on the user stack. An appropriate subroutine is given in Fig. 5.8. If the sum of the odd integers up to N - 2 is not available in R2, the subroutine continues to call itself. Before it does this, it must place the new argument, which is 2 less than the previous input argument, on the user stack. When the input argument becomes negative, a value of 0 is returned in R2, and then all the intermediate sums are computed and returned in R2. After the last exit from the subroutine, both the system stack pointer (R6) and the user-defined stack pointer (R1) have returned to the values they had at the beginning of the test program, and the result is returned in R2.

For readers who have not previously been introduced to recursive routines, this sample program may be confusing. Figure 5.9 presents a *trace* of the functioning of this routine when the number 9 (or 11_8) is entered as the input argument in the test program. This trace was run on a PDP-11 simulator. Careful inspection of this trace should clarify the function of this recursive routine.

Label	Location	Symbolic Code	Machine Code	Comments
RECUR:	1000	TST (R1)	005711	;Is argument positive?
	1002	BPL UP	100003	;Yes
	1004	MOV (R1)+,R2	012102	;No. Remove argument from the user stack.
	1006	CLR R2	005002	
	1010	RTS PC	000207	;Exit. Argument is negative
UP:	1012	MOV (R1),−(R1)	011141	;Put new argument on the user stack
	1014	SUB #2,(R1)	162711 000002	
	1020	JSR PC,RECUR	004767 17775	; Invoke self!!!!
	1024	ADD (R1)+,R2	062102	
	1026	RTS PC	000207	
******* START TEST *********************************				******************
START:	1030	MOV #RECUR,SP	012706 001000	;Load system stack pointer
	1034	MOV #2000,R1	012701 002000	;Load user stack pointer
	1040	MOV #11,−(R1)	012741 000011	;Put 9 on user stack
	1044	JSR PC,RECUR	004767 177730	
DONE:	1050	HALT	000000	

Figure 5.8   A solution to Example 5.25

```
       TIME   IADR   INST   OP   PTNZVC   RS     R0/4   R1/5   R2/6   R3/7
       ====== ====== ====== ==== ====== ====== ====== ====== ====== ======

       000000 000000 000000 HALT 000000 000000 000000 000000 000000 000000
                                               000000 000000 000000 001030
       000001 001030 012706 MOV  000000 000000 000000 000000 000000 000000
                                               000000 000000 001000 001034
       000002 001034 012701 MOV  000000 000000 000000 002000 000000 000000
                                               000000 000000 001000 001040
       000003 001040 012741 MOV  000000 000000 000000 001776 000000 000000
                                               000000 000000 001000 001044
       000004 001044 004767 JSR  000000 000000 000000 001776 000000 000000
                                               000000 000000 000776 001000
       000005 001000 005711 TST  000000 000000 000000 001776 000000 000000
                                               000000 000000 000776 001002
       000006 001002 100003 BPL  000000 000000 000000 001776 000000 000000
                                               000000 000000 000776 001012
       000007 001012 011141 MOV  000000 000000 000000 001774 000000 000000
                                               000000 000000 000776 001014
       000008 001014 162711 SUB  000000 000000 000000 001774 000000 000000
                                               000000 000000 000776 001020
       000009 001020 004767 JSR  000000 000000 000000 001774 000000 000000
                                               000000 000000 000774 001000
       000010 001000 005711 TST  000000 000000 000000 001774 000000 000000
                                               000000 000000 000774 001002
       000011 001002 100003 BPL  000000 000000 000000 001774 000000 000000
                                               000000 000000 000774 001012
       000012 001012 011141 MOV  000000 000000 000000 001772 000000 000000
                                               000000 000000 000774 001014
       000013 001014 162711 SUB  000000 000000 000000 001772 000000 000000
                                               000000 000000 000774 001020
       000014 001020 004767 JSR  000000 000000 000000 001772 000000 000000
                                               000000 000000 000772 001000
       000015 001000 005711 TST  000000 000000 000000 001772 000000 000000
                                               000000 000000 000772 001002
       000016 001002 100003 BPL  000000 000000 000000 001772 000000 000000
                                               000000 000000 000772 001012
       000017 001012 011141 MOV  000000 000000 000000 001770 000000 000000
                                               000000 000000 000772 001014
       000018 001014 162711 SUB  000000 000000 000000 001770 000000 000000
                                               000000 000000 000772 001020
       000019 001020 004767 JSR  000000 000000 000000 001770 000000 000000
                                               000000 000000 000770 001000
       000020 001000 005711 TST  000000 000000 000000 001770 000000 000000
                                               000000 000000 000770 001002
       000021 001002 100003 BPL  000000 000000 000000 001770 000000 000000
                                               000000 000000 000770 001012
       000022 001012 011141 MOV  000000 000000 000000 001766 000000 000000
                                               000000 000000 000770 001014
       000023 001014 162711 SUB  000000 000000 000000 001766 000000 000000
                                               000000 000000 000770 001020
       000024 001020 004767 JSR  000000 000000 000000 001766 000000 000000
                                               000000 000000 000766 001000
       000025 001000 005711 TST  000000 000000 000000 001766 000000 000000
                                               000000 000000 000766 001002
       000026 001002 100003 BPL  000000 000000 000000 001766 000000 000000
                                               000000 000000 000766 001012
       000027 001012 011141 MOV  000000 000000 000000 001764 000000 000000
                                               000000 000000 000766 001014
       000028 001014 162711 SUB  001001 000011 000000 001764 000000 000000
                                               000000 000000 000766 001020
       000029 001020 004767 JSR  001001 000011 000000 001764 000000 000000
                                               000000 000000 000764 001000
       000030 001000 005711 TST  001000 000010 000000 001764 000000 000000
                                               000000 000000 000764 001002
       000031 001002 100003 BPL  001000 000010 000000 001764 000000 000000
                                               000000 000000 000764 001004
```

Figure 5.9   Step-by-step trace of the recursive program in Fig. 5.9

TIME	IADR	INST	OP	PTNZVC	RS	R0/4	R1/5	R2/6	R3/7
000032	001004	012102	MOV	001000	000010	000000	001766	177777	000000
						000000	000000	000764	001006
000033	001006	005002	CLR	000100	000004	000000	001766	000000	000000
						000000	000000	000764	001010
000034	001010	000207	RTS	000100	000004	000000	001766	000000	000000
						000000	000000	000766	001024
000035	001024	062102	ADD	000000	000000	000000	001770	000001	000000
						000000	000000	000766	001026
000036	001026	000207	RTS	000000	000000	000000	001770	000001	000000
						000000	000000	000770	001024
000037	001024	062102	ADD	000000	000000	000000	001772	000004	000000
						000000	000000	000770	001026
000038	001026	000207	RTS	000000	000000	000000	001772	000004	000000
						000000	000000	000772	001024
000039	001024	062102	ADD	000000	000000	000000	001774	000011	000000
						000000	000000	000772	001026
000040	001026	000207	RTS	000000	000000	000000	001774	000011	000000
						000000	000000	000774	001024
000041	001024	062102	ADD	000000	000000	000000	001776	000020	000000
						000000	000000	000774	001026
000042	001026	000207	RTS	000000	000000	000000	001776	000020	000000
						000000	000000	000776	001024
000043	001024	062102	ADD	000000	000000	000000	002000	000031	000000
						000000	000000	000776	001026
000044	001026	000207	RTS	000000	000000	000000	002000	000031	000000
						000000	000000	001000	001050

TIME	IADR	INST	OP	PTNZVC	RS	R0/4	R1/5	R2/6	R3/7
000045	001050	000000	HALT	000000	000000	000000	002000	000031	000000
						000000	000000	001000	001052

Figure 5.9   (*cont.*)

Example 5.26

Design a subroutine that moves a block of words from one specified area of memory to another specified area of memory.

Solution   Three arguments will be carried into this subroutine: the block size, the address of the source block, and the address of the destination block. We will carry these arguments into the routine by placing them on a user-defined stack identified by (R5). This will be done prior to calling the subroutine. The destination block address will first be placed on this stack. Then the source block address and the block size will be pushed on the user stack. An appropriate subroutine and a test program are given in Fig. 5.10.

Example 5.27

Design a subroutine that adds each element of an array of *N* elements to the corresponding element in another array of *N* elements.

Solution   We will develop a subroutine that "pulls in" a *value* corresponding to the array size and *addresses* identifying the source array and destination array. When calling the subroutine, arguments corresponding to the address at which the array size is stored and the addresses of the arrays will be placed on a user-defined stack. A solution to this example is given in Fig. 5.11.

Label	Location	Symbolic Code	Machine Code	Comments
MOVE:	1000	MOV (R5)+,R1	012501	;Get arguments from the user stack.
	1002	MOV (R5)+,R2	012502	
	1004	MOV (R5)+,R3	012503	
BACK:	1006	MOV (R2)+,(R3)+	012223	;Move block
	1010	SOB R1,BACK	077102	
	1012	RTS PC	000207	
;****** START TEST PROGRAM **********************				******************
START:	1014	MOV #MOVE,SP	012706 001000	;Load system stack pointer
	1020	MOV #MOVE-100,R5	012705 000700	;Load user stack pointer
	1024	MOV #2000,-(R5)	012745 002000	;Push destination pointer
	1030	MOV #1000,-(R5)	012745 001000	;Push source pointer
	1034	MOV #30,-(R5)	012745 000030	;Block size = 24
	1040	JSR PC,MOVE	004767 177734	
DONE:	1044	HALT	000000	

Figure 5.10   A solution to Example 5.26

Label	Location	Symbolic Code	Machine Code	Comments
;****** START TEST PROGRAM ****************				
START:	1000	MOV #START,SP	012706 001000	;Load system SP
	1004	MOV #700,R5	012705 000700	;Load user SP
	1010	MOV #DEST,-(R5)	012745 001062	;Put addresses on
	1014	MOV #SORCE,-(R5)	012745 001050	stack
	1020	MOV #NUM,-(R5)	012745 001046	
	1024	JSR PC, MATADD	004767 000002	;Call MATADD
	1030	HALT	000000	
;****** SUBROUTINE MATADD BEGINS ***********************				***************
MATADD:	1032	MOV @(R5)+,R1	013501	;Get value of NUM
	1034	MOV (R5)+,R2	012502	;Get addresses of
	1036	MOV (R5)+,R3	012503	arrays
LOOP:	1040	ADD (R2)+,(R3)+	062223	;Add arrays
	1042	SOB R1,LOOP	077102	;Proceed until done
	1044	RTS PC	000207	;Exit
; ****** TEST DATA FOLLOWS *****************************				**************
NUM:	1046		000005	;Array size = 5.
SORCE:	1050		000005	;Source array be-
	1052		000004	gins
	1054		000003	
	1056		000002	
	1060		000001	;Source array ends
DEST:	1062		000001	;Destination array
	1064		000002	begins
	1066		000003	
	1070		000004	
	1072		000005	;Destination array ends

Figure 5.11   A solution to Example 5.27

The PDP-11 instruction set is very convenient for locating information stored in *tables*. This can be illustrated by using a *jump table* as an example. Consider the standard FORTRAN "computed GO TO" statement. This has a form similar to the following example:

```
GO TO (100,250,326,500,1102) N
```

The transfer of control depends on the value of *N*. In this example, if *N* has a value of 1, control transfers to statement 100. Similarly, if *N* has a value of 2, control is transferred to line 250. In this example, valid values of *N* range from 1 to 5.

Example 5.28

Suppose the number in R1 has a value between 1 and 5. Formulate a program segment that branches to octal memory locations 100, 250, 326, 500, or 1002, depending on whether the argument stored in R1 is 1, 2, 3, 4, or 5.

Solution   A solution is given in Fig. 5.12. The addresses identifying the locations to which control transfers may be made are stored in a table starting at location 2000. In the program segment, the number in R1 is doubled because an address entry requires 2 bytes of memory. The displacement used in the second program statement identifies the location of the jump table. The sum of the displacement plus the adjusted argument in R1 uniquely identifies the location of the destination address.

Label	Location	Symbolic Code	Machine Code	Comments
SEGMENT:	1000	ADD R1,R1	060101	;Double number in R1
	1002	JMP @TABLE-2(R1)	000171 001776	;Move address to PC
;	....			
;	******* JUMP TABLE FOLLOWS ***********************			*****************
TABLE:	2000		000100	;Destination addresses
	2002		000250	
	2004		000326	
	2006		000500	
	2010		001002	

Figure 5.12   A solution to Example 5.28

Review

1. Refer to Fig. 5.6. After the test program has been executed, what number will be in memory location, **(a)** 2040 or **(b)** 2042?

2. Refer to the test program in Fig. 5.8. After this program has been executed, what number will be in **(a)** R6, **(b)** R1, **(c)** R2?

3. Refer to the test program in Fig. 5.8. When this program is executed for the specified data, how many *bytes* of memory are required for
   (a) system stack space?
   (b) user stack space?

4. What modifications are required for the subroutine in Fig. 5.8 so that it will function in the same manner if an *even* positive integer is the input argument?

5. When a subroutine AVE4 is called, this routine is to find the average of the four signed numbers stored immediately after the calling statement. Develop and test an appropriate subroutine. Assume that the magnitude of each of the data numbers never exceeds the base-10 number 8000. (That is, overflow will not occur.)

REFERENCES

ECKHOUSE, R. H., and R. L. MORRIS, *Minicomputer Systems*. Englewood Cliffs, N.J.: Prentice-Hall, 1975.

FRANK, T. S., *Introduction to the PDP-11 and Its Assembly Language*. Englewood Cliffs, N.J.: Prentice-Hall, 1983.

GILL, A., *Machine and Assemble Programming of the PDP-11*. Englewood Cliffs, N.J.: Prentice-Hall, 1979.

Microcomputer Processors. Maynard, Mass.: Digital Equipment Corporation, 1979.

EXERCISES

1. Translate each of the following instructions into PDP-11 machine code.
   (a) BIC #1024,R0
   (b) TSTB @#177756
   (c) ASR @R1
   (d) ROL R3

2. Refer to Exercise 1. Prior to execution of each of these commands, the CPU registers and designated memory registers contain the indicated numbers.

   (R0) = 1276   (R1) = 2000   (R7) = 1000   (2000) = 3250   (177756) = 160000

   After each of the statements has been executed, what number will be in each of the locations?

3. What addressing modes available on the PDP-11 may be properly classified as *indirect* addressing modes?

4. Prior to execution of each of the following commands, the designated numbers are stored in the indicated locations.

   (R0) = 700   (R1) = 102345   (R2) = 2000   (R3) = 3002   (R6) = 7000
                 (R7) = 1234   (2000) = 3000   (3000) = 132076

   The following labels are associated with numbers as indicated:

   FISH = 1000   DOG = 2000   CAT = 3000   MOUSE = 3002

   Translate each of the following instructions into machine code.

    (a) JMP@#DOG

    (b) ADD DOG,CAT

    (c) SUB (R2)+,−(R3)

    (d) CMP R0,SP

5. Refer to the information given in Exercise 4. Translate each of the following instructions into machine code.

    (a) BIS #17324,1300(R0)

    (b) XOR R0,@1300(R0)

    (c) BVC FISH

    (d) SOB R0,FISH

6. Refer to Exercise 4. After each of these commands is executed, what number will be in each of the registers identified in the exercise?

7. Refer to Exercise 5. After each of these commands is executed, what number will be in each of the designated registers?

8. Refer to Exercises 1 and 2. For each of the specified commands, identify the values of the status bits after execution of the command is completed.

9. Refer to Exercise 4. For each of the specified commands, identify the values of the status bits that result from execution of the corresponding command.

10. Refer to Exercise 5. For each command, identify the values of the status bits that result from execution of the corresponding instruction.

11. Translate each of the following machine code instructions into symbolic code.

    (a) 012546

    (b) 162444

    (c) 012737   001234   004000

    (d) 150001

12. What types of addressing tend to support development of position-independent code?

The following program, written in symbolic code, refers to Exercises 13–16.

Label	Location	Symbolic Code	Data	Comments
START:	1000	MOV #START,SP		;Load stack pointer
	1004	JSR R4,SUBR		;CALL SUBR
NUMBER:	1010		000006	;Count value
DATA:	1012		000010	;Data value
	1014	HALT		
; ***** START SUBROUTINE SUBR **********				
SUBR:	1016	MOV (R4),R0		;Get arguments
	1020	MOV 2(R4),R1		
BACK:	1024	DEC R1		;DONE?
	1026	BNE UP		No
WHAT:	1030	CMP (R4)+,(R4)+		;Yes
	1032	RTS R4		;Exit
UP:	1034	ADD R1, 2(R4)		
	1040	BR BACK		

13. Translate this program into machine code.

14. What does this subroutine do? What are the practical limits to the values in the argument list for use with this subroutine?

15. Refer to the specified test data. After this program has been executed, what number will be in each of the following locations?
    (a) R0
    (b) R1
    (c) R6
    (d) R7
    (e) memory location 1012

16. What is the purpose of the command stored in the memory location labeled WHAT?

17. What is meant by each of the following terms?
    (a) a *reentrant* subroutine
    (b) a *recursive* procedure
    (c) position-independent code

18. Refer to the program in Fig. 5.8. Refer to the line identified by location number 1040. The substring "11" occurs three times in this line. Suppose the characters 11 are changed to the characters 15, and then this program is executed. When program execution is completed, what number will be in R2?

19. Refer to Exercise 18. How many *words* of *user stack* space were required during program execution?

20. Refer to the program in Fig. 5.13. Fill in the missing machine codes.

21. Suppose the program in Fig. 5.13 is stored in computer memory. The following sequence of ODT commands is entered. Indicate the numbers printed by the computer after each ODT command is entered.
    (a) 1010/
    (b) (LF)

Label	Location	Symbolic Code	Machine Code	
START:	1000	MOV #START,SP	?	?
	1004	MOV #5,R1	012701 000005	
	1010	JSR R5,SUBR	004567	?
	1014	HALT	000000	
	1016	HALT	000000	
	1020	HALT	000000	
;********SUBROUTINE STARTS***				
SUBR:	1022	MOV (R5)+,@#2000	012537 002000	
	1026	BR UP	?	
	1030	HALT	000000	
	1032	HALT	000000	
UP:	1034	CLR R3	005003	
HERE:	1036	CLR R2	005002	
BACK:	1040	MOV #2000,R4	012704 002000	
	1044	MOV R4,(R4)+	010424	
	1046	INC R3	005203	
	1050	SOB R1,BACK	?	
	1052	RTS R5	000205	

Figure 5.13 Program for Exercises 20, 21, and 22

(c) ←
(d) 1000G
(e) P

22. Prior to execution of this program, (R5) = 002004. After this program has been executed, what number will be in each of the CPU registers?

23. When a subroutine AVE8 is called, this routine is to find the average of eight *unsigned* numbers. The value of each of the data numbers is less than the base-10 number 8000. The argument list is to follow the statement that calls the subroutine. Develop and test a program for each of the following two cases.
(a) The *values* of the numbers immediately follow the JSR or CALL statement.
(b) The *addresses* of the numbers immediately follow the JSR or CALL statement.

24. A subroutine is to accept a value X and return a value Y whenever it is invoked. The specific relationship is $Y = 4X + 7$. Develop and test an appropriate subroutine. Assume numerical overflow will not occur.

The following information refers to Exercises 25 through 29.

Data *records* are stored in computer memory beginning at location 2000. Each record contains 16 bytes of information. Thus, the first record is stored at an address identified by the pointer 2000, the second record is identified by the pointer 2020, and so on. Each record is associated with a particular student. The first byte of each record specifies the gender of a student. Positive numbers specify female students, and negative numbers specify male students. The next 4 bytes in each record are ASCII characters identifying the student's name. The ninth byte in each record (i.e., memory location 2010 is the address of the ninth byte of the first record) is used to specify the ASCII repre-

Location	Data	Location	Data
2000	046600	2050	027106
2002	051101	2052	010456
2004	027113	2054	054130
2006	027056	2056	054130
2010	027102	2060	041200
2012	021056	2062	046111
2014	054103	2064	027114
2016	054130	2066	027056
2020	046000	2070	027101
2022	041525	2072	040056
2024	027131	2074	054130
2026	027056	2076	054130
2030	027104	2100	045002
2032	012456	2102	047101
2034	054130	2104	027105
2036	054130	2106	027056
2040	046401	2110	027103
2042	051101	2112	015056
2044	027131	2114	054130
2046	027056	2116	054130

Figure 5.14   Data for Exercises 25 through 29

sentation of a student's grade in a particular course. The twelfth byte of each record is used to specify a student's age. A set of *test data* for a collection of records is given in Fig. 5.14.

25. A student named MARY wishes to identify the starting address of her student record. Develop and test a subroutine that returns the starting address of her records.

26. A student named MARY wishes to compensate for errors made by her senile instructor. In particular, if her teacher has awarded her a grade of D or F, she wishes to change it to a B. If a grade of B or C has been entered in her record, she wishes to change it to an A. Develop and test appropriate software. The data contained in Fig. 5.14 may be used for testing this program.

27. A student wishes to search *K* records, each having 2L bytes, beginning at even-numbered memory location *N* in an attempt to locate the starting address of her or his record. In addition to the values of *K, L* and *N* being placed in the argument list, 5 additional bytes of information are to be included. These correspond to the sex of the student and the name of the student. Develop and test a subroutine that returns the corresponding record address if the name is located, and returns a number having a value of 0 otherwise.

28. Develop and test a program that searches five data records beginning at memory location 2000 and returns the address of the record or the oldest male student.

29. Generalize the program developed in Exercise 28.

30. (Major Project) Using a high-level language, design a PDP-11 emulator. Include in this emulator the capability to enter and display data in a manner similar to using ODT commands.

6

Assembly-Language Programming

Computer programs can be classified into one of two broad categories: *application* programs and *system* programs. In general, application programs involve tasks that are independent of the machine being utilized. For example, many business and scientific programs may be run on any machine as long as the necessary data are provided. Such programs should be written in *high-level languages,* such as COBOL, FORTRAN, or Pascal.

Some programs involve control of a particular machine or system. As a special case, consider a computer that is used to *monitor* and *control* an intensive care unit in a hospital. Such a program must address, modify, and monitor particular system components. Use of a high-level language may not be convenient for developing the required software. Thus, a large number of system programs are developed using *low-level languages.*

Programming at the *machine-language* level is convenient if we are monitoring or controlling specific bits of information or small groups of binary characters. Disadvantages of developing machine-language programs include the following:

1. It is difficult to associate binary or octal numbers with specific computer instructions.
2. Documentation of machine-language programs is awkward.
3. The readability attribute, which is important in developing good programs, cannot be realized when writing a program using machine codes.

4. Computation of branching displacements and relative addresses is awkward and can easily lead to addressing errors.

These obvious shortcomings, however, may be alleviated if we develop programs in *symbolic code* that corresponds directly to machine-language instruction codes. Assembly-language programming enables us to achieve the desired goals.

6.1 INTRODUCTION

An *assembly-language* program is written in symbolic code. The instructions or commands are simple mnemonics associated with particular machine-language instructions. An *assembler* is a program that converts a user-developed assembly-language program either into machine code or into a form closely resembling machine code. Figure 6.1 illustrates the function of an assembler.

The output of an assembler is referred to as *object code*. The object code produced by some assemblers is identical to machine-language code and is assigned to specific memory addresses. This code needs no further processing. However, some assemblers produce output code in which memory addressing has not yet been assigned. Furthermore, it may be necessary to *link* this code with similar code segments produced by previously assembling various subroutines. A *file* containing such previously assembled subroutines is called a *library*. If an assembler does not produce the final version of machine code, another program must be executed in order to connect the various program segments, to assign memory addresses to the

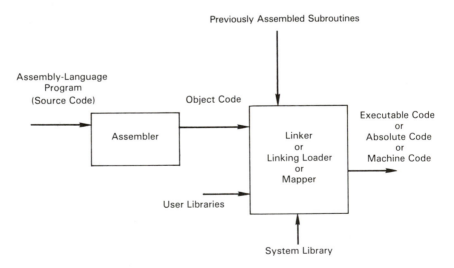

Figure 6.1 Developing machine code using an assembler

resulting program, and to produce the complete machine-language program. Such a program is called a linker, a mapper, or a relocatable linking loader.

We are concerned here with developing PDP-11 programs. The specific assembler that we will discuss is the MACRO-11 assembler. It is properly classified as a *macro assembler*. A macro assembler performs all the functions of an assembler. In addition, it allows a user to create her or his own mnemonics. That is, names corresponding to desired machine-language instructions may be created, and *sequences* of machine-language codes are associated with the user-defined names or macros. Use of macro instructions is illustrated in Section 6.4. The MACRO-11 assembler does not convert source code directly into executable or absolute code. Rather, the output of this assembler is processed by a *linking loader* in order to produce absolute or machine-language code.

Typical assembly-language program lines are composed of four sections or *fields*—a *label* field, a *command* field, an *operand* field, and a *comment* field. Not all of these fields are required in each line. For example, one line may consist of just a comment field, and another line may consist of just a command and an appropriate operand. Some assemblers reserve specific columns for each of the fields. Typical assemblers are either *format free* or nearly format free. That is, specific columns are not designated for each of the fields. Generally, the various fields are separated, or *delimited* by inserting at least one space between fields.

The MACRO-11 assembler does not require rigid formatting of input lines. Usually labels are started in column 1, and labels must be terminated with a colon. All comments must be preceded by a semicolon. The form of the operand depends on the particular command that is being used. Figure 6.2 illustrates a PDP-11 assembly-language program. This is essentially the same program as in Example 5.23.

In order to *assemble* this program, the program should be placed in a file; the MACRO-11 assembler should be run, and it should read this user program as input data. The output of the assembler should be the corresponding object code, and this output will usually be placed in an appropriate file. For benefit of the programmer, a printed listing of the assembler output will also be produced. The printed listing corresponding to the assembler output for the program shown in Fig. 6.2 is given in Fig. 6.3.

```
        HOW=2040
        LOW=2042
        TEN=10.
        PTR=2000
START:  MOV #10,RO      ;PUT COUNTER INTO RO
        CLR HOW         ;CLEAR MEMORY REGISTERS
        CLR LOW
        MOV #PTR,R1     ;LOAD POINTER
BACK:   ADD (R1)+,LOW
        BCC UP          ;IS THERE A CARRY?
        INC HOW         ;YES
UP:     SOB RO,BACK     ;LOOP UNTIL DONE
QUIT:   HALT
        .END QUIT
```

Figure 6.2 Assembly-language program

```
.MAIN.   MACRO V03.02B 00:04:25 PAGE 1


     1            002040                          HOW=2040
     2            002042                          LOW=2042
     3            000012                          TEN=10.
     4            002000                          PTR=2000
     5 000000     012700     000010     START:    MOV #10,R0      ;PUT COUNTER INTO R0
     6 000004     005067     002040               CLR HOW         ;CLEAR MEMORY REGISTERS
     7 000010     005067     002042               CLR LOW
     8 000014     012701     002000               MOV #PTR,R1     ;LOAD POINTER
     9 000020     062167     002042     BACK:     ADD (R1)+,LOW
    10 000024     103002                          BCC UP          ;IS THERE A CARRY?
    11 000026     005267     002040               INC HOW         ;YES
    12 000032     077006                UP:       SOB R0,BACK     ;LOOP UNTIL DONE
    13 000034     000000                QUIT:     HALT
    14            000034'                          .END QUIT
.MAIN.   MACRO V03.02B 00:04:25 PAGE 1-1
SYMBOL TABLE

BACK      000020R         LOW   = 002042         QUIT      000034R        TEN   = 000012
HOW   = 002040            PTR   = 002000         START     000000R
                                                                         UP        000032R

. ABS.    000000         000
          000036         001
ERRORS DETECTED:  0

VIRTUAL MEMORY USED:  283 WORDS   ( 2 PAGES)
DYNAMIC MEMORY AVAILABLE FOR  18 PAGES
DK:1,TT:1=DK:1.MAC

ERRORS DETECTED:  0
```

Figure 6.3   Printed output of assembler for program in Fig. 6.2

The manner in which the MACRO-11 assembler is run depends on the software available with a particular system. If a modern operating system is utilized, typical commands for initiating the assembly process are

```
MACRO/LIST:TT: MYFILE.MAC
```

if an output listing is desired, and

```
MACRO MYFILE.MAC
```

if no output listing is desired. Use of these commands requires that the source code be accessible in a file called MYFILE.MAC, and the assembler will place the resulting object code in a file called MYFILE.OBJ.

Refer to the assembly-language program in Fig. 6.2. The first four lines and the last line in the program do not correspond to executable PDP-11 commands. These lines are merely *directives* to the assembler, and are referred to as *pseudo-instructions*. The first four lines may be classified as EQUATE-type pseudo instructions. These commands are used merely to assign meaningful names to numerical quantities. Then these names can be used throughout the program to represent the corresponding numbers or addresses. This significantly improves the *readability* of the program. In line 3 of the program, observe that the number 10 is followed by a period. This means that the number is a base-10 number instead of a base-8 number.

Refer to the last line of the program. The .END statement is used to terminate the assembly-language program. The operand following this directive is used to identify the *starting address* or *entry point* for the program. When this program is initially run, the entry point or starting address will be at the memory location labeled QUIT. Just one program statement, the HALT command, will be executed. Then program control will pass to ODT microcode. ODT commands may then be used to enter data required by this program. After this is completed, the program can be initiated by typing the ODT command 1000G. The number 1000 is used because the linking loader generally assigns the first executable statement in a program to memory location 1000.

Now refer to the printed output of the assembler in Fig. 6.3. Observe that the symbolic code has been translated into appropriate machine code and that branching displacements have been properly computed by the assembler. Note that the executable statements of this program correspond to the statements between lines 5 and 13. The command codes are assigned to memory locations beginning at location 000000 and ending at location 000034.

Programs generally are not stored in these memory locations. Low-numbered memory locations are usually reserved for very special purposes. Recall that *trap* and *interrupt* vectors must be stored in specific low-numbered memory locations. Consequently, the addresses assigned by the assembler for program storage are considered to be *relative* addresses. Observe that the numbers stored in the symbol table corresponding to the labels BACK, QUIT, START, and UP have an *R* appended to their numerical addresses. This implies that the addresses are relative rather than absolute. When the object code is entered into the linking loader, true addresses will be assigned. For this example, true addresses will correspond to the relative addresses plus the octal number 1000. A listing of the machine-code program placed in its actual memory addresses is given in Fig. 6.4.

A typical command for entering the linking loader program is

```
LINK MYFILE.OBJ.
```

This command will cause the appropriate object code to be read by the linking loader. The linking loader will process this information and create a new file, MY-FILE.SAV. This new file will contain the machine code for the program. The ma-

```
.E 1000-1034
012700 000010 005067 001030 005067 001026 012701 002000
062167 001016 103002 005267 001006 077006 000000
.E 2000-2022
177777 000001 000001 000001 000001 000001 000001 000001
000001 177777
```

Figure 6.4 Machine-code program for assembly-language program in Fig. 6.2 (data values are included)

chine code will be assigned to an appropriate area of memory, and information related to the entry point will also be included in this file. If the program references subroutines that are not included in the file containing the program's object code, files containing the object code for the required subroutines must be read by the linking loader. A command similar to the following command is used to enter such object modules:

```
LINK MYFILE.OBJ, SUBS1.OBJ, SUBS2.OBJ
```

Only the first-named file may contain an entry point, and the absolute or executable program will be placed in a file called MYFILE.SAV. To initiate execution of the corresponding machine-language program, the operating system command

```
RUN MYFILE
```

may be given. It is unnecessary to specify a suffix for the designated file, as only executable modules can actually be run. Examples of other operating system commands are given in Section 6.2.

The MACRO-11 assembler has a considerable number of options and capabilities. It is not within the scope of this textbook to enumerate all of these capabilities. Similarly, there are a considerable number of pseudo instructions that may be useful to a programmer. Several of these directives will be introduced throughout the following sections.

Example 6.1

Using assembly language, develop a subroutine that finds the average of the four signed numbers immediately following the statement that calls the subroutine. The answer should be returned in R0. After this subroutine has been assembled, write a program that can be used to test the subroutine. Indicate how to execute this test program.

Solution   A subroutine satisfying the given requirements is given in Fig. 6.5. Observe that a new pseudo-instruction is introduced—the .GLOBL instruction, followed by an

```
        .GLOBL AVE4
        ;THIS SUBROUTINE PULLS IN THE 4 SIGNED NUMBERS
            ;IMMEDIATELY FOLLOWING THE CALL STATEMENT.  IT
            ;RETURNS THE AVERAGE VALUE OF THE NUMBERS IN R0.
            ;WE ASSUME OVERFLOW WILL NOT OCCUR.
            ;REGISTER R5 IS THE LINKING REGISTER.
AVE4:   CLR R0              ;CLEAR RUNNING SUM

        MOV #4,R1           ;SET COUNTER
BACK:   ADD (R5)+,R0
        SOB R1,BACK         ;BRANCH UNTIL DONE
        ASR R0              ;FIND AVERAGE
        ASR R0
        RTS R5
        .END
```

Figure 6.5   Subroutine for Example 6.1

operand AVE4. This indicates that a subroutine named AVE4 may be referenced by separately compiled modules. Suppose this subroutine is stored in a file called AVE4.MAC. Then, after it is assembled, the object code will be stored in a file called AVE4.OBJ.

A test program for this subroutine is given in Fig. 6.6. Observe that the subroutine AVE4 is again declared a global variable by the statement .GLOBL AVE4. Had this variable not been declared as shown, the assembler would have displayed an error message, as a program statement, JSR R5,AVE4, would have referred to an undefined variable.

Another pseudo–instruction appears in this program. The directive .WORD appears four times. This command directs the assembler to store the designated word in the address corresponding to the current line of the program. Thus, four words are stored in memory immediately after the statement that calls the subroutine.

Suppose the test program has been stored in a file called TEST.MAC. After this program has been assembled, its object code will probably be stored in a file called TEST.OBJ. To link the required files, we can give the command

```
LINK TEST.OBJ,AVE4.OBJ
```

To execute the program, the following operating system command may be given:

```
RUN TEST.
```

Review

1. Refer to the machine-language code in Fig. 6.4 and to the data in the figure. If program execution is started at memory location 1000, what number will appear in each of the following locations after program execution has been completed?
   (a) R7
   (b) memory location 2040
   (c) memory location 2042

2. Suppose the program corresponding to the code in Fig. 6.6 is executed. When program execution is completed, what number will be in R0?

3. Design and test a subroutine that accepts an argument list consisting of three 16-bit positive numbers. The subroutine returns the largest of these three numbers in R0.

```
        ,GLOBL START
        ,GLOBL AVE4
        ;TEST SUBROUTINE AVE4
START:  JSR R5,AVE4
        ,WORD   -75,    ;ENTER ARGUMENT LIST
        ,WORD   60,
        ,WORD   25,
        ,WORD   6
        HALT
        ,END START
```

Figure 6.6   Test program for Example 6.1

6.2 THE RT-11 OPERATING SYSTEM

An *operating system* is a *computer program* that performs certain specified tasks. Although some modern operating systems are implemented in microcode, it is still valid to visualize an operating system as a program. Computer systems based on a particular processor may include a variety of physical components as well as a variety of software packages. During the *system generation* phase of developing an operating system, it is important to *configure* the system for its specific components.

An operating system is frequently a large program. However, it is not essential that all of the system be resident in computer memory at all times. The operating system may require support from other programs. These programs may reside in secondary storage devices such as hard disks or flexible diskettes. However, this supporting software should be readily accessible to the operating system.

Some operating systems support multiuser and multitasking computer systems. Other operating systems have been developed primarily to support single-user online (or real-time) program development and operation. The major functions of such single-user operating systems include the following:

1. To interpret and execute user directives (command interpretation).
2. To provide file maintenance support. *Note:* A typical system supports operations on many types of files. Generally, files are classified by suffixes, such as MAC, OBJ, BAK, BAS, SAV, TXT, or SYS. These suffixes refer to the following types of files: macro assembler programs, object code files, backup files, BASIC programs, executable modules, text listings, and system programs.
3. To provide *input/output handlers*. An operating system generally provides software or interrupt processing routines that support I/O transfers for the various system devices.
4. The operating system should provide support for various language processors. Such support should include access to a *system library*.
5. An operating system should include access to certain user-support utility software packages. This set of packages should include a *text editor* and software to assist in *program debugging*.

We are discussing operating systems only because readers will utilize some capabilities of an operating system in developing and testing PDP-11 assembly-language programs. Typical operating systems used in the development of PDP-11 programs are the multiuser operating systems RSX-11M and RSX-11D and the relatively small single-user operating system RT-11. We will offer a very brief introduction to certain commands and capabilities available in the RT-11 operating system. From the perspective of a user, the RT-11 operating system may appear similar to popular operating systems used with microcomputers, such as DOS or CPM.

The RT-11 prompt character is a period. The form of a typical RT-11 command using an input file and an output file is the following:

```
COMMAND/OPTION INPUTFILE OUTPUTFILE
```

To be more specific, consider the following command:

```
COPY DX0:MYFILE.MAC DX1:YOURFILE.MAC
```

In this example, the COPY command is used, and no options are specified. The prefix for the first specified file is DX0. A *prefix* is used to specify a particular input/output storage device, sometimes referred to as a *volume*. Such devices include flexible disk drives, hard disk drives, and magnetic tape devices. The prefix DX0 refers to flexible disk drive 0. The example operating system command will result in a file MYFILE.MAC being copied to another file, YOURFILE.MAC, on a flexible disk located on disk drive 1.

Note: Operating system commands can perform the desired functions only if the particular software package required to execute this command is stored on the *system* volume. The system volume is the secondary storage device that is assigned to the operating system. When user files are stored on the system device, use of the volume prefix is not required. For example, frequently DX0 is the system device for systems using flexible disk drives. To access files contained on a floppy disk located on this unit, it is not necessary to specify the file prefix DX0.

Some RT-11 commands require the specification of just *input* files. For example, consider the following command:

```
MACRO/LIST:TT: FILE1.MAC,FILE2.MAC
```

Both files are input files. The command will cause the source programs contained in two different files to be assembled and listed. Two different object files, FILE1.OBJ and FILE2.OBJ, will be created. Because no file prefix has been specified, all files are accessed from the *system volume* or that physical device that is associated with the operating system.

Figure 6.7 is a listing of certain RT-11 operating system commands that may be useful for development of PDP-11 assembly-language programs. The purpose or function of each command is listed. Use of some of these commands has already been illustrated.

The *deposit* command, D, and the *examine* command, E, are useful for testing and debugging assembly-language programs. The deposit command may be used for inserting data into memory. For example, the command D 2000 = 1,2,7,177776 will cause the octal numbers 000001, 000002, 000007, and 177776 to be inserted, respectively, into memory locations 2000, 2002, 2004, and 2006. Similarly, the command E 1000–1020 will produce a listing of the words stored in memory locations

Command	Operand	Function or comment
FILE MANIPULATION COMMANDS		
1. DIR	Device Name:	List files on specified device. If no device is specified, list files on system device.
2. COPY	SRCFILE DSTFILE	Make a copy of a file.
3. EDIT	FILENAME	Use RT-11 text editor to create or modify a text file.
4. DELETE	FILENAME	Purge file.
5. TYPE	FILENAME	Type specified text file on the console printer.
PROCESSOR COMMANDS		
6. MACRO	FILENAME	Run MACRO-11 to assemble the source program in FILE-NAME. Create corresponding object file.
7. LINK	FILENAMES	Link and relocate object modules. First-named module should have an entry point.
8. RUN	FILENAME	Execute an absolute module.
COMMANDS USEFUL FOR DEBUGGING		
9. D	ADDRESS-DATA LIST	Deposit specified numbers in memory beginning at specified address.
10. E	ADDRESS-ADDRESS	Examine contents of memory between specified addresses.
11. B	ADDRESS	Add specified base address to addresses specified in subsequent D and E commands.

Figure 6.7 Some RT-11 commands useful for developing assembly-language programs

1000 to 1020. The B command is used to add displacements to addresses specified by subsequent examine or deposit commands. For example, the command

```
B 1000
```

will cause the octal number 1000 to be added to addresses specified in subsequent deposit or examine commands.

The RT-11 text editor may be used for building or modifying text files, such as PDP-11 assembly-language programs. When you wish to create a new text file, an RT-11 command similar to the following may be given.

```
EDIT/CREATE MYFILE.MAC
```

R: Read page of file text buffer.

xL: List, list, from the pointer, x lines of text

xN: Next; write the contents of the text buffer to the output file, clear the text buffer, and read into it the next page from the input file; perform this write/read sequence x times.

V: Verify; list the current line (the line containing the pointer) on the terminal.

xD: Delete; erase x characters to the right (or left) of the pointer.

I text (ESC) : Insert; insert text into the text buffer at the present pointer position.

xK: Kill; erase x lines of text, beginning at the pointer.

xA: Advance; move the pointer to the beginning of the xth line from the current pointer position.

B: Beginning; move the pointer to the beginning of the text buffer.

xJ: Jump; move the pointer forward or backward by x characters

xG text: Get; search the text buffer, beginning at the pointer, for the x occurrence of the indicated text string and leave the pointer at the end of the text string.

CTRL/L: Insert a form feed. The form feed character is used to delimit pages of text in a file (introduced as part of text by the Insert command).

EX: Exit; terminate editing, transfer the contents of the text buffer and the remainder of input file to the output file; close input and output files; return to monitor command mode.

Figure 6.8   Some RT-11 EDITOR commands (Copyright Digital Equipment Corporation, 1978. All rights reserved. Reprinted by permission.)

A listing of some RT-11 EDITOR commands is given in Fig. 6.8. These individual commands may be cascaded into strings of commands. Each command is terminated by typing the ESCAPE key after the command is typed. A command or a string of commands is executed only when ESCAPE is pressed again. When this editor is invoked, it responds and requests commands by typing an asterisk as a prompt character. Then it is very easy for a user to enter a program and store it in a text file.

First the insert command, I, is entered. This is followed by typing in the required lines of text. After the text has been entered, the insert command is terminated by pressing the ESCAPE key. Pressing the ESCAPE key once again causes the insert command to be executed. After this is done, the specified lines of text are stored in the editor's text buffer. Use of the command EX followed by typing two ESCAPE characters will result in the contents of the text buffer being stored in the newly created file.

The following sequence of commands illustrates creating and storing a simple assembly-language program. Underlined symbols are those typed by the computer.

```
.EDIT/CREATE MYFILE.MAC (RET)
*    ;SAMPLE PDP-11 PROGRAM (RET)
START:        MOV R2,R3 (RET)
              HALT (RET)
              .END START (RET)
(ESC) (ESC)
*EX (ESC) (ESC)
.
```

It appears to be very easy to create a textfile just by using the I and the EX editor commands. However, most of the time, mistakes will be included in the initial version of a text file. Therefore, it is necessary to edit files that have already been created and to correct the mistakes found in such files. AN RT-11 command of the form

```
EDIT OLDFILE.MAC
```

is used to initiate editing of a previously created file. Then the command R, or *read page of file into text buffer,* must be given. Then editor commands such as those shown in Figure 6.8 are used to make corrections to the file in the text buffer.

Elements of a text file are referred to relative to an *invisible pointer.* This pointer may identify the beginning of any line in the text buffer. Similarly, it may be positioned between any two characters in a line. In order to make corrections or insertions, this pointer must be positioned in the proper location. Example 6.2 illustrates modification of a text file using RT-11 editor commands.

Example 6.2

Suppose the following RT-11 command is given:

```
EDIT MYFILE.MAC
```

After the editor prompt symbol is displayed, suppose the following command string is entered:

```
R (ESC) 20L (ESC) (ESC)
```

In response to this command, suppose the following lines are printed:

```
START:    MOV R22,R3      ;MOVE R2 TO R3
          CRL R4          ;CLEAR R4
          NOPP
          HLT             ;HALT
          .END START
```

There are syntax errors in each of the first four lines. Use strings of editor commands to correct each of these errors.

Solution   To correct the first error, we will move the pointer just to the right of the string R22 and then delete one character to the left of the pointer. This can be done with the following string of editor commands:

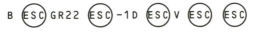

B (ESC) GR22 (ESC) -1D (ESC) V (ESC) (ESC)

To correct the error in line 2, we will delete the characters RL and insert the characters LR.

B (ESC) GCRL (ESC) -2D (ESC) ILR (ESC) V (ESC) (ESC)

We will delete the third line and insert a new line with the correct mnemonic for a NOP instruction.

B (ESC) 2A (ESC) 1K (ESC) I   NOP (RET) (ESC) (ESC)

We can use the following string of commands to correct the error in the mnemonic in the fourth line, to display the entire program, and to save the corrected text buffer in the file MYFILE.MAC.

B (ESC) GH (ESC) IA (ESC) B (ESC) 10L (ESC) EX (ESC) (ESC)

Review

1. Which of the following RT-11 commands is a valid command? Explain.
   (a) TYPE MYFILE.OBJ
   (b) TYPE MYFILE.SAV
   (c) TYPE MYFILE.TXT

2. Suppose the following sequence of RT-11 commands is entered.

```
D 1000 = 2,3,776,124
D 2000 = 3,776,2,124
B 1000
E 1000 - 1004
```

What numbers will be printed?

3. Suppose the RT-11 editor has been entered, and the following command string has been typed.

R (ESC) B (ESC) 20L (ESC) (ESC)

Then, in response to this command string, the following lines are printed.

```
START:  MOVE R1, R2
        ADD R2,R3
        SWAB R3
        NOOP        ;NOP COMMAND
        .END SATRT
```

There are three syntactical errors in this text. Formulate command strings to correct each of the errors.

6.3 DEVELOPING AND DEBUGGING PROGRAMS

The concepts in Chapter 2 relating to development of programs apply to development of assembly-language programs as well as to programs written in high-level languages. It is especially important that programs written in lower-level languages be developed in relatively small independent modules. The number of lines in an assembly-language program can become quite large in comparison to the number of lines required for a program written in a high-level language. Thus, the task of program debugging can be very tedious unless care is taken in the initial program development phase.

Even when program segments are carefully written and tested individually, difficulties still arise in locating logic errors in a program. It is very convenient if we can stop program execution at selected points and inspect the contents of the internal registers and selected memory locations. If the values in these locations are satisfactory, we can continue program execution until we reach another selected point in our program. If certain values are not satisfactory, we have identified a relatively small region within our program in which errors probably exist.

Program development packages are available on many computer systems. On PDP-11 systems, a *software* package called ODT may be used for debugging either assembly-language programs or FORTRAN programs. (ODT is an acronym used for online debugging technique, octal debugging technique, or online debugging tool.) The ODT software package is quite similar to the console ODT that is implemented in microcode, but it is considerably more powerful. The ODT object code may be linked to user object code by using the following RT-11 directive:

```
LINK/MAP:TT:/DEBUG MYFILE.OBJ,MYSUBS.OBJ
```

The MAP option results in a map being printed on the console. This map identifies the location of all global variables after the linking operation has been completed. When the command RUN MYFILE is given, program control passes to the ODT software. The ODT prompt * is printed, and then ODT commands may be entered to run and debug the user program under ODT control.

The console ODT commands given in Fig. 5.5 are almost a proper subset of the commands available with ODT software. In addition, there are several other commands that are useful in program development. Some of these commands are given in Fig. 6.9.

One of the most useful functions of ODT is the capability to set breakpoints at selected memory locations. Breakpoints may be set at any address in which the first word of a valid machine-language instruction is stored. Then, if a program is executed under ODT control, program execution proceeds up to the memory address at which the first breakpoint is set. Control then reverts back to ODT. At this point, CPU registers or memory locations may be inspected. Then the *proceed* command (;P) is given, and program execution continues until the next breakpoint is encountered.

	Command	Name	Function or Comment
1.	CTRL/C	Control C	Return to RT-11
2.	NUMBER0;B	Set Breakpoint	Set Breakpoint 0
	NUMBER1;B		Set Breakpoint 1
	NUMBER2;B		Set Breakpoint 2
3.	NUMBERX;NB	Reset Breakpoint	Reset Breakpoint n to address NUMBERX
4.	;NB	Remove Breakpoint	Delete Breakpoint N
5.	;B	Clear Breakpoints	Remove all Breakpoints
6.	NUMBER;G	GO	Run program beginning at NUMBER
7.	NUMBER\	Display byte	Open byte location NUMBER. Display the contents of this location in octal and as the corresponding ASCII character.

Note: Most console ODT commands such as given in Figure 5.5 are also valid.

Figure 6.9   Some useful commands available in the ODT software package

Example 6.3

Refer to the assembly-language program in Fig. 6.6 and to the subroutine in Fig. 6.5. Suppose the corresponding object modules are stored in the files TEST.OBJ and AVE4.OBJ, and the following ODT directive is given.

```
LINK/MAP:TT:/DEBUG TEST.OBJ,AVE4.OBJ
```

In response to this directive, a file TEST.SAV is created, and the *map* shown in Fig. 6.10 is printed. The command RUN TEST is then entered, and the computer responds with an ODT prompt.

(a) Suppose the following ODT command is given: 7106\. What ASCII character will be printed?

(b) Suppose the following sequence of commands is given. (*Note:* Underlined text refers to responses given by the ODT software.) What number will be printed in response to the last ODT command that is entered?

```
*7116;B
*7120;B
*7124;B
*7100;G
B0;007116
*;P
B1;007120
*;P
B2;007124
*;P
B2;007124
*;P
B2;007124
*;P
B2;007124
*$0/        (What will be the response?)
```

```
RT-11 LINK  V05.04A     Load Map
TEST .SAV       Title:  ODT      Ident:

Section   Addr    Size    Global  Value   Global  Value   Global  Value

. ABS.   000000  001000   (RW,I,GBL,ABS,OVR)
         001000  006136   (RW,I,LCL,REL,CON)
                          O.ODT   001232  START   007100  AVE4    007116

Transfer address = 001232, High limit = 007136 =   1939, words
```

Figure 6.10   Load map produced by linker for Example 6.3

Solution   **(a)** The number $60_{10} = 000074_8 = 0000000000111100_2$ is stored at word address 7106. This implies that the number $00111100_2 = 3C_{16}$ is stored at byte address 7106. Referring to Appendix A, it is seen that this is the ASCII code for the character $<$.

(b) When breakpoint 2, corresponding to the label BACK, is encountered for the fourth time, the operation stored at this location has been performed three times. Thus, the base-10 number 10 is stored in R0. The response to the last ODT command will be 000012.

Review

1. Refer to the program in Example 6.3. At which of the following memory locations may valid breakpoints be set?
   (a) 7114
   (b) 7116
   (c) 7122
   (d) 7126
   (e) 7130

2. Refer to the program in Example 6.3. After the RT-11 command RUN TEST is given, the following ODT command is entered: 7125\. What ASCII character will be printed?

3. Refer to the program in Example 6.3. Suppose the following sequence of ODT commands is given:

```
*7116;B
*7120;B
*7124;B
*;B
*7132;B
*7100;G
(Computer response)
*$0/
```

What will be the response to the last ODT command?

6.4 USE OF MACRO INSTRUCTIONS

An assembler is a program that translates simple mnemonics into the corresponding machine codes. There is a one-to-one relationship between a mnemonic and the corresponding machine-language instruction. Some assemblers allow users to create names for mnemonics and to use these names to represent corresponding *sequences* of instructions. Then, whenever the newly created name is referenced in an assembly-language program, the assembler translates this name into the corresponding sequence of instructions. The names that correspond to sequences of machine-language instructions are referred to as *macros* or *macroinstructions*. Assemblers that permit the use of macros are referred to as *macro assemblers*. MACRO-11 is a macro assembler.

Macros may be classified into two general categories: *user macros* and *system macros*. System macros are generally macroinstructions that have been supplied with the system software. They are stored in a *macro library* that is accessible to the operating system. The RT-11 system macro library is identified by the file name SYSMAC.SML. A significant number of system macros are stored in this library file. In particular, several macros useful for *input/output* operations are contained in this file. For many applications it is suggested that users perform all input/output operations using system macros. I/O operations are discussed in more detail in Chapters 8 and 9.

A user may generate his or her own macroinstructions. Such macros may be included as part of an assembly-language program, or they may be placed in a macro library. If any macroinstruction is utilized in an assembly-language program but is not explicitly defined in that module, the macro name must be identified. This is analogous to the way in which global variables are identified in program modules. Then, when the macro assembler is invoked, the particular library names must be identified. It is not necessary to identify explicitly the system macro library SYS-MAC.SML.

The program in Fig. 6.11 illustrates the use of two system macros. These are the .PRINT and the .EXIT macros. In order to identify these two *external* macros, the .MCALL statement followed by the specific macro names is used before either of the two macros appears in the program. The .PRINT macro initiates printing of a designated character string. Printing continues until a terminating character ap-

```
          .MCALL  .EXIT,.PRINT
          CR = 15              ;CARRIAGE RETURN
          LF = 12              ;LINE FEED
          FIN = 200
START:    NOP
          .PRINT #MYMES
          .EXIT
MYMES:    .ASCII /THIS PROGRAM ILLUSTRATES THE USE OF MACROS/<CR><LF>
          .ASCII /MESSAGE IS TERMINATED WITH OCTAL NUMBER 200/<FIN>
          .END START
```

Figure 6.11 Program illustrating use of system macroinstructions

pears. The octal number 200 is a terminating character for the routine defined by this macro. Observe that octal numbers corresponding to the codes for *carriage return* and *line feed* are inserted after the first line of the character string. The particular character string to be printed by this macro is identified by the word .MYMES. This argument is the address at which the character string to be printed begins.

The .EXIT macro is used to return program control to the RT-11 operating system. When system macros are used for I/O operations, generally program control should be returned to the operating system rather than to console ODT at the conclusion of the program. I/O operations differ from other types of computer operations. Other computer operations are initiated and completed before the following step in a sequence of instructions is initiated. I/O operations are initiated by an appropriate command such as a .PRINT macro. However, such operations are generally not completed until many other computer operations have been performed. In the example shown in Fig. 6.11, program control will be returned to RT-11 before printing of the character string has been completed. However, printing will continue until the terminating character is encountered, and then the RT-11 prompt will be printed. The functioning of such *interrupt-driven* routines will be discussed in more detail in Chapter 9.

Figure 6.12 illustrates the use of a *user-defined* macro, and Figure 6.13 is the corresponding assembler output. The user-defined macro PACK has two arguments. These correspond to a source pointer and a destination pointer. This macro will copy a character in a source string to a destination location and increment the pointers unless the character is the ASCII representation of a *space* or a *blank*. In this case, it will not copy the character, and will increment only the source pointer. Observe that the macro defined as PACK contains an internal *label,* UP.

```
        ;******************  USER DEFINED MACRO  *****************
        ;   ELIMINATE SPACE CHARACTER (ASCII 40)
        .MACRO PACK A,B
        SPACE = 40
        CMPB #SPACE,@A
        BEQ UP
        MOVB @A,@B
        INC B
UP:     INC A
        .ENDM
        ;****** TEST MACRO ********
START:  MOV #SOURCE,R0
        MOV #12.,R1      ;SET COUNTER
BACK:   PACK R0,POINT
        SOB R1,BACK
        HALT
SOURCE: .ASCII /HOW ARE YOU?/
        .EVEN
POINT:  .WORD DESTIN
DESTIN: .BLKW 6.
        .END START
```

Figure 6.12 Program illustrating use of a user-defined macroinstruction

The test program in Fig. 6.12 illustrates use of this macro. Refer to the corresponding assembler output in Fig. 6.13. In line 14 of this listing, observe that relative memory space between locations 000010 and 000026 has been reserved for insertion of the codes corresponding to the macro PACK. Also observe, from inspection of the symbol table, that the relative value of the label UP is 000026, which corresponds to the location of the last statement in the macro. During the linking operation, the codes for the macroinstruction will be inserted in the memory locations actually used in the machine-language program.

The example shown in Fig. 6.12 utilizes two assembler directives or pseudo-instructions that have not previously been used. The .EVEN directive informs the assembler to start the next executable command or memory storage directive at an *even-numbered* address. When strings of bytes are inserted within the program text, they may not occupy an integral number of words. Use of this directive ensures that the next memory location will correspond to an even address. In this program use of the .EVEN directive is not essential. However, sometimes it is necessary to use this directive because *instructions can be fetched only from even-numbered locations.*

Use of the .BLKW directive followed by the number N will direct the assembler to reserve space for a *block* of N words. In this example, space for a block of six words is reserved. A similar directive is .BLKB N. This pseudo–instruction causes the assembler to reserve space for a *block* of N bytes.

Use of the macro PACK in Figs. 6.12 and 6.13 is satisfactory only because the macro is invoked just once by the actual program. Generally, a macro is invoked more than once by a program. Suppose that PACK is invoked twice. The first time it is used, the label UP will be defined to correspond to a relative memory location. The second time it is used, the label UP will be assigned to a *different* memory location. Thus, the same label will be defined twice. This necessarily results in an assembler error. Thus, care must be taken when using labeled statements as part of user-defined macros.

There are two valid ways in which labeled statements may be incorporated within user-defined macros. The label name may be included as part of the macro argument list. Each time the macro is called, a different name may be used. This technique is illustrated in Fig. 6.14. In this example, the macro PACK is used twice, and the distinct label names are DOG and CAT. A second technique is to direct the macro to select different label identifiers each time it is invoked. This may be done by using a statement of the following form:

```
.MACRO PACK A,B,?C
```

In this example, the label name is *C*. Each time the macro is used, a different identifier is internally selected for the label *C*. A label identifier is *not* used when this macro is invoked. That is, only arguments corresponding to character strings *not* preceded by a question mark are transmitted to the macro.

```
.MAIN.  MACRO  V03.02B 02:07:16 PAGE  1

    1                      ;********************** USER DEFINED MACRO **********
    2                      ;     ELIMINATE SPACE CHARACTER (ASCII 40)
    3                      .MACRO PACK A,B
    4                      SPACE = 40
    5                      CMPB #SPACE,@A
    6                      BEQ UP
    7                      MOVB @A,@B
    8                      INC B
    9      UP:            INC A
   10                      .ENDM
   11                      ;****** TEST MACRO ********
   12  000000  012700  000034'   START:  MOV #SOURCE,R0
   13  000004  012701  000014            MOV #12,R1     ;SET COUNTER
   14  000010                    BACK:   PACK R0,POINT
   15  000030  077111                    SOB R1,BACK
   16  000032  000000                    HALT
   17  000034  110  117  127     SOURCE: .ASCII /HOW ARE YOU?/
       000037  040  101  122
       000042  105  040  131
       000045  117  125  077
   18                            POINT:  .EVEN
   19  000050  000052'           DESTIN: .WORD DESTIN
   20  000052                            .BLKW 6.
   21  000000'                           .END START

.MAIN.  MACRO  V03.02B 02:07:16 PAGE  1-1
SYMBOL TABLE

BACK   000010R    POINT   000050R    SPACE = 000040    START  000000R
DESTIN 000052R    SOURCE  000034R                      UP     000026R

. ABS.  000000    000
        000066    001
ERRORS DETECTED: 0

VIRTUAL MEMORY USED:  406 WORDS   ( 2 PAGES)
DYNAMIC MEMORY AVAILABLE FOR  18 PAGES
DK:PACK,TT:PACK=DK:PACK.MAC

ERRORS DETECTED: 0
```

Figure 6.13 Output of assembler for program in Fig. 6.12

```
    1                        ;******************** USER DEFINED MACRO ***************
    2                        ;    ELIMINATE SPACE CHARACTER (ASCII 40)
    3                        .MACRO PACK A,B,C
    4                        SPACE = 40
    5                        CMPB #SPACE,@A
    6                        BEQ C
    7                        MOVB @A,@B
    8                        INC B
    9                        INC A
   10                    C:  .ENDM
   11                        ;****** TEST MACRO ********
   12  000000 012700 000054'  START:  MOV #SOURCE,R0
   13  000004 012701 000014           MOV #12.,R1  ;SET COUNTER
   14  000010                 BACK:   PACK R0,POINT,DOG
   15  000030 077111                  SOB R1,BACK
   16  000032                         PACK R0,POINT,CAT
   17  000052 000000                  HALT
   18  000054 110 117 127   SOURCE:  .ASCII /HOW ARE YOU?/
       000057 040 101 122
       000062 105 040 131
       000065 117 125 077
   19                                 .EVEN
   20  000070 000072'        POINT:   .WORD DESTIN
   21  000072                DESTIN:  .BLKW 6.
   22  000072 000000'                 .END START
```

```
.MAIN.   MACRO  VO3.02B  00:06:38  PAGE  1-1
SYMBOL TABLE

BACK   000010R      DESTIN 000072R      POINT  000070R      SPACE = 000040
CAT    000050R      DOG    000026R      SOURCE 000054R      START  000000R
. ABS. 000000   000
       000106   001
ERRORS DETECTED: 0

VIRTUAL MEMORY USED: 419 WORDS  ( 2 PAGES)
DYNAMIC MEMORY AVAILABLE FOR 18 PAGES
DK:PACK1,TT:PACK1=DK:PACK1.MAC

ERRORS DETECTED: 0
```

Figure 6.14 Program illustrating transmittal of label names into a macro

Review

1. Refer to the program illustrated in Figs. 6.12 and 6.13. When this program is executed, to which byte address is the ASCII code corresponding to the character *Y* moved?

2. Refer to the program illustrated in Figs. 6.12 and 6.13. Suppose the assembler directive .BLKW is changed to .BLKB. What is the smallest value of an argument that can follow this directive in order that adequate space be reserved for the destination string in the test program?

3. Refer to Fig. 6.14. Suppose the following statement is inserted just above the HALT statement:

```
PACK R2,POINT,MOUSE
```

   (a) At what relative address will the program sequence corresponding to this macro begin?

   (b) To what relative address will the label MOUSE be assigned?

4. Refer to the macro PACK defined in Fig. 6.14. After the macro definition, suppose the following program is written:

```
START:  PACK R1,2000,LAB1
        PACK R2,2100,LAB2
        PACK R3,2200,LAB3
        HALT
        .END START
```

   How many words of program storage space are required for this program?

5. Design and test a macro that increments a pointer by 2 and decrements a counter by 1. Arguments corresponding to the pointer and counter are to be contained in the argument list of the statement invoking the macro.

6.5 ILLUSTRATIVE PROGRAMS

In this section we will give several examples illustrating assembly-language programming of PDP-11 computers. In Chapter 7 examples related specifically to numerical operations are presented. Programs illustrating use of input/output operations are developed in Chapters 8 and 9.

Example 6.4

Develop and test a subroutine that counts the number of times the ASCII representation for the letter *A* is stored in a specified block of memory.

Solution   A solution is given in Fig. 6.15. Refer to the statement labeled AGAIN. The letter *A* is preceded by an apostrophe. This directs the assembler to use the ASCII representation for this character. Refer to the line immediately following the statement labeled START. The number corresponding to the expression DONE-DATA is computed and then assigned to this memory location, which can be identified as START

```
                ;SUBROUTINE STARTS HERE
                ;POINTER TO ARGUMENT LIST IS IN LINKING REGISTER, RO
                ;SUBROUTINE COUNTS NUMBER OF  'A' S IN AN ARRAY OF N BYTES
                ;ARGUMENT LIST:  ARRAY SIZE,ARRAY ADDRESS
   COUNT:  MOV (RO)+,R1    ;PUT COUNTER IN R1
           MOV (RO)+,R2    ;PUT ARRAY POINTER IN R2
           CLR R3  ;INITIALIZE COUNT
   AGAIN:  CMPB #'A,(R2)+
           BNE UP
           INC R3  ;INCREMENT COUNTER IF CHARACTER IS AN A
   UP:     DEC R1  ;DONE?
           BNE AGAIN       ;NO
           RTS RO  ;YES
   ;************START TEST PROGRAM ******************
   START:  JSR RO,COUNT
           .WORD   DONE-DATA       ;ARRAY SIZE
           .WORD   DATA    ;ARRAY ADDRESS
           HALT
   DATA:   .ASCII /MERRY CHRISTMAS/
           .ASCII /HAPPY NEW YEAR/
   DONE:   .BYTE   0
           .END START
```

Figure 6.15   A solution to Example 6.4

+ 4. It is convenient to let the assembler perform such computations. Even though the programmer may know neither the address corresponding to the label DATA nor the address corresponding to the label DONE, it is clear that the difference of these two relative addresses is identical to the number of characters in the character strings identified by the two .ASCII statements.

Example 6.5

Design and test a subroutine that determines the sum of two 32-bit signed integers. Assume that the answer will always be expressible as a 32-bit signed integer. That is, neglect the possibility of overflow.

Solution   A solution is given in Fig. 6.16. Observe that the subroutine requires that the two integers be stored in consecutive memory spaces. Since each integer requires 4 bytes of memory, a total of 8 memory bytes is required. Execution of the subroutine does not change the value of the first integer. However, the value of the second integer is replaced with the value of the sum.

Example 6.6

Suppose an object file DATA.OBJ contains two global variables, DATA and DONE. Starting at memory location DATA, a set of 25 four-character strings is stored in this file. The label DONE identifies the memory location immediately following the last character string stored in this file. An example of a source program for the file DATA.OBJ is given in Fig. 6.17. Develop and test a subroutine that accepts an argument corresponding to a particular four-character string and returns a number indicating how many times this particular name appears in the file DATA.OBJ.

Solution   A subroutine satisfying the specified requirements is given in Fig. 6.18. Let us assume that this subroutine is stored in a file called COUNT.MAC. A program that invokes this subroutine is shown in Fig. 6.19. We will assume that this program is stored

```
                 ;SUBROUTINE ADDINT.  PC IS THE LINKING REGISTER.
                 ;OPERANDS ARE 32-BIT SIGNED INTEGERS.  THE MOST
                 ;  SIGNIFICANT WORD OF EACH INTEGER IS STORED FIRST.
                 ;THE POINTER IN R1 IDENTIFIES THE FIRST INTEGER.
                 ;(R1) + 4 IDENTIFIES THE SECOND INTEGER.
                 ;THE 32-BIT SUM IS PLACED IN MEMORY STARTING AT LOCATION
                 ;  (R1) + 4.
                 .GLOBL BEGIN,ADDINT,FIRST
        ADDINT:  ADD 2(R1),6(R1)
                 ADC 4(R1)
                 ADD(R1),4(R1)
                 RTS PC
        ;$$$$$    START TEST PROGRAM $$$$$$$$$$$$$$$$$
        BEGIN:   MOV #FIRST,R1
                 JSR PC,ADDINT
        ;$$$$DO ANOTHER TEST $$$$$$$$$$$$$$$$$$$$$$$$$$
                 MOV #OTHER,R1
                 JSR PC,ADDINT
                 HALT
        FIRST:   .WORD 177777,-3
                 .WORD 177777,-4
        OTHER:   .WORD 001234,155555
                 .WORD 017762,007777
                 .END BEGIN
```

Figure 6.16   Solution to Example 6.5: addition of two 32-bit signed integers

```
                 .GLOBL DATA
                 .GLOBL DONE
        DATA: .ASCII /MARYMARKLISABILLMARYTERILUCYMIKEMA/
              .ASCII /RYBILLBILLLISANUTSMARYLIS/
              .ASCII /ALISALISARUNTHELPMARYMARKLINNHOWAREYOU???/
        DONE:    .BYTE 200
                 .END
```

Figure 6.17   Source code for the file DATA.OBJ described in Example 6.6

```
                 ;THIS SUBROUTINE COUNTS THE NUMBER OF TIMES A PARTICULAR
                 ;  STRING OF FOUR ASCII CHARACTERS APPEARS IN AN ARRAY OF SUCH STRINGS.
                 ;  THE ARRAY OF STRINGS CONTAINS EXACTLY 'SIZE' ELEMENTS, WHERE THE
                 ;  NUMBER SIZE IS DEFINED WITHIN THE SUBROUTINE.
                 ;THE ARGUMENT STRING IS PLACED IMMEDIATELY AFTER THE STATEMENT THAT
                 ;  INVOKES THIS ROUTINE.  THE ANSWER IS RETURNED IN R0.
                 ;R1 IS THE LINKING REGISTER
                 .GLOBL COUNT,DATA
                 SIZE = 25.
        COUNT:   MOV #DATA,R2            ;INIT BLOCK PTR
                 CLR R0
                 MOV #SIZE,R3                 ;INIT BLOCK COUNTER
        BACK:    MOV R1,R4              ;INIT DATA PTR
                 MOV R2,R5                  ;INIT BYTE FILE PTR
                 CMPB (R5)+,(R4)+           ;IS FIRST LETTER PRESENT
                 BNE UP
                 CMPB (R5)+,(R4)+
                 BNE UP
                 CMPB (R5)+,(R4)+
                 BNE UP
                 CMPB (R5)+,(R4)+
                 BNE UP
                 INC R0
        UP:      ADD #4,R2              ;ADJUST BLOCK POINTER
                 DEC R3                 ;DONE?
                 BNE BACK               ;NO
                 ADD #4,R1
                 RTS R1                 ;YES
                 .END
```

Figure 6.18   Subroutine for Example 6.6

160

```
            ,GLOBL DATA,COUNT,DONE
START:      JSR R1,COUNT                    ;LET COUNT RETURN ANSWER
            ,ASCII/BILL/                    ;IN R0
            MOV R0,DONE                     ;SAVE B COUNT
            JSR R1,COUNT
            ,ASCII/LISA/
            MOV R0,DONE+2
            JSR R1,COUNT
            ,ASCII/MARY/
            MOV R0,DONE+4
            HALT
            ,END START
```

Figure 6.19   Test program for subroutine developed in Example 6.6

in a file called TEST.MAC. After the assembly process is completed, we may obtain an absolute module by giving the following directive to the linker:

```
LINK TEST.OBJ,COUNT.OBJ,DATA.OBJ
```

Then we may run the machine-language program stored in the file TEST.SAV. The three results computed by this test program will be stored in memory locations DONE, DONE + 2, and DONE + 4. Unfortunately, the person executing this program probably does not know the numerical identity of these addresses. These locations can be identified if the MAP option is used with the LINK command:

```
LINK/MAP:TT: TEST.OBJ,COUNT.OBJ,DATA.OBJ
```

An *array* or a *data array* can be visualized as a set of binary numbers stored in contiguous memory locations. An *element* of the array is identified by the contents of either one or a relatively small group of contiguous memory locations in the array. A variety of element *types* may be defined. For example, 8-bit integers, 16-bit integers, real numbers or floating points, or character strings can all be defined as elements of an array. Generally, all elements of a particular array are of the same type. Frequently, computer routines are required that perform operations on arrays of elements.

Example 6.7

Develop and test a subroutine that adds together the corresponding elements of two arrays of N elements and places the resulting elements in a third array of N elements. Assume the elements are 16-bit signed integers. If any addition operation produces numerical overflow, have the routine display an appropriate message.

Solution   A subroutine satisfying the problem requirements and a corresponding test program are given in Fig. 6.20.

We have discussed use of the .PRINT system macro for displaying character strings, but we have not yet introduced any method for *reading* characters from a system console. Although input/output operations are not formally discussed in

```
        .MCALL .EXIT,.PRINT
        ;SUBROUTINE MATADD
        ;THIS ROUTINE ADDS TWO ARRAYS OF N ELEMENTS AND
        ;    PLACES THE RESULT IN A THIRD ARRAY.
        ;THAT IS;    ARRAY A + ARRAY B => ARRAY C.
        ;THE ARGUMENT LIST FOLLOWS THE INVOKING STATEMENT.
        ;   ARGUMENT LIST:    N, A, B, C
        ; N IS A VALUE, AND A, B AND C ARE ADDRESSES.
        ;THE ELEMENTS OF THE ARRAYS ARE 16-BIT SIGNED INTEGERS.
        ;EACH TIME ADDITION OF ANY TWO ELEMENTS PRODUCES AN OVERFLOW,
        ;    AN APPROPRIATE MESSAGE IS PRINTED.
        ;R1 IS THE LINKING REGISTER.
        CR = 15
        LF = 12
        FIN = 200
OFMES:  .ASCII /WARNING!!!  OVERFLOW HAS OCCURRED !!!!!!/<CR><LF><FIN>
        .EVEN
MATADD: NOP       ;GET ARGUMENTS
        MOV (R1)+,R2      ;COUNTER
        MOV (R1)+,R3      ;SOURCE A POINTER
        MOV (R1)+,R4      ;SOURCE B POINTER
        MOV (R1)+,R5      ;DESTINATION POINTER
BACK:   MOV (R4)+,(R5)    ;ADD ARRAYS
        ADD (R3)+,(R5)+
        BVC UP  ;CHECK FOR OVERFLOW
        .PRINT #OFMES
UP:     SOB R2,BACK       ;LOOP UNTIL DONE
        RTS R1
;$$$$$$$$$$$$    START TEST PROGRAM    $$$$$$$$$$$$$$$$$$
        SIZE = 5
GO:     JSR R1,MATADD
        .WORD SIZE      ;N = SIZE
        .WORD AMAT      ;ADDRESSES
        .WORD BMAT
        .WORD CMAT      ;ADDRESS OF ANSWER
        .EXIT
AMAT:   .WORD -3,177776,77770,4,-8.
BMAT:   .WORD 9.,-3,12,3,7.
CMAT:   .BLKW 5
        .END GO
```

Figure 6.20 A solution to Example 6.7

detail until Chapters 8 and 9, it is convenient if we have at least one method of reading characters from the console keyboard. Use of the system macro .TTYIN provides a method for reading the ASCII representation of characters entered on the console keyboard.

The macroinstruction .TTYIN is used to *read* a character entered on the console keyboard. Typical I/O operations read characters into buffers or print characters that are contained in buffers. A *buffer* is merely a set of contiguous memory locations. Execution of the .TTYIN command will cause the next 7-bit ASCII character in the input buffer to be read into register R0.

The character is right justified; that is, it occupies the seven least significant bit positions of R0. Each time the .TTYIN command is encountered, the next character in the buffer will be read into R0. Suppose there are no characters in the input buffer. Then execution of the .TTYIN command will essentially cause a pause in program execution until the buffer is loaded. A user loads the input buffer by typing a string of characters on the console keyboard and then entering a valid terminating character, such as a carriage return or a line feed.

Example 6.8

Write a program that requests the user to enter a four-character password. If the correct password is entered, an appropriate message is printed. If an incorrect password is entered, the HALT statement is executed.

Solution   A solution is given in Fig. 6.21. The main program, which starts at the statement labeled GO, carries the correct password into the subroutine LOOK. This subroutine reads four characters that are entered from the console keyboard. If this character string is identical to the designated password, a 0 is stored in location FLAG when program control reverts back to the main program. Otherwise, a 1 is carried back in location FLAG, and the HALT mode is entered.

In this chapter we have introduced concepts related to assembly-language programming. Specifically, we have introduced assembly-language programming of the PDP-11 using the MACRO-11 assembler. We have presented just a brief introduction to the capabilities of the RT-11 operating system. The full capabilities of this system and of the related software are provided in the manufacturers' supporting documentation.

```
        ;THIS PROGRAM RESPONDS FAVORABLY IF THE
        ;   PROPER PASSWORD IS ENTERED.
        .MCALL  .TTYIN,.EXIT,.PRINT
GO:     .PRINT #MES
        JSR R2,LOOK
        .ASCII /HELP/
        TST FLAG
        BNE UP
        .PRINT #HELLO
        .EXIT
UP:     CLR FLAG        ; INCORRECT PASSWORD
        HALT
MES:    .ASCII /ENTER SECRET PASSWORD!!!!/<15><12><12><200>
HELLO:  .ASCII /YOUR PASSWORD IS CORRECT/<15><12>
        .ASCII /WELCOME TO RT-11   !!!!!/<15><12><200>
        .EVEN
;       $$$$$$$$$$$$$$ SUBROUTINE LOOK ****************
FLAG:   .BLKW 1
LOOK:   CLR FLAG
        MOV #4,R1            ;COUNTER
BACK:   .TTYIN R0
        CMPB R0,(R2)+
        BEQ AHEAD
        MOV #1,FLAG
AHEAD:  SOB R1,BACK
        RTS R2
        .END GO
```

Figure 6.21   Program that enters the HALT mode unless correct password is entered

Review

1. Refer to Example 6.4 and to the solution in Fig. 6.15. Prior to execution of this program, assume that each of the CPU registers contains the octal number 1000. After execution of the program is completed, what number will be in each of the following registers?
   (a) R0
   (b) R1
   (c) R3
   (d) R6

2. Refer to Example 6.5 and the solution in Fig. 6.16. After the test program has been executed, what octal number will be in each of the following specified word addresses?
   (a) FIRST
   (b) FIRST + 2
   (c) FIRST + 4
   (d) FIRST + 6
   (e) OTHER + 4
   (f) OTHER + 6

3. Refer to Example 6.6, to the test data in Fig. 6.17, and to the solution and test program in Figs. 6.18 and 6.19. During the linking operation, the map in Fig. 6.22 is produced. After the test program has been executed, what number will be in memory location 1272_8?

4. Refer to Example 6.6 and to the format of the file containing the four-letter character strings. Suppose this file is to be expanded so that it contains N character strings, where the value of N is not known to the programmer. The global labels DATA and DONE still bracket the strings. Modify the subroutine in Fig. 6.18 so it will work with the new data file.

5. Refer to Example 6.7 and to the solution and test program in Fig. 6.20. When this source program is assembled, the following symbol table is produced.

```
AMAT     000124R      CMAT     000150R     GO     000106R
BACK     000066R      CR    =  000015      LF  =  000012
BMAT     000136R      FIN   =  000200
     MATADD   000054R      SIZE   =  000005
     OFMES    000000R      UP        000102R
```

When the corresponding object program is processed by the linking loader, the absolute code is assigned to memory starting at octal location 1000.
(a) When the program is being executed, how many times will the overflow message be printed?

```
RT-11 LINK  V05.04A    Load Map
TEST  .SAV      Title:  .MAIN.  Ident:

Section  Addr   Size    Global  Value   Global  Value   Global  Value

. ABS.  000000  001000   (RW,I,GBL,ABS,OVR)
        001000  000272   (RW,I,LCL,REL,CON)
                         COUNT   001046  DATA    001124  DONE    001270

Transfer address = 001000, High limit = 001272 =   349, words
```

Figure 6.22   Map produced by linker in Example 6.6 (see Review question 3)

After program execution is completed, what number will be in each of the following memory locations?

(b) 1126; **(c)** 1140; **(d)** 1150; **(e)** 1160

REFERENCES

ECKHOUSE, R. H., and R. L. MORRIS, *Minicomputer Systems*. Englewood Cliffs, N.J.: Prentice-Hall, 1975.

FRANK, T. S., *Introduction to the PDP-11 and Its Assembly Language*. Englewood Cliffs, N.J.: Prentice-Hall, 1983.

GILL, A., *Machine and Assembly Language Programming of the PDP-11*. Englewood Cliffs, N.J.: Prentice-Hall, 1979.

IAS/RXS-11 MACRO-11 Reference Manual. Order #DEC-11-OIMRA-BD. Maynard, Mass.: Digital Equipment Corporation, 1976.

PDP-11 Software Handbook. Maynard, Mass.: Digital Equipment Corporation, 1980.

RT-11 System Users Guide. Order #DEC-11-ORGDA-A-D. Maynard, Mass.: Digital Equipment Corporation, 1977.

RT-11 The Advanced Programmers Guide. AA-5280B-TC. Maynard, Mass.: Digital Equipment Corporation, 1978.

EXERCISES

1. Identify at least five different MACRO-11 pseudo-instructions or assembler directives.

2. Refer to the assembler output in Fig. 6.3.
   (a) How many different *relative* addresses are identified in the symbol table?
   (b) If the assembler output from this program is the only input to the linking loader, what will be the true addresses corresponding to the variable names START, BACK, and QUIT?

3. What are advantages and disadvantages of using an assembler such as MACRO-11 to develop machine-language software rather than developing the corresponding code without the use of an assembler?

4. Which memory locations available on PDP-11 systems are generally not used for program storage? Explain.

5. What is a major advantage of creating the absolute code for a machine-language program using a linking loader rather than creating the machine code directly as the output of an assembler?

6. Develop and test a subroutine that accepts an argument corresponding to the address of an array of unsigned 16-bit numbers and another argument corresponding to the size of the array. The subroutine computes the sum of the elements in the array and returns the high-order word in global memory location SUM and the low-order word in SUM + 2.

7. Design and test a subroutine that accepts an argument list consisting of a value N followed by an address of an array of N 16-bit signed integers. The subroutine returns the largest of these integers in R0 and the smallest in R1.

8. Identify several different types of files in the RT-11 operating system.

The following information refers to Exercises 9, 10, and 11. When in the RT-11 EDIT mode, the following command is entered:

R (ESC) B (ESC) 20L (ESC) (ESC)

In response to this command, the following program is printed:

```
        ; MULTIPLY NUMBER BY COUNT
        .GLOBL ANSWER
        COUNT = 25.
        NUMBER = 16.
BEGIN:  MOVE #COUNT,R0
        CLEAR R1
BACK:   ADD #NUMBER,R1
        SOB R0,AGAIN
        HALT
        .END START
```

9. Formulate an editor command or a sequence of editor commands that will correct the errors in this program.

10. After the syntax and labeling errors have been corrected in the program, it is observed that the result has not been stored in the global address ANSWER. Use an appropriate string of editor commands to insert a statement that will cause the answer to be placed in this memory location.

11. Suppose the program has been corrected, assembled, linked, and executed. At the conclusion of execution, what octal number will be in each of the following locations?
    (a) R0
    (b) R1
    (c) memory location ANSWER

12. Refer to the program in Fig. 6.16. Suppose you wish to run this program in a *debug mode* by linking it with the ODT software.
    (a) What additional statement should be added to the source program?
    (b) After the source program has been assembled, the corresponding object code is placed in a file called ADDINT.OBJ. What command can be given to link this program to the ODT software?

13. Refer to Exercise 12. Suppose the following load map has been obtained and the command RUN ADDINT is entered.

```
RT-11 LINK   V05.04A     Load Map
ADDINT.SAV       Title: ODT      Ident:
Section   Addr   Size    Global Value     Global Value     Global Valu
ABS.      000000 001000   (RW,I,GBL,ABS,OVR)
          001000 006162   (RW,I,LCL,REL,CON)
                          O.ODT   001232  ADDINT 007100 BEGIN   0071
                          FIRST   007142
Transfer address = 001232, High limit = 007162 = 1849. words
```

After this command is entered, the computer responds with the ODT prompt *.
   (a) What command can now be given to set a breakpoint at the address corresponding to the source code statement ADC 4(R1)?
   (b) What command will cause program execution to be initiated?
   (c) When the breakpoint is first encountered, what octal number will be in each of the following locations?
      R1
      FIRST + 4
      FIRST + 6

14. Refer to Exercise 13. Which of the following addresses may serve as valid breakpoints?
   (a) 7102; (b) 7104; (c) 7110; (d) 7122; (e) 7123; (f) 7126

15. What is a major difference between using a macro to perform a task and calling a corresponding subroutine to perform the task?

16. Develop and test a macro that produces the commands to print a line consisting of 5 spaces followed by 20 asterisks. Then the macro causes a carriage return and two line feeds to be performed.

17. A subroutine is to search a character string starting at the address that is carried into the routine in R1. The search is to continue until the string terminator, octal number 200, is encountered. During the search, each time a capital letter between A and Z is encountered, it is to be replaced with the ASCII representation of the corresponding small letter. Develop and test an appropriate subroutine.

18. Refer to Example 6.8 and to the solution in Fig. 6.21. Modify this program so that a user will be given three chances to enter the correct password.

19. Refer to Example 6.8 and to the solution in Fig. 6.21. Modify the program and the subroutine LOOK so that the password may be changed from HELP to TIGERS.

20. Refer to the source code for the data file in Fig. 6.17. The file contains 25 four-letter names. Write a program segment that reads each of these names from the file and then *prints* each name on a separate line.
   Hint: To print each name, you may wish to develop a program segment such as the following:

```
PNTLN:  .ASCII /          /  ;SOME SPACES
NAME:   .BLKB    4           ;RESERVE SPACE FOR NAME
TERM:   .BYTE   12,15,200    ;LF,CR, TERMINATOR
        .EVEN
```

   Then, 4 bytes corresponding to a name can be read and stored in locations NAME, NAME +1, NAME +2, and NAME +3, and the command .PRINT #PNTLN can be given.

21. Refer to Exercise 20. Develop a corresponding program segment that reads N four-character names from a data file containing N names and prints each of these names on a separate line.

22. Develop a subroutine that
   (a) Sorts an array of four-character names into alphabetical order.
   (b) Prints the array of sorted names.

23. Refer to Exercise 22. Modify the specifications stated in part (b) so that no duplicate names will be printed. That is, each name will be printed only once.

24. Refer to Exercise 21. Do the corresponding tasks for an array of 16-character names.

25. Refer to Exercises 22 and 23. Do the corresponding tasks for an array of 16-character names.

26. A program segment is to employ the .TTYIN macro to read a line of text consisting of just capital letters terminated with a *carriage return*. Develop and test a program segment that reads this line and then prints the corresponding line using small letters.

7

Numerical Operations

Some digital computers are dedicated for use with business applications; others are used primarily for scientific applications. Many minicomputers, such as the PDP-11, are frequently utilized to monitor and control external systems. Regardless of the particular computer application, extensive use of arithmetic numerical *operations* is almost always required. The capability of a computer to perform such operations efficiently is sometimes referred to as the *number-crunching* capability.

The general-purpose microcomputers that were introduced in the 1970s and became very popular in the early 1980s had little hardware support for numerical operations. Machine-language instructions were generally available just for adding and subtracting relatively small numbers. Even the newer 16-bit microprocessors offered only limited number-crunching capabilities. Furthermore, these machine capabilities were generally restricted to performing arithmetic operations on integers.

When machines have limited number-crunching capabilities, it is necessary to provide suitable software so that operations on sufficiently large integers as well as operations on *floating-point numbers* may be performed. Such software includes addition, subtraction, multiplication, and division subroutines for both integers and real numbers or floating points. Many applications require the use of standard numerical functions, such as the *trigonometric functions*. Software required to implement these functions is generally stored in a system library. The functions are implemented by use of approximations involving rapidly converging power series. Developing software to implement such approximations is not difficult, provided that we have access to hardware or software that performs standard arithmetic operations on either integers or real numbers.

7.1 EXTENDED-PRECISION ARITHMETIC

A minimal PDP-11 configuration provides machine-language instructions for addition and subtraction of 16-bit signed integers. It is relatively easy to use these 16-bit operations as tools for performing corresponding arithmetic operations on multiword numbers. In addition, certain instructions are included in the PDP-11 instruction set that primarily facilitate certain extended-precision operations. These instructions are ADC or ADD CARRY, SBC or SUBTRACT BORROW, and the SIGN EXTEND instruction.

The ADC and SBC instructions are useful when we wish to perform operations on 32-bit integers. Refer to Example 6.5 and to the solution in Fig. 6.16. This example illustrates the use of the ADC command in performing operations on 32-bit integers. However, this command is not particularly useful for performing addition on integers containing more than 32 bits.

When we wish to perform addition on integers containing multiple words, we must first add corresponding words and then determine if there is a *new carry* to the next significant word position. Then we must add the previous value of the carry to the sum just computed and once again check to see if a new carry is being propagated. This technique is illustrated in Example 7.1.

Example 7.1

Develop and test a subroutine that adds together two multiword signed integers. Neglect the possibility that overflow may occur.

Solution   A solution is given in Fig. 7.1. The corresponding test program illustrates addition of two 80-bit integers. Observe that the two pointers brought into the subroutine are adjusted so that they point to the word position just past the least significant words of the multiword integers. However, also observe that the autodecrement mode of addressing is used. Therefore, before the initial addition operation actually occurs, the pointers identify the least significant words of the two operands.

The subroutine MPADD does not check to see if numerical overflow occurs as the result of the addition operation. In order to check for overflow, we can first see if the most significant bit of the first multiword term is the same as the most significant bit of the second term. If these bits are not the same, then we are adding together a positive number and a negative number, and there is no possibility that overflow can occur. If the most significant bits of the two terms are identical, we should also check the most significant bit of the result. If the result has the same sign as that of the two terms, overflow has not occurred. Otherwise, overflow has occurred. If there was numerical overflow, the subroutine should return this information to the invoking program. One way to do this is to set the overflow flag just prior to exiting from the subroutine.

```
                    ;THIS SUBROUTINE ADDS TWO MULTI-WORD SIGNED
                    ;   INTEGERS,  THE NUMBER OF WORDS IN AN INTEGER,
                    ;   N, IS CARRIED INTO THE SUBROUTINE IN R1.
                    ;A POINTER TO THE MOST SIGNIFICANT WORD OF THE
                    ;   FIRST NUMBER IS CARRIED INTO THE ROUTINE IN R2.
                    ;A POINTER TO THE SECOND NUMBER AND TO THE RESULTING
                    ;   SUM IS IN R3.
        MPADD:      ADD R1,R2          ;SET POINTERS PAST END OF NUMBERS
                    ADD R1,R2
                    ADD R1,R3
                    ADD R1,R3
                    CLR CAROLD         ;CLEAR PREVIOUS CARRY
        BACK:       CLR CARNEW         ;CLEAR NEXT CARRY
                    ADD -(R2),-(R3)
                    BCC UP
                    MOV #1,CARNEW
        UP:         ADD CAROLD,(R3)
                    BCC UP1
                    MOV #1,CARNEW
        UP1:        MOV CARNEW,CAROLD
                    SOB R1,BACK
                    RTS PC
        CARNEW:     .BLKW   1
        CAROLD:     .BLKW   1
        ;$$$$$$$$$$$$$$    START TEST PROGRAM   $$$$$$$$$$$$$$$$$
        ;$$$    ADD TWO 80-BIT INTEGERS    $$$$$$$
        START:      MOV #5,R1
                    MOV #FIRST,R2
                    MOV #SECOND,R3
                    JSR PC ,MPADD
                    HALT
        FIRST:      .WORD   012345,123454,165473,0,177760
        SECOND:     .WORD   043652,133333,144444,177777,177760
                    .END START
```

Figure 7.1   Subroutine for addition of multiword integers

In order to perform multiword subtraction operations, it is convenient first to compute the twos-complement of the multiword subtrahend. Use of the ADC operation can facilitate this computation. Then a subroutine, such as MPADD in Fig. 7.1, can be used to complete the subtraction operation.

Example 7.2

Develop and test a subroutine that replaces a multiword integer with its twos-complement.

Solution   A solution and a corresponding test program are given in Fig. 7.2. The result is computed by taking the ones-complement of the argument and then adding 1 to this number. Recall that binary numbers containing K bits can be used to represent integers in the range

$$-2^{K-1} < = \text{integer} < = 2^{K-1} - 1$$

Suppose we take the twos-complement of the negative number having the largest magnitude. Then

$$-(-2^{K-1}) = 2^{K-1}$$

However, the resulting positive number cannot be represented by a K-bit signed binary number. Thus, whenever we attempt to take the twos-complement of the smallest signed number, overflow occurs. The subroutine TWCMP prints an appropriate message if overflows occurs.

```
              .MCALL  .EXIT,.PRINT
              ;THIS SUBROUTINE REPLACES A MULTI-WORD INTEGER
              ;  WITH ITS TWOS COMPLEMENT.  THE NUMBER OF
              ;  WORDS IN THE INTEGER, N, IS CARRIED
              ;  INTO THE ROUTINE IN R1.  THE ADDRESS OF THE MOST
              ;  SIGNIFICANT WORD OF THE INTEGER IS IN R2.
              ;$$$$$$$$$$$$$$$$$$$$$$$$$$$$$$$$$$$$$$$$$$$$$$$$$$
TWCMP:        MOV  R1,R3
              ADD  R1,R2          ;MOVE POINTER PAST LAST WORD
              ADD  R1,R2
BACK:         COM  -(R2)          ;GET ONES COMPLEMENT
              SOB  R3,BACK
              ADD  R1,R2
              ADD  R1,R2
              MOV  R1,R3
              SEC
AGAIN:        ADC  -(R2)          ;GET TWOS COMPLEMENT
              SOB  R3,AGAIN
              ;CHECK FOR OVERFLOW !!!
              CMP  #100000,(R2)+
              BNE  DONE
              DEC  R1
              BEQ  AHEAD          ;OVERFLOW FOR SINGLE PRECISION CASE
MORE:         TST  (R2)+
              BNE  DONE
              SOB  R1,MORE
AHEAD:        .PRINT #MES
DONE:         RTS  PC
MES:          .ASCII /         OVERFLOW !!!/<15><12><200>
              .EVEN
;$$$$$$$$$      START TEST PROGRAM$$$$$$$$$$$$$$$$$$$$
START:        MOV  #4,R1
              MOV  #FIRST,R2
              JSR  PC,TWCMP
              MOV  #1,R1
              MOV  #SECOND,R2
              JSR  PC,TWCMP
              MOV  #5,R1
              MOV  #THIRD,R2
              JSR  PC,TWCMP
              MOV  #1,R1
              MOV  #LAST,R2
              JSR  PC,TWCMP
              .EXIT
FIRST:        .WORD   123456,0,52,0
SECOND:       .WORD   012345
THIRD:        .WORD   100000,0,0,0,0
LAST:         .WORD   100000
              .END START
```

Figure 7.2 Subroutine that returns the twos-complement of a multiword integer

Multiprecision addition and subtraction operations have been developed using operations on 16-bit words. Similarly, multiprecision multiplication and division routines may be developed using corresponding routines that operate on words that have a smaller number of bits.

Review

1. Refer to the subroutine in Fig. 7.1. Modify this routine so that when the RTS PC command is executed, the overflow flag will be up if and only if overflow has occurred in the multiword operation.

2. Refer to the test program in Figure 7.1 and to the following symbol table.

```
SYMBOL TABLE
BACK      000014R  CAROLD 000062R  MPADD   000000R
CARNEW 000060R  FIRST   000106R  SECOND 000100R

START   000064R  UP1       000046R
UP        000032R
```

After execution of this program is completed, what octal number will be in each of the following memory locations?
(a) 1120; **(b)** 1122; **(c)** 1124; **(d)** 1126; **(e)** 1130

3. Refer to the test program in Fig. 7.2 and to the following symbol table.

```
SYMBOL TABLE
AGAIN    000022R  DONE   000054R  MES   000056R
AHEAD    000046R  FIRST  000166R  MORE  000040R
BACK     000006R  LAST    000212R
SECOND 000176R  THIRD 000200R
START    000104R  TWCMP 000000R
```

(a) When this test program is being executed, how many times will the overflow message be printed?
   After execution of this program has been completed, what number will be in each of the following memory locations?
(b) 1166; **(c)** 1170; **(d)** 1176; **(e)**1202; **(f)** 1212

4. Suppose the subroutines in Figs. 7.1 and 7.2 are separately assembled. These routines are to be used with other software that will be separately assembled. In order to do this, a pseudo–instruction must be added to the source code of each of these routines. Identify the statement that must be added to each of these routines.

7.2 *SOFTWARE MULTIPLICATION AND DIVISION*

If machine-language instructions are not available for integer multiplication and division, then software must be developed to implement these operations. Multiplication may be done by using one of the factors as a counter, adding the value of the other factor to a double-length register, decrementing the counter, and repeating this procedure until the counter is 0. Division may be performed in a similar manner using the subtraction operation instead of the addition operation. However, this brute-force type of technique can be extremely time consuming. Unsigned 16-bit numbers may have values between 0 and 65,535. If the factors are randomly selected, a typical 16-bit multiplication operation would require more than 32,000 addition operations if performed in this manner.

When a software multiplication routine is required, it is frequently implemented by using a *shift and add* technique. Consider the illustration of a typical longhand multiplication operation on two unsigned binary numbers shown in Fig. 7.3. We make the following observations about this example.

1. Both the multiplicand and the multiplier are 4-bit numbers. However, the product cannot be expressed as a 4-bit number. In general, if we use N-bit registers for the multiplier and the multiplicand, two N-bit registers are required to store the product.

2. In binary multiplication we can only multiply by the 1 character or by the 0 character.

3. Multiplication starts at the rightmost bit of the multiplier. Then the operation proceeds from right to left.

4. Refer to lines 3 to 7 in Fig. 7.3. Each of these intermediate results is shifted one bit position to the left of the preceding result. An alternate way of expressing this is to say that each intermediate result is shifted one bit position to the right of the successor result.

5. To obtain the product, we must add the four intermediate results identified by lines 3 to 6. Generally, a computer ALU can add together just two numbers at a time. Therefore, we first place a 0 in a register and then add each of the four intermediate results to this register.

6. After line 3 is determined, the least significant bit of the product is known, and no further operations are required on this bit. Similarly, after each successive intermediate result is obtained and added to the running sum, the value of the next most significant bit of the product is known.

We can summarize these observations and formulate a plan for implementing multiplication of two unsigned N-bit numbers. Assume that we are using a machine that performs operations on numbers that are stored in N-bit registers. Suppose two N-bit registers are cascaded and are used to store the resulting product. A plan for the corresponding multiplication is given in Fig. 7.4. A corresponding flowchart is given in Fig. 7.5.

```
1. MULTIPLICAND:        0100
2. MULTIPLIER:          1011
3.                      0100
4.                      0100
5.                      0000
6.                      0100
7. PRODUCT:          00101100
```

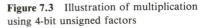

Figure 7.3 Illustration of multiplication using 4-bit unsigned factors

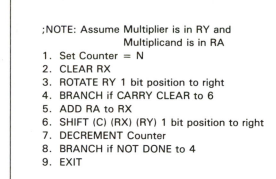

;NOTE: Assume Multiplier is in RY and
                   Multiplicand is in RA
1. Set Counter = N
2. CLEAR RX
3. ROTATE RY 1 bit position to right
4. BRANCH if CARRY CLEAR to 6
5. ADD RA to RX
6. SHIFT (C) (RX) (RY) 1 bit position to right
7. DECREMENT Counter
8. BRANCH if NOT DONE to 4
9. EXIT

Figure 7.4 Plan for multiplication of two unsigned *N*-bit integers

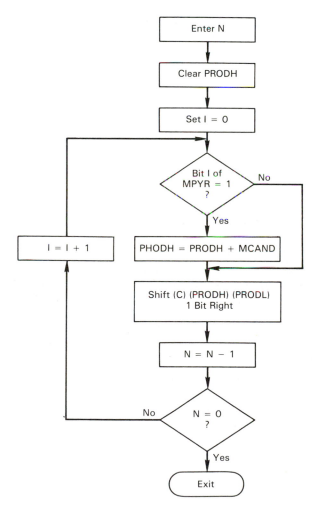

Figure 7.5 Flowchart for multiplication of two *N*-bit unsigned numbers

It is easy to implement multiplication of 16-bit unsigned numbers on the PDP-11. If the program plan in Fig. 7.4 is used, then step 6 requires a shift operation to be performed on a 32-bit register. Although there are no 32-bit registers available, we can easily implement this operation using a pair of 16-bit registers.

Example 7.3

Develop a program segment that shifts the 32-bit word in the register pair consisting of R2 and R3 one bit to the right. Let the routine shift the initial value of the carry bit into the most significant bit of R2.

Solution   The following two operations will produce the desired results:

```
ROR R2
ROR R3
```

The first rotation command places the least significant bit of R2 in the carry bit, and the second ROR command moves this bit into the most significant bit position of R3.

Once a subroutine has been developed that will perform multiplication on pairs of *unsigned* numbers, it is relatively easy to use this subroutine to develop a routine that operates on *signed* integers. This can be done in the following manner.

1. Determine if either or both of the factors are negative integers. If neither or both are negative, clear a software flag. If just one is negative, set this software flag.
2. Replace each negative factor with its twos-complement.
3. Use the *unsigned* multiplication routine to obtain a product.
4. If the *software flag is set,* replace this *product* with its twos-complement.

Development of software to perform division on unsigned numbers is straightforward. However, the division operation is slightly more involved than the multiplication operation. Because division is the *inverse* operation of multiplication, both the *divisor* and the *quotient* should be N-bit numbers, and the *dividend* should be a $2N$-bit number. That is, if the divisor and the quotient each occupy a single register, then a pair of registers is needed for the dividend. Execution of the division operation can produce a *remainder.* The remainder is always smaller than the divisor, so it can be stored in a single N-bit register.

When division is being performed on a computer, there is a possibility that overflow will occur. Division by 0 always results in an overflow. Other instances of overflow may also occur. Overflow occurs whenever it is impossible to represent the corresponding quotient as the correct N-bit number.

Example 7.4

Suppose we wish to perform unsigned division on 4-bit numbers. That is, the divisor and the quotient are represented as 4-bit numbers, and the dividend is an 8-bit number.

Which of the following operations will result in overflow?

(a) 1101 $\sqrt{11011010}$
(b) 0000 $\sqrt{00000000}$
(c) 0001 $\sqrt{00000000}$
(d) 0010 $\sqrt{11010000}$
(e) 0010 $\sqrt{00100000}$

Solution   All of the examples, except for case (c), will result in overflow. Each of the quotients in cases (a), (b), (d), and (e) requires at least 5 bits.

From the above example, we may infer the following rule: When an unsigned $2N$-bit number is divided by an unsigned N-bit number, numerical overflow occurs unless the N-bit divisor is *greater than* the first N bits of the dividend. When we develop a routine for performing division, we should first check to see if overflow will occur. If overflow does not occur, we should proceed in virtually the same manner as if we were performing the calculation longhand.

Example 7.5

Develop and test a subroutine that performs division between an unsigned 16-bit divisor and an unsigned 32-bit dividend.

Solution   A subroutine and a corresponding test program are given in Fig. 7.6. In order to use this test program, a divisor is placed in memory location 2000, and a dividend is placed in locations 2002 and 2004. The test program places the quotient and remainder in the next two memory locations.

Consider the subroutine for unsigned 16-bit division shown in Fig. 7.6. Observe that in the first three lines of the subroutine, starting at the statement labeled DIVD, a check is made to determine if overflow will occur. If overflow occurs, a message is printed, and control exits from the subroutine. In this case, neither the value of the divisor nor the value of the dividend is changed. If overflow does not occur, a counter is set, and the 32-bit dividend is shifted one bit position to the left. If the 16-bit divisor is greater than the 17-bit word consisting of the carry bit followed by the new contents of R2, then the high-order bit of the quotient is 0. If not, the high-order bit of the quotient is 1. If the high-order bit is 1, then 1 times the divisor must be subtracted from the 17-bit word consisting of the carry bit followed by the contents of R2. The result of this subtraction operation can never have more than 16 significant bits. The counter is then decremented. This entire procedure is repeated 15 more times.

Refer to the statement labeled AHEAD. During each cycle of the division operation the 32-bit logic shift operation performed on the dividend places a 0 in the rightmost bit of R3. Then, if the divisor "fits" into the 17-bit segment of the dividend, a 1 is placed in this bit position. By the time execution of the subroutine is completed, the dividend has been destroyed, the quotient has been properly shifted into R3, and the remainder is in R2.

```
                          .MCALL .EXIT,.PRINT
                  SIZE = 16.
                  CR = 15
                  LF = 12
                  TERM = 200
                  ;UNSIGNED DIVISION SUBROUTINE
                  ;POINTER TO DIVISOR IS CARRIED INTO ROUTINE IN R1
                  ;DIVIDEND IS IN R2 AND R3
                  ;QUOTIENT IS RETURNED IN R3
                  ;REMAINDER IS RETURNED IN R2
                  ;IF OVERFLOW OCCURS, DIVIDEND IS NOT CHANGED
         MES:     .ASCII/DIVISION OVERFLOW!!!/<CR><LF><TERM>
                  .EVEN
         DIVD:    CMP (R1),R2        ;CHECK FOR OVERFLOW
                  BHI UP             ;NO OVERFLOW
                  .PRINT #MES        ;OVERFLOW
                  RTS PC
         UP:      MOV #SIZE,R4
         BACK:    ASL R3   ;SHIFT LEFT
                  ROL R2
                  BCS AHEAD
                  CMP (R1),R2
                  BLOS AHEAD
         BACK1:   DEC R4   ;DONE?
                  BNE BACK           ;NO
                  RTS PC   ;YES
         AHEAD:   BIS #1,R3          ;DIVISOR FITS INTO PARTIAL DIVIDEND
                  SUB (R1),R2
                  BR BACK1
         ;$$$$$$$$$$$$$$$$$$ START TEST PROGRAM $$$$$$$$$$$$$$$$$$$$$$$$$$$$
         START:   MOV #DVSOR,R1
                  MOV HIGH,R2
                  MOV LOW,R3
                  JSR PC,DIVD
                  MOV R3,ANSWER
                  MOV R2,REMAINDER
                  .EXIT
         DVSOR = 2000
         HIGH = 2002
         LOW = 2004
         ANSWER = 2006
         REMAINDER = 2010
                  .END START
```

Figure 7.6   Subroutine and test program for 16-bit unsigned division

This subroutine may be used as a tool or a working routine if you wish to perform division on 16-bit *signed* numbers. Signed division can be performed in the following manner.

1. Determine if either the divisor or the dividend is a negative number. If neither is negative or if both are negative, clear a software flag. If just one is negative, set the software flag.
2. Replace each negative quantity with its twos-complement.
3. Use the *unsigned* division subroutine to obtain a quotient and a remainder.
4. If the software flag is set, replace the quotient and remainder found in step 3 with their twos-complements.

Review

1. Develop and test a subroutine that performs multiplication of two 16-bit unsigned numbers.

2. Refer to the subroutine and test program in Fig. 7.6. For each of the following cases, suppose that prior to execution of the test program the specified octal numbers are contained in memory locations 2000, 2002, and 2004. After the test program has been executed, identify the octal numbers that will be in memory locations 2006 and 2010.
   (a) 2,0,7
   (b) 41,41,03456
   (c) 42, 41, 03456
   (d) 0,0,0
   (e) 1,0,0

3. Refer to the five sets of numbers given in Review question 2. Suppose the test program is run for each of these sets of data. How many times will the overflow message be printed?

7.3 *USING AN EXTENDED INSTRUCTION SET*

Although early versions of the PDP-11 did not necessarily possess the machine-language instructions for performing integer multiplication, integer division, and floating-point operations, most modern implementations do have these capabilities. The commands that perform integer multiplication, integer division, and certain shifting operations are said to be part of an *extended instruction set.* Specifically, the extended instruction set includes the instructions listed below. The symbol REVEN refers to any even-numbered CPU register.

Instruction	Function
1. MUL SRC,REVEN	Multiply the 16-bit signed source operand by the signed contents of the specified register. *Note:* Any mode of addressing may be used for the source operand. *Note:* The product is returned in REVEN and REVEN + 1.
2. DIV SRC,REVEN	Divide the signed source operand into the 32-bit register consisting of REVEN and REVEN + 1. The signed quotient is returned in REVEN. The remainder, having the same sign as the dividend, is returned in REVEN + 1.
3. ASH SRC,R	Arithmetic shift the number in R N bits to the left or right, where $-16 <= N <= 16$ is specified by the source operand. *Note:* positive number $=>$ left shift; negative number $=>$ right shift.
4. ASHC SRC,REVEN	Arithmetic shift the 32-bit number in REVEN and REVEN + 1 N bits, where $-32 <= N <= 31$. *Note:* Positive number $=>$ left shift; negative number $=>$ right shift.

This summary does not include the full capabilities of each of these commands. The commands are defined in detail in Appendix B.

In addition to being useful for number crunching, these instructions also facilitate other computer operations, as illustrated in Examples 7.6 and 7.7.

Example 7.6

Develop a subroutine that converts a 16-bit unsigned number to the octal representation of the number expressed by the corresponding string of ASCII characters.

Solution A subroutine that perfoms this function will be useful if we wish to display the contents of any 16-bit CPU register or any memory location. The numerical operand will be converted to the corresponding character string. Then it is relatively easy to print this character string. A solution is given in Fig. 7.7. The subroutine converts the number in R1 to a string of ASCII characters and then stores the characters in memory locations BUFFER to BUFFER + 5. The test program prints in a suitable format the character string that identifies the number in R1. The first character in the octal representation of the 16-bit number is either a 0 or a 1. The first few steps in the subroutine are used to determine the corresponding ASCII character. Then the ASHC command is used in the subroutine loop to shift the contents of R1 3 bits to the left in order to isolate the various numbers corresponding to the octal characters.

Example 7.7

Develop a subroutine that converts a 16-bit unsigned number to a corresponding string of base-10 ASCII characters.

Solution A solution is given in Fig. 7.8. The *division* command is used to produce the base-10 digits. First, observe that no more than five base-10 numbers are ever re-

```
        .MCALL  .EXIT,.PRINT
        ;THIS SUBROUTINE CONVERTS THE UNSIGNED OCTAL
        ;   NUMBER IN R1 TO A CORRESPONDING STRING
        ;    OF ASCII CHARACTER CODES.
MES:    .ASCII /            /
BUFFER: .BLKB   6
TERM:   .BYTE   15,12,200          ;CR,LF AND TERM
        .EVEN
FILBUF: MOV #5,R4
        MOV #BUFFER,R5
        CLR R0
        ASHC  #1, R0       ;GET FIRST OCTAL CHARACTER
        ADD #60,R0         ;CONVERT TO ASCII
        MOVB R0,(R5)+
BACK:   ASHC #3,R0
        BIC #177770,R0     ;GET OCTAL CHARACTER
        ADD #60,R0         ;CONVERT TO ASCII
        MOVB R0,(R5)+      ;PUT IN BUFFER
        SOB R4,BACK
        RTS PC
; $$$$$$    START TEST PROGRAM     $$$$$$$$$$$$$$
START:  MOV #123456,R1
        CALL FILBUF        ;CALL => JSR PC
        .PRINT #MES
        .EXIT
        .END START
```

Figure 7.7 Subroutine that converts a 16-bit unsigned number to an octal character string

```
                    ;THIS SUBROUTINE CONVERTS THE UNSIGNED NUMBER IN R1
                    ;  TO A CORRESPONDING STRING OF BASE-10 ASCII CHARACTERS.
                    .MCALL .EXIT,.PRINT
MES:        .ASCII      /       /
BUF10:      .BLKB   4
TERM:       .BYTE   15,12,200
            .EVEN
FBUF10:     MOV #4,R4
            MOV #TERM,R5
BACK:       CLR R0
            DIV #16.,R0
            ADD #60,R1          ;CONVERT TO ASCII
            CMP R1,#'9          ;NUMERIC CHARACTER:
            BLE UP  ;YES
            ADD #7,R1           ;NO.  CONVERT TO ALPHABETICAL CHARACTER
UP:         MOVB R1,-(R5)       ;PUT IN BUFFER
            MOV R0,R1           ;PREPARE FOR NEXT DIVISION
            SOB R4,BACK
            RTS PC
;  $$$$$$       START TEST PROGRAM       $$$$$$$$$$$$$$$$
START:      MOV #123456,R1
            CALL FBUF10
            .PRINT #MES
            .EXIT
            .END START
```

Figure 7.8   Subroutine that converts a 16-bit unsigned number to a base-16 character string

quired to represent an unsigned 16-bit binary number. In order to obtain the corresponding base-10 digits, the 16-bit number is divided by the base-10 number 10. The remainder corresponds to the least significant digit of the base-10 representation of the number. Then the quotient just obtained is divided by 10 to obtain the next least significant digit. The process continues until five digits are obtained. The test program prints the character string corresponding to the number.

The commands MUL and DIV are convenient for 16-bit multiplication and division operations on *signed* integers. The solution to Review question 1 in Section 7.2 provides a subroutine for multiplication of 16-bit *unsigned* numbers. This routine can also be used for multiplication of positive signed numbers. A subroutine that performs operations on unsigned numbers is useful if we wish to perform the corresponding operation on signed numbers.

Refer to Fig. 7.9. This figure illustrates implementation of the multiplication operation on two-word operands. Suppose either a command or a subroutine is available that performs the multiplication operation on single-word unsigned numbers. Then this subroutine can be invoked four times to obtain the four 32-bit intermediate products corresponding to BD, BC, AD, and AC, as shown in Fig. 7.9. In order to obtain the final 64-bit product, the intermediate products may be shifted and added, as illustrated.

If multiple precision multiplication operations are to be performed on *signed* integers, we first check the sign of each factor. Then the negative factors can be converted to corresponding positive numbers. A subroutine that multiplies unsigned multiple precision numbers can then be invoked. When the output of this subroutine

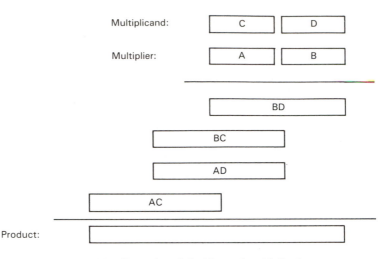

Figure 7.9 Illustration of double-word multiplication

is obtained, it should be negated if and only if exactly one of the factors was negative.

Review

1. Refer to Example 7.6 and to the subroutine developed in Fig. 7.7. Modify this subroutine so that it converts the unsigned 16-bit argument to a corresponding string of four hexadecimal characters.

2. Refer to Example 7.7 and to the subroutine developed in Fig. 7.8. Modify this subroutine so that it converts the unsigned 16-bit argument to a corresponding string of four hexadecimal characters.

3. What character string will be printed by
   (a) the test program in Fig. 7.7?
   (b) the test program in Fig. 7.8?

7.4 THE PDP-11 FLOATING POINT

In Section 3.6, the ANSI standard floating point was discussed. This is not the only popular representation of a real number or floating point. The method of representing floating points that is commonly used on PDP-11 computers is not only popular but is quite similar to recently defined floating-point standards.

Recall that the most significant bit is used to represent the sign of the number in an ANSI floating point. The next 8 bits are used to specify a biased value of the characteristic, and the final 23 bits are used to represent a normalized *significand* or *mantissa*. The characteristic of an ANSI floating point is represented in *excess-64* code, and the value of the base is 16. In representing the PDP-11 32-bit floating point, the most significant bit is also used to specify the sign of the number. The next 8 bits are used to represent the biased characteristic, and 24 bits are used to specify the value of the mantissa.

It appears we have made an error in counting the bits constituting a PDP-11 floating point. However, this is not the case. The normalized significand of this floating point always has a value

$$0.5 < = \text{significand} < 1.0$$

The implied binary point is always just to the left of the most significant bit of the significand. Because the normalization criterion is always used, it is not necessary to store the most significant bit of the significand, as it is *always* a 1. Consequently, the known bit is not included as part of the 24-bit mantissa, but must be reinstated when actual computations are performed. Because this bit does not appear as part of the floating-point representation, it is often referred to as a *hidden bit*.

The characteristic used with the PDP-11 floating point is represented in *excess-128* code, and the *base* used is *2*. Thus, the range of the magnitude of this particular floating point is

$$0.5 \times 2^{-128} \leq \text{FP} \leq 2^{127}$$

Because there is always a *hidden bit* in the PDP-11 representation of a floating point, the number 0 cannot be represented exactly. Generally, a number with a very small magnitude is interpreted to be 0. This is illustrated in Section 7.5.

Example 7.8

Represent each of the following decimal numbers as PDP-11 floating points. Write your answers as two 16-bit words expressed in octal.
(a) 93.5
(b) -157.03125

Solution   (a) $93.5_{10} => 1011101.1 = .10111011 \times 2^7$
The sign bit is 0, the biased exponent is $128 + 7 = 135$, and the 24-bit mantissa with the most significant bit suppressed is 011101100000000000000000. Expressed as two 16-bit words
$93.5_{10} => 0100001110111011 \quad 0000000000000000$
$=> 041673_8 \quad 000000_8$
(b) 142035   004000

Example 7.9

The following octal numbers are used to represent floating points. Identify the value of each floating point.
(a) 042017   010000
(b) 142400   114000

Solution   (a) The 32-bit binary representation of the floating point is
0 10001000 00011110001000000000000. The sign bit indicates that the number is positive, and the biased exponent is 136. Thus, the true ex-

ponent is 8. Reinstating the hidden bit, it is seen that the value of the floating point is

$$FP = 0.1000111110001 \times 2^8 = 10001111.0001 = 143.0625_{10}$$

(b) -514.375

It is easy to define an extended-precision floating point. Frequently, an extended-precision floating point is defined by addending one or more words to the mantissa of a single-precision floating point. The PDP-11 double-precision floating point is a 64-bit word in which the mantissa has 56 bits. As in the single-precision floating-point representation, one of the bits, the most significant bit, is always a 1 and therefore is not expressed as part of the representation of the floating point.

Conversion of numbers to their floating-point representations can be tedious. Fortunately, use of the MACRO-11 assembler facilitates this task. The following pseudo–operations are available for conversion of numbers to their floating-point representations.

```
.FLT2 NUMBER
.FLT4 NUMBER
```

The first command causes the specified number to be converted to a two-word or 32-bit floating point and placed in the memory address specified by the location of this instruction. The second command causes the specified number to be converted to a double-precision or 64-bit floating point. Typical examples of the use of these pseudo–instructions are

```
FIRST:   .FLT4 -3.14159
SECOND:  .FLT2 1.9E-12
```

Example 7.10 further illustrates use of this type of pseudo–instruction.

Example 7.10

Develop a subroutine that accepts one of the base-10 character values 0 to 9 and returns the corresponding floating-point value.

Solution A solution is given in Fig. 7.10. Floating-point numbers between 0.0 and 9.0 are stored in consecutive 32-bit memory locations starting at the location labeled FTABLE. When an argument, 0 to 9, is carried into the routine in R1, it is multiplied by 4. Then indexed addressing is used to retrieve the appropriate floating-point value from the table. The address of the appropriate table entry is FTABLE + the adjusted value in R1. The subroutine FPGET along with the corresponding conversion table will be useful for other numerical conversions.

Review

1. Convert each of the following base-10 numbers to PDP-11 floating points. Express each result as a pair of 16-bit numbers expressed in octal.
   (a) -229.0; **(b)** 876.125; **(c)** 3.14159

```
                ,GLOBL FPGET
FTABLE:              ,FLT2  0,0
                     ,FLT2  1,0
                     ,FLT2  2,0
                     ,FLT2  3,0
                     ,FLT2  4,0
                     ,FLT2  5,0
                     ,FLT2  6,0
                     ,FLT2  7,0
                     ,FLT2  8,0
                     ,FLT2  9,0
;    THIS SUBROUTINE CONVERTS A BASE-10 DIGIT VALUE TO A CORRESPONDING
;        FLOATING POINT.  THE VALUE OF THE DIGIT IS CARRIED INTO
;        THE ROUTINE IN R1.  THE FLOATING POINT IS RETURNED TO
;        THE ADDRESS IDENTIFIED BY THE CONTENTS OF R2.
FPGET:   ASL R1   ;MULTIPLY BY 4 FOR TABLE LOOKUP
         ASL R1
         MOV FTABLE(R1),(R2)+    ;TABLE LOOKUP
         MOV FTABLE+2(R1),(R2)
         RTS PC
         ,END



; $$$   TEST PROGRAM FOR FPGET SUBROUTINE   $$$$$
         ,GLOBL FPGET
         ,MCALL ,EXIT
START:   MOV #5,R1
         MOV #2000,R2
         CALL FPGET
         ,EXIT
         ,END START
```

Figure 7.10   Subroutine that converts an integer digit to the corresponding floating-point value

2. What decimal number is represented by each of the following 32-bit PDP-11 floating points? (*Note:* Each word is expressed in octal.)
   (a) 041466   000000
   (b) 143346   012400

3. Refer to the test program in Fig. 7.10. After this program has been run, what octal number will be in each of the following memory locations?
   (a) 2000; **(b)** 2002

7.5 USING THE FLOATING-POINT INSTRUCTION SET

It is not necessary to have floating-point hardware available on a computer. Floating-point operations may be implemented through use of appropriate software. This was illustrated in Section 3.6. However, if a significant number of floating-point operations are required, use of software results in a relatively slow processing time. Many modern computers have machine capabilities for performing at least some operations on floating points.

Even modest implementations of the PDP-11 frequently contain a *floating-point instruction set,* sometimes referred to as an *FIS.* The following instructions are included in the floating-point instruction set.

Instruction	Function
FADD R	A + B = > B
FSUB R	B − A = > B
FMUL R	A * B = > B
FDIV R	B ÷ A = > B

Each floating-point command has a single operand that must be a CPU register. The two floating-point numerical operands must be stored in consecutive 32-bit memory locations. A pointer to the first floating-point operand must be placed in the operand register prior to execution of a floating-point command. After the command is executed, the value of the first operand is unchanged. The calculated value of the result replaces the second operand, and the pointer in the register now identifies the memory location at which the result is stored.

As an example, suppose the following sequence of commands is given:

```
MOV    #2000,R1
FADD R1
```

This command will produce the sum of two floating points. The first of these two operands is stored in memory locations 2000 and 2002, and the second operand is stored in 2004 and 2006. After execution of the command is completed, the sum will be stored in 2004 and 2006, and the number 2004 will be in R1.

Example 7.11

Develop a subroutine that determines the mean squared value of two real arguments. That is, the subroutine computes the average value of the squares of two numbers.

Solution A solution and a corresponding test program are given in Fig. 7.11. The two user-defined macros, MOVFP and MOVMFP, are convenient for moving 32-bit words. Observe that it is necessary to position the floating-point operands properly before the floating-point operations can be performed.

Example 7.12

Develop a subroutine that accepts two floating-point arguments A and B, and computes and returns the quantity

$$(A^2 + 2AB + B^2)/A$$

If the value of A is approximately 0, the computations are bypassed, and an appropriate message is printed.

Solution A solution and a test program are given in Fig. 7.12. The real number A may be considered approximately 0.0 if the true characteristic has a value of −128. In the solution shown, a floating point is considered to have a value of 0.0, provided that the 15 least significant bits of its most significant word are all zeros. The true value of such a number is approximately 0.5×2^{-128}.

```
                    ;THIS  SUBROUTINE COMPUTES THE MEAN SQUARED
                    ;  VALUE OF TWO FLOATING POINTS.
                    ;  A POINTER TO THE TWO-ELEMENT INPUT ARRAY IS
                    ;  CARRIED INTO THE SUBROUTINE IN R1.
                    ;  THE SUBROUTINE RETURNS A POINTER TO THE ANSWER IN R1.
                    .MCALL .EXIT
                    .MACRO  MOVFP REG,Y
                    MOV (REG)+,Y
                    MOV (REG)+,Y+2
                    .ENDM
                    .MACRO MOVMFP   MEM1,MEM2
                    MOV MEM1,MEM2
                    MOV MEM1+2,MEM2+2
                    .ENDM
X:                  .BLKW  4
Y:                  .BLKW  4
TWO:                .FLT2 2.0
;$$$$$     START SUBROUTINE   $$$$$$$$$$$$$$$
MSQR:               MOVFP R1,X
                    MOVMFP X,X+4
                    MOVFP R1,Y
                    MOVMFP Y,Y+4      ;ARGUMENTS HAVE BEEN POSITIONED
                    MOV #X,R1         ;GET X*X
                    FMUL R1
                    MOV #Y,R1         ;GET Y*Y
                    FMUL R1
                    MOVFP R1,X
                    MOV #X,R1         ;GET SUM OF SQUARES
                    FADD R1
                    MOVMFP TWO,X
                    MOV #X,R1         ;GET MEAN SQUARED VALUE
                    FDIV R1
                    RTS PC
;    $$$$$          START TEST PROGRAM        $$$$$$$$
START:  MOV #ARRAY,R1
        CALL MSQR
        MOVFP R1,2000
        .EXIT
ARRAY:  .FLT2  -3.0
        .FLT2 5.0
        .END START
```

Figure 7.11 A subroutine that computes the mean squared value of two real numbers

Example 7.13

Develop and test a subroutine that converts a 16-bit unsigned binary number to the corresponding floating point.

Solution A subroutine and a test program are given in Fig. 7.13. There are several different ways in which the corresponding subroutine can be developed. In this particular routine, the value of a running sum is initially set to 0.0. Within the computation loop, the running sum is multiplied by 4.0. Then the two most significant bits of the operand are inspected. These two bits are converted to a floating point corresponding to a base-4 character and then added to the running sum. This sequence of steps is repeated seven more times.

The computation technique used in the solution of Example 7.13 can be used to convert a string of base-10 characters entered from a console to the corresponding

```
                .MACRO MOVFP REG,X
                MOV (REG)+,X
                MOV (REG)+,X+2
                .ENDM
  ;   $$$$$$$$$$$$$$$$$$$$$$$$$$$$$$$$$$$$$$$$$$$$$$$$$$$$$
                .MACRO MOVMFP P,Q
                MOV P,Q
                MOV P+2,Q+2
                .ENDM
                ;THIS SUBROUTINE RETURNS THE VALUE:
                ;    (A*A + 2*A*B + B*B)/A
                ;A MESSAGE IS PRINTED IF DIVISION BY 0 IS ATTEMPTED.
                ;A POINTER TO THE ARRAY OF TWO FLOATING-POINT
                ;   ARGUMENTS IS CARRIED INTO THE ROUTINE IN R1.
                ;A POINTER TO THE ANSWER IS RETURNED IN R1.
                .MCALL .EXIT,.PRINT
  ; $$$$$$    STORAGE SPACE   $$$$$$$$$$$$$
  A:        .BLKW 2
  B:        .BLKW 2
  ATEMP:    .BLKW 2
  ; $$$$$$   START SUBROUTINE   $$$$$$$$$$$$$$$
  SUBR:     MOVFP R1,A        ;GET ARGUMENTS
            MOVFP R1,B
            MOV A,R0          ;TEST FOR ZERO DIVISOR
            BIC #100000,R0    ;STRIP OFF SIGN BIT
            TST R0   ;IS DIVISOR APPROXIMATELY ZERO?
            BNE AHEAD         ;NO
            .PRINT #DZERO     ;YES. PRINT MESSAGE AND EXIT
            RTS PC
  AHEAD:    MOVMFP A,ATEMP
            MOV #A,R1
            FADD R1
            MOVFP R1,A
            MOV #A,R1
            FMUL R1 ;(A + B)**2
            MOVMFP ATEMP,A
            MOV #A,R1
            FDIV R1 ;GET RESULT
            RTS PC
  DZERO:    .ASCII /DIVISION BY ZERO IS NOT ALLOWED/<15><12><200>
            .EVEN
  ; $$$$$$   START TEST PROGRAM   $$$$$$$$$
  START:    MOV #ARRAY,R1
            CALL SUBR
            MOVFP R1,2000
            MOV #ARRAY+8.,R1
            CALL SUBR
            .EXIT
  ARRAY:    .FLT2 4.0
            .FLT2 2.0
            .FLT2 0.0
            .FLT2 0.0
            .END START
```

Figure 7.12   A solution to Example 7.12

floating-point representation. This can be accomplished by the following sequence
of steps:

1. Set a running sum to 0.0.
2. Get a character that is entered on the console.
3. Exit the routine if this character is a terminator.
4. Strip the nonnumeric information from the character.

```
        ;MCALL .EXIT
        ;THIS SUBROUTINE CONVERTS THE UNSIGNED
        ;  NUMBER IN R3 TO THE CORRESPONDING
        ;  FLOATING POINT.  A POINTER TO THE ANSWER
        ;  IS RETURNED IN R5.  THIS ROUTINE REQUIRES THE USE OF
        ;  THE SUBROUTINE, FPGET WHICH WAS DEFINED EARLIER.
        .GLOBL FPGET
FOUR:   .FLT2 4.0
ANS:    .BLKW 2
TEMP:   .BLKW 2
;   $$$$$START SUBROUTINE   $$$$$$$$$$$
FIXFLT: MOV #0,R1
        MOV #ANS,R2
        CALL FPGET          ;INITIALIZE RUNNING SUM
        MOV # 8.,R4          ;COUNTER
BACK:   CLR R2
        ASHC #2,R2           ;GET BASE-4 CHARACTER
        MOV #FOUR,R5
        FMUL R5             ;MULTIPLY RUNNING SUM BY 4.
        MOV R2,R1
        MOV #TEMP,R2
        CALL FPGET
        FADD R5             ;ADD BASE-4 CHARACTER
        MOV TEMP,ANS
        MOV TEMP+2,ANS+2      ;KEEP RUNNING SUM IN ANS
        SOB R4,BACK
        SUB #4,R5           ;ADJUST POINTER TO IDENTIFIER ANSWER
        RTS PC
;   $$$$$$$$$$$     START TEST PROGRAM     $$$$$$$$$$$$$$$$$$$
START:  MOV #38569.,R3
        CALL FIXFLT
        MOV (R5)+,2000
        MOV (R5)+,2002
        .EXIT
        .END START
```

Figure 7.13   Subroutine that converts a 16-bit binary number to a floating point

5. Convert this number to a floating point. (*Note:* Use a subroutine such as FPGET.)

6. Multiply the running sum by 10.0.

7. Add the value obtained in step 5 to the running sum.

8. Go to step 2.

This procedure is useful for converting whole numbers to the corresponding floating points. Suppose we wish to enter a decimal number with an expressed decimal point and convert it to the corresponding floating-point representation. The sequence of steps can easily be expanded to accomplish this task by inserting the following steps:

1a. Set POINT FLAG to 0.

3a. If character is a period, raise the POINT FLAG and go back to step 2.

7a. If POINT FLAG is up, divide the running sum by 10.0.

Further enhancements of routines that convert character strings to the corresponding floating points are easily implemented. Illustrations are given in the Review questions and exercises at the end of this chapter.

Review

1. Refer to the test program in Fig. 7.11. After this test program has been executed, what octal number will be in each of the following memory locations?
   (a) 2000; **(b)** 2002

2. Refer to the test program in Fig. 7.12.
   (a) As the program is being executed, how many times will the DIVIDE BY ZERO message be printed?
   After execution of this program has been completed, what octal number will be in each of the following memory locations?
   (b) 2000; **(c)** 2002

3. Refer to the test program in Fig. 7.13. After this test program has been executed, what octal number will be in each of the following memory locations?
   (a) 2000; **(b)** 2002

4. Refer to the following program:

```
START:  MOV #YUK,R1
        FSUB R1
        FMUL R1
        HALT
YUK:    .FLT2 3.0
BAD:    .FLT2 5.0
DIM:    .FLT2 6.0
POOR:   .FLT2 3.14159
        .END START
```

   After the program has been assembled, linked, and executed, identify the value of the floating point in each of the following memory locations:
   (a) YUK; **(b)** BAD; **(c)** DIM; **(d)** POOR
   (e) Identify the label corresponding to the number that will be in R1.

5. Design and test a subroutine that accepts a string of base-10 characters that are entered using the .TTYIN macro. The string of base-10 characters is to be terminated by striking the line feed key. The string of ASCII characters is to be converted to the corresponding floating point.

REFERENCES

ECKHOUSE, R. H., and R. L. MORRIS, *Minicomputer Systems.* Englewood Cliffs, N.J.: Prentice-Hall, 1975.

FRANK, T. S., *Introduction to the PDP-11 and Its Assembly Language.* Englewood Cliffs, N.J.: Prentice-Hall, 1983.

GILL, A., *Machine and Assembly Language Programming of the PDP-11.* Englewood Cliffs, N.J.: Prentice-Hall, 1979.

HASTINGS, CECIL JR., *Approximations for Digital Computers*. Princeton, N.J.: Princeton University Press, 1955.

JERMANN, W. H., *The Structure and Programming of Microcomputers*. Palo Alto, Calif.: Mayfield, 1982.

Microcomputer Processors. Maynard, Mass.: Digital Equipment Corporation, 1979.

EXERCISES

1. Develop and test a PDP-11 subroutine that adds together two 24-bit unsigned numbers.

2. Develop and test a PDP-11 subroutine that adds together two 24-bit signed numbers.

3. Formulate a program segment that converts an 8-bit signed integer to a 16-bit signed integer having the same value.

4. Formulate a program segment that converts a 16-bit signed integer to a 32-bit signed integer having the same value.

5. Develop and test a subroutine that performs *signed* multiplication on two 16-bit integers. Assume no EIS commands are available. Your subroutine may invoke the subroutine for unsigned multiplication that was developed as the solution to Review question 1 in Section 7.2.

6. Refer to the subroutine and test program in Fig. 7.6. Suppose prior to execution of this test program, the octal numbers specified below are stored in memory locations 2000, 2002, and 2004. For which sets of data will the overflow message be printed?
   (a) 1000,100,1000
   (b) 0,0,700
   (c) 1000,1000,100
   (d) 700,0,700
   (e) 177777,177777,177776

7. Develop and test a subroutine that performs division between a signed 16-bit divisor and a signed 32-bit dividend. Assume no EIS commands are available.

8. Refer to the following program segment:

```
MOV #77766,R2
MUL #8.,R2
```

   After execution of this program segment, what number will be in
   (a) R3? (b) R2?

9. Refer to the following program segment:

```
CLR R0
MOV #10001,R1
MUL #16.,R1
```

   After execution of this program segment, what number will be in
   (a) R0? (b) R1?

10. Refer to the following program segment:

```
MOV #177776,R2
MUL #2,R2
```

After execution of this program segment, what number will be in
(a) R2? **(b)** R3?

11. Refer to the following program segment:

```
MOV #177777,R2
MOV #17760,R3
DIV #7,R2
```

After execution of this program segment, what number will be in
(a) R2? **(b)** R3?

12. Develop and test a subroutine that converts the *signed octal* number in R1 to a corresponding string of ASCII character codes.

13. Develop and test a subroutine that converts the *signed* number in R1 to a corresponding ASCII sign character followed by a string of base-10 ASCII characters.

14. Develop and test a subroutine that finds the product of two unsigned 32-bit factors.

15. Develop and test a subroutine that finds the product of two signed 24-bit factors.

16. Represent each of the following base-10 numbers as PDP-11 floating points.
(a) 42; **(b)** 571.25; **(c)** −4097.125

17. Represent each of the following base-10 numbers as PDP-11 floating points.
(a) 0.1; **(b)** $2^{18} - 1$; **(c)** -4×10^4

18. What base-10 real number is represented by each of the following PDP-11 32-bit floating points?
(a) 041160   000000
(b) 141334   000000
(c) 042513   114000

19. Develop and test a subroutine that accepts three floating-point arguments *A, B,* and *C* and computes and returns the value of the function $B^2 - 4AC$.

20. Which of the following PDP-11 32-bit floating points, expressed in octal, has a value that is approximately 0.0?
(a) 100007   123456
(b) 040000   000000
(c) 040000   000001
(d) 140000   000000

21. Develop and test a subroutine that converts a 32-bit signed integer to the corresponding floating point.

22. Design and test a subroutine that accepts a string of base-10 ASCII characters that are entered using the .TTYIN macro. The string consists of several base-10 characters followed by a period and then followed by several more base-10 characters. For example, 157.37 or 3.14159 are typical strings that may be entered. Each string is terminated with a *line feed* character. The subroutine translates the string to the corresponding floating point.

23. Modify the subroutine developed in Exercise 22 so that the string may be preceded by either a plus or a minus sign. If there is no prefix, it is assumed that a positive number is entered.

24. Modify the subroutine developed in Exercise 22 so that the suffix EMN may be addended to the string. The letter E corresponds to the number 10, and M and N are base-10 characters. For example, the character string 4.5E15 corresponds to the number 4.5×10^{15}.

25. Modify the subroutine developed in Exercise 24 so that a sign character may be inserted in front of the digits following the symbol E.

26. Develop a program plan for converting a PDP-11 floating point to an appropriate ASCII character string.

27. Develop and test a subroutine that converts a PDP-11 32-bit floating point to a corresponding ASCII character string.

28. The following series can be used to approximate the function $\sin \frac{\pi}{2} X$, where $-1 <= X <= 1$.

$$\sin\tfrac{\pi}{2} X = C_1 X + C_3 X^3 + C_5 X^5$$

where $C_1 = 1.5706268$, $C_3 = -0.6432292$, and $C_5 = 0.0727102$. Develop and test a PDP–11 subroutine that computes $\sin\Theta$, where

$$-\tfrac{\pi}{2} \text{ radians} \leq \Theta \leq \tfrac{\pi}{2} \text{ radians}$$

8

Input/Output Operations

Computer programs that are ready to be executed are stored in the *primary,* or *main,* computer memory. The computer processor or CPU fetches and decodes instructions and produces the necessary control signals in order that sequences of commands may be properly executed. Frequently, the computer memory, along with the CPU and the required control devices, are classified as a *digital computer.* These devices may even be packaged and sold as a *computer* or as a *computer system.*

In order for a computer system to have any real value, it must be able to *communicate* with other devices. *Input/output* operations may be defined as the link between these peripheral devices and the computer. Some input/output devices are considered to be closely related to computer hardware. For example, programs may be read into primary memory from hard magnetic disks, flexible diskettes, cassettes, cards, keyboards, or punched paper tapes. The corresponding input/output devices are frequently considered to be integral parts of specific computer systems. Other media for input/output operations may not be considered as parts of the computer system. Translation or synthesis of human voices, outputs from transducers and electromechanical devices, and generation and interpretation of graphical displays are somewhat removed from the normal functioning of digital computers.

Communication between computer systems and external devices involves the transmission of *binary words. Serial communication* is the transmission of words one bit at a time. Serial devices are very commonly used. *Parallel* transmission consists of transmitting the bits of a binary word simultaneously. Clearly, parallel trans-

194

mission is faster than serial transmission of data. However, it also requires the use of *parallel communication channels*. For example, suppose we wish to communicate with a computer through a phone line. In particular, suppose we are sending and receiving 8-bit words. Serial communication requires the use of just one phone line, whereas parallel communication requires eight lines.

Communication between a computer CPU and computer primary memory during execution of instructions is relatively simple. However, communication with peripheral devices is much more involved. Generally, peripheral devices operate at significantly *different rates* than the computer CPU. For example, a CPU may fetch a new instruction once every microsecond, whereas a printer may operate a rate of 10 characters per second. Furthermore, input/output operations from peripheral devices may be sporadic. Characters may be transmitted before the CPU is ready to process the related information. There may be long intervals in which there is no input/output activity. Then there may be other intervals in which several peripheral devices are active simultaneously. This chapter and chapter 9 introduce techniques related to computer input/output operations, specifically, for I/O operations on PDP-11 computer systems.

8.1 CONTROLLING PERIPHERAL DEVICES

There are different ways in which communication between a computer CPU and peripheral devices is initiated. Some computers possess special instructions for input and output commands. For example, an IN command may be used to read a number from a register of an I/O device to an internal CPU register. When this command is given, an address must be specified to identify the location of the peripheral register, and appropriate I/O control signals must be generated. Because I/O control signals rather than *memory addressing* control signals are generated, the same addresses may be used to identify memory locations as are used to identify locations of peripheral registers.

Some computers do not have unique commands for input/output operations. Instead, the registers of peripheral devices are assigned to the same address space as that used for primary memory. Such computers are said to have *memory-mapped* input/output devices. In PDP-11 systems, the highest 4096 word addresses are reserved for input/output devices. An advantage of memory-mapped I/O is that the capability of the entire instruction set is available for use with registers assigned to peripheral devices.

The manner in which data transfers are made between primary memory and peripheral devices can be categorized under three general headings:

1. Programmed data transfers
2. Interrupt-driven data transfers
3. Block data transfers implemented through the use of DMA (direct memory access) word transfers.

This chapter is concerned primarily with *programmed data transfers*. The other two categories are discussed in Chapter 9.

A typical peripheral device contains several registers that are addressable by the CPU. These registers generally include

1. One or more *command* registers
2. One or more *data* registers
3. One or more *status* registers

A device is generally programmed and controlled by writing appropriate words into one or more *command* registers. The CPU receives information from a peripheral device by reading information from a status register and interpreting various bits of status words. Data transfers to or from peripheral devices are implemented through the use of data registers assigned to the specified peripherals.

In order to appreciate more fully the functioning of input/output operations, let us consider some typical peripheral devices.

A *hard disk* or a *floppy diskette* may be used as a mass storage device. Suppose we wish to transfer a block of data from such a device to the primary computer memory. In order to initiate this transfer, we must first place appropriate words in the peripheral device command register. These commands must identify the particular unit that is to be used and must specify the direction of the data transfer. An address corresponding to the initial memory address must be included as part of the command information. Likewise, we must specify the location of the block of memory that is resident on the disk.

Addresses of words stored on disks are sometimes identified with respect to one of several *concentric tracks* and one of several *wedge-shaped sectors*. Within the confines of each sector and track, a number of words, sometimes referred to as a *block,* will be stored. In order to identify the location of a particular word, it is necessary to identify a specific track and sector and the relative location of the particular word in this block. This information may be mapped into a *disk address space*. In any event, it is required to identify the disk location or address at which data transfers are to start.

The *mode* of a data transfer should be included as part of a command word. For example, the specified mode may relate to whether the transfer is a *programmed, interrupt-driven,* or *DMA* data transfer. Further refinements may be addended to the mode specification. Once the full specification of the desired data transfer is loaded into the appropriate command registers, a command to actually initiate the corresponding data transfer must be placed in a command register.

During *programmed* data transfers, the CPU generally monitors the information in one or more status registers. One bit of a status word is generally used to indicate whether or not a data word is in a data register ready to be transferred into memory. It may be a relatively long time until a word is ready to be transferred. A *read head* must first be moved radially until it is positioned over the specified track. Similarly, the disk must revolve until the specified sector is reached and the desired word in this particular block is located.

Once the word to be transferred is in the appropriate data register, it may be transferred to a CPU register or a memory location. However, in any operation involving the use of peripheral devices, there are many possibilities for malfunction of the equipment. Suppose we are in the process of reading a word from a flexible diskette in a particular disk drive unit. Suppose we have initiated the data transfer, but there is no disk in this particular unit. Clearly, a valid data word will never be placed in the corresponding data register.

Once an attempt has been made to read a data word, the peripheral device will become aware that something is wrong. A logic bit will be placed in one of the status register bit positions indicating that an error has occurred. At least one other bit position in a status register will probably be used to identify the nature of the error.

In any input/output transaction, a number of errors may occur. For example, consider the situation just described in which we wanted to transfer a block of data from a flexible diskette to memory. The following are some possible sources of error.

1. Either the specified memory address or the specified disk address may not be within the range of the equipment being used.

2. There may be a *parity error*. That is, after a word representation is read from the disk, the total number of binary 1s in the word representation may not correspond to the specified parity state (odd or even).

3. The read operation may not have been properly performed. This may be due to lack of a disk in the unit, improper insertion of the disk, or magnetic faults within certain areas of the disk.

4. The specified unit may not exist on the particular system.

5. A new data word may be placed in the data register before the old data word was read. This is referred to as an *overrun error*.

6. The specified block size may be too large.

For relatively sophisticated peripheral devices, a variety of error situations are possible. It is important to identify these errors by setting appropriate bits in the status registers.

Let us consider in more detail peripheral devices used in LSI-11 implementations of the PDP-11. For some relatively simple devices, use of an 8-bit command register and an 8-bit status register is sufficient. For other devices, several 16-bit registers may be required. Let us consider two relatively simple peripheral devices, the *console keyboard* and the *console printer,* or *typewriter*. Up to this point, a user may have considered these devices to be a single device. However, they clearly function as two separate devices. Each device possesses the following set of registers:

An 8-bit control register
An 8-bit status register
An 8-bit data register

The control register and the status register for a specific device may have identical addresses because the control register is always identified as a *destination operand,* and the status register is always indentified as a *source operand.* That is, we always *read* from a *status register* but *write* into a *command* or *control register.* The normal addresses for the corresponding registers are the following:

Peripheral Register	Address
Keyboard command register	177560
Keyboard status register	177560
Keyboard data register	177562
Printer command register	177564
Printer status register	177564
Printer data register	177566

The 8-bit command or control registers for the console keyboard and the console printer may be programmed in the following manner.

1. Placing all zeros in a command register causes the corresponding device to operate in a *programmed* mode.
2. Placing a 1 in bit 6 of a command register causes the device to operate in an *interrupt-driven* mode. That is, the device will actively request service from the computer when it is ready to make a data transfer.

So far, the only input/output commands we have used are the .TTYIN and the .PRINT macros. These commands produce interrupt-driven data transfers. The RT-11 operating system generally uses interrupt-driven data transfers. If we wish to utilize *programmed transfers* on our console devices, we must first program these devices accordingly.

Bit 7 of a status register is frequently used to inform the CPU if the corresponding device is ready to participate in a data transfer. It is convenient to use bit 7 of an even-numbered address because this is the *sign designator* for both a byte operand and a word operand. When a device is ready to participate in a data transfer, bit 7 of the corresponding status register becomes 1. Once the actual data transfer is made, generally this bit is automatically cleared.

Example 8.1

Develop subroutines that will *read* and *print* characters using programmed data transfers.

Solution   Corresponding READ and WRITE subroutines are given in Fig. 8.1. For these subroutines to function properly, both the keyboard and the printer must be programmed to accommodate *programmed data transfers.* The data transfers are called programmed data transfers because they are completely under control of the corresponding subroutines. That is, the subroutines monitor the status ports until a status bit indicates a transfer is ready to be made and then perform the desired data transfer

```
          .GLOBL READ,WRITE
          TKS=177560       ;ADDRESS OF KEYBOARD COMMAND AND STATUS REGISTERS
          TKB=177562       ;ADDRESS OF KEYBOARD DATA REGISTER
          TPS=TKS+4        ;ADDRESS OF PRINTER COMMAND AND STATUS REGISTERS
          TPB=TPS+2        ;ADDRESS OF PRINTER DATA REGISTER
READ:     BITB #200,@#TKS        ;IS THERE A CHARACTER IN THE KEYBOARD BUFFER?
       ;TO PUT A CHARACTER IN THE KEYBOARD BUFFER, PRESS THE DESIRED KEY!
          BPL READ         ;NO.  WAIT FOR BIT 7 TO COME UP.
          MOVB @#TKB,R0    ;YES.  READ THE CHARACTER IN THE BUFFER.
                    ;THIS WILL CLEAR BIT 7 IN THE STATUS REGISTER.
          BIC #177600,R0   ;KEEP 7 BITS CORRESPONDING TO ASCII CODE.
          RTS PC
     ;   $$$$$$    END OF CHARACTER READ ROUTINE   $$$$$$$$$$$$$$$$
WRITE:    BITB #200,@#TPS  ;IS PRINTER BUFFER READY TO RECEIVE A CHARACTER?
          BPL WRITE        ;NO.  WAIT FOR BIT 7 TO COME UP.
          MOVB R0,@#TPB          ;YES.  MOVE CHARACTER TO PRINTER BUFFER.
                    ;CHARACTER WILL THEN BE PRINTED.
          RTS PC
    ;  $$$$$$$$$      END OF WRITE ROUTINE   $$$$$$$$$$$$$$$$$$$

          .END
```

Figure 8.1   READ and WRITE subroutines for programmed data transfers

operation. Observe that only the least significant 7 bits of the word read from the keyboard buffer are retained. The MOVB operation that transfers this byte to R0 transfers an 8-bit word. Because the input device produces a code for a 7-bit ASCII character, the value of the most significant bit of this byte is not specified. It is dangerous to assume that this most significant bit is a 0.

Example 8.2

Develop a subroutine that prints the *successor* of the character that is entered on the keyboard. For example, if CNF is typed, DOG will be printed. Exit from the subroutine if and only if the character Z is typed.

Solution   A solution is given in Fig. 8.2. The READ and WRITE subroutines developed in Example 8.1 are utilized.

```
          ;THIS SUBROUTINE ECHOES THE SUCCESSOR OF
          ;   THE CHARACTER THAT IS TYPED.   ENTER A Z
          ;   TO EXIT FROM THE ROUTINE.
          ,GLOBL READ,WRITE
BADNEWS:      CALL READ          ;ENTER CHARACTER
          CMP #'Z,R0       ;DONE?
          BNE UP           ;NO
          RTS PC           ;YES
UP:       INC R0
          CALL WRITE       ;PRINT SUCCESSOR
          BR BADNEWS
   ;  $$$$$$$$$$$$$   START TEST PROGRAM   $$$$$$$$$$$$$$$$

START:    CLR @#177560     ;PROGRAM CONSOLE
          CLR 177564
          CALL BADNEWS
          HALT
          .END START
```

Figure 8.2   A solution to Example 8.2

Example 8.3

Develop a subroutine that prints a string of characters. Printing is to terminate when the octal number 200 is encountered. The printer should operate in the programmed mode of operation.

Solution   A solution and a corresponding test program are given in Fig. 8.3.

Review

1. Define or describe the following terms:
   (a) serial communication
   (b) parallel communication
   (c) status register
   (d) control register
   (d) overrun error

2. Which of the following octal addresses may identify peripheral device registers on a PDP-11 system?
   (a) 077776; (b) 177560; (c) 167776; (d) 170426

3. Develop and test a macro called PRINT that performs essentially the same function as the system macro .PRINT. The only significant difference is that the macro PRINT is to operate in the programmed mode rather than in the interrupt-driven mode.

4. Develop and test a subroutine that will accept a string of octal characters entered from the keyboard. The character string is to be terminated by striking the *carriage return* key. When control exits from the subroutine, the octal number corresponding to the last six characters entered will be in R1.

```
         .GLOBL PNTMES,WRITE
         ;THIS SUBROUTINE PRINTS A CHARACTER STRING.
         ;THE STARTING ADDRESS OF THE STRING MUST BE IN R1.
         ;THE OCTAL NUMBER 200 IS USED AS A STRING TERMINATOR.
PNTMES:  MOVB (R1)+,R0
         CMPB #200,R0      ;DONE?
         BNE UP            ;NO
         RTS PC            ;YES

UP:      CALL WRITE
         BR PNTMES
; $$$$$$$$$      START TEST PROGRAM      $$$$$$$$$$$$$$$$$$
START:   CLR 177560
         CLR 177564
         MOV #MYMES,R1
         CALL PNTMES
         HALT
MYMES:   .ASCII /      MERRY CHRISTMAS     /<12><15>
         .ASCII /              AND         /<12><15>
         .ASCII /      HAPPY NEW YEAR!!!!   /<12><15><200>
         .END START
```

Figure 8.3   Subroutine that prints a character string in the programmed mode

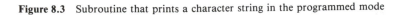

8.2 *DIGITAL INPUTS AND OUTPUTS*

Large mainframe computers are primarily used for computational data manipulations and for information storage and retrieval. Smaller computers are very commonly used to *monitor* and *control* the activities of *external systems*. By external systems, we refer to systems or components that are not considered an integral part of the computer. For example, magnetic tapes drives and hard disk units are peripheral devices that are generally considered to be components of a computer system. External activities, such as monitoring patients in an intensive care unit, controlling the sequencing of traffic lights, or controlling a manufacturing operation, may be fully linked to the operation of a computer. However, these activities and the associated hardware are not part of the computer itself.

In order to monitor and control external devices, it is generally necessary to provide *digital inputs* to the computer and *digital outputs* from the computer. That is, binary characters or *flags* must be *read* in from external input lines, and binary characters or *logic outputs* must be made available for use with external systems. Consider the illustrations in Fig. 8.4. Through use of appropriate parallel interfac-

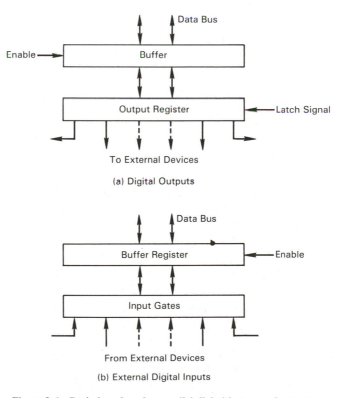

(a) Digital Outputs

(b) External Digital Inputs

Figure 8.4   Basic interface for parallel digital inputs and outputs

ing devices, an entire word may be read into a computer register. Similarly, a word may be sent out from a computer register, and the various bits may be used to control peripheral devices.

Refer to Fig. 8.4a. This particular type of interface is used to transfer logic signals to external devices. A word is moved from either a CPU register or from memory to the data bus. Then the word is moved through a buffer register to an output register and is *latched*. Although the particular word may appear on the data bus for only a fraction of a microsecond, it remains in the output register until another word is moved into this register.

The logic signals in the output register are accessible to the system user. The voltage levels of these logic signals are generally *TTL logic levels*. That is, logic ones have values in the neighborhood of 5 volts, and logic zeros have voltage levels in the neighborhood of 0 volts. Each of the logic signals in the output register may be used separately. Some examples of possible use of these signals follow.

1. Signals may be connected to external logic devices, such as *logic gates* or *flip-flops*.
2. Logic outputs may be used to control the operation of electromechanical relays. Electromechanical relays come in a wide variety of sizes and types. In many cases, a single TTL logic output does not possess sufficient power to activate a relay. In these cases, the logic output is connected to the relay coil through a *power amplifier* or a *driver*.
3. Logic outputs may be connected to other electromechanical devices, such as digitally controlled valves.
4. These outputs may be connected to the control inputs of display devices, such as oscilloscopes, plotters, or the various segments of light-emitting diode (LED) display units.

The wide range of potential applications of digital outputs is apparent. Based on decision-making algorithms contained within the computer software, individual logic outputs may be used to energize or deenergize large motors, activate emergency systems, sound alarms, or provide proper sequencing of operations required for sophisticated manufacturing operations.

Refer again to Fig. 8.4a. Observe the dotted arrows pointing upward into the buffer register. These arrows indicate that in some implementations the logic values contained in the output register can be sensed or read back by the computer CPU. If this capability is not present, then the output register may be referred to as a *write-only* register. If the output register can be read by the CPU, the same address is generally used for reading from the register as is used for writing into the register. If this capability exists, then arithmetic and logic operations may be performed on the logic outputs. For example, a command may be given to complement the logic outputs. The *read* capability is needed to implement directly such a command, as all arithmetic and logic operations are performed within the CPU. That is, either an operand or a pair of operands is first *read* into ALU registers. Then the operation is performed, and the result is routed to the destination register.

Refer to Fig. 8.4b. *Binary inputs* or *flags* may be read into a computer register through an input buffer register. This is a *unidirectional* operation. Furthermore, the external inputs are generally not latched. That is, the values that are read when the corresponding command is executed are identical to the values connected to the input lines at that particular instant.

Let us summarize the various ways that registers associated with peripheral devices may be accessed.

1. At a particular address associated with a peripheral device, there may be just a *read-only* register.

2. At a particular address associated with a peripheral device, there may be just a *write-only* register.

3. At a particular address, there may be an output register whose current contents may be accessed or read by the CPU.

4. At a particular address, there may be two distinct registers associated with a peripheral device. One of these is accessed during an input cycle and the other during an output cycle.

5. At a particular address associated with a peripheral device, some of the logic lines or bits may be input lines and others may be output lines. It is convenient to visualize this situation as if there were two distinct registers at this particular location. However, this is different from case 4, because if bit *K* is an input bit, then this same bit position cannot be used for an output line. The command and status registers associated with the console printer and the console keyboard are examples of this case. Similarly, the command and status register for the analog-to-digital converter (described in the following section) allocates certain bit positions for command or output use and other bit positions for status or input use.

The *DRV11 parallel line unit* is used to provide digital inputs and outputs for LSI-11 implementations of PDP-11 systems. If a system contains just one parallel line unit, the three addresses associated with the device registers are generally 167770, 167772, and 167774. The first of these addresses identifies a 16-bit command and status register. The second address identifies a 16-bit *output port*. The contents of this port may be read by the CPU. The highest of the three addresses identifies a 16-bit *input port*. When this parallel line unit is used for just digital inputs and outputs in a programmed mode, there is no need to access the status register. In order to operate the digital input lines and the digital output lines in the programmed mode, all zeros may be loaded into the command register.

Example 8.4

A PDP-11 is monitoring and controlling an external system through the use of a DRV11 parallel line unit. If either input line 9 or input line 2 is set, a 1 is to be sent out on line 3 of the output port. If both bit 14 and bit 0 of the input port are logic ones, the value of the logic output sent out on line 6 of the output port is to be *changed*. Develop a subroutine that satisfies these specifications.

Solution   A solution is given in Fig. 8.5. Refer to the second to the last line in the subroutine MONIT. Execution of the code corresponding to this statement requires the capability to *read* the bits stored in the output port. After these values have been read, the EXCLUSIVE OR operation is performed, and the results are sent out to the logic lines of the output port.

The DRV11 devices are not the only standard devices used for digital outputs in LSI-11 systems. Channel 3 of a standard LSI-11 digital-to-analog converter unit is frequently used when just a small number of digital output lines is required. This particular device is described in more detail in the following section. When this particular device is available, the register in which the digital output lines reside is frequently assigned to address 170446. Logic outputs are available in just bit positions 0, 1, 2, and 3 of the 16-bit register identified by this address. The values of the bits stored in the output registers may be accessed by the CPU.

Example 8.5

Refer to the diagram in Fig. 8.6. When a logic 1 is present on bit 3 of the output port, current flows through coil *A,* and the *normally open* contact *A* closes. When contact *A* closes, the red light is turned on. Similarly, when a logic 1 is present on bit 1 of the output port, the white light is turned on. Develop a program that accepts, echoes, and interprets each of the following commands that may be entered from the console key board.

```
        .MCALL .EXIT
        ;THIS ROUTINE PERFORMS THE MONITORING
        ;    AND CONTROL REQUIREMENTS THAT
        ;    ARE SPECIFIED IN EXAMPLE 8-4.
        MASK = 001004          ;BITS 9 AND 2
        CNTPORT = 167770
        INPORT = 167774
        OUTPORT = 167772
MONIT:  BIT @#INPORT,#MASK     ;CHECK BITS 9 AND 2
        BEQ NEXT        ;NEITHER IS SET
        MOV #4,@#OUTPORT        ;AT LEAST 1 IS SET.  SEND 1 OUT.
NEXT:   BIT @#INPORT,#40000    ;BIT 14 SET?
        BNE UP          ;YES
        RTS PC          ;NO
UP:     BIT @#INPORT,#1        ;BIT 1 SET?
        BNE UP1         ;YEP
        RTS PC          ;NOPE
UP1:    MOV #000100,R0  ;BITS 14 AND 1 ARE BOTH SET
        XOR R0,@#OUTPORT        ;CHANGE BIT 6 OF OUTPUT PORT
        RTS PC
; $$$$$$$$$$  START TEST PROGRAM  $$$$$$$$$$$$$$$$$$$$$$
GO:     CLR @#CNTPORT          ;PROGRAM THE I/O DEVICE
        CALL MONIT
        .EXIT
        .END GO
```

Figure 8.5   Solution to Example 8.4

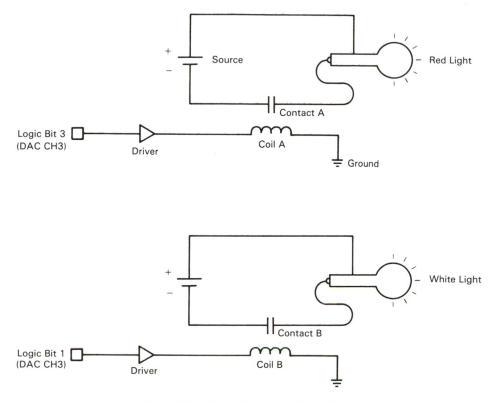

Figure 8.6   Circuit diagram for Example 8.5

Command	Function
RED	Turn red light on.
WHT	Turn white light on.
NRD	Turn red light off.
NWT	Turn white light off.
OFF	Turn both lights off.
BYE	Exit from program.

Note: If any other three-character command is entered, an appropriate message is to be printed.

Solution   A solution is given in Fig. 8.7. Initially, the keyboard and the printer console typewriter are configured for programmed operation and zeros are placed in register R5. This register is used to store the current data word associated with the output port. Then the subroutine GET is invoked. This subroutine uses the routines READ and WRITE that we have previously developed. The subroutine GET is used for entry of three characters from the keyboard. These characters are then stored in a 3-byte buffer identified by the label BUFFER.

The subroutine CHECK is used to determine if the three-character string in the buffer is identical to the subroutine argument that immediately follows the invoking

```
                  ;SOLUTION TO EXAMPLE 8-5
          .GLOBL READ,WRITE
          CPTR=0
          CKBD=0
          PKS=177560
          TKB=177562
          PTS=177564
          TPD=177566
          START:  CLR PKS
                  CLR PTS                   ;PROGRAMMED INPUT AND OUTPUT
                  CLR R5                    ;DAC WORD
          RUN:    JSR PC,GET                ;READ  3 CHARACTERS INTO BUFFER
                  JSR R4,CHECK              ;RED?
                  .ASCII /RED/
                  .EVEN
                  BEQ RED
                  JSR R4,CHECK              ;WHITE?
                  .ASCII /WHT/
                  .EVEN
                  BEQ WHT
                  JSR R4,CHECK              ;TURN RED OFF?
                  .ASCII /NRD/
                  .EVEN
                  BEQ NRD
                  JSR R4,CHECK              ;TURN WHITE OFF?
                  .ASCII /NWT/
                  .EVEN
                  BEQ NWT
                  JSR R4,CHECK              ;BOTH LIGHTS OFF?
                  .ASCII /OFF/
                  .EVEN
                  BEQ OFF
                  JSR R4,CHECK              ;EXIT FROM PROGRAM?
                  .ASCII /BYE/
                  .EVEN
                  BEQ BYE
                  MOV #MES,R1               ;INVALID INPUT.
                  CALL MESAGE
                  JMP RUN
          MES:    .ASCII /THIS IS NOT A COMMAND!!!/<15><12><200>
                  .EVEN
          ; $$$$$$$$$$$     SUBROUTINES START HERE    $$$$$$$$$$$$$$$$$$$$$
          MESAGE: CMPB #200,(R1)            ;TERM?
                  BNE AHEAD
                  RTS PC
          AHEAD:  MOVB (R1)+,R0
                  CALL WRITE
                  BR MESAGE
          ; ************* WHICH COMMAND WAS TYPED? *******************
          RED:    BIS #10,R5       ;RED?
                  MOV R5,@#170446
          JMP RUN
                  JMP RUN
          WHT:    BIS #2,R5        ;WHITE?
                  MOV R5,@#170446
                  JMP RUN
          NRD:    BIC #10,R5       ;RED OFF?
                  MOV R5,@#170446
                  JMP RUN
          NWT:    BIC #2,R5        ;WHITE OFF?
                  MOV R5,@#170446
                  JMP RUN
          OFF:    BIC #12,R5       ;BOTH LIGHTS OFF?
                  MOV R5,@#170446
                  JMP RUN
          BYE:    HALT
```

Figure 8.7   Solution to Example 8.5

```
;            $$$$$$$$$$$$    DEFINE MACRO    $$$$$$$$$$$$$$$$
.MACRO RETLF
MOVB #15,R0                  ;CARRIAGE RETURN
CALL WRITE
MOVB #12,R0                  ;LINE FEED
CALL WRITE
.ENDM
BUFFER:  .BLKB 3
         .EVEN
GET:     MOV #BUFFER,R1
         MOV #3,R2
BACK:    CALL READ
         CALL WRITE
         MOVB R0,(R1)+
         SOB R2,BACK
         RETLF
         RTS PC
CHECK:   MOV R4,R3                  ;FIRST LETTER OF COMMAAND
         ADD #4,R4
         MOV #BUFFER,R1
         CMPB (R1)+,(R3)+
         BEQ UP
         RTS R4
UP:      CMPB (R1)+,(R3)+          ;SECOND LETTER
         BEQ UP1
         RTS R4
UP1:     CMPB (R1)+,(R3)+
         RTS R4
         .END START
```

Figure 8.7   (*cont.*)

statement. If the string stored in the buffer matches the argument string, program control exits from the subroutine with the zero flag raised. Otherwise, program control exits from the subroutine with the zero flag cleared. If the string in the buffer matches an argument, program control is routed to the appropriate program segment. If the string entered does not match one of the arguments, the related message is printed. If a light is to be turned on, a logic 1 corresponding to the location of the output line is ORED with the control word. If a light is to be turned off, a logic 0 corresponding to the location of the particular output line is ANDed to the control word.

Review

1. Suppose a PDP-11 system is monitoring and controlling an external system through the use of a DRV11 parallel line unit. Develop a subroutine that sends logic 1s out on all odd-numbered output lines if and only if bit 2 of the input port and either bit 4, 5, or 9 of the input port are all logic 1s.

2. Refer to Example 8.5 and to the solution in Fig. 8.7. Modify this program so that it includes one additional command, CHG. When CHG is entered, the state of both of the lights is to be *changed*. That is, if a light was on, it is to be turned off, and if a light was off, it is to be turned on.

3. Suppose a DRV11 parallel line unit is being used, and the following EQUATE statements are included in the related program:

```
INPORT = 167774
OUTPORT = 167772
```

Which of the following commands are invalid?

(a) TST INPORT
(b) TST OUTPORT
(c) ADD INPORT,OUTPORT
(d) ADD OUTPORT,INPORT
(e) COM INPORT
(f) NEG OUTPORT

8.3 HYBRID COMPONENTS

When digital input lines are monitored by a computer system, only simple yes-no types of decisions can be made about the signal connected to an input line. Similarly, when a logic signal is sent out on an output line, it can only be used to activate or to deactivate some external component.

Logic signals are represented by two distinct voltage levels, referred to as a *high* level and a *low* level. When a system of logic components uses the high level as a logic 1 and the low level as a logic 0, then the system is said to employ *positive logic* devices. Likewise, when just these two voltage levels are used, the system is said to be a *discrete* system or a *digital* system. For many applications it is convenient to use voltage values that vary continuously. That is, meaningful voltage values may range anywhere between a lower bound and an upper bound. Systems in which voltages have meaningful values within defined intervals are said to be *continuous* or *analog* systems.

Suppose a computer is to monitor the temperature of a room. External hardware can easily be configured such that a logic 1 is applied to an input line of the computer if and only if the room temperature is greater than some predefined temperature such as 90°. For some system requirements, this may yield sufficient information. However, for other system requirements, a more precise measure of the actual temperature may be required. A temperature *transducer* may be used to convert the temperature to a corresponding voltage value. Then, if the computer system can identify the particular voltage value, a precise measure of temperature will be available for use with the computer software.

A wide variety of transducers are commercially available. In general, a *transducer* is a device that converts a measure of some physical parameter to a corresponding voltage value. Values of temperature, pressure, mechanical strain, fluid flow, velocity, acceleration, relative position, and other physical quantities can be readily converted to corresponding voltage values through the use of appropriate transducers. If the value of the voltage can be converted to a corresponding binary representation or binary number, it can easily be sensed by a digital computer.

A device that converts a voltage to a corresponding binary number is called an *analog-to-digital* converter, also referred to as an ADC or an A/D. An analog-to-digital converter is referred to as a *hybrid* peripheral device because the input to the device is an *analog* signal or a voltage, and the output is a set of binary or discrete signals called a *digital* word. The range of voltages used with typical ADCs is generally, between -10 volts and $+10$ volts. Frequently, a 5-volt range is utilized. Some typical word sizes available on commercial ADCs are 8 bits, 10 bits, and 16 bits.

Analog-to-digital converters generally possess a straight-line relationship between their input voltage and the binary number represented by the digital output. Thus, it is necessary only to specify the digital output for two values of input voltage in order to characterize the behavior of the device over the entire range of input voltages.

The range of inputs to an analog-to-digital converter consists of a continuum of voltage levels. However, the output of the device is represented by the contents of a finite-length register. Thus, it is impossible to specify exactly the values of all voltages within the voltage range. For example, suppose an analog-to-digital converter can accept a voltage within the range of 0 to 10 volts. Further suppose that the output register for this device is a 12-bit register. Thus, for a 10-volt range, there are 2^{12} possible output values. For this device there are exactly 4096 possible output values, and each of these can be used to specify a voltage within a $10/4096 = 0.0024414$-volt interval. The limitations inherent in fabricating the analog-to-digital converter may result in voltage errors as large as the theoretical quantizing-type of error mentioned above.

Another hybrid device is a *digital-to-analog* converter, commonly called a DAC or a D/A. This type of device converts an N-bit binary number to a corresponding voltage. There is generally a straight-line relationship between the value of the binary number and the corresponding voltage. The voltage range and the number of bits in the input register are generally comparable to the corresponding quantities on an analog-to-digital converter. Digital-to-analog converters are required when it is necessary for a varying voltage to be applied to a peripheral device. DACs are frequently used with continuous-type display devices, such as ink plotters or storage oscilloscopes. On these devices, one DAC is used to control the horizontal motion of a beam or a pen and another is used to control the vertical motion.

Digital-to-analog converters are among the simplest of peripheral devices. Generally, no control or status registers are required. When a binary number is sent to a DAC, this number is generally latched. The output voltage remains constant until a new value is latched at the input to the digital-to-analog converter.

The AAV11-A digital-to-analog converter is commonly used with LSI-11 implementations of PDP-11 systems. This unit contains four digital-to-analog converters, commonly referred to as DAC0, DAC1, DAC2, and DAC3. The DAC channels are located at four contiguous word addresses. During installation of this device, the system user may specify the addresses of these channels and select one of several voltage ranges. If just one of these units is used, the following are the recommended addresses for those 12-bit DACs.

DAC0	170440
DAC1	170442

DAC2   170444

DAC3   170446

The fourth channel, DAC3, also has four logic output lines available to users. These correspond to bits 0 to 3 of the output 12-bit register. Using these output lines does affect the output voltage produced by DAC3. However, because only the four least significant bits of a 12-bit DAC are used as logic output lines, the effect of using these bits as logic outputs produces an error of only $16/4096 = 0.39\%$ in comparison with the full-scale voltage range of the DAC. However, if voltages corresponding to a relatively small number of significant bits are to be output on a DAC channel, then DAC3 should not be used for this purpose.

Several different voltage ranges are available with this particular unit. We will assume that this DAC unit has been configured to produce a bipolar voltage output in the radius of -5.12 volts to $+5.12$ volts. For such a configuration, the 12-bit input binary number 0000_8 will produce an output voltage of -5.12 volts, and the number 4000_8 will produce an output voltage of 0 volts.

Example 8.6

Develop a program segment that causes 2.3 volts to be sent out on DAC1.

Solution   The following equation characterizes the behavior of the digital-to-analog converter that we have been discussing.

$$\text{number} = m \times \text{voltage} + b$$

In order to solve for m and b, we can use the information provided with the digital-to-analog converter. For the configuration that we have discussed, the following equations can be formulated.

$$0000_8 = m \times (-5.12) + b$$
$$4000_8 = m \times 0 + b$$

It is convenient to use just one number system in the set of equations. Using the base-10 number system, the equations may be rewritten as

$$0 = -5.12\,m + b$$
$$2048 = 0\,m + b$$

Solving these equations, it is seen that $b = 2048$ and $m = 400$. Thus, for an output voltage of 2.3 volts

$$\text{number} = m \times \text{voltage} + b = 400 \times 2.3 + 2048 = 2968$$

The following program segment will satisfy the program requirements.

```
VOUT = 2968.
DAC1 = 170442
MOV #VOUT,@#DAC1
```

Example 8.7

   Refer to Fig. 8.8. Develop a program that requests an input in the form $X.Y$, where $0.0 \le X.Y \le 5.1$. That is, $0 \le X \le 5$, and $0 \le Y \le 9$. If $X = 5$, then Y can have a value of just 0 or 1. The numerical voltage that is entered on the keyboard is to be displayed on the voltmeter, and a new input is to be requested. In addition, if the most recent valid value that has been requested is greater than 4 volts, the red light is to be illuminated. The program is to terminate if and only if the character Q is entered on the console keyboard.

   Solution   A solution is given in Fig. 8.9. After the keyboard and the printer have been configured for programmed operation, the number corresponding to a DAC output of 0 volt is placed in R2. Then the subroutine GETCHR is invoked. If a Q is entered, the program enters the HALT mode. Assume a valid character, that is, a number between 0 and 5, is entered. Then the corresponding numerical value is stripped from the ASCII representation, converted to a corresponding voltage increment, and added to the running sum in R2. Then GETCHR is again invoked. If a period is not entered at this time, an appropriate error message is printed, and program control reverts back to START. If a period is entered, then GETCHR is again invoked. The number entered is converted to a proper voltage increment and added to the running sum. Then the least significant bit of the running sum is erased. If the value entered from the keyboard is greater than 4.0 volts, the least significant bit of the running sum is set to 1 before the running sum is output to DAC3.

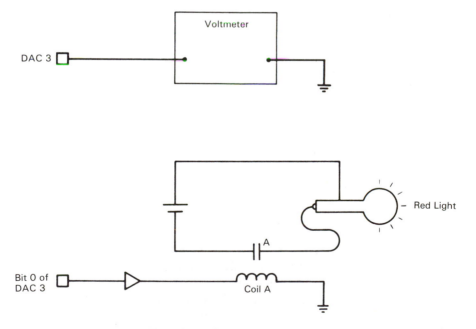

Figure 8.8   Diagram for Example 8.7

```
;THIS PROGRAM REQUESTS AN INPUT IN THE FORM OF
;X.Y, WHERE 0.0<X.Y<5.1 AND ENDS WHEN A "Q" IS TYPED.
          .GLOBL  READ,WRITE
          DAC3=170446
          CPNTR=0
          CKBD=0
          TKS=177560
          FOURVT=3648.       ;FOUR VOLTS
          TPS=177564
BEGIN:    MOV #CPNTR,@#TPS                   ;PROGRAM PRINTER
          MOV #CKBD,@#TKS                    ;PROGRAM KEYBOARD
START:    MOV #4000,R2             ;PUTS ZERO IN R2
          MOV #MESS,R1
          CALL PNTMES
          CALL GETCHR
          BIC #177760,R0
          MOV R0,R3
          MUL #400.,R3            ;MULTIPLY INPUT BY 1 VOLT
          ADD R3,R2              ;ADDS TO RUNNING SUM
          CALL GETCHR
          BIC #177760,R0
          MOV R0,R3
          MUL #40.,R3            ;MULTIPLIES INPUT BY .1 VOLT
          ADD R3,R2             ;ADDS TO RUNNING SUM
          BIC #1,R2             ;TURNS OFF LIGHT
          CMP R2,#FOURVT        ;GREATER THAN FOUR VOLTS?
          BLOS SET             ;NO
          BIS #1,R2            ;YES.  TURN ON LIGHT.
SET:      MOV R2,DAC3          ;SENDS OUT RUNNING SUM
          JMP START
GETCHR:   CALL READ
          CALL WRITE
          CMP #'Q,R0             ;IS INPUT A Q?  THEN STOP
          BNE UP
          HALT
UP:       RTS PC
PNTMES:   CMPB #200,(R1)
          BNE OUT
          RTS PC
OUT:      MOVB (R1)+,R0
          CALL WRITE
          BR PNTMES
MESS:     .ASCII <15><12>/ENTER A VOLTAGE VALUE IN THE FORM X.Y/<15><12><200>
          .EVEN
AWAY:     .ASCII <15><12>/IMPROPER DATA ENTRY!!  TRY AGAIN!!/<15><12><200>
          .EVEN
FAR:      MOV #AWAY,R1
          CALL PNTMES
          JMP START
          .END BEGIN


TYPE E87.MAC
```

Figure 8.9   A solution to Example 8.7

The ADV11-A *analog-to-digital* converter is commonly used with LSI-11 implementations of the PDP-11. This unit contains a 12-bit ADC and 16 analog input channels. Any of these channels may be selected for a voltage conversion. Two contiguous word addresses are utilized with this A/D unit. During installation or system modification, a user may specify these addresses. If just a single ADC unit is used, the following are the recommended word addresses.

ADC control register   170400
ADC status register   170400
ADC data register   170402

Note: The 12-bit data word is stored in bit position 11 to bit position 0.

Some of the lines located at address 170400 are control lines and some are status lines. Figure 8.10 identifies these logic lines. If the ACD operates in a range between −5.12 and +5.12 volts, then the 12-bit number 0000_8 represents −5.12 volts, and 4000_8 represents 0 volts. In subsequent discussions and examples, we will assume that the ADC is operating over this voltage range.

For the present, we will just illustrate use of this device in the *programmed mode* of operation. When a 1 is applied to bit 0 of the command register, a conversion of the voltage applied to the specified channel is initiated. When the conversion has been completed, the start signal applied to bit position 0 will be cleared, and the conversion complete flag located in bit position 7 of the status register will be raised. If bit 3 in the command register is set, then bit 12 in the data register will also become 1 when the conversion is completed.

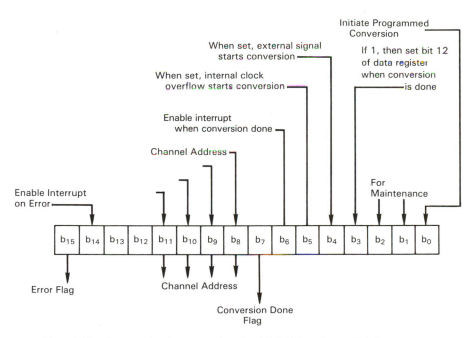

Figure 8.10   Command and status register for ADV-11A analog to digital converter (Courtesy of Digital Equipment Corporation)

Example 8.8

Suppose a voltage source is connected to channel 5 of the ADC that we have just described. Develop a subroutine that

(a) Reads and converts the voltage value if and only if the word GO is entered on the console keyboard.

(b) Each time a voltage is converted, it is printed in the form $X.Y$, where $0 \leq X \leq 5$ and $0 \leq Y \leq 9$. *Note:* The maximum value of voltage to be converted and printed is 5.1.

(c) After printing the value of a voltage, the program waits for a new input from the console.

(d) Control exits from the subroutine if and only if EX is entered on the keyboard.

Solution   A solution is given in Fig. 8.11. Beginning at the statement labeled GO, the conversion is initiated. Then the converted voltage value is moved into R3. Because the minimum value of voltage to be used is 0 volt, the number 4000 is subtracted from the converted value. Division of this adjusted value by the base-10 number 400 yields the integral number of volts applied. Division of the remainder by the base-10 number 40 yields the number of tenths of a volt.

Review

1. Modify the program in Fig. 8.9 so that it functions properly for values of $X.Y$ in the following range:

$$-5.1 \leq X.Y \leq 5.1$$

Negative quantities are entered by typing a minus sign just prior to entering the value of X.

2. An oscilloscope is adjusted so that the beam is in the lower left-hand corner when 0 volt is applied to both the horizontal and vertical input terminals. The scope is calibrated so that the horizontal input produces a deflection of 1 cm for each 0.5 volt applied. The input to the vertical terminal produces a deflection of 1 cm per volt applied. Suppose DAC0 is connected to the horizontal input, and DAC1 is connected to the vertical input of the scope. Develop a program segment that moves the beam 4 cm to the right and 3 cm in the upward direction.

3. Modify the program in Fig. 8.11 so that it functions properly if the input is connected to ADC channel 13 instead of ADC channel 5.

4. Refer to the program in Fig. 8.11. Suppose the input voltage is connected to ADC channel 5, but the ADC command word is specified as

```
CWORD = 2411
```

What additional program modifications are now required for the program to function properly?

5. Give at least one example of a way in which an error in using the ADC might occur, and thus produce a 1 in bit 15 of the status register.

```
;  THIS SUBROUTINE READS AND PRINTS THE
;     VOLTAGE CONNECTED TO CHANNEL 5 OF THE
;     ADC IF AND ONLY IF THE COMMAND 'GO' IS
;     ENTERED ON THE CONSOLE.
;       EXIT FROM ROUTINE BY TYPING "EX"
              .GLOBL READ,WRITE
              .MACRO PRINT MES
              MOV MES,R1
              CALL PNTMES
              .ENDM
              CWORD = 2401      ;ADC COMMAND WORD
              ADCCMD = 170400 ;COMMAND AND STATUS REGISTER
              ADCDAT = 170402 ;DATA REGISTER
RTLF:         .ASCII <15><12>/     /<200>
              .EVEN
ERROR:        .ASCII /*** INVALID COMMAND ***/<15><12><200>
              .EVEN
START:        CALL READ          ;GET INPUT STRING
              CMPB #'G,R0
              BNE EX
              CALL READ
              CMPB #'O,R0
              BEQ GO             ;IF 'GO START CONVERSION
BAD:          PRINT #ERROR
              BR START
EX:           CMPB #'E,R0
              BNE BAD
              CALL READ
              CMPB #'X,R0
              BNE BAD
              RTS PC             ;EXIT IF 'EX' IS ENTERED
GO:           MOV #CWORD,@#ADCCMD      ;START CONVERSION
BACK:         TSTB @#ADCCMD            ;CONVERSION DONE?
              BPL BACK                 ;NO
              MOV @#ADCDAT,R3          ;READ VOLTAGE
              SUB #4000,R3             ;BIAS VOLTAGE VALUE
              CLR R2                   ;PREPARE TO DIVIDE
              DIV #400.,R2             ;GET NUMBER OF VOLTS
              MOV R2,R0
              ADD #60,R0               ;CONVERT TO ASCII
              CALL WRITE
              CLR R2                   ;KEEP JUST THE REMAINDER
              MOV #'.,R0
              CALL WRITE
              DIV #40.,R2              ;GET TENTHS OF VOLT
              MOV R2,R0
              ADD #60,R0               ;CONVERT TO ASCII
              CALL WRITE
              PRINT #RTLF
              JMP START
;$$$  END SUBROUTINE $$$
PNTMES:       CMPB #200,(R1)
              BNE AHEAD
              RTS PC
AHEAD:        MOVB (R1)+,R0
              CALL WRITE
              BR PNTMES
;$$$$$ START TEST PROGRAM $$$$$
RUN:          CLRB @#177560           ;PROGRAMMED INPUT AND OUTPUT
              CLRB @#177564
              PRINT #RTLF
              CALL START
              HALT
              .END RUN
```

Figure 8.11   Subroutine and test program illustrating use of an ADC

8.4 COMPUTER CONTROLLED SYSTEMS

Through the use of a few peripheral devices, a computer may have the capability to monitor and control a relatively sophisticated external system. However, care must be taken when using a computer to control a system. Before the system components are assembled and before any software is developed, the system planner should be sure to define all of the requirements of the external system to be controlled. In addition, contingency plans should be made in case the system does not function as expected. In modern computer-controlled systems, diagnostic checks are frequently made during system initialization and at regular intervals during system operation.

Use of a programmed mode of operation is generally not sufficient for monitoring and controlling complex external activities. However, use of a programmed mode of operation may be satisfactory for controlling a very simple system that employs a minimal number of computer components. Control of a very simple system is illustrated in Example 8.9.

Example 8.9

Consider the diagram defining system components in Fig. 8.12 and the system requirements in Fig. 8.13. Formulate a subroutine that will satisfy these system requirements. Assume that a PDP-11 system is available with the peripheral devices that have been described in this chapter.

Solution   A subroutine that satisfies the specified requirements is given in Fig. 8.14. This subroutine requires the use of several other routines designed to do specific tasks. These working routines are given in Figs. 8.15 and 8.16.

Refer to Fig. 8.14. The number stored in LOGWRD is used to update the digital outputs. These outputs are used to determine the direction of rotation of the motor, to apply a brake to the motor shaft, to activate the grappler relay, and to activate the alarm. To *set* a single bit in this register, the BIS command may be used. The BIC command is used when a single bit is to be *cleared*. Several working routines are employed by the subroutine TASK. The routine CHKPOS is used to determine if the grappler mechanism is in the correct initial position. CHKTMP is used to sense if the temperature has reached the desired level. When this is accomplished, MOTRUN is used to move the grappler arm, and BRAKE is used to stop this movement. CHECK is used to determine if the grappler is over the bucket position. If the grappler overshoots the correct bucket position, the routine MOTBCK is called. If the grappler again overshoots the desired position, no further attempts are made to properly position the device. The subroutine ALARM is used to sound the alarm and to identify sources of difficulty.

Refer to Fig. 8.15. The macro CHINTV is used to implement the subroutines CHKPOS and CHECK, as well as the working routine LOOK that is used by the subroutine BRAKE. Refer to Fig. 8.16. The two subroutines used to control the

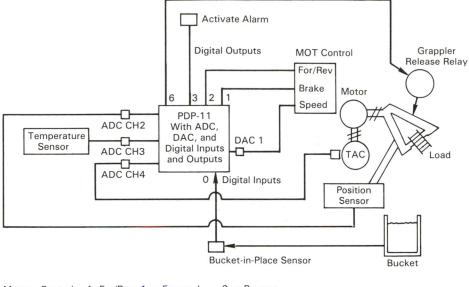

Motor   Control: 1. For/Rev: 1 → Forward   0 → Reverse
                         NOTE: Reverse motion is initially required
                      2. Brake: 1 → Apply Brake   0 → Release Brake
                      3. Speed: 3 Volts → Fast
                            0 Volts → Stop   2 Volts → Slow   1 Volt → Very Slow

Tachometer Output: 5 Volts → 600 RPM, − 5 Volts → − 600 RPM

Temperature Sensor: T = 200° → 5 Volts, T = 300° → 3 Volts

Position Sensor: When 1.9 ≤ V ≤ 2.0, Grappler is over bucket position

Grappler Release Relay: 1 → Open Grappler and Release Load
                         0 → Close Grappler

Alarm Control: 1 → Sound Alarm

Bucket in Place Sensor: 1 → Bucket in Place

Figure 8.12   Computer system controlling a robot arm

motor are shown in this figure. The macro DRIVE is used to operate the motor at a given forward speed until a specified boundary is reached.

This software will serve to perform the desired operation only if no serious difficulties are encountered. In real-world situations, however, such difficulties will generally be encountered at least once in a while. Suppose, for example, that program control has been passed to the subroutine CHKTMP. Control will exit from this routine only if the temperature being monitored exceeds 280°. In the particular process being controlled, perhaps a heating unit is being used to raise the measured temperature to this level. Suppose the heating unit is not functioning properly. Then

Initial conditions when routine is entered for this particular phase of a control operation:

(a) Motor is off.

(b) Brake is on.

(c) Position of grappler should be $4.5 \leq V \leq 5.0$ volts

(d) Reverse operation of motor required to move grappler to bucket position.

Task of this routine:

Wait until temperature $\geq 280°$. Then move grappler to bucket position and drop load into bucket.

System requirements and limitations:

(a) Motor may operate at high speed until position sensor indicates $V < 3$ volts.

(b) Motor must operate at very low speed for $V < 2.5$ volts.

(c) Motor and load are large and cannot stop instantenously.

(d) Drop load into bucket only if motor is off, brake is on, and indicated motor speed is less than 1 rpm. Exit from routine after dropping load.

(e) Do not drop load unless all conditions are met. If there is difficulty, sound alarm, send message to operator, and exit from routine.

Figure 8.13 System requirements for Example 8.9

program control may *never* exit from this routine. Furthermore, no alarm will be activated, and no message suggesting a system malfunction will be transmitted. This is not a very good situation. There are several other places in the control software that the program can "hang up" if the system is not functioning properly.

There are several ways in which the software can be modified to avoid such undesirable situations. For example, consider the CHKTMP routine. This routine can be rewritten so that if the temperature does not increase after a specified number of readings, program control will exit from the subroutine and appropriate action will be initiated. Alternately, a *time interval* may be *programmed* or specified. If a desired action does not occur within this time interval, control will exit from the routine.

In order to develop useful software for the control of any system, we must know *precisely* how the system is to function and what must be done in the event of a system malfunction. This is the *most important consideration* in the development of a computer-controlled system. System requirements should be thoroughly studied and understood before computer components are selected and before any software is developed.

Determination of *time intervals* is frequently required in the implementation of computer-controlled systems. For example, we may wish to initiate an analog-to-digital conversion every millisecond, or we may wish to terminate a process if a temperature does not reach a certain level within 10 minutes. A commonly used peripheral device that facilitates determination of such intervals is called a *real-time clock*. A real-time clock commonly used with LSI-11 implementations of PDP-11 systems is the KWV11-A programmable real-time clock. This is a powerful periph-

```
                    ,GLOBL CHKPOS,ALARM,CHKTMP,MOTRUN,BRAKE
                    .GLOBL CHECK,LOGWRD,POSFLG,CHKFLG,MOTBCK,TASK
        ; *** THIS ROUTINE PERFORMS THE REQUIREMENTS
        ;         SPECIFIED IN FIGURE 8-13   ***
                    GRAPCT = 100       ;GRAPPLER CONTROL BIT
                    LOGREG = 167772 ;ADDRESS OF LOGIC OUTPUTS
                    BUKMSK = 1         ;MASK FOR BUCKET-IN-PLACE SENSOR
                    FLGREG = 167774 ;ADDRESS OF FLAG REGISTER
        LOGWRD:  .WORD  0            ;CONTROL WORD FOR LOGIC OUTPUTS
        POSFLG:  .WORD  0
        CHKFLG:  .WORD  0
        TASK:    CALL CHKPOS        ;CHECK INITIAL POSITION
                 TST POSFLG         ;WITHIN SPECIFICATIONS?
                 BEQ UP             ;YES
                 JSR R1,ALARM       ;NO
                 .ASCII /GRAPPLER IS NOT IN CORRECT POSITION/<200>
                 .EVEN
        UP:      CALL CHKTMP;       RETURNS WHEN T>=280 DEGREES
                 CALL MOTRUN        ;RETURNS WHEN POSITION < 2 VOLTS
                 CALL BRAKE         ;RETURNS WHEN SPEED < 1 RPM
                 CALL CHECK         ;CHECK DESIRED POSITION
                 TST CHKFLG         ;IN CORRECT POSITION?
                 BNE UP1            ;NOT IN POSITION
                 BIT #BUKMSK,@#FLGREG      ;BUCKET THERE?
                 BNE UP2            ;YES
        NOBUCK:  JSR R1,ALARM
                 .ASCII /LOAD IN POSITION BUT BUCKET NOT THERE/<200>
                 .EVEN
        UP2:     BIS #GRAPCT,LOGWRD       ;DROP LOAD
                 MOV LOGWRD,@#LOGREG
                 RTS PC             ;MISSION ACCOMPLISHED
        UP1:     NOP                ;TRY AGAIN
                 CALL MOTBCK        ;RETURN WHEN POSITION >1.9 VOLTS
                 CALL BRAKE
                 CALL CHECK
                 TST CHKFLG
                 BNE DONE
                 BIT #BUKMSK,@#FLGREG
                 BEQ NOBUCK
                 BR UP2
        DONE:    JSR R1,ALARM
                 .ASCII /CANNOT POSITION GRAPPLER PROPERLY/<200>
                 .EVEN
                 .END
```

Figure 8.14   Subroutine for the task described in Fig. 8.13

eral device, and we shall not attempt to describe its full capabilities. However, we will illustrate its use in determining time intervals.

The KWV11-A programmable real-time clock contains two 16-bit registers located at contiguous word addresses. Suggested addresses are 170420 and 170422. The lower address identifies the location of the *command and status register,* and the higher address identifies a *buffer preset register* or a *counter register.* If this device is used to measure time intervals, the twos-complement of the number of clock pulses to be counted is loaded into the counter register. Then an appropriate command is loaded into the control register. The functions of the command and status register are shown in Fig. 8.17. We will only illustrate the use of mode 0, or the single interval timing mode.

Suppose, for example, that we wish to measure an interval of 50 microseconds. We may choose a clock rate of 1 megahertz and count 50 clock pulses. After 50

```
          DAC1 = 170442    ;ADDRESS OF DAC1
          T280 = 3408.     ;TEMPERATURE = 280 DEGREES
          RDCH4 = 002001   ;READ CHANNEL 4
          RDCH3 = 001401   ;READ CHANNEL 3
          RDCH2 = 001001   ;READ CHANNEL 2
          ADCCAS = 170400  ;ADC CMD AND STATUS REG
          ADCDAT = 170402  ;ADC DATA REGISTER
          VOLT19 = 2808.   ;1.9 VOLTS
          VOLT2 = 2848.    ;2 VOLTS
          VOLT45 = 3848.   ;4.5 VOLTS
          VOLT5 = 4048.    ;5 VOLTS
          ALRM = 8.        ;ALARM CONTROL BIT
          BRAKBT = 2       ;BRAKE CONTROL BIT
          LOGREG = 167772  ;ADDRESS OF DIGITAL OUTPUTS
          .MCALL .PRINT
          .GLOBL CHKPOS,ALARM,CHECK,CHKTMP
          .GLOBL POSFLG,CHKFLG,LOGWRD,BRAKE
;  *** SUBROUTINES CHKPOS,ALARM,CHECK,CHKTMP AND BRAKE
          .MACRO CHINTV FLAG,COMAND,LOW,HIGH,?BAD,?BACK
;   RETURNS WITH 0 IN FLAG IFF VOLTAGE IS WITHIN SPECIFIED LIMITS
          CLR FLAG
          MOV #COMAND,@#ADCCAS      ;LOAD ADC CD REGISTER
BACK:     TSTB @#ADCCAS   ;CONVERSION COMPLETE?
          BPL BACK        ;NO
          CMP #HIGH,@#ADCDAT        ;GREATER THAN HIGH?
          BCS BAD                   ;YES
          CMP @#ADCDAT,#LOW         ;LESS THAN LOW?
          BCS BAD                   ;YES
          RTS PC
BAD:      COM FLAG
          RTS PC
          .ENDM
CHKPOS:   CHINTV POSFLG,RDCH2,VOLT45,VOLT5
ALARM:    ADD #2,SP       ;ADJUST STACK POINTER
          .PRINT R1
          BIS #BRAKBT,LOGWRD
          MOV LOGWRD,@#LOGREG       ;SOUND ALARM
          RTS PC
CHECK:    CHINTV CHKFLG,RDCH2,VOLT19,VOLT2
CHKTMP:   MOV #RDCH3,@#ADCCAS       ;CHECK TEMP
AGAIN:    TSTB @#ADCCAS
          BPL AGAIN
          CMP #T280,@#ADCDAT        ;TEMP > 280 DEGREES?
          BCS CHKTMP                ;NO. WAIT
          RTS PC
BRAKE:    MOV #4000,@#DAC1          ;TURN OFF MOTOR
          BIS #BRAKBT,LOGWRD        ;APPLY BRAKE
          MOV LOGWRD,@#LOGREG
;  *** WAIT UNTIL MOTOR NEARLY STOPS ***
WAIT:     CALL LOOK
          TST POSFLG
          BNE WAIT
          RTS PC
LOOK:     CHINTV POSFLG,RDCH4,2045.,2051.
          .END
```

Figure 8.15 Utility routines required for control routine in Fig. 8.14

clock pulses have been counted, the counter will overflow, and the counter overflow flag will be raised. In order to realize this interval using a programmed mode of operation, we first place the twos-complement of the base-10 number 50, or 177716_8, in the buffer preset register. Then we load an appropriate command word such as 000011_8 into the command register, and then monitor bit 7 of the status register until the counter overflow flag is raised.

```
        LOGREG = 167772 ;ADDRESS OF LOGIC OUTPUT REGISTER
        RDCH2 = 1001    ;READ CHANNEL 2
        ADCCAS = 170400
        ADCDAT = 170402
        BRAKBT = 2        ;BRAKEBIT
        FORREV = 4        ;FORWARD/REVERSE BIT
        DAC1 = 170442
        VOLT3 = 3248.   ;3 VOLTS
        VOLT25 = 3048.  ;2.5 VOLTS
        VOLT2 = 2848.   ;2 VOLTS
        VOLT19 = 2808.
        VOLT1 = 2448.
        .GLOBL MOTRUN,MOTBCK,LOGWRD
; *** SUBROUTINES MOTRUN AND MOTBCK ***
        .MACRO DRIVE SPEED,BOUND,?BACK,?RADC
        MOV #SPEED,@#DAC1           ;SEND OUT SPEED SETTING
RADC:   MOV #RDCH2,@#ADCCAS        ;READ POSITION
BACK:   TSTB @#ADCCAS
        BPL BACK
        CMP @#ADCDAT,#BOUND        ;POSITION LESS THAN BOUND?
        BCC RADC                   ;NO
        .ENDM
MOTRUN: BIC #BRAKBT,LOGWRD         ;RELEASE BRAKE
        BIS #FORREV,LOGWRD         ;FORWARD
        MOV LOGWRD,@#LOGREG
        DRIVE VOLT3,VOLT3          ;HIGH SPEED
        DRIVE VOLT2,VOLT25         ;LOW SPEED
        DRIVE VOLT1,VOLT2          ;VERY LOW SPEED
        RTS PC
MOTBCK: BIC #BRAKBT,LOGWRD         ;RELEASE BRAKE
        BIC #FORREV,LOGWRD         ;REVERSE
        MOV LOGWRD,@#LOGREG
        MOV #VOLT1,@#DAC1          ;RUN BACKWARDS
RADC:   MOV #RDCH2,@#ADCCAS        ;READ POSITION
BACK:   TSTB @#ADCCAS
        BPL BACK
        CMP #VOLT19,@#ADCDAT       ;POSITION GREATER THAN BOUNDARY?
        BCC RADC                   ;NO
        RTS PC                     ;YES
        .END
```

Figure 8.16   Control subroutines required for routine in Fig. 8.14

Example 8.10

Develop a program segment that causes a bell to be rung every minute. This program is to be terminated when a key is pressed on the console keyboard.

Solution   A solution is given in Fig. 8.18. The 100 Hz clock is selected in the programmable real-time clock module, and the base-10 number -6000 is loaded into the counter register. After 6000 clock pulses, the counter overflows, the overflow flag is raised, and the bell ringing is initiated. Then the entire process is repeated. *Note:* The time required to initiate the bell ringing process, which corresponds to the statement CALL BELL, is very small in comparison with a 60-second interval.

Review

1. **(a)**   Develop a *main program* for executing the software developed for the solution of Example 8.9.
   (b)   Suppose the main program has been assembled and stored in a file called TEST.OBJ. Likewise, suppose the object programs for the program segments shown in Figs. 8.14,

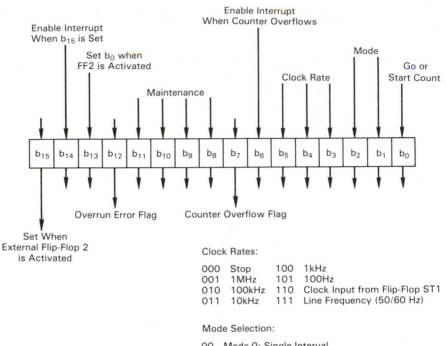

Clock Rates:

000	Stop	100	1kHz
001	1MHz	101	100Hz
010	100kHz	110	Clock Input from Flip-Flop ST1
011	10kHz	111	Line Frequency (50/60 Hz)

Mode Selection:

00	Mode 0: Single Interval
01	Mode 1: Repeated Interval
10	Mode 2: External Event Timing
11	Mode 3: External Event Timing From Zero Base

Figure 8.17 Command and status register for KWV11-A real-time clock (Copyright Digital Equipment Corporation, 1978. All rights reserved. Reprinted by permission.)

```
            .MCALL  .EXIT,.PRINT
RING:       .ASCII  <7><7><7><7><7><7><7><7><200>
            .EVEN
BELL:       .PRINT  #RING
            RTS PC
            TKS = 177560
            TPS = 177564
            MINUTE = -6000.
            CONTRL = 51         ;100 HZ CLOCK
            CSREG = 170420      ;CLOCK CONTROL REGISTER
            CLKDAT = 170422     ;CLOCK DATA REGISTER
START:      CLR TKS
BACK:       MOV #MINUTE,CLKDAT       ;SET COUNT
            MOV #CONTRL,CSREG
AGAIN:      TSTB TKS            ;DONE?
            BMI DONE            ;YES
            TSTB CSREG          ;CLOCK OVERFLOW?
            BPL AGAIN           ;NO
            CALL BELL           ;END OF CLOCKED INTERVAL
            BR BACK
DONE:       TKS+2,TPS+2
            MOV #100,TKS        ;PREPARE TO REENTER RT-11
            .EXIT
            .END START
```

Figure 8.18 Command and status registers for ADV-11A analog-to-digital converter (Copyright Digital Equipment Corporation, 1978. All rights reserved. Reprinted by permission.)

8.15, and 8.16 are stored, respectively, in files called TASK.OBJ, SUBS.OBJ, and MO-TOR.OBJ. What RT-11 command is required to produce the absolute code for this system software?

2. Suppose the absolute module referred to in Review question 1 is available, and the required analog-to-digital converter, digital-to-analog converter, and digital input and output lines are available as part of the system. However, suppose that none of the hardware or sensors shown in Fig. 8.12 are currently available for use with the computer system. How can the system software be tested?

3. Refer to Example 8.9 and to the system requirements given in Fig. 8.13. Suppose that these system requirements are modified so that the motor is to operate at *high* speed until the position sensor indicates a voltage of 2.5 volts. Modify the software accordingly.

4. Modify the program in Fig. 8.18 so that the bells will be rung once every hour.

5. Refer to the third to the last line in the program in Fig. 8.18. Why is this statement required?

8.5 ILLUSTRATIVE EXAMPLE

In this section we will illustrate the use of a particular peripheral device. We will discuss and illustrate the use of a digital-to-analog converter module as the interface required for producing graphical displays. The system of interest can be used to produce graphical displays either on a storage oscilloscope or on an *X-Y* plotter that uses an inkpen. We will generally assume that we are using a relatively high-quality storage oscilloscope, referred to as a *display scope*.

Refer to Fig. 8.19. Observe that analog signals are connected to the *X* and *Y* inputs of this device through the use of DAC channels 0 and 1. Also observe that two logic outputs or digital signals are connected to this device. Some display scopes use several logic signals. Other display devices, such as ink plotters, may require just a single logic input to raise or lower the pen. In this particular device, the beam will be on if and only if a logic 1 is present on bit 2 of the logic output register. The screen will be cleared if a logic 1 is applied to bit position 0 for a sufficiently long duration.

In order to produce graphs on a display device, it is necessary to generate small *line segments*. Then software can be developed that interconnects the line segments in the desired manner. It is convenient to develop a *software package* that includes the capability of connecting *straight lines* between any two specified points. We shall discuss and illustrate the development of such software.

Before developing such software, we must know the specifications and calibration of the display device being used. For the device shown in Fig. 8.19, we will assume that if the voltage levels output on DAC0 and on DAC1 are both -5.12 volts, the beam will be positioned in the lower left-hand corner. If both DAC channels output voltages having values of $+5.12$ volts, the beam will be positioned in the upper right-hand corner of the screen. We will also assume that the required logic levels are standard TTL signals such as produced in bit positions 0 and 1 of DAC3.

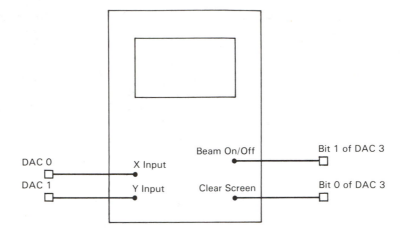

Figure 8.19　Interface connections for graphics display device

Suppose the beam is initially positioned at coordinates (x_0, y_0). That is, a value of x_0 volts is being sent out on DAC0, and a value of y_0 volts is being sent out on DAC1. Suppose we wish to draw a straight-line segment between this point and another point specified by the coordinates (x_f, y_f). Then we might consider implementing the following sequence of events.

1. Turn on the beam.
2. Send out a binary number corresponding to x_f volts on DAC0.
3. Send out a binary number corresponding to y_f volts on DAC1.

This sequence of operations will not generate the desired line segment. The three steps listed are generally executed in just a few microseconds. Prior to execution of the corresponding commands, the beam will be at the position identified by coordinates (x_0, y_0). After execution of these commands, the beam will be at position (x_f, y_f). However, the beam will change positions so rapidly that there will be no visible path between the two points. If the screen of a display scope *could* respond at such a rapid speed, then the display generated would not be a straight line between the two points but rather a horizontal line segment followed by a vertical line segment.

Suppose the sequence of steps is applied to the interface outputs that are connected to an ink-plotting device. In step 2 of the sequence, a voltage is applied to the horizontal drive of the plotter. Before the pen-driving mechanism can accelerate in the x direction, a voltage is applied to the vertical drive of the plotter. The pen will very rapidly proceed to (and probably overshoot) the coordinates (x_f, y_f), but there will not be sufficient time for any ink to be released from the pen.

In order to produce a visible line between the two points, the beam or inkpen must be slowly "walked" between the two points. Consider that an invisible line segment connects the two points, and suppose that this line segment has a slope of at least 1. Then the following sequence of events will generate a visible line segment.

1. Apply a small voltage increment to the x input.
2. Continue to apply identical voltage increments to the y input until the beam has reached or crossed the imaginary line.
3. Implement a time-delay routine so that the beam has sufficient time to discharge a visible line increment on the scope.
4. Terminate this process if the final or destination point has been reached. If not, go back to step 1.

If small steps are utilized, by the time this sequence of events is completed, it will appear that a continuous line has been drawn between the two points. If the slope of the line is an integer, then the line segment will appear to be a straight line. Suppose the slope of the line has a nonintegral value such as 2.5. If this technique is used, the first portion of the line segment will have a slope of 3, and the latter portion of the line segment will have a slope of 2. This is not a very good approximation for a straight line. A better approximation can be obtained by employing the following modification of this technique.

Suppose the L section obtained by first stepping once in the x direction and then one or more times in the y direction does not exactly meet the true invisible line connecting the two points. Then if the last L section that did not exactly touch the true line crossed over the line, then the present L section approximation should stop just short of the true line. Similarly, if the last L section stopped just short of the true line and the present L section does not exactly terminate at the true line, then this L section should pass over the line.

Although there are algorithms that yield better approximations to straight-line segments, this technique is very easy to program. In order to see if a particular L-shaped segment meets or passes over the true line, let us first formulate the following definitions.

$$XD = x_f - x_0 \quad \text{(horizontal displacement)}$$
$$YD = y_f - y_0 \quad \text{(vertical displacement)}$$
$$\Delta X = \text{horizontal step size} \quad \text{(usually} \quad 1)$$
$$\Delta Y = \text{vertical step size} \quad \text{(usually} \quad 1)$$

Then, to determine if the L-shaped step has touched or passed over the true line segment, we can perform the following sequence of steps. *Note:* Assume that initially $x = x_0$ and $y = y_0$.

1. Add ΔX to the value of x.
2. Add ΔY to the value of y.
3. Subtract XD from YD. That is, $YD = YD - XD$.
4. If YD is less than or equal to 0, exit from this sequence. If not, go back to step 2.

A flow diagram for the generation of a line segment with a slope greater than or equal to 1 is given in Fig. 8.20. If a line segment has a slope less than 1, the walking procedure is implemented by first taking a step in the y direction and then taking one or more steps in the x direction. Suppose we refer to the subroutine illustrated in Fig. 8.20 as YPLOT. Then we can develop a similar routine for cases in which the slope of a line has a magnitude less than 1. We will refer to this subroutine as XPLOT. Using these two subroutines, we can easily implement a routine for drawing a line between any two points. Such a routine must also be capable of drawing vertical and horizontal line segments. A flowchart for such a routine is given in Fig. 8.21.

Suppose we have developed software to implement the routine in Fig. 8.21. Then we can use this software to interconnect line segments and to draw desired graphs and pictorial displays. In many cases, it is also desirable to have the capability to intersperse alphanumeric information with graphical displays. That is, we would like our display software package to have capabilities of producing text strings. This is relatively easy to implement if we formulate characters using a *dot-matrix grid*.

Refer to Fig. 8.22a. A 6 × 8 dot matrix is illustrated in this figure, and the various dot positions are identified. In order to represent a character in this grid, the beam is turned off and then positioned to point 1. At this position, the beam is either left off or is turned on for a brief interval. Then the beam is moved to position 2, and a similar function is performed. The character generation routine traverses the beam to all 48 positions of the grid. At each position the beam is either left off or turned on for a brief interval depending on the value of a particular data bit. Because there are 48 dots in the grid, three words of data information are required to specify each character.

Refer to Fig. 8.22b. Formulation of the character R corresponding to the ASCII code 122 is illustrated. The state of the beam at each dot position is specified by the three octal words 177220, 114224, and 061000.

PDP-11 software required to implement the plotting routines just discussed is shown in Figs. 8.23 to 8.28. In order to implement efficiently plotting and character generation operations, the software is written to function as a *command interpreter*. That is, after the plotting routine is invoked, subsequent data words are interpreted as *plotting commands*. This is similar to use of an interpretive language, such as most implementations of BASIC. If the data word immediately following the JSR R5,PLOT statement that calls this routine is a 0, then the sequence of plotting commands immediately follows this word. If it is not a 0, it is considered to be the address at which the plotting commands begin.

Fig. 8.23 shows the command interpreter portion of the software package. Observe that there are 14 different commands that may be given. These correspond to the octal numbers between 0 and 15 inclusive. A table is used to route a specific command to the corresponding processing routine. The main portion of each of the processing routines is shown in Fig. 8.24. The function of each of these routines is also defined in this figure. For example, the octal command 0 is used to exit from

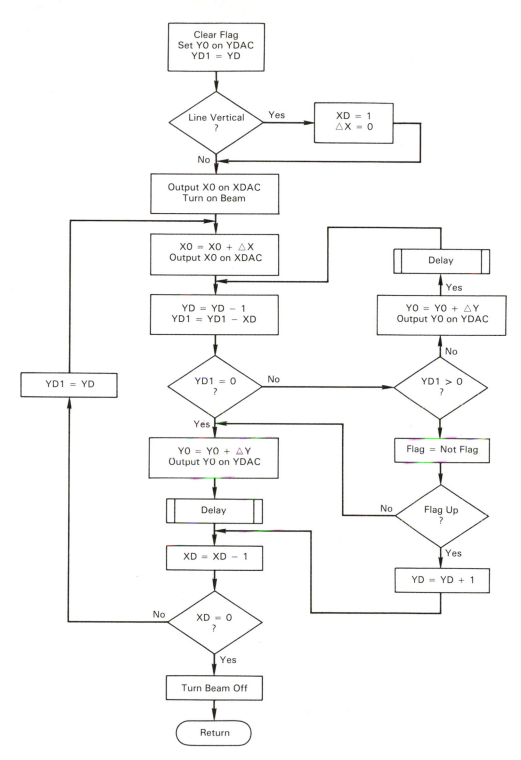

Figure 8.20 Flowchart for generation of a line segment for slope ≥ 1 (Courtesy of Mayfield Publishing Company)

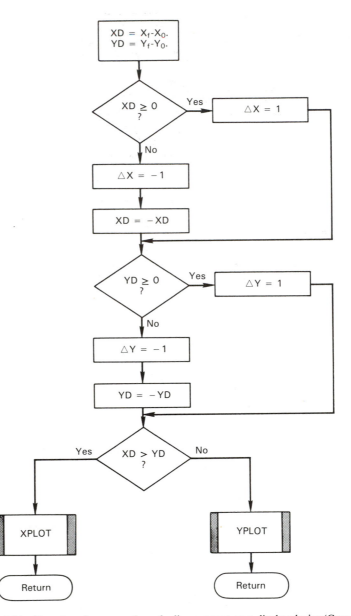

Figure 8.21 Flowchart for generation of a line segment on a display device (Courtesy of Mayfield Publishing Company)

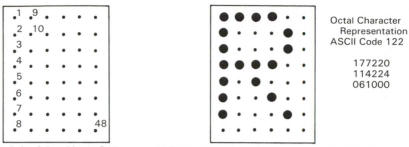

(a) A 6 x 8 Dot Matrix Grid   (b) Formulation of the Character R in a 6 x 8 Grid

Octal Character
Representation
ASCII Code 122

177220
114224
061000

Figure 8.22   (a) A 6×8 dot-matrix grid; (b) Formulation of the character R in a 6×8 grid

```
        .GLOBL  CTBL
        .GLOBL  PLOT
        XDAC = 170440
        YDAC = 170442
        CBITS = 170446
    ;                               THIS SUBROUTINE PLOTS POINTS, LINES,
    ;                               AND CHARACTERS USING TWO DACS.
    ;
    ;                               THE FOLLOWING SECTION SAVES ALL OF
    ;                               THE REGISTERS THAT ARE ALTERED BY
    ;                               THIS SUBROUTINE AND PUTS THE
    ;                               RETURN ADDRESS IN SR5 IF A
    ;                               DEFERRED COMMAND TABLE IS USED.
PLOT:   MOV   R0,SR0
        MOV   R1,SR1
        MOV   R2,SR2
        MOV   R3,SR3
        MOV   R4,SR4
        MOV   (R5)+,R4
        MOV   R5,SR5
        CMP   #0,R4
        BNE   MP1
        MOV   #0,SR5
        BR    STP
MP1:    MOV   R4,R5
STP:    MOV   (R5)+,R2          ;THIS SECTION GETS ONE COMMAND
        MOV   #TABL,R3          ;WORD FROM THE COMMAND TABLE AND
        CLC                     ;BRANCHES TO THE PROPER SUBROUTINE.
        ROL   R2
        ROL   R2
        ADD   R2,R3
        JMP   (R3)
TABL:   JMP   CMD0
        JMP   CMD1
        JMP   CMD2
        JMP   CMD3
        JMP   CMD4
        JMP   CMD5
        JMP   CMD6
        JMP   CMD7
        JMP   CMD8
        JMP   CMD9
        JMP   CMD10
        JMP   CMD11
        JMP   CMD12
        JMP   CMD13
```

Figure 8.23   Command interpreter for plotting software package

```
CMD0: MOV   SR0,R0        ;RESTORE ALL REGISTERS AND RETURN
      MOV   SR1,R1        ;TO CALLING PROGRAM THRU R5 IF A
      MOV   SR2,R2        ;DIRECT TABLE WAS USED OR THRU
      MOV   SR3,R3        ;SR5 IF A DEFERRED TABLE WAS USED.
      MOV   SR4,R4
      CMP   #0,SR5
      BEQ   CM01
      MOV   SR5,R5
CM01: RTS   R5
CMD1: BIS   #2,@#CBITS    ;TURN ON BEAM
      JMP   STP
CMD2: BIC   #2,@#CBITS    ;TURN OFF BEAM
      JMP   STP
CMD3: BIC   #1,@#CBITS    ;ERASE SCREEN
      JSR   PC,WAIT
      BIS   #1,@#CBITS
      MOV   #100000,CNT1
HLDE: DEC   CNT1
      BNE   HLDE
      JMP   STP
CMD4: BIC   #10,@#CBITS   ;TURN ON SCREEN VIEW
      JMP   STP
CMD5: BIS   #10,@#CBITS   ;TURN OFF SCREEN VIEW
      JMP   STP
CMD6: MOV   (R5)+,SPR1    ;SET BEAM - LOAD SPR1 AND SPR2
      MOV   (R5)+,SPR2    ;WITH X AND Y COORDINATES
      JMP   STP           ;OF NEW BEAM LOCATION.
CMD7: MOV   (R5)+,R2      ;SET BEAM - SAME AS ABOVE EXCEPT
      MOV   (R2)+,SPR1    ;COORDINATES ARE LOADED FROM THE
      MOV   (R2),SPR2     ;ADDRESS GIVEN AFTER THE COMMAND
      JMP   STP
CMD8: MOV   (R5)+,EPR1    ;DRAW LINE - DRAWS A LINE FROM THE
      MOV   (R5)+,EPR2    ;CURRENT BEAM POSITION TO THE POSITION
      JMP   DRAW          ;GIVEN BY THE NEXT TWO WORDS
CMD9: MOV   (R5)+,R2      ;DRAW LINE - SAME AS ABOVE EXCEPT
      MOV   (R2)+,EPR1    ;COORDINATES ARE LOADED FROM THE
      MOV   (R2),EPR2     ;ADDRESS GIVEN AFTER THE COMMAND
      JMP   DRAW
CMD10: MOV  R5,R2         ;WRITE TEXT ACROSS - ASCII TEXT FROM
       JSR  PC,WTA        ;THE COMMAND TABLE IS WRITTEN IN A
       MOV  R2,R5         ;HORIZONTAL LINE STARTING FROM THE
;CURRENT BEAM POSITION.    THE FIRST CHARACTER OF THE STRING
       JMP  STP           ;INDICATES WHAT CHARACTER WILL BE
                          ;USED AS A STRING TERMINATOR.
CMD11: MOV  (R5)+,R2      ;WRITE TEXT ACROSS - SAME AS ABOVE
       JSR  PC,WTA        ;EXCEPT THE TEXT IS LOADED FROM THE
       JMP  STP           ;ADDRESS GIVEN AFTER THE COMMAND.
CMD12: MOV  R5,R2         ;WRITE TEXT DOWN - SAME AS WRITE
       JSR  PC,WTD        ;TEXT ACROSS EXCEPT TEXT IS WRITTEN
       MOV  R2,R5         ;DOWN A VERTICAL LINE FROM THE CURRENT
       JMP  STP           ;BEAM POSITION.
CMD13: MOV  (R5)+,R2      ;WRITE TEXT DOWN - SAME AS ABOVE
       JSR  PC,WTD        ;EXCEPT TEXT IS LOADED FROM THE
       JMP  STP           ;ADDRESS GIVEN AFTER THE COMMAND.
```

Figure 8.24 Commands for plotting software package

the plotting package. The octal command 3 is used to erase the screen, and the octal command 10 is used to connect a line segment between the present position of the beam and the position specified by the next two data words.

The line generation working routines are shown in Fig. 8.25. These correspond to the algorithms illustrated in the flowcharts in Figs. 8.20 and 8.21.

Software required for character generation is shown in Fig. 8.26. Some work-

```
DRAW: MOV   SPR1,XO      ;THIS SECTION COMPUTES THE DIFFERENCE
      MOV   SPR2,YO      ;IN THE X AND Y COORDINATES AND
      MOV   EPR1,XF      ;THEN SELECTS THE PROPER PLOT ROUTINE.
      MOV   EPR2,YF      ;LINES WHOSE SLOPE ARE BETWEEN -1 AND +1
      CMP   XO,XF        ;ARE PLOTTED IN XPLT.
      BGE   DRW1 ;OTHER LINES ARE PLOTTED IN YPLT.
      MOV   XF,XD
      SUB   XO,XD
      MOV   #1,DX
      BR    DRW2
DRW1: MOV   XO,XD
      SUB   XF,XD
      MOV   #177777,DX                   YPLT: CLR   FLG
DRW2: CMP   YO,YF                              MOV   YD,YD1
      BGE   DRW3                               MOV   YO,@#YDAC
      MOV   YF,YD                              CMP   XO,XF
      SUB   YO,YD                              BNE   PY1
      MOV   #1,DY                              MOV   #1,XD
      BR    DRW4                               MOV   #0,DX
DRW3: MOV   YO,YD                        PY1:  MOV   XO,@#XDAC
      SUB   YF,YD                              BIS   #2,@#CBITS
      MOV   #177777,DY                   PY2:  ADD   DX,XO
DRW4: CMP   XD,YD                              MOV   XO,@#XDAC
      BGT   XPLT                         PY3:  DEC   YD
      BR    YPLT                               SUB   XD,YD1
XPLT: CLR   FLG   ;LINE DRAWING ROUTINES       BNE   PY6
      MOV   XD,XD1                        PY4:  ADD   DY,YO
      MOV   XO,@#XDAC                           MOV   YO,@#YDAC
      CMP   YO,YF                               JSR   PC,WAIT
      BNE   PX1                           PY5:  DEC   XD
      MOV   #1,YD                               BEQ   FINP
      MOV   #0,DY                               MOV   YD,YD1
PX1:  MOV   YO,@#YDAC                           BR    PY2
      BIS   #2,@#CBITS                   PY6:  ADD   #0,YD1
PX2:  ADD   DY,YO                               BMI   PY7
      MOV   YO,@#YDAC                           BEQ   PY7
PX3:  DEC   XD                                 ADD   DY,YO
      SUB   YD,XD1                             MOV   YO,@#YDAC
      BNE   PX6                                JSR   PC,WAIT
PX4:  ADD   DX,XO                              BR    PY3
      MOV   XO,@#XDAC                    PY7:  MOV   #1,R1
      JSR   PC,WAIT                            XOR   R1,FLG
PX5:  DEC   YD                                BEQ   PY4
      BEQ   FINP                               INC   YD
      MOV   XD,XD1                             BR    PY5
      BR    PX2                         FINP: BIC   #2,@#CBITS
PX6:  ADD   #0,XD1                            MOV   EPR1,SPR1
      BMI   PX7                               MOV   EPR2,SPR2
      BEQ   PX7                               JMP   STP
      ADD   DX,XO
      MOV   XO,@#XDAC
      JSR   PC,WAIT
      BR    PX3
PX7:  MOV   #1,R1
      XOR   R1,FLG
      BEQ   PX4
      INC   XD
      BR    PX5
```

Figure 8.25   Line generation portion of plotting software package

```
WTD:    MOVB  (R2),R3       ;WRITE TEXT DOWN
        BIC   #177600,R3    ;GET FIRST BYTE AND SAVE AS TERMINATOR
        INC   R2
WTD1:   MOVB  (R2),R4       ;GET A CHARACTER.  IF NOT THE TERMINATOR,
        BIC   #177600,R4    ;CALL THE WRITE CHARACTER ROUTINE.
        INC   R2
        CMP   R3,R4
        BNE   WTD2
        INC   R2
        BIC   #1,R2
        RTS   PC
WTD2:   JSR   PC,WTC        ;MOVE THE BEAM POSITION TO THE PROPER
        MOV   RES,R1        ;POSITION FOR THE NEXT CHARACTER.
        CLC
        ROL   R1
        ROL   R1
        ROL   R1
        SUB   R1,SPR2
        MOV   RES,R0
        CLC
        ROL   R0
        SUB   R0,R1
        SUB   R1,SPR1
        BR    WTD1
WTC:    MOV   R4,R1         ;WRITE CHARACTER - THE CHARACTER TO BE
        CLC                 ;WRITTEN IS IN R4.  THIS NUMBER IS
        ROL   R1            ;MULTIPLIED BY 6 AND USED AS AN
        ROL   R4            ;INDEX TO THE TABLE WHICH CONTAINS
        ROL   R4            ;THE CHARACTER DEFINITIONS.
        ADD   R1,R4
        MOV   #CTBL,R1
        ADD   R1,R4
        MOV   #3,CNT1
WTC1:   MOV   (R4)+,R1
        MOV   #10,CNT2
WTC2:   JSR   PC,WTDT       ;R1 CONTAINS 1/3 OF THE CHARACTER
        DEC   CNT2          ;DEFINITION.
        BNE   WTC2          ;AFTER EACH DOT IS WRITTEN, THE BEAM
        MOV   RES,R0        ;POSITION IS MOVED TO THE LOCATION
        CLC                 ;OF THE NEXT DOT.
        ROL   R0
        ROL   R0
        ROL   R0
        ADD   R0,SPR2
        ADD   RES,SPR1
        MOV   #10,CNT2
WTC3:   JSR   PC,WTDT
        DEC   CNT2
        BNE   WTC3
        MOV   RES,R0
        CLC
        ROL   R0
        ROL   R0
        ROL   R0
        ADD   R0,SPR2
        ADD   RES,SPR1
        DEC   CNT1
        BNE   WTC1
        RTS   PC
```

Figure 8.26   Character generation routines for plotting software package

```
WTDT:  ROL   R1              ;WRITE DOT - R1 IS ROTATED LEFT AND
       BCC   WTT1            ;IF A 1 ROLLS INTO THE CARRY FLAG,
       MOV   SPR1,@#XDAC     ;A DOT IS PLACED AT THE CURRENT BEAM
       MOV   SPR2,@#YDAC     ;POSITION.
       BIS   #2,@#CBITS
       JSR   PC,WAIT
       JSR   PC,WAIT
       JSR   PC,WAIT
       BIC   #2,@#CBITS
WTT1:  SUB   RES,SPR2
       RTS   PC
WTA:   MOVB  (R2),R3         ;GET FIRST BYTE AND SAVE AS TERMINATOR
       BIC   #177600,R3
       INC   R2
WTA1:  MOVB  (R2),R4         ;GET A CHARACTER.  IF NOT THE TERMINATOR,
       BIC   #177600,R4      ;CALL THE WRITE CHARACTER ROUTINE.
       INC   R2
       CMP   R3,R4
       BNE   WTA2
       INC   R2
       BIC   #1,R2
       RTS   PC
WTA2:  JSR   PC,WTC
       BR    WTA1
WAIT:  MOV   #15,TEST        ;THE FOLLOWING SECTION IS A SHORT
WAIT1: DEC   TEST ;DELAY LOOP USED FOR LINE DRAWING
       BNE   WAIT1           ;AND CHARACTER GENERATION
       RTS   PC
SPR1:  .WORD  0              ;CURRENT X COORDINATE
SPR2:  .WORD  0              ;CURRENT Y COORDINATE
EPR1:  .WORD  0              ;ENDING X COORDINATE
EPR2:  .WORD  0              ;ENDING Y COORDINATE
XD:    .WORD  0              ;DIFFERENCE IN X COORDINATES
YD:    .WORD  0              ;DIFFERENCE IN Y COORDINATES
XO:    .WORD  0              ;STARTING X
YO:    .WORD  0              ;STARTING Y
XF:    .WORD  0              ;ENDING X
YF:    .WORD  0              ;ENDING Y
XD1:   .WORD  0
YD1:   .WORD  0
DX:    .WORD  0              ;X AXIS INCREMENT
DY:    .WORD  0              ;Y AXIS INCREMENT
FLG:   .WORD  0
TEST:  .WORD  0
RES:   .WORD 17
CNT1:  .WORD 0
CNT2:  .WORD 0
SR0:   .WORD 0
SR1:   .WORD 0
SR2:   .WORD 0
SR3:   .WORD 0
SR4:   .WORD 0
SR5:   .WORD 0
       .END
```

Figure 8.27 Utility subroutines and storage allocations for plotting software package

```
.GLOBL  CTBL
CTBL:   .BLKW   96.
.WORD   0           ;SPACE
.WORD   0
.WORD   0
.WORD   0           ;!
.WORD   175000
.WORD   0
.WORD   000340      ;"
.WORD   000340
.WORD   0
.WORD   024376      ;#
.WORD   024376
.WORD   024000
.WORD   022124      ;$
.WORD   177124
.WORD   044000
.WORD   143310      ;%
.WORD   010046
.WORD   143000
.WORD   006162      ;&
.WORD   115144
.WORD   005000
.WORD   000040      ;'
.WORD   040200
.WORD   0
.WORD   000070      ;(
.WORD   042202
.WORD   0
.WORD   000202      ;)
.WORD   042070
.WORD   0
.WORD   024020      ;*
.WORD   176020
.WORD   024000
.WORD   010020      ;+
.WORD   076020
.WORD   010000
.WORD   001014      ;,
.WORD   0
.WORD   0
.WORD   010020      ;-
.WORD   010020
.WORD   010000
.WORD   001000      ;.
.WORD   0
.WORD   0
.WORD   003010      ;/
.WORD   010040
.WORD   140000
.WORD   076212      ;0
.WORD   111242
.WORD   076000
.WORD   000102      ;1
.WORD   177002
.WORD   0
.WORD   107222      ;2
.WORD   111222
.WORD   061000
.WORD   042202      ;3

.WORD   111222
.WORD   066000
.WORD   014050      ;4
.WORD   044376
.WORD   004000
.WORD   162242      ;5
.WORD   121242
.WORD   116000
.WORD   036122      ;6
.WORD   111222
.WORD   006000
.WORD   103210      ;7
.WORD   110240
.WORD   140000
.WORD   066222      ;8
.WORD   111222
.WORD   066000
.WORD   060222      ;9
.WORD   111224
.WORD   074000
.WORD   000154      ;:
.WORD   066000
.WORD   0
.WORD   000332      ;;
.WORD   156000
.WORD   0
.WORD   000020      ;<
.WORD   024104
.WORD   101000
.WORD   024050      ;=
.WORD   024050
.WORD   024000
.WORD   101104      ;>
.WORD   024020
.WORD   0
.WORD   040200      ;?
.WORD   115140
.WORD   0
.WORD   046222      ;@
.WORD   117202
.WORD   076000
.WORD   037110      ;A
.WORD   104110
.WORD   037000
.WORD   177222      ;B
.WORD   111222
.WORD   066000
.WORD   076202      ;C
.WORD   101202
.WORD   042000
.WORD   177202      ;D
.WORD   101104
.WORD   134000
.WORD   177222      ;E
.WORD   111202
.WORD   101000
.WORD   177220      ;F
.WORD   110200
.WORD   100000
.WORD   076202      ;G

.WORD   101222
.WORD   117000
.WORD   177020      ;H
.WORD   010020
.WORD   177000
.WORD   000202      ;I
.WORD   177202
.WORD   0
.WORD   002002      ;J
.WORD   001002
.WORD   176000
.WORD   177020      ;K
.WORD   024104
.WORD   101000
.WORD   177002      ;L
.WORD   001002
.WORD   001002
.WORD   177100      ;M
.WORD   030100
.WORD   177000
.WORD   177100      ;N
.WORD   020020
.WORD   177000
.WORD   076202      ;O
.WORD   101202
.WORD   076000
.WORD   177220      ;P
.WORD   110220
.WORD   060000
.WORD   076202      ;Q
.WORD   105204
.WORD   075000
.WORD   177220      ;R
.WORD   114224
.WORD   061000
.WORD   042242      ;S
.WORD   111212
.WORD   042000
.WORD   100200      ;T
.WORD   177200
.WORD   100000
.WORD   176002      ;U
.WORD   001002
.WORD   176000
.WORD   160030      ;V
.WORD   003030
.WORD   160000
.WORD   177004      ;W
.WORD   104004
.WORD   177000
.WORD   143050      ;X
.WORD   010050
.WORD   143000
.WORD   140040      ;Y
.WORD   017040
.WORD   140000
.WORD   103212      ;Z
.WORD   111242
.WORD   141000
.BLKW   111.
.END
```

Figure 8.28 Character table for plotting software package

```
        .GLOBL  PLOT
START:  NOP
        CLR  R0
        JSR  R5,PLOT
        .WORD  0
        .WORD  3              ;ERASE SCREEN
        .WORD  6              ;SET BEAM                           .WORD  6        ;SET BEAM
        .WORD  420                                                .WORD  7500
        .WORD  2100                                               .WORD  5000
        .WORD  10             ;DRAW LINE                          .WORD  14       ;WRITE TEXT DOWN
        .WORD  420                                                .ASCII "?STAR?"
        .WORD  3140                                               .EVEN
        .WORD  10             ;DRAW LINE                          .WORD  0
        .WORD  1250                                               HALT
        .WORD  3770                                               DPT:   .WORD  2310
        .WORD  10             ;DRAW LINE                                 .WORD  1250
        .WORD  2310                                               DPT1:  .WORD  4210
        .WORD  3770                                                      .WORD  3140
        .WORD  10             ;DRAW LINE                           DTXT:  .ASCII"QDEMONSTRATION PROGRAMQ"
        .WORD  3140                                                      .EVEN
        .WORD  3140                                                      .END START
        .WORD  10             ;DRAW LINE
        .WORD  3140
        .WORD  2100
        .WORD  11             ;DRAW LINE (DEFERRED)
        .WORD  1220              ;ADDRESS OF DPT
        .WORD  10             ;DRAW LINE
        .WORD  1250
        .WORD  1250
        .WORD  10             ;DRAW LINE
        .WORD  420
        .WORD  2100
        .WORD  7              ;SET BEAM (DEFERRED)
        .WORD  1224              ;ADDRESS OF DPT1
        .WORD  10             ;DRAW LINE
        .WORD  7350
        .WORD  3140
        .WORD  10             ;DRAW LINE
        .WORD  4630
        .WORD  1250
        .WORD  10             ;DRAW LINE
        .WORD  5670
        .WORD  3770
        .WORD  10             ;DRAW LINE
        .WORD  6740
        .WORD  1250
        .WORD  10             ;DRAW LINE
        .WORD  4210
        .WORD  3140
        .WORD  6
        .WORD  1600
        .WORD  6000
        .WORD  13             ;WRITE TEXT ACROSS (DEFERRED)
        .WORD  1230              ;ADDRESS OF DTXT
        .WORD  6              ;SET BEAM
        .WORD  5
        .WORD  5000
        .WORD  14             ;WRITE TEXT DOWN
        .ASCII "!OCTAGON!"
        .EVEN
```

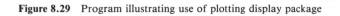

Figure 8.29 Program illustrating use of plotting display package

DEMONSTRATION PROGRAM

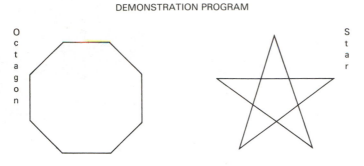

Figure 8.30 Display generated by program in Fig. 8.29

ing routines as well as required space allocations for data storage are shown in Fig. 8.27. A table defining the subset of ASCII characters that may be displayed is given in Fig. 8.28.

It is relatively easy to use this plotting package. A program illustrating its use is given in Fig. 8.29, and the display obtained by executing this program is given in Fig. 8.30. Although this package is easy to use, some modifications or extensions may be desired. Certain extensions are suggested in the Review questions and exercises at the end of this chapter.

Review

1. Refer to the following program. After this program has been executed, what geometric shape will be present on the display device?

```
          .GLOBL PLOT
  START:  CLR R0 ;R0 MUST BE CLEARED WHEN ENTERING PLOT!
          JSR R5,PLOT
          .WORD 0,3,6,4000,4000    ;SET BEAM
          .WORD 11,FIGURE,11,FIGURE+4,11,FIGURE+8.,0
  FIGURE: .WORD 5000,6000,6000,4000,4000,4000
          .END START
```

2. Refer to the 6 × 8 dot matrix in Fig. 8-22a. Identify the character corresponding to each of the following 48-bit words.
   (a) 042202   111222   066000
   (b) 177004   104004   177000
   (c) 177020   010020   017000

3. The software package discussed in this section does not have a routine for connecting several points together. Suppose two such routines, LINE and LINED, are developed. When the routine LINE is executed, the points immediately following the LINE command are connected together until a data word corresponding to a negative 16-bit number is encountered. The command LINED works in a similar manner except that the word following this command identifies the *address* of an array of data points. After each of these routines is executed, program control is to revert to the statement labeled STP. The interpreter command for LINE is to be the octal number 16, and the command for

LINED is to be the octal number 17. Modify the command interpreter shown in Fig. 8.23 to accommodate these new commands.

REFERENCES

ADV11-A, KWV11-A, AAV11-1, DRV11 Users Manual. EK-ADV11-OP-002. Maynard, Mass.: Digital Equipment Corporation, 1977.

ECKHOUSE, R. H., and R. L., MORRIS, *Microcomputer Systems.* Englewood Cliffs, N.J.: Prentice-Hall, 1975.

JERMANN, W. H., *The Structure and Programming of Microcomputers.* Palo Alto, Calif.: Mayfield Publishing Company, 1982.

Microcomputer Interfaces Handbook. Maynard, Mass.: Digital Equipment Corporation, 1981.

SHERR, SOL, *Electronic Displays.* New York: John Wiley, 1979.

EXERCISES

1. Develop and test a subroutine that prints the unsigned number stored in R1 by typing the corresponding six octal characters.

2. Develop and test a macro called TXTIN that functions in the following manner. When the program statements produced by this macro are executed, a string of characters entered on the console will be read (using the programmed mode) and stored in a buffer. Control will exit from this routine only if the carriage return key is pressed.

3. Formulate and test a macro TXTIN that has an argument TERM. When the program corresponding to this macro is executed, a string of characters entered on the console will be read and stored in the buffer using programmed input operations. Control will exit from this routine only if a key whose ASCII representation is identical to the value of the argument is pressed.

4. Refer to the subroutine CHECK in Fig. 8.7. Modify this subroutine so it will check to see if a particular four-character string is in the input buffer.

5. Refer to Exercise 4. Modify CHECK so it will accept an argument N. Then the routine will check to see if a particular N-character string is in the input buffer.

6. Refer to Exercise 5. Modify this routine so that the *address* of the source string rather than the string itself immediately follows the invoking statement.

7. Refer to Fig. 8.6. Design a system similar to the one shown in the figure that satisfies the following requirements.
   (a) A red light and a white light are to be controlled as specified in Example 8.5.
   (b) In addition, a motor is to be digitally controlled.
   (c) The motor will be turned on if and only if the word MOT is entered when the white light is on and the red light is off.
   (d) When the motor is running, it can be turned off by changing the state of either or both lights.

8. Refer to Example 8.5 and to the solution given in Figs. 8.6 and 8.7. Modify this solution so that both lights will be turned on if the word TWO is entered.

9. A 12-bit analog-to-digital converter operates over a range between 0 and 10 volts. A value of 10 volts corresponds to the octal number 0000, and a value of 0 volt corresponds to the octal number 7777. What octal number will be produced by the ADC when a voltage level of 3.2 volts is being read?

10. Suppose a 12-bit analog-to-digital converter operates over a range from -10.24 to $+10.24$ volts. Within what voltage interval does a particular binary number on the output lines of this device specify the value of a voltage?

11. Suppose the following command is executed on a PDP-11 computer that has an AAV11-A digital-to-analog converter such as described in Section 8.3.

```
MOV #3217.,DAC2
```

What voltage level will be sent out on DAC channel 2?

12. Design a PDP-11 program segment that requests a DAC channel number and a voltage. If a valid channel number and voltage value are entered, the corresponding voltage will be sent out on the designated channel. If an invalid entry is made, an error message will be printed.

13. Develop a subroutine that reads each of the 16 input channels on an ADV11-A analog-to-digital converter module. The routine prints a channel number corresponding to a channel in which the highest value of voltage is read.

14. A temperature transducer has a straight-line relationship between the temperature sensed and its output voltage. A temperature of 32° produces an output voltage of 3 volts, and a temperature of 100° produces an output voltage of -1 volt. The output of this transducer is connected to ADC multiplexer channel 5. What is the temperature when a conversion is made and the octal number 1234 is read on channel 5?

15. Refer to the specifications and system requirements given in Example 8.9. Suppose that after the subroutine MOTBCK has been executed the grappler mechanism still has overshot the desired position. Modify the software so that one more attempt will be made to correctly position the grappler arm. During this attempt, the nearly linear control motor is to be operated at approximately half of the very slow speed setting.

16. Refer to Review question 4 in Section 8.4 and to the corresponding solution given in Appendix D. Suppose the specifications given in the problem statement are truly desired. What is wrong with implementing the solution as shown?

17. Refer to the plotting package given in Section 8.5 Extend this package so that the small letters *a, b, c,* and *d* are included as part of the character set that can be displayed.

18. Refer to Review question 8.3 in Section 8.5. Develop the routines LINE and LINED as specified in this problem statement.

9

Efficient Implementation of Input/Output Activities

In Chapter 8, the use of programmed input/output operations was discussed. In most cases, this involves sensing a flag in a status register until the state of that flag indicates that a peripheral device has responded to a request. If extensive use is made of *programmed data transfers,* then most of the computer CPU cycles are waiting in loops for responses from external devices. This is not a very efficient use of the capabilities of a computer.

In this chapter we discuss *interrupt-driven* input/output data transfers. These differ significantly from programmed data transfers. When an external device is ready to participate in a data transfer activity, the device actively requests service. Therefore, it is not necessary for a program to consume computer cycles in a non-productive loop while waiting for peripherals to respond.

We also introduce concepts related to the efficient transfer of *blocks* of data. This is generally implemented through the use of *direct memory access* (DMA) data transfers. DMA data transfers are made directly between memory and peripheral storage systems. After a block transfer has been initiated, no active CPU intervention is required to complete the transfer. It is merely necessary to ensure that the system buses are performing no more than a single task at any one time.

9.1 PROGRAMMED INTERRUPTS AND TRAPS

Before discussing data transfers that are initiated through the use of *external interrupts,* let us first consider certain programmed operations that function in a similar manner. These commands are referred to as *software-interrupt* or *programmed trap* commands. These commands were introduced in Section 5.3.

As discussed in Section 5.3, there are four software-interrupt or trap-type commands—EMT, BPT, IOT, and TRAP. The mnemonic relationships of the first three commands refer to the phrases EMulator Trap, BreakPoint Trap, and Input/Output Trap. Each of these commands is encoded as a 16-bit or one-word command. However, only the most significant 8 bits of the TRAP and EMT commands are used to specify the command completely. Any 8-bit word may be placed in the least significant byte of each of these two commands. This byte is frequently used as a *data byte* or as an *identifier* related to a specific routine.

Each of these trap commands has a unique *vector* associated with it. The vector consists of two words: the *address* of a trap processing routine and a new *value* to be placed in the processor status word. Whenever one of these commands is being executed, the following sequence of events occurs:

1. The current number in the processor status register is pushed onto the stack.
2. The number in the program counter is pushed onto the stack.
3. The first word of the particular trap vector is placed in the program counter.
4. The second word of the particular trap vector is placed in the processor status register.

After this particular trap-type command has been executed, program control branches to the memory location identified by the first word of the trap vector. After the trap processing routine has been executed, program control normally reverts to the command immediately following the command that invoked the trap operation. This is accomplished by execution of either an RTI or an RTT command. Each of these commands will cause the two words on top of the stack to be popped into the program counter and processor status register, respectively. Identification of the various programmed trap vector locations is given in Section 5.3 and Appendix B.

It appears that the EMT command and the TRAP command serve identical functions. Users are generally encouraged to use the TRAP command if the user programs are to operate under a particular operating system, such as RT-11. If the operating system is to be used only to develop software dedicated to specific real-time applications, then the user may utilize EMT commands. Care should be taken, however, if system macros are included as part of the user's software package.

When an EMT command is being executed, program control will branch to the address specified by the word stored in octal location 30. A new number will be loaded into the PSW register from memory location 32. When system routines are utilized, the pointer in location 30 identifies the entry point to the system software package. Then the byte stored in the lower half of the word corresponding to the EMT command is used to identify the particular system routine that is being invoked. If an RT-11 system routine requires a data list, a pointer to this list is generally loaded into R0.

```
HI:       .ASCII /HI/<200>
          .EVEN
HOW:      .ASCII / HOW/<200>
          .EVEN
AREYOU:   .ASCII / ARE YOU?/<200>
          .EVEN
          .MCALL .PRINT,.EXIT
START:    .PRINT #HI
          MOV #HOW,R0              ;*** SAME AS THE
          EMT 351                  ;MACRO  .PRINT #HOW ***
          MOV #AREYOU,R0
          EMT 351
          .EXIT
          .END START
```

Figure 9.1   Program segment illustrating use of the EMT command

Refer to the program in Fig. 9.1. The .PRINT macro is invoked in this program segment. The .PRINT macro is translated into two machine-language commands. Refer to the two statements immediately following the statement START. These two lines of assembly-language code are translated into exactly the same machine code as if they were replaced with the statement .PRINT #HOW. When the EMT 351 command is executed, program control is transferred to the address contained in memory location 30. Here an EMT processing routine identifies the data byte that has an octal value of 351 and branches to an appropriate printing routine. This service routine transfers the characters to be printed to an output buffer and initiates printing using an interrupt-driven mode of operation.

Example 9.1

Develop and test an EMT processing routine. This routine checks the byte addended to the EMT command. If this byte has a value of 1, a message related to the EMT 1 command is to be printed. If this byte has a value of 2, a message related to an EMT 2 command is printed. If the byte has any other value, an error message is printed.

Solution   In order to implement the required software, the address of the user processing routine must be loaded into octal memory location 30. Then a corresponding processing routine must be developed. This routine will first check the value appended to the related EMT command and then invoke the corresponding service routine. Each service routine merely prints an appropriate message. An easy and efficient way to print a message is to use the system macro .PRINT.

However, as we may have observed from the previous discussion and inspection of Fig. 9.1, the .PRINT macro uses an emulator trap command. Therefore, the EMT address vector stored in location 30 must identify the entry point to the RT-11 software package. This seems to be a problem, as only one value can be stored in location 30 at any instant of time.

This difficulty is rather easy to resolve. Refer to Fig. 9.2. In the statement START, the address of the system EMT processing routine is stored in location ENTVTR. Then the address of the user EMT processing routine is loaded into location 30. When the first EMT command is executed, program control will branch to location 2000. At this step, the system EMT processing address is loaded into location 30. Then the argument of the EMT command is identified, and the appropriate service routine is called. After execution of this routine, the user EMT vector is restored, and control reverts to the

```
          .MCALL .EXIT,.PRINT
EMTVTR:   .BLKW                  ;SYSTEM EMT ADDRESS VECTOR
MYEMT:    .WORD 2000             ;USER EMT ADDRESS VECTOR
START:    MOV 30,EMTVTR          ;SAVE RT-11 EMT VECTOR
          MOV MYEMT,30           ;SET UP USER EMT VECTOR
          EMT 1
          EMT 47
          EMT 2
          MOV EMTVTR,30          ;RESTORE RT-11 EMT ADDRESS VECTOR
          .EXIT
.=EMTVTR+1000      ;EMT PROCESSING ROUTINE STARTS AT 2000
;** START USER EMT PROCESSING ROUTINE **
          MOV EMTVTR,30          ;SET UP RT-11 EMT VECTOR
          MOV (SP),R5            ;GET RETURN ADDRESS
          SUB #2,R5              ;POINT TO EMT COMMAND
          CMPB #1,(R5)           ;EMT 1 COMMAND?
          BNE UP                 ;NO
          CALL SERV1             ;YES
          BR DONE
UP:       CMPB #2,(R5)           ;EMT 2 COMMAND?
          BNE UP1                ;NO
          CALL SERV2             ;YES
          BR DONE
UP1:      CALL BAD
DONE:     MOV MYEMT,30           ;RESTORE USER EMT VECTOR
          RTI                    ;RETURN  FROM TRAP PROCESSING ROUTINE
;*** TRAP SERVICE ROUTINES START HERE ***
SERV1:    .PRINT #MES1
          RTS PC
SERV2:    .PRINT #MES2
          RTS PC
BAD:      .PRINT BADMES
          RTS PC
; ***    START MESSAGES   ***
MES1:     .ASCII /USER EMT 1 COMMAND!!!/<15><12><200>
          .EVEN
MES2:     .ASCII /USER EMT 2 COMMAND!!!!!/<12><15><200>
          .EVEN
BADMES:   .WORD NEXT
NEXT:     .ASCII /THIS EMT COMMAND IS NOT DEFINED./<12><15><200>
          .END START
```

Figure 9.2   A solution to Example 9.1

main program. Prior to execution of the .EXIT command, the system EMT vector is restored.

If a programmer does not know how the .PRINT macro is implemented, more than likely considerable difficulty will be encountered in developing a program to satisfy the specifications given in the problem statement of Example 9.1. In general, novices should avoid the EMT command and use the TRAP command instead.

The IOT and BPT commands also produce programmed traps. The BPT, or breakpoint trap, functions with its vector located at octal memory locations 14 and 16. When the T bit in the processor status word is set, a *breakpoint* trap using this same vector occurs at the end of execution of *each* instruction. Users should exercise caution in employing the BPT command when internal breakpoint traps are permitted to occur. Such internal traps are used by debugging packages, such as the ODT software package.

Review

1. Suppose you wish to locate the machine code used in implementing RT-11 system software that includes the code for the .PRINT macro. How can you locate the entry point into this software package?

2. Refer to Fig. 9.2. What output will be printed when this program is executed?

3. Refer to Example 9.1. Replace the word EMT with the word TRAP in the statement of program requirements. Modify and simplify the solution in Fig. 9.2 to satisfy the new program requirements.

9.2 USE OF INTERRUPT-DRIVEN I/O DEVICES

In Section 9.1, we introduced the use of programmed trap instructions. Now we will consider such operations when they are not programmed. Suppose an external device is ready to participate in a data transfer operation. Or suppose an external component in a computer-controlled system has an immediate need for service. This device will send a logic signal to the computer CPU. If the computer is in a state in which it is receptive to an interrupt request, it first completes the instruction that is currently being executed. Then it essentially executes a trap-type instruction using a vector that is associated with the particular device that is requesting the interrupt. This results in program control *vectoring* to an interrupt processing routine that will service the interrupting device.

Let us consider this situation in more detail. Suppose an external interrupt has occurred. At the completion of execution of the current instruction, program control will vector to an appropriate processing routine. The current contents of the processor status register, as well as the expected return address, will be stored on the stack. Then the interrupt processing routine is entered to service the requesting device.

In some hardware configurations, when an external interrupt signal is acknowledged and control is passed to an interrupt processing routine, the logic signal requesting service is automatically cleared. In other configurations, this request signal may not be cleared until the requesting device is actually serviced. In this situation, an external interrupt request is still active when program control is passed to the interrupt processing routine. It is important that this signal is not again acknowledged; otherwise an infinite loop situation will arise. The new word that is placed in the processor status register when an external interrupt is acknowledged establishes a new *operating state* for the computer. Generally, only an external device that is assigned a priority *higher* than that of the present operating state of the computer may produce an external interrupt.

There is one major task that an interrupt processing routine should accomplish: It should provide appropriate service to the device requesting the interrupt. When servicing is completed, program control returns to the program sequence being executed at the time the interrupt was first acknowledged. This is done by execution of either an RTI command or an RTT command. If an interrupting device has not been properly serviced, and if the interrupting signal was not cleared when the interrupt was first acknowledged, the device will still be requesting service. Because the original PSW is restored by execution of a return from interrupt command, program control will again pass immediately to the interrupt processing routine. Clearly, this results in an *infinite loop* situation.

A *trap* is very similar to an external interrupt. One difference is that a trap emanates from within the computer, and an interrupt is originated by an external device. Devices such as console keyboards, printers, mass storage devices, analog-to-digital converters, and programmable real-time clocks are external devices. The computer CPU, memory, and buses are generally internal devices. Various trap and interrupt vector locations for LSI-11 implementations of PDP-11 systems are given in Fig. 9.3.

Refer to Fig. 9.3. If an instruction attempts to access an invalid address, or if an invalid instruction such as JMP R5 is attempted to be executed, a trap to the address located in memory location 004 will occur. Similarly, if a binary number that is not a valid operation code for any computer instruction is fetched and placed in the instruction register, a trap to the address stored in location 010 will occur. An external device with a high priority is generally connected to an internal line

Reserved Interrupt and Trap Locations		
Identification		Vector addresses
Illegal Address and Invalid Instruction Trap		004 and 006
Illegal Instruction Trap		010 and 012
Breakpoint or T-bit Trap and BPT Command Trap		014 and 016
IOT Command Trap		020 and 022
Power Fail Trap		024 and 026
EMT Command Trap		030 and 032
Console Input Device Interrupt		060 and 062
Console Output Device Interrupt		064 and 066
External Event Line Interrupt		100 and 102
Floating Point Instruction Traps		244 and 246
Suggested Interrupt Vector Addresses for Peripherals:		
DRV11 Parallel Line Unit:	Interrupt A	300 and 302
	Interrupt B	304 and 306
ADV11-A Analog-to-Digital Converter	Conversion Done:	400 and 402
	Error	404 and 406
KWV11-A Real-Time Clock:	Clock Overflow	440 and 442
	ST2 Signal	444 and 446

Figure 9.3 Certain reserved and suggested locations for LSI-11 traps and interrupts

called the *event line*. Generally this device is a *line-time clock*. This produces an interrupt request every 1/60 of a second. Each interrupt causes a time-of-day counter to be updated. If floating-point operations produce an overflow, or if division by zero is attempted, a floating-point trap will occur.

The processor status register of a PDP-11 computer contains a 16-bit processor status word. Bits 7, 6, and 5 of this word are used to specify the current state of the machine. It is possible for a PDP-11 CPU to operate in one of eight different states identified by the numbers 0 to 7. Not all implementations of the PDP-11 can operate in eight meaningful distinct states. In particular, the LSI-11 implementation of the PDP-11 operates in just two states. These states may be referred to as state 0 and state 4.

Suppose an external device is requesting service from a PDP-11 CPU. The service request will be acknowledged if and only if the device has a priority *higher* than that of the current state of the CPU. On LSI-11 implementations, all external devices are considered to have a priority 4 level. Thus, if a machine is to be receptive to external interrupt requests, then the current state of the machine, as specified by the PSW, must be less than 4. Once an external interrupt has been acknowledged, it is generally not desired to have the current processing of the interrupting device interrupted by any device that does not have a *higher* priority. Therefore, when an interrupt is acknowledged in an LSI-11 system, the priority bits in the *new* processor status word should specify a priority of at least level 4. The M68000 processor described in Chapter 11 functions in a manner similar to a PDP-11 system that operates within all of the specified priority levels.

If a trap occurs, it will be processed regardless of which priority level is specified. If more than one trap request is present at any one instant, a set of priorities determines which trap is to be processed first. This differs with various implementations of PDP-11 systems.

There may be several external devices with the same priority level that are simultaneously requesting service. The priority in which these devices will be serviced generally depends on the relative positions in which they are connected to the system bus. Thus, the priorities may be selected by the system user.

Example 9.2

Develop and test an interrupt service routine that accepts characters from the console keyboard, echoes these characters, and stores them in a memory buffer.

Solution   A solution is given in Fig. 9.4. The test program begins at the line labeled START. The keyboard is programmed for interrupt-driven operations, and the operating system keyboard vector is saved on the stack. The test program terminates when the ASCII representation for a question mark is loaded into the buffer. Then the operating system keyboard vector is restored before program control reverts to the operating system.

Refer to the interrupt processing routine in Fig. 9.4. The first step in this routine reads the keyboard data register and loads it into the memory buffer. After

```
          .MCALL .EXIT
          TKS = 177560
START:    MOVB #100,TKS      ;SET KEYBOARD FOR INTERRUPT OPERATION
          MOV 62,-(SP)       ;SAVE RT-11 KB VECTOR
          MOV 60,-(SP)
          MOV #PROCES,60     ;SET USER KB VECTOR
          MOV #200,62        ;PRIORITY 4
BACK:     MOV BUFFER,R1      ;START TEST PROGRAM
          CMPB #'?,-(R1)     ;QUIT?
          BNE BACK           ;NO
          MOV (SP)+,60       ;RESTORE RT-11 VECTOR
          MOV (SP)+,62
          .EXIT
;**** USER KEYBOARD INTERRUPT PROCESSING ROUTINE ****
PROCES:   MOVB @#TKS+2,@BUFFER    ;READ KEYBOARD BUFFER
          BICB #200,@BUFFER       ;7-BIT ASCII CODE
          MOVB @BUFFER,@#TKS+6    ;ECHO
          INC BUFFER              ;ADVANCE BUFFER POINTER
          RTI
BUFFER:   .WORD BUFFER+2          ;BUFFER POINTER
          .BLKB 100
          .END START
```

Figure 9.4 Illustration of a keyboard interrupt service routine

the most significant bit is stripped from the input byte, the character is echoed. If it is valid to assume that the output device can respond as fast as a user can enter characters, there is no need to employ *handshaking* when sending characters to the printer buffer register.

Example 9.3

Develop and test a subroutine that initiates a string of 128 analog-to-digital conversions. Once initiated, the voltage inputs are to be sampled every 100 microseconds by the output of a real-time clock. The ADC is to operate in an interrupt-driven mode, and the results of the conversions are to be stored in a 128-word buffer.

Solution We will use the KWV11-A real-time clock described in Fig. 8.17 to initiate the conversions. We will use this device in the repeated-interval mode, and will employ a 1-megahertz clock rate. The conversions will be taken from the voltage input connected to multiplexer channel 13 of an ADV-11A analog-to-digital converter such as described in Fig. 8.10. An appropriate subroutine, interrupt handler, and test program are shown in Fig. 9.5.

Refer to Fig. 9.5. The subroutine identified by the label RDCH13 is used to initiate the conversion process. Just before the ADC is programmed for interrupt-driven operations, the ADC conversion complete flag is cleared. This is done by accessing the ADC data register. If this is not done, an interrupt will occur before the first conversion is actually performed. The entry point of the interrupt service routine is identified by the label ADCSRV. This routine reads the ADC data register, stores the value in a 256-word buffer, and tests to see if the buffer is full.

Refer to the test program beginning with the label START. When the routine RDCH13 is invoked, the real-time clock is programmed and started, and the analog-to-digital converter is programmed for interrupt-driven operations. Then control reverts back to the next step of the main program. For our example, this is the .TTYIN macro, but in general, any sequence or instructions may be placed here.

```
                      ;THIS SUBROUTINE SAMPLES CHANNEL 13 EVERY
            ;100 MICROSECONDS FOR 12800 MICROSECONDS.  THE
            ;VALUES OF THE SAMPLED POINTS ARE STORED IN A 128-WORD
            ;BUFFER.  THE REAL-TIME CLOCK IS USED TO INITIATE
            ;CONVERSIONS.  COMPLETED CONVERSIONS INITIATE INTERRUPTS.
            ;  THE HANDLER, ADCSRV, SERVICES THESE INTERRUPTS.
                      .MCALL .TTYIN,.EXIT
                      .GLOBL RDCH13,MYBUF        ;ENTRY POINT AND BUFFER
                      CLCNTR = 13       ;REPEATED INTERVAL OVERFLOW STARTS ADC
                      COUNT = -100.
                      ADCSTR = 6540   ;START ADC.  DRIVEN BY CLOCK OVERFLOW
                      ADCBUF = 170402 ;ADC DATA REG
                      ADCCSR = 170400 ;ADC C/S REG
                      ADCOFF = 0
                      CLKCS = 170420  ;CLOCK C/S REG
                      CLKBUF = 170422 ;CLOCK DATA REG
                      CLKOFF = 0
            RDCH13:   MOV #200,402      ;NEW PSW
                      MOV #ADCSRV,400 ;IDENTIFY ADC SERVICE ROUTINE
                      MOV #COUNT,CLKBUF        ;LOAD COUNT INTERVAL
                      MOV #CLCNTR,CLKCS        ;PROGRAM REAL-TIME CLLOCK
                      MOV #MYBUF,MYPTR        ;IDENTIFY BUFFER
                      TST ADCBUF              ;CLEAR ADC INTERRUPT FLAG
                      MOV #ADCSTR,ADCCSR      ;START CONVERSION OPERATION
                      RTS PC
            ADCSRV:   MOV ADCBUF,@MYPTR       ;READ DATA.  PUT IN BUFFER
                      ADD #2,MYPTR            ;UPDATE BUFFER POINTER
                      CMP MYPTR,#MYBUF+26.    ;BUFFER FULL?
                      BEQ UP            ;YES
                      RTI               ;NO
            UP:       MOV #CLKOFF,CLKCS       ;STOP CONVERSION PROCESS
                      MOV #ADCOFF,ADCCSR
                      RTI
            MYPTR:    .WORD  MYBUF    ;BUFFER POINTER
            MYBUF:    .BLKW  128.     ;BUFFER
            ;$$$$$$$$$$$$$$  START TEST PROGRAM  $$$$$$$$$$$$$$$$$$$$$
            START:    CALL RDCH13
                      .TTYIN
                      .EXIT
                      .END START
```

Figure 9.5   A solution to Example 9.3

Suppose the .TTYIN macro is replaced by a more meaningful sequence of instructions. These commands will be fetched and executed at the same time that the clock is operating and initiating conversions. Likewise, as conversions are being performed, commands will continue to be fetched and executed. This process will be interrupted only when a conversion is completed. Then the interrupt service routine will read and store the converted voltage value and return control to the main program.

Observe that the computing activities and the input-output activities occur simultaneously. This phenomenon is referred to as *concurrency*. Concurrent operations result in efficient use of computer resources. A number of different I/O operations may be in progress at the same time that computer instructions are being fetched and executed.

In modern computer systems, not only is there concurrency between the functioning of the processor and the I/O devices, but several processors connected to the same bus may be contributing to the performance of the same task. This type of processor concurrency is referred to as *parallel processing*.

Review

1. Modify the interrupt processing routine in Fig. 9.4 so that an appropriate message will be printed if the capacity of the input buffer is exceeded.
2. Develop and test a trap processing routine that prints an appropriate message whenever execution of an illegal instruction is attempted.
3. Develop and test a trap processing routine that prints an appropriate message if and only if floating-point division by zero is attempted. *Note:* When a floating-point trap occurs, the carry flag will be set if and only if this trap is caused by a division by zero operation.

9.3 DEVELOPMENT OF INTERRUPT AND TRAP HANDLERS

Interrupt service routines that perform the actual transfer of data to and from peripheral devices are referred to as *device handlers*. These routines are usually initiated as the result of a data transfer request. Operating systems such as RT-11 usually have a set of device handlers. A single device handler may include several subroutines, and the subroutines may be shared by different device handlers.

Operating systems frequently provide support for adding user-generated devices to a system, with specific commands for their installation. Specific information related to adding such software to an operating system is usually contained in the documentation describing the function of the particular operating system.

We will generalize the concept of a *device handler* and consider formulation of *interrupt* and *trap handlers*. Such handlers will be defined as the set of software required to service a particular interrupt or trap. In general, such handlers should possess the following attributes:

1. A handler should properly service the particular interrupt or trap request.
2. After service is completed, program control should resume with the contents of internal registers the same as before the exception occurred.
3. Unless specifically requested, the contents of the PSW should be identical to its value just before exception processing was initiated.

In addition to these requirements, a user must ensure that a proper interrupt vector identifies the particular interrupt service routine. These concepts are illustrated in Example 9.4, servicing trace traps. Recall that when the T bit in the processor status word is set, a trap occurs at the conclusion of execution of each instruction.

Example 9.4

Develop a trap handler that prints the contents of R1 and the contents of the program counter whenever a *trace trap* occurs.

Solution   Two main tasks are associated with developing a satisfactory solution to this problem. First, convenient software should be developed for initiating and terminating a trace. Then an appropriate handler should be written to satisfy user requirements. The user requirements stated in the specifications of this example are very simple. In order to implement a reasonably useful trace-trap handler, a considerable number of additions to this software package would be required.

Refer to the macros TRON and TROFF defined in Fig. 9.6. Also refer to the test program that uses these macros. The TRON macro is used to identify the trap handler and to set the T bit in the PSW. There is no explicit command available for setting this bit, so it must be set indirectly. The octal number 20 and the address CONT+2 are pushed onto the stack. The RTT command pops the address CONT+2 into the program counter, and pops the octal number 20 into the processor status word. Starting at the instruction stored in location CONT+2, a trace trap will occur after the execution of each instruction.

The macro TROFF is used to terminate the trace mode of operation. Execution of this macro results in a 0 being placed in the T bit of the PSW. If a user wishes to obtain a trace of a certain program segment, it is expected that just a trace of the user-generated program would be desired. It would be confusing to a user if the trace included the directives internal to the TROFF macro. In order to inhibit a trace of the instructions contained in this macro, a software flag TFLAG is cleared when initiating the trace and set when terminating the trace. When the trap handler finds that this flag is set, the trace display segment of this routine will be bypassed.

```
        .GLOBL MYHNDR,TFLAG
        .MCALL .EXIT,.PRINT
;THIS MACRO IS USED TO SET THE T BIT AND TO DEFINE A TRACE HANDLER
;A TRACE TRAP WILL VECTOR TO THNDLR
        .MACRO TRON THNDLR,?CONT
        MOV #THNDLR,14   ;SET TRACE VECTOR
        MOV #340,16
        MOV #20,-(SP)    ;SET T BIT
        MOV #CONT+2,-(SP)        ;PUSH STARTING TRACE ADDRESS
        CLR TFLAG               ;CLEAR TRACE FLAG
CONT:   RTT              ;SET T BIT AND START TRACE
        .ENDM
;$$$$$$$$$$$$$$$$$$$$$$$$$$$$$$$$$$$$$$$$$$$$$$$$$$$$$$$$$$$$$$$$
;TROFF IS USED TO CLEAR T BIT AND STOP TRACE
        .MACRO TROFF,?NEXT
        INC TFLAG        ;SET TRACE FLAG
        MOV #0,-(SP)
        MOV #NEXT+2,-(SP)
NEXT:   RTT      ;CLEAR T BIT
        .ENDM
;$$$$$$$$$$$$$$$$$$$$$$$$$$$$$$$$$$$$$$$$$$$$$$$$$$$$$$$$$$$$$$$$$$$$
;*** THIS PROGRAM TESTS THE TRON AND TROFF MACROS.
;    IT ALSO TESTS THE TRACE-TRAP HANDLER, MYHNDR
START:  NOP
        TRON MYHNDR      ;TURN ON TRACE.  USE MYHNDR
        MOV #6,R1
BACK:   NOP
        SOB R1,BACK
        TROFF    ;TURN OFF TRACE
        NOP
        NOP
        .EXIT
        .END START
```

Figure 9.6 Test program for trace-trap handler. TRON and TROFF macros are included

Refer to the test program in Fig. 9.6. The TRON statement defines the name of the handler to be used, which is MYHNDR. Execution of each subsequent step is traced until the TROFF statement is encountered.

Refer to the trap handler MYHNDR shown in Fig. 9.7. Initially, TFLAG is tested. If this flag is up, program control reverts to the program being traced through use of the RTT command. Note that it is essential to use the RTT command rather than the RTI command. A trace trap will *not* occur at the completion of an RTT command even though the T bit in the PSW is once again set. A trace trap will occur at the completion of an RTI instruction. Thus, if this routine is terminated with an RTI command, program control will immediately return to MYHNDR, resulting in an infinite loop.

Suppose, now, that the TFLAG is not up when MYHNDR is entered. Then the contents of registers R1 to R5 are saved on the stack. The number previously contained in R1 is pulled off the stack and placed in R3. This value and an appropriate address

```
            .GLOBL MYHNDR,TFLAG
            .MCALL .PRINT
;MYHNDR IS A TRACE-TRAP HANDLER
MYHNDR:  TST TFLAG
         BNE UP
         ;THIS ROUTINE PRINTS CONTENTS OF R1 AND PC.
         MOV R2,-(SP)
         MOV R3,-(SP)
         MOV R4,-(SP)
         MOV R5,-(SP)
         MOV R1,-(SP)
         MOV (SP),R3        ;GET CONTENTS OF R1
         MOV #FIRST,R4      ;LOCATION POINTER
         CALL LOAD
         MOV 10.(SP),R3     ;GET CONTENTS OF USER PC FROM STACK
         MOV #SECOND,R4     ;LOCATION
         CALL LOAD
         .PRINT #MES
         MOV (SP)+,R1       ;RESTORE REGISTERS
         MOV (SP)+,R5
         MOV (SP)+,R4
         MOV (SP)+,R3
         MOV (SP)+,R2
UP:      RTT
COUNT:   .BLKW 1
TFLAG:   .BLKW 1
MES:     .ASCII <12><15>/  R1 CONTAINS /
FIRST:   .BLKB 6
         .ASCII /.   THE PC CONTAINS /
SECOND:  .BLKB 6
FIN:     .ASCII /./<12><15><200>
LOAD:    MOV #5,COUNT
         CLR R2
         ASHC #1,R2         ;GET MOST SIGNIFICANT CHARACTER
         ADD #60,R2         ;CONVERT TO ASCII
         MOVB R2,(R4)+      ;PUT IN BUFFER
BACK:    CLR R2             ;GET REST OF CHARACTERS
         ASHC #3,R2
         ADD #60,R2
         MOVB R2,(R4)+      ;PUT IN BUFFER
         DEC COUNT
         BNE BACK
         RTS PC
         .END
```

Figure 9.7   Trap handler for Example 9.3

are used as arguments when the subroutine LOAD is invoked. The number previously in R1 is then converted to a string of six ASCII characters and stored in a data array. Similarly, the number in the program counter prior to execution of the trap is fetched from the stack, converted to an ASCII string, and stored in a data array. The .PRINT macro is used to display the array. Then the pretrap contents of the registers are restored, and program control exits from the trap handler.

There are some limitations to the use of the trace handler illustrated in Figs. 9.6 and 9.7. Both the TRON and TROFF macros modify the contents of the current PSW. Therefore, these macros should be used only when there is no harm done in modifying the contents of the current PSW. Clearly, neither the TRON nor the TROFF command should be used just prior to a conditional branch instruction.

The TRON and TROFF commands can be rewritten so that they do not change any bits of the PSW other than the T bit. One way to do this is to utilize programmed trap commands to implement each of these macros. After a programmed trap corresponding to the TRON command is executed, a BIS command can be used to place a 1 in the T bit of the PSW that has just been stored on the stack. Similarly, it is convenient to use a BIC command when it is necessary to clear the T bit of a PSW that is stored on the stack.

If TRON and TROFF commands such as suggested above are to be developed, either another macro or a subroutine, perhaps named TINIT, should be formulated. This program segment would be invoked before any TRON or TROFF commands are used, and would set an appropriate trap vector and identify the location of the programmed trap service routine.

The trace-trap handler shown in Fig. 9.7 generally will not trace any interrupt or trap service operations. If it is desired to trace such activities, the processor status word portions of the designated vectors should be modified so that each contains a 1 in the T bit location.

During a trace operation, it may be desired to pause after each trap and request user intervention. Facilities for inspecting any register, the PSW, or any memory location may be included as part of the trace-trap software package. Likewise, the user may be given an option to either continue or discontinue the trace mode of operation.

Developing handlers for sophisticated input/output devices requires precise information related to the functioning of the particular devices. Mass storage devices generally employ direct memory access data transfers (discussed in Section 9.4). In order to facilitate use of I/O devices, system macros related to specific devices may be included with operating system software. A brief introduction related to the use of such macros in conjunction with RT-11 device handlers is given in Section 9.5.

Review

1. Refer to the program in Fig. 9.6 and to the related trap handler in Fig. 9.7. When this program is executed, how many lines of output text will be printed?

2. Modify the trap handler shown in Fig. 9.7 so that the contents of the PSW rather than the contents of R1, as well as the contents of the PC, will be printed.

3. Refer to Fig. 9.6. Rewrite the macros TRON and TROFF so that they will not modify any bits of the current PSW other than the T bit. It is suggested that trap commands be used to implement these requirements. Also develop a subroutine TINIT that loads the appropriate trap vector. Be sure a routine is available to service the programmed traps.

9.4 DMA AND BLOCK DATA TRANSFERS

Programmed data transfers require monitoring and control of each byte or word of data that is transferred between memory and a peripheral device. Clearly, this is not an effective use of the capabilities of a digital computer. Interrupt-driven data transfers are much more efficient. When a byte or word is ready to be transferred, an interrupting signal generally results in control being passed to an appropriate service routine. Then the contents of certain registers are saved, the data are either read from or placed in a memory buffer, the contents of the registers that have been used are restored, and control reverts back to the pre-interrupt state. Even when interrupt-driven transfers are implemented, execution of several machine-language instructions is required just to transfer a single byte or word of data.

Although interrupt-driven data transfers are more efficient than programmed data transfers, such transfers are still not very efficient for moving *blocks* of data. A *block* of data consists of a set of contiguous data bytes or words. These words are stored in consecutive storage locations either in primary computer memory or on some secondary storage device, such as a disk or a magnetic tape. A block transfer consists of moving the entire set of *data* words. The word *data* may be slightly misleading. Words that are considered to be data during a transfer operation may actually be the statements of a computer program.

Block data transfers are normally implemented through the use of *direct memory access* (DMA) techniques. When a DMA transfer is made, it is done directly between memory and a peripheral device. No active CPU intervention is required. All the CPU does is release or give up control of the system bus long enough for the data transfer to be implemented. Then the CPU continues its normal operation. In some cases just a single machine cycle is required for the DMA transfer. The manner in which block data transfers are initiated is summarized in the following sequence of statements.

1. Under program control, command words are written into one or more device control registers. For example, suppose a block data transfer is to be made between a floppy disk unit and primary memory. Then the following information must be loaded into appropriate command registers:

   a. The identity of the particular unit of the peripheral device. *Note:* This may be uniquely associated with the particular address.

   b. The disk drive number.

    c. The direction of the data transfer. For example, is the transfer to memory or from memory?

    d. The course to be taken if errors occur. That is, if an error occurs, should this produce an interrupt?

    e. Specification of the track and sector of the disk and possibly identification of a starting address within this region.

    f. The interrupt state when the block transfer is completed. For example, will completion of a block transfer produce an interrupting signal?

2. A *current address register* is loaded. The contents of this register determine the starting address of the memory buffer used in the DMA data transfer.

3. A *word count* register is loaded. The quantity placed in the word count register identifies the *size* of the block of words to be transferred. In some systems a positive number is placed in a word count register. Frequently, a *negative* number or the twos-complement of a corresponding positive number is placed in the word count register.

4. A directive to *start* the block data transfer is loaded into an appropriate command register. This is the last programmed step related to the block data transfer.

After this sequence of events has been completed, a block data transfer between a peripheral device and memory will have been initiated. The computer CPU and the peripheral device essentially operate in parallel during the interval in which the transfer is being made. The parallel functioning ceases only during the brief intervals when the peripheral device requires immediate use of the system buses. The process is described by the following sequence of statements.

Suppose, for example, that a block of words is being transferred from a disk to memory, and the DMA block data transfer has been properly initiated. Then

1. The peripheral device retrieves a data word and places it in a data register that can be addressed by the CPU.

2. After the word is placed in the data register, the peripheral device sends a logical signal, frequently referred to as a HOLD signal, to the CPU.

3. When the CPU receives the HOLD request, it completes the current *machine cycle. Note:* A machine cycle is a portion of an instruction cycle. It generally consists of one memory reference cycle or the equivalent.

4. At the completion of this machine cycle, the CPU *floats* the *data bus,* the *address bus,* and, in some configurations, certain control lines. Floating these lines means that the CPU essentially disconnects itself from the lines. Technically, it may be said that the lines are placed in the *high impedance state.* Then the CPU sends out a logical signal sometimes referred to as a HOLD ACKNOWLEDGE signal.

5. When the peripheral device receives this logic signal, it uses the address bus and the data bus to transfer the word in the data register to the memory lo-

cation specified by the contents of the memory address register. Then the HOLD request is negated.

6. The current address register is incremented.

7. The word count register is decremented. *Note:* If a negative number is used in this register, the contents of this register are incremented instead.

> *Note:* Steps 5, 6, and 7 may be implemented in a single machine cycle.

8. After the HOLD request is negated, the CPU regains control of its buses and continues its normal functioning until the next HOLD request is made.

9. When the word count register *overflows,* the block data transfer is completed. An appropriate status bit is then raised in the device status register. If a suitable command was used in initiating the block data transfer, an interrupt signal will also be activated at this time.

DMA techniques are very efficient in implementing block data transfers. Such techniques are now commonly used even in small microcomputer systems. A single large-scale integrated circuit commonly referred to as a DMA controller is sufficient to interface appropriate devices to a computer system.

Review

1. Cite at least one major difference between interrupt-driven data transfers and DMA block data transfers.

2. Define or describe each of the following phrases:
   (a) floating or high impedance state
   (b) current address register
   (c) word count register

3. Suppose a block of 8-bit words is being transferred from an external device to a memory buffer. In this particular system, suppose that only negative numbers are loaded into the word count register. Just prior to initiation of the block data transfer, the octal numbers 012346 and 177400 are loaded into the memory address register and the word count register, respectively. After the block transfer is completed
   (a) How many bytes will have been transferred?
   (b) What octal number will be in the current address register?
   (c) What number will be in the word count register?

9.5 THE RT-11 INPUT/OUTPUT PROGRAMMING SYSTEM

In Chapter 8 and the first four sections of this chapter, we discussed techniques for implementing input and output data transfers. Most of these techniques require precise knowledge about the particular hardware being utilized. Routines that implement certain input or output activities were specially developed for particular applications. Such input/output activities are satisfactory when a computer system is dedicated to a single specific function. However, on more generally used and complex computer systems, users are seldom permitted to program specific input/output operations.

One function of an *operating system* is to control input and output activities. The software used for these activities may be referred to as an *input/output programming system.*

We already introduced in Chapter 6 two RT-11 macros that are used for I/O activities: the .PRINT macro and the .TTYIN macro. These macros facilitate certain input and output activities, and do not require any specific knowledge about the console keyboard or the console printer. Use of such commands presents certain advantages to a programmer. Some of these advantages are listed below.

1. These commands facilitate programming. Programmers do not have to identify various status and control registers, nor be aware of the significance of various bits in these registers. Instead, attention can be dedicated to the primary programming task.
2. Generally, system software is better written than user-developed software. Furthermore, certain working routines are used by a variety of devices.
3. Programs written using system routines are readily transportable to other environments. Programs can be written that are device independent.

RT-11 macro instructions used in conjunction with controlling peripheral devices are generally translated into *emulator trap,* or EMT, commands. Recall that an EMT command requires just 8 bits to implement, and the other 8 bits of the command word may be used as an argument to assist in specifying the precise directive.

The capabilities of the device handlers of the RT-11 operating system are quite extensive. It is not within the scope of this textbook to describe these capabilities fully or to describe the conventions required for their use. For these details, the reader is referred to the appropriate RT-11 documentation. We will, however, briefly introduce these capabilities and the techniques for using them.

Consider the sample program in Fig. 9.8. This program illustrates the use of an RT-11 device handler. In particular, the disk device handler software DX is utilized. This software must be resident in memory when the sample program is being executed. If a disk unit is being used as the *system volume,* this software should already be resident in memory. If not, the device handler must be loaded into memory. This can be done by using the RT-11 command INSTALL DX or the Macro-11 command .FETCH DX. Of course, it is required that the device handler that is being fetched actually be stored on the system volume. Handlers are generally not self-contained software packages, but require use of routines resident in the monitor portion of the operating system.

The example program in Fig. 9.8 illustrates renaming of a file stored on disk unit number 1 (DX1). *Linkage* between the user program and the device handler is through the use of system macros that are usually encoded as EMT commands. These macros must first be declared using the .MCALL assembler directive. This

```
;NOTE:      .MCALL .RENAME,.EXIT,.PRINT
START:      DX DEVICE HANDLER MUST BE RESIDENT IN MEMORY!
            .RENAME #AREA,#5,#BLOCK
            BCC DONE
            .PRINT #NOT
DONE:       .EXIT
NOT:        .ASCII /FILE NOT FOUND/<12><15><200>
            .EVEN
BLOCK:      .RAD50 /DX1/
            .RAD50 /SALLY/
            .RAD50 /MAC/
            .RAD50 /DX1/
            .RAD50 /BILL/
            .RAD50 /MAC/
AREA:       .BLKW 6
            .END START
```

Figure 9.8   Program illustrating the use of the RT-11 DX device handler

is an essential part of the necessary *preamble* required in the use of a handler. In the present example, only one system macro, .RENAME, is utilized in conjunction with the desired operation.

The task of the program in Fig. 9.8 is to rename a disk file. A file BILL.MAC is to be renamed SALLY.MAC. Observe that the program portion of the listing contains just four lines, and the specified task is accomplished through use of the single system macro .RENAME. This is just one of several powerful macros available for use with the DX device handler. This particular macro contains three arguments. In this example the argument list consists of

```
#AREA, #5, #BLOCK
```

Because system macros are implemented with EMT commands, provisions must be made for storing and accessing the specified argument list. This is done by placing the arguments in a data array. In this example, the location of the array is identified by the label AREA. When implementing the macro, the address corresponding to AREA is first placed in R0 before the emulator trap command is coded.

The second argument used by .RNAME identifies a *logical* channel number associated with this particular input/output activity. Any octal number between 0 and 377 may be selected, and this number is stored in 1 byte of the first word of the argument list. The other word of this argument list identifies the address of the block of data required for this particular activity.

In order to change a file name, both the old file name and the new file name are required. Such names could be specified as strings of ASCII characters. In RT-11 systems, such strings are usually represented in a more compact code referred to as a RADIX-50 code. This code permits a subset of the ASCII character set to be stored using a smaller number of bits of storage space. In particular, three characters rather than just two characters can be packed into a single 16-bit word. When performing a conversion to RADIX-50 code, strings are often specified in multiples of three characters. If they are not specified in such a manner, the .RAD50 assembler directive addends blanks to the strings until the number of characters is divisible by three.

Use of the .RNAME directive and the DX device handler greatly facilitates implementation of the desired operation. It is unnecessary for a programmer to make provisions for loading command registers or current address and word count registers. It is not necessary to formulate program segments required for monitoring status information or for loading vectors. Knowledge of the physical characteristics of the input/output device is not required. The particular routine that was employed even provides for the possibility that the source file name may not be present. If the source file name is located, program control resumes with the carry bit cleared. If it is not located, program control resumes with the carry bit set.

Use of the .RNAME macro is just one special example of the use of system macros available for use with the DX device handler. System macros are available for use with various device handlers that perform the following general functions:

1. Opening and closing files
2. Reading and writing files
3. General control of such input and output activities

A somewhat typical system macro is the .WRITE directive. This directive has the following format:

```
.WRITE area,channel,buffer,wordcount,block
```

where the elements of the argument list are defined as follows.

Area	The address of the array used to store the macro arguments.
Channel	An 8-bit logical channel number. The other byte of the first word of the argument block is used to store a *function* number. This number is used to assist in identifying the particular function (i.e., WRITE) by the EMT processing routine.
Buffer	The address of the memory buffer to be written on the storage device.
Wordcount	The number of words in the buffer.
Block	The block number on which the buffer is to be written. *Note:* A terminating word is required for the data list for this command. It has a value of 1.

A number of details must be attended to when utilizing RT-11 I/O macros in conjunction with specific device handlers. Users of these systems are encouraged first to consult the appropriate sections of the RT-11 system user's manual.

The program in Fig. 9.9 illustrates the use of an RT-11 disk handler. Various system macros are used to support writing a block of words on a floppy diskette. The program in Fig. 9.10 illustrates use of the device handler and related system macros for reading a block of words from a diskette. We shall not elaborate on the

```
;THIS PROGRAM ILLUSTRATES THE USE OF AN RT-11 DISK HANDLER.
;NUMBERS STORED IN BUFF ARE WRITTEN TO SECTOR 3 TRACK 2 OF A DISK.
          .MCALL .LOOKUP,.SPFUN,.PRINT,.EXIT,.WAIT,.FETCH,.CLOSE
START:    .FETCH #HSPC,DX ;FETCH DISK HANDLER
          .LOOKUP #AREA,#5,#DBLK  ;OPEN CHANNEL 5
          BCS LKERR           ;BRANCH ON ERROR IN CHANNEL
          .SPFUN #AREA,#5,#376,#BUFF,#3,#2,#0
                      ;WRITE (CODE 376) A 65-WORD BLOCK.
                      ;FIRST WORD IS A FLAG.  MUST BE 0.
          BCS SPERR         ;BRANCH ON ERROR
          .PRINT #DONE
          .WAIT #5          ;WAIT FOR I/O COMPLETION ON CHANNEL 5
          .CLOSE #5
          .EXIT
;
LKERR:    .PRINT #LKMSG
          .EXIT
SPERR:    .PRINT #SPMSG
          .EXIT
;
DX:       .RAD50 /DX/
SPMSG:    .ASCII /  SPECIAL FUNCTION ERROR  /<12><15><200>
          .EVEN
LKMSG:    .ASCII /  FILE ERROR  /<12><15><200>
          .EVEN
;
AREA:     .BLKW 10
DBLK:     .RAD50 /DX1/
          .WORD 0,0,0         ;FOR NON-FILE STRUCTURE
BUFF:     .WORD 0,1,2,3,4,5,6,7,10
DONE:     .ASCII /$$$ WELL DONE $$$$$$/<12><15><200>
          .EVEN
HSPC =.
          .END START
```

Figure 9.9   Program illustrating writing a block of words on diskette

specifics involved in utilizing these macros, as they are described in detail in appropriate RT-11 documentation.

Block data transfers such as those resulting from execution of the programs shown in Figs. 9.9 and 9.10 are generally DMA data transfers. Once initiated, I/O actions proceed concurrently with other currently active I/O devices as well as with processor activities. Suppose some computation-related commands are placed immediately above the .WAIT #5 command in the program in Fig. 9.9. The processor will execute these commands *concurrently* with the interrupt-driven printing activity initiated by the .PRINT #DONE command and the DMA block transfer activity initiated by the .SPFUN macro.

Review

1. Refer to the statement AREA in Fig. 9.8. The assembler directive .BLKW is used to reserve six words.
   (a) What is the minimum number of words that must be reserved in this array?
   (b) Identify the address that will be stored in the second word of the array.

```
;THIS PROGRAM ILLUSTRATES THE USE OF AN RT-11 DISK HANDLER.
;THE CONTENTS OF TRACK 3 SECTOR 2 OF THE DISK IN DX1 ARE
;READ INTO A MEMORY BLOCK OF 65 WORDS STARTING AT BUFF.
          .GLOBL BUFF,AREA
          .MCALL .LOOKUP,.SPFUN,.PRINT,.EXIT,.WAIT,.FETCH,.CLOSE
START:    .LOOKUP #AREA,#5,#DBLK  ;OPEN CHANNEL 5
          BCS LKERR        ;BRANCH ON ERROR IN CHANNEL
          .SPFUN #AREA,#5,#377,#BUFF,#3,#2,#0
                    ;READ (CODE 377) A 65-WORD BLOCK.
                    ;FIRST WORD IS A FLAG.  MUST BE 0.
          BCS SPERR        ;BRANCH ON ERROR
          .PRINT #DONE
          .WAIT #5          ;WAIT FOR I/O COMPLETION ON CHANNEL 5
          .CLOSE #5
          .EXIT
;
LKERR:    .PRINT #LKMSG
          .EXIT
SPERR:    .PRINT #SPMSG
          .EXIT
;
DX:       .RAD50 /DX/
SPMSG:    .ASCII /  SPECIAL FUNCTION ERROR  /<12><15><200>
          .EVEN
LKMSG:    .ASCII /  FILE ERROR  /<12><15><200>
          .EVEN
;
AREA:     .BLKW 10
DBLK:     .RAD50 /DX1/
          .WORD 0,0,0      ;FOR NON-FILE STRUCTURE
BUFF:     .BLKW 65.
DONE:     .ASCII /$$$ WELL DONE $$$$$$/<12><15><200>
          .END START
```

Figure 9.10   Program illustrating reading a block of words from diskette

2. The system macro .RNAME in Fig. 9.8 is implemented using two lines of code. The second line is an EMT command. What is the assembly-language statement corresponding to the first line of code?

3. Refer to Fig. 9.8. How many *words* of storage space are required in the list identified by the label BLOCK? That is, how many words of storage are used by the .RAD50 directives?

REFERENCES

ECKHOUSE, R. H., and R. L. MORRIS, *Minicomputer Systems.* Englewood Cliffs, N.J.: Prentice-Hall, 1975.

JERMANN, W. H., *The Structure and Programming of Microcomputers.* Palo Alto, Calif.: Mayfield Publishing Company, 1982.

IAS/RSX-11 MACRO-11 Reference Manual. Order No DEC-11-OIMRA-B-C. Maynard, Mass.: Digital Equipment Corporation, 1976.

RT-11 Advanced Programmers Guide. AA-5280B-TC. Maynard, Mass.: Digital Equipment Corporation, 1978.

EXERCISES

1. Suppose a programmed TRAP command is permitted to have an argument between 0 and 15_{10}. Develop and test an appropriate trap processing routine that reads the A/D channel corresponding to the trap argument and returns the value read in register R1.

2. Develop and test an IOT processing routine that functions in the following manner.
   (a) When the routine is entered, the word in the memory location identified by the contents of R0 is checked. If the number in this location has a value of 0, the command is considered to be an input directive. Characters are to be entered on the console keyboard and stored in the buffer identified by the contents of R0. This IOT procedure is to terminate when a *carriage return* is entered.
   (b) If the word in the memory location identified by the contents of R0 does not have a value of 0, the command is an output directive. The byte string in the corresponding buffer is to be printed. The string is terminated with a byte having a value of 0.

3. Develop and test a printer interrupt service routine that prints the contents of an output buffer identified by the pointer in R0. The string is terminated by a byte having a value of 0. When the terminating byte is encountered, the service routine reprograms the printer to operate in the *programmed* mode rather than in the *interrupt-driven* mode of operation.

4. Develop and test an analog-to-digital converter service routine that reads a converted number and places it in an input buffer.

5. Modify the routine developed in Exercise 4 so that a maximum buffer size is specified. If the maximum buffer size is exceeded, an appropriate message is to be printed.

6. Develop and test a trap processing routine that prints an appropriate message if a floating-point trap is produced by some floating-point error other than division by zero.

7. Develop and test a trace-trap processing routine that prints the value that is in *R6* just prior to the trap.

8. Develop and test a trace-trap routine that prints the contents of each of the eight general-purpose registers following execution of each user-defined instruction.

9. Develop a trace-trap routine that pauses and requests an input after each trap. The following are valid inputs: *P, Q,* and *R.*
   (a) If the input is *P,* the program is to proceed to the next step.
   (b) If the input is *Q,* the program should exit from the trace mode, and program execution should resume.
   (c) If the input is *R,* the contents of the eight registers should be printed, and another input should be requested.

10. Modify the program developed in Exercise 9 so that an *M* option is included. If the character *M* is entered, then the routine requests an octal address. When this address is entered, its contents should be displayed, and another input should be requested.

11. Suppose several different input/output devices employing DMA capabilities are contained in a computer system. Explain why the use of DMA data transfers significantly enhances the capabilities of this system.

12. Cite both advantages and disadvantages of using *system device handlers* and *system macros* as opposed to using user-generated input/output operations.

10

The 8086 Microprocessor

In Chapters 5 through 9, the architecture and instruction set of a particular computer were emphasized. The attributes discussed were common to a particular family of computers, the PDP-11 family. Inexpensive implementations of this computer CPU have been available for many years. The LSI-11 microprocessor consists of a PDP-11 central processing unit fabricated on either four or five large-scale integrated circuits. More recently, this CPU has been fabricated on a single chip. One version of this implementation is referred to as the T11, and another version of this microprocessor is called the F11. These chips are intended to be competitive with newer 16-bit machines.

The nomenclature PDP-11 represents a computing system that includes a PDP-11 processor, memory, control devices, and input/output devices. There are several popular models of this computing system. Furthermore, models with identical nomenclature may differ significantly. The peripheral devices and system software characterize a particular computer installation. The thread of commonality among PDP-11 computing systems is that each PDP-11 processor is capable of executing the same basic instruction set.

Until the beginning of the 1980s, 16-bit computers were associated with processors designed and manufactured by the company marketing the related minicomputers. Thus, entire systems were developed, marketed, and supported by a single company. Development of microprocessors caused a distinct change in direction in the computer industry. No longer was it practical for a single manufacturer to develop hardware, software, and supporting components for relatively inexpensive 16-bit computing systems. Even IBM, the giant in the computing industry, entered the personal computer market using a processor, supporting components, and system software developed and produced by separate organizations.

In order to study modern 16-bit machines, it is no longer practical to consider families of machines built and supported by a single organization. Rather, one should study the popular 16-bit microprocessors that serve as central processors for a number of computing systems.

One of the very early 16-bit microprocessors was the PACE, manufactured by National Semiconductor. Shortly afterward, Texas Instruments Corporation introduced its 16-bit machine, the TMS9900. More recently, three 16-bit microprocessors have been introduced. All three employ a relatively modern fabrication technology referred to as HMOS, or high-density metal oxide semiconductor, technology. This technology enables more components to be fabricated on a chip, and results in a faster operating speed.

The first of the three relatively modern 16-bit HMOS machines to be introduced was the 8086. This device and its supporting family of components was developed by the Intel Corporation. The CPU was developed with the constraint that it would, in some sense, be upward compatible with the very popular 8-bit machines, the 8080 and the 8085. The 8086 was developed using on-chip firmware. Then the Zilog Corporation developed its entry into the 16-bit market. Its chip, the Z8000, appears to be an enhancement of the 8086. Finally, Motorola developed a 16-bit machine that performs some operations on 32-bit words. Its entry into the 16-bit market, the M68000, is probably the most powerful of the three 16-bit HMOS microprocessors. However, new machines and enhancements of the earlier machines are continuously being developed.

At the time this textbook was being prepared, the 8086 family was the most popular of the newer 16-bit machines. The decision by IBM to utilize an 8088 microprocessor in its own entry into the personal computer market probably contributed to the popularity of the 8086 architecture. The 8088 microprocessor is a device that has 8086 architecture but just an 8-bit data bus.

Based on current trends, it appears that families of processors based on the 8086/88 and the M68000 will be widely used in the implementation of modern 16-bit computers. We shall introduce the attributes of each of these processors.

10.1 ORGANIZATION OF THE 8086

The 8086 microprocessor is a 40-pin large-scale integrated circuit. It utilizes a 16-bit data bus and a 20-bit address bus. Thus, it can address up to 2^{20} bytes of memory (more than 1 million bytes) without using memory management hardware. The 8086 function has two parallel units: the *bus interface unit* and the *execution unit*. Figure 10.1 illustrates the components of these two units.

The execution unit proceeds with execution of its current instruction while the bus interface unit continues to fetch instructions until the 6-byte instruction queue

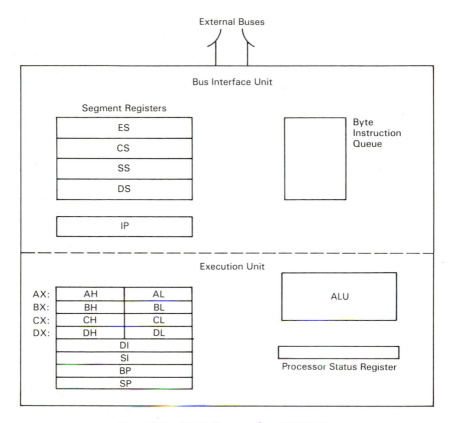

Figure 10.1   Block diagram of an 8086 CPU

is filled. This parallel operation enhances the overall speed of the processor. This process may be considered analogous to the use of a *cache memory*. Cache memory is a block of memory that has a very fast access speed. It is loaded with instructions (or with data) whose addresses are in the neighborhood of those currently being accessed by the processor. As long as memory references are currently being made within this neighborhood, all memory access operations can be done very rapidly using the cache memory with its rapid access capability. When a target address is not contained in the cache memory, the cache memory is reloaded from the slower primary memory.

The five registers shown in the bus interface unit are 16-bit registers. The IP register is the instruction pointer. This register is very similar to the program counter in the PDP-11. It is used in conjunction with another 16-bit register to provide the 20-bit address of the next instruction to be fetched. Its component of the address is referred to as the *offset*. The four remaining 16-bit registers are referred to as *segment* registers. CS, DS, SS, and ES refer, respectively, to the code segment, data segment, stack segment, and extra segment registers.

The numbers stored in each of the segment registers are used to identify a particular segment (or paragraph) of memory. The contents of a segment register can be used to identify a particular 64K-byte block of memory. (*Note:* 64K-bytes = 65,536 bytes.) The contents of a segment register are combined with an offset in a related register to produce a true 20-bit memory address. For example, the true address of an instruction to be fetched consists of the sum of the unsigned number stored in the instruction pointer and 16 times the number stored in the code segment register. Memory addressing is discussed in more detail in Section 10.2.

In Chapters 5 through 9, operations on 16-bit machines were discussed. The octal, or base-8, number system was used to identify numbers stored in memory or in the internal registers. This number system was used so that we would be consistent with the literature and specifications produced by the manufacturers of PDP-11 systems. However, most modern computer systems do not represent register contents and machine-language instructions using the octal number system. Instead, the base-16, or hexadecimal, number system is utilized (see Section 3.1). The hexadecimal number system will be utilized throughout Chapters 10 and 11.

Example 10.1

Suppose the contents of the 16-bit registers on a bus interface unit of an 8086 CPU are the following:

(CS) = $4A1B$ (DS) = 2222 (SS) = $ABCD$ (ES) = 047E (IP) = A832

From which address will the next instruction be fetched?

Solution   Recall that multiplying a binary number by 2 corresponds to shifting a string of binary characters one position to the left. Similarly, multiplying a hexadecimal number by the base-10 number 16 corresponds to shifting the string of hexadecimal characters one position to the left. Therefore, the address of the next instruction is 4A1B0 + A832 = 549E2.

The execution unit on the 8086 chip includes a set of eight 16-bit registers. These are not general-purpose registers, such as those included in the PDP-11 architecture. Four of the registers can be utilized either as 16-bit registers or as pairs of 8-bit registers. These are the AX, BX, CX, and DX registers. The second letter *H* or *L* appended to the register label refers to high-order or low-order byte of the register. This register group is sometimes referred to as a general register group.

The labeled names on each register group are significant. Although many common operations can be performed on each of these registers, the various registers also possess some individual attributes. The AX register can be used as a true *accumulator*. The results of certain operations must be stored in the accumulator. For certain commands, the BX register is used to store pointers, sometimes referred to as *base* pointers. Likewise, certain operations imply that a *counter* be stored in the CX register and *data* be stored in the DX register.

The remaining four 16-bit registers are used for various *pointers*. The SP register contains a 16-bit stack pointer. It is used in conjunction with the stack segment register to identify the top of the stack. A 20-bit address is used to identify the stack structure in memory. The contents of the stack segment register identify the general segment in memory, and the contents of the stack pointer identify the offset of this 20-bit address. The BP, or *base pointer,* register generally is also used in conjunction with the stack segment register. Access can be made to contents of a primary stack without changing the contents of the stack pointer register. The base pointer register is frequently used to identify local variable lists stored on the stack.

The SI and DI registers are used for indexed addressing. Source index addressing and destination index addressing may be accomplished using these registers and their corresponding segment registers. Generally, the contents of the source index register are used with the contents of the data segment register to obtain a true memory address. The contents of the destination index register are frequently used with the contents of the extra segment register in order to obtain a true 20-bit address. The index registers are also used for primitive string operations. For most cases these primitive string operations merely result in the contents of the corresponding index registers being automatically incremented or decremented.

Example 10.2

Suppose the contents of the various registers on an 8086 CPU are as follows:

$$(CS) = ABCD \quad (DS) = BCDE \quad (ES) = 8ABC \quad (SS) = 78AB$$
$$(IP) = 2222 \quad (SP) = FFFF \quad (BP) = 2345 \quad (SI) = 3333 \quad (DI) = 4444$$

Identify
(a) The address of the next instruction to be fetched.
(b) The address of the top of the stack.
(c) The address of the next source operand to be acquired using indexed addressing.

Solution   Address of the next instruction is ABCD0 + 2222 = ADEF2. Top of stack is 78AB0 + FFFF = 88AAF. Next source operand is BCDE0 + 3333 = C0113.

The 16-bit flag register is used to store the current status of the various control and status bits. The contents of this register are illustrated in Fig. 10.2.

The zero flag (Z), the carry flag (C), and the sign flag (S) perform the same functions as the corresponding flags on the PDP-11. The overflow flag (O) performs the same function as the V flag on the PDP-11. Recall that this flag is raised if the result of an operation on signed numbers cannot be properly specified due to the finite size of the registers. In an arithmetic operation, if a carry propagates into the high-order bit but not out of it, or vice versa, then the overflow flag will be set. Overflow of signed numbers was discussed in detail in Section 3.3.

The parity flag (P) is set if the low-order byte of a result has an even number

X	X	X	X	O	D	I	T	S	Z	X	A	X	P	X	C

Figure 10.2   8086 status flag register

of ones. The direction flag (D) is either set or cleared by a program command. If it is set, the contents of the source and destination index registers are automatically decremented after they are utilized for string operations. If the data direction bit is cleared, these registers are automatically incremented. The auxiliary or half-carry bit (A) is used only in conjunction with binary coded decimal operations. Such operations were described in Section 3.5. Recall that the auxiliary carry bit is raised if an arithmetic operation causes a carry to be produced out of the lowest nibble (half-byte) of the result.

The interrupt bit (I) and the trap bit (T) are similar to the corresponding control bits in the PDP-11 processor status word. A 1 in the I bit permits external interrupts to be processed. A 0 in this bit disables all interrupts except nonmaskable interrupts. If a 1 is placed in the T bit, just a single instruction is executed before a trap occurs. This mode of operation is used for program debugging. There are 7 unspecified bits in the flag register. Generally, these bit positions are occupied by logic zeros.

Example 10.3

An 8086 instruction has just been executed. This instruction added together the following two numbers: $7F3A$ and $6ABC$. The processor is programmed to accept interrupts and is not in a single-step mode. Index registers are to be incremented during string operations. What number is in the flag register immediately after the addition instruction is completed?

Solution From the problem conditions, the interrupt flag is set, the data direction bit is cleared, and the trap bit is cleared. The sum of $A + C$ produces a carry, so the auxiliary carry bit is set. The sum of two positive numbers produces a negative number. Thus, the overflow bit and the sign bit are set, and the zero flag and the carry flag are cleared. The sum of the lower bytes produces the number $F6$. When expressed in the binary number system, this number has an even number of ones. Thus, the parity bit is set. The resulting number in the flag register is 0000101010010100 (base-2) = $0A94$ (base-16).

Review

1. List similarities and differences between the 8086 architecture and the PDP-11 architecture.

2. Suppose an 8086 processor is executing a jump-type instruction. What must be done with the contents of the instruction queue located in the bus interface unit?

3. The registers on an 8086 CPU contain the following numbers

$$(CS) = A11B \quad (DS) = B22A \quad (SS) = C339$$
$$(ES) = 2EA0 \quad (IP) = 789A \quad (AX) = 3456$$
$$(BX) = 2305 \quad (CX) = 4567 \quad (DX) = 789A$$
$$(SP) = 1579 \quad (BP) = 268A \quad (SI) = 1111 \quad (DI) = 2222$$

(a) From which address will the next instruction be fetched?
(b) What address identifies the top of the stack?

(c) What 20-bit address is identified by the contents of the base-pointer register?

(d) What 20-bit address is identified by the contents of the source index register?

4. Refer to Review question 3. Suppose that prior to execution of an instruction, the flag register contains all zeros. Then an instruction is executed. The instruction adds the number *E20A* to the accumulator. After the instruction is completed

(a) What number will be in register AX?

(b) Which register in the bus interface unit will have its contents changed?

(c) What will be the new contents of the flag register?

5. Refer to Review questions 3 and 4. After the addition operation is performed, a primitive string operation is performed. This operation moves a byte from one memory location to another memory location. (*Note:* Index addressing is used for string operations.)

(a) What is the address of the source operand?

(b) What is the address of the destination operand?

(c) What numbers will be in the source index register and in the destination index register after the instruction is completed?

10.2 ADDRESSING TECHNIQUES FOR THE 8086

The registers available to a programmer on the 8086 CPU are 16-bit registers. Each memory address is a 20-bit address. As discussed in the previous section, addresses are obtained by combining a segment identifier stored in an appropriate segment register with a 16-bit offset. Unless specifically overridden, certain registers are assigned corresponding segment registers. For example, an instruction address is always obtained by combining the number stored in the instruction pointer with the number stored in the code segment register. The assignment of the code segment register to specify an instruction address can never be overridden. Assignments of other segment registers generally can be overridden by specifying an appropriate prefix to an instruction.

A variety of addressing modes are available on the 8086. These modes may be summarized under the following classifications:

1. Immediate addressing
2. Direct addressing
3. Relative addressing
   a. With a specified displacement
   b. With no specified displacement
4. Stack addressing

The addressing modes associated with the 8086 CPU are relatively easy to understand. However, descriptive terminology used to classify these modes can become quite confusing. We shall avoid much of this descriptive terminology.

The modes of addressing on the PDP-11 are very systematic and well ordered. All 16-bit registers are general-purpose registers. The only inherent assignments require that R7 be the program counter and R6 the system stack pointer. All addressing modes are general. That is, any register can be used like any other register. Immediate, absolute, and relative addressing are special cases of the general addressing modes. For example, there are no special instruction codes or special restrictions when using immediate addressing. The instruction MOV #5, R3 not only satisfies the definition of immediate addressing but is also an application of mode 2, register 7 addressing. The instruction MOV R3, #5 is equally valid, but it is difficult to interpret in terms of immediate addressing.

The modes of addressing on the 8086 are very powerful. However, they are considerably less general than those used on the PDP-11. Instructions utilizing immediate addressing have a different operation code from those not using immediate addressing. Most two-operand instructions involve one word (or byte) that is stored in one of the registers on the execution unit and one word (or byte) that is stored either in one of these registers or in memory. For most instructions, the destination operand can be placed in any register or memory location. For some instructions, the various registers have well-defined uses. These uses were outlined in the previous section.

Recall that all primary memory addresses on an 8086 system are 20-bit addresses. The true address of an instruction is obtained by adding the 16-bit offset to 16 times the number stored in a related segment register. For instruction addresses the instruction pointer is always used with the code segment register. The stack pointer is always used with the stack segment register. Similarly, when primitive string operations are used, the contents of the destination index register are always used in conjunction with the contents of the extra segment register. All other addresses may be determined by explicitly assigning a segment register to be used with operand addressing. If an explicit assignment is not made, certain default segment registers are used. These default registers are as follows. Data references involving use of the base pointer (BP) use the stack segment register. All other data references are determined using the data segment register.

There are some complexities associated with use of segment registers and 20-bit addresses. There are 2^{16} memory addresses within a segment. However, many more memory addresses are not within the segment. Addresses that can be obtained within a segment are referred to as *intrasegment* operands. The operand is said to be of NEAR type. Operands that cannot be obtained unless the contents of a segment register are changed may be referred to as *intersegment* operands. They are referred to as FAR-type operands. If a program segment does not involve any operations on segment registers, then it is very easy to execute this program from any area of memory. Such program segments are said to be *dynamically relocatable*.

A general format for an 8086 instruction is given in Fig. 10.3. Addressing on the 8086 CPU is determined primarily by the contents of the address byte. This byte specifies how an address offset is determined. The contents of this byte are specified by the following fields:

Mode (2 bits)	Register (3 bits)	Register or Memory (3 bits)

[PFX1],[PFX2],[PFX3],CODE,[ADDR],[DISPL],[DISPH],[IMML],[IMMH]

Notes:

0. If direct addressing is used, DISPL and DISPH specify the address.

1. Bytes enclosed within brackets are either optional or required only for specific instructions.

2. The CODE byte specifies the instruction. In some cases certain bits of the address byte are used to refine the instruction further.

3. The displacement bytes are used for relative addressing. If 2 bytes are used, the low-order byte precedes the high-order byte.

4. Immediate operands follow displacement bytes. If 2 bytes are used, the low-order byte precedes the high-order byte.

5. Instruction prefix bytes are sometimes used to refine instructions. These prefix bytes can be used for:
   a. Segment override
   b. Causing repetition of a string instruction
   c. Locking out or preventing external devices from gaining control of the sytem bus until the instruction is completed.

Figure 10.3   Instruction format for an 8086 instruction

This byte is usually specified using the following abbreviations:

mod	reg	r/m

It is generally the second byte of an instruction. Any bytes preceding the operation code are referred to as instruction prefixes.

The register assignments are not always needed in a two-operand instruction. For example, when an immediate operand is used, the r/m bits specify the second or destination operand. In this case the 3 bits stored in the register field may be used for instruction refinement. When the register bits are needed, the contents of the register field are interpreted as shown in Fig. 10.4.

2-byte operand (w = 1)		1-byte operand (w = 0)	
Designation	Register	Designation	Register
000	AX	000	AL
001	CX	001	CL
010	DX	010	DL
011	BX	011	BL
100	SP	100	AH
101	BP	101	CH
110	SI	110	DH
111	DI	111	BH

Figure 10.4   Designation for register field of address byte

r/m	mod 00	mod 01	mod 10	mod 11
000	BX + SI	BX + SI + DISPL	BX + SI + DISP	Note 1
001	BX + DI	BX + DI + DISPL	BX + DI + DISP	
010	BP + SI	BP + SI + DISPL	BP + SI + DISP	
011	BP + DI	BP + DI + DISPL	BP + DI + DISP	
100	SI	SI + DISPL	SI + DISP	
101	DI	DI + DISPL	DI + DISP	
110	DISP	BP + DISPL	BP + DISP	
111	BX	BX + DISPL	BX + DISP	

Notes:
  1. Operand is in register. For mode 11, register designators as given in Fig. 10–4 specify operand.
  2. For mode 01, displacement is an 8-bit signed displacement.
  3. Mode 00,r/m 110 is referred to as direct addressing.

Figure 10.5   Specification of offset by contents of address byte

The addressing modes are specific interpretations of the contents of the address byte of an instruction. These are defined as shown in Fig. 10.5. The 16-bit offset identified by the contents of the table in Fig. 10.5 is frequently referred to as an effective address.

Note from Fig. 10.5 that the difference between mode 01 and mode 10 involves the size of the displacement. In mode 01, the displacement is an 8-bit signed word.

In order to illustrate the various addressing modes, we will use two 8086 instructions, a MOVE instruction and an ADD instruction. The code for a register to memory/register or a memory/register to register MOVE operation is the binary number

$$1 \quad 0 \quad 0 \quad 0 \quad 1 \quad 0 \quad d \quad w.$$

The least significant bit, w, indicates whether the operands are bytes or words. A value $w = 1$ indicates word operands, and a value $w = 0$ indicates byte operands. The bit labeled d indicates the direction of the operation. If $d = 0$ the contents of the specified register are the source operand. If $d = 1$ the specified register is the destination.

Example 10.4

For each of the following instructions, indicate the location of the source operand and the location of the destination operand. Prior to instruction execution, the following hexadecimal numbers are contained in the various registers.

(CS) = 1111   (DS) = 2222   (SS) = 3333   (ES) = 4444
(AX) = 5555   (BX) = 6666   (CX) = 7777   (DX) = 8888
(SI)   = 9999   (DI) = 1234   (BP) = BBBB   (SP) = CCCC

Note: Assume the above conditions hold prior to execution of each of the following instructions.

Instruction (binary)						Instruction (hexadecimal)
(a) 10001001	01	110	110	00000001		89 76 01
(b) 10001011	00	001	010			8B 0A
(c) 10001011	01	000	001	11111110		8B 41 FE
(d) 10001001	10	111	011	00011111	10101010	89 BB 1F AA
(e) 10001010	00	110	110	00011111	10101010	8A 36 1F AA
(f) 10001000	11	010	111			88 D7

Solution   **(a)** Word operand. Source operand is in source index register. Offset for destination address is BBBB + 01 = BBBC. Segment register is the stack segment register. Therefore, the destination address is 3EEEC. *Note:* This means that the low-order byte of the word will be moved to 3EEEC, and the high-order byte to memory location 3EEED.

   (b) Word operand. Destination is the CX register. Offset for the source operand is the 16-bit sum of BBBB + 9999, which is 5554. Because the base pointer was used, the appropriate segment register is the stack segment register. Therefore, the source address is 38884.

   (c) Word operand. Destination is the AX register. Offset for source operand is 6666 + 1234 + signed displacement. The signed displacement expressed as a 16-bit word is FFFE. The data segment register is used. Therefore, the address of the source operand is 29AB8.

   (d) Word operation. Source operand is in DI register. Offset for destination address is (BP) + (DI) + AA1F = 780E. The destination address is 3AB3E.

   (e) Byte operation. The mode of addressing is direct addressing. Destination is the DH register. Offset for source address is AA1F, and the source address is 2CC3F. *Note:* The byte stored in this address is the source operand.

   (f) Byte operation. This instruction moves the number stored in the DL register into the BH register.

If an instruction utilizes immediate addressing, then only a destination operand is required. There is no need for a direction bit in the operation code. Consider the code for the ADD IMMEDIATE operation.

```
1 0 0 0 0 0 s w     mod 000 r/m
```

There is no need to specify a register. If a register is the desired destination, then mode = 11 can be used, and the last 3 bits of the address byte are used to specify the destination register. Therefore, the 3 bits normally used for register specification are used to complete the operation code for the ADD IMMEDIATE instruction. The least significant bit, w, in the command is used as before to indicate whether the operand is a byte or a word operand. Suppose the operation is a word operation. Further suppose the immediate operand is either a small positive number or a negative number having a small magnitude. It is not practical to specify the immediate operand as a 2-byte word. If s is set equal to 1, then such an operand is expressed using just a single byte.

Example 10.5

Prior to execution of each of the following instructions, assume the contents of the CPU registers are the same as specified in Example 10.4. What is done by each of the following instructions?

(a) 10000001   10   000   100   00110100   00010010   01111000   01010110
     or expressed in hexadecimal: 81   84   34   12   78   56

(b) 10000000   11   000   000   00010010
     or expressed in hexadecimal: 80   *C*0   12

(c) 10000011   11   000   000   11110101
     or expressed in hexadecimal: 83   *C*0   *F*5

     Solution   (a) The hexadecimal number 5678 is added to the word identified by the address 2CDED.

                (b) The hexadecimal number 12 is added to the contents of the AL register.

                (c) The number *FFF*5 is added to the AX register.

As shown in Fig. 10.3, instructions may be preceded by one or more instruction prefixes. One instruction prefix is referred to as a *segment override* prefix. If an instruction prefix is used, the default segment registers are no longer used in computing a true 20-bit address. Recall that the code segment register is always used with the instruction pointer in determining instruction addresses. Similarly, the stack pointer is always used with the stack segment register. In string operations, the destination index register is always used with the extra segment register. Other default segment register assignments may be overridden in an instruction by use of a segment override prefix. The format for this 1-byte command is

```
001 reg 110
```

where one of the following codes is used to specify the desired segment register.

```
ES:00 CS:01 SS:10 DS:11
```

Example 10.6

Prior to execution of each of the following instructions, assume the contents of each of the CPU registers are the same as specified in Example 10.4. What is done by each of the following instructions?

(a) 001   01   110   10000001   10   000   100   00110100
     00010010   01111000   01010110
     or expressed in hexadecimal: 2*E*   81   84   34   12   78   56

(b) 001   11   110   10001011   00   001   010
     or expressed in hexadecimal: 3*E* 8*B* 0*A*

(c) 001   00   110   10001000   01   110   110   00000001
     or expressed in hexadecimal: 26   89   36   01

Solution   **(a)** The hexadecimal number 5678 is added to the word stored in address 1BCDD. (*Recall*: Low-order byte is in 1BCDD and high-order byte is in 1BCDE.)
(b) The word stored in location 27774 is moved into the CX register.
(c) The number in the source index register is moved to address 4FFFC.

The addressing modes enumerated at the beginning of this section are immediate, direct, relative, and stack addressing. The first three modes of addressing have been illustrated. Stack addressing merely indicates that operations are being performed on the stack. Examples of such commands are PUSH and POP commands.

Review

1. Compare and contrast addressing modes used on the 8086 CPU with those used on the PDP-11.

   The following information refers to Review questions 2, 3, and 4. Prior to execution of each instruction, suppose that the registers on an 8086 CPU contain the following hexadecimal numbers:

(CS)	= *CFFF*	(DS) = 8000	(SS)	= 4000	(ES)	= 0000
(IP)	= 0000	(AX) = 1122	(BX)	= 3344	(CX)	= 5566
(DX)	= *FF*00	(BP) = 99*AA*	(SP)	= *BBCC*	(SI)	= *DDEE*
(DI)	= *FF*00					

Also suppose that the following numbers are stored in the indicated memory addresses.

Memory Range	Number Stored (hexadecimal)
00000-3FFFF	12 is stored in odd addresses
	13 is stored in even addresses
40000-7FFFF	56 is stored in odd addresses
	78 is stored in even addresses
80000-BFFFF	9*A* is stored in odd addresses
	BC is stored in even addresses
C0000-CFFEF	*DE* is stored in odd addresses
	*F*0 is stored in even addresses
D0010-FFFFF	*DE* is stored in odd addresses
	*F*0 is stored in even addresses

2. For each of the following commands, identify the location of the source operand and the location of the destination operand.
   (a) 10001001   01   001   011   01111111
   (b) 001   00   110   10001011   01   011   010   10001111
   (c) 10001001   00   001   110   00001111   00010010

3. What is done by each of the following instructions?
   (a) 001   01   110   10000000   00   000   001   01100111
   (b) 10000001   10   000   000   00000001   00000010   00000011   00000100
   (c) 00000000   00000000

4. Execution of each of the following instructions will change the contents of some registers and/or some memory locations. For each of the following instructions, identify those locations in which the contents will be changed. What are the new contents of each of these locations?
   (a) 10001011   11   110   011
   (b) 10000011   00   000   111   10000000
   (c) 001   00   110   00000001   01   001   100   11111110

5. Refer to the register and memory assignments for Review questions 2, 3, and 4. Why were the contents of memory not specified between memory locations CFFF0 and D000F?

10.3 THE 8086 INSTRUCTION SET

To a large extent, the relative value of a microprocessor is closely related to the capabilities of its instruction set. Some computers—sometimes referred to as reduced instruction set computers—possess very weak instruction sets. For very specific applications it may be beneficial to use computers with these limited instructions. However, for most general-purpose applications, powerful instruction sets facilitate both software development and the overall development of computer-controlled systems.

A complete listing of an 8086 instruction set may be obtained from the manufacturer or an authorized representative. We shall not attempt to illustrate all of these instructions. Many of the instructions are very similar to those used on the PDP-11, others are relatively simple and need no clarification or discussion. We will discuss those instructions that are somewhat different from those previously encountered.

The instructions may be classified under the following categories:

1. Move-type instructions
2. Arithmetic and logic operations
3. Decimal adjust commands
4. Stack operations
5. Input/output commands
6. Shift and rotate commands
7. String operations
8. Control transfer instructions
9. Processor control operations
10. Special instructions

Move-type instructions are similar to those used on the PDP-11. The source operand is moved to the destination address, but the contents of the source address are not changed. The XCHG, or exchange, instruction moves the source operand to the destination location and the destination operand to the source location. The second byte of these instructions is the address byte discussed in the previous section. Therefore, at least one of the operands must be located in a register.

Load and store commands are also move-type commands. Recall that an address is defined by both a segment and an offset. Therefore, to load or store a true address, two words are involved. For example, the LDS command loads a word from memory into the specified register and then loads the following word into the DS segment register. The LES command performs a similar function but uses the ES segment register. Corresponding store commands are not available. To store a true address in memory, two move register to memory commands may be utilized.

Example 10.7

What function is performed by each of the following instructions?

	Mnenomic	Code
(a)	LES DI,[BX]	11000100 00 111 111
(b)	XCHG AH,AL	10000110 11 000 100

Solution (a) The word identified by the segment in the DS register and the offset in the BX register is loaded into the destination index register. The word stored in the next memory location is loaded into the extra segment register. *Note:* The proper assembly-language syntax for this command is LES DI, DWORD PTR [BX]. The text DWORD PTR indicates that the operand in memory is a double word, or 4 bytes.

(b) The byte in the AH register is exchanged or swapped with the byte in the AL register.

Note: When mnemonics are used to describe operations with double operands, the destination operand precedes the source operand.

A variety of arithmetic and logic operations are available in the 8086 instruction set. Many of these are very similar to instructions that have previously been discussed and illustrated. Such arithmetic instructions are the following:

ADD	Addition
SUB	Subtraction
INC	Increment or add 1
DEC	Decrement or subtract 1
NEG	Negate or take twos-complement
CMP	Compare or subtract and discard results

Similarly, logic instructions that have previously been discussed or illustrated for the PDP-11 are the following:

NOT	Complement or take ones-complement
AND	Logic AND operation
OR	Logic OR operation
TEST	Logic AND operation and discard result
XOR	Logic EXCLUSIVE OR operation

Several of the arithmetic and logic operations are different from those previously discussed. The ADC, or add with carry, operation performs a conventional ADD operation. In addition, it adds the value of the previous carry bit to the result. The SBB, or subtract with borrow, command performs a similar function. Hardware fixed-point multiplication and division commands are also available in the 8086 instruction set. Both unsigned operations MUL and DIV and signed operations IMUL and IDIV are available. The results of multiplying 8-bit operands are always stored in the AX register. The results of multiplying 16-bit operands are always stored in the 32-bit register obtained by concatenating the DX register with the AX register. Division operations are defined such that they are inverse operations as compared to multiplication operations.

Recall that numbers transmitted between computers and external devices frequently are representations of base-10 or decimal numbers. Such numbers may be represented as strings of ASCII characters or as strings of binary coded decimal numbers. Such representations were discussed in Section 3.4. Some computers require that these numbers first be converted to binary numbers. Then operations are performed on the binary numbers, and the results are converted back to ASCII or BCD format before they are output to peripheral devices. Most modern microprocessors as well as some of the early mainframe computers permit some operations to be performed directly on decimal representations of numbers.

Example 10.8

Consider the following commands:

```
ADD  AL,CL
DAA
```

Suppose, initially, the number in the AL register is 27H (the hexadecimal number 27) and the number in the CL register is 55H. These are BCD representations for the base-10 numbers 27 and 55. What number will be in the AL register at the conclusion of the two commands?

Solution After the first command is executed, the number 7CH will be in the AL register. This is not a valid BCD number. After the DAA (decimal adjust operation) is performed, the number 82H will be in the AL register. This is not only a valid BCD number but is the correct result for addition of the two BCD numbers.

The decimal adjust-type commands that are available on the 8086 are the following:

AAA	ASCII adjust for addition
DAA	Decimal adjust for addition
AAS	ASCII adjust for subtraction
DAS	Decimal adjust for subtraction
AAM	ASCII adjust for multiplication
AAD	ASCII adjust for division

These commands are described in detail in instruction sets furnished by the manufacturer.

There are several 8086 commands that result in operations on the system stack. We are referring to the stack that is defined by the segment value in the SS register and the offset in the SP register. There are just four commands that explicitly operate on the stack. These commands are the following:

PUSH	Pushes a register or memory word onto stack
POP	Pops top word of stack into a register or memory location
PUSHF	Pushes flag register onto stack
POPF	Pops top of stack into flag register

Several other commands also implicitly affect the stack. The CALL and RET commands result in words being pushed on or popped from the stack. Similarly, the programmable interrupt commands, INT and INTO, as well as the return from interrupt command IRET, result in stack operations.

On some computer systems there are no explicit commands for input or output operations. Recall that on the PDP-11 certain memory addresses are reserved for input and output devices. Thus the mechanics of programming input and output operations are identical to those of programming memory reference operations. Some computers have special commands for input/output operations. The 8086 microprocessor is such a machine. When these commands are executed, special internal signals associated with input or output operations are generated. The 8086 instruction set has two such commands, IN and OUT. Either 8-bit or 16-bit words may be transferred between the CPU and peripheral devices. Commands for input from external devices are the following:

IN AL,DX	Input to AL from external port specified by (DX)
IN AX,DX	Input to AX from external port specified by (DX)
IN AL,PORT8	Input to AL from the 8-bit port specified by PORT8
IN AX,PORT16	Input to AX from the 16-bit port specified by address, PORT16

Similar output commands are available using the OUT command.

A variety of rotate and shift commands are available on the 8086. The RAL and RAR commands are used to rotate an 8-bit number or a 16-bit number 1 or more bits to the left or to the right. The command RAR DX rotates the number in the DX register 1 bit to the right. The command RAL DX,CL rotates the word in the DX register N bits to the left, where N is the number stored in the CL register. Similarly, the RCL and RCR commands are used to rotate 9-bit or 17-bit words. These words consist of the carry bit concatenated with the specified operand.

In addition to the rotate-type commands, both arithmetic and logic shift commands are available. These commands have the same format as the rotate commands. For example, the machine code for the arithmetic shift right command SAR is

```
110100vw mod 111 r/m
```

The symbol w indicates whether the operand is a byte or a word operand. If v = 0, a 1-bit shift is performed. If v = 1, an N-bit shift is performed, where N is the number stored in the CL register.

Example 10.9

Prior to execution of each of the following program segments, assume that the CPU registers contain the following hexadecimal numbers:

$$(AH) = 39 \quad (AL) = 62 \quad (DX) = ABCD \quad (CX) = 1E04$$

	Mnemonic	Code
(a)	SUB AL, AH	00101000 11 100 000
	DAS	00101111
(b)	IN,AL,DX	11101100
(c)	SHL AX,CL	11010011

What will be the contents of the AX register after each of the commands is executed?

Solution (a) The hexadecimal number 39 is subtracted from the hexadecimal number 62. The difference, $29H$, is placed in the AL register. After the DAS command is performed, the number $23H$ will be in the AL register. The content of the AH register is not changed.

(b) The 8-bit number in input port CDH is read into AL. The content of AH is not changed.

(c) The contents of the AX register are shifted 4 bits to the left. The new number in AH is $96H$, and the new number in AL is $20H$.

The following string operations are available in the 8086 instruction set:

Mnemonic	Function
MOVSB or MOVSW	Move byte or move word
LODSB or LODSW	Load byte into AL or load word into AX
STOSB or STOSW	Store AL or AX in memory
CMPSB or CMPSW	Compare destination operand with source operand (DST − SRC). Do not save result
SCASB or SCASW	Compare destination operand with AL or AX
REP	Repeat prefix is added to instruction

When string operations are utilized, pointers in the SI and/or DI registers are used to identify memory operands. After each instruction has been executed, these pointer values are either increased or decreased, depending on whether the data direction flag is cleared or set. The pointers are increased (or decreased) by 1 for byte operations and by 2 for word operations.

The REP, or REPEAT, prefix can be used in conjunction with string operations. If the REP prefix is used with an LODS, STOS, or MOVS string operation, then

1. The string operation is executed.
2. The number in the CX register is decremented.
3. The string operation is executed again unless (CX) = 0.

The machine code for the REP prefix is

1111001z

The last bit of this instruction is meaningful if a string-compare (CMPS) or a string-scan (SCAS) operation follows the instruction prefix. If one of these operations is performed and a REP prefix is used, then the string operation is repeatedly performed until either the contents of the CX register are zero or until the value of the zero flag resulting from the operation does not match the least significant bit of the instruction prefix.

Example 10.10

Prior to execution of each of the following instructions, suppose the following CPU registers contain these hexadecimal numbers:

$$(DS) = 1111 \quad (ES) = 2222 \quad (SI) = 1230 \quad (DI) = 4440$$
$$(CX) = 0010 \quad (AX) = 00FF \quad (\text{flag register}) = 0000$$

What is done by each of the following commands?

	Mnemonic	Code
(a)	REP MOVSW	1111001x 10100101
(b)	REPZ CMPSB	11110011 10100110
(c)	REPNZ SCASB	11110010 10101110

Solution   The data direction flag is cleared, so pointers in the index registers will be incremented.

(a) A block of 16 words starting at location 12340 will be copied into memory beginning at location 26660. After this block move operation is completed, the number in the SI register will be 1250H, and the number in the DI register will be 4460H.

(b) A 16-byte string starting at location 12340 is compared with a 16-byte string starting at location 26660. If the strings are identical, then the zero flag will be up at the completion of the operation, 1240H will be in the source index register, and 4450 will be in the destination index register. If the strings are not identical, the zero flag will be down at the completion of the operation.

(c) Up to 16 bytes, beginning at location 26660, are checked to see if one of these bytes has a value of *FF*. If none of these bytes has a value of *FF*, the zero flag will be down at the completion of the operation. If at least 1 byte in the string has a value of *FF*, the zero flag will be up, and the number in the destination index register will point to the successor of the first byte in the string that has a value of *FF*.

There are several 8086 instructions that may be classified as processor control instructions. These instructions are used to set or clear flags or to perform similar processor operations. No further discussion of these operations is warranted.

Certain instructions do not fit well into any formal category. We have classified these as special instructions. The LOCK and ESC instructions are used to control information on the data bus. They are relevant only if supported by external hardware. The CBW instruction is used to convert the byte in the AL register to a word. This is done by extending its sign bit into the 8 bits of the AH register. Similarly, the CWD or convert word to double-word command is used to extend the sign bit of the word in the AX register into the 16 bits of the DX register. This is useful for programming 32-bit arithmetic.

The XLAT, or table-lookup, instruction is a powerful command. It adds the unsigned number in the AL register to the contents of the BX register to obtain an offset. Then it uses this offset to address a memory byte. The contents of this memory byte are returned in the AL register. The number originally stored in the BX register remains in the BX register.

Example 10.11

Suppose the following binary to BCD table is stored in 100 bytes of memory.

Memory Location	Contents
10000H	00H
10001H	01H
–	–
–	–
10009H	09H
1000AH	10H
–	–
–	–
10063H	99H

Prior to execution of an instruction, the internal registers contain the following hexadecimal numbers:

$$(AX) = AB2C \quad (BX) = 0004 \quad (DS) = 1000$$

What is done by the following instruction?

XLAT

Solution   Observe that the table starts at $10000H$, but the sum of $16*(DS)+BX$ is $10004H$. Thus, a BCD number 4 larger than the table entry argument in AL will be returned, provided that the number in AL is less than the base-10 number 96. After the above instruction is executed, the number 48*H* will be in AL.

The final class of instructions to be discussed consists of control transfer instructions. These instructions include the following types of commands.

Mnemonic	Comment
CALL	Call a subroutine
JMP	Unconditional branch
JMP__	Branch if condition on status flags (or CX register) is satisfied
LOOP__	Similar to branch on condition, but CX is decremented
INT_	Programmed interrupt
RET or IRET	Return from subroutine or return from interrupt

The addressing modes for control transfer instructions are somewhat different from those described in Section 10.2. For example, some jump commands and all jump on condition commands are 2-byte commands. The first byte specifies the command and the second byte contains a signed displacement. Suppose such a jump-type instruction within a code segment is stored in a memory location identified by (IP). Then the target address is identified by the offset

$$\text{Offset} = (\text{IP}) + 2 + \text{signed displacement}$$

The reason 2 is added to the contents of the instruction pointer is that the contents of the instruction pointer have been incremented twice before the actual branch command is executed.

Example 10.12

Prior to execution of an instruction, the designated hexadecimal numbers are in the following registers:

$$(\text{CS}) = 1111 \quad (\text{IP}) = 2220 \quad (\text{flag register}) = 0001$$

The following command is fetched and executed:

Mnemonic	Code	Comment
JC BACK	01110010 11111000	Jump to BACK if CARRY is set

Solution   Because the carry flag is set, the conditional jump operation is performed. The offset is 2222 + *FFF*8 = 221*A*. Therefore, the target address identified by the label BACK is 1332*A*.

In general, CALL and JUMP type operations can be either intrasegment or intersegment operations. For intersegment operations, the destination operand consists of two words, an offset and a 16-bit segment identifier. There are two general ways in which this 32-bit operand may be referenced. Frequently, these two ways are called DIRECT and INDIRECT addressing. However, these addressing mode designators are not too meaningful for control transfer operations. When the mode of addressing classified as direct is used, the operand is an immediate operand. During instruction execution, the two words of this operand are moved into the IP and CS registers. When the mode of addressing classified as indirect is used, the operand in memory is identified by an offset. This offset is identified by the mod and r/m designators in the address byte of the instruction. During CALL operations, the return address is placed on the stack. For intersegment operations, this address consists of two numbers, a segment and an offset. The segment identifier is pushed on the stack first.

Example 10.13

Prior to execution of each of the following instructions, the indicated hexadecimal numbers are contained in the internal registers as shown below.

$$(CS) = 1234 \quad (IP) = 5678 \quad (SP) = 2224 \quad (SS) = A000$$
$$(BX) = 3332 \quad (DS) = 4444$$

and MOUSE is a FAR-type procedure identified by SEGMENT 4567 and OFFSET 2346.

(*Note*: MOUSE => ADDRESS 479B6.)

Identify all changes made after each of the following instructions is executed.

	Mnemonic	Code
(a)	JMP MOUSE	EAH 46H 23H 67H 45H
(b)	CALL MOUSE	9AH 46H 23H 67H 45H
(c)	CALL DWORD PTR [BX]	11111111B 00 011 111B

Solution (a) After this intersegment jump operation is executed, the number in IP will be 2346H and the number in CS will be 4567H.

(b) This instruction execution will result in the same numbers being in CS and in IP as in part (a). However, the return address will now be stored on the stack. Offset for the return address is 5678H + 5 = 567DH. Therefore, the new numbers placed on the stack are as follows.

Memory Address	Content
A2220H	7DH
A2221H	56H
A2222H	34H
A2223H	12H

(c) In order for this CALL instruction to function properly, a double-word pointer must first be stored in memory. The starting address of this pointer is

$$(DS)*16 + (BX) = 47772H$$

The pointer must identify the offset and the segment of MOUSE. This is shown below.

Data Memory Address	Content
47772H	46H
47773H	23H
47774H	67H
47775H	45H

After this instruction is performed, the changes will be the same as described in part (b), except that the contents of memory location A2220H will now be 7AH.

The return from subroutine command, RET, performs the inverse operation of the CALL statement. Care must be taken, however, to match the type of return statement to the type of call statement. For example, if an intersegment call is made to a subroutine, then there must be an intersegment return from the subroutine.

The final control transfer command to be discussed is the software-interrupt command. There are two such commands. One of the software-interrupt commands, INT, is an unconditional command. The other interrupt command, INTO, is executed only if the overflow flag is set. A programmed interrupt command performs the following functions.

1. The flag register is pushed onto the stack.
2. The T and I bits in the flag register are cleared.
3. The contents of CS and the offset to the next instruction are pushed onto the stack.
4. Program control is transferred to an interrupt processing routine identified by one of 256 possible two-word interrupt vectors.

Interrupt commands are illustrated by the following example.

Example 10.14

Refer to the following interrupt commands. To which address is control transferred?

	Mnemonic	Code
(a)	INT 21 or INT 15H	11001101 00010101
(b)	INT	11001100
(c)	INTO	11001110

Solution (a) The interrupt vector is stored at an address corresponding to the immediate operand times 4. Expressed in binary

$$10101 * 100 = 1010100 => 54H$$

Thus the double-word interrupt vectors are stored in memory locations 00054H to 00057H. The first word of this vector identifies the offset of the interrupt processing routine, and the second word identifies the code segment of the routine.

(b) Same as INT 3. That is, two-word vector is stored in memory starting at 0000CH.

(c) Same as INT 4. Vector is stored starting at 00010H.

In order to exit properly from an interrupt routine, the IRET command must be executed.

Review

1. Refer to either the LEA, LDS, or LES command. For example, the LES command is encoded as

$$11000100 \quad mod \ reg \ r/m$$

Which mod designator is invalid for this command? Explain.

2. Refer to the mnemonic and the code in Example 10.7b. What other code will perform the same function?

Prior to each part of Review questions 3, 4, and 5, assume that the CPU and memory registers contain the following hexadecimal numbers:

(CS) = 1111   (DS) = 2222   (ES) = 2221   (IP) = 0000   (AX) = 2305
(SS) = 4945   (BX) = 5555   (CX) = 0003   (SI) = 5556
(DI) = 5568   (flag register) = 00C0   (SP) = 0000

Memory Data Storage (Hexadecimal)

Location	Number	Location	Number
27775	2	2777A	7
27776	3	2777B	8
27777	4	2777C	9
27778	5	2777D	A
27779	6	2777E	B

3. Suppose the following command is executed: XLAT.
   (a) Which registers will have their contents changed?
   (b) What numbers will be in these registers after the command has been executed?

4. For each of the following commands, identify which registers or memory locations will have their contents changed.
   (a) LODSB
   (b) STOSW
   (c) REP MOVSB
   (d) REP CMPSB
   (e) JNZ BACK ; (*Note:* BACK is an intrasegment or NEAR-type label
                ; identified by an offset of 60H.)
   (f) JNC BACK
   (g) CALL EXIT ; (EXIT is a FAR-type label identified by segment
                ; 0100H and offset AAAAH.)

5. Refer to Review question 4. Identify the new contents of each of the registers or memory locations.

10.4 PROGRAMMING WITH AN 8086 ASSEMBLER

In Chapters 6 through 9, use of the PDP-11 Macro-11 assembler was illustrated. Recall that this assembler translated PDP-11 assembly-language code into a relocatable object code. Then a linking loader was used to link this object code with external references and to provide absolute addressing. The output of the linking loader was an absolute or an executable module. The assembly process for 8086-based systems is very similar.

The macro assembler available on the IBM personal computer was used for all examples given in this chapter. This assembler operates under the DOS operating system. Source modules were developed using the EDLIN editor. Programs were tested and debugged using the DOS DEBUG program. However, concepts related to 8086 assembly-language programming developed in this chapter do not depend on the use of this particular software package.

A minimal requirement for a good assembler is that it gives the user access to the complete instruction set. This criterion is satisfied by the 8086 macro assembler. Furthermore, use of assembler directives and pseudo instructions facilitates the development of software and even encourages good programming techniques. There are a considerable number of such directives available on the 8086 macro assembler. It is beyond the scope of this textbook to describe and illustrate all of them. However, discussion of the capabilities of the assembler will be sufficient so that the reader will be able to develop reasonably efficient assembly-language programs.

Refer to the assembly-language program in Fig. 10.6. This program merely illustrates linking with the DOS operating system. When an absolute module is executed under DOS, it is desired to return to the operating system at the conclusion of program execution. The starting address of DOS is always on a PARAGRAPH boundary. That is, its memory address is divisible by 16. Such addresses can be specified by placing an appropriate address in the CS register and using this address with an offset of 0000. Before DOS transfers control to an absolute or executable module, it places its address in the DS register.

```
STACK     SEGMENT PARA STACK 'STACK'
                  DB       64 DUP('STACK    ')
STACK             ENDS
;
WORKDATA          SEGMENT PARA PUBLIC 'DATA'
WORKDATA          ENDS
;
CSEG              SEGMENT PARA PUBLIC 'CODE'
START             PROC     FAR
                  ASSUME   SS:STACK. CS:CSEG. DS:WORKDATA. ES:WORKDATA
                  PUSH     DS
                  SUB      AX.AX
                  PUSH     AX
                  MOV      AX.WORKDATA
                  MOV      DS.AX
                  MOV      ES.AX
;
;PUT PROGRAM LINES HERE
;
                  RET
START             ENDP
CSEG              ENDS
                  END      START
```

Figure 10.6 A skeleton assembly-language program used for linking with DOS

The skeleton program in Fig. 10.6, or a similar skeleton, will be included as part of all assembly-language programs illustrated in this chapter. Refer to the assembly directive or pseudo operation SEGMENT. At run time, each instruction and each variable must be within a specified segment. Each segment is associated with a range of memory locations identified by the contents of a segment register. Therefore, all code-generating directives must be included within a segment. The identifier to the left of the word SEGMENT is a segment name. This name is used to identify the beginning and the end of a particular segment. The word PARA indicates the alignment of a particular segment. Other alignment options are BYTE, WORD, and PAGE. These four options indicate that the starting address of the segment must be divisible by either 16, 1, 2, or 256.

The option PUBLIC indicates that a segment of a particular name will be concatenated to others of the same name during the linking operation. The option STACK indicates that a particular segment is to be part of the run-time stack. The linking loader requires that one segment be given this option. The final entry in the SEGMENT directive is enclosed in half quotation marks. This 'class' entry is used to group various segments during the linking operation.

Observe that there are three segments defined in the example in Fig. 10.6. The names selected for these segments are STACK, WORKDATA, and CSEG. Refer to the segment named STACK. The DB, or DATA BYTE, directive is used in this segment. This command can be used to reserve and initialize one or more memory bytes. In this example, 512 data bytes are reserved and assigned initial values. The ASCII representations for S, P, A, C, E, Space, Space, and Space are stored in the first 8 bytes of the reserved space. Then this character string is duplicated until the entire 512 bytes of memory have been initialized. Putting initial values in stack memory is not necessary. It is, however, useful for debugging purposes. Initializing the stack memory makes it easy to locate and easy to identify the extent of its usage during program execution. At the beginning of program execution, the true value of the stack pointer will be 1 greater than the highest memory address reserved for stack usage.

The WORKDATA segment is associated with memory references. Names defined within this segment are variable names. Such names should be defined before they are used in a CODE segment. Similarly, subroutine names may be defined before they are used. Forward referencing is discouraged when developing 8086 assembly-language programs.

Refer to the CODE segment in the sample program. The name START identifies a PROCEDURE. Observe that the same name is used when terminating the procedure. Each CODE segment may include several procedures. These procedures are more general structures than subprograms or Pascal-type procedures. A procedure may be a subprogram and explicitly invoked by a CALL statement. It may just be a program block and may be executed without being explicitly invoked. Similarly, it is valid to jump or conditionally branch to the start of a procedure. A code segment may contain several procedure blocks. If a procedure is to be invoked by a command identified by a different value in the CS register, it must be assigned a FAR attribute. Any procedure accessed directly from the operating system must be given this attribute. If a procedure is given this attribute, RET statements included within the procedure will be intersegment commands.

The ASSUME directive tells the assembler which segment register is associated with which segment. In this program, for instance, the segment WORKDATA is associated with the DS segment register. This information is required for translation of certain assembler commands. However, this directive does not load the four segment registers.

When the DOS operating system transfers control to an executable module, it first places a number corresponding to its starting address in the DS segment register. In order for program control to return to DOS, this number must be placed in the CS register, and an offset of 0000 must be placed in the IP. Observe from the example in Fig. 10.6 that first the DOS code segment identifier is pushed on the stack. Then a value of 0000 is pushed on the stack. The segment value identified by the name WORKDATA is loaded into ES and DS for use in the user program. The user program is identified by the comment "PUT PROGRAM LINES HERE." Assume that at the conclusion of this user program the value of the stack pointer, identified by (SS) and (SP), has been returned to the same value that it had at the beginning of the program. Then the intersegment RET command pops the starting address of DOS back into the IP and CS registers.

The final assembler directive in this example is used to identify the starting address of the program. This is virtually the same command that was used on the PDP-11 Macro-11 assembler.

Refer to the sample program in Fig. 10.7. This program uses virtually the same skeleton as that used in the previous example. The line numbers given in this program are merely the line numbers used by the editor. The user program is located between lines 19 and 27. Observe that the variable names NAME1, NAME2, and NUMCHAR are defined within the WORKDATA segment. The variable NUMCHAR is a DW, or data word, variable. It is initialized to have a base-10 value of 8.

In line 20, the offset corresponding to the beginning of the first string is moved into the SI register. In line 21, the counter value is moved into the CX register. In line 22, the offset corresponding to the start of the second string is moved into the DI register. In line 23, a destination character is temporarily stored in AL. Then, in line 24, this destination character is replaced with the corresponding source character. In line 25, the corresponding source character is replaced with the byte stored in AL. The process is repeated until the counter becomes 0. An assembler output listing of this program is given in Fig. 10.8.

In order to develop and test an assembly-language program, the following steps are required.

1. Using an editor, build your source program.
2. Using the macro assembler, assemble your source program.

```
 1: STACK    SEGMENT PARA STACK 'STACK'
 2:                  DB        64 DUP('ABCDEFGH')
 3: STACK            ENDS
 4: WORKDATA         SEGMENT PARA PUBLIC 'DATA'
 5: NAME1    DB      'HENRY...'
 6: NAME2    DB      'MICHELLE'
 7: NUMCHAR  DW       8
 8: WORKDATA         ENDS
 9: :
10: CSEG             SEGMENT PARA PUBLIC 'CODE'
11: START            PROC    FAR
12:                  ASSUME  SS:STACK, CS:CSEG, DS:WORKDATA, ES:WORKDATA
13:                  PUSH    DS      ;SAVE RETURN SEGMENT
14:                  SUB     AX,AX
15:                  PUSH    AX      ;SAVE RETURN OFFSET
16:                  MOV     AX,WORKDATA     ;LOAD SEGMENT REGISTERS
17:                  MOV     DS,AX
18:                  MOV     ES,AX           ;SEGMENT REGISTERS ARE LOADED
19: :
20:                  MOV SI,OFFSET NAME1
21:                  MOV CX,NUMCHAR
22:                  MOV DI,OFFSET NAME2
23: AGAIN:           MOV AL,[DI]
24:                  MOVSB
25:                  MOV [SI-1],AL
26:                  LOOP AGAIN     ;BRANCH TO AGAIN UNTIL COUNTER = 0
27: :
28:                  RET
29: START            ENDP
30: CSEG             ENDS
31:                  END     START
```

Figure 10.7 Sample program illustrating exchange of two character strings

3. Using a relocatable linking loader, link your program with any required external modules.

4. Execute the absolute program. It may be desired to execute the program under a debug mode of operation.

To be more specific, suppose that you wish to assemble and run the program given in Fig. 10.7 on an IBM Personal Computer using the DOS operating system. Then the following commands are required.

1. **EDLIN MYNAME.ASM**
   Note: The EDLIN editor is used to create the source assembly-language program MYNAME.ASM. After the program is created, return to DOS.

2. **MASM**
   Note: The assembler will ask for information, such as the source program name and the object program name. If there are errors, a tabulation of errors will be given.

3. **LINK**
   Note: The linker will ask for information such as the names of the object modules and the name to be assigned to the absolute module.

```
0000                                    STACK     SEGMENT PARA STACK 'STACK'
0000      40 [                                    DB        64 DUP('ABCDEFGH')
              41 42 43 44
              45 46 47 48
                          ]

0200                                    STACK               ENDS
                                        :
0000                                    WORKDATA            SEGMENT PARA PUBLIC 'DATA'
0000      48 45 4E 52 59 2E             NAME1     DB        'HENRY...'
          2E 2E
0008      4D 49 43 48 45 4C             NAME2     DB        'MICHELLE'
          4C 45
0010      0008                          NUMCHAR   DW        8
0012                                    WORKDATA            ENDS
                                        :
0000                                    CSEG                SEGMENT PARA PUBLIC 'CODE'
0000                                    START               PROC    FAR
                                                            ASSUME  SS:STACK. CS:CSEG. DS:W
                                        ORKDATA. ES:WORKDATA
0000      1E                                                PUSH    DS      :SAVE RETURN SEG
                                        MENT
0001      2B C0                                             SUB     AX.AX
0003      50                                                PUSH    AX      :SAVE RETURN OFF
                                        SET
0004      B8   ---- R                                       MOV     AX.WORKDATA   :LOAD SE
                                        GMENT REGISTERS
0007      8E D8                                             MOV     DS.AX
0009      8E C0                                             MOV     ES.AX         :SEGMENT
                                         REGISTERS ARE LOADED
                                        :
000B      BE 0000 R                                         MOV SI.OFFSET NAME1
000E      8B 0E 0010 R                                      MOV CX.NUMCHAR
0012      BF 0008 R                                         MOV DI.OFFSET NAME2
0015      8A 05                         AGAIN:              MOV AL.[DI]
0017      A4                                                MOVSB
0018      88 44 FF                                          MOV [SI-1].AL
001B      E2 F8                                             LOOP AGAIN   :BRANCH TO AGAIN U
                                        NTIL COUNTER = 0
                                        :
001D      CB                                                RET
001E                                    START               ENDP
001E                                    CSEG                ENDS
                                                            END     START
```

	N a m e	Size	align	combine	class
CSEG		001E	PARA	PUBLIC	'CODE'
STACK.		0200	PARA	STACK	'STACK'
WORKDATA		0012	PARA	PUBLIC	'DATA'

Symbols:

	N a m e	Type	Value	Attr	
AGAIN.		L NEAR	0015	CSEG	
NAME1.		L BYTE	0000	WORKDATA	
NAME2.		L BYTE	0008	WORKDATA	
NUMCHAR.		L WORD	0010	WORKDATA	
START.		F PROC	0000	CSEG	Length =001E

```
Warning  Severe
Errors   Errors
0        0
```

Figure 10.8   Output listing of program given in Fig. 10.7

4. **MYNAME** or **DEBUG MYNAME.EXE**

Note: If it is desired to inspect the contents of registers or memory, to trace the individual steps of a program, or to insert and remove breakpoints, the program should be executed under the DEBUG mode.

Refer to the program illustrated in Figs. 10.7 and 10.8. Figure 10.9 illustrates execution of this program under the DEBUG mode. The first DEBUG command

```
-T

AX=0000  BX=0000  CX=0000  DX=0000  SP=01FE  BP=0000  SI=0000  DI=0000
DS=049F  ES=049F  SS=04B1  CS=04AF  IP=0001   NV UP DI PL NZ NA PO NC
04AF:0001 2BC0          SUB     AX,AX
-T

AX=0000  BX=0000  CX=0000  DX=0000  SP=01FE  BP=0000  SI=0000  DI=0000
DS=049F  ES=049F  SS=04B1  CS=04AF  IP=0003   NV UP DI PL ZR NA PE NC
04AF:0003 50           PUSH    AX
-T

AX=0000  BX=0000  CX=0000  DX=0000  SP=01FC  BP=0000  SI=0000  DI=0000
DS=049F  ES=049F  SS=04B1  CS=04AF  IP=0004   NV UP DI PL ZR NA PE NC
04AF:0004 B8D104       MOV     AX,04D1
-T

AX=04D1  BX=0000  CX=0000  DX=0000  SP=01FC  BP=0000  SI=0000  DI=0000
DS=049F  ES=049F  SS=04B1  CS=04AF  IP=0007   NV UP DI PL ZR NA PE NC
04AF:0007 8ED8         MOV     DS,AX
-T

AX=04D1  BX=0000  CX=0000  DX=0000  SP=01FC  BP=0000  SI=0000  DI=0000
DS=04D1  ES=049F  SS=04B1  CS=04AF  IP=0009   NV UP DI PL ZR NA PE NC
04AF:0009 8EC0         MOV     ES,AX
-D 04D1:0000
04D1:0000   48 45 4E 52 59 2E 2E 2E-4D 49 43 48 45 4C 4C 45   HENRY...MICHELLE
04D1:0010   08 00 00 00 00 00 00 00-00 00 00 00 00 00 00 00   ................
04D1:0020   00 00 00 00 00 00 00 00-00 00 00 00 00 00 00 00   ................
04D1:0030   00 00 00 00 00 00 00 00-00 00 00 00 00 00 00 00   ................
04D1:0040   00 00 00 00 00 00 00 00-00 00 00 00 00 00 00 00   ................
04D1:0050   00 00 00 00 00 00 00 00-00 00 00 00 00 00 00 00   ................
04D1:0060   00 00 00 00 00 00 00 00-00 00 00 00 00 00 00 00   ................
04D1:0070   00 00 00 00 00 00 00 00-00 00 00 00 00 00 00 00   ................
-G

Program terminated normally
-D0  04D1:0000
04D1:0000   4D 49 43 48 45 4C 4C 45-48 45 4E 52 59 2E 2E 2E   MICHELLEHENRY...
04D1:0010   08 00 00 00 00 00 00 00-00 00 00 00 00 00 00 00   ................
04D1:0020   00 00 00 00 00 00 00 00-00 00 00 00 00 00 00 00   ................
04D1:0030   00 00 00 00 00 00 00 00-00 00 00 00 00 00 00 00   ................
04D1:0040   00 00 00 00 00 00 00 00-00 00 00 00 00 00 00 00   ................
04D1:0050   00 00 00 00 00 00 00 00-00 00 00 00 00 00 00 00   ................
04D1:0060   00 00 00 00 00 00 00 00-00 00 00 00 00 00 00 00   ................
04D1:0070   00 00 00 00 00 00 00 00-00 00 00 00 00 00 00 00   ................
-D 04AF:0000
04AF:0000   1E 2B C0 50 B8 D1 04 8E-D8 8E C0 BE 00 00 8B 0E   .+ƆP8Ð.Ɏ.Ɏ.Ⱦ...
04AF:0010   10 00 BF 08 00 8A 05 A4-88 44 FF E2 F8 CB 00 00   ..?....$.D.bxK..
04AF:0020   41 42 43 44 45 46 47 48-41 42 43 44 45 46 47 48   ABCDEFGHABCDEFGH
04AF:0030   41 42 43 44 45 46 47 48-41 42 43 44 45 46 47 48   ABCDEFGHABCDEFGH
04AF:0040   41 42 43 44 45 46 47 48-41 42 43 44 45 46 47 48   ABCDEFGHABCDEFGH
04AF:0050   41 42 43 44 45 46 47 48-41 42 43 44 45 46 47 48   ABCDEFGHABCDEFGH
04AF:0060   41 42 43 44 45 46 47 48-41 42 43 44 45 46 47 48   ABCDEFGHABCDEFGH
04AF:0070   41 42 43 44 45 46 47 48-41 42 43 44 45 46 47 48   ABCDEFGHABCDEFGH
-Q
```

Figure 10.9   Execution of the exchange program under the DEBUG mode

given is a T command. This trace instruction causes a single instruction of the program to be executed. Then the contents of all internal registers are displayed. Observe that the absolute addresses of the various program segments are now available to the programmer.

The D DEBUG command is used to display a data block. This block contains the two data strings before they have been exchanged. The G command causes program execution until either a breakpoint has been encountered or until normal termination. Because no breakpoints were defined, execution proceeds until the program is completed. However, program control remains under the DEBUG mode. The next DEBUG command displays a data memory block after the strings have been exchanged. The final D command is used to display a CODE block. Note that a portion of the stack is also identified. The last DEBUG command, Q, causes program control to exit from the DEBUG mode.

Review

1. Refer to the program illustrated in Figs. 10.7, 10.8, and 10.9. What is the true address identified by the stack pointer? Which ASCII character is stored in the address corresponding to the offset [SP-4]?

   The program in Fig. 10.10 is used for questions 2, 3, and 4.

2. There are two invalid commands in this program. Identify these two commands.

3. Which commands in this program use each of the following modes of addressing?
   (a) direct addressing
   (b) relative addressing
   (c) immediate addressing
   (d) stack addressing

4. Refer to the executable commands in this program. Which of these instructions are
   (a) 1-byte commands?
   (b) 2-byte commands?
   (c) 3-byte commands?

5. Write an assembly-language program that will add together the 16-bit variables NUMB1, NUMB2, and NUMB3 and place the answer in the variable name ANS. Assume that the answer will fit in a 16-bit word. Test your program by adding together the following 3 base-10 numbers: 45, 156, and −15.

10.5 PROGRAMMING EXAMPLES

In order to illustrate capabilities of the 8086 macro assembler, certain selected examples are discussed in this section.

Example 10.15

Write a program that finds the prime numbers between 0 and 99. Recall that a prime number is a number that is divisible only by itself and by 1.

```
 1:  :@@@@@@@@@@@@@@@@@@@@@@@@@@@@@@@@@@@@@@@@@@@@@@@@@@@@@@@@@
 2:  :@                                                      @
 3:  :@                                                      @
 4:  :@                                                      @
 5:  :@   REVIEW QUESTIONS 10-2. 10-3 AND 10-4               @
 6:  :@   THIS ASSIGNMENT DEMONSTRATES VARIOUS MOVE          @
 7:  :@   INSTRUCTIONS.  NOTE THAT TWO OF THE MOVE           @
 8:  :@   INSTRUCTIONS DEMONSTRATED ARE ILLEGAL              @
 9:  :@                                                      @
10:  :@@@@@@@@@@@@@@@@@@@@@@@@@@@@@@@@@@@@@@@@@@@@@@@@@@@@@@@@@
11:  :
12:  :
13:  :
14:  :
15:  STACK    SEGMENT PARA STACK 'STACK'
16:           DB 15 DUP ('RAYMOND ')
17:  STACK    ENDS
18:  :
19:  :
20:  WDATA    SEGMENT PARA PUBLIC 'DATA'
21:  ARRAY    DW 2222H
22:  MAMA     DW 1111H
23:  WDATA    ENDS
24:  :
25:  :
26:  CSEG     SEGMENT PARA PUBLIC 'CODE'
27:  MAIN     PROC FAR
28:           ASSUME  CS:CSEG.DS:WDATA.SS:STACK,ES:NOTHING
29:           PUSH DS
30:           SUB AX.AX
31:           PUSH AX
32:           MOV AX.WDATA
33:           MOV DS.AX
34:  :
35:  :START PROGRAM ......
36:  :
37:           MOV DI.0
38:           MOV SI.0
39:           MOV AX.1111H
40:           MOV BX.02H
41:  :
42:  :        GROUP A MOVE
43:  :
44:           MOV AX.BX
45:           MOV AX.[BX]
46:           MOV [AX].BX
47:           MOV [AX].[BX]
48:  :
49:  :        GROUP B MOVE
50:  :
51:           MOV AX,ARRAY
52:           MOV AX.OFFSET ARRAY
53:           MOV AX.ARRAY
54:           RET
55:  MAIN     ENDP
56:  CSEG     ENDS
57:           END MAIN
```

Figure 10.10   Program for Review questions 2, 3, and 4

Solution   A solution is given in Fig. 10.11. Several new concepts are also illustrated in this program.

Refer to the segment WDATA. A variable name ARRAY is used in this segment. This variable is a word-byte variable. The offset associated with ARRAY

```
 1: *:@@@@@@@@@@@@@@@@@@@@@@@@@@@@@@@@@@@@@@@@@@@@@@@@@@@@@@@@@@
 2: :@                                                         @
 3: :@                  PRIME NUMBER GENERATION                @
 4: :@                                                         @
 5: :@                                                         @
 6: :@                                                         @
 7: :@      10-07-85                                           @
 8: :@                                                         @
 9: :@@@@@@@@@@@@@@@@@@@@@@@@@@@@@@@@@@@@@@@@@@@@@@@@@@@@@@@@@@@@
10: :
11: :
12: :
13: STACK    SEGMENT PARA STACK 'STACK'
14:          DB 16 DUP ('RAYMOND ')
15: STACK    ENDS
16: :
17: :
18: WDATA    SEGMENT PARA PUBLIC 'DATA'
19: ARRAY    DW 100 DUP (1)
20: WDATA    ENDS
21: :
22: :
23: CSEG     SEGMENT PARA PUBLIC  'CODE'
24: MAIN     PROC FAR
25:          ASSUME CS:CSEG, DS:WDATA, SS:STACK, ES:NOTHING
26:          PUSH DS
27:          SUB AX,AX
28:          PUSH AX
29:          MOV AX,WDATA
30:          MOV DS,AX
31:          MOV DI,0                  ;SET DATA POINTER
32:          MOV AX,1H                 ;FIRST PRIME NUMBER
33:          MOV DS:ARRAY[DI],AX       ;STORE #
34:          ADD DI,TYPE ARRAY         ;INCREMENT DI
35:          MOV AX,2H                 ;SECOND PRIME #
36:          MOV DS:ARRAY[DI],AX       ;STORE #
37:          ADD DI,TYPE ARRAY
38:          MOV CL,3H
39: UP:      MOV AL,CL                 ;LOAD AL WITH TEST #
40:          MOV AH,0                  ;MAKE AX A 16-BIT WORD
41:          MOV CH,2H                 ;LOAD DIVIDER
42: BACK:    DIV CH                    ;DIVIDE AX BY CH
43:          CMP AH,0                  ;REMAINDER(AH) ?
44:          JZ DOWN                   ;NO
45:          INC CH                    ;INCREMENT THE DIVISOR
46:          CMP CH,CL                 ;CHECK FOR FINISH
47:          MOV AL,CL                 ;RELOAD TEST #
48:          MOV AH,0
49:          JNZ BACK                  ;JUMP NOT ZERO TO BACK
50:          MOV AL,CL
51:          MOV AH,0
52:          MOV DS:ARRAY[DI],AX       ;STORE PRIME #
53:          ADD DI,TYPE ARRAY         ;INCREMENT DI
54: DOWN:    INC CL
55:          CMP CL,63H                ;CHECK FOR TERMINATION
56:          JNZ UP
57: TERM:    RET
58: MAIN     ENDP
59: CSEG     ENDS
60:          END MAIN
```

Figure 10.11   A solution to Example 10.15

identifies the first word in a group of 100 words. The word ARRAY is a meaningful name because in this example the results are to be stored in an array-type data structure identified by this name. Refer to line 33. The destination operand illustrates the use of a segment override prefix. However, in this example, it is not necessary to use the segment override prefix as part of the variable name DS:ARRAY, as DS is the default segment register.

Refer again to line 33. The offset for the destination address is determined by adding the 16-bit number corresponding to the offset of ARRAY to the number in the destination index register. Because the number in DI has been set to 0, the effective address in which 1 is stored corresponds to the name ARRAY. Refer to line 34. TYPE ARRAY is added to the number in DI. Because ARRAY is a word-type variable (2 bytes), the number 2 is added to the contents of the DI register. Now ARRAY[DI], which is a valid representation for the offset [DI + ARRAY], identifies the next address in the array-type data structure.

The remainder of the program given in Fig. 10.11 is self-explanatory. A number is placed in the AX register and divided by N, where N is initially 2. Then the divisor may be incremented, and division again performed. The process may continue until the divisor and the dividend are identical. If at any stage in the process a remainder of 0 is obtained, the number in AX is not prime, and no further testing of this number is required. If the process continues until the divisor and the dividend have the same value, the number is prime and is stored in the array.

One attribute of a macro assembler is that it allows the user to create her or his own commands or macros. This is illustrated in Fig. 10.12. There are three macros defined in this program; PUT, INST, and STORE. Each macro uses at least one dummy argument. When the first macro is invoked, it moves the numbers 0, 1, 2, . . . F into memory locations N, $N + 1$, . . . $N + 15$, where $N = 16*ES +$ OFFSET BLOC. Similar move-type commands are performed by the second and third macros.

Refer to statement 37 in Fig. 10.12. Observe that the MOVS, or string move, command has two operands. These are dummy operands that are used to improve the readability of the program. The destination operand is always identified by the ES segment and the offset in the DI register. The source operand is generally identified by the DS segment and the offset in the SI register.

```
 1:  ;&&&&&&&&&&&&&&&&&&&&&&&&&&&&&&&&&&&&&&&&&&&&&&&&&&&&&&&&&&&&&&&&
 2:  ;&                                                            &
 3:  ;&                                                            &
 4:  ;&                                                            &
 5:  ;&              THIS PROGRAM DEMONSTRATES THE                 &
 6:  ;&              USE OF MACRO INSTRUCTIONS.                    &
 7:  ;&                                                            &
 8:  ;&&&&&&&&&&&&&&&&&&&&&&&&&&&&&&&&&&&&&&&&&&&&&&&&&&&&&&&&&&&&&&&&
 9:  ;
10:  ;
11:  ;
12:  ;   CAUTION!!!
```

Figure 10.12   Program illustrating the use of macro instructions

```
13: PUT      MACRO    S1        ;PUT NUMBER MACRO
14:          MOV CX,10          ;LOAD COUNTER
15:          MOV DI,S1          ;LOAD DESTINATION INDEX
16:          MOV AX,0           ;LOAD FIRST NUMBER
17: BACK:    MOV ES:BLOC[DI],AL      ;MOV # INTO MEMORY
18:          INC AX             ;NEXT NUMBER
19:          INC DI             ;NEXT MEMORY LOCATION
20:          LOOP BACK          ;LOOP BACK UP
21:          ENDM
22: ;
23: ; DANGER!!!
24: INST     MACRO S2,S1        ;INSERT ROUTINE
25:          MOV DI,S2          ;S2 IS 2ND MEM BLK LOC
26:          MOV SI,S1          ;S1 IS 1ST MEM BLK LOC
27:          MOV CX,5           ;SET COUNTER
28: BAC1:    MOVS BLOC,BLOC     ;MOV MEMORY
29:          LOOP BAC1          ;INTO MEMORY(DI)
30:          MOV AX,0AH         ;LOAD FIRST # TO BE INSERTED
31: BAC2:    MOV ES:BLOC[DI],AL    ;INSERT MEMORY
32:          INC AX             ;NEXT #
33:          INC DI             ;NEXT MEM LOC
34:          CMP AX,0FH         ;CHECK FOR FINISH
35:          JNZ BAC2           ;IF NOT, INSERT MORE
36:          MOV CX,5           ;LOAD COUNTER
37: UP:      MOVS BLOC,BLOC     ;MOVE MEMORY
38:          LOOP UP
39:          ENDM               ;END MACRO
40: ;
41: ; BEWARE !!!!!
42: STORE    MACRO S2,S3        ;STORE MEMORY ROUTINE
43:          MOV SI,S2          ;SET POINTER
44:          MOV DI,S3          ;DITTO
45:          MOV DX,48          ;SET COUNTER
46: BAC3:    MOVS BLOC,BLOC     ;COPY MEMORY BLOCK
47:          LOOP BAC3
48:          ENDM
49: ;
50: ;
51: ;
52: STACK    SEGMENT PARA STACK 'STACK'
53:          DB 32 DUP ('RAYMOND ')
54: STACK    ENDS
55: ;
56: WDATA    SEGMENT PARA PUBLIC 'DATA'
57: BLK      DB 200 DUP (0)
58: WDATA    ENDS
59: ;
60: EXTRA    SEGMENT PARA PUBLIC 'XSEG'
61: BLOC     DB 200 DUP (0)
62: EXTRA    ENDS
63: ;
64: CSEG     SEGMENT PARA PUBLIC 'CODE'
65: MAIN     PROC FAR
66:          ASSUME CS:CSEG,DS:WDATA,SS:STACK,ES:EXTRA
67:          PUSH DS
68:          SUB AX,AX
69:          PUSH AX
70:          MOV AX,WDATA
71:          MOV DS,AX
72:          PUT 80H            ;INVOKE PUT MACRO
73:          INST 90H,80H       ;INVOKE INST MACRO
74:          STORE 90H,0A0H     ;INVOKE STORE MACRO
75:          RET
76: MAIN     ENDP
77: CSEG     ENDS
78:          END MAIN
```

Figure 10.12   *(cont.)*

Observe the comments in lines 12, 23, and 41. Recall that when a macro is invoked, the assembler code is effectively placed in the position at which the macro is invoked. Observe that each macro uses at least one label. If a macro is invoked more than once in a program, the same label will appear in at least two places. This results in an assembly error. Recall that a similar problem exists when using the PDP-11 Macro-11 assembler. If the pseudo operation LOCAL is placed in the first line after a macro definition, then new labels will be generated each time the macro is invoked.

Refer to the program in Fig. 10.13 and to the output of the assembler for this program in Fig. 10.14. The data word identified by the name FIRST is not to be initialized to any specified value. Therefore, a question mark is used after the DW directive. However, immediately after this word, four data words are to be initialized. This is done by using the IRP directive, which is terminated by the ENDM command. The assembler translates the DW directive for each number in the argument list. Refer to the next IRP-ENDM block. This directive causes eight double words (4-byte words) to be initialized. Observe that the first seven of these words are floating-point values. The assembler translates these numbers into 32-bit floating points. The last word is an integer. The assembler translates this into a 32-bit integer. Observe that all of these words are stored with the least significant byte first.

In order to perform input/output operations on an 8086-based system, addresses of input and output devices must be known. Then appropriate control and status words are used to control programmed input and output operations. If we are using a computer system that is under the control of an operating system, we may use the resident operating system's I/O routines. Recall that the RT-11 IOPS, or input/output programming system, commands are available to the programmer. Similarly, DOS input and output routines are available to users of this operating system.

In order to illustrate input/output operations using an 8086-based system, four DOS I/O functions will be discussed. To utilize any of these functions, an INT 21H command is executed. The number in the AH register when this routine is entered

```
LIFO    SEGMENT PARA STACK 'STACK
        DB 20 DUP ('HELLO')
LIFO ENDS
MYDATA  SEGMENT    PARA  PUBLIC 'DATA'
FIRST   DW  ?
IRP     MYWORDS.<1,47H,56,-2>
        DW MYWORDS
        ENDM
;
        IRP MYFLOATS.<1.0,3.0,0.03125,-3.0,4.0,-7.0,1.06E-19,-4>
;  NOTE.  LAST WORD IS AN INTEGER, NOT A FLOATING POINT!
        DD MYFLOATS      ;FOUR-BYTE WORDS
        ENDM
MYDATA  ENDS
        END
```

Figure 10.13 Program illustrating IRP command and assembler data translation

```
The IBM Personal Computer MACRO Assembler 01-01-99        PAGE    1-1


0000                                      LIFO    SEGMENT PARA STACK 'STACK'
0000    14 [                                      DB 20 DUP ('HELLO')
           48 45 4C 4C
           4F
              ]

0064                                      LIFO ENDS
0000                                      MYDATA  SEGMENT    PARA  PUBLIC 'DATA'
0000    ????                              FIRST   DW   ?
                                          IRP     MYWORDS.<1,47H,56,-2>
                                                  DW MYWORDS
                                                  ENDM
0002    0001                       +              DW 1
0004    0047                       +              DW 47H
0006    0038                       +              DW 56
0008    FFFE                       +              DW -2
                                          :
                                          IRP MYFLOATS,<1.0,3.0,0.03125,-3.0,4.0,
                                          -7.0,1.06E-19,-4>
                                          : NOTE.  LAST WORD IS AN INTEGER, NOT A FLOATI
                                          NG POINT!
                                                  DD MYFLOATS     ;FOUR-BYTE WORDS
                                                  ENDM
000A    00 00 00 81                +              DD 1.0  ;FOUR-BYTE WORDS
000E    00 00 40 82                +              DD 3.0  ;FOUR-BYTE WORDS
0012    00 00 00 7C                +              DD 0.03125      ;FOUR-BYTE WORDS
0016    00 00 C0 82                +              DD -3.0 ;FOUR-BYTE WORDS
001A    00 00 00 83                +              DD 4.0  ;FOUR-BYTE WORDS
001E    00 00 E0 83                +              DD -7.0 ;FOUR-BYTE WORDS
0022    12 49 7A 41                +              DD 1.06E-19     ;FOUR-BYTE WORDS
0026    FC FF FF FF                +              DD -4   ;FOUR-BYTE WORDS
002A                               MYDATA ENDS
                                          END
```

Figure 10.14   Assembler output for program in Fig. 10.13

identifies the particular I/O command. Arguments carried into these routines are frequently carried into the routine in the DX register. When the routine is completed, program control returns to the next executable statement. The following listing identifies four DOS I/O functions.

Function	ARG in AH	Description
1. Character input	7	Waits for character input from console. Character is returned in AL.
2. Character output	2	Character in DL is output to the display.
3. String output	9	String identified by address DS:DX is printed on display. Printing continues until string terminator. '$', is encountered.
4. String input	10 or 0AH	String typed in on console is stored in a buffer. String is terminated when enter key is pressed. Buffer is part of a data structure identified by DS:DX. The first byte of this structure contains the maximum buffer size. The buffer begins at the third byte of the structure. The number of characters entered, excluding the terminator, is returned in the second byte.

Example 10.16

Write a program that accepts characters from the keyboard but echoes their successors. For example, if a 'P' is entered, a 'Q' will be displayed. The program should terminate when a 'Z' is entered.

Solution   A solution is given in Fig. 10.15.

Use of the DOS string-input and string-output functions is illustrated in Fig. 10.16. In this example, first a string is printed and then a string is entered from the console and stored in a message buffer. This string is then printed. In this example, the STRUC pseudo operation is introduced. This is used to define the structure required for the string-input routine. In line 26, this structure is loaded into a data segment.

Review

1. Refer to Fig. 10.12. What operations are performed by the macros INST and STORE as they are used in this example?

2. Let a data segment contain space for two 5-element arrays. An element is to be a signed 32-bit integer. Write a program that adds the source array to the destination array. Test your program for the following two arrays: S = [101   −45   15   872   0]   and   D = [−321   −4   −615   41245   87].

```
 1: STACK             SEGMENT  PARA   STACK   'STACK'
 2:                   DB    120   DUP  ('HELP')
 3: STACK   ENDS
 4: EMPTY_BOX         SEGMENT  PARA   PUBLIC 'DATA'
 5: EMPTY_BOX  ENDS
 6: RUN_SEG           SEGMENT PARA PUBLIC 'CODE'
 7: BEGIN             PROC    FAR
 8:                   ASSUME DS:EMPTY_BOX,CS:RUN_SEG,SS:STACK,ES:NOTHING
 9:                        PUSH DS
10:                        XOR AX,AX
11:                        PUSH AX
12: COMMENT *     THIS PROGRAM ILLUSTRATES USE OF TWO DOS INPUT-
13:               OUTPUT ROUTINES.  THE CHARACTER IN AND THE CHARACTER
14:               PRINT ROUTINES ARE ILLUSTRATED. *
15:                        CLI
16:               BACK:    MOV AH,7
17:                        INT 33         ;GET A CHARACTER
18:                        CMP AL,'Z'     ;TERMINATOR?
19:                        JE UP          ;YES
20:                        INC AL         ;NO
21:                        MOV DL,AL
22:                        MOV AH,2       ;SET UP OUTPUT ROUTINE
23:                        INT 21H        ;PRINT CHARACTER
24:                        JMP SHORT BACK
25:               UP:      NOP
26:                        RET
27: BEGIN   ENDP
28: RUN_SEG ENDS
29:         END BEGIN
```

Figure 10.15   Solution to Example 10.16

```
 1: RETLF                    MACRO
 2: ;THIS MACRO CAUSES A RETURN AND A LINE FEED ON THE SCREEN.
 3:                          MOV DX,OFFSET LFRET
 4:                          MOV AH,9        ;GET DOS PRINT STRING ROUTINE
 5:                          INT 21H
 6:                          ENDM
 7: ;    USE EQUATE STATEMENTS
 8: CR     EQU               0DH;    ASCII FOR CARRIAGE RETURN
 9: LF     EQU               0AH
10: BUFFER_SIZE             EQU        30
11: ;         NOW DEFINE A STRUCTURE
12: MYSTRUCT                 STRUC
13: SIZE     DB              BUFFER_SIZE
14: NOT_USED                DB    ?
15: MESSAGE_BUFFER          DB    BUFFER_SIZE DUP ('$')
16: MESSAGE_TERMINATOR      DB    '$'
17: ;         STRUCTURE HAS BEEN DEFINED
18: MYSTRUCT                 ENDS
19: ;
20: STACK    SEGMENT   PARA  STACK     'STACK'
21:             DB         65 DUP ('TIGER')
22: STACK ENDS
23: ;
24: MYDATA  SEGMENT   PARA  PUBLIC    'DATA'
25: ;PUT STRUCTURE IN DATA SEGMENT
26: IOSTRUCT                MYSTRUCT<>
27: MESSOUT                 DB    'PLEASE TYPE IN A ONE LINE MESSAGE$'
28: LFRET                   DB    CR,LF,'$'
29: MYDATA  ENDS
30: ;
31: GO    SEGMENT   PARA PUBLIC 'CODE'
32: FIRST    PROC      FAR
33:          ASSUME CS:GO,SS:STACK,DS:MYDATA,ES:NOTHING
34:                    PUSH DS
35:                    MOV AX,0
36:                    PUSH AX
37:                    MOV AX,MYDATA
38:                    MOV DS,AX
39: ;          BEGIN USER PROGRAM!!!!!!!!!!!!!!!!
40:                    RETLF
41:                    RETLF
42:                    MOV AH,9
43:                    MOV DX,OFFSET MESSOUT
44:                    INT 21H        ;SEND MESSAGE
45:                    RETLF
46:                    RETLF
47: ;NOW GET CHARACTER STRING AND PUT IN INPUT BUFFER!!
48:                    MOV DX, OFFSET IOSTRUCT
49:                    MOV AH,0AH
50:                    INT 21H
51:                    RETLF
52:                    RETLF
53: ;
54: ;NOW PRINT THIS MESSAGE
55:                    MOV AH,9
56:                    MOV DX,OFFSET MESSAGE_BUFFER
57:                    INT 21H
58:                    RET
59: FIRST ENDP
60: GO      ENDS
61: END     FIRST
```

Figure 10.16   Program illustrating use of DOS string-input and string-output functions

3. Let a data segment contain an array of ten positive 16-bit numbers. Write a program that sorts the elements of this array in ascending order. Test your program using the following set of numbers: {4310,97,1,432,97,15,3118,2,87,4}.

4. Write and test a program that prints the message, 'I AM A DOG' if and only if the three characters CAT are entered in succession on the keyboard. Use at least one-user defined macro in your program.

5. Write and test a program that prints the unsigned number stored in DX
   (a) as a hexadecimal number.
   (b) as a base-10 number.

   Use at least one macro in your program.

REFERENCES

IBM Personal Computer Macro Assembler. Boca Raton, Fla.: International Business Machines Corporation, 1981.

Intel iAPX 86/89, 186/188 User's Manual. Santa Clara, Calif.: Intel Corporation, May 1983.

Intel ASM 86 Language Reference Manual, rev 1. Santa Clara, Calif.: Intel Corporation, 1981.

Intel ASM-86 Macro Assembler Operating Instructions for 8086-Based Systems, rev 3. Santa Clara, Calif.: Intel Corporation, 1982.

MORGAN, C. L., and M. WAITE, *8086/8088 16-Bit Microprocessor Primer.* Hightstown, N.J.: Byte/McGraw-Hill, 1982.

RECTOR, R., and G. ALEXY, *The 8086 Book.* Berkeley, Calif.: Osbourne/McGraw-Hill, 1980.

EXERCISES

1. Refer to the Review questions in Section 10.1. Prior to execution of an instruction, the flag register contains all zeros. Then an instruction is executed. The instruction adds 23F4 to the number in AX. After the execution of the instruction is completed
   (a) What number will be in AX?
   (b) What will be the new contents of the flag register?

2. Refer to Exercise 10.1. What number is stored in each of the following memory locations?
   (a) A8A4A
   (b) A8A4B
   (c) A8A4C

3. Refer to Exercise 10.1. Suppose that the following command is fetched and executed: MOVSB.
   (a) What is the address of the source operand?
   (b) What is the address of the destination operand?

4. Refer to Exercise 10.3. Identify which internal registers have their contents changed by execution of this instruction. What is the new number in each of these registers?

5. Refer to the information in Review question 1 in Section 10.2. For each of the following commands, identify the location of the source operand and the destination operand.
   (a) 001 00 110 10001001 01 010 010 10000001
   (b) 10001011 01 010 011 00000011
   (c) 10001001 11 101 010

6. Refer to the information in Review question 1 in Section 10.2. For each of the following instructions, identify the registers or memory locations in which values will be changed.
   (a) 00000000 11 000 001
   (b) 10000001 01 000 001 00000001 00000010 00000011

7. Translate each of the following mnemonics into machine code.
   (a) REP MOVS
   (b) MOV [BX + 13],AX
   (c) ADD DL, [BP + SI]

8. What function is performed by each of the following instructions?
   (a) XOR DX, [BP + 5]
   (b) IMUL AL,CH
   (c) CBW

9. What is done by each of the following instructions?
   (a) LEA BX,[BP + DI]
   (b) SUB AX,[BP]
   (c) CMP 3[BP],CX

10. Suppose that at the beginning of each instruction, registers and memory locations have the values given in Review question 1 in Section 10.2. Identify the location of the destination operand and its new value for each instruction in Exercise 10.7.

11. Repeat Exercise 10.10 for each instruction in Exercise 10.8.

12. Repeat Exercise 10.10 for each instruction in Exercise 10.9.

13. Consider the following program segment:

```
MOV AL,93H
ADD AL,87H
DAA
```

At the conclusion of execution of this segment, what number will be in AL?

14. Refer to Exercise 10.13. Suppose that ADD is replaced by SUB and DAA by DAS. At the conclusion of execution of this segment, what number will be in AL?

15. Refer to the following program segment:

```
MOV AX,0F3H
MOV CX,05H
SHR AX,CL
```

At the conclusion of execution of this segment, what number will be in AX?

16. Refer to Exercise 10.15. Suppose that SHR is replaced by SAR. At the conclusion of execution of this program segment, what number will be in AX?

17. Refer to the conditions given in Review question 1 in Section 10.2. For the specified conditions, what will be in AX after the following commands are executed?

```
AND CL,OFH
ROL AX,CL
```

18. Suppose that the ROL command in Exercise 10.17 is replaced with an RCR command. At the conclusion of execution of this segment, what number will be in AX?

19. Express the program segment given in Exercise 10.17 in machine code.

20. Consider the following program segment.

Label	Location (Offset)	Command
BACK	1200	NOP
	.	
	.	
	.	
HERE	1276	JNC BACK

What is the code for the statement at location HERE?

21. Refer to Exercise 10.20. Suppose that your program is fetching instructions starting at location 1B03. You wish to branch to BACK if and only if the carry bit is cleared. Indicate a proper sequence of instructions.

22. Refer to the assembly-language program in Fig. 10.7. Convert this program to a subroutine. Prior to calling this subroutine, the source and destination addresses are to be placed in the SI and DI registers. The number of characters in the string is to be placed in the CX register. Test your subroutine.

23. Refer to Exercise 10.22. Rewrite the subroutine so that it "pulls in" the three arguments. The 16-bit offsets identifying the starting addresses of the strings are to be placed immediately after the CALL statement. The 16-bit character count is to follow immediately the offsets.

24. Refer to Problem 23. Redo Exercise 10.23 so that both segments and offsets are pulled into the subroutine. When exiting from the subroutine, the segment registers should contain the same numbers as when the routine was entered.

25. Write and test a subroutine that returns the average of three 16-bit signed numbers. Clearly identify the method used for transmitting arguments between the main program and the subroutine. Test your subroutine.

26. Refer to the floating points illustrated in Fig. 10.14. Using the same type of representation, indicate the hexadecimal representation for each of the following floating points.
    (a) 17.0
    (b) -31.0
    (c) 4.625

27. Write and test a subroutine that sorts N 16-bit signed numbers in ascending order.

28. Write and test a subroutine that sorts N 32-bit signed integers in ascending order.

29. Write and test a subroutine that sorts N 32-bit floating points in ascending order.

30. Write a subroutine that pulls in an offset X and a 16-bit number N. Then the subroutine displays in hexadecimal notation the words stored in locations X, X + 2, . . . X + 2 $(N - 1)$.

31. Modify the subroutine described in Exercise 10.30 so that both a segment and an offset are pulled into the subroutine in order to identify a starting address.

32. The 1-byte code for an 8086 instruction is to be carried into a subroutine. The instruction is to be a valid code for one of the following commands:

```
LAHF
SAHF
PUSHF
POPF
```

Note: Any other 8-bit codes are considered to be invalid instructions.

Write a subroutine that acts as a disassembler. That is, it prints out one of the above mnemonics or an invalid code message depending upon which operation code is carried into the subroutine.

33. Write and test a subroutine that returns the product of two 32-bit floating points.

34. Write an interpreter that fetches and interprets a command string that uses the following commands:

CMD	Function
CLR	Clears AX and BX
INA	Increments AX
INB	Increments BX
ADD	BX + AX = > AX
END	Prints END message and returns to DOS

Test your interpreter using the following program.

```
CLR
INA
INB
ADD
INB
ADD
END
```

11

The M68000 Microprocessor

Modern microprocessors are designed so that they may readily support powerful high-level languages and popular operating systems. The M68000 microprocessor, developed by the Motorola Corporation, was clearly designed with such tasks considered. Furthermore, this processor was given hardware and software attributes that facilitate its incorporation as a component of a multiprocessor system.

In order to support modern operating systems, the M68000 contains a set of *privileged* instructions. These instructions can be executed only when the CPU is in a privileged, or supervisory, mode of operation. A vectored priority interrupt capability assists in supporting such systems. The powerful instruction set, wide range of addressing modes, and large number of internal registers—in particular, 32-bit registers and instructions with 32-bit operands—facilitate the implementation of modern high-level languages.

11.1 ORGANIZATION OF THE M68000

The M68000 is a large-scale integrated circuit that has 64 external pin connections. Voltages representing one of the two logic levels are associated with most of these pins. If a label identifying a pin has a bar drawn over it, the function of the pin is active when associated with a low voltage level, or a logic 0. Figure 11.1 is a representation of the M68000 microprocessor. Observe that there are 23 address lines, enabling approximately 8 million words of memory to be addressed directly. Each

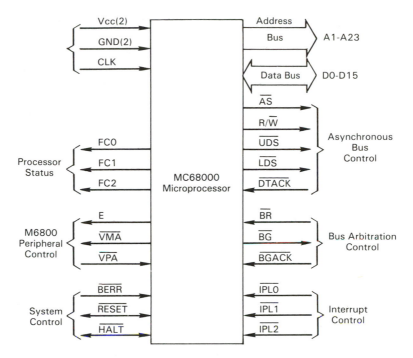

Figure 11.1   M68000 pin connections (Courtesy of Motorola, Inc.)

memory word is accessed by way of the 16-bit data bus. If a byte operand is desired, appropriate bus control signals are generated. The $\overline{UDS}$ and $\overline{LDS}$ (upper data strobe and lower data strobe) pins are used for this purpose. The $\overline{AS}$ signal becomes active when there is a valid address on the address bus. Similarly, appropriate bus control signals are generated to specify read or write operations. A data acknowledge signal may be used for memory or I/O handshaking.

Bus request, bus grant, and bus acknowledge signals are used if the M68000 is part of a multiprocessor system sharing a common bus. These three signals are part of a bus arbitration circuit to determine which device will be a bus master device.

A seven-level vectored priority interrupt is available on the M68000 processor. External devices can be grouped into seven different categories. Each category is associated with a 3-bit word. This word is related to the logic signals connected to $\overline{IPL2}$, $\overline{IPL1}$, and $\overline{IPL0}$. No interrupt is requested if logic 1s are connected to each of these pins. Because in this case, three inactive signals are connected to the three pins, this interrupt level is referred to as level 0. If logic 0s are connected to $\overline{IPL2}$ and $\overline{IPL1}$, and a logic 1 is connected to $\overline{IPL0}$, this interrupt level is referred to as level 6. The highest interrupting level, level 7, produces a nonmaskable interrupt. If the level of an interrupt occurring during execution of an instruction is greater than the 3-bit interrupt mask stored in the status register, an interrupt will occur at the conclusion of the present instruction. Otherwise, an external interrupt will not be processed.

Refer to the left portion of Fig. 11.1. Two pins on this chip are used for the 5-volt power supply, and two pins are used for a ground connection. One input line is required for the system clock. The three pins FC0, FC1, and FC2 are used to communicate the information about the internal state of the processor to external devices. It is especially important for peripherals to know whether or not the processor is in a supervisory state. Certain external components should remain inactive unless the processor is in a supervisory state.

The enable pin E, valid memory address pin $\overline{\text{VMA}}$, and valid peripheral address pin $\overline{\text{VPA}}$ facilitate use of standard components that were developed for an earlier microprocessor, the 8-bit M6800. The bus-error pin $\overline{\text{BERR}}$ is used to accept a signal input if a valid number is not on a bus during a designated interval. This signal may be used to produce a trap to an appropriate processing routine. The $\overline{\text{RESET}}$ and $\overline{\text{HALT}}$ pins are used for bidirectional signals. The processor may be externally reset, or it may generate a reset signal that is sent to peripheral devices. Similarly, the processor may output a signal on the $\overline{\text{HALT}}$ pin indicating that it is in the halt mode. An external device, such as a device producing direct memory access data transfers, may send a signal to the $\overline{\text{HALT}}$ pin. If this is done, the processor halts at the conclusion of its current machine cycle and floats its buses.

A complete description of the control signals and their timing relationships is not within the scope of this textbook. Interested readers are referred to the appropriate manufacturer's literature.

Figure 11.2 displays a representation of the internal registers available to a programmer of the M68000. There are eighteen 32-bit registers and one 16-bit register. The first eight registers shown are *data registers*. They may be used for either 8-bit (byte), 16-bit (word), or 32-bit (long word) operations. The next set of registers is referred to as *address registers*. These registers may be used as base registers for addressing or even for ''user'' stack pointers. Word or long-word operations may be performed on the contents of these registers. Because these registers are intended to be used in conjunction with addresses rather than with data, operations on the contents of these registers do not affect the status flags. Any of the data or address registers may be used as index registers. In addition to these registers, there are two 32-bit system stack pointers. One of these defines the system stack pointer available in the *user* mode of operation. The other register contains the system stack pointer available when operating in the *supervisory* mode.

The 16-bit status register is divided into two segments: a supervisor segment and a user segment. The user segment is frequently called a condition codes register. Figure 11.3 defines the various bits in the status register.

The four bits N, Z, V, and C in the condition codes register are the sign bit, zero bit, overflow bit, and carry bit. The functions of these bits are essentially the same as those of the corresponding flags on either a PDP-11 or an 8086 processor. The X bit is very similar to the carry bit. Arithmetic operations affect this bit in the same way that the carry bit is affected. However, this bit is not cleared by logic

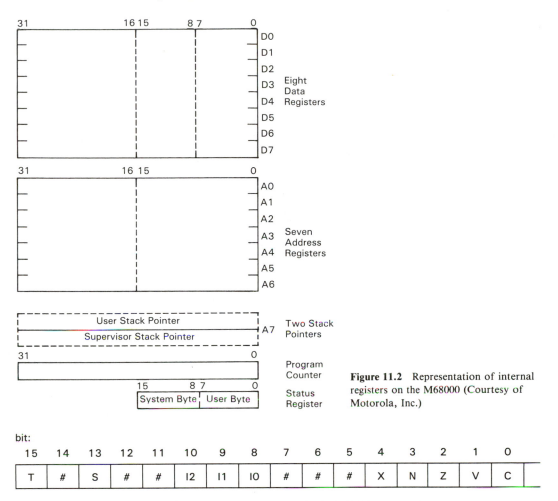

Figure 11.2 Representation of internal registers on the M68000 (Courtesy of Motorola, Inc.)

Figure 11.3 Bit assignments in the M68000 status register

operations. It is used for extended precision arithmetic operations. As an example, the ADDX command performs virtually the same function as the ADC or add with carry command that is used on 8086-based systems.

If the T bit is set when an instruction is fetched, an internal interrupt or trap will be executed at the conclusion of the instruction. The value stored in the S bit determines the mode of operation of the processor. If the S bit is 1, the processor is in the supervisory state. All computer instructions can be executed from this state. If the S bit is 0, the processor is in the user state. Certain instructions cannot be executed while in the user state. Examples of such instructions are the STOP and RESET instructions and any instructions that can change bits of the high-order byte of the status register. When in the user mode, only an external reset signal, an interrupt, or a trap can cause the processor to return to the supervisory mode. Furthermore, external status information is provided by the processor to indicate when the processor is in the supervisory mode. This information can be used to activate certain portions of memory or certain I/O devices only when the system is in the supervisory state. Thus, internal security can easily be maintained.

Refer again to Fig. 11.3. A 3-bit interrupt mask consists of bits I2, I1, and I0. The 3-bit number defined by these bits determines the current priority of the system. In general, only an interrupting signal having a priority higher than the number currently stored in the interrupt mask will activate an interrupt processing routine. There is one exception to this rule. Suppose the interrupt mask contains the number 7. If the signal connected to pins $\overline{IPL2}$, $\overline{IPL1}$, and $\overline{IPL0}$ changes from a lower priority to a priority 7 interrupt, the interrupt will be processed. Thus, a level 7 interrupt is considered to be a nonmaskable interrupt.

Suppose that an external interrupt of higher priority than that specified in the interrupt mask occurs during the execution of an instruction. Then, when the instruction is completed, the following sequence of events will occur:

1. A replica will be made of the status register.
2. The T bit in the status register is set to 0, and the S bit is set to 1. The 3-bit interrupt mask is updated to correspond to the level of the current interrupting signal.
3. The 32-bit "return address" is pushed onto the supervisory stack. Then the replica of the status register is pushed onto the supervisory stack.
4. An 8-bit interrupt vector number is either fetched from the lower half of the data bus or is generated internally.
5. The interrupt vector number is used to identify a 4-byte block of memory under supervisory mode control. The address of an appropriate interrupt processing routine is fetched from this block (called the interrupt vector) and placed in the program counter.
6. Control transfers to the interrupt processing routine. At the conclusion of this routine, an RTE, or return from exception, instruction is executed. This restores the previous program status word and causes a return to the previously interrupted program segment.

External interrupts are just one type of *exception* processing. Application of a reset signal or encountering an addressing error or a bus error produces an exception having a higher priority than external interrupts. Execution of TRAP-type instructions has a lower priority than external interrupts. All of these "exception-type" operations require use of an interrupt-type vector. The addresses associated with these vectors should be stored in memory that is accessible only when the processor is in the supervisory mode of operation.

The M68000 has a 32-bit program counter and 32-bit address registers. Yet internal pin connections representing the address bus can identify only 2^{23} different addresses. Enhancements of the M68000 are now available that will enable the processor to access easily a full range of memory addresses. The most recent of these, the M68020, is a realization of a true 32-bit machine. An 8-bit version, the 68008, is also available. This machine uses the same instruction set as the 68000 but provides only an 8-bit data bus that is useful for smaller applications.

Review

1. The 8086 utilizes a 40-pin integrated circuit, whereas the M68000 utilizes a 64-pin chip. Cite advantages and disadvantages of the two configurations.
2. Refer to Fig. 11.1. In order to protect information in memory from *user* access and modification, certain information is required from the processor. Which pins supply the required information?
3. Suppose the interrupt mask is set to level 7. An external interrupt will occur only if the input on the appropriate pins *changes* from a lower level to level 7. Why is a change required just for this particular case?
4. Prior to the execution of a NOP instruction, the hexadecimal number in the status register is 5DF8. (Assume that the unspecified bits in the status register are all 1s.) During execution of this instruction, the following logic levels are applied to pins $\overline{IPL2}$, $\overline{IPL1}$, and $\overline{IPL0}$: high, low, high. When the subsequent instruction is fetched, what number will be in the status register?
5. Refer to Review question 4. Suppose that the logic levels applied to pins $\overline{IPL2}$, $\overline{IPL1}$, and $\overline{IPL0}$ are, respectively, low, low, high. When the subsequent instruction is fetched, what number will be in the status register?

11.2 ADDRESSING TECHNIQUES FOR THE M68000

There is a similarity between addressing modes on PDP-11 computers and those on the M68000. It is convenient for a programmer if the modes of addressing used for one type of instruction are all available for any similar type of instruction. Clearly, attempts have been made to realize this attribute for the M68000 instruction set. As a practical matter, however, such generality is not maintained over the entire instruction set.

Instructions, word data, and long-word data may be addressed only from even-numbered addresses. Unlike 8086-based systems, the high-order byte of a word is stored in the lower or even-numbered address. Similarly, for double words the most significant word is stored in an even-numbered memory location identified by an address that is 2 less than that of the least significant word. Figure 11.4 illustrates the general format of an M68000 instruction.

| Command word | IMM OPND | IMM OPND | SOURCE ADDR EXTEN | SOURCE ADDR EXTEN | DESTIN ADDR EXTEN | DESTIN ADDR EXTEN |

Figure 11.4 Instruction format for an M68000 instruction

Notes:

1. Each component of the instruction is a 16-bit word.
2. The COMMAND word specifies the instruction.
3. Words within brackets are either optional or required only for specific instructions.
4. Two words are required if an immediate operand is a long word or if a 32-bit address extension is needed.

Although the M68000 addressing modes were designed so that a certain amount of regularity would be obtained, this goal was not achieved in the same manner as it was for the basic PDP-11 instruction set. However, the efforts made toward this regularity do facilitate the development of programs.

Figure 11.5 illustrates a typical format for a two-operand instruction. Figure 11.6 illustrates eight modes of addressing. The ADD instruction is used to illustrate these modes of addressing. The modes of addressing refer to the modes of computing the effective address of an operand that may be located in a register or in memory. The addressing modes defined are reasonably general. However, there are some exceptions for virtually all instructions that use these modes to compute the effective address of an operand.

Note: The data register refers to D0 to D7. The OP-modes are defined as follows:

1. Bit 8 is a direction bit.
   0 = > Data register defines destination
   1 = > Data register defines source
2. Bits 7 and 6 define word length.
   00 = > byte   01 = > word   10 = > long word   11 = > undefined

Notes:

0. ADD.B, ADD.W, or ADD.L is used to specify byte, word, or long-word operation. If the suffix is omitted, the word operation is the default operation.
1. The effective address cannot specify a data register as a destination register.
2. If an address register is the destination register, then the ADDA command rather than the ADD command must be used.

b15 b14 b13 b12 b11	b10 b9 b8 b7 b6	b5 b4 b3	b2 b1 b0
Command	Data Register Register Op-Mode	Effective Mode	Address Reg

Figure 11.5 A typical double-operand instruction

THE ADD INSTRUCTION ADD DN,<EA> OR ADD <EA>,DN MODES FOR DETERMINING EFFECTIVE ADDRESS

Mode	Name	Examples	Notes
000	Data register direct	ADD DN,DM ADD DM,DN	1
001	Address register direct	ADD DN,AM ADD AM,DN	2
010	Address register deferred	ADD DN,(AM) ADD (AM),DN	3,4
011	Address register deferred with postincrement	ADD DN,(AM)+ ADD (AM)+,DN	4,5
100	Address register deferred with predecrement	ADD DN,−(AM) ADD −(AM),DN	6,7
101	Address register deferred with displacement	ADD DN,d16(AM) ADD d16(AM),DN	8,9
110	Address register deferred with index register and with displacement	ADD DN,d8(AM,RI.X) ADD d8 (AM,RI),DN	10,11
111	Special cases		12

Figure 11.6   Effective addressing modes illustrated for a typical two-operand instruction

3. Effective memory address is identified by the contents of AM.

4. Alternate notation for (AM) is AM@.

5. After identifying operand, AM is incremented by 1, 2, or 4, depending on whether instruction operates on bytes, words, or long words.

6. Prior to operand identification, AM is decremented by either 1, 2, or 4. Then it is used to identify appropriate operand in memory.

7. Another commonly used notation for −(AM) is AM@−.

8. Address of operand is the contents of AM plus the 16-bit word immediately following the instruction operation code. The sign of this word is extended.

9. Another common notation for d16(AM) is AM@(d16).

10. The subsequent word identifies one of 16 possible index registers and a sign-extended 8-bit displacement. The effective address is the contents of AM plus the contents of index register plus sign-extended 8-bit displacement. Figure 11.7 identifies the subsequent word when indexed addressing is used.

11. An alternate notation for d8(AM,RI.X) is AM@(d8,RI.X), where

    $X => W$ implies index is 16-bit sign extended word.
    $X => L$ implies index is 32-bit word.
    Suffix omitted $=> X = W$.

12. Several special addressing modes are defined using this operation code.

b15	b14 b13 b12	b11	b10 b9 b8	b7 b6 b5 b4 b3 b2 b1 b0
D/A	Register	W/L	0 0 0	Displacement

Note: Bit 15: 1 => address register   0 => data register
       Bit 11: 1 => long word   0 => sign-extended word

Figure 11.7 Definition of subsequent word used with indexed addressing

Example 11.1

Translate each of the following mnemonics into appropriate operation codes. Express your answers using the hexadecimal number system.

(a) ADD.W D7,(A5)+

(b) ADD.L −(A4),D1

(c) ADD.B −7(A4,A5.W),D2

(d) ADD 25(A3),D3

Solution   **(a)** The effective address is the destination address. Mode 3 addressing is utilized. Therefore, the operation code is DF5D.

(b) Mode 4 is utilized. The operation code is D2A4.

(c) Because mode 6 is used, a 16-bit word must be addended to the instruction. The resultant code is D434   D0F9.

(d) The resultant code is D66B   0019.

Example 11.2

Translate each of the following machine-language instructions, expressed in hexadecimal, into appropriate mnemonics.

(a) *DC4D*

(b) *DC*65

(c) *DE6C*   0102

(d) *D*664

(e) *D*55A

(f) *D*273   28*F*2

Solution   **(a)** Expressed in binary, the command is 1101   110   001   0   01   101. Therefore, the data register D6 is the destination register. Mode 1 is used in conjunction with address register 5. Therefore, the command is ADD A5,D6.

(b) ADD −(A5),D6

(c) ADD 258(A4),D7

(d) ADD −(A4),D3

(e) ADD D2,(A2)+

(f) Expressed in binary, the command is

1101   001   001   110   011   0   010   1   000   11110010

Mode 6 refers to indexed addressing. The full 32-bit D2 register is used as the index register, and the displacement is −14. Therefore, the command is ADD −14(A3,D2.L),D1

Example 11.3

Explain what is done by each of the commands used in Example 11.1.

Solution (a) The least significant 16 bits of the number in D7 are added to the memory word identified by the address in A5. Then the number in A5 is incremented by 2.

(b) The number 4 is subtracted from the number in A4. Then the 32-bit word identified by the new address is added to D1.

(c) The word consisting of the lower 16 bits in A5 is sign extended. Then this 32-bit word, the 32-bit word in A4, and the 32-bit representation of -7 are added together to obtain a new 32-bit address. The byte stored at this address is added to the least significant byte of the number stored in D2.

Warning: Recall that in the direct implementation of instructions on the basic M68000 machine, the high-order address byte is not placed on the external address bus.

(d) An address that is 25 larger than the number stored in A3 is used to identify a 16-bit word. This word is added to the low-order word stored in D3.

When the 3-bit MODE segment of the effective address field of an instruction contains all logic 1s, a special addressing mode is defined. There are five such addressing modes. The 3-bit REGISTER segment of the effective address field is used to identify these special addressing modes. Figure 11.8 illustrates these special addressing modes.

ADD INSTRUCTION IS USED TO ILLUSTRATE SPECIAL MODES
ADD DN,<EA> OR ADD <EA>,DN
THE MODE SEGMENT OF THE EFFECTIVE ADDRESS FIELD CONTAINS THE FOLLOWING
BINARY DIGITS: 1   1   1

Register designator	Name	Example	Notes
000	Absolute short addressing	ADD d16,DN ADD DN,d16	1
001	Absolute long addressing	ADD d32,DN ADD DN,d32	2
010	Relative addressing	ADD RELd16,DN	3,4,5,6
011	Relative indexed addressing	ADD RELd8(RI.L),DN ADD RELd8(RI.W),DN	5,6 7,8
100	Immediate addressing	ADD.B #d8,DN ADD.W #d16,DN ADD.L #d32,DN	6,9

Figure 11.8   Special addressing modes illustrated for a typical two-operand instruction

Notes:

1. An alternate notation for ADD d16,DN is ADD d.W,DN. The 16-bit operand, sign extended, is the effective address.

2. An alternate notation is ADD d.L,DN. The 32-bit word is the effective address.

3. An alternate notation is ADD PC@(d16),DN. The alternate notations that have been used to represent effective addresses are referred to as RTL, or register transfer language, representations of addressing modes.

4. The effective address is the sum of the number in the program counter plus the sign-extended 16-bit displacement. The number in the program counter changes during execution of the instruction. The value used is the number corresponding to the address of the displacement word. This may be represented as (PC) + 2, where (PC) identifies the address of the corresponding instruction command.

5. The prefix REL indicates that the 16-bit number must be identified in a manner such that relative addressing is selected. See Example 11.4 for an illustration of this syntax.

6. The effective address cannot be used as a destination operand for this particular instruction.

7. Using RTL, the syntax for this instruction is

   ```
   ADD PC@(d8,RI.W) or ADD PC@(d8,RI.L)
   ```

8. Suppose the instruction is stored in an address identified by (PC). Then the effective address of the operand is (PC) + 2 + number in the index register + sign-extended 8-bit displacement. If the number in the index register is a 16-bit number, it is sign extended.

9. An alternate way to perform this operation is to use the ADDI or ADDQ commands. Most assemblers automatically select these alternate forms. Instructions such as these are illustrated in Section 11.3.

Example 11.4

Refer to the following assembly-language program. The first statement is the RORG directive. This indicates that the initial location counter is relative. That is, the program is intended to be relocatable or position independent. The instructions labeled C, D, E, and F could be interpreted in two different ways. Because they follow the RORG assembler directive, they are interpreted as relative addressing instructions. Translate instructions A, B, C, D, E, and F into machine code and indicate what each instruction does.

```
RORG $1000
```

*   *Note:* The $ prefix is used to represent a hexadecimal number.

A: ADD 20,D0
B: ADD $10000,D1
C: ADD *+6,D2

*   *Note:* The notation *+ indicates the operand is to have an address 6 greater than the address of the instruction.

D: ADD UP,D2
E: ADD *+$0ABC,D2
F: ADD UP(A2),D3
                ADD.B #10,D2   IMMEDIATE ADDRESSING!!
                ADD #10,D2   WORD OPERAND!!!
UP: NOP
                END

Solution   **(a)** The hexadecimal code is D078   0014. The command causes the word stored in location $00000014 to be added to the low-order word stored in D0.

(b) The code is $D279   0001   0000. The command will add the word stored in $00010000 to the low-order word in D1.

(c) Relative addressing is used. The desired operand is stored at an address that is 6 greater than the address of the instruction, or 4 greater than (PC) + 2. The code is $D47A   0004.

(d) The address corresponding to the label UP is $14 greater than the address of the instruction. Thus the command code is $D47A   0012. The instruction will cause the word stored at location UP to be added to the low-order word in D2.

(e) The word whose address is $0ABC larger than the address of the instruction is added to the low-order word in D2. The code is $D47A   0ABA.

(f) This is relative indexed addressing. The label UP corresponds to an address that is 12 larger than the address of the instruction. The code is $D67B   A00A. When executed, this instruction will add the word stored in location UP to the low-order word in D3 if and only if the current value of the low-order word in A2 is 0.

The 12 modes of addressing that have been discussed are used in single-operand as well as double-operand instructions. Frequently, literature on the M68000 indicates that there are 14 modes of addressing. The two modes of addressing that have not yet been discussed are referred to as quick immediate addressing and inherent addressing. Inherent addressing implies that the instruction itself determines the mode of addressing. Examples of inherent addressing are stack operations and branch instructions. Quick immediate addressing implies that the immediate operand is contained as part of the 16-bit command code. Both of these modes of addressing are discussed in the following section.

Review

1. Refer to Fig. 11.6 and to its Note 1. Why was this stipulation made by the designers of the M68000?

2. Refer to Example 11.2. What does each of these instructions do?

3. Prior to execution of each of the following instructions, suppose the designated registers contain the following hexadecimal numbers:

   (D0) = 0000FFFE   (A0) = 0000FFFE   (D1) = 00000003   (D2) = 0000FFFE

   What number will be in the destination register after each of the following instructions is executed?
   (a) ADD.B D1,D0
   (b) ADD.W D1,D2
   (c) ADD.W D1,A0

4. Refer to Example 11.4. Suppose the assembler directive RORG $1000 is changed to ORG $1000. What will be the new operation codes for the instructions identified by the labels C, D, E, and F?

5. Refer to the following assembly-language program. Translate each step into machine code, and indicate what is done by each statement during program execution.

   ```
              ORG $1000
              ADD D4,-(A5)
              ADD D0,$0123(A2)
              RORG $1006
              ADD AHEAD(A6),D3
   AHEAD:     ADD.L (A4)+,D0
              END
   ```

11.3 CAPABILITIES OF THE M68000 INSTRUCTION SET

In comparison to earlier microprocessors, the M68000 contains a powerful instruction set. A listing and description of these instructions are presented in Appendix C. In this section, instructions that are somewhat different from those previously encountered will be discussed.

The M68000 instructions may be classified under the following categories:

1. Move-type instructions
2. Arithmetic and logic operations
3. Decimal or binary coded decimal commands
4. Stack operations
5. Shift and rotate commands
6. Control transfer instructions

7. Processor control operations

8. Bit operations

9. Special instructions, including those that are valid only in the supervisory mode of operation.

The move-type commands consist of a variety of MOVE commands, the MOVEP command, the LEA command, and the EXG command. Recall that most M68000 commands can operate either on bytes, words, or long words, where a long word consists of 4 bytes. MOVE commands have the capability to operate on two memory operands. That is, both the source and the destination operand may be stored in memory. The EXG, or exchange, command may be used to exchange two operands. However, this command may operate only on the contents of data registers. A data register may be loaded using a 16-bit MOVEQ or MOVE QUICK command. The immediate operand is a signed number represented by the last 8 bits of the operation code. This number is sign extended before being placed in a 32-bit data register.

The LEA command is used to load an address register with the effective address of its operand. The MOVEP commands are intended to facilitate input/output operations. Frequently 8-bit command registers and status registers are located at even-numbered addresses. Several registers may be loaded with a single MOVEP command. Similarly, the contents of several status registers may be moved using a single MOVEP command.

Example 11.5

Suppose the console keyboard and printer control registers are located at the same addresses as those typically found on small PDP-11 systems. Similarly, suppose these peripherals operate in the same manner as the PDP-11 peripherals that have previously been discussed in this textbook. It is intended to program the keyboard for interrupt-driven operation and the printer for programmed input/output. Write an M68000 program segment that will do this.

Solution   Recall that if all zeros are placed in the command register, the device operates in a programmed mode. If a logic 1 is placed in bit-6 of the corresponding command register, the device operates in an interrupt-driven mode. Also recall that the keyboard command register is located at octal address 177560 and the printer command register is located at octal address 177564. The following program segment satisfies the requirements.

```
MOVEA.L    #$0000FF60,A1
MOVE.L     #$40000000,D1
MOVEP.L    D1,$10(A1)
```

Another variation of the MOVE command is the MOVEM, or move-multiple, registers command. This instruction is used to move a set of registers into consecutive memory locations.

Example 11.6

Write and decode an M68000 instruction that moves the 32-bit contents of the registers D0, D4, D7, A3, and A5 into consecutive memory locations starting at location F000. Assume that the number 0000F000 is stored in A4.

Solution Refer to the MOVEM command in Appendix C. The mnemonic is

```
MOVEM.L   D0/D4/D7/A3/A5,(A4)
```

The machine-language code for this command, expressed in base-16, is 48D4 2891.

Most of the arithmetic and logic commands available on the M68000 are similar to commands already discussed. These include variations of the ADD, SUB, CMP, EOR, AND, NEG, NOT, and OR commands. The TST command subtracts 0 from the operand and sets the sign and zero flags accordingly. The CLR command places all zeros in the bits of the destination operand. There are no increment or decrement commands. The ADDQ and SUBQ commands are used in lieu of these commands. The ADDQ or ADD QUICK command is a 16-bit command that is used to add a number between 1 and 8 to the destination operand. The SUBQ command subtracts a number between 1 and 8 from the destination operand. The MULS and MULU commands perform either signed or unsigned multiplication of 16-bit operands. The DIVS and DIVU commands are used for the corresponding inverse operations.

Certain arithmetic operations may be performed on 8-bit packed binary coded decimal numbers. These operations are handled somewhat differently on the M68000 than they are on the 8086 microprocessor. The following commands are available.

ABCD	SRC + DST + X => DST	Decimal adjust DST
SBCD	DST − SRC − X => DST	Decimal adjust DST
NBCD	0 − DST − X => DST	Decimal adjust DST

Two modes of addressing are available for use with the above instructions. In one mode, both of the byte operands are stored in data registers. In the other mode, both byte operands are stored in memory, and the autodecrement mode of addressing is utilized. This mode of addressing facilitates the implementation of addition and subtraction of multiple-precision decimal operands.

Other than jump to subroutine, trap-type and return-type commands, there are just three M68000 commands that inherently operate on the run-time stack. The PEA command pushes the 32-bit effective address of the operand on the stack. The UNLK (unlink) command loads the stack pointer from an address register and then pops the top of the stack into that address register. The LINK command pushes the contents of a specified address register onto the stack, loads the updated stack pointer into the specified address register, and changes the value in the updated stack pointer by a signed 16-bit displacement, d. Frequently, the value of d is negative. This has the effect of reserving or allocating stack space, and is commonly used by compilers of higher-level languages in the allocation of local variable space.

Example 11.7

Write a program statement that pushes D5 onto the stack.

Solution   None of the commands discussed above is needed. The following command will achieve the desired results.

```
MOVE.L   D5,-(A7)
```

The rotate and shift commands on the M68000 are very similar to those on the 8086. Bytes, words, and long words may be rotated or shifted. There is an 8086 command for rotating bytes or words through the carry bit. Similarly, bytes, words, and long words on M68000-based systems may be rotated through the extend bit, X. Operands stored in memory must be words and may be rotated or shifted just 1 bit. Operands stored in a data register may be bytes, words, or long words. These operands may be shifted or rotated more than one bit.

Control transfer instructions consist of the following types of instructions:

Bcc	Branch on condition code values.
BRA	Unconditional branch.
BSR	Branch to subroutine. Store return address on stack.
DBcc	Test condition codes, decrement contents of specified data register, and branch to destination address if either the specified conditions are satisfied or if the number in the specified register is -1.
JMP	Unconditional transfer. Address range is not limited.
JSR	Jump to subroutine. Store return address on stack. Address range is not limited.
RTR	Return and restore condition codes.
RTS	Return from subroutine.

All TRAP instructions.

The branch instructions are similar to the jump on condition instructions used on the 8086. Relative addressing is employed on all branch-type instructions. However, the signed displacement may be a 16-bit word. The destination address is (PC) + 2 + signed displacement, where (PC) identifies the location of the branch-type instruction. If the displacement can be expressed as an 8-bit signed integer, a branch instruction consists of just a 16-bit word that includes an 8-bit displacement. If it is required to have a 16-bit displacement, a two-word instruction is required. In this case, the 8 displacement bits of the first word are all zeros, and the subsequent word defines the 16-bit displacement.

The JMP and JSR instructions can access any memory address. The RTS command pops the return address into the program counter. The RTR command first pops a 16-bit word into the status register. However, it does not change the value of the supervisor status bit.

Execution of TRAPS results in exception processing. When a TRAP is executed, the machine enters the supervisory state, stores the old processor status word on the stack, stores the return address on the stack, and branches to a routine whose starting address is stored in an appropriate TRAP vector location. These locations are identified on the last page of Appendix C.

Example 11.8

A 20-digit BCD number is stored in memory beginning at hexadecimal location 2000. Another 20-digit BCD number is stored in memory beginning at hexadecimal location 3000. Write a program that adds the first number to the second number. *Note:* We will represent base-16 numbers by prefixing them with a dollar sign.

Solution

```
          MOVE      #0,CCR       ;CLEAR EXTEND BIT
          MOVEA.L   #$200A,A1    ;SET SOURCE POINTER
          MOVEA.L   #$300A,A2    ;SET DESTINATION POINTER
          MOVE.B    #9,D0        ;SET COUNTER
  BACK:   ABCD      -(A1),-(A2)
          DBRA  D0,BACK
          . . . . . . . . . . . . . . . . . .
```

Example 11.9

For each of the following commands, program execution will continue at an address that is stored in a particular memory location. Identify the address of each location at which the starting address of the corresponding TRAP processing routine is stored.
(a) TRAPV
(b) ILLEGAL
(c) TRAP #5

Solution   Refer to the last page of Appendix C.
(a) Space for the TRAP-ON-OVERFLOW vector starts at location 01C.
(b) 010
(c) This uses vector number 37. Space starts at hexadecimal location $080 + 5(4) = 094$. (*Note:* Arithmetic is in base-16!)

Certain instructions may be considered as processor control instructions. The MOVE TO CCR instruction permits any combination of status flags to be modified by a single instruction. The two privileged instructions STOP and RESET may be considered as processor control instructions. The RESET instruction may be used to send out an active signal on the processor reset line. In a typical configuration this will cause all external peripherals connected to this line to be reset. Execution of the STOP command causes termination of normal bus cycles. These may resume if an external interrupt signal, a trace exception, or an external reset signal is asserted.

The TAS command may also be considered a processor control signal. The TAS command tests the contents of a byte of memory, adjusts the zero flag and the sign flag accordingly, sets the most significant bit of the operand, and replaces it in memory. This is all done in one indivisible operation. This instruction is used to provide a form of communication in a multiprocessor environment called a *binary semaphore*. Because the location is tested and updated in one indivisible operation, the programmer is guaranteed that another processor cannot change the contents of this location between the time it has been tested and the time it is updated. This is essential in developing *synchronization primitives* used in multiprocessor operating systems, something that was very difficult to accomplish using earlier microprocessors that did not provide this feature.

Four commands may be used for single-bit operations: BCHG, BCLR, BSET, or BTST. Each of these commands can be used in either of two ways. Either a bit in the long word in a data register is tested or a bit in a byte stored in memory is tested. If the designated bit is 0, the zero flag comes up. If the designated bit is not 0, the zero flag goes down. Then the bit tested is allowed to remain the same, changed, set, or cleared, depending on whether the command is BTST, BCHG, BSET, or BCLR. Such commands are very useful when the processor is sensing a flag on a peripheral device. As soon as the flag is asserted, it can be cleared and program control can be transferred to an appropriate service routine.

The remaining M68000 commands may be classified as special commands. The NOP and EXT (sign extend) commands require no further explanation. The CHK command is used to ensure that values of operands are within specified limits. If not, a CHECK TRAP occurs. This command is especially useful for checking bounds either during compilation or run time for strongly typed languages, such as Ada or Pascal.

The SWAP command is used to interchange two words in a data register. The Scc commands are used to establish a static flag in memory based on conditions of the dynamic flags at some particular instant during program execution. This is especially useful for languages that allow evaluation of Boolean expressions, such as C. All privileged instructions may also be considered to be special instructions. These instructions relate to major processor control operations or modification of the status of the machine.

Review

1. Write a single instruction that will push the contents of the following 32-bit registers onto the stack: D0,D1,D2,A3,A4,A5.
2. Write a single program statement that will
   (a) Set the carry flag
   (b) Clear the zero flag
   (c) Clear the overflow flag
   (d) Set the extend flag
   (e) Set the sign flag

3. At a particular point during program execution it is desired to set the 8-bit number in memory location FLAG to the value 1 if and only if either the carry flag or the zero flag is set. If neither flag is set, the value in FLAG is to be set to 0. Write a program consisting of just two statements that satisfies these requirements.

4. Suppose a status register of a peripheral device is located at hexadecimal address 2000. Write a program segment that monitors bit 5 of this 8-bit register until bit 5 becomes a logic 1. Then the procedure SERVICE is invoked.

5. List all of the privileged instructions. Why is the MOVE USP instruction useful?

11.4 USE OF AN M68000 CROSS ASSEMBLER AND SIMULATOR

Programs for first-generation microprocessors were frequently developed in machine language. Due to the large number of addressing modes and to the diversity of the instruction set, it would be quite difficult to develop M68000 programs directly in machine code. Motorola has developed a cross assembler and a simulator to assist in M68000 software development. Both software packages are written in FORTRAN and are easily transportable to different host machines. The specific programs that were used in this chapter for developing assembly-language programs are the M68KXASM(D3) Cross Macro Assembler and the M68K0SIM(D2) Simulator. These packages are furnished to educational institutions at a nominal cost.

It is not within the scope of this textbook to illustrate the full capabilities of the cross macro assembler and the simulator. However, they will be discussed in sufficient detail to enable the reader to use these tools for M68000 software development.

Refer to the assembly-language program in Fig. 11.9. This program computes the sum of four 16-bit unsigned numbers. It is possible that the sum of the four numbers will be too large to express as a 16-bit number. Therefore, the result is placed in two 16-bit locations referred to as HIGH__ANS and LOW__ANS. These

```
100 *        ADD FOUR 16-BIT UNSIGNED NUMBERS.
110 *        PUT HIGH-ORDER WORD OF ANSWER IN HIGH_ANS.
120 *        PUT LOW-ORDER WORD OF ANS IN LOW_ANS.
130               ORG    $1000
140 START         MOVEQ  #4,D0
150               MOVEA.L #FIRST,A1
160               MOVEA.L #0,A2
170        BACK:  ADDA   (A1)+,A2
180               SUBQ   #1,D0      DECREMENT COUNTER.
190               BNE    BACK       NOT DONE
200               MOVE.L A2,HIGH_ANS    SAVE ENTIRE ANSWER!!!
210               STOP   #0
220 FIRST:        DC.W   1
230               DC.W   2,$7FFF,$7FFF
240 HIGH_ANS      DS     1
250 LOW_ANS       DS     1
260          END
```

Figure 11.9   An M68000 assembly-language program

locations contain, respectively, the high-order and the low-order words of the answer.

Any full-line comments must be preceded by an asterisk in column 1, as illustrated by the comments in lines 100, 110, and 120. *Note:* The line numbers are *not* part of the assembly-language program. For statements related to machine-language commands, there are four fields in each line. These are the *label, command, operand,* and *comment* fields. A valid symbol beginning in column 1 (other than an asterisk) is considered to be the first character of a label. Strings representing labels may not exceed 30 characters. If a label starts in a column other than column 1, it must be terminated with a colon.

An assembly-language program contains both mnemonics and assembler directives or pseudo instructions. Some assembler directives are simply internal instructions to the assembler. In Fig. 11.9, two such commands are the ORG and the END directives. The ORG directive defines an initial or current value of a location counter. The number $1000 following the ORG command indicates that the program is to start at the hexadecimal memory location 1000. Any number of ORG or RORG directives may be used in a program. Instructions following an RORG, or relative origin, directive are translated into position-independent code, when possible. That is, relative addressing rather than absolute addressing is utilized. The single END directive is used to indicate termination of the program.

Other assembler directives are used for data storage. These directives may have labels. The *data constant* directive in line 220 is used to place the hexadecimal number 0001 in a 16-bit memory location identified by the label FIRST. Similarly, the subsequent command is used to store 2 at FIRST + 2, 7FFF at FIRST + 4, and 7FFF at FIRST + 6. The DS directive is used to reserve data space. Each DS directive in this program is used to reserve 2 bytes of storage space.

Recall that the program in Fig. 11.9 adds together a set of positive 16-bit numbers. The result consists of a high-order and a low-order word. Normally, when such a program is written, a 16-bit number is added to a running sum. If a carry is produced, the high-order word is incremented. In this example, it is not necessary to perform this incrementation on the high-order word. An address register is used to contain the running sum. Recall that any word that is added to an address register automatically affects the entire 32-bit contents of the register. The traditional method of incrementing the high-order word if the carry flag is set cannot be used if the destination operand is in an address register. When operations are performed on address registers, generally status flags are not affected.

Figure 11.10 illustrates the output of the assembler for this particular program. Observe that the assembler output includes a symbol table. In addition to this output, it is also desired to produce an output that may be used as an input either to a simulator or to an M68000 developmental system. Such an output is illustrated in Fig. 11.11.

After a program has been assembled, it is necessary to test (and usually to debug) the program. The M68000 simulator is a useful tool for initial testing and debugging of software. The M68000 cross assembler places a coded version of the

```
MC68000 ASM REV:  1.51- COPYRIGHT  MOTOROLA 1978
  1                        *       ADD FOUR 16-BIT UNSIGNED NUMBERS.
  2                        *       PUT HIGH-ORDER WORD OF ANSWER IN HIGH_ANS.
  3                        *       PUT LOW-ORDER WORD OF ANS IN LOW_ANS.
  4         00001000               ORG     $1000
  5 001000 7004        START       MOVEQ   #4,D0
  6 001002 227C0000101C            MOVEA.L #FIRST,A1
  7 001008 247C00000000            MOVEA.L #0,A2
  8 00100E D4D9            BACK:    ADDA    (A1)+,A2
  9 001010 5340               SUBQ    #1,D0       DECREMENT COUNTER.
 10 001012 66FA               BNE    BACK         NOT DONE
 11 001014 21CA1024           MOVE.L A2,HIGH_ANS      SAVE ENTIRE ANS
 12 001018 4E720000           STOP #0
 13 00101C 0001        FIRST:   DC.W      1
 14 00101E 0002                 DC.W      2,$7FFF,$7FFF
 15 001024 0002        HIGH_ANS DS        1
 16 001026 0002        LOW_ANS  DS        1
 17                               END

****** TOTAL ERRORS    0--    0 -- TOTAL LINES   14


APPROX  2114 UNUSED SYMBOL TABLE ENTRIES

BACK     00100E FIRST    00101C HIGH_ANS 001024 LOW_ANS   001026 START    001000
```

Figure 11.10   Output of assembler for program in Fig. 11.9

```
1 S00600004844521B
2 S11310007004227C0000101C247C00000000D4D951
3 S11310105340066FA21CA10244E72000000010002F7
4 S10710207FFF7FFFCC
5 S9030000FC
```

Figure 11.11   Coded output of assembler for program in Fig. 11.9

machine-language program into a file that is accessible by the simulator. Then appropriate simulator commands are given in order to test the program.

Figure 11.12 illustrates a typical set of simulator commands. All commands must begin in column 1, and the line number is not part of a command. The first command, IM, is the input memory command. This causes the most recent program output from the assembler to be read into the simulated memory. The DM command given in line 110 is the display memory command. All numerical operands are hexadecimal operands. This command causes the simulator to print the contents of 8 bytes of memory beginning at memory location 101C. Recall from the results displayed in Fig. 11.10 that 101C is the address of the first data word. The SR, or set register, command is used to initialize the internal registers. In this example, two internal registers are initialized. The hexadecimal number 1000 is placed in the pro-

```
100 IM
110 DM 101C,8
120 SR P1000,CC2700
130 R 20
140 DM 1024,4
150 SR P1000,CC2700
160 T 20
170 EX
```

Figure 11.12   A set of simulator commands for program in Fig. 11.9

gram counter. Likewise, the status register is initialized. The binary digits 111 are placed in bits 10, 9, and 8 of the status register. This causes the simulated machine to operate at a priority 7 level. Likewise, a 1 is placed in bit 13 of the status register. Thus, the simulated machine is operating in the supervisory mode. All machine instructions can be executed while the machine is in the supervisory mode of operation.

The R command in line 130 causes the simulator to run the program. The operand used indicates that the simulator is to fetch and execute 32 instructions. Fewer instructions will be executed if a STOP command is encountered. Similarly, the program will terminate on certain TRAP commands unless valid trap vectors are specified. If no operand is included with the run command, the program will execute until a STOP command or certain TRAP operations are encountered.

The DM command in line 140 is used to display the 4 bytes containing the answer for the sample program. Then, in line 150, the program counter and the status registers are reset to their previous values. The command given in line 160 is the TRACE command. This causes the contents of each register to be printed at the conclusion of each instruction. The operand indicates the number of instructions to be traced. The command in line 170 causes program control to exit from the simulator.

Figure 11.13 is the simulator output obtained from the program illustrated in Fig. 11.9 using the simulator commands shown in Fig. 11.12. Each question mark is a prompt for a simulator command. If operating in a time-sharing mode, the appropriate simulator command may be typed in following this prompt character. In the example illustrated, the entire set of simulator commands was placed in a file. For each prompt encountered, the appropriate simulator command was read from the file.

Use of the M68000 simulator significantly facilitates software development. In addition to the simulator commands illustrated in the previous example, several other simulator commands are useful for program development. Refer to the output display that was obtained when executing a TRACE instruction or displaying registers (see Fig. 11.13). All data registers, all address registers, the instruction code, the contents of the program counter and status register, and the accumulated number of clock cycles are all displayed. For many programs, not all of this information is needed. The programmer may set the desired display by using the SD simulator command followed by an argument list. The argument list indicates which parameters are to be displayed. An illustration is contained in the solution to Example 11.10.

In order to facilitate debugging of programs, *breakpoints* can be set. These can be set at any valid instruction address, and up to ten breakpoints may be set. The format of the command for setting breakpoints is BP N1, N2, ... The NI are the instruction addresses at which the breakpoints are set. The command BC may be used to clear all breakpoints. The command BD is used to display the addresses corresponding to all breakpoints that are currently set. Another useful command is the TB NUM trace command. This is a TRACE ON BRANCH command.

```
MACSS SIMULATOR - REL 1.5
?
?
101C 00 01 00 02 7F FF 7F FF ........
?
?
MACHINE HALTED DUE TO STOP STATEMENT.
 D0=0 D1=0 D2=0 D3=0 D4=0 D5=0 D6=0 D7=0 A0=0 A1=1024 A2=10001 A3=0 A4=0
A5=0 A6=0 A7=0 I=1018=STOP P=101C=ORI  C=0 T=42
?
1024 00 01 00 01 ....
?
?
 D0=4 D1=0 D2=0 D3=0 D4=0 D5=0 D6=0 D7=0 A0=0 A1=1024 A2=10001 A3=0 A4=0
A5=0 A6=0 A7=0 I=1000=LDQ  P=1002=MOVE C=SI(7)=2700 T=44
 D0=4 D1=0 D2=0 D3=0 D4=0 D5=0 D6=0 D7=0 A0=0 A1=101C A2=10001 A3=0 A4=0
A5=0 A6=0 A7=0 I=1002=MOVE P=1008=MOVE C=SI(7)=2700 T=4A
 D0=4 D1=0 D2=0 D3=0 D4=0 D5=0 D6=0 D7=0 A0=0 A1=101C A2=0 A3=0 A4=0
A5=0 A6=0 A7=0 I=1008=MOVE P=100E=ADD  C=SI(7)=2700 T=50
 D0=4 D1=0 D2=0 D3=0 D4=0 D5=0 D6=0 D7=0 A0=0 A1=101E A2=1 A3=0 A4=0
A5=0 A6=0 A7=0 I=100E=ADD  P=1010=SUBQ C=SI(7)=2700 T=54
 D0=3 D1=0 D2=0 D3=0 D4=0 D5=0 D6=0 D7=0 A0=0 A1=101E A2=1 A3=0 A4=0
A5=0 A6=0 A7=0 I=1010=SUBQ P=1012=BNE  C=SI(7)=2700 T=56
 D0=3 D1=0 D2=0 D3=0 D4=0 D5=0 D6=0 D7=0 A0=0 A1=101E A2=1 A3=0 A4=0
A5=0 A6=0 A7=0 I=1012=BNE  P=100E=ADD  C=SI(7)=2700 T=5B
 D0=3 D1=0 D2=0 D3=0 D4=0 D5=0 D6=0 D7=0 A0=0 A1=1020 A2=3 A3=0 A4=0
A5=0 A6=0 A7=0 I=100E=ADD  P=1010=SUBQ C=SI(7)=2700 T=5F
 D0=2 D1=0 D2=0 D3=0 D4=0 D5=0 D6=0 D7=0 A0=0 A1=1020 A2=3 A3=0 A4=0
A5=0 A6=0 A7=0 I=1010=SUBQ P=1012=BNE  C=SI(7)=2700 T=61
 D0=2 D1=0 D2=0 D3=0 D4=0 D5=0 D6=0 D7=0 A0=0 A1=1020 A2=3 A3=0 A4=0
A5=0 A6=0 A7=0 I=1012=BNE  P=100E=ADD  C=SI(7)=2700 T=66
 D0=2 D1=0 D2=0 D3=0 D4=0 D5=0 D6=0 D7=0 A0=0 A1=1022 A2=8002 A3=0 A4=0
A5=0 A6=0 A7=0 I=100E=ADD  P=1010=SUBQ C=SI(7)=2700 T=6A
 D0=1 D1=0 D2=0 D3=0 D4=0 D5=0 D6=0 D7=0 A0=0 A1=1022 A2=8002 A3=0 A4=0
A5=0 A6=0 A7=0 I=1010=SUBQ P=1012=BNE  C=SI(7)=2700 T=6C
 D0=1 D1=0 D2=0 D3=0 D4=0 D5=0 D6=0 D7=0 A0=0 A1=1022 A2=8002 A3=0 A4=0
A5=0 A6=0 A7=0 I=1012=BNE  P=100E=ADD  C=SI(7)=2700 T=71
 D0=1 D1=0 D2=0 D3=0 D4=0 D5=0 D6=0 D7=0 A0=0 A1=1024 A2=10001 A3=0 A4=0
A5=0 A6=0 A7=0 I=100E=ADD  P=1010=SUBQ C=SI(7)=2700 T=75
 D0=0 D1=0 D2=0 D3=0 D4=0 D5=0 D6=0 D7=0 A0=0 A1=1024 A2=10001 A3=0 A4=0
A5=0 A6=0 A7=0 I=1010=SUBQ P=1012=BNE  C=SI(7)Z=2704 T=77
 D0=0 D1=0 D2=0 D3=0 D4=0 D5=0 D6=0 D7=0 A0=0 A1=1024 A2=10001 A3=0 A4=0
A5=0 A6=0 A7=0 I=1012=BNE  P=1014=MOVE C=SI(7)Z=2704 T=7B
 D0=0 D1=0 D2=0 D3=0 D4=0 D5=0 D6=0 D7=0 A0=0 A1=1024 A2=10001 A3=0 A4=0
A5=0 A6=0 A7=0 I=1014=MOVE P=1018=STOP C=SI(7)=2700 T=83
MACHINE HALTED DUE TO STOP STATEMENT.
 D0=0 D1=0 D2=0 D3=0 D4=0 D5=0 D6=0 D7=0 A0=0 A1=1024 A2=10001 A3=0 A4=0
A5=0 A6=0 A7=0 I=1018=STOP P=101C=ORI  C=0 T=84
?
```

Figure 11.13 Output of simulator for program in Fig. 11.9. Simulator commands shown in Fig. 11.12 are used.

Like the TRACE command, this command traces the next NUM instructions. However, the designated registers are displayed only immediately after a BRANCH command is executed.

Example 11.10

Write and test a subroutine that "pulls in" the four 32-bit signed integers that are stored immediately after the statement that invokes the subroutine. The subroutine is to return the average value (fixed-point or integer average) of these four numbers. The answer is to be returned in D0.

Solution   A solution is given in Fig. 11.14. The solution presented is the output of the cross assembler after the appropriate program has been entered into the assembler. Refer to the subroutine AVE. The UNLK command is used to pop the data pointer from the user stack into A0. This pointer is used to fetch the data, and is incremented accordingly. The LINK command is used to place the true return address back on top of the stack. Observe that relative addressing is used in this program. No executable termination statement is used in this example.

A set of simulator commands used for testing this program is given in Fig. 11.15. The corresponding printed output is given in Fig. 11.16. Observe that the subroutine is tested for two different sets of data.

Additional examples of the use of the M68000 cross assembler and simulator are given in the following section.

Review

1. Refer to the program in Fig. 11.9. Instead of using an address register to accumulate the running sum, suppose that a data register is used. Rewrite the program for this situation.
2. Refer to the program in Fig. 11.9. Instead of testing this program for the data 1, 2, $7FFF, and $7FFF, test the program for the following sets of data:
   (a) 1, 2, 3, 4

```
MC68000 ASM REV:  1.51- COPYRIGHT  MOTOROLA 1978
   1         00001000              RORG $1000
   2                       *  START SUBROUTINE.  AVERAGE IS RETURNED IN D0.
   3                       *     THIS SUBROUTINE COMPUTES THE AVERAGE OF FOUR SI
   4                       *     32-BIT INTEGERS.  DATA FOLLOWS THE CALL INSTRUC
   5 001000 304F       AVE        MOVEA A7,A0
   6 001002 4E58                  UNLK A0        GET DATA POINTER
   7 001004 323C0004              MOVE #4,D1
   8 001008 4240                  CLR D0
   9 00100A D098       BACK:      ADD.L (A0)+,D0
  10 00100C 5341                  SUBQ #1,D1
  11 00100E 66FA                  BNE BACK
  12 001010 E440                  ASR #2,D0
  13 001012 4E500000              LINK A0,#0
  14 001016 4E75                  RTS
  15                       *  **************************************************
  16                       *     START TEST PROGRAM
  17 001018 3E7C1000   FIRST:     MOVEA #$1000,A7
  18 00101C 4EBAFFE2              JSR AVE
  19 001020 0000000A   DATA:      DC.L  10
  20 001024 FFFFFFFB              DC.L  -5
  21 001028 0000001B              DC.L  27
  22 00102C 0000000F              DC.L  15
  23 001030 4E71       TERM:      NOP
  24                              END

****** TOTAL ERRORS    0--    0 -- TOTAL LINES    24


APPROX  2115 UNUSED SYMBOL TABLE ENTRIES

AVE      001000 BACK     00100A DATA     001020 FIRST    001018 TERM     001030
```

Figure 11.14 A solution for Example 11.10

```
100 IM
110 DM 1000,32
120 SR P 1018
130 BP 1030
140 BD
150 SD PICTADO,D1
160 R
170 BC
180 SR P1018
190 BP 1000,1030
200 SM 1020,00,00,00,46,0FF,0FF,0FF,00,00,00,00,12,00,00,00,0AB
210 T1
220 DM 1020,10
230 R
240 R
250 EX
```

Figure 11.15   Simulator commands used for Example 11.10

```
MACSS SIMULATOR - REL 1.5
?
?
1000 30 4F 4E 58 32 3C 00 04 42 40 D0 98 53 41 66 FA 00NX2<..B@..SA..
1010 E4 40 4E 50 00 00 4E 75 3E 7C 10 00 4E BA FF E2 .@NP..N.>...N...
1020 00 00 00 0A FF FF FF FB 00 00 00 1B 00 00 00 0F ................
1030 4E 71 N.
?
?
?
001030
?
?
BREAKPOINT.
 D0=B D1=0 A0=FFC A1=0 A2=0 A3=0 A4=0 A5=0 A6=0 A7=1000 I=1016 P=1030
C=XC=11 T=65
?
?
?
?
?
 D0=B D1=0 A0=FFC A1=0 A2=0 A3=0 A4=0 A5=0 A6=0 A7=1000 I=1018 P=101C
C=XC=11 T=69
?
1020 00 00 00 46 FF FF FF 00 00 00 00 12 00 00 00 AB ...F............
?
BREAKPOINT.
 D0=B D1=0 A0=FFC A1=0 A2=0 A3=0 A4=0 A5=0 A6=0 A7=FFC I=101C P=1000
C=XC=11 T=72
?
BREAKPOINT.
 D0=0 D1=0 A0=FFC A1=0 A2=0 A3=0 A4=0 A5=0 A6=0 A7=1000 I=1016 P=1030
C=XZC=15 T=CA
?
```

Figure 11.16   Output of simulator for Example 11.10 using simulator commands
in Fig. 11.15

(b) 1, $7000, $7100, $0

(c) $6ABC, $7CDE, $77FF, 24556

Without rewriting the program, formulate a set of simulator commands that will test the program for these data.

3. Refer to the simulator commands in Fig. 11.15 and to the simulator output in Fig. 11.16.

The subroutine AVE was tested for a second set of numbers. Identify these numbers as base-10 integers, and identify the number returned from the subroutine.

4. Refer to the solution to Example 11.10. Correct answers will not be obtained for all sets of integers.

   (a) For which of the following sets of integers, expressed as hexadecimal numbers, will correct answers be obtained?

   (1) *FFFFFFFF, FFFFFFFE, FFFFFFFD, FFFFFFFC*
   (2) 60000000, 70000000, 80000000, 90000000
   (3) 60000000, 80000000, 70000000, 90000000
   (4) 20000000, 20000000, 20000000, 20000000
   (5) 00000000, 00000003, *FFFFFFFF, 7FFFFFFF*

   (b) What statement can be added to the subroutine to assist a user of this routine to find out when her or his results are correct?

5. Write and test a subroutine that pulls in 8 bytes of data. Each byte is a positive number. The subroutine returns the smallest byte in D0 and the largest byte in D7.

11.5 ILLUSTRATIVE EXAMPLES

In this section, examples illustrating certain attributes of the M68000 instruction set are given.

Exception processing constitutes a major effort in the development of most software packages. Recall that during exception processing, both the previous contents of the status register and the apparent return address are saved on the stack identified by the supervisory stack pointer. Then an appropriate vector or address is placed in the program counter, and the processor continues execution in the supervisory mode. During the initiation of an exception processing action, 6 bytes of information are stored on the supervisory stack. Thus, the supervisory stack pointer is decremented by 6.

The supervisory stack pointer can be loaded only by a programmed command when the processor is operating in the supervisory mode. Yet, to transfer control from the user mode to the supervisory mode of operation, it is required that an appropriate number first be placed in the supervisory stack pointer register. This results in somewhat of a dilemma. Use of a RESET signal and an appropriate reset vector can resolve this dilemma. When an active signal is applied to the reset pin of an M68000 microprocessor, the long word in memory addresses 000 to 003 is loaded into the supervisory stack pointer. During this interval, the output of the status pins indicates that the CPU is in the supervisory state. The reset signal also produces the following effects. The processor interrupt mask is set to priority level 7, the supervisory bit in the status register is set, and nothing is saved on the stack. The number stored in memory locations 004 to 007 is placed in the program counter, and program execution continues at this address.

There is no realistic way to simulate a hardware reset signal using an M68000 simulator. Example 11.11 illustrates use of an exception processing routine and a method of setting the supervisory stack pointer.

Example 11.11

Write an exception processing routine that will execute the STOP command if a TRAP #0 command is encountered.

Solution   Figure 11.17 illustrates such a routine. The simulator commands in Fig. 11.18 illustrate a method of setting the supervisory stack pointer and then executing the source program from the user mode of operation. When the TRAP #0 command is executed, the processor proceeds to the appropriate exception processing routine. A trace of the program execution for the simulator commands in Fig. 11.18 is given in Fig. 11.19.

A very useful attribute of the M68000 microprocessor is its ability to manipulate 32-bit words. Furthermore, automatic incrementation and decrementation can be done in steps of 4 bytes. This is illustrated in Example 11.12.

```
100 *      NOTE:   THE RESET VECTOR IS NORMALLY USED TO LOAD THE
110 *              SUPERVISORY STACK POINTER.  SINCE WE CANNOT
120 *              SIMULATE A RESET, WE WILL INITIALLY LOAD THE
130 *              SUPERVISORY STACK POINTER USING APPROPRIATE SIMULATOR
140 *              COMMANDS.  WE WILL LOAD THE SUPERVISORY STACK
150 *              POINTER TO 0FE0.
160 *     IN THIS PROGRAM, WE WILL LET A 'TRAP 0' COMMAND VECTOR
170 *         OUR PROGRAM TO A STOP ROUTINE.
180                    ORG $2000
190 *      THIS IS OUR STOP ROUTINE!!!
200 QUIT:          STOP #0
210                RTE
220 *      WE MUST SET OUR TRAP-0 VECTOR
230                ORG $80
240                DC.L QUIT        VECTOR IS SET TO $2000
250                ORG $1000
260 SUBR:          NOP         NEAT SUBROUTINE!!!!
270                RTS         END OF NEAT SUBROUTINE
280 *      START TEST PROGRAM
290 START:         MOVEA #$1000,A7      LOAD USER STACK POINTER
300                JSR SUBR
310                TRAP #0
320 *      NEXT, WE WILL RESERVE SPACE FOR BOTH THE USER STACK AND
330 *             THE SUPERVISORY STACK
340                ORG $0FC0
350                DS  $40
360                END
```

Figure 11.17   Solution to Example 11.11

```
100 IM
110 SR CC2000
120 SR A7,0FE0
130 SR CC0
140 SR P1004
150 T50
160 DM 0FC0,40
170 EX
```

Figure 11.18   Simulator commands used for Example 11.11

```
MACSS SIMULATOR - REL 1.5
?
?
?
?
?
?
 D0=0 D1=0 D2=0 D3=0 D4=0 D5=0 D6=0 D7=0 A0=0 A1=0 A2=0 A3=0 A4=0 A5=0
A6=0 A7=1000 I=1004=MOVE P=1008=JSR  C=0 T=4
 D0=0 D1=0 D2=0 D3=0 D4=0 D5=0 D6=0 D7=0 A0=0 A1=0 A2=0 A3=0 A4=0 A5=0
A6=0 A7=FFC I=1008=JSR  P=1000=NOP  C=0 T=C
 D0=0 D1=0 D2=0 D3=0 D4=0 D5=0 D6=0 D7=0 A0=0 A1=0 A2=0 A3=0 A4=0 A5=0
A6=0 A7=FFC I=1000=NOP  P=1002=RTS  C=0 T=E
 D0=0 D1=0 D2=0 D3=0 D4=0 D5=0 D6=0 D7=0 A0=0 A1=0 A2=0 A3=0 A4=0 A5=0
A6=0 A7=1000 I=1002=RTS  P=100C=TRAP C=0 T=16
 D0=0 D1=0 D2=0 D3=0 D4=0 D5=0 D6=0 D7=0 A0=0 A1=0 A2=0 A3=0 A4=0 A5=0
A6=0 A7=FDA I=100C=TRAP P=2000=STOP C=S=2000 T=1C
MACHINE HALTED DUE TO STOP STATEMENT.
 D0=0 D1=0 D2=0 D3=0 D4=0 D5=0 D6=0 D7=0 A0=0 A1=0 A2=0 A3=0 A4=0 A5=0
A6=0 A7=1000 I=2000=STOP P=2004=RTE  C=0 T=1D
?
OFCO 00 00 00 00 00 00 00 00 00 00 00 00 00 00 00 00 ................
OFD0 00 00 00 00 00 00 00 00 00 00 00 00 00 00 10 0E ................
OFE0 00 00 00 00 00 00 00 00 00 00 00 00 00 00 00 00 ................
OFF0 00 00 00 00 00 00 00 00 00 00 00 00 00 00 10 0C ................
?
```

Figure 11.19   Simulator output for program in Example 11.11

Example 11.12

Write and test an M68000 subroutine that "pulls in" the number of elements in an array and the starting address of the array. The elements of the array consist of 32-bit unsigned integers. The subroutine sorts the elements of this array in ascending order.

Solution   An appropriate subroutine and a test program that invokes the subroutine are given in Fig. 11.20.

The assemblers previously discussed in this textbook were macro assemblers. That is, user-defined macros can be formulated and referred to during the assembly process. Similarly, macros may be used with the M68000 assembler (already discussed). These macros are developed in a similar manner. Argument lists may be carried into a macro, and unique labels may be generated within a macro. In addition, the suffixes B, L, or W may be carried into a macro.

Refer to lines 180 to 220 in Fig. 11.21. The macro PNT is defined within these lines. Refer to line 190. The suffix "\0" is used to indicate a type of operand. The type may be byte, word, or long word. The other variables carried into the macro are identified by the order in which they appear in the call list. Thus, \1 refers to the first argument in the call list and \2 to the second argument. The label within the macro is represented by \@. Each time the macro is referred to by the assembler, a different label is generated. Refer to line 350. The first time the macro PNT is invoked, the suffix L is specified, and the call list consists of the numbers 1 and $20. Observe that the macro is called four times. Refer to the assembler output in Fig. 11.22. The translations for each macro call are shown. Observe that four different labels are generated.

```
*    THIS PROGRAM SORTS N 32-BIT WORDS.
*    THE SUBROUTINE PERFORMS A BUBBLE SORT ON THE
*    NUMBERS.  SINCE THE PROGRAM IS TO BE STORED
*    IN ROM, THE SUBROUTINE USES REGISTERS FOR
*    FLAGS AND COUNTERS, ETC.
*    BEGINNING OF SUBROUTINE SORT
          ORG   $1000
SORT:     MOVE  A7,A0
          UNLK  A0
          MOVEQ.B #0,D4     CLEAR FLAG
          MOVE  (A0)+,D0     GET N
          SUBQ  #1,D0
          MOVE.L (A0)+,A2     GET STARTING ADDRESS OF DATA
          LINK  A0,#0          PUSH TRUE RETURN ADDRESS ON STACK
TOP:      MOVE.L A2,A1
          MOVE.L A1,A0
          ADDQ  #4,A0
          MOVE  D0,D1
BACK:     CMPM.L (A1)+,(A0)+
          BHI   DOWN          NO SWAP NEEDED
          MOVE.L -(A1),D2     PERFORM THE SWAP
          MOVE.L -(A0),D3
          MOVE.L D3,(A1)+
          MOVE.L D2,(A0)+
          MOVEQ.B #1,D4       SET FLAG
DOWN:     SUBQ.B #1,D1        ADJUST COUNT
          BNE   BACK          IF NOT TO END OF NUMBERS, DO AGAIN
          CMP   #0,D4         IF FLAG NOT SET, THEN RETURN
          BEQ   DONE
          MOVEQ.B #0,D4       CLEAR FLAG
          SUBQ  #1,D0         N = N - 1
          BNE   TOP           CONTINUE
DONE:     RTS
*         BEGIN MAIN PROGRAM
          ORG   $2000
START:    MOVE.L #$1000,A7   LOAD STACK POINTER
          JSR   SORT
          DC.W   25           NUMBER OF DATA ELEMENTS
          DC.L   $3000        STARTING ADDRESS
          STOP  #0
          ORG   $0FC0         AREA FOR STACK
          DS   $40
          ORG   $3000         ARRAY OF 32-BIT NUMBERS
          DC.L    5,4,3,2,1,$10,$40,3,2,0,$41,$20,$35,$90,$200000
          DC.L    4,9,$0A,$0F,3,2,5,7,9,$0C
          END START
```

Figure 11.20 Solution to Example 11.12

The M68000 simulator provides some facilities for simulating input and output operations. These are summarized below.

Command	Input/Output Function
JSR $10000	Input from Console
	(A5) = > Starting address of input buffer
	(A6) = > The address of the last CHAR entered +1
JSR $10002	Output to Console
	(A5) = > Starting address of output buffer
	(A6) = > Address of last CHAR + 1 in buffer
JSR $10004	Read Record from File (Unit #2) *
	(A5) = > Start of Input Buffer
	(A6) = > Address of last CHAR + 1 in buffer

```
100          ORG $1000
110          TTL  CAT AND MOUSE PROGRAM
120 *    EQUATE AND SET STATEMENTS ARE ILLUSTRATED.
130 *    IF  STRING IS 'SET' TO A NUMBER, THIS ASSIGNMENT MAY
140 *    BE CHANGED LATER DURING THE ASSEMBLY LANGUAGE PROGRAM.
150 STRING_IN    EQU     $10000
160 STRING_OUT   SET     $10002
170 *    THE FOLLOWING MACRO PRINTS A STRING OF N IDENTICAL CHARACTERS, X.
180 PNT    MACRO
190          MOVE.\0  #\1,D7
200          MOVEA.L   #XBYTE,A5
210          MOVEA.L   A5,A6
220 \@       MOVE.B    #\2,(A6)+
230          DBCS      D7,\@
240          MOVE.B    #$20,D7
250          MOVE.B    D7,XBYTE
260          JSR     STRING_OUT
270          ENDM
280 XBYTE:   DS $60
290 MICE:    DC.B 'MICE'
300 STOP:    DC.B 'STOP'
310 MES:     DC.B ' I AM A HUNGRY CAT!!!'
320 MESEND:  DC.B '!!!'
330          DS     1          ESTABLISH EVEN BOUNDARY!!!
340 BEGIN:   MOVEA #1000,A7    LOAD STACK POINTER
350 FIRST:   PNT.L 1,$20        DO TWO LINE FEEDS
360          PNT.L 1,$20
370          PNT.L 50,'*'       PRINT 50 ASTERISKS!
380          PNT.L 79,'$'
390 START:   MOVEA.L #XBYTE,A5
400          JSR STRING_IN
410          MOVE.L STOP,D4
420          CMP.L XBYTE,D4
430          BEQ DONE           IF STOP THEN BRANCH TO DONE
440          MOVE.L MICE,D4
450          CMP.L XBYTE,D4
460          BNE START
470          MOVEA.L #MES,A5
480          MOVEA.L #MESEND,A6
490          JSR STRING_OUT
500          BRA FIRST
510 DONE     STOP #0
520          END
```

Figure 11.21 Solution to Example 11.13

JSR $10006   Write Record to File (Unit #2) *
                        (A5) = > Starting address of output buffer
                        (A6) = > The address of the last CHAR entered +1

Note: In some systems, it is convenient to use a FORTRAN unit number other than Unit #2.

   The above input/output routines that are included in the M68000 simulator are FORTRAN routines. Thus, the various steps in these routines cannot be traced using the M68000 simulator trace command. Use of two of these subroutines is illustrated in Example 11.13.

Example 11.13

   Write and test an M68000 program that accepts a string of four characters from a console. Program execution terminates if the string corresponds to the word STOP. If the string input corresponds to the word MICE, then an appropriate message is printed. For any other string input, no action is performed, and a new string must be entered.

```
MC68000 ASM REV: 1.51- COPYRIGHT  MOTOROLA 1978
   1          00001000            ORG  $1000
   3                          *   EQUATE AND SET STATEMENTS ARE ILLUSTRATED.
   4                          *   IF  STRING IS 'SET' TO A NUMBER, THIS ASSIGNMENT
   5                          *   BE CHANGED LATER DURING THE ASSEMBLY LANGUAGE PRO
   6          00010000        STRING_IN     EQU    $10000
   7          00010002        STRING_OUT    SET    $10002
   8                          *   THE FOLLOWING MACRO PRINTS A STRING OF N IDENTICA
   9                          PNT     MACRO
  10                                  MOVE.\0    #\1,D7
  11                                  MOVEA.L    #XBYTE,A5
  12                                  MOVEA.L    A5,A6
  13                          \@      MOVE.B     #\2,(A6)+
  14                                  DBCS       D7,\@
  15                                  MOVE.B     #$20,D7
  16                                  MOVE.B     D7,XBYTE
  17                                  JSR        STRING_OUT
  18                                  ENDM
  19 001000 00C0              XBYTE:  DS  $60
  20 0010C0 4D                MICE:   DC.B 'MICE'
  21 0010C4 53                STOP:   DC.B 'STOP'
  22 0010C8 20                MES:    DC.B ' I AM A HUNGRY CAT!!!'
  23 0010DD 21                MESEND: DC.B '!!'
  24 0010E0 0002              DS  1                ESTABLISH EVEN BOUNDARY!!!
  25 0010E2 3E7C03E8          BEGIN:  MOVEA #1000,A7   LOAD STACK POINTER
  26                          FIRST:  PNT.L 1,$20            DO TWO LINE FEEDS
  26 0010E6 7E01                      MOVE.L #1,D7
  26 0010E8 2A7C00001000              MOVEA.L #XBYTE,A5
  26 0010EE 2C4D                      MOVEA.L A5,A6
  26 0010F0 1CFC0020          @001 MOVE.B #$20,(A6)+
  26 0010F4 55CFFFFA                  DBCS D7,@001
  26 0010F8 1E3C0020                  MOVE.B #$20,D7
  26 0010FC 11C71000                  MOVE.B D7,XBYTE
  26 001100 4EB900010002              JSR STRING_OUT
  27                                  PNT.L 1,$20
  27 001106 7E01                      MOVE.L #1,D7
  27 001108 2A7C00001000              MOVEA.L #XBYTE,A5
  27 00110E 2C4D                      MOVEA.L A5,A6
  27 001110 1CFC0020          @002 MOVE.B #$20,(A6)+
  27 001114 55CFFFFA                  DBCS D7,@002
  27 001118 1E3C0020                  MOVE.B #$20,D7
  27 00111C 11C71000                  MOVE.B D7,XBYTE
  27 001120 4EB900010002              JSR STRING_OUT
  28                                  PNT.L 50,'*'        PRINT 50 ASTERISKS!
  28 001126 7E32                      MOVE.L #50,D7
  28 001128 2A7C00001000              MOVEA.L #XBYTE,A5
  28 00112E 2C4D                      MOVEA.L A5,A6
  28 001130 1CFC002A          @003 MOVE.B #'*',(A6)+
  28 001134 55CFFFFA                  DBCS D7,@003
  28 001138 1E3C0020                  MOVE.B #$20,D7
  28 00113C 11C71000                  MOVE.B D7,XBYTE
  28 001140 4EB900010002              JSR STRING_OUT
  29                                  PNT.L 79,'$'
  29 001146 7E4F                      MOVE.L #79,D7
  29 001148 2A7C00001000              MOVEA.L #XBYTE,A5
  29 00114E 2C4D                      MOVEA.L A5,A6
  29 001150 1CFC0024          @004 MOVE.B #'$',(A6)+
  29 001154 55CFFFFA                  DBCS D7,@004
  29 001158 1E3C0020                  MOVE.B #$20,D7
  29 00115C 11C71000                  MOVE.B D7,XBYTE
  29 001160 4EB900010002              JSR STRING_OUT
  30 001166 2A7C00001000 START:    MOVEA.L #XBYTE,A5
  31 00116C 4EB900010000              JSR STRING_IN
  32 001172 283810C4                  MOVE.L STOP,D4
  33 001176 B8B81000                  CMP.L XBYTE,D4
  34 00117A 67000022                  BEQ DONE           IF STOP THEN BRANCH TO DO
  35 00117E 283810C0                  MOVE.L MICE,D4
```

Figure 11.22   Assembler output for Example 11.13

```
36  001182  B8B81000                    CMP.L XBYTE,D4
37  001186  66DE                        BNE START
38  001188  2A7C000010C8                MOVEA.L #MES,A5
39  00118E  2C7C000010DD                MOVEA.L #MESEND,A6
40  001194  4EB900010002                JSR STRING_OUT
41  00119A  6000FF4A                    BRA FIRST
42  00119E  4E720000      DONE          STOP #0
43                                      END

****** TOTAL ERRORS    0--     0 -- TOTAL LINES    43


APPROX   2101 UNUSED SYMBOL TABLE ENTRIES

@001    0010F0 @002    001110 @003    001130 @004    001150 BEGIN   0010E2
DONE    00119E FIRST   0010E6 MES     0010C8 MESEND  0010DD MICE    0010C0
START   001166 STOP    0010C4 STRING_I 010000 STRING_O 010002 XBYTE  001000
```

Figure 11.22   (*cont.*)

Solution   A solution is given in Fig. 11.21. The assembler output for this solution is given in Fig. 11.22. A sample set of simulator commands is given in Fig. 11.23, and the simulator output for these commands is given in Fig. 11.24.

```
100 IM
110 SR P10E2
120 R
130 DOGS
140 CATS
150 MISE
160 RATS
170 MICE
180 MICE
190 STOP
200 EX
```

Figure 11.23   Simulator commands for Example 11.13

```
MACSS SIMULATOR - REL 1.5
?
?
?


**************************************************
$$$$$$$$$$$$$$$$$$$$$$$$$$$$$$$$$$$$$$$$$$$$$$$$$$$$$$$$$$$$$$$$$$$$$$$$$$$$$$$$$$$$
I AM A HUNGRY CAT!!!


**************************************************
$$$$$$$$$$$$$$$$$$$$$$$$$$$$$$$$$$$$$$$$$$$$$$$$$$$$$$$$$$$$$$$$$$$$$$$$$$$$$$$$$$$$
I AM A HUNGRY CAT!!!


**************************************************
$$$$$$$$$$$$$$$$$$$$$$$$$$$$$$$$$$$$$$$$$$$$$$$$$$$$$$$$$$$$$$$$$$$$$$$$$$$$$$$$$$$$
PRIVILEDGED INSTRUCTION TRAP ADDRESS IS ZERO.
 D0=0 D1=0 D2=0 D3=0 D4=53544F50 D5=0 D6=0 D7=FFFFFF20 A0=0 A1=0 A2=0
 A3=0 A4=0 A5=1000 A6=1004 A7=3E8 I=119E=STOP P=11A2=ORI  C=Z=4 T=149C
?
```

Figure 11.24   Output of simulator for Example 11.13

```
100                          RORG   $1000
110 MESS_OUT                 EQU    $10002
120 *    THIS ROUTINE ADDS TWO ONE-DIMENSIONAL ARRAYS OF INTEGERS.
130 *    THE SUM IS PLACED IN A THIRD ARRAY.
140 *    THE ARGUMENT LIST IS AS FOLLOWS
150 *    N     A 16-BIT NUMBER IDENTIFYING THE ARRAY SI*E
160 *    A AND B    THE ADDRESSES OF THE SOURCE ARRAYS
170 *    C          THE ADDRESS OF THE DESTINATION ARRAY
180 *    NOTE:  THE VALUES OF N, A, B, AND C ARE PLACED IMMEDIATELY
190 *           AFTER THE INVOKING COMMAND. (THE JSR COMMAND)
200 MATADD:    MOVEA  A7,A0
210            UNLK  A0       GET ARGUMENT LIST POINTER
220            MOVE.W  (A0)+,D7    PUT COUNTER IN D7
230            MOVEA.L  (A0)+,A1   GET A-POINTER
240            MOVEA.L  (A0)+,A2   GET B-POINTER
250            MOVEA.L  (A0)+,A3   GET C-POINTER
260            LINK  A0,#0        PUT RETURN ADDRESS ON STACK
270 *    ARGUMENTS HAVE BEEN PULLED IN.
280   BACK:    CLR.L  D6
290            MOVE.L  (A1)+,D6
300            MOVE.L  (A2)+,(A3)
310            ADD.L  D6,(A3)+
320            TRAPV
330            SUBQ #1,D7       DONE?
340            BNE BACK         NO.
350            RTS              YES
360 *    TRAP MESSAGE
370            ORG $1200
380 TMESS:     DC.B  ' LOOK TURKEY!!  YOU ARE USING NUMBERS'
390            DC.B  ' WHOSE MAGNITUDES ARE TOO LARGE!!!!!'
400 ENDT       DC.B  '!!'
410            DS  1      USED TO ENSURE EVEN BOUNDARY!!
420 TRAPMES:   MOVEA #TMESS,A5
430            MOVEA #ENDT,A6
440            JSR MESS_OUT     PRINT MESSAGE
450            RTE              BACK TO THE USER PROGRAM
460            ORG $01C
470 *    SET TRAP-ON-OVERFLOW VECTOR
480            DC.L  TRAPMES
490            ORG $1500
500 *    START TEST PROGRAM
510 START:     MOVEA #$1000,A7
520            JSR MATADD
530 NUM:       DC.W   5
540 AMAT:      DC.L   FIRST
550 BMAT:      DC.L   SECOND
560 CMAT:      DC.L   THIRD
570 TERM:      NOP
580            STOP #0
590            ORG $2000
600 FIRST:     DC.L   1,-15,25,415,0
610            DS  20
620 SECOND:    DC.L   -2,12,25,45,13
630            DS  20
640 THIRD:     DS  40
650            ORG  $0FC0
660 *    RESERVE STACK SPACE
670 *    WE WILL ASSUME SUPERVISORY STACK POINTER TO BE SET AT 0FE0.
680            DS  40
690            END
```

Figure 11.25 Solution to Example 11.14

Example 11.14

Consider three one-dimensional arrays of N 32-bit signed integers. Write and test a subroutine that adds the corresponding elements of two of the arrays together and places the results in the third array. If numerical overflow should occur during any addition operation, a trap is to be executed and an appropriate message is to be printed.

Solution   A solution is given in Fig. 11.25. The resulting symbol table and a set of simulator commands are given in Fig. 11.26. The output of the simulator for this set of simulator commands is given in Fig. 11.27.

The input/output subroutines provided as part of the M68000 simulator help facilitate the development of practical input/output service routines. Generally, it is desired to have I/O activities performed at a higher privilege level than is available for the execution of user programs. Yet users must have access to these routines. Frequently, users access I/O handlers through the use of programmed TRAP or INTERRUPT commands. These concepts are illustrated in the following examples.

Example 11.15

Suppose the console READ and console WRITE routines entered at $10000 and $10002, respectively, can be accessed only when the processor is in the supervisory mode. Develop a console device handler that is invoked from user programs using a TRAP #2 command. Arguments required by this handler are to be transmitted by placing them on the user stack.

Solution   A solution is given in Fig. 11.28. The solution shown includes an I/O handler and a test program. Simulator commands used in running this program are also shown.

```
                        SYMBOL TABLE ENTRIES

AMAT      00150A BACK     001010 BMAT     00150E CMAT     001512 ENDT     001249
FIRST     002000 MATADD   001000 MESS_OUT 010002 NUM      001508 SECOND   00203C
START     001500 TERM     001516 THIRD    002078 TMESS    001200 TRAPMES  00124E


100 SR CC2000
110 SR A7,0FE0
120 SR CC0
130 IM
140 SR P1500
150 DM 2000,14
160 DM 203C,14
170 DM 2078,14
180 R
190 DM 2078,14
200 SR P1500
210 SM 2000,80,00,00,01
220 SM 1508,00,03
230 SM 1512,00,00,20,8C
240 DM 2000,0C
250 DM 203C,0C
260 R
270 DM 208C,0C
280 EX
```

Figure 11.26   Symbol table and set of simulator commands for Example 11.14

```
MACSS SIMULATOR - REL 1.5
?
?
?
?
?
?
2000 00 00 00 01 FF FF FF F1 00 00 00 19 00 00 01 9F ...............
2010 00 00 00 00 ....
?
203C FF FF FF FE 00 00 00 0C 00 00 00 19 00 00 00 2D ..............-
204C 00 00 00 0D ....
?
2078 00 00 00 00 00 00 00 00 00 00 00 00 00 00 00 00 ...............
SAME PATTERN
?
PRIVILEDGED INSTRUCTION TRAP ADDRESS IS ZERO.
 D0=0 D1=0 D2=0 D3=0 D4=0 D5=0 D6=0 D7=0 A0=FFC A1=2014 A2=2050 A3=208C
A4=0 A5=0 A6=0 A7=1000 I=1518=STOP P=151C=ORI  C=Z=4 T=F9
?
2078 FF FF FF FF FF FF FF FD 00 00 00 32 00 00 01 CC ..........2....
2088 00 00 00 0D ....
?
?
?
?
?
2000 80 00 00 01 FF FF FF F1 00 00 00 19 ............
?
203C FF FF FF FE 00 00 00 0C 00 00 00 19 ............
?
 LOOK TURKEY!!  YOU ARE USING NUMBERS WHOSE MAGNITUDES ARE TOO LARGE!!!!!
PRIVILEDGED INSTRUCTION TRAP ADDRESS IS ZERO.
 D0=0 D1=0 D2=0 D3=0 D4=0 D5=0 D6=19 D7=0 A0=FFC A1=200C A2=2048 A3=2098
A4=0 A5=1200 A6=1249 A7=1000 I=1518=STOP P=151C=ORI  C=Z=4 T=1C8
?
208C 7F FF FF FF FF FF FF FD 00 00 00 32 ..........2
?
```

Figure 11.27 Output of simulator for Example 11.14

Use of TRAP commands to implement I/O operations may present difficulties for novice computer users. It may be beneficial to have easy-to-use macros available for I/O operations.

Example 11.16

Develop and test two macros that use the device handler developed in Example 11.15. The available I/O operations are implemented by using one of the two macros shown below.

```
GET ----- ,              ;Gets a record entered from the console
                             and places it ;in a buffer.
                      PRINT ----- , ----- ;Prints a record
                           of specified size located ;in a
                           designated buffer.
```

Solution A solution is given in Fig. 11.29. Observe that these macros are similar to the .PRINT and .TTYIN system macros discussed in Chapters 6 and 7.

```
*    M68000 CONSOLE INPUT/OUTPUT ROUTINES.
*    ASSUME SIMULATOR SUBROUTINES LOCATED AT $10000 AND $10002
*       ARE ACCESSIBLE FROM JUST THE SUPERVISORY STATE.
*  TRAP #2 COMMAND INVOKES CONSOLE I/O
*  ARGUMENTS ARE CARRIED INTO HANDLER ON TOP OF USER STACK.
*
*    TOP WORD:        ODD=>READ RECORD      EVEN=>WRITE RECORD
*    NEXT LONG WORD:   ADDRESS OF BUFFER     ADDRESS OF BUFFER
*    NEXT WORD:                              BUFFER SI*E
*    WHEN CONTROL IS RETURNED FROM HANDLER, ALL REGISTERS
*    EXCEPT A6 HAVE CONTENTS THAT EXISTED PRIOR TO PROGRAMMED TRAP.
*    ARGUMENTS ARE DISCARDED FROM USER STACK.
              ORG $88
              DC.L  CONSOL         CONSOLE DEVICE HANDLER
              ORG $2000
CONSOL        MOVEM.L  D0/A0/A5,-(A7)
              MOVE USP,A0          ;GET USER STACK POINTER
              MOVE (A0)+,D0         ;GET READ-WRITE FLAG
              MOVEA.L (A0)+,A5      ;GET BUFFER POINTER
              CMP.B  #1,D0          ;READ?
              BEQ READ              ;YES
WRITE         MOVE.L A5,A6          ;NO
              ADDA (A0)+,A6
              JSR $10002            ;INVOKE WRITE ROUTINE
              BRA DONE
READ          JSR $10000
DONE          MOVE A0,USP           ;CLEAN UP USERS STACK
              MOVEM.L (A7)+,A5/A0/D0   ;RESTORE USERS REGISTERS
              RTE
*             START TEST PROGRAM
              ORG $1000
START         MOVEA.L #START,A7
              MOVE.L #BUFFER,-(A7)      ;PUT ARGUMENTS ON STACK
              MOVE #1,-(A7)
              TRAP #2                 ;TEST READ ROUTINE
              SUBA #BUFFER,A6
              MOVE A6,-(A7)           ;PUT ARGUMENTS ON STACK
              MOVE.L #BUFFER,-(A7)
              MOVE #0,-(A7)
              TRAP #2                 ;TEST WRITE ROUTINE
              STOP #0
BUFFER        DS.B    90
              END


IM
SR CC 2000
SR A7 0500
SR CC 0000
SR P 1000
R2000
MERRY CHRISTMAS ANS A HAPPY NEW YEAR!!!!!!!!!!!!!!!!!!
EX
```

Figure 11.28 I/O handler, test program, and simulator commands for Example 11.15

Review

1. Refer to Example 11.12 and to the solution in Fig. 11.20. Modify this program so that it will sort *signed* 32-bit integers.

2. Refer to the assembly-language program in Fig. 11.30. What function is served by the statement given in line 250?

```
*     THIS PROGRAM DEFINES READ AND WRITE MACROS.   THE HANDLER DEFINED
*      IN THE PREVIOUS EXAMPLE MUST BE AVAILABLE.
*   DEFINE THE READ MACRO
GET       MACRO
          MOVE.L \1,-(A7)
          MOVE.W #1,-(A7)
          TRAP #2
              ENDM
*   DEFINE WRITE MACRO
PRINT       MACRO
          MOVE.W \2,-(A7)
          MOVE.L \1,-(A7)
          MOVE #0,-(A7)
          TRAP #2
          ENDM
*
*
*
*    START TEST PROGRAM
          ORG $1000
START     MOVEA.L #START,A7
*   TEST GET AND PRINT MACROS !!!!!
          GET #BUFFER
          SUBA #BUFFER,A6
          PRINT #BUFFER,A6
          STOP #0
BUFFER    DS.B    90
          END
```

Figure 11.29

3. Refer to the program in Fig. 11.30 and to the symbol table and set of simulator commands given in Fig. 11.31. The program is run for five sets of data. Two RUN commands are required to complete program execution for the first set of data.

   (a) The *test program* for the subroutine starts at the memory location identified by which alphanumeric label?

   (b) Refer to the simulator commands and to the first run. The first breakpoint is set to an address corresponding to which label?

   (c) The second breakpoint in the first run has been set to a breakpoint corresponding to which label?

   (d) During program execution, suppose the first breakpoint is encountered. What hexadecimal number is in D6 at this time?

   (e) During run 1, the second breakpoint is encountered. What hexadecimal number will be in D6?

   (f) During which run is the "CHECK" message printed for the first time?

   (g) During which run is the "CHECK" message printed for the final time?

   (h) What hexadecimal number will be in D6 at the conclusion of the last run?

4. Write and test a program that reads and prints records from a file. Program execution is to terminate if and only if the first four characters in a record are DONE.

5. Design and test a subroutine that computes the positive integer K MOD(N), where K and N are positive integers carried into the subroutine.

```
100        ORG  $1000
110 STUDENT_AGES  DC.B  99,13,6,83,15,11,37,1,8,$97,1,2,3
120        DS  20
130 NICE    DC.B   ' USE HONEST AGES, STUPID!!'
140 NICER   DC.B   '!'
150        DS  1
160 *  THE FOLLOWING SUBROUTINE COMPUTES THE AVERAGE AGE OF A
170 *     GROUP OF N STUDENTS.  N IS CARRIED INTO THE ROUTINE IN D7.
180 *     THE AVERAGE AGE IS RETURNED IN D6.
190 AVE_AGE          CLR.W  D6
200              MOVE.B  D7,D5
210              MOVE #105,D3      UPPER AGE BOUND
220              MOVEA.L  #STUDENT_AGES,A1      POINTER
230      BACK:    MOVE.B  (A1)+,D4
240              EXT.W  D4          EXTEND TO A WORD
250              CHK D3,D4          CHECK BOUNDS
260              ADD D4,D6
270              SUBQ #1,D5
280              BNE BACK
290              AND.L #$0FFFFF,D6
300              EXT.W D7
310              DIVU  D7,D6       GET AVERAGE
320      DOG:     NOP
330              AND.L #$0FFFF,D6   MASK OUT REMAINDER
340              RTS
350 *    SET VECTOR
360              ORG $18
370              DC.L  CHECK
380              ORG $1200
390 CHECK:       MOVEA #NICE,A5
400              MOVEA #NICER,A6
410              JSR $10002
420              RTE
430 NUM          DC.B  3
440              DS 1
450 DUCK:        MOVEA  #$1000,A7
460              MOVE.B  NUM,D7
470              JSR AVE_AGE
480 TERM         NOP
490              STOP #6
500          END
```

Figure 11.30

REFERENCES

M68000 Cross Macro Assembler Reference Manual, 3rd ed. Austin, Tex.: Motorola, Inc., 1979.

MC68000 Educational Computer Board User's Manual, 2nd ed. Tempe, Ariz.: Motorola, Inc., 1982.

M68000 Simulator Reference Manual, 2nd ed. Austin, Tex.: Motorola, Inc., 1980.

MC68000 16-Bit Microprocessor User's Manual, 3rd ed. Motorola, Inc. Englewood Cliffs, N.J.: Prentice-Hall, 1982.

STARNES, THOMAS, "Design Philosophy Behind Motorola's MC68000, Part 1," *BYTE,* 8, no 4 (April 1983): 70–92.

———, "Design Philosophy Behind Motorola's MC68000, Part 2," *BYTE,* 8, no 5 (May 1983): 342–367.

```
****** TOTAL ERRORS    0--    0 -- TOTAL LINES    41

APPROX  2111 UNUSED SYMBOL TABLE ENTRIES

AVE_AGE  001054 BACK    001062 CHECK    001200 DOG      001078 DUCK    001214
NICE     001036 NICER   001050 NUM      001210 STUDENT_ 001000 TERM    001220
```

```
100 IM
110 SR CC 2000
120 SR A7,0FE0
130 SR CC0
140 SR P1214
150 BP 1078,1220
160 R                      <- RUN 1
170 R                      <- RUN 1 (CONTINUED)
180 BC
190 BP 1220
200 BD
210 SM 1210,0C
220 SR P1214
230 R                      <- RUN 2
240 SR P 1214
250 SM 1210,5
260 SM 1007,7E
270 R                      <- RUN 3
280 SR P1214
290 SM 1210,9
300 R                      <- RUN 4
310 SM 1210,2
320 SR P1214
330 R                      <- RUN 5
340 EX
```

Figure 11.31

EXERCISES

1. Suppose an active signal is applied to the RESET pin of an M68000 chip for a sufficiently long interval. What happens within the CPU?

2. Devices A, B, and C are peripheral components that request service by producing interrupts. When one of these devices is to request service, it sends the following signals to pins $\overline{IPL2}$, $\overline{IPL1}$, and $\overline{IPL0}$, respectively.

Device	Signals
A	low, high, low
B	low, low, high
C	high, low, low

Which device or devices will have their service requests granted if the current contents of the processor status word are

   (a) 0F3D?
   (b) 43AB?
   (c) 321F?

3. Prior to the execution of an instruction, suppose that the number in the status register

is *5DF*8, the number in the program counter is 00001*F*22, and the number in D0 is 6*A*5*C*. The machine code corresponding to the following command is fetched and executed.

```
ADD.B  #0A1,D0
```

What will be the new number in
(a) the program counter?
(b) the status register?
(c) D0?

4. Suppose that it is desired to enter a TRACE mode when a TRAP #0 instruction is executed and to exit from the TRACE mode when a TRAP #1 command is executed. Formulate appropriate software. Do not write the TRACE routine.

5. Write a program statement that when executed will load the number $1120 into the program counter.

6. Translate each of the following instructions into machine code:
   (a) SUBQ.B   #1,D0
   (b) ADDA   #$0F3,A5
   (c) ASL.L   #7,D4

7. Translate each of the following M68000 commands into machine code:
   (a) BCHG   #5,(A6)
   (b) MOVE.B D0,(A5)+
   (c) MOVEM.L A1/A2,−(A3)
   (d) MOVE   −(A2),(A2)+

8. Translate each of the following machine-language instructions into appropriate mnemonics. (*Note:* The instructions are all move-type instructions.)
   (a) 243C   ABD4   5612
   (b) 267C   0000   1014
   (c) 2682

9. Translate each of the following machine-language instructions into appropriate mnemonics. (*Note:* The instructions are all add-type instructions.)
   (a) D279   0001   0000
   (b) D478   1010
   (c) D66A   1022

10. Refer to the following program. Translate each line into machine code.

```
            RORG   $1000
    BACK:   ADD.B  FISH(A3),D2
            BMI BACK
    FISH:   TRAP #9
            END
```

11. Refer to the program in Exercise 10. Suppose initially the number 0 is stored in both A3 and D2. After execution of this program is completed, what number will be in D2?

12. Formulate an instruction that places the contents of all data registers and all address registers except A7 on the stack.

13. Refer to Exercise 12. Write a command that properly restores the values back into these registers.

14. A 20-digit BCD number is stored in memory beginning at hexadecimal location 2000. Another 20-digit BCD number is stored in memory beginning at location 3000. The second number has a value less than that of the first number. Write a program that subtracts the second number from the first number and places the result in the locations previously occupied by the minuend.

15. Design and test a subroutine that converts a two-digit BCD number to the corresponding binary number.

16. Design and test a subroutine that converts a four-digit BCD number to the corresponding binary number.

17. Design and test a subroutine that converts a binary number whose value is less than 100 to a corresponding two-digit BCD number.

18. Design and test a subroutine that converts a binary number whose magnitude is less than 10,000 to a corresponding four-digit packed BCD number.

19. Design and test a subroutine that accepts two two-digit BCD numbers and returns a four-digit BCD number corresponding to their product.

20. Suppose the ILLEGAL instruction is executed. Write and test an appropriate exception processing routine that prints a nasty message each time this instruction is executed.

21. Write a single program statement that will
    (a) Clear the carry flag
    (b) Set the zero flag
    (c) Set the overflow flag
    (d) Clear the sign flag
    (e) Clear the extend flag

22. Formulate a macro that senses bit K in a data register. If bit K = 1, the words in the data register are swapped. The value of the bit sensed is not to be changed.

23. Write and test a subroutine that prints the contents of D0 as an eight-character hexadecimal number.

24. Design and test a subroutine that prints the low-order byte in D1 as a two-character hexadecimal number.

25. Design and test a subroutine that accepts a 32-bit argument. The subroutine prints this address as a hexadecimal number. Then the contents of this memory location and the next seven consecutive bytes of memory are printed.

26. Design and test a subroutine that accepts N four-character strings from the console. Then these strings are sorted in alphabetical order and stored in a file.

27. Repeat Exercise 26 for eight-character strings.

28. Repeat Exercise 26 for 16-character strings.

29. Write and test a subroutine that returns the product of two 24-bit unsigned numbers.

30. Using 32-bit floating points such as those used on the PDP-11, design and test a subroutine that returns the normalized product of two floating points.

31. Design and test an appropriate trap processing routine that prints a suitable message when division by zero is attempted.

32. Design and test a TRACE routine that prints the address of the next command that is executed. When testing this routine, use a technique such as developed in Exercise 4 to enter into and exit from the TRACE mode of operation.

12

A Look at 16-Bit Machines

Small computer systems developed in the 1960s were perhaps the first very popular 16-bit machines. Examples of such systems include the PDP-11 and the NOVA families of computers. The word *minicomputer* was first used to describe such systems. The advent of microprocessors in the 1970s led to extensive use of 4-bit machines and 8-bit machines. By the end of this decade, 16-bit microprocessors had been introduced and were becoming popular. It was only a relatively short period of time before 32-bit microprocessors were proposed and developed. It is interesting to speculate on the relative importance that 16-bit machines may have in future applications.

12.1 CLASSIFICATION AND USE OF SMALL COMPUTERS

The phrase *small computer* is usually associated with a computer not classified as a mainframe computer. Traditionally, a mainframe computer is one that is supported by a full-time staff. Such a computer usually includes a variety of relatively modern peripheral devices, and serves the need of a group or organization. It is virtually impossible to give a time-invariant definition of a mainframe computer in terms of computing power, memory capacity, or even in terms of data throughput. Classification in terms of these technical parameters does not have significant value because many modern microcomputers easily outperform some of the older mainframe computers.

At one time there appeared to be reasonably well-defined lines of demarcation between minicomputers and microcomputers. These classifications no longer appear to be useful. A 12-bit machine, the PDP-8, is still being manufactured. Through tradition this machine is called a minicomputer. Even though this machine has a relatively primitive architecture, it is still an important and useful device. It is supported by massive amounts of software that have been developed by users over the past two decades. Yet, at the present time, there are multiuser microcomputers supported by sophisticated operating systems that are vastly superior in terms of computing power.

Traditionally, machines have been classified according to a specified number of bits. Popular classifications have included 4-bit, 8-bit, 12-bit, 16-bit, 18-bit, 32-bit, 36-bit, and 64-bit machines. The first microprocessors to obtain important commercial use were 4-bit machines. Popular 4-bit machines included the Intel 4004 and 4040 and the Rockwell PPS-4. These machines were popular because there were many new applications related to input, manipulation of, and output of binary coded decimal numbers. Such applications include computer-controlled cash registers, monitored weighing units, and other point-of-sale terminals. In addition, 4-bit machines were more than adequate for use as programmable replacements for many digital logic circuits.

At the same time that 4-bit machines were achieving very important commercial usage, 8-bit machines were being enhanced and applied to a wider variety of problems. Although many considered these machines as digital logic replacement devices, it was soon apparent that computer applications that had not previously been conceived would soon be implemented. Because 8-bit machines operate on bytes, and because byte information could now easily be manipulated, it was apparent that general-purpose 8-bit computers would soon be implemented. The relatively early entries into the personal or home computer market included the Commodore Pet, the Radio Shack TRS 80 , and the Apple-II computers. New uses for general-purpose computers were found. Vast amounts of software were developed for the popular 8-bit general purpose computers. Similarly, de facto industry standard operating systems such as CPM emerged.

It was certainly not surprising that 16-bit microprocessors would be developed or that personal computers based on these microprocessors would rapidly emerge. The IBM Personal Computer based on the Intel 8088 microprocessor was introduced in late autumn of 1981. Within one year, this personal computer achieved a strong position within the small computer market.

Early in the 1980s, 32-bit miroprocessors were developed for commercial usage. With this inception, the gap between the computing capabilities of mainframe computers and microcomputers became narrow. It is evident that technology exists to expand further the capabilities of microcomputers.

The concepts associated with classification of machines as 4-bit, 8-bit, 16-bit, or 32-bit are not unique. At one time a machine was considered to be an N-bit machine if its accumulator or accumulators were N-bit registers. Modern machines do not uniquely assign specified registers to be accumulators. This definition could be extended so that a machine would be considered to be an *N*-bit machine if its general-purpose registers were *N*-bit registers. Using this definition, the 8085 could be called a 16-bit machine and the M68000 a 32-bit machine. It is reasonable to classify a machine according to the width of its data bus. Using this definition, the 8088 would be an 8-bit machine.

Perhaps the most popular means of classifying machines is in relationship to the size of the internal data buses. The time required for the execution of an instruction largely depends on the time required for internal data movements. Consider a fictitious machine with a 32-bit ALU and an 8-bit internal data bus. Clearly, the time required to perform a 32-bit arithmetic or logic operation depends significantly on the time required to transfer information to and from the ALU. These sequential operations include the requirements of loading the ALU registers 1 byte at a time and transferring the results to a destination register 1 byte at a time.

Even use of the size of internal data buses as a means of classifying computers may not be too meaningful. Modern systems may employ simultaneous parallel operations on words of various sizes.

Just as the first microprocessors and their supporting components were considered as replacements for mechanical or electronic logic components, the earlier minicomputers were considered by many individuals primarily for use in real-time applications. Use of minicomputers in monitoring and controlling external systems is extensive. New applications are still being developed.

However, both minicomputers and general-purpose microcomputers are widely used for computational activities. These include both business-oriented and scientific applications. Huge volumes of software have been developed for operation on various minicomputer systems. Similarly, the growth of software packages for use on general-purpose microcomputers has been phenomenal. This includes development of new compilers, word processing systems, spreadsheet programs, graphics packages, database management systems, integrated office management systems, and communication and networking systems.

Review

1. Suppose that it is desired to classify a small computer as an 8-bit, a 16-bit, or a 32-bit machine. Why is the size of each of the following components relatively insignificant in determining this classification?
   (a) the memory address register
   (b) the ALU registers
   (c) the program counter

12.2 *COMPARISON OF 16-BIT MACHINES*

Three different 16-bit machines have been discussed in this textbook. Attributes common to the PDP-11 family of computers have been introduced. Similarly, attributes of two 16-bit microprocessors, the 8086/88 and the M68000, have been discussed. Although there are certain similarities among these machines, each possesses certain attributes that are somewhat unique.

Enhancements of each of these machines are either already being marketed or will be available in the near future. The VAX-11 minicomputer family is an extension of the PDP-11 family. Both of these computer families are properly classified as *systems* rather than as microprocessors. The 8086 and M68000 machines are microprocessors. Both are supported by a wide variety of peripheral devices. Modern enhancements of both of these machines are very powerful. Perhaps certain enhancements should not even be classified as 16-bit machines. All three of these machines can be readily enhanced because the machine architecture is defined by the microcode associated with the machine. Machines whose internal control units consist of hard-wired electronic components are not as easy to refine or enhance.

It is of interest to compare the architecture of these three basic machines. Although it is a relatively old machine, the PDP-11 possesses attributes that may make it very attractive to a programmer. For the basic single-operand and double-operand instructions, *all* addressing modes are permitted. An exception is that meaningless instructions such as JMP TO A REGISTER are not allowed. Registers, including the program counter, are truly general-purpose registers. True indirect addressing is available on the PDP-11 but not on either the M68000 or the 8086.

The M68000 and the 8086 are competitive 16-bit microprocessors. The development of both of these machines was influenced by the PDP-11 architecture. This is especially apparent with respect to the M68000. Both of these modern machines include machine-language instructions for fixed-point multiplication and division operations. Similarly, both machines have instructions that support binary coded decimal operations and multibit shift and rotation operations. Both instruction sets include instructions that readily support implementation of modern structured languages, such as Pascal and Ada. Both machines include control signals and machine-language instructions that facilitate the use of parallel processors and the formulation of computer networks. Floating-point coprocessors are available for use with these machines.

The 8086 may be characterized by its use of segment registers for identifying blocks of program, data, and stack operands. It may also be characterized by use of byte instructions. At times, use of byte commands, one or more byte prefixes and byte-sized addressing operands seems awkward. On the other hand, it offers certain efficiency in that instructions need not be excessively long. Use of a 40-pin chip offers economical advantages for users of low-end 16-bit microprocessors. Operation of the machine in a minimal mode configuration further offers the possibility of cost reduction for relatively modest applications. Yet the capability of operating in the maximal mode permits the use of parallel processing and operation within a network.

A fundamental management decision in developing the 8086 microprocessor was to make it reasonably upward compatible with the older 8-bit machines, the 8080 and the 8085 microprocessors. This was not a primary decision in the development of the M68000. Instead, it appears that the machine was developed as a base machine with future enhancements in mind. In particular, it appears that the machine architecture of the M68000 can easily be extended to a true 32-bit machine.

Use of a 64-pin chip for implementation of the M68000 appears to lessen its competitiveness for low-end 16-bit applications. It does offer greater possibilities for developing more sophisticated machines that are upward compatible with the M68000. The M68000 may be characterized by its implementation of 32-bit operations and by its use of eight general-purpose address registers and eight general-purpose data registers. Use of privileged instructions while in a supervisory state and the availability of seven priority interrupt levels facilitate certain applications.

There are advantages associated with use of the newer 16-bit machines. However, the use of the various addressing modes and efficient use of the instruction sets do not appear to be simple. The availability of relatively good assemblers appears to compensate at least partially for the difficulties encountered in selecting appropriate instructions and addressing modes.

Review

1. Identify at least two significant characteristics or attributes of each of the three machines discussed in this textbook.
2. List some similarities between the PDP-11 architecture and the M68000 architecture.
3. It is desired to develop the following M68000 command to implement indirect addressing on an M68000-based system.

```
MOVIND.X   SOURCE,DEST
```

That is, when the command is given, the operand stored in the address that is stored at locations SOURCE to SOURCE +3 is moved into the location identified by DEST. Write and test the corresponding macro.

12.3 APPLICATIONS OF 16-BIT MACHINES: PAST, PRESENT, AND FUTURE

The early popular 16-bit machines included the PDP-11 family of computers manufactured by the Digital Equipment Corporation. The NOVA family, manufactured by the Data General Corporation, was another popular family of 16-bit machines. These minicomputers included the NOVA, the SUPERNOVA, and the ECLIPSE. Enhancements of these families resulted in powerful 32-bit machines. The VAX11 (Virtual Addressing Extended) family and the MV8000 system are machines with extended and improved systems in comparison with their 16-bit prototypes.

The 16-bit machines have been used for a variety of applications, including

Control of machine tools and processes
Instrumentation and control of experiments

Implementation of automatic testing systems

Control of manufacturing operations

Monitoring and control of data acquisition systems

Interactive graphics systems

Speech analysis systems

Image processing systems

The use of 16-bit processors for applications involving the analysis and synthesis of analog signals is convenient. For typical applications, hybrid components (analog-to-digital and digital-to-analog converters) involve the use of registers having no more than 16 bits. Examples of such devices and their uses were given in Section 8.3.

The 16-bit minicomputers clearly exhibited a major impact related to real-time computer applications. Shortly after the development of 4-bit and 8-bit microprocessors, the first 16-bit microprocessor was introduced. This was the PACE manufactured by the National Semiconductor Corporation. Its relatively good "number-crunching" capabilities enabled it to be suitable for numerical control operations. This was perhaps the first 16-bit microcomputer to perform tasks previously relegated to minicomputers.

In 1975, the Digital Equipment Corporation introduced the LSI-11 minicomputer. This implementation of PDP-11 architecture consisted of a CPU implemented on either four or five chips. The five-chip version included microcode required for implementation of an extended instruction set. During the same time, Texas Instruments introduced the TMS9900. This was probably the first single-chip microprocessor whose capabilities were competitive with existing minicomputers. Single-chip versions of the NOVA were also developed during this period.

The development of the three HMOS microprocessors—the 8086, Z8000, and M68000—had a significant impact on the use of 16-bit machines. Clearly, these machines are capable of supporting sophisticated multiuser systems. The 8086 (and the 8088) and the M68000 became quite popular within a short time. These machines are used both as dedicated logic components and as central processors or coprocessors for both single-user and multiuser systems.

At present, the three 16-bit processors discussed in this textbook are widely used. Even though 32-bit machines with similar architectures already either exist or are in late stages of development, it is anticipated that use of 16-bit machines will continue to expand, at least for a while. The expansion of the use of 8-bit microprocessors did not seem to have a serious impact on the use of 4-bit machines. The price of one very popular 8-bit microprocessor dropped to less than $3 per unit when purchased in large lots. However, the price of a very popular 4-bit machine dropped below $1. Just based upon cost considerations, it appears that use of 16-bit machines will not seriously diminish the use of 8-bit machines. Similarly, the emerging 32-bit microprocessors will probably not have an immediate impact on the use of 16-bit machines.

Perhaps the most significant factor related to continued usage of the PDP-11 family is the vast library of software that operates under RT-11 or RSX-11 operating systems. Similarly, large investments have been made in software for microcomputers operating under either the IBM DOS operating system or under CMP-86. Several current general-purpose microcomputers utilizing the M68000 operate under UNIX-like operating systems. Thus, significant software is already available.

The top-of-the-line general-purpose microcomputers introduced in 1982 and 1983 generally utilized 16-bit processors. A considerable number of such microcomputers were introduced in Japan during this period. Most of these computers were based on 8086 or 8088 microprocessors. This suggests that these microprocessors or upward compatible enhancements of these machines will be widely used in the future.

Significant enhancements of computing machines are likely to continue. The capability of implementing more than 1 million electronic components on a single silicon chip will soon be realizable in a practical manner. Clearly, there will be innovations in instruction sets and new programing concepts and languages developed. Already technology exists to incorporate significant extensions in computer architecture. It is rather simplistic to visualize the development of 64-bit, 128-bit, and 256-bit microprocessors. Although advances in computer technology will occur, the development of such devices may be of very little value for general-purpose applications.

Instead of increasing word sizes, there are probably better methods of seeking improved machine performances. Increased use of parallel processors offers the possibility of significantly increasing performance of a system without significantly increasing component costs.

Perhaps some of the tacit assumptions related to implementation and use of computers will be challenged. By discussing 8-bit, 16-bit, and 32-bit machines, we imply that the concept of bit is fundamental in the operation or classification of computers. In the past, components of computers have been two-state or binary devices. Use of such devices is both economical and highly reliable. Use of just two logic levels is also consistent with simple propositional logic concepts developed more than 2,000 years ago. Simple declarative sentences were formulated and classified as either true or false. Functions of these statements could be similarly classified.

To this date, virtually all digital computers have used binary devices. Even computers that have been called decimal computers actually perform manipulations on sets of binary numbers. The technology exists to classify reliably voltages to be within one of several distinct levels. For example, suppose that it is desired to have a true decimal computer. It is conceivable that each register cell and each memory cell could store a voltage value that is within one of ten distinct intervals. Similarly, arithmetic and logic devices that operate on such levels can be formulated.

Based on current technologies, implementation of such a machine would be very expensive. Initially, there would be serious problems related to achieving suitable reliability. On the positive side, perhaps millions of person-hours could be saved both in educational institutions and in software development organizations. The problems associated with converting a number from one number system or binary representation to a different number system or representation would no longer be present.

It is not suggested that use of binary signals for implementing computer hardware be abandoned. Rather, it is suggested that future progress in developing computer systems should not be limited to simple extensions of what has traditionally been done.

REFERENCES

ECKHOUSE, R., and L. MORSE, *Minicomputer Systems; Organization, Programming and Applications* (PDP-11), Englewood Cliffs, N.J.: Prentice-Hall, 1979.

JERMANN, W., *The Structure and Programming of Microcomputers.* Palo Alto, Calif.: Mayfield Publishing Company, 1982.

KORN, G., *Minicomputers for Scientists and Engineers,* New York: McGraw-Hill, 1973.

Lemmons, Phil, "New Japanese Microcomputers," *BYTE,* 8, no. 4 (April 1983): 110–28.

MAYOH, B., *Solving Problems with ADA.* Chichester, England: John Wiley, 1982.

Microcomputers and Memories. Maynard, Mass: Digital Equipment Corporation, 1981.

OSBORNE, A., *An Introduction to Microcomputers,* vol. II. *Some Real Products.* Berkeley, Calif.: Adam Osborne and Associates, 1976.

A

Table of ASCII Codes

ASCII Code	Character	ASCII Code	Character	ASCII Code	Character
00	NUL	2B	+	56	V
01	SOH	2C	,	57	W
02	STX	2D	-	58	X
03	ETX	2E	.	59	Y
04	EOT	2F	/	5A	Z
05	ENQ	30	0	5B	[
06	ACK	31	1	5C	\
07	BEL	32	2	5D	]
08	BS	33	3	5E	$\wedge(\uparrow)$
09	HT	34	4	5F	$-(\leftarrow)$
0A	LF	35	5	60	\
0B	VT	36	6	61	a
0C	FF	37	7	62	b
0D	CR	38	8	63	c
0E	SO	39	9	64	d
0F	SI	3A	:	65	e
10	DLE	3B	;	66	f

(continued)

Note: Table yields 7-bit ASCII code expressed in hexadecimal. Most significant bit is set to 0.

Source: Lance A. Leventhal, *Introduction to Microprocessors*. Software, Hardware, Programming. ©1978, p. 545. Reprinted by permission of Prentice-Hall, Inc., Englewood Cliffs, N.J.

ASCII Code	Character	ASCII Code	Character	ASCII Code	Character
11	DC1 (X-ON)	3C	<	67	g
12	DC2 (TAPE)	3D	=	68	h
13	DC3 (X-OFF)	3E	>	69	i
14	DC4	3F	?	6A	j
15	NAK	40	@	6B	k
16	SYN	41	A	6C	1
17	ETB	42	B	6D	m
18	CAN	43	C	6E	n
19	EM	44	D	6F	o
1A	SUB	45	E	70	p
1B	ESC	46	F	71	q
1C	FS	47	G	72	r
1D	GS	48	H	73	s
1E	RS	49	I	74	t
1F	US	4A	J	75	u
20	SP	4B	K	76	v
21	!	4C	L	77	w
22	"	4D	M	78	x
23	#	4E	N	79	y
24	$	4F	O	7A	z
25	%	50	P	7B	{
26	&	51	Q	7C		
27	'	52	R	7D	} (ALT MODE)
28	(	53	S	7E	–
29	)	54	T	7F	DEL (RUB OUT)
2A	*	55	U		

B

A PDP-11 Instruction Set[1]

SYMBOLS:

( ) = contents of

SS or src = source address

DD or dst = destination address

loc = location

← = becomes

↑ = "is popped from stack"

↓ = "is pushed onto stack"

∧ = boolean AND

∨ = boolean OR

∀ = exclusive OR

~ = boolean NOT

Reg or R = register

B = Byte

$\blacksquare = \begin{cases} 0 \text{ for word} \\ 1 \text{ for byte} \end{cases}$

, = concatenated

Notes:

1. This is the instruction set for the LSI-11 processor. Instructions are listed in alphabetical order. *Exception:* Instructions involving setting or clearing status flags are all listed with the CLN mnemonic.

2. The extended arithmetic option (EIS and floating-point) instructions are not included with all LSI-11 processors. These instructions are MUL, DIV, ASH, ASCH, FADD, FSUB, FMUL, AND FDIV.

[1]Copyright, Digital Equipment Corporation, 1976. All rights reserved. Reprinted by permission.

ADC   add carry   ■055DD
ADCB

Operation: (dst) ← (dst) + (C bit)   **Condition Codes:**   N: set if result < 0;
Adds the contents of the C-bit into the desti-   cleared otherwise
nation. This permits the carry from the addi-   Z: set if result = 0;
tion of the low-order words to be carried into   cleared otherwise
the high-order result.   V: set if (dst) was 077777
Byte: Same   and (C) was 1; cleared
                                                                      otherwise
                                                                      C: set if (dst) was 177777
                                                                      and (C) was 1; cleared
                                                                      otherwise

ADD   add src to dst   06SSDD

Operation: (dst) ← (src) + (dst)   **Condition Codes:**   N: set if result < 0;
Adds the source operand to the destination   cleared otherwise
operand and stores the result at the destination   Z: set if result = 0;
address. The original contents of the destina-   cleared otherwise
tion are lost. The contents of the source are   V: set if there was arith-
not affected. Two's complement addition is   metic overflow as a result
performed.   of the operation; that is
Note: There is no equivalent byte mode.   both operands were of the
                                                                      same sign and the result
                                                                      was of the opposite sign;
                                                                      cleared otherwise
                                                                      C: set if there was a carry
                                                                      from the most significant
                                                                      bit of the result; cleared
                                                                      otherwise

ASH   shift arithmetically   072RSS

Operation: R ← R Shifted arithmetically NN   **Condition Codes:**   N: set if result < 0;
              places to right or left, where NN   cleared otherwise
              = low order 6 bits of source   Z: set if result = 0;
The contents of the register are shifted right or   cleared otherwise
left the number of times specified by the shift   V: set if sign of register
count. The shift count is taken as the low or-   changed during shift;
der 6 bits of the source operand. This number   cleared otherwise
ranges from −32 to +31. Negative is a right   C: loaded from last bit
shift and positive is a left shift.   shifted out of register

ASHC   arithmetic shift combined   073RSS

Operation: R, Rv1 ← R, Rv1 Double word   **Condition Codes:**   N: set if result < 0;
              shifted NN places to the right or   cleared otherwise
              left, where NN = low order six   Z: set if result = 0;
              bits of source   cleared otherwise

The contents of the register and the register ORed with one are treated as one 32 bit word; R + 1 (bits 0–15) and R (bits 16–31) are shifted right or left the number of times specified by the shift count. The shift count is taken as the low order 6 bits of the source operand. This number ranges from −32 to +31. Negative is a right shift and positive is a left shift. When the register chosen is an odd number the register and the register ORed with one are the same. In this case the right shift becomes a rotate (for up to a shift of 16). The 16–bit word is rotated right the number of bits specified by the shift count.

V: set if sign bit changes during the shift; cleared otherwise
C: loaded with the high-order bit when left shift; loaded with the low-order bit when right shift (loaded with the last bit shifted out of the 32-bit operand)

ASL
ASLB

arithmetic shift left

■063DD

Operation: (dst) ← (dst) shifted one place to the left
Word: Shifts all bits of the destination left one place. Bit 0 is loaded with a 0. The C-bit of the status word is loaded from the most significant bit of the destination. ASL performs a signed multiplication of the destination by 2 with overflow indication.

Condition Codes: N: set if the high-order bit of result is set (result < 0); cleared otherwise
Z: set if result = 0; cleared otherwise
V: loaded with the exclusive OR of the N-bit and C-bit (as set by the completion of the shift operation)
C: loaded with the high-order bit of the destination

ASR
ASRB

arithmetic shift right

■062DD

Operation: (dst) ← (dst) shifted one place to the right
Word: Shifts all bits of the destination right one place. Bit 15 is reproduced. The C-bit is loaded from bit 0 of the destination. ASR performs signed division of the destination by two.

Condition Codes: N: set if the high-order bit of the result is set (result < 0); cleared otherwise
Z: set if result = 0; cleared otherwise
V: loaded from the Exclusive OR of the N-bit and C-bit (as set by the completion of the shift operation)
C: loaded from the low-order bit of the destination

BCC   branch if carry is clear   103000 Plus offset

Operation: PC ← PC + (2 × offset) if
      C = 0

Condition Codes: Unaffected

Tests the state of the C-bit and causes a
branch if C is clear. BCC is the complementary operation to BCS.

BCS   branch if carry is set   103400 Plus offset

Operation: PC ← PC + (2 × offset) if
      C = 1

Condition Codes: Unaffected

Tests the state of the C-bit and causes a
branch if C is set. It is used to test for a carry
in the result of a previous operation.

BEQ   branch if equal (to zero)   001400 Plus offset

Operation: PC ← PC + (2 × offset) if
      Z = 1

Condition Codes: Unaffected

Tests the state of the Z-bit and causes a
branch if Z is set.

BGE   branch if greater than or equal   002000 Plus offset
                            (to zero)

Operation: PC ← PC + (2 × offset) if
      N ∀ V = 0

Condition Codes: Unaffected

Causes a branch if N and V are either both
clear or both set. BGE is the complementary
operation to BLT. Thus BGE will always cause
a branch when it follows an operation that
caused addition of two positive numbers. BGE
will also cause a branch on a zero result.

BGT   branch if greater than (zero)   003000 Plus offset

Operation: PC ← PC + (2 × offset) if
      Z v(N ∀ V) = 0

Condition Codes: Unaffected

Operation of BGT is similar to BGE, except
BGT will not cause a branch on a zero result.

BHI   branch if higher   101000 Plus offset

Operation: PC ← PC + (2 × offset) if
      C = 0 and Z = 0

Condition Codes: Unaffected

Causes a branch if the previous operation
caused neither a carry nor a zero result. This
will happen in comparison (CMP) operations
as long as the source has a higher unsigned
value than the destination.

BHIS   branch if higher or same   **103000 Plus offset**

Operation: PC ← PC + (2 × offset) if   **Condition Codes:** Unaffected
        C = 0
BHIS is the same instruction as BCC. This
mnemonic is included only for convenience.

BIC   bit clear   **■4SSDD**
BICB

Operation: (dst) ← ~(src) ∧ (dst)   **Condition Codes:** N: set if the high–order
Clears each bit in the destination that corre-   bit of result set; cleared
sponds to a set bit in the source. The original   otherwise
contents of the destination are lost. The con-   Z: set if result = 0;
tents of the source are unaffected.   cleared otherwise
                                                                      V: cleared
                                                                      C: not affected

BIS   bit set   **■5SSDD**
BISB

Operation: (dst)← (src) v (dst)   **Condition Codes:** N: set if the high-order bit
Performs "Inclusive OR" operation between   of result set, cleared
the source and destination operands and leaves   otherwise
the result at the destination address; that is,   Z: set if result = 0;
corresponding bits set in the source are set in   cleared otherwise
the destination. The contents of the destina-   V: cleared
tion are lost.   C: not affected

BIT   bit test   **■3SSDD**
BITB

Operation: (src) ∧ (dst)   **Condition Codes:** N: set if the high-order bit
Performs logical "AND" comparison of the   of result set; cleared
source and destination operands and modifies   otherwise
condition codes accordingly. Neither the   Z: set if result = 0;
source nor destination operands are affected.   cleared otherwise
The BIT instruction may be used to test   V: cleared
whether any of the corresponding bits that are   C: not affected
set in the destination are also set in the source
or whether all corresponding bits set in the
destination are clear in the source.

BLE   branch if less than or equal   **003400 Plus offset**
                                         (to zero)

Operation: PC ← PC + (2 × offset) if   **Condition Codes:** Unaffected
        Z v(N ∀ V) = 1
Operation is similar to BLT but in addition
will cause a branch if the result of the previous operation was zero.

BLO   branch if lower   103400 Plus offset

Operation: PC ← PC + (2 × offset) if   **Condition Codes:** Unaffected
            C = 1
BLO is the same instruction as BCS. This
mnemonic is included only for convenience.

BLOS   branch if lower or same   101400 Plus offset

Operation: PC ← PC + (2 × offset)   **Condition Codes:** Unaffected
            if C v Z = 1
Causes a branch if the previous operation
caused either a carry or a zero result. BLOS is
the complementary operation to BHI. The
branch will occur in comparison operations as
long as the source is equal to, or has a lower
unsigned value than the destination.

BLT   branch if less than (zero)   002400 Plus offset

Operation: PC ← PC + (2 × offset) if   **Condition Codes:** Unaffected
            N $\veebar$ V = 1
Causes a branch if the "Exclusive OR" of the
N and V bits is 1. Thus BLT will always
branch following an operation that added two
negative numbers, even if overflow occurred.
In particular, BLT will always cause a branch
if it follows a CMP instruction (even if overflow occurred). Further, BLT will never cause
a branch when it follows a CMP instruction
operating on a positive source and negative
destination. BLT will not cause a branch if the
result of the previous operation was zero
(without overflow).

BMI   branch if minus   100400 Plus offset

Operation: PC ← PC + (2 × offset) if   **Condition Codes:** Unaffected
            N = 1
Tests the state of the N-bit and causes a
branch if N is set. It is used to test the sign
(most significant bit) of the result of the previous operation, branching if negative. BMI is
the complementary function of BPL.

BNE   branch if not equal (to zero)   001000 Plus offset

Operation: PC ← PC + (2 × offset) if   **Condition Codes:** Unaffected
            Z = 0
Tests the state of the Z-bit and causes a
branch if the Z-bit is clear. BNE is the complementary operation to BEQ.

BPL branch if plus 100000 Plus offset

Operation: $PC \leftarrow PC + (2 \times \text{offset})$ if $N = 0$

Tests the state of the N-bit and causes a branch if N is clear, (positive result). BPL is the complementary operation to BMI.

Condition Codes: Unaffected

BPT breakpoint trap 000003

Operation:
$\downarrow (SP) \leftarrow PS$
$\downarrow (SP) \leftarrow PC$
$PC \leftarrow (14)$
$PS \leftarrow (16)$

Performs a trap sequence with a trap vector address of 14. Used to call debugging aids. The user is cautioned against employing code 000003 in programs run under these debugging aids.
(No information is transmitted in the low byte.)

Condition Codes:
N: loaded from trap vector
Z: loaded from trap vector
V: loaded from trap vector
C: loaded from trap vector

BR branch (unconditional) 000400 Plus offset

Operation: $PC \leftarrow PC + (2 \times \text{offset})$
Provides a way of transferring program control within a range of -128_{10} to $+127_{10}$ words with a one–word instruction.

Condition Codes: Unaffected
New PC address = updated PC + (2 × offset)
Updated PC = address of branch instruction + 2

BVC branch if overflow is clear 102000 Plus offset

Operation: $PC \leftarrow PC + (2 \times \text{offset})$ if $V = 0$

Tests the state of the V-bit and causes a branch if the V–bit is clear. BVC is the complementary operation to BVS.

Condition Codes: Unaffected

BVS branch if overflow is set 102400 Plus offset

Operation: $PC \leftarrow PC + (2 \times \text{offset})$ if $V = 1$

Tests the state of the V-bit (overflow) and causes a branch if the V–bit is set. BVS is used to detect arithmetic overflow in the previous operation.

Condition Codes: Unaffected

CLN	SEN
CLZ	SEZ
CLV	SEV
CLC	SEC
CCC	SCC

condition code operators   **0002XX**

0	0	0	0	0	0	0	0	1	0	1	O/I	N	Z	V	C
15											5	4	3	2	1	0

NOP No operation   000240
Combinations of the above set
or clear operations may be ORed
together to form combined instructions.

Set and clear condition code bits. Selectable
combinations of these bits may be cleared or
set together. Condition code bits corresponding to bits in the condition code operator (bits
0–3) are modified according to the sense of bit
4, the set/clear bit of the operator, i.e., set the
bit specified by bit 0, 1, 2, or 3, if bit 4 is a 1.
Clear corresponding bits if bit 4 = 0.

SCC	Set all CC's	000277
CCC	Clear all CC's	000257

CLR
CLRB

clear destination   **■050DD**

Operation: (dst)← 0
Word: Contents of specified destination are
replaced with zeroes.
Byte: Same

Condition Codes: N: cleared
Z: set
V: cleared
C: cleared

CMP
CMPB

compare src to dst   **■2SSDD**

Operation: (src) − (dst)
Compares the source and destination operands
and sets the condition codes, which may then
be used for arithmetic and logical conditional
branches. Both operands are unaffected. The
only action is to set the condition codes. The
compare command is customarily followed by
a conditional branch instruction. Note that
unlike the subtract instruction the order of operation is (src) − (dst), not (dst) − (src).

Condition Codes: N: set if result < 0;
cleared otherwise
Z: set if result = 0;
cleared otherwise
V: set if there was arithmetic overflow; that is,
operands were of opposite
signs and the sign of the
destination was the same
as the sign of the result;
cleared otherwise
C: cleared if there was a
carry from the most significant bit of the results; set
otherwise

COM
COMB

complement dst   **■051DD**

Operation: (dst)← ~(dst)
Replaces the contents of the destination address by their logical complement. (Each bit

Condition Codes: N: set if most significant
bit of result is set; cleared
otherwise

equal to 0 is set and each bit equal to 1 is cleared.)
Byte: Same

Z: set if result = 0;
cleared otherwise
V: cleared
C: set

DEC
DECB

decrement dst

■053DD

Operation: (dst) ← (dst) − 1
Word: Subtract 1 from the contents of the destination
Byte: Same

Condition Codes: N: set if result < 0;
cleared otherwise
Z: set if result = 0;
cleared otherwise
V: set if (dst) was 100000;
cleared otherwise
C: not affected

DIV

divide

071RSS

Operation: R, Rv1 ← R, Rv1 /(src)
The 32-bit two's complement integer in R and Rv1 is divided by the source operand. The quotient is left in R; the remainder in Rv1. Division will be performed so that the remainder is of the same sign as the dividend. R must be even.
Assembler format for all EIS instruction is:
OPR src, R

Condition Codes: N: set if quotient < 0,
cleared otherwise
Z: set if quotient = 0;
cleared otherwise
V: set if source = 0 or if the absolute value of the register is equal to or larger than the absolute value of the source. (In this case the instruction is aborted because the quotient would exceed 15 bits.)
C: set if divide by 0 attempted; cleared otherwise

EMT

emulator trap

104000–104377

Operation: ↓ (SP) ← PS
↓ (SP) ← PC
PC ← (30)
PS ← (32)

All operation codes from 104000 to 104377 are EMT instructions and may be used to transmit information to the emulating routine (e.g., function to be performed). The trap vector for EMT is at address 30. The new PC is taken from the word at address 30; the new processor status (PS) is taken from the word at address 32.

Condition Codes: N: loaded from trap vector
Z: loaded from trap vector
V: loaded from trap vector
C: loaded from trap vector
Caution: EMT is used frequently by DEC system software and is therefore not recommended for general use.

FADD   floating add   **07500R**

Operation: [(R)+4, (R)+6]← [(R)+4,
      (R)+6]+[(R),(R)+2]
Adds the A argument to the B argument and
stores the result in the A argument position on
the stack. General register R is used as the
stack pointer for the operation.
A← A+B

Condition Codes: N: set if result < 0;
cleared otherwise
Z: set if result = 0;
cleared otherwise
V: cleared
C: cleared

FDIV   floating divide   **07503R**

Operation: [(R)+4,(R)+6]←
      [(R)+4,(R)+6]/[(R),(R)+2]
Divides the A argument by the B argument
and stores the result in the A argument position on the stack. If the divisor (B argument)
is equal to zero, the stack is left untouched.
A← A/B

Condition Codes: N: set if result < 0;
cleared otherwise
Z: set if result = 0;
cleared otherwise
V: cleared
C: cleared

Note

Unlike the PDP-11/40 (and the PDP-11/35),
the LSI-11 processor pushes one word onto
the stack during execution of FMUL and
FDIV instructions and pops the word from the
stack when completed. Thus, the SP (R6) must
point to a read/write memory location; otherwise, a bus error (timeout) will occur.

FMUL   floating multiply   **07502R**

Operation: [(R)+4, (R)+6]← [(R)+4,
      (R)+6]×[(R), (R)+2]
Multiplies the A argument by the B argument
and stores the result in the A argument position on the stack.
A← A×B

Condition Codes: N: set if result < 0;
cleared otherwise
Z: set if result = 0;
cleared otherwise
V: cleared
C: cleared

FSUB   floating subtract   **07501R**

Operation: [(R)+4, (R)+6]← [(R)+4,
      (R)+6]−[(R), (R)+2]
Subtracts the B argument from the A argument and stores the result in the A argument
position on the stack.
A← A−B

Condition Codes: N: set if result < 0;
cleared otherwise
Z: set if result = 0;
cleared otherwise
V: cleared
C: cleared

HALT   halt   **000000**

Causes the processor to leave RUN mode. The
PC points to the next instruction to be executed. The processor goes into HALT mode.
The contents of the PC are displayed on the
console terminal and the console mode of operation is enabled.

Condition Codes: not affected

INC   increment dst   **■052DD**
INCB

Operation: (dst)← (dst)+1
Word: Add one to contents of destination
Byte: Same

Condition Codes: N: set if result < 0;
cleared otherwise
Z: set of result = 0;
cleared otherwise
V: set if (dst) held 077777;
cleared otherwise
C: not affected

IOT   input/output trap   **000004**

Operation: ↓ (SP) ← PS
↓ (SP) ← PC
PC← (20)
PS← (22)
Performs a trap sequence with a trap vector
address of 20.
(No information is transmitted in the low
byte.)

Condition Codes: N: loaded from trap vector
Z: loaded from trap vector
V: loaded from trap vector
C: loaded from trap vector

JMP   jump   **0001DD**

Operation: PC ← (dst)
JMP provides more flexible program branching than provided with the branch instructions. Control may be transferred to any
location in memory (no range limitation) and
can be accomplished with the full flexibility of
the addressing modes, with the exception of
register mode 0. Execution of a jump with
mode 0 will cause an "illegal instruction" condition, and will cause the CPU to trap to vector address 4.

Condition Codes: unaffected

JSR   jump to subroutine   **004RDD**

Operation: (tmp) ← (dst) (tmp is an internal
            processor register)
            ↓ (SP)← reg (push reg contents
            onto processor stack)
            reg← PC (PC holds location fol-
            lowing JSR; this address now put
            in reg)
            PC← (dst) (PC now points to sub-
            routine destination)
In execution of the JSR, the old contents of
the specified register (the "LINKAGE
POINTER") are automatically pushed onto
the processor stack and new linkage information placed in the register.

MARK   mark   **0064NN**

Operation: SP← updated PC + 2 + 2n   **Condition Codes:**   unaffected
            n = number of parameters
            PC← R5
            R5← (SP)↑
Used as part of the standard PDP-11 subroutine return convention. MARK facilitates the
stack clean up procedures involved in subroutine exit. Assembler format is: MARK N

MFPS   move byte from processor   **1067DD**
                         status word

Operation: (dst)← PSW   **Condition Codes**
            dst lower 8 bits   **Bits:** N = set if PSW bit 7 = 1; cleared
The 8–bit contents of the PS are moved to the   otherwise
effective destination. If the destination is   Z = set if PS ⟨0:7⟩ = 0; cleared
mode 0, PS bit 7 is sign extended through the   otherwise
upper byte of the register. The destination op-   V = cleared
erand address is treated as a byte address.   C = not affected

MOV   move source to destination   **■1SSDD**
MOVB

Operation: (dst)← (src)   **Condition Codes:** N: set if (src) <0; cleared
Word: Moves the source operand to the desti-   otherwise
nation location. The previous contents of the   Z: set if (src) = 0; cleared
destination are lost. The contents of the source   otherwise
address are not affected.   V: cleared
Byte: Same as MOV. The MOVB to a register   C: not affected
(unique among byte instructions) extends the

most significant bit of the low order byte (sign extension). Otherwise MOVB operates on bytes exactly as MOV operates on words.

MTPS   move byte to processor status   **1064SS**
                                        word

Operation: PSW ← (src)
The 8 bits of the effective operand replace the current contents of the PSW. The source operand address is treated as a byte address. Note that the T bit (PSW bit 4) cannot be set with this instruction. The src operand remains unchanged. This instruction can be used to change the priority bit (PSW bit 7) in the PSW.

Condition Codes: Set according to effective SRC operand bits 0–3

Note: When executing the MTPS instruction, the LSI-11 processor fetches the source operand via the DATIO bus cycle, rather than the DATI bus cycle. If the source operand is contained in a PROM or ROM location, a bus error (timeout) will occur because the processor will attempt to write into the addressed location after fetching the operand.

MUL   multiply   **070RSS**

Operation: R, Rv1 ← R x(src)
The contents of the destination register and source taken as two's complement integers are multiplied and stored in the destination register and the succeeding register (if R is even). If R is odd only the low-order product is stored. Assembler syntax is: MUL S,R.
(Note that the actual destination is R,Rv1 which reduces to just R when R is odd.)

Condition Codes: N: set if product < 0; cleared otherwise
Z: set if product $= 0$; cleared otherwise
V: cleared
C: set if the result is less than -2^{15} or greater than or equal to $2^{15}-1$.

NEG   negate dst   **■054DD**
NEGB

Operation: (dst) ← – (dst)
Word: Replaces the contents of the destination address by its two's complement. Note that 100000 is replaced by itself (in two's complement notation the most negative number has no positive counterpart).
Byte: Same

Condition Codes: N: set if result < 0; cleared otherwise
Z: set if result $= 0$; cleared otherwise
V: set if the result = 100000; cleared otherwise
C: cleared if the result = 0; set otherwise

RESET   reset external bus   **000005**

Sends INIT on the BUS for 10 μsec. All de-   **Condition Codes:** not affected
vices on the BUS are reset to their state at
power-up. The processor remains in an idle
state for 90 μsec following issuance of INIT.

ROL   rotate left   ■**061DD**
ROLB

Operation: (dst)← (dst)   **Condition Codes:** N: set if the high-order bit
           rotate left one place   of the result word is set
Word: Rotate all bits of the destination left   (result < 0); cleared
one place. Bit 15 is loaded into the C-bit of   otherwise
the status word and the previous contents of   Z: set if all bits of the re-
the C-bit are loaded into bit 0 of the destina-   sult word = 0; cleared
tion.   otherwise
Byte: Same   V: loaded with the Exclu-
                                                                    sive OR of the N-bit and
                                                                    C-bit (as set by the com-
                                                                    pletion of the rotate oper-
                                                                    ation)
                                                                    C: loaded with the high-
                                                                    order bit of the destination

ROR   rotate right   ■**060DD**
RORB

Operation: (dst)← (dst)   **Condition Codes:** N: set if the high-order bit
           rotate right one place   of the result is set (result
Rotates all bits of the destination right one   < 0); cleared otherwise
place. Bit 0 is loaded into the C-bit and the   Z: set if all bits of result
previous contents of the C-bit are loaded into   = 0; cleared otherwise
bit 15 of the destination.   V: loaded with the Exclu-
Byte: Same   sive OR of the N-bit and
                                                                    C-bit (as set by the com-
                                                                    pletion of the rotate oper-
                                                                    ation)
                                                                    C: loaded with the low-or-
                                                                    der bit of the destination

RTI   return from interrupt   **000002**

Operation: PC← (SP)↑   **Condition Codes:** N: loaded from processor
           PS← (SP)↑   stack.
Used to exit from an interrupt or TRAP ser-   Z: loaded from processor
vice routine. The PC and PS are restored   stack
(popped) from the processor stack. If a trace   V: loaded from processor
trap is pending, the first instruction after RTI   stack
will not be executed prior to the next T traps.   C: loaded from processor
                                                                    stack

RTS   **return from subroutine**   00020R

Operation: PC ← (reg)
                  (reg) ← (SP)↑
Loads contents of register into PC and pops
the top element of the processor stack into the
specified register.

RTT   **return from interrupt**   000006

Operation: PC← (SP)↑   **Condition Codes:**   N: loaded from processor
                  PS← (SP)↑   stack
Operation is the same as RTI except that it in-   Z: loaded from processor
hibits a trace trap while RTI permits trace   stack
trap. If new PS has T bit set, trap will occur   V: loaded from processor
after execution of first instruction after RTT.   stack
                                                                     C: loaded from processor
                                                                     stack

SBC   **subtract carry**   ▪056DD
SBCB

Operation: (dst)← (dst)−(C)   **Condition Codes:**   N: set if result < 0;
Word: Subtracts the contents of the C-bit   cleared otherwise
from the destination. This permits the carry   Z: set if result = 0;
from the subtraction of two low-order words   cleared otherwise
to be subtracted from the high–order part of   V: set if (dst) was 100000;
the result.   cleared otherwise
Byte: Same   C: set if (dst) was 0 and C
                                                                     was 1; cleared otherwise

SOB   **subtract one and branch**   077RNN
                                    (if ≠ 0)

Operation: (R) ← (R) − 1; if this result ≠ 0   **Condition Codes:**   unaffected
                  then PC ← PC − (2 × offset) if
                  (R) = 0; PC ← PC
The register is decremented. If it is not equal
to 0, twice the offset is subtracted from the
PC (now pointing to the following word). The
offset is interpreted as a 6-bit positive number.
This instruction provides a fast, efficient
method of loop control. Assembler syntax is:

                  SOB R,A

where A is the address to which transfer is to
be made if the decremented R is not equal to
0. Note that the SOB instruction cannot be
used to transfer control in the forward direction.

SUB

subtract src from dst

16SSDD

Operation: (dst) ← (dst) − (src)
Subtracts the source operand from the destination operand and leaves the result at the destination address. The original contents of the destination are lost. The contents of the source are not affected. In double-precision arithmetic the C-bit, when set, indicates a "borrow."

Condition Codes: N: set if result < 0; cleared otherwise
Z: set if result = 0; cleared otherwise
V: set if there was arithmetic overflow as a result of the operation, that is, if operands were of opposite signs and the sign of the source was the same as the sign of the result; cleared otherwise
C: cleared if there was a carry from the most significant bit of the result; set otherwise

SWAB

swap bytes

0003DD

Operation: Byte 1/Byte 0 ← Byte 0/Byte 1
Exchanges high-order byte and low-order byte of the destination word (destination must be a word address).

Condition Codes: N: set if the high-order bit of the low-order byte (bit 7) of the result is set; cleared otherwise
Z: set if the low-order byte of the result = 0; cleared otherwise
V: cleared
C: cleared

SXT

sign extend

0067DD

Operation: (dst) ← 0 if N-bit is clear
(dst) ← −1 N-bit is set
If the condition code bit N is set then a −1 is placed in the destination operand: if N bit is clear, then a 0 is placed in the destination operand. This instruction is particularly useful in multiple precision arithmetic because it permits the sign to be extended through multiple words.

Condition Codes: N: unaffected
Z: set if N-bit clear
V: cleared
C: unaffected

TRAP

trap

104400 − 104777

Operation: ↓ (SP)← PS
↓ (SP)← PC
PC← (34)
PS← (36)
Operation codes from 104400 to 104777 are TRAP instructions. TRAPs and EMTs are

Condition Codes: N: loaded from trap vector
Z: loaded from trap vector
V: loaded from trap vector

identical in operation, except that the trap vector for TRAP is at address 34.

C: loaded from trap vec-
tor

TST
TSTB

test dst   ■057DD

Operation: (dst)← (dst)
Word: Sets the condition codes N and Z according to the contents of the destination address, contents of dst remains unmodified
Byte: Same

Condition Codes: N: set if result < 0;
cleared otherwise
Z: set if result = 0;
cleared otherwise
V: cleared
C: cleared

WAIT

wait for interrupt   000001

Provides a way for the processor to relinquish
use of the bus while it waits for an external interrupt request.

Condition Codes: not affected

XOR

exclusive OR   074RDD

Operation: (dst)← Rv(dst)
The exclusive OR of the register and destination operand is stored in the destination address. Contents of register are unaffected.
Assembler format is: XOR R,D

Condition Codes: N: set if result < 0;
cleared otherwise
Z: set if result = 0;
cleared otherwise
V: cleared
C: unaffected

C

An M68000 Instruction Set[1]

EFFECTIVE ADDRESSING MODE CATEGORIES

Addressing Mode	Mode	Register	Addressing Categories				Assembler Syntax
			Data	Mem	Cont	Alter	
Data Reg Dir	000	reg no.	X	–	–	X	Dn
Addr Reg Dir	001	reg no.	–	–	–	X	An
Addr Reg Ind	010	reg no.	X	X	X	X	(An)
Addr Reg Ind w/Postinc	011	reg no.	X	X	–	X	(An)+
Addr Reg Ind w/Predec	100	reg no.	X	X	–	X	–(An)
Addr Reg Ind w/Disp	101	reg no.	X	X	X	X	d(An)
Addr Reg Ind w/Index	110	reg no.	X	X	X	X	d(An,Ri)
Absolute Short	111	000	X	X	X	X	XXX
Absolute Long	111	001	X	X	X	X	XXXXXX
Prog Ctr w/Disp	111	010	X	X	X	–	d(PC)
Prog Ctr w/Index	111	011	X	X	X	–	d(PC,Ri)
Immediate	111	100	X	X	–	–	#XXX

[1]Courtesy of Motorola, Inc.

Notes:

1. Instruction Fields:
   Register field—Specifies any of the eight data registers.
   Op-Mode field—

Byte	Word	Long	Operation
000	001	010	$(<Dn>)+(<ea>)\rightarrow\ <Dn>$
100	101	110	$(<ea>)+(<Dn>)\rightarrow\ <ea>$

2. If the effective address is a destination address, then mode 0 and mode 1 cannot be used. Likewise, the special modes 010, 011, and 100 cannot be used.

3. Mode 1 and the special modes 010, 011, and 100 cannot be used.

4. The special modes 010, 011, and 100 cannot be used.

5. Mode 1 is not permitted.

6. Mode 0 cannot be used.

7. Size: 00 $\rightarrow$ byte 01 $\rightarrow$ word 10$\rightarrow$ long word

8. Size: 01 $\rightarrow$ byte 11$\rightarrow$ word 10$\rightarrow$ long word

9. Size: 11 $\rightarrow$ word 10$\rightarrow$ long word

ABCD   Add Decimal with Extend

Operation: $(Source)_{10}+(Destination)_{10}$
$+X\rightarrow$ Destination

Assembler ABCD Dy, Dx
Syntax: ABCD $-(Ay), -(Ax)$
Attributes: Size = (Byte)
Description: Add the source operand to the destination operand along with the extend bit, and store the result in the destination location. The addition is performed using binary coded decimal arithmetic. The operands may be addressed in two different ways:
1. Data register to data register: The operands are contained in the data registers specified in the instruction.
2. Memory to memory: the operands are addressed with the predecrement addressing mode using the address registers specified in the instruction.

Condition Codes:

X	N	Z	V	C
*	U	*	U	*

Instruction Format:

15	14	13	12	11 10 9	8	7	6	5	4	3	2 1 0
1	1	0	0	Register Rx	1	0	0	0	0	R/M	Register Ry

Instruction Fields:
Register RX field—Specifies the destination register:
If R/M = 0, specifies a data register.

If R/M = 1, specifies an address register for the predecrement addressing mode.

R/M field—Specifies the operand addressing mode:

0—The operation is data register to data register.

1—the operation is memory to memory.

Register Ry field—Specifies the source register:

If R/M = 0, specifies a data register.

If R/M = 1, specifies an address register for the predecrement addressing mode.

ADD   Add Binary

Operation: (Source) + (Destination)
                → Destination

Assembler ADD <ea>, DN

Syntax: ADD <ea>, Dn

Attributes: Size = (Byte, Word, Long)

Condition Codes:

X	N	Z	V	C
*	*	*	*	*

Instruction Format:

15	14	13	12	11	10	9	8	7	6	5	4	3	2	1	0
1	1	0	1	Register			Op-Mode			Effective Address Mode			Register		

Notes: 1,2

ADDA   Add Address

Operation: (Source) + (Destination)
                → Destination

Assembler

Syntax: ADD <ea>, An

Attributes: Size = (Word, Long)

Description: Add the source operand to the destination address register, and store the result in the address register. The size of the operation may be specified to be word or long. The entire destination address register is used regardless of the operation size.

Condition Codes: Not affected

Instruction Format:

15	14	13	12	11	10	9	8	7	6	5	4	3	2	1	0
1	1	0	1	Register			Op-Mode			Effective Address Mode			Register		

Instruction Fields:

Register field—Specifies any of the eight address registers. This is always the destination.

Op-Mode field—Specifies the size of the operation:

011—word operation. The source operand is sign-extended to a long operand and the operation is performed on the address register using all 32 bits.
111—long operation.

ADDI   Add immediate

Operation: Immediate Data +
                 (Destination)→ Destination
Assembler
Syntax: ADDI #<data>,<ea>
Attributes: Size = (Byte, Word, Long)

Condition Codes:

X	N	Z	V	C
*	*	*	*	*

Instruction Format:

15	14	13	12	11	10	9	8	7	6	5	4	3	2	1	0
0	0	0	0	0	1	1	0	Size		Effective Address Mode | Register					
Word Data (16 bits)								Byte Data (8 bits)							
Long Data (32 bits, including previous word)															

Note: 3
00→ Byte 01→ Word 10→ L. Word

ADDQ   Add Quick

Operation: Immediate Data +
                 (Destination)→ Destination
Assembler
Syntax: ADDQ # <data>, <ea>
Attributes: Size = (Byte, Word, Long)
Note: 4,7
Description: Add the immediate data to the operand at the destination location. The data range is from 1 to 8. The size of the operation may be specified to be byte, word, or long. Word and long operations are also allowed on the address registers and the condition codes are not affected. The entire destination address register is used regardless of the operation size.

Condition Codes:

X	N	Z	V	C
*	*	*	*	*

The condition codes are not affected if an addition to an address register is made.

Instruction Format:

15	14	13	12	11	10	9	8	7	6	5	4	3	2	1	0
0	1	0	1	Data			0	Size		Effective Address Mode | Register					

Data 1 to 8
000 → 8

ADDX

Add Extended

Operation: (Source) + (Destination)
+X→ Destination

Assembler ADDX Dy, Dx
Syntax: ADDX −(Ay), −(Ax) *Note:* 7

Attributes: Size = (Byte,Word,Long)

Condition Codes:

X	N	Z	V	C
*	*	*	*	*

Instruction Format:

15	14	13	12	11 10 9	8	7 6	5	4	3	2 1 0
1	1	0	1	Register Rx	1	Size	0	0	R/M	Register Ry

Register Rx field—Specifies the destination register:
If R/M = 0, specifies a data register.
If R/M = 1, specifies an address register for the predecrement addressing mode.

AND

AND Logical

Operation: (Source)∧(Destination)
→ Destination

Assembler AND <ea>, Dn
Syntax: AND Dn, <ea>
Attributes: Size = (Byte,Word,Long)

Condition Codes:

X	N	Z	V	C
—	*	*	0	0

Notes: 1,2,5

Instruction Format:

15	14	13	12	11 10 9	8 7 6	5 4 3	2 1 0
1	1	0	0	Register	Op-Mode	Effective Address Mode	Register

ANDI

AND Immediate

Operation: Immediate Data∧(Destination)
→ Destination

Assembler
Syntax: ANDI # <data>, <ea>
Attributes: Size = (Byte,Word,Long)

Condition Codes:

X	N	Z	V	C
—	*	*	0	0

15	14	13	12	11	10	9	8	7 6	5 4 3	2 1 0
0	0	0	0	0	0	1	0	Size	Effective Address Mode	Register
Word Data (16 bits)								Byte Data (8 bits)		
Long Data (32 bits, including previous word)										

Notes: 3,7

ANDI
to CCR

AND Immediate to Condition Codes

Operation: (Source)∧CCR → CCR

Assembler
Syntax: ANDI #xxx, CCR

Attributes: Size = (Byte)

Condition Codes:

X	N	Z	V	C
*	*	*	*	*

Instruction Format:

15	14	13	12	11	10	9	8	7	6	5	4	3	2	1	0
0	0	0	0	0	0	1	0	0	0	1	1	1	1	0	0
0	0	0	0	0	0	0	0	Byte Data (8 bits)							

ANDI
to SR

AND Immediate to the Status Register (Privileged Instruction)

Operation: If supervisor state
then (Source)∧SR → SR
else TRAP

Assembler
Syntax: ANDI #xxx, SR

Attributes: Size = (Word)

Condition Codes:

X	N	Z	V	C
*	*	*	*	*

Instruction Format:

15	14	13	12	11	10	9	8	7	6	5	4	3	2	1	0
0	0	0	0	0	0	1	0	0	1	1	1	1	1	0	0
Word Data (16 bits)															

ASL,ASR

Arithmetic Shift

Operation: (Destination) Shifted by
<count> → Destination

Assembler   ASd Dx, Dy
Syntax: ASd #<data>, Dy
ASd <ea>

Attributes: Size = (Byte,Word,Long)

Condition Codes

X	N	Z	V	C
*	*	*	*	*

V Set if the most significant bit
is changed at any time during
the shift operation. Cleared
otherwise.

Instruction Format (Memory Shifts):

15	14	13	12	11	10	9	8	7	6	5	4	3	2	1	0
1	1	1	0	0	0	0	dr	1	1	Effective Address Mode			Register		

Note: Operand is word. *Notes:* 3,6,7 1-bit
shift

Instruction Format (Register Shifts):

15	14	13	12	11	10	9	8	7	6	5	4	3	2	1	0
1	1	1	0	Count/ Register			dr	Size		i/r	0	0	Register		

dr = 0 → sh rgt. dr = 1 → sh lft. i/r = o
→ immediate shift count. Count = 1 to 8.
i/r = 1 → shift count is in specified data register.

Bcc   **Branch Conditionally**

Operation: If (condition true)
then PG + d → PC

Assembler
Syntax: Bcc <label>
Attributes: Size = (Byte, Word)

Condition Codes: Not affected.
Instruction Format:

15	14	13	12	11	10	9	8	7	6	5	4	3	2	1	0
0	1	1	0	Condition				8-bit Displacement							
16-bit Displacement if 8-bit Displacement = 0															

CC	carry clear	0100	$\overline{C}$		LS	low or same	0011	$C + Z$
CS	carry set	0101	C		LT	less than	1101	$N \cdot \overline{V} + \overline{N} \cdot V$
EQ	equal	0111	Z		MI	minus	1011	N
GE	greater or equal	1100	$N \cdot V + \overline{N} \cdot \overline{V}$		NE	not equal	0110	$\overline{Z}$
GT	greater than	1110	$N \cdot V \cdot \overline{Z} + \overline{N} \cdot \overline{V} \cdot \overline{Z}$		PL	plus	1010	$\overline{N}$
HI	high	0010	$\overline{C} \cdot \overline{Z}$		VC	overflow clear	1000	$\overline{V}$
LE	less or equal	1111	$Z + N \cdot \overline{V} + \overline{N} \cdot V$		VS	overflow set	1001	V

+ → or   • → and

BCHG   **Test a Bit and Change**

Operation: ~(<bit number> OF Destination)→ Z;
~(<bit number> OF Destination)→ <bit number> OF Destination

Assembler   BCHG Dn, <ea>
Syntax: BCHG #<data>, <ea>
Attributes: Size = (Byte, Long) *Note:* 3
Description: A bit in the destination operand is tested and the state of the specified bit is reflected in the Z condition code. After the test, the state of the specified bit is changed in the destination. If a data register is the destination, then the bit numbering is modulo 32, allowing bit manipulation on all bits in a data register. If a memory location is the destination, a byte is read from that location, the bit operation performed using the bit number modulo 8, and the byte written back to the location with zero referring to the least-significant bit. The bit number for this operation may be specified in two different ways:

Condition Codes:

X	N	Z	V	C
—	—	*	—	—

Instruction Format (Bit Number Static):

15	14	13	12	11	10	9	8	7	6	5	4	3	2	1	0
0	0	0	0	Register			1	1	0	Effective Address Mode | Register					

Instruction Format (Bit Number Dynamic):

15	14	13	12	11	10	9	8	7	6	5	4	3	2	1	0
0	0	0	0	1	0	0	0	1	0	Effective Address Mode | Register					
0	0	0	0	0	0	0	0	bit number							

1. Immediate—the bit number is specified in a second word of the instruction.

2. Register—the bit number is contained in a data register specified in the instruction.

BCLR   **Test a Bit and Clear**

Operation: ~(<bit number>) OF Destination)→ Z;
0→ <bit number> OF Destination

Assembler BLCR Dn, <ea>
Syntax: BCLR #<data>, <ea>
Attributes: Size = (Byte,Long)

Instruction Format (Bit Number Dynamic):

15	14	13	12	11	10	9	8	7	6	5	4	3	2	1	0
0	0	0	0	Register			1	1	1	Effective Address Mode | Register					

Instruction Format (Bit Number Static):

15	14	13	12	11	10	9	8	7	6	5	4	3	2	1	0
0	0	0	0	1	0	0	0	1	0	Effective Address Mode | Register					
0	0	0	0	0	0	0	0	bit number							

Note: see BCHG

BRA   **Branch Always**

Operation: PC + d → PC
Assembler
Syntax: BRA <label>
Attributes: Size = (Byte,Word)

Condition Codes: Not affected.
Instruction Format:

15	14	13	12	11	10	9	8	7	6	5	4	3	2	1	0
0	1	1	0	0	0	0	0	8-bit Displacement							
16-bit Displacement if 8-bit Displacement = 0															

BSET   **Test a Bit and Set**

Operation: ~(<bit number>) OF Destination → Z
1→ <bit number> OF Destination

Assembler BSET Dn, <ea>
Syntax: BSET #<data>, <ea>
Attributes: Size = (Byte,Long)
Note: See BCHG

Instruction Format (Bit Number Static):

15	14	13	12	11	10	9	8	7	6	5	4	3	2	1	0
0	0	0	0	1	0	0	0	1	1	Effective Address Mode | Register					
0	0	0	0	0	0	0	0	bit number							

Instruction Format (Bit Number Dynamic):

15	14	13	12	11	10	9	8	7	6	5	4	3	2	1	0
0	0	0	0	Register			1	1	1	Effective Address Mode | Register					

BSR   Branch to Subroutine

Operation: PC → −(SP); PC + d → PC

Assembler
Syntax: BSR <label>

Attributes: Size = (Byte, Word)

Instruction Format:

15	14	13	12	11	10	9	8	7	6	5	4	3	2	1	0
0	1	1	0	0	0	0	1	8-bit Displacement							
16-bit Displacement if 8-bit Displacement = 0															

BTST   Test a Bit

Operation: ~(<bit number> OF Destination) → Z

Assembler BTST Dn, <ea>
Syntax: BTST # <data>, <ea>

Attributes: Size = (Byte, Long)

Note: See BCHG

Instruction Format (Bit Number Static):

15	14	13	12	11	10	9	8	7	6	5	4	3	2	1	0
0	0	0	0	1	0	0	0	0	0	Effective Address Mode | Register					
0	0	0	0	0	0	0	0	bit number							

Instruction Format (Bit Number Dynamic):

15	14	13	12	11	10	9	8	7	6	5	4	3	2	1	0
0	0	0	0	Register			1	0	0	Effective Address Mode | Register					

CHK   Check Register Against Bounds

Operation: If Dn < 0 or Dn > (<ea>) then TRAP

Assembler
Syntax: CHK <ea>, Dn

Attributes: Size = (Word)

Note: 5

Condition Codes:

X	N	Z	V	C
—	*	U	U	U

N Set if Dn < 0; cleared if Dn > (<ea>). Undefined otherwise.

Instruction Format:

15	14	13	12	11	10	9	8	7	6	5	4	3	2	1	0
0	1	0	0	Register			1	1	0	Effective Address Mode | Register					

CLR   Clear an Operand

Operation: 0 → Destination

Assembler
Syntax: CLR <ea>

Note: 3

Attributes: Size = (Byte, Word, Long)

Condition Codes:

X	N	Z	V	C
—	0	1	0	0

Instruction Format:

15	14	13	12	11	10	9	8	7	6	5	4	3	2	1	0
0	1	0	0	0	0	1	0	Size		Effective Address Mode | Register					

CMP   Compare

Operation: (Destination) − (Source)
Assembler
Syntax: CMP < ea >, Dn
Attributes: Size = (Byte,Word,Long)

Condition Codes:

X	N	Z	V	C
—	*	*	*	*

Instruction Format:

15	14	13	12	11	10	9	8	7	6	5	4	3	2	1	0
1	0	1	1	Register			Op-Mode			Effective Address Mode			Register		

CMPA   Compare Address

Operation: (Destination) − (Source)
Assembler
Syntax: CMPA < ea >, An
Attributes: Size = (Word,Long)

Condition Codes:

X	N	Z	V	C
—	*	*	*	*

Instruction Format:

15	14	13	12	11	10	9	8	7	6	5	4	3	2	1	0
1	0	1	1	Register			Op-Mode			Effective Address Mode			Register		

Note: See ADDA

CMPI   Compare Immediate

Operation: (Destination) − Immediate Data
Asssembler
Syntax: CMPI #< data >, < ea >
Attributes: Size = (Byte,Word,Long)

Condition Codes:

X	N	Z	V	C
—	*	*	*	*

Instruction Format:

15	14	13	12	11	10	9	8	7	6	5	4	3	2	1	0
0	0	0	0	1	1	0	0	Size		Effective Address Mode			Register		
Word Data (16 bits)								Byte Data (8 bits)							
Long Data (32 bits, including previous word)															

Notes: 3,7

CMPM   Compare Memory

Operation: (Destination) − (Source)
Assembler
Syntax: CMPM (Ay) +, (Ax) +
Attributes: Size = (Byte,Word,Long)
Note: 7

Condition Codes:

X	N	Z	V	C
—	*	*	*	*

Instruction Format:

15	14	13	12	11	10	9	8	7	6	5	4	3	2	1	0
1	0	1	1	Register Rx			1	Size		0	0	1	Register Ry		

DBcc   **Test Condition, Decrement, and Branch**

Operation: If (condition false)
then Dn − 1 → Dn
If (Dn ≠ − 1)
then PC + d → PC
else PC + 2 → PC
(Fall through to next instruction)

Condition Codes: Not affected.

Instruction Format:

15	14	13	12	11	10	9	8	7	6	5	4	3	2	1	0
0	1	0	1	Condition			1	1	0	0	1	Register		
				Displacement											

Assembler
Syntax: DBcc Dn, <label>
Attributes: Size = (Word)

CC	carry clear	0100	$\overline{C}$		LS	low or same	0011	$C + Z$
CS	carry set	0101	C		LT	less than	1101	$N \cdot \overline{V} + \overline{N} \cdot V$
EQ	equal	0111	Z		MI	minus	1011	N
F	false	0001	0		NE	not equal	0110	$\overline{Z}$
GE	greater or equal	1100	$N \cdot V + \overline{N} \cdot \overline{V}$		PL	plus	1010	$\overline{N}$
GT	greater than	1110	$N \cdot V \cdot \overline{Z} + \overline{N} \cdot \overline{V} \cdot \overline{Z}$		T	true	0000	1
HI	high	0010	$\overline{C} \cdot \overline{Z}$		VC	overflow clear	1000	$\overline{V}$
LE	less or equal	1111	$Z + N \cdot \overline{V} + \overline{N} \cdot V$		VS	overflow set	1001	V

DIVS   **Signed Divide**

Operation: (Destination)/(Source)
→ Destination

Assembler
Syntax: DIVS <ea>, Dn
Attributes: Size = (Word)
Description: Divide the destination operand
by the source operand and store
the result in the destination.
The destination operand is a
long operand (32 bits) and the
source operand is a word oper-
and (16 bits). The operation is
performed using signed arithmetic. The result is a 32-bit result such that:
1. The quotient is in the
lower word (least significant 16 bits).
2. The remainder is in the
upper word (most signifi-
cant 16 bits).
The sign of the remainder
is always the same as the
dividend unless the remain-

Condition Codes:

X	N	Z	V	C
—	*	*	*	0

V Set if division overflow is detected. Cleared
otherwise. Overflow occurs if the quotient is
larger than a 16-bit signed integer.

Instruction Format:

15	14	13	12	11	10	9	8	7	6	5	4	3	2	1	0
1	0	0	0	Register				1	1	1	Effective Address				
											Mode			Register	

der is equal to zero.
Two special conditions
may arise:
1. Division by zero causes a
   trap.
2. Overflow may be detected
   and set before comple-
   tion of the instruction. If
   overflow is detected, the
   condition is flagged but
   the operands are
   unaffected.

DIVU   Unsigned Divide

Operation: (Destination)/(Source)   *Note:* See Divs
                  → Destination
                                                Instruction Format:
Assembler

15	14	13	12	11	10	9	8	7	6	5	4	3	2	1	0
1	0	0	0	Register			0	1	1	Effective Address Mode | Register					

Syntax: DIVU <ea>, Dn
Attributes: Size = (Word)

EOR   Exclusive OR Logical

Operation: (Source) ⊕ (Destination)   **Condition Codes:**
                  → Destination

X	N	Z	V	C
—	*	*	0	0

Assembler
Syntax: EOR Dn, <ea>   *Notes:* 1,2,5
Attributes: Size = (Byte,Word,Long)
                                                Instruction Format:

15	14	13	12	11	10	9	8	7	6	5	4	3	2	1	0
1	0	1	1	Register			Op-Mode			Effective Address Mode | Register					

EORI   Exclusive OR Immediate

Operation: Immediate Data ⊕ (Destination)   **Condition Codes:**
                  → Destination

X	N	Z	V	C
—	*	*	0	0

Assembler
Syntax: EORI #<data>, <ea>
Attributes: Size = (Byte,Word,Long)
Note: 3
                                                Instruction Format:

15	14	13	12	11	10	9	8	7	6	5	4	3	2	1	0
0	0	0	0	1	0	1	0	Size		Effective Address Mode | Register					
Word Data (16 bits)								Byte Data (8 bits)							
Long Data (32 bits, including previous word)															

EORI
to CCR

Exclusive OR Immediate to Condition Codes

Operation: (Source) $\oplus$ CCR $\rightarrow$ CCR

Assembler
Syntax: EORI #xxx, CCR
Attributes: Size = (Byte,)

Condition Codes:

X	N	Z	V	C
*	*	*	*	*

Instruction Format:

15	14	13	12	11	10	9	8	7	6	5	4	3	2	1	0
0	0	0	0	1	0	1	0	0	0	1	1	1	1	0	0
0	0	0	0	0	0	0	0				Byte Data (8 bits)				

EORI
to SR

Exclusive OR Immediate to the Status Register
(Privileged Instruction)

Operation: If supervisor state
then (Source) $\oplus$ SR $\rightarrow$ SR
else TRAP

Assembler
Syntax: EORI #xxx, SR
Attributes: Size = (Word)

Condition Codes:

X	N	Z	V	C
*	*	*	*	*

Instruction Format:

15	14	13	12	11	10	9	8	7	6	5	4	3	2	1	0
0	0	0	0	1	0	1	0	0	1	1	1	1	1	0	0
					Word Data (16 bits)										

EXG

Exchange Registers

Operation: Rx $\leftrightarrow$ Ry
Assembler
Syntax: EXG Rx,Ry
Attributes: Size = (Long)

Condition Codes: Not affected.
Instruction Format:

15	14	13	12	11 10 9	8	7 6 5 4 3	2 1 0
1	1	0	0	Register Rx	1	Op-Mode	Register Ry

Op-Mode field—Specifies whether exchanging:
01000—data registers.
01001—address registers.
10001—data registers and address registers.

EXT

Sign Extend

Operation: (Destination) Sign-extended
$\rightarrow$ Destination
Assembler
Syntax: EXT Dn
Attributes: Size = (Word,Long)

Condition Codes:

X	N	Z	V	C
—	*	*	0	0

Instruction Format:

15	14	13	12	11	10	9	8 7 6	5 4 3	2 1 0
0	1	0	0	1	0	0	Op-Mode	0 0 0	Register

Instruction Fields:
Op-Mode Field—Specifies the size of the
sign-extension operation:

010—Sign-extend low-order byte of data register to word.
011—Sign-extend low-order word of data register to long.

ILLEGAL

Illegal Instruction

Operation: PC → −(SSP); SR → −(SSP)
(Illegal Instruction Vector) → PC

Attributes: None

Condition Codes: Not affected

Instruction Format:

15	14	13	12	11	10	9	8	7	6	5	4	3	2	1	0
0	1	0	0	1	0	1	0	1	1	1	1	1	1	0	0

JMP

Jump

Operation: Destination → PC

Assembler Syntax: JMP <ea>

Attributes: Unsized

Instruction Fields:
Effective Address field—Specifies the address of the next instruction. Only control addressing modes are allowed as shown:

Condition Codes: Not affected.

Instruction Format:

15	14	13	12	11	10	9	8	7	6	5 4 3	2 1 0
0	1	0	0	1	1	1	0	1	1	Effective Address Mode	Register

Addressing Mode	Mode	Register	Addressing Mode	Mode	Register
Dn	—	—	d(An, Xi)	110	register number
An	—	—	Abs.W	111	000
(An)	010	register number	Abs.L	111	001
(An)+	—	—	d(PC)	111	010
−(An)	—	—	d(PC, Xi)	111	011
d(An)	101	register number	Imm	—	—

JSR

Jump to Subroutine   *Note:* Same addressing modes as JMP

Operation: PC → −(SP); Destination → PC

Assembler Syntax: JSR <ea>

Attributes: Unsized

Condition Codes: Not affected.

Instruction Format:

15	14	13	12	11	10	9	8	7	6	5 4 3	2 1 0
0	1	0	0	1	1	1	0	1	0	Effective Address Mode	Register

LEA

Load Effective Address   *Note:* Same addressing modes as JMP

Operation: Destination → An

Assembler Syntax: LEA <ea>, An

Attributes: Size = (Long)

Condition Codes: Not affected.

Instruction Format:

15	14	13	12	11 10 9	8	7	6	5 4 3	2 1 0
0	1	0	0	Register	1	1	1	Effective Address Mode	Register

LINK   Link and Allocate

Operation: An → −(SP); SP → An;
              SP + d → SP

Assembler

Syntax: LINK An, #<displacement>

Attributes: Unsized

Description: The current content of the specified address register is pushed onto the stack. After the push, the address register is loaded from the updated stack pointer. Finally, the 16-bit sign-extended displacement is added to the stack pointer. The content of the address register occupies two words on the stack. A negative displacement is specified to allocate stack area.

Condition Codes: Not affected.

Instruction Format:

15	14	13	12	11	10	9	8	7	6	5	4	3	2	1	0
0	1	0	0	1	1	1	0	0	1	0	1	0	Register		
Displacement																

LSL, LSR   Logical Shift

Operation: (Destination) Shifted by <count> → Destination

Assembler LSd Dx, Dy

Syntax: LSd #<data>, Dy
           LSd <ea>   *Note:* 7

Attributes: Size = (Byte, Word, Long)

Note: See ASL, ASR

Condition Codes:

X	N	Z	V	C
*	*	*	0	*

Instruction Format (Memory Shifts):

15	14	13	12	11	10	9	8	7	6	5	4	3	2	1	0
1	1	1	0	0	0	1	dr	1	1	Effective Address Mode		Register		

Instruction Format (Register Shifts):

15	14	13	12	11	10	9	8	7	6	5	4	3	2	1	0
1	1	1	0	Count/ Register		dr	Size		i/r	0	1	Register		

MOVE   Move Data from Source to Destination

Operation: (Source) → Destination

Assembler

Syntax: MOVE <ea>, <ea>   *Note:* 8

Attributes: Size = (Byte, Word, Long)

Note: All addressing modes are permitted for source operand. For destination operand, see note 3.

Condition Codes:

X	N	Z	V	C
—	*	*	0	0

Instruction Format:

15	14	13	12	11	10	9	8	7	6	5	4	3	2	1	0
0	0	Size		Destination Register		Mode		Source Mode		Register	

MOVE
to CCR

Move to Condition Codes

Operation: (Source)→ CCR
Assembler
Syntax: MOVE <ea>, CCR
Note: 5
Attributes: Size = (Word)

Condition Codes:

X	N	Z	V	C
*	*	*	*	*

Instruction Format:

15	14	13	12	11	10	9	8	7	6	5	4	3	2	1	0
0	1	0	0	0	1	0	0	1	1	\multicolumn{6}{}{Effective Address}

Effective Address: Mode | Register

MOVE
to SR

**Move to the Status Register
(Privileged Instruction)**

Operation: If supervisor state
then (Source) → SR
else TRAP
Assembler
Syntax: MOVE <ea>, SR
Attributes: Size = (Word)
Note: 5

Condition Codes: Set according to
the source operand.

Instruction Format:

15	14	13	12	11	10	9	8	7	6	5	4	3	2	1	0
0	1	0	0	0	1	1	0	1	1	\multicolumn{6}{}{Effective Address}

Effective Address: Mode | Register

MOVE
from SR

Move from the Status Register

Operation: SR → Destination
Assembler
Syntax: MOVE SR, <ea>
Attributes: Size = (Word)
Note: 3

Condition Codes: Not affected.

Instruction Format:

15	14	13	12	11	10	9	8	7	6	5	4	3	2	1	0
0	1	0	0	0	0	0	0	1	1	\multicolumn{6}{}{Effective Address}

Effective Address: Mode | Register

MOVE
USP

**Move User Stack Pointer
(Privileged Instruction)**

Operation: If supervisor state
then USP → An; An → USP
else TRAP
Assembler MOVE USP, An
Syntax: MOVE An, USP
Attributes: Size = (Long)

Condition Codes: Not affected.

Instruction Format:

15	14	13	12	11	10	9	8	7	6	5	4	3	2	1	0
0	1	0	0	1	1	1	0	0	1	1	0	dr	\multicolumn{3}{}{Register}

dr = 0 → An is Source
dr = 1 → An is Destin

MOVEA   Move Address

Operation: (Source) → Destination
Assembler
Syntax: MOVEA <ea>, An
Attributes: Size = (Word,Long)
Note: 9

Condition Codes: Not affected.
Instruction Format:

15	14	13	12	11	10	9	8	7	6	5	4	3	2	1	0
0	0	Size		Destination Register			0	0	1	Source Mode			Register		

MOVEM   Move Multiple Registers

Operation: Registers → Destination
                (Source) → Registers
Assembler MOVEM <register list>, <ea>
Syntax: MOVEM <ea>, <register list>
Attributes: Size = (Word,Long)
Description: Selected registers are transferred to or from consecutive
memory locations starting at
the location specified by the effective address. A register is
transferred if the bit corresponding to that register is set
in the mask field. The instruction selects how much of each
register is transferred; either the
entire long word can be moved
or just the low–order word. In
the case of a word transfer to
the registers, each word is sign-
extended to 32 bits (also data
registers) and the resulting long
word loaded into the associated
register.
MOVEM allows three forms of
address modes: the control
modes, the predecrement mode,
or the postincrement mode. If
the effective address is in one
of the control modes, the registers are transferred starting at
the specified address and up
through higher addresses. The
order of transfer is from data
register 0 to data register 7,
then from address register 0 to
address register 7.

Condition Codes: Not affected.
Instruction Format:

15	14	13	12	11	10	9	8	7	6	5	4	3	2	1	0
0	1	0	0	1	dr	0	0	1	Sz	Effective Address Mode			Register		
Register List Mask															

dr = 0 → r to m
dr = 1 → m to r
sz = 0 → word
sz = 1 → long word

If the effective address is in the predecrement mode, only a register to memory operation is allowed. The registers are stored starting at the specified address minus two and down through lower addresses. The order of storing is from address register 7 to address register 0, then from data register 7 to data register 0. The decremented address register is updated to contain the address of the last word stored.

If the effective address is in the postincrement mode, only a memory to register operation is allowed. The registers are loaded starting at the specified address and up through higher addresses. The order of loading is the same as for the control mode addressing. The incremented address register is updated to contain the address of the last word loaded plus two.

Note: For m to r transfers, modes 0,1,4, and the special mode 100 are not permitted. For r to m transfers, modes 0,1,3, and the special modes 010, 011, and 100 are not permitted.

Register List Mask field—Specifies which registers to be transferred. The low–order bit corresponds to the first register to be transferred; the high bit corresponds to the last register to be transferred. Thus, both for control modes and for the postincrement mode addresses, the mask correspondence is

15	14	13	12	11	10	9	8	7	6	5	4	3	2	1	0
A7	A6	A5	A4	A3	A2	A1	A0	D7	D6	D5	D4	D3	D2	D1	D0

while for the predecrement mode addresses, the mask correspondence is

15	14	13	12	11	10	9	8	7	6	5	4	3	2	1	0
D0	D1	D2	D3	D4	D5	D6	D7	A0	A1	A2	A3	A4	A5	A6	A7

MOVEP   Move Peripheral Data

Operation: (Source) → Destination
Assembler MOVEP Dx,d(ay)
Syntax: MOVEP d(Ay), Dx
Attributes: Size = (Word,Long)
Instruction Fields:

Data Register field—Specifies the data register to or from which the data is to be transferred.

Op-Mode field—Specifies the direction and size of the operation:

    100—transfer word from memory to register.
    101—transfer long from memory to register.
    110—transfer word from register to memory.
    111—transfer long from register to memory.

Address Register field—Specifies the address register which is used in the address register indirect plus displacement addressing mode.

Displacement field—Specifies the displacement which is used in calculating the operand address.

Condition Codes: Not affected.
Instruction Format:

15	14	13	12	11 10 9	8 7 6	5	4	3	2 1 0
0	0	0	0	Data Register	Op-Mode	0	0	1	Address Register
Displacement									

Example: Long transfer to/from an even address.
Byte organization in register

31 24	23 16	15 8	7 0
hi-order	mid-upper	mid-lower	low-order

Byte organization in memory (low address at top)

15 14 13 12 11 10 9 8	7 6 5 4 3 2 1 0
hi-order	
mid-upper	
mid-lower	
low-order	

Example: Word transfer to/from an odd address.
Byte organization in register

31 24	23 16	15 8	7 0
		hi-order	low-order

Byte organization in memory (low address at top)

15 14 13 12 11 10 9 8	7 6 5 4 3 2 1 0
	hi-order
	low-order

MOVEQ   Move Quick

Operation: Immediate Data → Destination
Assembler
Syntax: MOVEQ #<data>, Dn
Attributes: Size = (Long)
Description: Move immediate data to a data register. The data is contained in an 8-bit field within the operation word. The data is sign-extended to a long operand and all 32 bits are transferred to the data register.

Condition Codes:

X	N	Z	V	C
—	*	*	0	0

Instruction Format:

15	14	13	12	11 10 9	8	7 6 5 4 3 2 1 0
0	1	1	1	Register	0	Data

MULS

Signed Multiply

Operation: (Source)*(Destination)
 → Destination

Assembler
Syntax: MULS <ea>, Dn
Attributes: Size = (Word)
Note: 5

Condition Codes:

X	N	Z	V	C
—	*	*	0	0

Instruction Format:

15	14	13	12	11 10 9	8	7	6	5 4 3	2 1 0
1	1	0	0	Register	1	1	1	Effective Address Mode	Register

MULU

Unsigned Multiply

Operation: (Source)*(Destination)
 → Destination

Assembler
Syntax: MULU <ea>, Dn
Attributes: Size = (Word)
Note: 5

Condition Codes:

X	N	Z	V	C
—	*	*	0	0

Instruction Format:

15	14	13	12	11 10 9	8	7	6	5 4 3	2 1 0
1	1	0	0	Register	0	1	1	Effective Address Mode	Register

NBCD

Negate Decimal with Extend

Operation: $0 - (\text{Destination}) 10 - X$
 → Destination

Assembler
Syntax: NBCD <ea>
Attributes: Size = (Byte)
Description: The operand addressed as the
 destination and the extend bit are
 subtracted from zero. The operation is performed using decimal
 arithmetic. The result is saved in
 the destination location. This instruction produces the tens complement of the destination if the
 extend bit is clear, the nines complement if the extend bit is set.
 This is a byte operation only.

Note: 3

Condition Codes:

X	N	Z	V	C
*	U	*	U	*

Instruction Format:

15	14	13	12	11	10	9	8	7	6	5 4 3	2 1 0
0	1	0	0	1	0	0	0	0	0	Effective Address Mode	Register

NEG   Negate

Operation: $0 - (\text{Destination}) \rightarrow \text{Destination}$
Assembler
Syntax: NEG <ea>
Attributes: Size = (Byte,Word,Long)
Notes: 3,7

Condition Codes:

X	N	Z	V	C
*	*	*	*	*

Instruction Format:

15	14	13	12	11	10	9	8	7	6	5	4	3	2	1	0
0	1	0	0	0	1	0	0	Size		Effective Address					
										Mode			Register		

NEGX   Negate with Extend

Operation: $0 - (\text{Destination}) - X$
              $\rightarrow \text{Destination}$
Assembler
Syntax: NEGX <ea>
Attributes: Size = (Byte,Word,Long)
Notes: 3,7

Condition Codes:

X	N	Z	V	C
*	*	*	*	*

Instruction Format:

15	14	13	12	11	10	9	8	7	6	5	4	3	2	1	0
0	1	0	0	0	0	0	0	Size		Effective Address					
										Mode			Register		

NOP   No Operation

Operation: None
Assembler
Syntax: NOP
Attributes: Unsized

Condition Codes: Not affected.
Instruction Format:

15	14	13	12	11	10	9	8	7	6	5	4	3	2	1	0
0	1	0	0	1	1	1	0	0	1	1	1	0	0	0	1

NOT   Logical Complement

Operation: $\sim (\text{Destination}) \rightarrow \text{Destination}$
Assembler
Syntax: NOT <ea>
Attributes: Size = (Byte,Word,Long)
Notes: 3,7

Condition Codes:

X	N	Z	V	C
—	*	*	0	0

Instruction Format:

15	14	13	12	11	10	9	8	7	6	5	4	3	2	1	0
0	1	0	0	0	1	1	0	Size		Effective Address					
										Mode			Register		

OR   Inclusive OR Logical

Operation: (Source) v (Destination)
                 → Destination
Assembler OR <ea>, Dn
Syntax: OR Dn, <ea>
Attributes: Size = (Byte,Word,Long)
Notes: 1,2,5

Condition Codes:

X	N	Z	V	C
—	*	*	0	0

Instruction Format:

15	14	13	12	11	10	9	8	7	6	5	4	3	2	1	0
1	0	0	0	Register			Op-Mode			Effective Address Mode | Register					

ORI   Inclusive OR Immediate

Operation: Immediate Data v (Destination)
                 → Destination
Assembler
Syntax: ORI #<data>, <ea>
Attributes: Size = (Byte,Word,Long)
Notes: 3,7

Condition Codes:

X	N	Z	V	C
—	*	*	0	0

Instruction Format:

15	14	13	12	11	10	9	8	7	6	5	4	3	2	1	0
0	0	0	0	0	0	0	0	Size		Effective Address Mode | Register					
Word Data (16 bites)								Byte Data (8 bits)							
Long Data (32 bits, including previous word)															

ORI   Inclusive OR Immediate to
to CCR   Condition Codes

Operation: (Source) v CCR → CCR
Assembler
Syntax: ORI #xxx, CCR
Attributes: Size = (Byte)

Condition Codes:

X	N	Z	V	C
*	*	*	*	*

Instruction Format:

15	14	13	12	11	10	9	8	7	6	5	4	3	2	1	0
0	0	0	0	0	0	0	0	0	0	1	1	1	1	0	0
0	0	0	0	0	0	0	0	Byte Data (8 bits)							

ORI   Inclusive OR Immediate to the Status Register
to SR   (Privileged Instruction)

Operation: If supervisor state
                 then (Source) v SR → SR
                 else TRAP
Assembler
Syntax: ORI #xxx, SR
Attributes: Size = (Word)

Condition Codes:

X	N	Z	V	C
*	*	*	*	*

Instruction Format:

15	14	13	12	11	10	9	8	7	6	5	4	3	2	1	0
0	0	0	0	0	0	0	0	0	1	1	1	1	1	0	0
Word Data (16 bits)															

PEA

Push Effective Address

Operation: Destination → −(SP)

Assembler
Syntax: PEA <ea>

Attributes: Size = (Long)

Instruction Fields:
Effective Address field—Specifies the address to be pushed onto the stack. Only control addressing modes are allowed as shown:

Condition Codes: Not affected.

Instruction Format:

15	14	13	12	11	10	9	8	7	6	5 4 3	2 1 0
0	1	0	0	1	0	0	0	0	1	Effective Address Mode	Register

Addressing Mode	Mode	Register	Addressing Mode	Mode	Register
Dn	—	—	d(An, Xi)	110	register number
An	—	—	Abs.W	111	000
(An)	010	register number	Abs.L	111	001
(An)+	—	—	d(PC)	111	010
−(An)	—	—	d(PC, Xi)	111	011
d(An)	101	register number	Imm	—	—

RESET

Reset External Devices
(Privileged Instruction)

Operation: If supervisor state
then Assert RESET Line
else TRAP

Assembler
Syntax: RESET

Attributes: Unsized

Condition Codes: Not affected.

Instruction Format:

15	14	13	12	11	10	9	8	7	6	5	4	3	2	1	0
0	1	0	0	1	1	1	0	0	1	1	1	0	0	0	0

ROL
ROR

Rotate (without Extend)

Operation: (Destination) Rotated by
<count> → Destination

Assembler ROd Dx, Dy
Syntax: ROd # <data>, Dy
ROd <ea>

Attributes: Size = (Byte, Word, Long)

Description: Rotate the bits of the operand in the direction specified. The extend bit is not included in the rotation.

See ASL, ASR

Condition Codes:

X	N	Z	V	C
—	*	*	0	*

C Set according to the last bit shifted out of the operand. Cleared for a shift count of zero.

Instruction Format (Register Rotate):

15	14	13	12	11 10 9	8	7 6	5	4 3	2 1 0
1	1	1	0	Count/ Register	dr	Size	i/r	1 1	Register

Instruction Format (Memory Rotate):

15	14	13	12	11	10	9	8	7	6	5 4 3	2 1 0
1	1	1	0	0	1	1	dr	1	1	Effective Address Mode	Register

ROXL
ROXR

Rotate with Extend   The extend bit is included as part of the rotated register.

Operation: (Destination) Rotated by
                 <count> → Destination

Assembler   ROXd Dx, Dy
Syntax: ROXd #<data>, Dy
                 ROXd <ea>

See ASL, ASR

Attributes: Size = (Byte, Word, Long)

Condition Codes:

X	N	Z	V	C
*	*	*	0	*

Instruction Format (Memory Rotate):

15	14	13	12	11	10	9	8	7	6	5	4	3	2	1	0
1	1	1	0	0	1	0	dr	1	1	Effective Address Mode			Register		

Instruction Format (Register Rotate):

15	14	13	12	11	10	9	8	7	6	5	4	3	2	1	0
1	1	1	0	Count/ Register			dr	Size		i/r	1	0	Register		

RTE

Return from Exception
(Privileged Instruction)

Operation: If supervisor state
                 then (SP) + → SR; (SP) +
                 → PC
                 else TRAP

Assembler
Syntax: RTE

Attributes: Unsized

Condition Codes: Set according to the content of the word on the stack.

Instruction Format:

15	14	13	12	11	10	9	8	7	6	5	4	3	2	1	0
0	1	0	0	1	1	1	0	0	1	1	1	0	0	1	1

RTR

Return and Restore
Condition Codes

Note: Does not affect S bit in SR.

Operation: (SP) + → CC; (SP) + → PC

Assembler
Syntax: RTR

Attributes: Unsized

Condition Codes: Set according to the content of the word on the stack.

Instruction Format:

15	14	13	12	11	10	9	8	7	6	5	4	3	2	1	0
0	1	0	0	1	1	1	0	0	1	1	1	0	1	1	1

RTS

Return from Subroutine

Operation: (SP) + → PC

Assembler
Syntax: RTS

Attributes: Unsized

Condition Codes: Not affected.

Instruction Format:

15	14	13	12	11	10	9	8	7	6	5	4	3	2	1	0
0	1	0	0	1	1	1	0	0	1	1	1	0	1	0	1

SBCD   Subtract Decimal with Extend

Operation: $(\text{Destination})_{10} - (\text{Source})_{10} - X$
$\rightarrow$ Destination

Assembler   SBCD Dy, Dx
Syntax: SBCD $-(\text{Ay})$, $-(\text{Ax})$

Attributes: Size = (Byte)

See ABCD

Condition Codes:

X	N	Z	V	C
*	U	*	U	*

Instruction Format:

15	14	13	12	11 10 9	8	7	6	5	4	3	2 1 0
1	0	0	0	Register Rx	1	0	0	0	0	R/M	Register Ry

Scc   Set According to Condition

Operation: If (Condition True)
then 1's $\rightarrow$ Destination
else 0's $\rightarrow$ Destination

Assembler
Syntax: Scc $<$ea$>$

Attributes: Size = (Byte)

Description: The specified condition code is tested; if the condition is true, the byte specified by the effective address is set to TRUE (all ones), otherwise that byte is set to FALSE (all zeroes). "cc" may specify the following conditions:
       See DBCC

Note: 3

Condition Codes: Not affected.

Instruction Format:

15	14	13	12	11 10 9 8	7	6	5 4 3	2 1 0
0	1	0	1	Condition	1	1	Effective Address Mode	Register

STOP   Load Status Register and Stop
                          (Privileged Instruction)

Operation: If supervisor state
then Immediate Data $\rightarrow$ SR;
STOP else TRAP

Assembler
Syntax: STOP #xxx

Attributes: Unsized

Condition Codes: Set according to the immediate operand.

Instruction Format:

15	14	13	12	11	10	9	8	7	6	5	4	3	2	1	0
0	1	0	0	1	1	1	0	0	1	1	1	0	0	1	0
Immediate Data																

SUB   Subtract Binary

Operation: $(\text{Destination}) - (\text{Source})$
$\rightarrow$ Destination

Assembler   SUB $<$ea$>$, Dn
Syntax: SUB Dn, $<$ea$>$

Attributes: Size = (Byte, Word, Long)

Notes: 1,2

Condition Codes:

X	N	Z	V	C
*	*	*	*	*

Instruction Format:

15	14	13	12	11 10 9	8 7 6	5 4 3	2 1 0
1	0	0	1	Register	Op-Mode	Effective Address Mode	Register

SUBA   Subtract Address

Operation: (Destination) − (Source)
                 → Destination

Assembler
Syntax: SUBS <ea>, An
Attributes: Size = (Word,Long)

Condition Codes: Not affected.
Instruction Format:

15	14	13	12	11 10 9	8 7 6	5 4 3	2 1 0
1	0	0	1	Register	Op-Mode	Effective Address Mode	Register

Op-Mode: 011 → word
111 → Long word

SUBI   Subtract Immediate

Operation: (Destination) − Immediate Data
                 → Destination

Assembler
Syntax: SUBI #<data>, <ea>
Attributes: Size = (Byte,Word,Long)
Notes: 3,7

Condition Codes:

X	N	Z	V	C
*	*	*	*	*

Instruction Format:

15	14	13	12	11	10	9	8	7 6	5 4 3	2 1 0
0	0	0	0	0	1	0	0	Size	Effective Address Mode	Register
Word Data (16 bits)									Byte Data (8 bits)	
Long Data (32 bits, including previous word)										

SUBQ   Subtract Quick

Operation: (Destination) − Immediate Data
                 → Destination

Assembler
Syntax: SUBQ #<data>, <ea>
Attributes: Size = (Byte,Word,Long)
Notes: 3,7

Description: Subtract the immediate data from the destination operand. The data range is from 1–8. The size of the operation may be specified to be byte, word, or long. Word and long operations are also allowed on the address registers and the condition codes are not affected. Word size source operands are sign extended to 32-bit quantities before the operation is done.

Condition Codes:

X	N	Z	V	C
*	*	*	*	*

Instruction Format:

15	14	13	12	11 10 9	8	7 6	5 4 3	2 1 0
0	1	0	1	Data	1	Size	Effective Address Mode	Register

Data: 1 → 8
000 → 8

SUBX

Subtract with Extend

Operation: (Destination) − (Source) − X
            → Destination

Assembler SUBX Dy, Dx

Syntax: SUBX − (Ay), − (Ax)

Attributes: Size = (Byte, Word, Long)

Note: 7

Condition Codes:

X	N	Z	V	C
*	*	*	*	*

Instruction Format:

15	14	13	12	11 10 9	8	7 6	5	4	3	2 1 0
1	0	0	1	Register Rx	1	Size	0	0	R/M	Register Ry

Note: See ADDX

SWAP

Swap Register Halves

Operation: Register [31:16] ↔ Register
          [15:0]

Assembler
Syntax: SWAP Dn

Attributes: Size = (Word)

Condition Codes:

X	N	Z	V	C
—	*	*	0	0

N Set if the most significant bit of the 32-bit result is set. Clear otherwise.

Instruction Format:

15	14	13	12	11	10	9	8	7	6	5	4	3	2 1 0
0	1	0	0	1	0	0	0	0	1	0	0	0	Register

TAS

Test and Set an Operand

Operation: (Destination) Tested → CC;
          1 → bit 7 OF Destination

Assembler
Syntax: TAS < ea >

Attributes: Size = (Byte)

Note: 3

Description: Test and set the byte operand addressed by the effective address field. The current value of the operand is tested and N and Z are set accordingly. The high-order bit of the operand is set. The operation is indivisible (using a read-modify-write memory cycle) to allow synchronization of several processors.

Condition Codes:

X	N	Z	V	C
—	*	*	0	0

Instruction Format:

15	14	13	12	11	10	9	8	7	6	5 4 3	2 1 0
0	1	0	0	1	0	1	0	1	1	Effective Address Mode	Register

TRAP   Trap

Operation: PC → −(SSP); SR → −(SSP);
          (Vector) → PC

Assembler
Syntax: TRAP #<vector>

Attributes: Unsized

Condition Codes: Not affected.
Instruction Format:

15	14	13	12	11	10	9	8	7	6	5	4	3	2	1	0
0	1	0	0	1	1	1	0	0	1	0	0		Vector		

TRAPV   Trap on Overflow

Operation: If V then TRAP
Assembler
Syntax: TRAPV
Attributes: Unsized

Condition Codes: Not affected.
Instruction Format:

15	14	13	12	11	10	9	8	7	6	5	4	3	2	1	0
0	1	0	0	1	1	1	0	0	1	1	1	0	1	1	0

TST   Test an Operand

Operation: (Destination) Tested → CC
Assembler
Syntax: TST <ea>
Attributes: Size = (Byte,Word,Long)
Notes: 3,7
Description: Compare the operand with zero.
No results are saved; however,
the condition codes are set according to results of the test. The
size of the operation may be
specified to be byte, word, or
long.

Condition Codes:

X	N	Z	V	C
—	*	*	0	0

Instruction Format:

15	14	13	12	11	10	9	8	7	6	5 4 3	2 1 0
0	1	0	0	1	0	1	0	Size		Effective Address	
										Mode	Register

UNLK   Unlink

Operation: An → SP: (SP) + → An
Assembler
Syntax: UNLK An
Attributes: Unsized
Description: The stack pointer is loaded
from the specified address register. The address register is
then loaded with the long word
pulled from the top of the
stack.

Condition Codes: Not affected.
Instruction Format:

15	14	13	12	11	10	9	8	7	6	5	4	3	2 1 0
0	1	0	0	1	1	1	0	0	1	0	1	1	Register

Register field—specifies the address register
through which the unlinking is to be done.

EXCEPTION VECTOR ASSIGNMENT

Vector Number(s)	Dec	Address Hex	Space	Assignment
0	0	000	SP	Reset: Initial SSP[2]
	4	004	SP	Reset: Initial PC[2]
2	8	008	SD	Bus Error
3	12	00C	SD	Address Error
4	16	010	SD	Illegal Instruction
5	20	014	SD	Zero Divide
6	24	018	SD	CHK Instruction
7	28	01C	SD	TRAPV Instruction
8	32	020	SD	Privilege Violation
9	36	024	SD	Trace
10	40	028	SD	Line 1010 Emulator
11	44	02C	SD	Line 1111 Emulator
12[1]	48	030	SD	(Unassigned, Reserved)
13[1]	52	034	SD	(Unassigned, Reserved)
14[1]	56	038	SD	(Unassigned, Reserved)
15	60	03C	SD	Uninitialized Interrupt Vector
16–23[1]	64	040	SD	(Unassigned, Reserved)
	95	05F		—
24	96	060	SD	Spurious Interrupt[3]
25	100	064	SD	Level 1 Interrupt Autovector
26	104	068	SD	Level 2 Interrupt Autovector
27	108	06C	SD	Level 3 Interrupt Autovector
28	112	070	SD	Level 4 Interrupt Autovector

(continued)

[1]Vector numbers 12, 13, 14, 16 through 23, and 48 through 63 are reserved for future enhancements by Motorola. No user peripheral devices should be assigned these numbers.

[2]Reset vector (0) requires four words, unlike the other vectors which only require two words, and is located in the supervisor program space.

[3]The spurious interrupt vector is taken when there is a bus error indication during interrupt processing.

EXCEPTION VECTOR ASSIGNMENT

Vector Number(s)	Dec	Address Hex	Space	Assignment
29	116	074	SD	Level 5 Interrupt Autovector
30	120	078	SD	Level 6 Interrupt Autovector
31	124	07C	SD	Level 7 Interrupt Autovector
32–47	128	080	SD	TRAP Instruction Vectors[4]
	191	0BF		
48–63[1]	192	0C0	SD	(Unassigned, Reserved)
	255	0FF		—
64–255	256	100	SD	User Interrupt Vectors
	1023	3FF		—

[4]TRAP #n uses vector number 32 + n.

D

Answers to Review Questions

CHAPTER 2

Section 2.1

1. The program would no longer be "transportable." That is, it would no longer run on systems that do not use this particular version of BASIC.
2. There are numerous ways to make the required changes. One way to do this is:
   Change "DECIMAL" to "PERCENT" in line 200.
   Change line 280 to:
      280 PRINT "ENTER THE PERCENT INTEREST ACCRUED"
   Change "100*I" to "I/100" in line 370
   Change "I1" to "I" in line 390
   Change "I" to "I1" in line 460
3. Insert line 231 to be:
      231 REM Y   THE YEAR DEPOSIT IS MADE
   Insert lines 331 and 332 to be:
      331 PRINT "ENTER THE YEAR IN WHICH DEPOSIT IS MADE"
      332 INPUT Y
   Change "ELAPSED TIME" to "CURRENT YEAR" in line 420
   Change line 440 to be:
      440 PRINT Y,P
   Change "I" to "I1" in line 460

Insert line 465 to be:
    465 Y = Y + 1
Change ''J'' to ''Y'' in line 470

Section 2.2

1. **(a)** The smallest element must be the last element of the array.
   (b) When the strings are already sorted at the beginning of program execution.
2. **(a)** 100 strings   **(b)** 32 characters
3. **(a)** In line 10 of PROCEDURE READ_NAMES, 16 characters are read.
   (b) Any valid character.
4. **(a)** Change line 170 to read: 170 DIM A(100). Also, change all string variables A$ to
      A. Related REM or Remark statements should also be modified.
   (b)
```
*        THIS PROGRAM READS A SET OF NON-NEGATIVE NUMS FROM A FILE CALLED
*           CLASSROLL.  THE NUMBERS ARE PRINTED.  THEN THE NUMBERS ARE
*           ARRANGED IN ALPHABETICAL ORDER AND ARE PRINTED AGAIN.  THE
*           NUMBER OF NUMBERS IS LIMITED TO 100.  THE LIST OF NUMBERS
*           IN CLASSROLL IS TERMINATED WITH A NEGATIVE NUMBER.
*     ###########   START MAIN PROGRAM  #######################
          DIMENSION NUMS(100)
          CALL GETDAT(NUMS,NUMBER)
          CALL PNTDAT(NUMS,NUMBER)
          CALL SORT(NUMS,NUMBER)
          WRITE(6,99)
99        FORMAT(//,'      SORTED NUMBERS')
          CALL PNTDAT(NUMS,NUMBER)
          STOP
          END
*     ***********************************************************
          SUBROUTINE GETDAT(N1,NUM)
          DIMENSION N1(100)
*         INTEGERS ARE IN I10 FORMAT.  MUST BE RIGHT JUSTIFIED.
*         READ IN DATA ON UNIT 10.  MUST ASSIGN CLASSROLL TO UNIT 10.
*         IF FORTRAN 77 IS USED, CAN USE 'OPEN' STATEMENT.
          I=1
99                READ(10,98) N1(I)
98                FORMAT (I10)
                  IF (N1(I).LT.0) RETURN
                  NUM = I
                  I=I+1
                  GO TO 99
                      END
*     ***********************************************************
          SUBROUTINE PNTDAT(N1,NUM)
          DIMENSION N1(100)
          WRITE(6,98)
98        FORMAT(/)
                  DO 99 I=1,NUM
99                WRITE (6,97) N1(I)
97        FORMAT(10X,I10)
          RETURN
          END
      ***********************************************************
          SUBROUTINE SORT(N1,NUM)
          DIMENSION N1(100)
          N=NUM-1
          IFLAG=1
97        IF (IFLAG.EQ.0) RETURN
          IFLAG = 0
                  DO 99 K=1,N
```

```
98              IF(N1(K).GT.N1(K+1)) CALL SWITCH(N1,K,IFLAG)
99              CONTINUE
                N=N-1
                IF (N.EQ.0) RETURN
                GO TO 97
     END
********************************************************************
     SUBROUTINE SWITCH(N1,I,IFLAG)
     DIMENSION N1(100)
     ITEMP=N1(I)
     N1(I)=N1(I+1)
     N1(I+1)=ITEMP
     IFLAG=1
     END
```

(c) (*** THIS PROGRAM READS, SORTS AND PRINTS A SET OF
        NON-NEGATIVE INTEGERS IN DESCENDING ORDER. ***)

```
PROGRAM SORT_NUMBERS(INPUT,OUTPUT,NUMBEROLL);
TYPE NUMBERS = INTEGER;
     LIST = PACKED ARRAY[1..100] OF NUMBERS;
     STATUS = PACKED ARRAY[1..2] OF CHAR;
VAR    N: INTEGER;
       ARRAY_OF_INTEGERS:  LIST;
       NUMBEROLL:   TEXT;
(*---------------- PROCEDURES _____*)
PROCEDURE READ_NUMBERS(VAR NUMBER_OF_NUMBERS:INTEGER
                            VAR NUMBERLIST: LIST);

VAR I,J: INTEGER;
    THIS_NUMBER:   NUMBERS;
    BEGIN
         J:=1;   NUMBER_OF_NUMBERS:=0;
       WHILE NOT EOF(NUMBEROLL) DO
             BEGIN
           READLN(NUMBEROLL,THIS_NUMBER);
           IF(THIS_NUMBER>=0) THEN BEGIN
                               NUMBER_OF_NUMBERS:=NUMBER_OF_NUMBERS+1;
                               NUMBERLIST[J]:=THIS_NUMBER;
                               J:=J+1;
                               END;
              END;
    END;
(**************************************************************)
PROCEDURE WRITE_NUMBERS(VAR NUMBER_OF_NUMBERS: INTEGER
                             VAR NUMBERLIST: LIST);

VAR I: INTEGER;
    BEGIN
           WRITELN;
           FOR I := 1 TO NUMBER_OF_NUMBERS DO
           WRITELN('       ', NUMBERLIST[I]);
    END;
(**************************************************************)
PROCEDURE SWITCH_NUMBERS(I:INTEGER VAR NUMBERLIST: LIST
                             VAR SWITCH_FLAG: STATUS);

VAR TEMP: NUMBERS;
     BEGIN
        SWITCH_FLAG :='UP';
        TEMP:=NUMBERLIST[I];
        NUMBERLIST[I]:=NUMBERLIST[I+1];
        NUMBERLIST[I+1]:=TEMP;
     END;
(**************************************************************)
PROCEDURE SORT_NUMBERS(VAR NUMBER_OF_NUMBERS: INTEGER;
                            VAR NUMBERLIST: LIST);
VAR  I,N: INTEGER;
     FLAG: STATUS;
     BEGIN
       N:= NUMBER_OF_NUMBERS-1;
           FLAG:='UP';
```

```
        REPEAT
            FLAG:='DN';
            FOR I:= 1 TO N DO
                IF NUMBERLIST[I]<NUMBERLIST[I+1] THEN
                    SWITCH_NUMBERS(I,NUMBERLIST,FLAG);
            N:=N-1;
        UNTIL ((N=0) OR (FLAG='DN'));
      END;
(*************** END PROCEDURES *******************************)
(*$$$$$$$$$$$$$$$$$$ START MAIN PROGRAM $$$$$$$$$$$$$$$$$$$$$$$$$*)
BEGIN
      RESET  (NUMBEROLL);
      READ_NUMBERS(N,ARRAY_OF_INTEGERS);
      WRITE_NUMBERS(N,ARRAY_OF_INTEGERS);
      SORT_NUMBERS(N,ARRAY_OF_INTEGERS);
      WRITELN;
      WRITELN('    SORTED LIST OF NUMBERS');
      WRITE_NUMBERS(N,ARRAY_OF_INTEGERS);
  END.
```

Section 2.3

1.

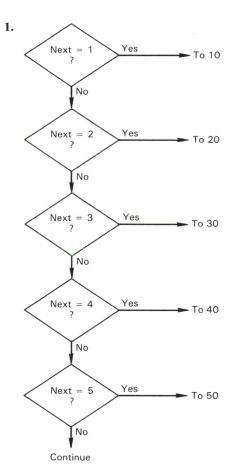

2. LAST + 2

3. (a) 5   **(b)** 5   **(c)** 11

4. (a) 1   **(b)** 0   **(c)** 2

Section 2.4

1. (a) 64   **(b)** 6

2.
```
PROGRAM EXAMPLE;
CONST LENGTH = 100;
TYPE  ALPHA = PACKED ARRAY[1..16] OF CHAR;
VAR LOW,HIGH,MID,INDEX: INTEGER;
    NAME: ALPHA;
    TABLE: ARRAY[1..LENGTH] OF ALPHA;

(*********************************************************************)
(*   PERFORM A BINARY SEARCH ON AN ALPHABETICALLY ORDERED          *)
(*   ARRAY OF 16 CHARACTER NAMES.  ASSUME THE TABLE OF NAMES       *)
(*   HAS BEEN READ INTO THE ARRAY, AND A SPECIFIC NAME HAS BEEN    *)
(*   ASSIGNED.  THEN IF THIS NAME IS FOUND IN THE ARRAY, THE       *)
(*   CORRESPONDING SUBSCRIPT IS PLACED IN A VARIABLE CALLED        *)
(*   "INDEX."  OTHERWISE, A VALUE OF 0 IS PLACED IN "INDEX."       *)
(*********************************************************************)
BEGIN (* EXAMPLE *)
   LOW := 1; (* FIRST SUBSCRIPT *)
   HIGH :=LENGTH;  (*LAST SUBSCRIPT*)
   REPEAT
      MID:=(LOW+HIGH) DIV 2;
      IF NAME<=TABLE[MID] THEN HIGH:=MID-1;
      IF NAME>=TABLE[MID] THEN LOW :=MID+1;
   UNTIL LOW > HIGH;
   IF LOW-1 > HIGH
        THEN INDEX:= MID      (*FOUND NAME IN TABLE*)
        ELSE INDEX:=0         (*NAME NOT IN TABLE*)
END.
```

3. In order to reduce the number of character string exchanges, when two alphabetized arrays are merged, they will not initially be concatenated. Instead, half of the source array will be placed in front of the destination array. The second half of the source array will be placed at the end of the destination array. Then the new array (the destination array) will be sorted. This process is illustrated by the following sequence of steps.

    1. For I = 1 to N/2, set TEMP (I) = FILE1 (I)

    2. For I = 1 to N, set TEMP (I + N/2) = FILE2 (I)

    3. For I = 1 to N/2, set TEMP (I + 3N/2) = FILE1 (I)

    4. SORT Temp. *Note:* Use a sorting routine such as developed in Chapter 2.

    The procedure described above will be given the name MERGE2. The following is a flowchart related to the stated problem.

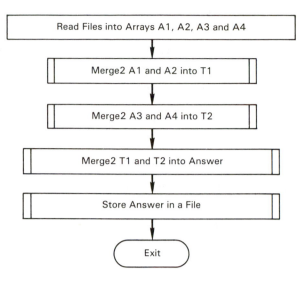

CHAPTER 3

Section 3.1

1. **(a)** 156   **(b)** 1196.75   **(c)** 28.625   **(d)** 26.875
2. **(a)** 15.324   **(b)** 35166.5655
3. **(a)** 2505   **(b)** 17003.4631   **(c)** 0.1024
4. **(a)** 928C   **(b)** A1C4.C   **(c)** 0.25A1
5.
```
PROGRAM CONVERT(INPUT,OUTPUT);
VAR   X,Y:  REAL;
         N:  INTEGER;
BEGIN
         READLN; (* INPUT A POSITIVE REAL NUMBER *)
         READ (X);
         N:=TRUNC(X);
         Y:= X-SQRT(N*N);
         WRITELN(X,N,Y)
END.
```

Section 3.2

1. **(a)** $B055_{16}$, C = 0   **(b)** $44F7_{16}$, C = 0   **(c)** 010710_8, C = 1   **(d)** $81D6_{16}$, C = 0
2. **(a)** $FEDC_{16}$ **(b)** 113456_8 **(c)** $43F7_{16}$ **(d)** 100063_8 **(e)** $AE11_{16}$
   (f) 164142_8
3. **(a)** 5660_{16} and C = 1   **(b)** $69F3_{16}$ **(c)** 0090_{16} **(d)** $2F81_{16}$

Section 3.3

1. (a) $-8 \leq \text{range} \leq 7$ (b) $-2^{31} \leq \text{range} \leq 2^{31} - 1$
2. (a) 0079   (b) FFE7   (c) FFBB   (d) 002B
3. (a) A, B, C, G *Note:* Subtracting 0 does not raise the carry flag on most modern computers.
   (b) D   (c) B, D, E, F,   (d) B, E   (e) D

Section 3.4

1. (a) HORSE   (b) BIRD   (c) GIRL
2. 0, 20, 270, 2760
3. (a) 0, 1, 26, 421, 6748, 107968, 1727488
   (b) 421.75

Section 3.5

1. 57_{16} 89_{16} 01_{16}
2. (a) AF = 0. Result is 81_{16}, and C = 0.
   (b) AF = 1. Result is 87_{16}, and C = 1.
   (c) AF = 0. Result is 01_{16}, and C = 1.
3. (a) AF = 0. Result is 13_{16}, and C = 0.
   (b) AF = 1. Result is 09_{16}, and C = 0.
   (c) AF = 0. Result is 81_{16}, and C = 1.

Section 3.6

1. (a) 12.0   (b) -3746.0 (c) .00012207
2. (a) 43219000_{16} (b) C1A4CCCC   (c) 3E10624D
3. (a) If the value of the resulting mantissa is $<0.0001_2$, normalization is required.
   (b) Shift mantissa 4 bits to the left and subtract 1 from the exponent.
4. (a) No overflow   (b) Overflow   (c) No overflow

CHAPTER 4

Section 4.1

1. (a) A machine in which instruction codes and data are stored in a common memory. Sequences of instruction codes are fetched and executed.
   (b) A set of logic lines connected to two or more components.
   (c) A state in which a logic line or a bus is essentially disconnected from a circuit.

(d) An interface that receives a word from the data bus, appends appropriate control bits, and sends the information out on a logic line one bit at a time. Likewise, a serial interface may receive bits serially from a logic line, remove control bits that have been appended, and send the word that has been collected to the data bus.

(e) An internal control program.

2. (a) Memory   (b) CPU   (c) Peripherals   (d) CPU

3. (a) Flag register or PSW
   (b) Instruction register
   (c) Program counter
   (d) Memory address register
   (e) Data register and memory address register
   (f) Accumulator

Section 4.2

1. 32
2. (a) 15   (b) 8
3. (a) Read only memory.
   (b) Disks, tapes, or other sequential storage devices.
   (c) Nonvolatile primary memory composed of magnetic cores or toroids.
   (d) Memory that loses its stored information when power is disconnected. Semiconductor memory.
   (d) Circuitry required to replace decaying charges that are stored in dynamic memory.

Section 4.3

1. Starting at memory location OEFA, the following hexadecimal numbers are stored in sequential order: 20,02,10,02,0A,BC.
2. (a) 440A (b) 09FE
   (c) $EFCD$ (d) 89AB

   Only locations 9FE and 9FF have their contents changed. AB is now stored in 9AE and 89 in 9FF.
3. (a) 7856   (b) $BC9A$ (c) 1006

Section 4.4

1. (R1) = 1000   (R2) = 0   (PC) = 1010
   If memory addresses identify 16-bit words, (SP) = 777. If memory addresses identify bytes, (SP) = 776.

2. A JUMP or a BRANCH command.

3. If we assume that the DEC command affects the carry flag, the number 31_{10} or 37_8 will be in R0.

4. (a) (R1) = 177654 and (C) = 0   (b) (R1) = 037530 and (C) = 1
   (c) (R1) = 175307 and (C) = 1   (d) (R1) = 077726 and (C) = 0

Section 4.5

1. 1) (PC) => MAR
   2) (MAR) => ADDRESS BUS
   3) Memory is addressed. INSTRUCTION WORD => DATA BUS
   4) (DATA BUS) => DATA REG
   5) (DATA REG) => INSTRUCTION REG
   6) Instruction is translated
   7) (PC) => ALU REG
   8) ALU increments operand
   9) Output of ALU => MAR
   10) (MAR) => ADDRESS BUS
   11) Memory is addressed. OPERAND WORD => DATA BUS
   12) (DATA BUS) => DATA REG
   13) (DATA REG) => PC

2. The sequence of steps that increments the program counter, steps 25 to 27, can be placed in other positions in the queue of events.

3. Increase the size of the program counter and the memory address register. It is convenient to let these be 16-bit registers. Then a memory space of 2^{16} bytes is available. Memory reference instructions will now contain 3 bytes, as addresses are specified by 16-bit words. The following changes must be made to the emulator:
   Line 3: Increase the size of the memory array. The maximum size that the array can be dimensioned is now 0:65535.
   Line 34: Change to: ADDRESS = MEMORY (PC+1) *256 + MEMORY (PC+2)
   Line 36: Change to: PC = PC + 3

4. 256 + 18 = <u>274</u>, which is the sum of 137 and 137.

5. (ACC) = 238　(PC) = 07　(C) = 1　(Z) = 0

CHAPTER 5

Section 5.1

1. Upward compatibility
2. $(3012) = 01100011_2 = 143_8$ $(3013) = 11100101_2 = 345_8$
3. 1001
4. R6 and R7. During CALL and INTERRUPT operations, *words* are stored on the stack. Instructions must begin at even-numbered memory locations.
5. **(a)** 000000 to 167776　　**(b)** 170000 to 177776

Section 5.2

1. **(a)** 060112　　**(b)** 005127
   (c) 062743　001234

    (d) 062765   000042   000056
    (e) 063727   000042   000056

2. **(a)** (R7) = 1002   (R1) = 1200   (R2) = 1402   (R3) = 1400   (1200) = 1300
    (1300) = 1400   (1400) = 2400
    (b) (R7) = 1002   (R3) = 001775   Others are unchanged.
    (c) (R7) = 1002   (R1) = 1201   (1200) = 1077
    (d) (R7) = 1006   (1400) = 1400
    (e) (R7) = 1006   (1200) = 1500

3. **(a)** (R7) = 1004   (R1) = 2000   (2200) = 2200
    (b) (R7) = 1002   (R6) = 1002   (R1) = 012601
    (c) (R7) = 1004   (R6) = 776   (776) = 123456

4. Address   Code
    1000   011537   002000
    1004   012700   001004
    1010   066274   000020   177776
    1016   000000

5. (R7) = 1020   (R0) = 1004   (R2) = 760   (R4) = 2002
    (R5) = 1006   (2000) = 1004   (1004) = 024437

Section 5.3

1. **(a)** 160102   (R2) = 103714   (NZVC) = 1011
   (b) 020102   (R2) = 013256   (NZVC) = 0010
   (c) 005702   (R2) = 013256   (NZVC) = 0000
   (d) 050102   (R2) = 117356   (NZVC) = 100_
   (e) 030102   (R2) = 013256   (NZVC) = 000_
   (f) 040102   (R2) = 010014   (NZVC) = 000_

2. **(a)** 102774   **(b)** 103100   **(c)** 077130   **(d)** 100421

3. **(a)** BR, BNE, BPL, BVC, BCS, BGE, BGT, BLOS, BLO
   (b) Same as in part **(a)**.
   (c) BR, BNE, BMI, BVC, BCC, BLT, BLE, BHIS, BHI

4. **(a)** 0000   **(b)** 774   **(c)** 2002   **(d)** (NZVC) = 1111

5. **(a)** 065302   C = 0
   (b) 015260   C = 1
   (c) 065303   C = 0
   (d) 115260   C = 1
   (e) 060465   C = 0

Section 5.4

1. **(a)** 017701   **(b)** R2/000000

2. **(a)** ←   **(b)** @

3. Between START and BACK

Section 5.5

1. **(a)** 4   **(b)** 2
2. **(a)** 001000   **(b)** 002000   **(c)** 000031
3. **(a)** 12   **(b)** 12
4. No modifications are needed.
5.

Label	Location	Symbolic Code	Machine Code	Comments
AVE4:	1000	CLR R0	005000	
	1002	ADD (R5)+,R0	062500	
	1004	ADD (R5)+,R0	062500	
	1006	ADD (R5)+,R0	062500	
	1010	ADD (R5)+,R0	062500	
	1012	ASR R0	006200	;Divide by 2
	1014	ASR R0	006200	;Divide by 2
	1016	RTS R5	000205	;EXIT
;****START TEST PROGRAM ********************				
START:	1020	MOV #1000,SP	012706 001000	;Load SP
	1024	JSR R5,@#AVE4	004537 001000	;Call AVE4
DATA:	1030		000005	;Data starts
	1032		000032	
	1034		177760	
	1036		000030	;Data ends
TERM:	1040	HALT	000000	

CHAPTER 6

Section 6.1

1. **(a)** 1036   **(b)** 2   **(c)** 6
2. 4
3.
```
         ;LET R5 BE THE LINKING REGISTER
   GETBIG:         MOV (R5)+,R0
                   CMP R0,(R5)+
                   BGT UP
                   TST -(R5)         ;DECREMENT POINTER
                   MOV (R5)+,R0
   UP:             CMP R0,(R5)+
                   BGT DONE
                   TST -(R5)
                   MOV (R5)+,R0
   DONE:           RTS R5
   ;******** START TEST PROGRAM **************
   START:          JSR R5,GETBIG
                   .WORD 45,173,52
                   HALT
                   .END START
```

Section 6.2

1. TYPE MYFILE.LST is valid. We can only list *textfiles* with the TYPE command.
2. 000003   000776   000002
3.

B (ESC) 1K (ESC) ISTART: MOV R1, R2 (RET) (ESC) V (ESC) (ESC)

GOO (ESC) – 1D (ESC) V (ESC) (ESC)

GSAT (ESC) – 2D (ESC) ITA (ESC) 10L (ESC) (ESC)

Section 6.3

1. All are valid except 7122.
2. e
3. 000010

Section 6.4

1. 1100
2. 10. or 12
3. **(a)** 000052   **(b)** 000070
4. 25
5.

```
        .MACRO IANDD PTR,CTR
        INC PTR
        INC PTR
        DEC CTR
        .ENDM
;********   START TEST PROGRAM   ******************
START:  MOV #2000,R0
        MOV #6,R1
        IANDD R0,R1
        IANDD POINT,COUNT
        HALT
POINT:  .WORD  2100
COUNT:  .WORD  5
        .END START
```

Section 6.5

1. **(a)** 1000   **(b)** 0   **(c)** 3   **(d)** 1000
2. **(a)** 177777   **(b)** 177775   **(c)** 177777   **(d)**177771   **(e)** 021216
    (f) 165554
3. 5

4. Delete the statement SIZE = 25.

   Change the statement MOV #SIZE, R3 to MOV #DONE-DATA, R3.

   Insert the statement .GLOBL DONE near the beginning of the program.

   Modify the comments.

5. **(a)** once   **(b)** 177776   **(c)** 177775   **(d)** 6   **(e)** 177777

CHAPTER 7

Section 7.1

1.
```
        .MCALL  .EXIT,.PRINT
        ;THIS SUBROUTINE ADDS TWO MULTI-WORD SIGNED
        ;   INTEGERS.  THE NUMBER OF WORDS IN AN INTEGER,
        ;   N, IS CARRIED INTO THE SUBROUTINE IN R1.
        ;A POINTER TO THE MOST SIGNIFICANT WORD OF THE
        ;   FIRST NUMBER IS CARRIED INTO THE ROUTINE IN R2.
        ;A POINTER TO THE SECOND NUMBER AND TO THE RESULTING
        ;   SUM IS IN R3.
        ;AN OVERFLOW CHECK IS INCLUDED.
MPADD:  CLR FLAG
        MOV (R2),R5
        MOV (R3),R4
        XOR R5,R4           ;OVERFLOW POSSIBLE?
        BMI GO              ;NO
        TST (R2)            ;YES.  FIND CORRECT SIGN
        BPL GO
        MOV#100000,FLAG
GO:     ADD R1,R2           ;SET POINTERS PAST END OF NUMBERS
        ADD R1,R2
        ADD R1,R3
        ADD R1,R3
        CLR CAROLD          ;CLEAR PREVIOUS CARRY
BACK:   CLR CARNEW          ;CLEAR NEXT CARRY
        ADD -(R2),-(R3)
        BCC UP
        MOV #1,CARNEW
UP:     ADD CAROLD,(R3)
        BCC UP1
        MOV #1,CARNEW
UP1:    MOV CARNEW,CAROLD
        SOB R1,BACK
                            ;CHECK FOR OVERFLOW
        TST R4              ;OVERFLOW POSSIBLE?
        BPL AHEAD           ;YES
        RTS PC              ;NO
AHEAD:  MOV (R3),R4
        XOR R4,FLAG         ;OVERFLOW?
        BPL DONE            ;NO
        SEV                 ;YES
DONE:   RTS PC
FLAG:   .BLKW  1
CARNEW: .BLKW  1
CAROLD: .BLKW  1
;***************  START TEST PROGRAM  *******************
;$$$   ADD TWO 80-BIT INTEGERS
START:  MOV #5,R1
        MOV #FIRST,R2
        MOV #SECOND,R3
        JSR PC,MPADD
        BVC THRU
        .PRINT #OMES
```

```
THRU:      .EXIT
OMES:      .ASCII /        OVERFLOW!!!!/<15><12><200>
           .EVEN
FIRST:     .WORD    072345,123454,165473,0,177760
SECOND:    .WORD    043652,133333,144444,177777,177760
           .END START
```

2. (a) 056220   (b) 057010   (c) 132140   (d) 000000   (e) 177740

3. (a) twice   (b) 54321   (c) 177777   (d) 165433   (e) 0   (f) 100000

4. .GLOBL MPADD and .GLOBL TWCMP

Section 7.2

1.
```
           ;SUBROUTINE FINDS PRODUCT OF TWO UNSIGNED
           ;  16-BIT INTEGERS.  FACTORS ARE IN R1 AND R3.
           ;HOW OF PROD RETURNED IN R2.  LOW RETURNED IN R3.
PROD:      MOV #16.,R4
           CLR R2
           ROR R3
BACK:      BCC UP          ;BIT = 1?
           ADD R1,R2       ;YES
UP:        ROR R2          ;NO.  SHIFT RIGHT
           ROR R3
           SOB R4,BACK     ;LOOP UNTIL DONE
           RTS PC
           ;$$$$$$$$$$$$$$ START TEST PROGRAM $$$$$$$$$$$$$$$$$$$$
           ;USE CONSOLE ODT TO LOAD FACTORS AND DISPLAY ANSWERS.
START:     JSR PC,PROD
QUIT:      HALT
           .END QUIT
```

2. (a) 3, 1   (b) 034567, 000041   (c) 175051, 000005   (d) 0, 0   (e) 0, 0

3. twice

Section 7.3

1.
```
FILBUF:    MOV #4,R4
           MOV #BUFFER,R5
           CLR R0
BACK:      ASHC #4,R0
           BIC #177760,R0  ;GET HEXADECIMAL VALUE
           ADD #60,R0      ;CONVERT TO ASCII
           CMP R0,#'9
           BLE UP
           ADD #7,R0
UP:        MOVB R0,(R5)+   ;PUT IN BUFFER
           SOB R4,BACK
           RTS PC
```

2.
```
FBUF10:    MOV #4,R4
           MOV #TERM,R5
BACK:      CLR R0
           DIV #16.,R0
           ADD #60,R1      ;CONVERT TO ASCII
           CMP R1,#'9      ;NUMERIC CHARACTER?
           BLE UP          ;YES
           ADD #7,R1       ;NO.  CONVERT TO ALPHABETICAL CHARACTER
UP:        MOVB R1,-(R5)   ;PUT IN BUFFER
           MOV R0,R1       ;PREPARE FOR NEXT DIVISION
           SOB R4,BACK
           RTS PC
```

3. (a) 123456   (b) 34567

Section 7.4

1. **(a)** 142145   000000   **(b)** 042533   004000   **(c)** 040511   007720
2. **(a)** 45.5   **(b)** −7362.625
3. **(a)** 040640   **(b)** 000000

Section 7.5

1. **(a)** 041210   **(b)** 000000
2. **(a)** once   **(b)** 041020   **(c)** 000000
3. **(a)** 044026   **(b)** 124400
4. **(a)** 3.0   **(b)** 2.0   **(c)** 12.0   **(d)** 3.14159   **(e)** DIM
5.

```
            .MCALL .TTYIN,.EXIT
            .GLOBL FPGET
TEN:        .FLT2 10.
ANS:        .BLKW 2
TEMP:       .BLKW 2
FLOTIN: MOV #0,R1
        MOV #ANS,R2
        CALL FPGET
BACK:   .TTYIN
        BIC #177760,R0
        CMP #12,R0
        BNE UP
        SUB #4,R5
        RTS PC
UP:     MOV #TEN,R5
        FMUL R5
        MOV R0,R1
        MOV #TEMP,R2
        CALL FPGET
        FADD R5
        MOV TEMP,ANS
        MOV TEMP+2,ANS+2
        BR BACK
;$$$$$ START TEST PROGRAM $$$$$$$$$$$$$$$
START:  CALL FLOTIN
        MOV (R5)+,2000
        MOV (R5)+,2002
        .EXIT
        .END START
```

CHAPTER 8

Section 8.1

1. **(a)** Transmission of binary characters one bit at a time.
   (b) Simultaneous transmission of bits of a word.
   (c) A peripheral register that can be read by the CPU and that contains information related to the current state of the peripheral device.

(d) A register in which command and control words related to the operation of a peripheral device can be entered under CPU control.

(e) A data register is reloaded before the previous word has been read.

2. b, c, and d

3.
```
          .GLOBL PNTMES
          .MACRO PRINT MESS
          MOV MESS,R1
          CALL PNTMES
          .ENDM
;  $$$$$$ START TEST PROGRAM $$$$$$$$$
START:    CLR 177564
          PRINT #NUTS
          HALT
NUTS:     .ASCII /NUTS TO YOU !!!!  /<200>
          .END START
```

4.
```
GETNUM:  CLR R1
BACK:    RETLF
         PROMPT
BACK1:   CALL READ
         CALL WRITE
         CMPB #15,R0
         BNE UP
         RETLF
         RTS PC
UP:      BIC #177770,R0
         MUL #8.,R1
         ADD R0,R1
         BR BACK1
;  $$$$$$$$  START TEST PROGRAM  $$$$$$$$$$$$$
START:   CLR 177560
         CLR 177564
         CALL GETNUM
         HALT
         .END START
```

Section 8.2

1.
```
          PCTR = 167770
          PTIN = 167774
          PTOUT = 167772
          ODD = 125252
          MASK = 001140    ;BITS 5, 6 AND 9
LOOK:     BIT @#PTIN,#MASK
          BNE UP
          RTS PC
UP:       BIT @#PTIN,#4
          BNE UP1
          RTS PC
UP1:      MOV #ODD,@#PTOUT
          RTS PC
;  $$$$$  START TEST PROGRAM  $$$$$$$
START:    CLR @#PCTR
          CALL LOOK
          HALT
          .END START
```

2. Refer to Fig. 8.7. Insert the following statements after the statement BEQ BYE:
```
JSR R4,CHECK
.ASCII /CHG/
.EVEN
BEQ CHG
```

Insert the following statements after the statement labeled BYE:

```
CHG:      MOV #12,R0
          XOR R0,R5
          MOV R5,@#170446
          JMP RUN
```

3. d and e

Section 8.3

1. Insert the following line just before BEGIN:

```
MFLAG:  .WORD  0          ;MINUS FLAG
```

Insert the following line just after BEGIN:

```
CLR MFLAG
```

Insert the following lines after the first CALL GETCHR statement:

```
HERE:    CMPB #'-,R0
         BNE AHEAD
         COM MFLAG
         BR HERE-4
AHEAD:   NOP
```

Insert the following lines just before the BIC #1, R2 statement:

```
         TST MFLAG
         BEQ UP1
         NEG R2
         BIC #170001,R2
         BR SET
UP1:     NOP
```

2. DACO = 170440
DAC1 = 170442
XOUT = 2848.
YOUT = 3248.
MOV #XOUT, @#DACO
MOV #YOUT, @#DAC1

3. Change CWORD = 2401 to CWORD = 6401 .

4. Insert the following line just after the line MOV @#ADCDAT, R3:

```
BIC #170000, R3
```

5. An overrun error occurs if a new conversion is initiated before the results of the previous conversion are read.

Section 8.4

1. (a)

```
.MCALL .EXIT
.GLOBL TASK
START: CALL TASK
.EXIT
.END START
```

(b) LINK TEST, TASK, SUBS, MOTOR

2. Connect variable voltage sources to the ADC input channels and a voltage corresponding to the desired logic level to the flag line. Use a voltmeter on the DAC1 output line, and monitor the logic output lines. Adjust the variable voltage sources and the flag input level to correspond to anticipated operational sequences.

3. Refer to Fig. 8.16. Change the first DRIVE command to

```
DRIVE VOLT3,VOLT25
```

Delete the second DRIVE command.

4. Refer to Fig. 8.18, and make the following modifications:
After the line labeled START, insert the following line:

```
INIT: CLR R1
```

Delete the line with the statement CALL BELL, and insert the following lines in its place:

```
    INC R1
    CMP #60.,R1
    BNE UP
    CALL BELL
    BR INIT
UP: NOP
```

5. RT-11 operates with the keyboard in an interrupt-driven mode.

Section 8.5

1. An isosceles triangle

2. (a) 3   **(b)** w   **(c)** h

3. Add the following two commands immediately after JMP CMD13:

```
JMP LINE
JMP LINED
```

CHAPTER 9

Section 9.1

1. Inspect memory location 30 when the operating system is resident in memory.

2.
```
USER EMT 1 COMMAND!!!
THIS EMT COMMAND IS NOT DEFINED.
USER EMT 2 COMMAND!!!!!
```

3.
```
        .MCALL .EXIT,.PRINT
START:  MOV #2000,34     ;SET UP USER TRAP VECTOR
        TRAP 1
        TRAP 47
        TRAP 2
        .EXIT
.=START+1000      ;TRAP PROCESSING ROUTINE STARTS AT 2000
;**   START USER TRAP PROCESSING ROUTINE **
        MOV (SP),R5      ;GET RETURN ADDRESS
        SUB #2,R5        ;POINT TO TRAP COMMAND
        CMPB #1,(R5)     ;TRAP 1 COMMAND?
        BNE UP           ;NO
        CALL SERV1       ;YES
        RTI
UP:     CMPB #2,(R5)     ;TRAP 2 COMMAND?
        BNE UP1          ;NO
        CALL SERV2       ;YES
        RTI
UP1:    CALL BAD
        RTI              ;RETURN FROM TRAP PROCESSING ROUTINE
; ** TRAP SERVICE ROUTINES START HERE **
SERV1:  .PRINT #MES1
        RTS PC
SERV2:  .PRINT #MES2
        RTS PC
BAD:    .PRINT BADMES
        RTS PC
;   START MESSAGES
MES1:   .ASCII /USER TRAP 1 COMMAND!!!/<15><12><200>
        .EVEN
MES2:   .ASCII /USER TRAP 2 COMMAND!!!!!/<12><15><200>
        .EVEN
BADMES: .WORD  NEXT
NEXT:   .ASCII /THIS TRAP COMMAND IS NOT DEFINED./<12><15><200>
        .END START
```

Section 9.2

1.
```
;*****  USER KEYBOARD INTERRUPT PROCESSING ROUTINE  ****
PROCES: MOVB @#TKS+2,@BUFFER              ;READ KEYBOARD BUFFER
        BICB #200,@BUFFER                 ;7-BIT ASCII CODE
        MOVB @BUFFER,@#TKS+6              ;ECHO
        INC BUFFER                        ;ADVANCE BUFFER POINTER
        CMP BUFFER,#BUFFER+103.
        BNE UP
        .PRINT #OVERFL
UP:     NOP
        RTI
BUFFER: .WORD   BUFFER+2                  ;BUFFER POINTER
        .BLKB 100
OVERFL: .ASCII /BUFFER HAS OVERFLOWED!!!/<200>
```

2.
```
            .MCALL .EXIT,.PRINT
   TEST:    MOV 10,-(SP)     ;SAVE SYSTEM VECTOR
            MOV #BADINS,10   ;USER VECTOR
            .WORD 177777,176543,176666      ;BAD INSTRUCTIONS
            MOV (SP)+,10     ;RESTORE SYSTEM VECTOR
            .EXIT
   BADINS:  .PRINT #BAD
            RTI
   BAD:     .ASCII /BAD INSTRUCTION!!!!/<12><15><200>
            .END TEST
```

3.
```
            .MCALL .EXIT,.PRINT
   DATA:    .FLT2 0.0
            .FLT2 1.0
   TEST:    MOV 244,-(SP)    ;SAVE SYSTEM VECTOR
            MOV #FPTRAP,244  ;USER VECTOR
            MOV #DATA,R1
            FDIV R1
            MOV  (SP)+,244   ;RESTORE SYSTEM VECTOR
            .EXIT
   FPTRAP:  MOV SP,R2
            BIT 2(R2),#1     ;CHECK CARRY
            BEQ UP
            .PRINT #ZERO
   UP:      RTI
   ZERO:    .ASCII /DIVISION BY ZERO/<200>
            .END TEST
```

Section 9.3

1. 13

2. Modify lines 6, 12, and MES in Fig. 9.6 to read as follows:

```
   ;THIS ROUTINE PRINTS CONTENTS OF THE PSW AND PC

            MOV 12.(SP),R3            ;GET CONTENTS OF THE PSW

   MES:     .ASCII <12><15>/    THE PSW CONTAINS /
```

3.
```
            .GLOBL  TINIT
            .MCALL .EXIT,.PRINT
            .MACRO TRON
            TRAP 0
            .ENDM
            .MACRO TROFF
            TRAP 1
            .ENDM
   ;*** THIS PROGRAM TESTS THE TRON AND TROFF MACROS.
   ;     IT ALSO TESTS THE TRACE-TRAP HANDLER, MYHNDR
   START:   CALL TINIT
            TRON ;TURN ON TRACE.  USE MYHNDR
            MOV #6,R1
   BACK:    NOP
            SOB R1,BACK
            TROFF    ;TURN OFF TRACE
            NOP
            NOP
            .EXIT
            .END START
```

```
          ,GLOBL TINIT,MYHNDR
TINIT:    MOV #THANDL,34            ;LOAD TRAP VECTOR
          MOV #340,36
          MOV #MYHNDR,14  ;LOAD TRACE-TRAP VECTOR
          RTS PC
THANDL:   MOV R1,-(SP)
          MOV R2,-(SP)
          MOV 4(SP),R1
          SUB #2,R1        ;POINT TO TRAP COMMAND
          MOVB (R1),R2     ;GET TRAP ARGUMENT
          ADD R2,R2        ;PREPARE FOR TABLE LOOKUP
          JMP @TABLE(R2)
DONE:     MOV (SP)+,R2     ;RESTORE AND RETURN
          MOV (SP)+,R1
          RTT
TABLE:    .WORD   TON      ;TURN ON TRACE BIT
          .WORD TOFF       ;TURN OFF TRACE BIT
          .BLKW 10         ;RESERVED FOR OTHER DIRECTIVES
TON:      BIS #20,6(SP)
          BR DONE
TOFF:     BIC #177760,6(SP)
          BR DONE
          .END
```

Section 9.4

1. In interrupt-driven transfers, the CPU performs the data transfer. In DMA transfers, the external device performs the data transfer.
2. (a) The bus is essentially disconnected and made available to another user.
   (b) Identifies memory address for DMA transfers.
   (c) Stores block size.
3. (a) 256   (b) 012746   (c) 000000

Section 9.5

1. (a) 2   (b) BLOCK
2. MOV #AREA, R0
3. 8

CHAPTER 10

Section 10.1

1. Each have 16-bit registers and are capable of either word or byte operations. The status flags are similar, although the 8086 has more flags. The 8086 has a 20-bit address register and has internal registers that are dedicated, at least for certain instructions. The 8086 uses segmented addressing.
2. The bytes stored in the queue are abandoned, and the queue is reloaded starting at the new address.
3. (a) A8A4A   (b) C4909   *Note:* Generally the top of the stack is identified by an even-numbered address.   (c) C5A1A   (d) B33B1

4. (a) 1660   **(b)** IP   **(c)** 0015
5. (a) B33B1   **(b)** 30C22   **(c)** 1112 and 2223

Section 10.2

1. There is greater use of "register" addressing on the 8086. There is no true indirect addressing on the 8086. The modes of addressing are more general on the PDP-11. Determination of true addresses on the 8086 requires the use of segment registers.
2. **(a)** CX, memory locations 49929 and 4992A
   (b) Memory locations 07727 and 07728, BX
   (c) CX, 8120F and 81210
3. **(a)** Add 67H to the number in location D3234.
   (b) Add 0403 to the word in location 81333 and 81334.
   (c) Add the byte in AL to the byte in location 81132.
4. **(a)** The new contents of SI will be 3344.
   (b) The new contents of location 83344 will be 3C. The new contents of 83345 will be 9B.
   (c) The new byte in DDEC is 79. The new byte in DDED is 67.
5. The program is stored in this area of memory.

Section 10.3

1. MOD 11 is invalid since a source address is needed.
2. 10000110   11   100   000
3. **(a)** AL and IP.
   (b) 7 will be in AL and 1 in IP.
4. **(a)** IP, AL and SI
   (b) IP, DI and locations 27778 and 27779
   (c) IP, SI, DI, CX and locations 27778, 27779 and 2777A
   (d) IP, SI, DI, CX and Flag register
   (e) IP   **(f)** IP
   (g) IP, SP, CS, and locations 5944C to 5944F
5. **(a)** 0001, 03, 5557
   (b) 0001, 556A, 05, 23
   (c) 0002, 5559, 556B, 0, 3, 4, and 3
   (d) 0002, 5559, 556B, 0 and (FLAG REGISTER) = 0091
   (e) 0002   **(f)** 1000
   (g) AAAA, FFFC, 0100, 05, 00, 11, 11

Section 10.4

1. 04D0E at the beginning of the program
   The ASCII character E is initially stored at [SP-4].
2. Lines 46 and 47

3. **(a)** Lines 51 and 53
   (b) Line 45. Register addressing is used in lines 30, 33, and 44.
   (c) Lines 32, 37, 38, 39, 40, and 52
   (d) Lines 29, 31, and 54

4. **(a)** Lines 29, 31, and 54
   (b) Lines 30, 33, 44, and 45
   (c) Lines 32, 37, 38, 39, 40, and 52

5.
```
0000                                    STACK     SEGMENT  PARA  STACK  'STACK'
0000      40 [                                    DB    64  DUP('ABCDEFGH')
             41 42 43 44
             45 46 47 48
                             ]

0200                                    STACK    ENDS
0000                                    WORKDATA          SEGMENT  PARA  PUBLIC  'DATA'
0000  002D                              NUMB1     DW     45
0002  009C                              NUMB2     DW     0156
0004  FFF1                              NUMB3     DW     -15
0006  ????                              ANS       DW     ?
0008                                    WORKDATA          ENDS
                                        ;
0000                                    CSEG     SEGMENT PARA     PUBLIC  'CODE'
0000                                    START     PROC    FAR
                                                  ASSUME SS:STACK, CS:CSEG, DS:WORKDATA,
                                        ES:WORKDATA
0000  1E                                          PUSH DS  ;SAVE RETURN SEGMENT
0001  2B C0                                       SUB AX,AX
0003  50                                          PUSH AX ;SAVE RETURN OFFSET
0004  B8   ---- R                                 MOV AX,WORKDATA ;LOAD SEGMENT REGISTERS
0007  8E D8                                       MOV DS,AX
0009  8E C0                                       MOV ES,AX        ;SEGMENT REGISTERS ARE
                                        LOADED
                                        ;
000B  33 C0                                       XOR AX,AX        ;CLEAR RUNNING SUM
000D  03 06 0000 R                                ADD AX,NUMB1
0011  03 06 0002 R                                ADD AX,NUMB2
0015  03 06 0004 R                                ADD AX,NUMB3
0019  A3 0006 R                                   MOV ANS,AX
                                        ;
                                        ;
001C  CB                                          RET
001D                                    START     ENDP
001D                                    CSEG      ENDS
                                                  END START
```

Section 10.5

1. INST merely illustrates various MOVE operations. First a block of five words starting
   at DS:S1 is moved to a block starting at ES:S2. Then the hexadecimal numbers *A, B,
   C, D,* and *E* are placed in memory locations ES:S2 + 10 + BLOC to ES:S2 + 14 + BLOC.
   Then a block of five words starting at DS:S1 + 10 is moved to a block starting at
   ES:S2 + 16.

   STORE moves a block of words starting at DS:S2 to a block starting at ES:S3.

2.
```
;****************************************************************
;*    AN 8086 ASSEMBLY LANGUAGE PROGRAM THAT ADDS THE SOURCE ARRAY    *
;*    TO THE DESTINATION ARRAY.   THE DATA SEGMENT CONTAINS SPACE     *
;*    FOR TWO 5-ELEMENT ARRAYS.   AN ELEMENT IS A SIGNED 32-BIT       *
;*    INTEGER.                                                        *
;****************************************************************
;
```

```
        STACK    SEGMENT PARA     STACK    'STACK'
                 DB       64 DUP('ASG#10..')
        STACK    ENDS
        ;
        WORKDATA           SEGMENT PARA PUBLIC      'DATA'
        ARRAYS DD       101,-45,15,872,0
        ARRAYD DD       -321,-4,-615,41245,87
        WORKDATA           ENDS
        ;
        CSEG     SEGMENT PARA     PUBLIC  'CODE'
        START    PROC    FAR
                 ASSUME SS:STACK,CS:CSEG,DS:WORKDATA,ES:WORKDATA
                 PUSH DS ;SAVE RETURN SEGMENT
                 SUB AX,AX
                 PUSH AX ;SAVE RETURN OFFSET
                 MOV AX,WORKDATA ;LOAD SEGMENT REGISTERS
                 MOV DS,AX
                 MOV ES,AX        ;SEGMENT REGISTERS ARE LOADED
        ;
                 SUB CX,CX       ;CLEAR COUNTER
                 CLD             ;CLEAR DIRECTION FLAG
                 MOV SI,OFFSET ARRAYS
                 MOV DI,OFFSET ARRAYD
        LOOP:    MOV AX,[SI]     ;LOOP TO ADD THE TWO ARRAYS
                 ADD [DI],AX
                 MOV AX,[SI+2]
                 ADC [DI+2],AX
                 ADD SI,4        ;INCREMENT SI & DI REGISTERS TO
                 ADD DI,4        ; OBTAIN THE NEXT 32-BIT INTEGERS
                 INC CX
                 CMP CX,5        ;CHECK TO SEE IF DONE
                 JNZ LOOP
                 RET
        START    ENDP
        CSEG     ENDS
                 END START

        B>A:DEBUG ASG10.EXE
        -D 04D2:0 L30
        04D2:0000  65 00 00 00 D3 FF FF FF-0F 00 00 00 68 03 00 00    e...S.......h...
        04D2:0010  00 00 00 00 BF FE FF FF-FC FF FF FF 99 FD FF FF    ....?~..\....}..
        04D2:0020  1D A1 00 00 57 00 00 00-00 00 00 00 00 00 00 00    .!..W...........
        -D SS:0 L30
        04B2:0000  41 53 47 23 31 30 2E 2E-41 53 47 23 31 30 2E 2E    ASG#10..ASG#10..
        04B2:0010  41 53 47 23 31 30 2E 2E-41 53 47 23 31 30 2E 2E    ASG#10..ASG#10..
        04B2:0020  41 53 47 23 31 30 2E 2E-41 53 47 23 31 30 2E 2E    ASG#10..ASG#10..
        -G

        Program terminated normally
        -D 04D2:0 L30
        04D2:0000  65 00 00 00 D3 FF FF FF-0F 00 00 00 68 03 00 00    e...S.......h...
        04D2:0010  00 00 00 00 24 FF FF FF-CF FF FF FF A8 FD FF FF    ....$...O...(}..
        04D2:0020  85 A4 00 00 57 00 00 00-00 00 00 00 00 00 00 00    .$..W...........
        -Q
```

```
3.  STACK    SEGMENT PARA     STACK    'STACK'
    DB       40      DUP('BIG_Z')
    STACK    ENDS
    WD       SEGMENT PARA     PUBLIC  'DATA'
             DW       0
    NUM      DW       4310    ;ENTERING THE NUMBERS TO BE SORTED
             DW       97
             DW       1
             DW       432
             DW       97
             DW       15
             DW       3118
             DW       2
             DW       87
             DW       4
```

```
WD        ENDS
CSEG      SEGMENT PARA    PUBLIC  'CODE'
BEGIN     PROC    FAR        ;BEGIN MAIN PROGRAM
          ASSUME CS:CSEG, DS:WD, SS:STACK, ES:NOTHING
          PUSH DS
          XOR AX,AX
          PUSH AX
          MOV AX,WD
          MOV DS,AX       ;MOV WORKDATA INTO DS
PUT           MACRO ;SWITCHES WORDS
          MOV BX,[SI]
          MOV DI,[SI+2]
          MOV [SI],DI
          MOV [SI+2],BX
ENDM
          MOV AX,10      ;NUMBER TO BE SORTED
NOSE:     MOV CX,9       ;LOAD COUNTED
          DEC AX
          JZ FIN
          MOV SI,OFFSET NUM-2
AGAIN:    ADD SI,2
          MOV DX,[SI]
          CMP DX,[SI+2]  ;NEED SWITCHING?
          JLE GO         ;NO
          PUT            ;YES
GO:       LOOP AGAIN
          JMP NOSE
FIN:      NOP
          RET
BEGIN     ENDP
CSEG      ENDS
          END BEGIN
```

4.
```
;THIS PROGRAM PRINTS 'I AM A DOG' IF AND ONLY IF
;THE THREE CHARACTERS 'CAT' ARE ENTERED IN SUCCESSION
;ON THE KEYBOARD.
FETCH           MACRO
;THIS MACRO READS A CHARACTER FROM THE KEYBOARD.
          MOV AH,7
          INT 33  ;GET A CHARACTER
ENDM
STACK     SEGMENT PARA    STACK  'STACK'
          DB      120 DUP ('ABCD')
STACK     ENDS
WORKDATA          SEGMENT PARA    PUBLIC  'DATA'
MESSAGE DB      'I AM A DOG$'
WORKDATA          ENDS
CSEG      SEGMENT PARA    PUBLIC  'CODE'
START     PROC    FAR
          ASSUME DS:WORKDATA,ES:WORKDATA,CS:CSEG,SS:STACK
          PUSH DS
          XOR AX,AX
          PUSH AX
;SKELETON COMPLETE.  PROGRAM BEGINS HERE.
          MOV AX,WORKDATA
          MOV DS,AX
          CLI
BACK:     FETCH
          CMP AL,'C'     ;IS CHARACTER A 'C'
          JE UP   ;YES
          JMP SHORT BACK ;NO
UP:       FETCH
          CMP AL,'A'     ;A?
          JE LAST        ;YES
          JMP SHORT BACK ;NO
LAST:     FETCH
          CMP AL,'T'     ;T?
          JE PRINT       ;YES
          JMP SHORT BACK ;NO
```

```
       PRINT:   MOV AH,9
                MOV DX,OFFSET MESSAGE
                INT 21H            ;SEND MESSAGE
                RET
       START    ENDP
       CSEG     ENDS
                END START
```

5.
```
    1: ;     SOLUTION TO REVIEW PROBLEM 10-5
    2: OUT             MACRO
    3: ;THIS MACRO PRINTS A CHARACTER
    4:                 MOV DL,AL
    5:                 MOV AH,2
    6:                 INT 21H
    7:                 ENDM
    8: RETLF           MACRO
    9: ; PRINT A RETURN AND A LINE-FEED
   10:                 MOV DX,OFFSET LFRET
   11:                 MOV AH,9
   12:                 INT 21H
   13:                 ENDM
   14: CR      EQU     0DH
   15: LF      EQU     0AH
   16: STACK   SEGMENT PARA    STACK   'STACK'
   17:         DB      20 DUP ('TIGERS')
   18: STACK   ENDS
   19: MYDATA  SEGMENT PARA    PUBLIC  'DATA'
   20: LFRET   DB      CR,LF,'$'
   21: SPACE   DB      10 DUP(?)
   22: SPACEND DB      ?
   23: MYDATA  ENDS
   24: CMDSEG  SEGMENT PARA    PUBLIC  'CODE'
   25: ASSUME  CS:CMDSEG, SS:STACK, DS:MYDATA, ES:NOTHING
   26: SUBR    PROC    FAR
   27:         MOV BX,DX
   28:         RETLF
   29:         MOV CX,4
   30: BACK:   ROL BX,1
   31:         ROL BX,1
   32:         ROL BX,1
   33:         ROL BX,1
   34:         MOV AX,BX
   35:         AND AX,000FH
   36:         CMP AL,10
   37:         JNC CHAR
   38:         ADD AX,30H
   39:         OUT     ;NOTE:  MACRO, NOT ASSEMBLY CODE!
   40:         JMP  UP
   41: CHAR:   ADD AX,41H
   42:         SUB AX,10
   43:         OUT
   44: UP:     LOOP BACK
   45:         RETLF
   46:         MOV DX,BX
   47:         RET
   48: SUBR    ENDP
   49: SUBR2   PROC    FAR
   50: ; PRINTS CONTENTS OF DX AS A POSITIVE BASE-10 NUMBER.
   51:         MOV CX,6
   52:         MOV SI,0
   53: BACK1:  MOV SPACE[SI],0
   54:         INC SI
   55:         LOOP BACK1
   56:                 MOV BX,DX
   57:                 MOV AX,DX
   58:                 MOV DX,0
   59:                 MOV CX,10
   60: AGAIN:          DIV CX
   61:                 DEC SI
```

```
62:                            MOV SPACE[SI],DL
63:                            CMP AX,0
64:                            JZ DONE
65:                            MOV DX,0
66:                            JMP AGAIN
67: DONE:                      MOV CX,6
68:                            MOV SI,OFFSET SPACE
69: OVER:                      MOV AL,[SI]
70:                            INC SI
71:                            ADD AL,30H
72:                            OUT
73:                            LOOP OVER
74:                            MOV DX,BX
75:                            RET
76: SUBR2     ENDP
77: FIRST     PROC    FAR
78:                            PUSH    DS
79:                            MOV AX,0
80:                            PUSH AX
81:                            MOV AX,MYDATA
82:                            MOV DS,AX
83: ;START TEST PROGRAM
84:                            MOV DX,4650H
85:                            CALL SUBR
86:                            CALL SUBR2
87:                            MOV DX,0AB5FH
88:                            CALL SUBR
89:                            CALL SUBR2
90:                            RET
91: FIRST     ENDP
92: CMDSEG    ENDS
93:                    END FIRST
```

CHAPTER 11

Section 11.1

1. A 40-pin chip is more economical, requires less board space, and uses a less expensive socket. A 64-pin chip offers greater enhancement possibilities. Because there is less multiplexing, a circuit with a smaller number of chips may be realized.

2. The processor status pins.

3. If level signals produce the interrupt, the processing routine would continuously be interrupted and never given the opportunity to process the interrupting device.

4. 5DF8

5. 7EF8

Section 11.2

1. This would be redundant. If a data register is to be a destination register, place a 0 in bit 8 of the command word and use mode 0 in the effective address field.

2. **(a)** Add the low-order word in A5 to the low-order word in D6.
   (b) Decrement A5 by 2. Then add the number in memory, identified by the new pointer in A5, to the low-order word in D6.

(c) The effective address is the contents of A4 + 258. Add the word stored at this address to the low-order word in D7.

(d) Decrement A4 by 2. Then add the number in memory, identified by the new pointer in A4, to the low-order word in D3.

(e) Add the low-order word in D2 to the word stored in memory that is identified by the pointer in A2. Then increment the pointer by 2.

(f) To get the pointer, add the 32-bit word in D2 and the 32-bit word in A3 together and obtain a 32-bit sum. Subtract 14 from this 32-bit pointer. Add the word stored in this location to the low-order word in D1.

3. (a) 0000FF01
   (b) 00000001
   (c) This is an invalid instruction. An assembler may translate this instruction to the code corresponding to the mnemonic ADDA.W D1,A0. In this case, the number in A0 will be 00010001.

4. C: D478 1010
   D: D478 1022
   E: D478 1ACE
   F: D66A 1022

5. (a) D965. Add the word in D4 to the word identified by (A5) -2. Decrement contents of A5 by 2.
   (b) D16A 0123.
   Add word in D0 to word in location (A2) + $0123.
   (c) D67B E002. Relative indexed addressing is used. The lower half of A6 is the index register. The word in AHEAD is added to the word in D3 if and only if the word in A3 has a value of 0.
   (d) D09C. Add the long word in address identified by contents of A4 to D0. Increment A4 by 4.

Section 11.3

1. `MOVEM.L D0/D1/D2/A3/A4/A5,-(A7)`

2. `MOVE #$19,CCR`

3. `SLS FLAG`
   `NEG FLAG`

4. `STATUS EQU $2000`
   `BACK: BCLR #5,STATUS ;CLEAR FLAG WHEN IT COMES UP`
   `      BEQ BACK`
   `      JSR SERVICE`

5. Privileged Instructions are

```
EORI #NUM, SR
MOVE <EA>,SR
MOVE USP, An or MOVE An,USP
ORI #NUM,SR
RESET
RTE
STOP XX
```

The MOVE USP,An and the MOVE An,USP instructions are needed because in a multitask or multiuser environment, the supervisor must have access to the user stack pointers. The user stack pointer from a task that is not completed must be saved before a new task is serviced.

Section 11.4

1.
```
        ORG  $1000
        MOVEQ #4,D0
        MOVEA.L  #FIRST,A1
        MOVE.L #0,D2
BACK:   MOVE (A1)+,D3
        EXT.L  D3
        ADD.L  D3,D2
        SUBQ  #1,D0
        BNE BACK
        MOVE.L D2,HIGH_ANS
        STOP #0
FIRST:  DC.W  1,2,$7FFF,$7FFF
HIGH_ANS   DS 4
        END
```

2.
```
IM
SR P1000
SM 101C 00 01 00 02 00 03 00 04
R
DM 1024,4
SR P1000
SM 101C,00 01 70 00 71 00 00 00
R
DM 1024,4
SR P1000
SM 101C,6A 0BC 7C 0DE 77 0FF 5F 0EC
R
DM 1024,4
EX
```

3. The base-10 numbers are 70, −256, 18, and 171. The fixed-point average is 0.

4. 1 and 3. Overflow occurs on sets 2, 4, and 5. A TRAPV statement can be inserted immediately after the ADD command. Then an overflow routine can be formulated to print an appropriate message.

5.
```
     ORG  $1000
*   FIND THE SMALLEST AND LARGEST UNSIGNED BYTE.
BIG   EQU  0
SMALL EQU  $0FF
*   START SUBROUTINE
FIND:   MOVE #8,D1     SET COUNTER
        MOVEA.L  (A7)+,A1     POP DATA POINTER FROM STACK
        MOVE.B   #BIG,D7
        MOVE.B   #SMALL,D0
BACK:   CMP.B  (A1),D0        SMALLER?
        BLS  UP               NO
        MOVE.B  (A1),D0       YES.  SET NEW SMALLEST.
UP:     CMP.B  (A1),D7        BIGGER?
        BCC UP1               NO
        MOVE.B (A1),D7        YES
UP1:    CMP.B (A1)+,D5        INCREMENT POINTER
        SUBQ #1,D1            DONE?
        BNE BACK             NO.
        MOVE.L A1,-(A7)       PLACE RETURN ADDRESS ON STACK
        RTS
*    START TEST PROGRAM
```

```
START:   MOVEA.L   #$1000,A7   LOAD STACK POINTER
         BSR FIND
DATA:    DC.B   7,253,4,19,$27,4,251,16
BPSET:   NOP
         STOP #0
     END
```

Section 11.5

1. Change BHI to BGE.

2. The statement checks to ensure that $0 <= AGE <= 105$. If not, A CHECK TRAP is encountered.

3. **(a)** DUCK   **(b)** DOG   **(c)** TERM   **(d)** 00010027

   (e) 27   **(f)** 2   **(g)** 4   **(h)** 38

4.
```
         ORG $1000
STRING:    DS   20
DONE:      DC.B   'DONE'
START:     MOVEA.L #$1000,A7
           MOVEA.L #STRING,A5
BACK:      JSR $10004
           JSR $10002
           MOVE.L DONE,D0
           CMP.L  (A5),D0
           BNE BACK
           STOP #0
         END
```

5.
```
*   SUBROUTINE MOD RETURNS N MOD (K) AS A WORD IN D0.
*     VALUES OF N AND K MUST FOLLOW INVOKING STATEMENT.
*     N IS A LONG WORD, AND K IS A WORD.
             ORG $1000
MOD:         MOVEA.L   (A7)+,A1
             MOVE.L    (A1)+,D0
             DIVU      (A1)+,D0
             MOVE.L    A1,-(A7)
             SWAP D0
             ANDI.L  #$0FFFF,D0
             RTS
*    #####    START TEST PROGRAM    ######
START:   MOVEA.L   #$1000,A7
         BSR   MOD
N:       DC.L   75
K:       DC.W   13
         STOP #0
         END
```

CHAPTER 12

Section 12.1

1. **(a)** Relates only to size of memory that can be "directly" addressed.
   (b) Large ALU registers do not significantly speed up operations unless the internal data buses are the same width.
   (c) The size of the program counter is generally a proper subset of address register size. It has very little effect on computing capabilities, especially if the internal data bus has smaller width.

Section 12.2

1. PDP-11: General-purpose registers including the PC. General-type addressing modes including indirect addressing

   8086: Segment registers facilitate implementation of multiuser systems. Byte instructions and use of byte prefixes. Compatibility with popular 8-bit machines.

   M68000: 32-bit registers and operations. Supervisory mode and extensive vectored priority interrupt capabilities. Large address space.

2. Similar status flags, processor status word, and priority interrupt system. Use of general-purpose registers. Very similar branch on condition instructions. Similar treatment of I/O operations.

3.
```
          ORG  $1000
MOVIND          MACRO
                MOVE.L  \1,A0
                MOVE.\0  (A0),\2
                ENDM
*  START TEST PROGRAM *************************
          MOVIND.B    BIRD,D5
          MOVIND.L    BIRD,BIRD
DONE:     NOP
          STOP #0
     ORG $2000
BIRD:     DC.L        FISH
     ORG $2100
FISH:     DC.B    $12,$34,$56,$78
     END
```

Index